PRINCIPLES

OF

TORT LAW

Second Edition

By

Marshall S. Shapo

Frederic P. Vose Professor
Northwestern University School of Law

CONCISE HORNBOOK SERIES®

THOMSON

WEST

Mat #18375389

Concise Hornbook Series, *WESTLAW* and West Group are
registered trademarks used herein under license.

COPYRIGHT © 1999 WEST GROUP

COPYRIGHT © 2003 By WEST GROUP
                       610 Opperman Drive
                       P.O. Box 64526
                       St. Paul, MN 55164–0526
                       1–800–328–9352

ISBN 0–314–25850–7

For Helene,
The Nonpareil

For Ben   For Nat

For Gabrielle

To the memory of my parents

Mitchell Shapo   Norma S. Shapo

*

iii

Preface

This book aims to capture the core of tort law for law students. It provides a critical summary and discussion of issues that, during more than a third of a century of torts teaching, have seemed to me the most troublesome to those first wrestling with the subject. The issues on which I focus here are those about which students most consistently seek aid during term time and especially in those days when examinations are imminent.

I have sought to maintain a tight focus on the things that appear to count the most in tort law. Rather than accumulating thousands of citations on quite particularized issues, I have tried to give a spare treatment of the law, selecting authorities aimed at evocative and graphic illustrations of the most challenging problems in torts.

Because lawyers speak in terms of legal doctrine, I write in those terms. Because a principal function of lawyers is to penetrate doctrine to reality, I have sought to go behind the labels of theory to what courts do in fact. Because American lawyers relate law to policy, I seek to identify the bases of tort law in those policy considerations that most often appear to engage courts, both consciously and subconsciously.

Tort law is a fascinating study. It is a means of dispute resolution, a body of rules for governing conduct, and a social symbol. I hope that this book captures these aspects of the law in a way that is informative to students, and indeed, to lawyers and judges.

*

Acknowledgments

This book is a personal benchmark after thirty-seven years of teaching torts. I can only begin to record the debts I have accumulated along the way to colleagues and students who have criticized my work, sympathized with it, and generally aided my understanding of the law.

It was my particular good fortune to begin professional life with two of the titans of the twentieth century in the field of torts, Leon Green and Page Keeton. Each—Green as my teacher at Miami and colleague at Texas, and Keeton as my dean and colleague at Texas —nurtured me with a sense of encouragement that would be fortunate for any young teacher. Another very distinguished colleague at Texas, Charles Alan Wright, also especially encouraged my scholarship in this field.

Many other people have provided creative irritants and general inspiration. These include my colleagues at Texas, Virginia, and for twenty-five years now at Northwestern, and the extended community of torts teachers across the country. I have profited always from discussions with them—sometimes fierce verbal battles—and those conversations have set rigorous standards for me. Without attempting to catalog individuals by name, I note my obligations to dozens of men and women whose criticism, challenges, and praise have contributed to my development as a teacher and scholar.

For research support that aided in the writing of this book, I thank the Northwestern University School of Law and the deans with whom I have served: David Ruder, Robert Bennett and David van Zandt. I acknowledge, in particular, support during my year as the Stanford Clinton Sr. Research Professor, and also grants from the Julius Rosenthal Fund, the Charles C. Linthicum Fund, the Seder Corporate Research Fund, the Edwin Walsh Fund, the Clemens and Jane Werner Faculty Enrichment Fund and the Corporate Counsel Center of Northwestern University School of Law.

Scholars run on fuel from libraries, and librarians I have known are among the best. Among Northwestern's splendid crew of reference librarians, Marcia Lehr has been stellar, and I appreciate also the consistent and cheerful aid of her colleagues, especially Pegeen Bassett and Irene Berkey. The librarians who run the ship set the course for their complicated institutions, and I have had good luck at my law schools from the initial stewardship of Roy Mersky through that of George Grossman and Chris Simone.

Thousands of students have served as sounding boards for my ideas about torts, and in turn have contributed ideas to me. Of the few dozen who have been my student assistants over the years, I particularly thank Cris Carmody, formerly editor-in-chief of the Northwestern University Law Review, for helpful criticism of the manuscript.

I am especially grateful to Derek Gundersen, my secretary, for his extensive labors on both editions of this work.

***   ***   ***

This book, and my study of tort law, represent a family project. More than forty years ago, in a gem of a letter, my father wrote me, "When I studied law, it was my ambition to fight injustice." Because tort law provides such a fine measure of our views about injustice, and justice, those words are a polestar for me.

My children, Ben and Nat, probably cannot count the times that I teased them with the *Palsgraf* case and other hypotheticals at dinner. Both now accomplished analysts—Nat of law and Ben of science—they have been teaching me about the fundamentals of my subject since they were very young.

Helene Shapo, my boon companion of forty-three years, is also a nonpareil among editors. Her sense of organization, her insistence on precision, and her moral authority as a critic have given this book much of whatever quality it has to offer.

Chicago and Evanston
January 2003

Summary of Contents

[Chapters 74–75 are reserved for supplementary
material.]

PART SIX.   TORT LAW AND ITS NEIGHBORS

Table of Contents

PRINCIPLES
OF
TORT LAW
Second Edition

*

Part One

INTRODUCTION

Section One

TORT LAW AND ITS PURPOSES

Chapter One

AN OVERVIEW OF TORT LAW

Analysis

¶ 1.01   The Province of Tort

Lay persons and beginning law students, who are lay persons themselves, want to know what a "tort" is. It is well to begin a treatise on tort law by giving at least a summary answer to that question.

A.   *The subjects of tort law*

Tort law, in simplified definition, consists of the rules governing civil suits for injuries caused by wrongs to others. Tort cases are as varied as human activities that create risks of injury. In a motoring society, vehicle accidents are ubiquitous. The product that explodes in someone's face, electrocutes its user, or cuts off a limb may become the subject of suit under a special classification in tort law, known as products liability. A doctor who provides substandard health care may face litigation under the law of medical

2

malpractice. A government that fails to give police protection to an informant might be subject to tort liability for the revenge killing of that person. When an airplane blows up, that occurrence may create a number of tort actions against defendants that include the carrier, the maker of the craft, and governments, both foreign and domestic. Even the most mundane of everyday incidents, including those literally in one's own backyard, may be torts. Limbs fall from one person's tree onto a neighbor's home. People slip and fall on oily substances on the supermarket floor. It is the job of tort law to sort out the justice of these cases within the complex and sometimes contradictory desires of the broad society, of various classes within society, and even of individuals themselves.

B. Working definition

A more sophisticated definition of a tort is an event, arising out of the action or omission of another party, which causes injury to the human body or personality, to property, or to economic interests, in circumstances where the law deems it just to require compensation from the person who has acted or failed to act.[1] When lawyers refer to tort law, they principally mean a body of judge-made law, that is, common law, that grows out of precedents derived from litigation about injuries.

Most frequently, the plaintiff is an individual, but business firms also may be tort plaintiffs, and defendants range from individuals to businesses to governments and government officials. Injury suits against officials, and sometimes governments, are often based on civil rights legislation that incorporates the federal constitution—the so-called "constitutional tort."[2] Legislatures have partially taken over some areas of tort law, passing statutes that supplant or modify the common law of subjects like products liability.

One way that lawyers distinguish torts from other parts of the law is to contrast torts with the subject of contracts. However, there is also significant overlap between those two great areas of the common law—enough overlap that in the 1970s, a leading scholar announced that contract was "being reabsorbed" into tort.[3] There are certain kinds of economic losses that courts classify only under the heading of contract. Apart from those types of cases, however, practically any injury that may be litigated at common

---

1. ABA, Special Committee on the Tort Liability System, *Towards a Jurisprudence of Injury: the Continuing Creation of a System of Substantive Justice in American Tort Law* 1–3 (M. Shapo, Rptr. 1984). Parts of this chapter draw generally on material in that volume.

2. 42 U.S.C. § 1983 (1994).

3. See Grant Gilmore, The Death of Contract (1970), e.g., at 87. Gilmore declared that "[w]e are fast approaching" a point where "there is really no longer any viable distinction between liability in contract and liability in tort." Id. at 88.

law—including some that are subject to contract suits—is likely to fit under the tort umbrella.

Lawyers also distinguish the criminal law from tort law. By definition, crimes involve wrongs against the state, and the person who brings the action is a public prosecutor rather than a private individual. This distinction is crucial, since the state may not only impose monetary penalties on criminal offenders—analogous to awards of civil damages in tort cases—but may also imprison those found guilty of crimes. Of course, the victim of a crime will often be a central actor in the criminal prosecution, both as a witness and as a party in an indirect moral capacity. And a crime victim may bring an individual tort action against the criminal, seeking personal compensation for the injuries inflicted by the crime. Yet, the concept of crime is conceptually distinct from that of tort because it is the state that brings the action, directly to vindicate the interests of society as a whole.

¶ 1.02 Competing Approaches to Tort Law

The stakes in tort law are so high, both socially and financially, and the subject is so interesting intellectually, that it is not surprising to find many arguments about its nature and premises. We summarize briefly some of these theoretical controversies.

A. Unification vs. pluralism

There is disagreement among scholars about whether it is possible to formulate a unified theory of tort law. Certainly, the recognition of torts as a separate subject occurred as early as 1859 with the publication of the first American torts treatise. The first torts casebook followed in 1874.[4] By 1924, Roscoe Pound had remarked that "[g]rowth of the law of torts has gone along with systematizing of the subject."[5]

Although the ordering of tort law has proceeded in a variety of treatises and many scholarly articles, one also must view torts as a highly pluralistic intellectual enterprise, a multifaceted response to a very varied set of problems. We already have indicated the variety of the subject areas that generate the injuries to which tort decisions must address themselves. The refinements in the spectrum of tort liability[6] further indicate how difficult it is to cabin this area of law as if in a periodic table of elements.

---

4. See, e.g., G. Edward White, The Intellectual Origins of Torts in America, 86 Yale L. J. 671, 671 (1977).

5. Roscoe Pound, Foreword to Harvard Law Review Ass'n, Selected Essays on the Law of Torts iii, iii (1924).

6. See ¶ 1.03(A) infra.

B. Doctrinal versus functional

Tort law features constant competition between doctrine and function. Legal doctrines are a shorthand, an intellectual currency, by which lawyers communicate among themselves. When lawyers call certain conduct a battery, or label it negligence, or talk about strict liability, they are speaking a highly compressed language that summarizes concepts they have developed to describe the legal consequences of injuries. At the same time, all lawyers recognize that law is a functional discipline, and must respond to particular features of various activities and situations. Thus, one may functionally view a vehicle accident case as an "automobile case" or view it doctrinally as a "negligence" case, and one may functionally describe a case involving injuries caused by a product as a "products liability" case or label it doctrinally as one of "strict liability," if that theory is used by the plaintiff. What lawyers and judges do is to combine function and doctrine in ways they hope will persuade one another, and also persuade the ultimate consumers of the justice system, those who are subject to its writ.

C. The practical and the theoretical

Tort law is an intensely practical subject, dealing as it does with the consequences of injuries to persons, their property and sometimes their economic interests. Tort law in action involves many hours of factual investigation, and often concentrates on issues of proof and damages. Academic tort commentary, by comparison, frequently indulges in theoretical disquisitions on subjects like duty and culpability. However, it is clear that academics cannot work without the fodder of the cases that tort litigation provides, as it is equally clear that practicing lawyers require the theoretical background that academic law provides.

D. The particular and the comprehensive

Tort law continues to progress along lines that flow from its common law roots. Judge-made law necessarily develops on a case-by-case basis. However, lawyers also have an instinct for codification and systematizing.[7] A set of significant enterprises aimed at reducing the principles of tort law to literally blackletter text are the successive Restatements of Torts. These volumes—the original Restatement of Torts was published in the 1930s[8]—are a product of the American Law Institute (ALI), an organization of judges, prac-

---

7. For a contrast between the "masculine" desire for comprehensive ordering of the law and "order in . . . the feminine sense" as emphasizing "particulars and concrete, specific facts," see Anita Bernstein, Restatement (Third) of Torts: *General Principles* and the Prescription of Masculine Order, 54 Vand. L. Rev. 1367, e.g., at 1392, 1399–1400, 1410–11 (2001).

8. Restatement of Torts, vols. 1 & 2 (1934); vol. 3 (1938); vol. 4 (1939).

ticing lawyers and law professors. The 951 sections of the current full set, the Restatement (Second) of Torts,[9] aim to provide guidance to courts faced with difficult issues in this area of the law. The ALI has now begun a Restatement (Third), whose first major project deals with products liability.[10] Since the ALI is a private organization, its Restatements are not binding on the courts, but represent an effort to establish plausible solutions to challenging problems.

More authoritatively, legislatures have passed statutes that codify and sometimes change tort law, for example in the fields of products liability and medical malpractice. In addition to making substantive rules governing specific activities, legislatures have passed statutes that affect the availability and amount of remedies for injury. A historic example is the statute of limitations, which sets limits on the time period during which claimants may sue. Recently, in addition to changing various aspects of these time limitations, legislatures have passed laws limiting the amount of damages that can be recovered, particularly for intangible harms. Statutes have also restricted the breadth of remedies available in cases where more than one defendant has contributed to an injury. We discuss below statutes that preempt tort law and replace it with comprehensive legislative solutions, the most prominent of which is workers' compensation legislation.[11]

¶ 1.03   Tort Doctrines

A.   *The culpability spectrum*

Tort law exists on a spectrum of culpability that ranges, in sometimes deceptively lay terminology, from intentional torts through negligence to strict liability. At one end of this spectrum is the category of torts known as intentional torts, although the definition of "intent" in that category does not necessarily require the desire or purpose that the lay connotations of the term would indicate. Most tort litigation involves negligence law. Although there are many academic definitions of negligence, most of them include the concept of conduct that is unreasonable under the circumstances. Strict liability doctrines impose tort liability regardless of culpability in the sense of either negligence or intentional acts as defined in the intentional torts. Strict liability torts comprise two major subcategories—for activities and for products—that courts refuse to commingle.

9. Restatement (Second) of Torts, vols. 1 & 2 (1965); vol. 3 (1977); vol. 4 (1979).

10. Restatement (Third) of Torts: Products Liability (1998).

11. See infra, ¶ 1.05.

Although courts firmly distinguish among the principal culpability categories, the spectrum moves gradually from one end to another. The intentional torts blend into a bridge category of wanton, willful, and reckless conduct, which itself merges into gross negligence. In turn, gross negligence blends into negligence, the doctrine most used in ordinary tort litigation, and negligence maintains a fuzzy border with strict liability.

B. A catalog of tort theories

Within each culpability category is a cluster of particular liability theories. Intentional torts to the person include assault, battery, false imprisonment, false arrest, malicious prosecution, and abuse of process. Intentional torts to property include trespass to real estate, conversion, and trespass to chattels. A group of other tort actions that loosely fulfill the definition of intentional torts includes intentional interference with contract and "insurer bad faith." The tort of fraud or deceit is an intentional tort heading that embraces deliberately or recklessly false statements on which people rely in commercial and consumer contexts. The tort of defamation, now redefined under First Amendment principles, spans intentional and negligent publications.

The general action for negligence is remarkably capacious, spanning accidents in every realm of life. But there are also subcategories of doctrine that include negligent interference with contract, negligent misrepresentation, and a medical malpractice doctrine of "informed consent" that straddles the categories of negligence and battery.

We have noted that strict liability has two distinct subclassifications, for abnormally dangerous activities and for products. The strict products liability category blends at its edges, and indeed rather substantially overlaps, with contract-based theories of implied warranty.

¶ 1.04 Rationales

Courts refer to a smorgasbord of rationales in deciding tort cases. Some theorists have insisted that the principal goal of tort law is to achieve corrective justice between individuals, without reference to broader social considerations.[12] This idea draws on the

---

12. A philosophical presentation of the idea appears in Ernest Weinrib, The Idea of Private Law (Harvard 1995). Weinrib summarizes the concept of corrective justice developed by Aristotle as one in which "quantitative equality pairs one party with another." In this view of the subject, "[c]orrective justice treats the defendant's unjust gain as correlative to the plaintiff's unjust loss. The disturbance of the equality [by an injury] connects two, and only two, persons. The injustice that corrective justice corrects is essentially bipolar." Id. at 64. A lengthy set of commentaries on the subject appears in Symposium: Correc-

concepts of justice, fairness, and morality that embody the avowed ethical basis of tort law.[13]

Besides concerning themselves with justice between individuals, courts refer to a number of so-called instrumental concerns, assessing the probable social and economic impact of their decisions. For example, courts sometimes may seek to achieve economic efficiency through their decisions. One famous formula would determine negligence according to whether the cost of avoiding an accident exceeds the cost of the accident.[14] Volumes of economic analysis have emphasized the search for the "cheapest cost avoider"—the party best situated to avoid injuries at the lowest cost—in situations that generate injury.[15] One implication of this form of analysis is that the person who conducts a harmful activity may not always be the most efficient avoider of loss. For example, although it might seem the just result to place liability on a polluter, it might also be the case that those who suffer from pollution can more cheaply avoid injury, as by taking self-protective measures, than can a polluter who might have to adopt prohibitively expensive technology.

Other courts, not focally concerned with efficiency, apparently seek to achieve accident reduction through tort law even if their decisions would drive the level of accidents below an efficient one. These courts seem to find an independent moral basis for achieving relatively high levels of safety, rather than seeking only economically optimal resource allocation. For example, in a case involving a rented motor vehicle, one court spoke of "maximum protection for the victims of defective rentals."[16] Language of this sort appears to declare a social policy preference for protecting life and bodily integrity beyond marketplace valuations; unconstrained by efficiency limitations, it may also line up in spirit with individualized notions of corrective justice that emphasize offsetting the losses of injured persons from the gains of injurers.

A relatively controversial rationale for tort law is loss spreading. The basic theory is that it is just to distribute among many others what may be the overwhelming burden of loss to an injured person. Law can effect this distribution by "spreading" the

tive Justice and Formalism—The Care One Owes One's Neighbors, 77 Iowa L. Rev. No. 2 (1992).

13. See, e.g., Towards a Jurisprudence of Injury, supra note 1, at 4–153—4–169.

14. United States v. Carroll Towing Co., 159 F.2d 169, 173 (2d Cir. 1947).

15. A seminal presentation of the idea is Ronald H. Coase, The Problem of Social Cost, 3 J. L. & Econ. 1, e.g., at 41 (1960). An important application of the idea in a concrete legal context, that of products liability, appears in Guido Calabresi and Jon M. Hirschoff, Toward a Test for Strict Liability, 81 Yale L. J. 1055 (1972).

16. Martin v. Ryder Truck Rental, Inc., 353 A.2d 581, 587 (Del.1976).

monetarily quantifiable part of that burden in the price paid by other users of the good or service that caused the injury, who presumably have benefited from that product or activity. Critics of loss spreading attack it as being judicial arrogation of a role that only legislatures should undertake, that of redistributing wealth on the basis of principles of justice or equity.

Besides these rationales, there are numerous other goals and purposes—sometimes conflicting ones—that courts take into consideration in deciding tort cases. These include the perceived need to respond to the dynamic nature of increasingly sophisticated technology, the desire to provide relatively clear standards of conduct, the goals of protecting expectations and of maintaining certainty and predictability in the law, and the reduction of administrative costs in the justice system itself.[17]

Indicative of the complex manner in which the rationales of tort law relate to one another is the way that both sides in injury disputes can use the same abstract moral and economic concepts. Illustratively, tort claimants may invoke the concept of individualism, emphasizing injury to their dignitary interests. At the same time, defendants who attribute the responsibility for injuries to claimants will rely on individualism by emphasizing that plaintiffs have made personal choices to confront risk. With that line of argument, they stress the autonomy of the individual. Another illustration of the way that both sides may use the same concept appears in the idea of communitarianism. Plaintiffs may stress the heightening of a sense of community when a personal injury verdict for culpable conduct "sends a message" that that type of conduct will not be tolerated. Defendants, melding economic theory with ideas of community, will argue that society as a whole will gain on occasions when the social benefits of risky conduct outweigh the losses such conduct causes to particular individuals.

¶ 1.04A Tort Law as a System

Tort law is not simply a collection of rules and doctrines. The administration of its legal principles exists within what is sometimes called the "tort liability system," a term that describes the institutional structures and processes by which courts and other agencies resolve disputes about personal injuries.[18] That system shares important practical elements with other litigation processes generally, notably the adversarial tradition that is common to all litigation. Distinguishing features of tort law include the facts that a very high percentage of tort cases is tried to juries, and that jury verdicts in tort cases seem to generate a relatively high amount of

---

17. See Towards a Jurisprudence of Injury, supra note 1, ch. 4, passim.

18. See Towards a Jurisprudence of Injury, supra note 1, at 1–3.

media coverage. By comparison with other systems of injury law like compensation systems and regulation,[19] but in common with litigation generally, tort law provides an individualized form of justice. The court resolves a concrete dispute between named parties—often, just two parties.[20] An important question with both philosophical and practical aspects is whether the individualization of justice produces significant social benefits by reinforcing individual responsibility.

¶ 1.05 Relation to Other Systems

Tort law exists as part of a much broader system that may be called injury law.[21] Some statutes have provided the basis for actions unknown to the common law that have tort-like features, and others liberalize common law liability doctrines in particular areas. Legislative enactments that create actions for injury range from the Federal Employers' Liability Act,[22] a statute that provides remedies for injured railroad employees, to a host of anti-discrimination statutes such as civil rights acts,[23] the Americans with

19. See infra ¶ 1.05.

20. In some situations—for example, class actions involving "mass torts"—the names of all the individuals whose rights may be at stake will not appear in the title of the case.

21. See generally Towards a Jurisprudence of Injury, supra note 1.

For another broad summary of the institutional framework that surrounds tort law, see Am. Law Inst., 1 Enterprise Liability for Personal Injury (Reporters' Study) 55–251 (1991). The Report "defend[s] the basic tort model as a valuable aspect of our personal injury system: this is the one institution which permits individual victims to call to account before a lay jury the enterprises whose activities have caused the victims harm." 2 id. at 579. The Report does take a "relatively skeptical view of tort litigation as an injury prevention mechanism" and gives "an even bleaker evaluation of the tort system as a compensatory mechanism." As to deterrence, however, it notes that sometimes it has taken "the threat of tort liability" to bring about "meaningful regulation" and says that "even with improvement," regulation will continue to have "many gaps and deficiencies." Concerning compensation, the Report opines that there is "no alternative but to attempt to coordinate in a more rational fashion the present mix of tort litigation and private

and social insurance, and to close some of the more glaring compensation gaps, particularly with respect to rehabilitation costs and income losses with long-term disabilities." 1 id. at 448.

A book review by a British author concisely summarizes broad issues concerning the rationales of tort law and the relationship of tort to other systems for regulating conduct and compensating for misfortune. Simon Deakin, The Evolution of Tort, 19 Oxford J. Legal Studies 537 (1999). Deakin encapsules "the most important theme" of a book by Peter Cane, The Anatomy of Tort Law, as being "the tension between corrective justice and the 'instrumental' goals of efficiency and redistribution"[see supra, this book, ¶ 1.04]. Deakin observes that "[t]he tort law of our own time, far from withering away along with the 'welfare state', is filling the spaces left by the dismantling of social insurance and universal health-care systems." He also says that "[t]ort law cannot operate in isolation from the growing body of economic regulation which is aimed not just at constituting markets, but also at controlling and mediating their effects." Id. at 545–46.

22. 45 U.S.C. §§ 51–60 (1994).

23. See, e.g., 42 U.S.C. §§ 2000a–2000b–3 (1994) (public accommodations and public facilities).

Disabilities Act,[24] and the Age Discrimination in Employment Act.[25]

Two major sets of legislatively created legal systems also coexist with torts, frequently driving toward the same goals, but sometimes diverging. One of these statutory schemes is compensation legislation, typified by workers' compensation. That legislation generally supersedes tort in the workplace, providing compensation for economic losses for persons injured in the scope of their employment, without requiring proof of fault on the part of the employer and without allowing defenses based on the employee's conduct.

In many states, automobile compensation plans provide a partial no-fault remedy for victims of motoring accidents. All the states have enacted statutes that make available some compensation to victims of crime, who in most cases will not be able successfully to sue the offender, and Congress has provided supplementary funding for these programs.[26] In addition to all these statutory compensation programs, general social legislation provides a partial "safety net" of economic relief for people who lose income because of injuries.

Second, a vast array of regulatory statutes seeks to reduce injuries at their source. The Occupational Safety and Health Act, complementing workers' compensation, provides regulatory tools aimed at reduction of accident levels in the workplace. Federal statutes enforced by the Food and Drug Administration seek to assure the purity of food, the safety and efficacy of drugs and devices, and the safety of cosmetics. Other statutes create a federal regulatory presence in areas as diverse as vehicle safety, cigarettes, flammable fabrics, and toys. The Consumer Product Safety Act covers a wide range of products that are not the subject of specific category regulation.

Alongside these regulatory regimes, often a part of them, stands the criminal law. Criminal sanctions in various regulatory statutes, including occupational safety and health legislation, create a significant overlap with tort remedies as well as with civil sanctions provided by the statutes themselves. The federal securities laws have occasionally provided a basis for jailing tycoons as well as more minor functionaries. An important decision of the Supreme Court in 1943 reinstated the conviction of a corporate president that effectively held him strictly liable for shipping adulterated and misbranded drugs.[27]

---

24. 42 U.S.C. §§ 12101–12213 (1994).

25. 29 U.S.C. §§ 621–634 (1994).

26. See Desmond Greer, A Transatlantic Perspective on the Compensation of Crime Victims in the United States, 85 J. Crim. L. & Criminology 333, 333–34 (1994).

27. United States v. Dotterweich, 320 U.S. 277 (1943).

Some prosecutions for behavior that may also be tortious invoke general criminal statutes, on occasion even seeking criminal sanctions against corporations. One well-publicized prosecution indicted the Ford Motor Company for reckless homicide in the design of a fuel tank on an automobile. Although the company was acquitted, a commentary emphasized that "the trial of a corporation for criminal homicide is a precedent-setting event in American jurisprudence."[28]

¶ 1.06   Tort Law and Society

The basic spectrum of tort liability with its tripartite classification system of intentional torts, negligence, and strict liability is relatively spare and comprehensible. The application of the law is sometimes complex, but this complexity arises from the fact-specific nature of tort law and from the variety and the complexity of life itself.

Because it deals every day with the entire range of injuries in society at ground level, tort law has distilled a rich set of lessons about society itself. Because it is down to earth and rooted in homely controversy, the precedents it generates comprise a cultural mirror. The mosaic of those precedents tells us much about our societal attitudes, and the values that are imbedded in them. It mirrors those values in decisions about disputes involving corporate exercise of power over individuals; it reflects our views about our relationship to governments and officials; it illustrates the complexities of our beliefs about the value of industrial production and the protection of the environment; it even informs us about our attitudes toward sports and games. In short, because of the intensity of the conflict that produces its decisions, tort law provides a remarkably accurate version of ourselves.[29]

[Chapters 2–5 are reserved for supplementary material.]

28. Victoria L. Swigert & Ronald A. Farrell, Corporate Homicide: Definitional Processes in the Creation of Deviance, 15 Law and Soc. Rev. 161, 163 (1980–81).

29. See generally Marshall S. Shapo, In the Looking Glass: What Tort Scholarship Can Teach us About the American Experience, 89 Nw. U. L. Rev. 1567 (1995).

Part Two

THEORIES OF LIABILITY
AND DEFENSES

Section Two
INTENTIONAL TORTS
Chapter Six
ASSAULT

Analysis

The assault tort is as basic a tort theory as there is, yet it is perhaps the least litigated of the major tort doctrines. A practical reason that it is not often a focus of lawsuits is that the tort, by itself, typically will not afford an economic basis to accept a case for claimants' lawyers who operate on contingency fees. Yet an analysis of the elements of the tort reveals bedrock qualities that symbolize how tort doctrines reflect tensions that infect all of injury law: tensions between personal dignity and freedom of movement; between objective and subjective tests; and concerning how far the law should go in protecting "mental," as contrasted with purely "physical" interests.

¶ 6.01 Definition

As is so with all the torts, assault does not have an absolutely standard definition. In fact, there is a particular confusion of labeling associated with the tort because frequently the term "assault" operates in the public and journalistic minds to denote a physical touching. Technical tort definitions, however, use the terminology of "battery," discussed below,[1] for physical touchings.

With some variation among jurisdictions, the elements that a plaintiff must prove are (1) an act by the defendant that

---

1. See Chapter 7 infra.

14

(2) intentionally (3) creates imminent apprehension in the plaintiff of (4) physical contact (5) that is harmful or (6) offensive. Thus, the assault tort requires that the plaintiff apprehended that the defendant would physically contact him, rather than that the defendant touched the plaintiff. Of course, an assault—that is, an act that causes the apprehension of a touching—may immediately precede a battery—the touching itself.

A. The act

The fine old case of *Read v. Coker*[2] teaches the basic lesson concerning the sort of "act" required for assault. In that case, which arose from the ashes of a failed business association between the litigants, the defendant's workmen "mustered round the plaintiff, tucking up their sleeves and aprons, and threatened to break his neck if he did not go out." As the court summarized the facts, the plaintiff departed, "fearing that the men would strike him if he did not do so." The court's judgment for the plaintiff, accompanied by nominal damages of one farthing, illustrates about as liberal a definition of "act" as one may find. The decision teaches that one does not even have to raise a fist to perpetrate an assault within the tort definition. Rolling up your sleeves will do, particularly if you have associates who are doing the same thing, and especially in the context of verbal threats.

Yet, threats by themselves will not carry a case for the plaintiff: "[N]o words can amount to an assault" was the formulation that the defendant in *Read v. Coker* quoted from an old text.[3] It is true that there are a lot of situations in which many people would take words alone to have an assaultive character, for example, especially threatening words uttered by a nearby person of menacing physique. But the need to have specific standards in the law has fenced out from the definition of assault even the vicious threat, so long as it is not accompanied by an act, although sometimes threatening words may subject the speaker to other tort actions, particularly the tort of intentional infliction of emotional distress.[4] The need to preserve leeway for speech, even at some expense to dignitary interests, further supports the formal requirement that the plaintiff must show an act to prove an assault.

---

2. 138 Eng.Rep. 1437 (1853).

3. Id., quoting Buller's Nisi Prius 15. A modern application of the principle is Raines v. Shoney's, Inc., 909 F.Supp. 1070, 1083 (E.D.Tenn.1995). The manager of a restaurant, in an effort to solve an apparent theft of $600, searched employees with the aid of police officers. An employee said that after the search was over, the manager told her "there would be some 'ass whippings' if a lawsuit was filed." In granting summary judgment to the defendant, the court said that although there was "a threat of harm to the person of another," the manager's statement did "not suggest the immediacy of harm necessary to constitute an assault."

4. See infra, Chapter 13.

Allied to these considerations is the problem of proof. It is easier for a court to enforce a liability rule if the defendant has actually made an overt movement, rather than having only glared or even uttered a threat. This is not to say that if a very mean-looking person glares menacingly or speaks threateningly to an ordinary or rather timid individual, that may not cause significant emotional effects. A good example is the case of men who make vulgar remarks to women passersby. There may be reasons why a legislature might wish to make this grounds for civil liability, but under the traditional judicial definition it does not qualify as the tort of assault.[5] In balancing the competing social interests that the tort of assault tries to sort out, the law has concluded that the plaintiff must prove an act.

B. Intent

We will defer fuller discussion of the intent element of assault to our discussion of battery below.[6] Presently, it is sufficient to say that the plaintiff must show that the defendant had a desire or purpose to place the plaintiff in apprehension of a harmful or offensive physical contact, or had knowledge with substantial certainty that his act would create that apprehension.

C. Apprehension

The plaintiff must apprehend an imminent harmful or offensive physical contact. The requirement of a perception of imminent contact rests on the idea that the plaintiff could not fairly apprehend a contact that was not about to happen. A pragmatic basis for the requirement is a judgment that typically there will be insufficient validation of injury if the defendant was not in a position to touch the plaintiff immediately.

One should note, however, that under this formula the plaintiff need not feel or exhibit fear, although much of the common law emerged from cases where the plaintiff in fact was afraid or feared the defendant.[7] The reason for allowing a tort action for intentionally caused apprehension, absent actual fear, lies in the dignitary foundations of the assault tort. Over the course of centuries, the law came to protect the interest in mental security, to a point that it would award damages for violation of the interest in being free from the perception that one is about to be touched against one's will. The tort of assault, therefore, is actually a modern creature in

---

5. See Cynthia Bowman, Street Harassment and the Informal Ghettoization of Women, 106 Harv. L. Rev. 517, 555 (1993).

6. See infra, ¶ 7.01(D).

7. See Read v. Coker, supra note 2.

terms of our collective psychological life as well as the history of the law.[8]

A modern statutory analogue of the assault tort is the offense of stalking. An example is the Wyoming stalking statute, which makes it both a crime and grounds for a civil suit to "engage[] in a course of conduct reasonably likely to harass" another. The statute defines "harass" to mean conduct that "includ[es] but [is] not limited to verbal threats, written threats, vandalism or nonconsensual physical contact, directed at a specific person" or that person's family, "which the defendant knew or should have known would cause a reasonable person to suffer substantial emotional distress, and which does in fact seriously alarm" that person. The Tenth Circuit concluded that a jury could have found this definition fulfilled in a civil case in which a funeral director told a competitor he would "ruin" him both financially and reputationally. There also was evidence that the defendant "either followed or placed [the plaintiff] under surveillance" on four occasions, that on another occasion he blocked the plaintiff's car to slow down his response to an ambulance call, and that he created a "remarkably complex diagram" of the plaintiff's relations with 14 other members of the community that the plaintiff claimed made him "the center of a point ... trying to make people come after me or that he's after me."[9] The elements of the crime differ somewhat from the assault tort, but its emphasis on protection of dignitary interests is similar.[10]

D. Harmful or offensive contact

In our discussion of battery, we will elaborate on the requirement of a contact, which is so central to the definition of a battery.[11] Here, we simply focus on the requirement that the intended contact be harmful or offensive. In the most typical assault case, like that of the missed punch, the intent to do harmful contact is straightforward enough.

However, it requires emphasis that a defendant may also be liable in assault for intending to cause apprehension of an offensive contact, even if he did not intend the contact itself. We already have implied the reason for this in our discussion of the apprehension element: Assault is a mental dignity tort. The interest it

---

8. See Roscoe Pound, Interests of Personality, 28 Harv. L. Rev. 343, 357 (1915) (after moving to protect "group interest[s] against insult" and "a social interest against disorder," and then individual interests against "physical injury" and "overcoming the will," "[f]inally the law begins to take account of purely subjective mental injuries to a certain extent and even to regard infringement of another's sensibilities").

9. Veile v. Martinson, 258 F.3d 1180 (10th Cir.2001).

10. For other material on stalking, in the context of the privacy tort of intrusion, see infra, ¶ 8.02.

11. See infra, ¶ 7.01(A).

protects is not an interest in not being physically injured. It is, simply, an interest in not apprehending an unwanted touching. Illustrations of how assault issues might arise in everyday modern situations appear in certain episodes of alleged sexual harassment. For example, if someone has made clear to another that she does not desire what the other subjectively may regard as an affectionate touching, the law of assault protects the first person's antipathy to even an attempt at that touch.

¶ 6.02   Policy Considerations

Like other tort doctrines, the law of assault must resolve competing social interests. We want to protect people against apprehensions of unwanted touchings, but we do not want jovial persons to shrink back in their shells at the prospect of a lawsuit for friendly gestures. In setting firmly in place a tort that protects a mental interest, the law of assault strikes something of a balance in favor of the desire to avoid perception of an unwanted contact and against subjective, if sincere, joviality.

One of the most fascinating theoretical questions about assault, which has not been resolved, is how objectively the law will judge a plaintiff's perceptions that a touch would be offensive. At some point the law draws a line in favor of objectivity: rejecting assault suits by unusually timid or withdrawn plaintiffs, it will effectively tell them that if they shrink from contact that most would consider normal, perhaps they should live in germ-free bubbles. But because of the dignitary roots of the doctrine, the tort provides some room for plaintiffs to prove their subjective reactions. To some extent, the plaintiff's own world-view, especially when announced to the world, will determine what kind of attempted touching is an offensive one.

Chapter Seven
BATTERY

Analysis

The tort of battery is simple in its general definition but profound in its theoretical implications. It is, indeed, one of the most powerful tools in the torts arsenal. One of the bedrock principles of the law of torts is that one shall not touch another intentionally without the other's consent, implied if not express, and without a privilege to do so.

¶ 7.01 Elements

It is relatively easy to set out the elements of battery, although those elements become intertwined in subtle ways. The basic definition is that a battery is an (1) intentional (2) contact with the person of another, (3) either harmful or offensive, that is (4) unconsented and (5) unprivileged. It is convenient to begin the discussion of these elements with the element of a contact, following that with an explanation of lack of consent and privilege, and then analyzing the concept of intent and the character of the touching.

A. *Contact*

It would seem that the requirement of a contact is so obvious as not to require explication. However, even this simple element exhibits some refinements, including the notion that a touching of the plaintiff's body may not be necessary if the defendant touched something that is closely connected with the plaintiff. Illustratively, a nineteenth century case indicated that one might be held for a battery if he struck a horse that drew a carriage in which the plaintiff was riding.[1]

A modern application of this extension of the contact element, with civil rights overtones, appeared in a Texas case in which a motel club manager refused service to an African–American guest, snatching a plate from the guest's hand. The plaintiff "testified that he was not actually touched, and did not testify that he suffered fear or apprehension of physical injury," but he did say that he had been "highly embarrassed and hurt" by the manager's conduct in front of his associates. While evincing a recognition that the essence of the plaintiff's claim arguably was for intentional infliction of emotional distress—a tort that had not yet been adopted in Texas—the Texas Supreme Court imposed liability for battery. The court employed precedents and commentary to support the conclusion that the plate was so closely associated with the plaintiff as to be part of his body, fixing on the "offensive manner" in which the motel employee engaged in the "forceful dispossession" of the plaintiff's plate. The court commented that "[p]ersonal indignity is the essence of an action for battery."[2]

An even less direct form of contact may also satisfy the requirements of the tort. In one well known case, the defendant allegedly pulled a chair out from under the plaintiff as she began to sit down. The court implicitly accepted that the plaintiff's fall to the ground was a contact for purposes of the law of battery.[3]

B. Unconsented

Lack of consent is a fundamental requirement of the battery tort. The baseline definition of consent, one intuitive to lay persons as well as to lawyers, is "willingness in fact for conduct to occur," which "may be manifested by action or inaction."[4] The element of lack of consent blends at its edges into the element of privilege, which is discussed below.[5] Theoretically, however, consent is personal to the plaintiff, and in that way differs from the classic idea of privilege as a permission that is socially conferred.

---

1. Marentille v. Oliver, 2 N.J.L. 379 (1808).

2. Fisher v. Carrousel Motor Hotel Inc., 424 S.W.2d 627, 629–30 (Tex.1967).

3. Garratt v. Dailey, 279 P.2d 1091 (Wash.1955), discussed infra, ¶ 7.01(D), text accompanying notes 15–18.

4. Restatement (Second) of Torts § 892 (1979). For elaboration on the basic definition, including the ways in which consent may be manifested, see ¶ 17.01 infra.

5. See ¶ 7.01(C) infra.

The consent requirement ties in with the fundamental proposition that every human being has a right to decide what happens to his or her own body, an idea that Justice Cardozo eloquently expressed in a medical maloccurrence case.[6] Medical malpractice law, in particular, now tends to chalk up consent issues under the doctrine of "informed consent,"which courts employ under both battery and negligence headings.[7] In its role as a fundamental element of the general definition of the battery tort, the consent element emphasizes each person's dignitary interest in freedom from invasion of his or her personal sphere.

C. Unprivileged

Another requirement for a battery claim is a showing that the contact was unprivileged. We have noted that there is an overlap between the concepts of lack of privilege and lack of consent, but a useful working distinction would view consent as granted by an individual and privilege as a kind of license granted by society.

The element of lack of privilege also overlaps with the requirement of intentionality, which is discussed below.[8] The famous decision on the second appeal in *Vosburg v. Putney*[9] illustrates the bridging of the two concepts. In that case, the almost twelve-year-old defendant kicked the fourteen-year-old plaintiff "a little below the knee" after the teacher had called the class to order. The jury found, on a special verdict, that the defendant did not intend to do the plaintiff "any harm." However, harm ensued, in the form of a disabling injury to the plaintiff's leg, which evidently was triggered, unforeseeably, by the defendant's kick. The case thus presented a classic example of an intended touching with an unintended result, a serious physical harm.

The Wisconsin Supreme Court's subtle analysis linked the privilege issue, defined in terms of unlawful conduct, with the defendant's intent. Declaring that a battery plaintiff "must show either that the intention was unlawful, or that the defendant is in fault," the court explained that "if the intended act is unlawful, the intention to commit it must necessarily be unlawful."

An important fact was that the defendant had kicked the plaintiff "after the regular exercises of the school had commenced." The court indicated that in the circumstances of the classroom, "no implied license to do the act complained of existed, and such act was a violation of the order and decorum of the school, and

---

6. Schloendorff v. Society of New York Hosp., 105 N.E. 92, 93 (N.Y.1914), quoted ¶ 27.03 infra, text accompanying note 20.

7. See ¶ 27.01 infra.

8. See ¶ 7.01(D) infra.

9. 50 N.W. 403 (Wis.1891).

necessarily unlawful.''[10] The court contrasted the situation that would have presented itself if the parties had been "upon the playgrounds of the school, engaged in the usual boyish sports."[11] The kick might not have been a tort at recess, for the intended act would not have violated the rules of that more boisterous environment. This analysis shows how social context defines privilege. It also demonstrates the inseparability of the privilege issue from the question of intent, to which we now turn.

D. Intentionality

A plaintiff suing for battery must show that the defendant's conduct was intentional, but the definition of intent for purposes of the intentional torts is rather technical. The first level of definition for the intent requirement of a battery under the Restatement (Second) requires that the defendant must act "intending to cause a harmful or offensive contact with the person of the other or a third person, or an imminent apprehension of such a contact."[12] Of course, intent to cause such a contact will fulfill the intent element if contact occurs. Beyond that, however, this definition makes clear that, at a minimum, all the defendant in a battery case need intend is an assault. If the defendant intends to place another in imminent apprehension of a harmful or offensive contact, even if he does not intend the contact itself, that will suffice for a battery if the contact ensues.[13]

Beyond that, the requirement of intention ties in with the defendant's desire or purpose to cause a harmful or offensive contact, or his knowledge that he is breaking the rules—the social rules. This is how intent may link up with the privilege element in close cases. When one person punches another, the case is an easy one, because the defendant clearly intends harm. In a *Vosburg*-type

10. Id. at 403–04.

11. An extraordinary monograph by Professor Zigurds Zile provides an exhaustive analysis of *Vosburg*. *Vosburg v. Putney:* A Centennial Story, 1992 Wis. L. Rev. 877. Professor Zile utilizes contemporary documents that include transcripts of the case, newspaper articles, and even tombstones to frame the facts and law of the case in its setting of local history and human interest.

12. Restatement (Second) of Torts § 13 (1965).

13. Illustrative is a case in which the defendant, returning shots from an auto, fired towards the car. One bullet from the exchange struck the plaintiff, who lived next to the defendant's house. The trial court gave judgment for the defendant on the ground that there was no evidence that he had intended to shoot the plaintiff. The appellate court reversed for findings on whether the defendant had fired the bullet that hit the plaintiff. It that were the case, the court indicated, the defendant could be held for a battery. The reason was that "by aiming and firing a loaded weapon at the automobile," even if he did so "for the stated purpose of protecting his house," the defendant "did intend to put the youths who occupied the vehicle in apprehension of a harmful or offensive bodily contact," which would "satisfy the intent requirement for battery against plaintiff." Hall v. McBryde, 919 P.2d 910, 914 (Colo.Ct.App.1996).

case,[14] the problem is more difficult; that case is harder because of the jury's finding that the defendant did not intend to harm the plaintiff, although he evidently intended to touch him.

Another much-discussed case involving a juvenile defendant further fleshed out the definition of intent, in a situation in which it also would have been difficult to find that the defendant actually intended to harm the plaintiff. In this case, *Garratt v. Dailey*,[15] the five-year-old defendant allegedly pulled a chair out from under the elderly plaintiff. In analyzing whether this act could be found to be a battery, the court drew on a comment in the first Restatement that defined intention in terms of whether the act was "done for the purpose of causing the contact or apprehension or with knowledge on the part of the actor that such contact or apprehension is substantially certain to be produced."[16] It remanded the case with instructions requiring "definite findings on the issue of whether [the defendant] knew with substantial certainty that the plaintiff would attempt to sit down where the chair which he moved had been."[17] This formulation further sharpens the definition of battery. Permitting a court to hold a five-year-old child for an "intentional tort" even though he may only have been engaged in a childish prank, the *Garratt* decision signals that so long as a child is old enough to understand a set of relevant social rules, his act that breaks those rules may be a battery.[18]

Particular contexts define the relevant rules, and may do so restrictively. Illustrative is a case in which a worker sued an

14. See supra, ¶ 7.01(C), text accompanying notes 9–11.

15. 279 P.2d 1091 (Wash.1955).

16. Id. at 1093, quoting Restatement of Torts § 13, comment a (1934). The Second Restatement has changed this formulation somewhat, defining intent as "denot[ing] that the actor desires to cause consequences of his act, or that he believes that the consequences are substantially certain to result from it." Restatement (Second) of Torts § 8A (1965).

Placing the Restatement phraseology in a theoretical context beyond legal doctrine is Anita Bernstein, Reciprocity, Utility, And the Law of Aggression, 54 Vand. L. Rev. 1, e.g., at 35–39 (2001), identifying the relational elements of "aggression" as residing in the sense that there has been a "violation" of the injured person and that the injurer has committed an "intentional trespass." Bernstein comments that the "substantially certain" language of the Restatement "implies an understanding of probable consequences, so that legal responsibility for the intentional causation of consequences (such as harmful bodily contact, or invasion of land, or severe emotional distress) depends on the actor's awareness of the boundary that is crossed." In Bernstein's definitional framework, "aggression" "requires the actor to know that her chosen behavior invades the territory of another." Id. at 39.

17. 279 P.2d at 1095.

18. Cf. Waters v. Blackshear, 591 N.E.2d 184 (Mass.1992) (defendant, apparently aged eight or nine, put firecracker in sneaker of seven-year-old playmate and lit it; plaintiff sued only for negligence; courts affirms defendant's verdict, saying that "[t]he defendant was not so young that a person of his age, experience and intelligence, would not have understood the harmful nature of [the] contact," and stressing that "[t]he defendant's conduct was a battery, an intentional tort").

employer and a utility for assigning him to work near an area "dangerously contaminated by radiation." The court concludes that this allegation "may have stated a claim for battery" but specifies that the plaintiff must plead "a violation of the regulations governing occupational dose limits" for those working in radiation areas.[19]

Application in workers' compensation. Although *Vosburg* and *Garratt* are the leading decisions on the definition of intentionality in intentional torts from a pedagogical standpoint, their factual profiles do not represent large numbers of reported cases. By comparison, one area where the definition has become quantitatively important is workers' compensation. In that body of law, claimants are typically limited to recovery for workplace injuries to the benefits provided by the statutory compensation scheme. However, under the workers' compensation statutes of a number of states, an exception to this general rule of "exclusivity" is for conduct labeled with terminology like "intentional wrongs." In those cases, the worker may sue an employer in tort.

The New Jersey Supreme Court employed the Restatement's "substantial certainty" test in a case in which the plaintiff employee worked on a rolling mill on which the safety guard had been disengaged by being "tied up" with a wire. The only time that the guard would be lowered into place was when inspectors for the Occupational Safety and Health Administration (OSHA) came to the plant, and as soon as they left, the guard would again be lifted out of place. There had been "close calls" for the plaintiff and a fellow employee whose gloves had been ripped off when they put their hands into the unguarded part of the machine. On three occasions "immediately preceding" his injury, the plaintiff had asked his supervisor to put the guard back into operation. The supervisor, walking away, replied that the matter was "not a problem." The employer admitted that "the guard was removed for 'speed and convenience.'" Given all this evidence, and obviously strongly influenced by the fact that the employer had "deliberately and systematically deceive[d] OSHA into believing that the machine [was] guarded," the court reversed a dismissal. Under a statutory provision that allowed employees to sue in tort for "intentional wrong[s]," it said that a jury could have found that the employer "knew that it was substantially certain that the removal of the safety guard would result eventually in injury to one of its employees."[20]

---

19. Corcoran v. N.Y. Power Auth., 935 F.Supp. 376, 387–88 (S.D.N.Y.1996). The court subsequently dismissed the battery claim under the statute of limitations. 1997 WL 603739 (S.D.N.Y.

1997), aff'd, 202 F.3d 530, 542 (2d Cir. 1999).

20. Laidlow v. Hariton Mach. Co., 790 A.2d 884, 897–98 (N.J.2002). See also, e.g., Swope v. Columbian Chems.

D–1. "Transferred intent"

The law may effect a "transfer" of intent from one party initially targeted by the defendant's tortious conduct to another to whom the defendant's act causes a harmful contact. Thus, where someone intends to effectuate even an assault on another, and his act causes a contact to a third person, the original actor may be liable to the third person for a battery.[21] Illustrative is a case involving a shootout in which A shot at a car in which others were riding, and during the exchange of gunfire a bullet struck A's neighbor. The court concluded that if the bullet had come from A's gun he could be held for a battery if he had intended to put the persons in the vehicle "in apprehension of a harmful or offensive bodily contact."[22]

E. The "everyday touching"

One implication of the principles we have discussed is that an "everyday touching" is not a battery. This is rather more of a common sense rule than a legalistic one. It simply summarizes the practical idea that when one bundles together the concepts of intent, lack of privilege, and lack of consent, there are certain kinds of touchings that the law will deem to be tolerated in everyday existence, like a touch to get someone's attention.[23]

F. "Harmful or offensive"

Consideration of the distinction concerning everyday touchings leads to analysis of the requirement that a touching be "harmful or offensive." A central lesson under this heading is that one person's pleasure may be another's disgust. The reaction of two Florida courts to the same fact situation provides an interesting spectrum of possibilities. The parties in this 1970s case, a man and a woman who were employees at the same plant, were having lunch at a worktable. The male defendant knew that the female plaintiff, his co-worker, was shy. Trying to tease her, he "pulled her head toward him" in a " 'friendly unsolicited hug.' "The plaintiff immediately felt sharp pains in the back of her neck and ear and in the

---

Co., 281 F.3d 185, 194, 201 (5th Cir. 2002) (employer "continually required [the plaintiff] to breathe ozone without protective respiratory equipment" for more than nine years; repeated episodes of respiratory discomfort for plaintiff and fellow employees; at least three workers "had passed out from breathing too much ozone," and on many occasions "employees had to flee the immediate vicinity ... because the ozone level had become intolerable"; jury could find that employer "knew to a substantial

certainty of plaintiff's exposure to "high levels of ozone" and that these exposures "would do gradual, but definite and repeated, bodily harm to him").

21. Restatement (Second) of Torts § 16.

22. Hall v. McBryde, 919 P.2d 910 (Colo.Ct.App.1996).

23. Coward v. Baddeley, 157 Eng. Rep. 927 (Excheq. 1859).

base of her skull and suffered paralysis on one side of her face and mouth.[24]

The intermediate appellate court viewed the action as one for assault and battery and barred it under the statute of limitations for those torts.[25] However, the Florida Supreme Court said that the case should have gone to the jury under a negligence count, for which the limitations period had not run. The supreme court concluded that "[i]t cannot be said that a reasonable man in this defendant's position would believe that the bizarre results ... were 'substantially certain' to follow," but it also stressed that this did "not mean that he does not become liable for such unanticipated results." Under negligence law, the supreme court observed, "a defendant becomes liable for reasonably foreseeable consequences, though the exact results and damages were not contemplated."[26]

It seems plausible that the fact that the plaintiff was barred by the battery statute of limitations pushed the Florida Supreme Court to consider a way to recognize a sympathetic claim. However, it is interesting to consider the case on its merits as a battery action, particularly with reference to the question of whether the contact, viewed by the defendant as "friendly," was "offensive." With respect to that issue, one should stress that the question of what an "offensive" contact is takes its answer from social and cultural contexts. Whatever room may have existed in decades past for unwanted hugs, such touchings are today "offensive" for the purposes of the law of battery. Somewhat analogously to *Vosburg*, a defendant may be liable for an intentional tort for even a touching subjectively intended to be playful, and even when it causes a "bizarre" harm to the recipient of the unwanted touch.

G. Comparison and overlaps with assault

It is worth noting how battery doctrine interacts with assault. The Restatement says that one may be liable for a battery if his act that causes a harmful touching had the intent to cause another person to have an imminent apprehension of a harmful or offensive bodily contact—that is, an assault.[27] A colorful example is a First Circuit case in which the defendant was a baseball pitcher who overreacted to hecklers in the stands next to the bullpen where he was warming up. He threw a ball in the direction of the hecklers,

---

24. Spivey v. Battaglia, 258 So.2d 815, 816 (Fla.1972).

25. Spivey v. Battaglia, 242 So.2d 477 (Fla.App.1970) (mem. per curiam). On the facts of the case, one may rationalize this conclusion on the basis that an "aggressor" "may believe that the target would welcome the initiative," and may "desire benefit for the target, or for other persons, or for society" but, as one

commentator has said, "[n]one of these motives precludes liability for an intentional tort." Bernstein, supra note 16, 54 Vand. L. Rev. at 39.

26. Spivey v. Battaglia, 258 So. 2d at 817.

27. Restatement (Second of Torts § 13 (1965).

who were seated behind a wire mesh screen, arguably intending to frighten them. The ball went through the screen and hit the plaintiff. Citing the Restatement provision just summarized, the court said that it was error to direct a verdict for the defendant on a battery count.[28] The gist of the decision is that in committing an assault—that is, doing something that would place the fans in apprehension of a harmful contact—the defendant ultimately committed a battery because his action resulted in a harmful contact.

An interesting comparison lies in the fact that it is possible to commit a battery without committing an assault. An example of this situation is where the defendant strikes a sleeping plaintiff. There is no assault because the plaintiff could not apprehend an harmful contact, but there is a battery because the contact occurred.

¶ 7.02   The Legal Consequences of a Battery

A.   *Unforeseen consequences*

Once a court characterizes a touching as a battery, the defendant will be liable for a relatively broad range of consequences. The *Vosburg* court put the principle in rather general terms, saying that "[t]he rule of damages in actions for torts" was "that the wrongdoer is liable for all injuries resulting directly from the wrongful act, whether they could or could not have been foreseen by him."[29] Courts sometimes apply even to negligence cases a principle of liability for unforeseeable consequences, utilizing the so-called "eggshell skull" rule, which makes a defendant "take his victim as he finds him," including the victim's unusual susceptibilities to injury. All we need emphasize here is that those who commit "intentional torts" are liable for unforeseeable harms.

B.   *Statutes of limitations; punitive damages*

The labeling of an act as an "intentional tort" may have other important practical consequences. One such result, which often may cut against plaintiffs, is to place a case within statutes of limitations for assault and battery, which tend to be relatively short, rather than those for negligence. Another, which invariably would cut in favor of plaintiffs, is that the intentional tort label will help to support a claim for punitive damages, which are occasionally awarded in tort cases in addition to compensatory damages. Punitive damages are designed to provide a punishment function in tort law, as well as to achieve more deterrence of especially culpable conduct than compensatory damages might achieve.[30] One should

---

28. Manning v. Grimsley, 643 F.2d 20, 22 (1st Cir.1981).

29. Vosburg, supra note 9, 50 N.W. at 404.

30. For a general discussion of punitive damages, see infra, Chapter 73.

note, however, that a plaintiff seeking a punitive award is likely to have to show that the defendant's conduct fell within the common connotations of the term "intent." That is, the plaintiff may have to prove purpose, or even malice in its common meaning, rather than fulfilling only the technical minimum definition of intent as "knowledge of substantial certainty" that a harmful or offensive contact will occur.[31]

¶ 7.03   Special Applications

A.   Domestic violence

A quantitatively large set of intentional torts appears in the domestic setting, with large numbers of batteries occurring between spouses and other domestic partners. The standard elements of battery are usually not difficult to establish in these cases, but they are often unreported[32] and seldom sued upon.[33] Critics have pointed out that ordinary tort law does not provide relief in any significant measure for victims, being ineffective both as to deterrence[34] and compensation.[35] At least one decision has fashioned a response to this kind of brutal activity, setting up a tort for "battered-woman's syndrome." It would limit the cause of action to "physical or psychological abuse ... over an extended period of time" within a "marital or marital-like relationship," which produces "recurring physical or psychological injury" in a situation where the plaintiff is not able "to take any action to improve or alter the situation unilaterally."[36] One proposal for legislative action would impose a requirement of coverage for domestic violence as a part of the mandatory liability insurance policy for autos.[37]

B.   The Federal Tort Claims Act

1.   Third party crimes

A small but interesting subset of cases involving intentional tort theories and legal characterization has developed under the Federal Tort Claims Act (FTCA). That legislation permits suits against the United States Government for the torts of its employ-

---

31. For a discussion of the verbal standards used for punitive damages, see infra, ¶ 73.03.

32. Cusseaux v. Pickett, 279 N.J.Super. 335, 340, 652 A.2d 789, 791 (1994), citing State v. Kelly, 97 N.J. 178 , 478 A.2d 364 (1984).

33. See Douglas D. Scherer, Tort Remedies for Victims of Domestic Abuse, 43 S.C. L. Rev. 543, 565 (1992).

34. See Jennifer Wriggins, Domestic Violence Torts, 75 So. Calif. L. Rev. 121, 144–46 (2001).

35. See id. at 146–47.

36. Cusseaux, supra note 32, 279 N.J.Super. at 344, 652 A.2d at 793–94 (1994).

37. See Wriggins, supra note 34, at 152–69.

ees, but specifically excludes claims based on several intentional-type torts, including "assault" and "battery."

A typical problem in this category arises when an employee of the Government commits what is clearly an intentional tort. The plaintiff, prevented by the statute from claiming against the Government for an intentional tort, sues it for its alleged negligence in not supervising or restraining the employee. In one case, the Supreme Court barred an action against the Government for the death of an off-duty army private who had been murdered by another soldier. The plaintiff, the decedent's mother and personal representative, argued that the Government was negligent in controlling the soldier who committed the murder because of the Government's knowledge of the murderer's previous conviction for manslaughter. Denying recovery, Chief Justice Burger wrote in the plurality opinion that the plaintiff could not evade the "assault and battery" exclusion in the legislation "by framing her complaint in terms of negligent failure to prevent the assault and battery."[38]

In a later case, however, the Court allowed a negligence suit against the Government when naval corpsmen failed to subdue a drunken medical aide who was packing a rifle, and did not notify authorities of the man's condition or the fact that he was armed. Later, the medical aide shot at a vehicle and wounded the plaintiff. The Government had adopted regulations barring firearms on naval bases and requiring that all personnel report the presence of firearms. Reversing a dismissal, Justice Stevens said that the fact that the shooter's behavior was "characterized as an intentional assault rather than a negligent act" was "irrelevant." He said it would be "odd to assume" that Congress meant to impose liability on the Government for breach of a duty to control "a foreseeably dangerous individual" when that individual "was merely negligent but not when he or she was malicious."[39]

2. Pranks

In a very different setting, the Second Circuit held that a prank was a battery and that therefore the plaintiff could not recover under the FTCA. In this case, a federal employee injured a co-worker when he came up behind him, yelled "boo!," pulled a stocking cap over his head and rode him piggyback. Although presumably all the mischievous employee intended was horseplay, the court found that he had committed a battery because of his intent to make contact and held the government immune.[40]

---

38. United States v. Shearer, 473 U.S. 52, 54–55 (1985).

39. Sheridan v. United States, 487 U.S. 392, 403 (1988).

40. Lambertson v. United States, 528 F.2d 441, 444 (2d Cir.1976).

C. Sexual harassment

Unwanted touchings may provide a basis for an independent claim of sexual harassment under Title VII. An example is a case in which the plaintiff testified that the defendant put his arm around her shoulder and said "in a suggestive manner 'I really like you Pat' and 'do you mind if I put my arm here.' " In the context of ensuing "arbitrary" employment actions by the defendant, eventuating in a discharge, the court ruled that a jury could "make a connection" between that incident and the discharge.[41]

¶ 7.04 Rationales

In reviewing the rationales of battery, including their moral elements and their assumptions about the effects of law on conduct, one is struck by their variety and the earnest search for justice that they reflect.

- Battery rationales generally emphasize the protection of dignitary interests, combined with a basic assumption that each person's body deserves protection against invasion by others.

- The battery tort sets social standards based on cultural norms and practical mores. Classic examples of this feature of the tort are the *Vosburg* decision,[42] with its emphasis on the fact that the classroom had been called to order when the defendant kicked the plaintiff, and *Garratt v. Dailey*, in which a little boy allegedly pulled a chair out from under an elderly woman.[43] These cases define the frontier of the tort by indicating that children, even very young children, must be taken to understand in some meaningful sense what is right and wrong from a social point of view. Indeed, some decisions, like those discussed above concerning the defendant who grabbed a plate[44] and the defendant who hugged a co-worker,[45] may place the court in the vanguard of describing new social norms rather than confirming entirely established ones.[46]

- Battery rules will at least indirectly influence behavior, deterring socially undesirable conduct. Communicated through cultural standards, they may even have an effect on the conduct of persons without the mental capacity to foresee the harmful consequences of their acts—that is, people like children who cannot legally or morally be judged negligent. Moreover, the

---

41. O'Donnell v. Coulson, 40 F. Supp.2d 446, 454 (N.D.Ohio 1998).

42. See text accompanying notes 9–11 supra.

43. See text accompanying notes 15–18 supra.

44. See text accompanying note 2 supra.

45. See text accompanying notes 24–26 supra.

46. I am grateful to Cris Carmody for a suggestion leading to this observation.

potential availability of punitive damages provides extra deterrent effect in the case of batteries that include a purpose to do harm.

● A moral feature of the battery tort becomes strikingly evident in situations in which the defendant is relatively innocent, at least as to the unforeseen consequences of his or her act. An example is the case in which a "friendly hug" caused paralysis to the person who was hugged.[47] Many people might be inclined to regard the paralysis as literally "accidental," and not proper grounds for a holding that the defendant has committed a civil wrong. And, as noted, the Florida Supreme Court viewed the proper classification of the case as negligence. Yet the defendant, although subjectively intending no harm, deliberately engaged in conduct that was against the wishes of the plaintiff and that violated at least developing social rules. As between the parties, a rule-breaking actor who acts intentionally and an entirely innocent person who suffers harm, the characterization of conduct as an intentional tort arguably would achieve justice.

By imposing liability for battery, decisions like *Vosburg* and *Garratt* teach an interesting lesson about the meaning of fault in tort law. Forced to make a choice between vexing alternatives—to call a subjectively innocent act a battery or to leave its completely faultless, injured target uncompensated—courts have opted to require compensation from the actor. They do so even though the actor's moral blameworthiness for the precise result would not justify the kind of community condemnation that would attach to acts like the brutal beating that is the ordinary connotation of the term "battery."

47. See text accompanying notes 24–26 supra.

Chapter Eight

INTRUSION

Analysis

¶ 8.01   Definition

The developing tort of intrusion, sometimes classified under the more general label of "invasion of privacy," represents a judicial effort to define personal spheres or zones that the law deems off limits to others. The key elements of the tort, which may vary somewhat from jurisdiction to jurisdiction, include the following: (1) intentional conduct that (2) intrudes upon (3) a sphere or zone of privacy in (4) a way that the law deems especially offensive.

The concepts of intrusion, a defined sphere of privacy, and culpable offensiveness are linked together. We specifically discuss methods of intrusion below.[1] With respect to the nature of the sphere of personal life that is protected, courts have often referred to a landmark article by Louis Brandeis and Samuel Warren that spoke of a right of every person to "determin[e], ordinarily, to what extent his thoughts, sentiments and emotions shall be communicated to others."[2] In a more slangy modern version, this appears to have become transmuted into notions of private "space," which may refer as much to psychological territory as to real estate.[3]

A principal battleground of the intrusion tort, focusing on the question of whether the defendant's conduct was so offensive that it should occasion tort liability, involves assessment of the social

---

1. See ¶ 8.02 infra.

2. Louis D. Brandeis & Samuel Warren, The Right to Privacy, 4 Harv. L. Rev. 193, 198 (!890).

3. See, e.g., Carter v. Innisfree Hotel, 661 So.2d 1174, 1178 (Ala.1995) ("Peeping Tom" spied on sexual intercourse through one-way mirror in de-fendant's hotel; reversing summary judgment for defendant, court refers to "intrusion upon a physical space, such as a trespass, or by an invasion of one's 'emotional sanctum,' "and says that the "law prohibits a wrongful intrusion into either of these areas of privacy").

acceptability of the acts at issue. An important dictum emphasizes that the defendant must be seeking information about the plaintiff "by improperly intrusive means."[4] Judgments about what is "improperly intrusive" may be highly subjective; one person's courting may be another person's stalking. The Restatement, in an effort to establish an objective standard, speaks of an intrusion that "would be highly offensive to a reasonable person."[5] Other authorities speak of the defendant using "improper means" to gather information[6] or emphasize that the defendant's conduct lacked "social or economic excuse or justification."[7] Language of this sort provides a rather flexible standard for courts to employ in capturing society's definition of the protected sphere and also its revulsion at certain kinds of conduct.

As to the intent element, it may be difficult in practice to distinguish the intention to commit an act the consequence of which is to fulfill the other elements of the tort—that is to intrude on a sphere of privacy in a way that is in fact offensive—from an intention to do something offensive. The basic definition of intention in the intentional torts requires that the defendant intend an act that violated a norm.[8] The case law on intrusion does not focus on this problem, but one might expect courts to straddle the issue. While they might focus on the question of whether the defendant's act in fact was offensive, they might require a showing of some knowledge by the defendant that his behavior was a serious violation of standards of decent conduct.

¶ 8.02   Methods of Intrusion

There are many ways in which one may intrude upon the privacy of another. One of the most clearcut, from a legal point of view, is through electronic means, for example, by wiretapping or by electronic eavesdropping. These were among the methods condemned in a suit against officials of the National Security Agency by the famous pediatrician-author, Dr. Benjamin Spock. The court rejected the defendant's motion to dismiss on Spock's allegations of "interception of . . . oral, wire, telephone and telegraph communications."[9] Given that phone tapping is an obvious form of intrusion, one may argue that a logical analogue of that rule is to make harassing phone calls an actionable invasion. Taking that position in a leading case, a concurring judge situated the defendant's

---

4. Pearson v. Dodd, 410 F.2d 701, 704 (D.C.Cir.1969) (dictum).

5. Restatement (Second) of Torts § 652B (1977).

6. Nader v. General Motors Corp., 255 N.E.2d 765, 769 (N.Y.1970) (characterizing precedents).

7. Id. at 772 (Breitel, J., concurring).

8. See supra, ¶ 7.01(C)-(F).

9. Spock v. United States, 464 F.Supp. 510, 512 (S.D.N.Y.1978).

harassing calls in the context of the plaintiff's allegations about other offensive acts.[10]

One also may interfere with another's privacy rights by frequent movements near and around the plaintiff with the intention of gathering information. The Second Circuit upheld an unusual grant of injunctive relief against a photographer who annoyingly took pictures of Jacqueline Kennedy Onassis and her children in all kinds of settings. For example, the defendant "jumped and postured around while taking pictures" of a party that Ms. Onassis gave at a theater opening, and he jumped out into the path of her son, John F. Kennedy Jr., as he rode his bicycle in Central Park. Referring to the trial court's finding that the defendant had "insinuated himself into the very fabric of Ms. Onassis' life," the appellate court concluded that injunctive relief was "sustainable under New York's proscription of harassment."[11] This 1973 decision provides an interesting American sidelight to the circumstances surrounding the death of Princess Diana in France in 1997.

The developing criminal statutory prohibition of conduct described as "shadowing" and "stalking" finds some reflection in intrusion-type privacy law. In an opinion that was otherwise relatively restrictive, the New York Court of Appeals declared that "surveillance may be so 'overzealous' as to render it actionable."[12] The occasion was a case in which Ralph Nader claimed that General Motors had "kept him under surveillance in public places for an unreasonable length of time."

In another case of stalking-type behavior, where the stalker's apparent motive was specifically to annoy rather than to get information, the plaintiff had broken off a "brief extra-marital affair" with the defendant. Angry, the defendant would appear several mornings a week at the plaintiff's home when he went to work, often turned up at his office when he went to lunch, and would follow him when he went out with his family. The defendant made "sexually vulgar remarks" to the plaintiff in settings where they could be overheard by others and delivered to him "numerous unwanted letters, cards and gifts." In affirming an award of money damages and injunctive relief for the plaintiff, the court rejected the defendant's argument that she was justified because the plaintiff's "own sexual immorality made him unworthy of judicial relief."[13]

10. Nader, supra note 6, 255 N.E.2d at 772 (Breitel, J., concurring).

11. Galella v. Onassis, 487 F.2d 986, 992–95 (2d Cir.1973).

12. Nader, supra note 6, 255 N.E.2d at 771.

13. Kramer v. Downey, 680 S.W.2d 524, 525–26 (Tex.Ct.App.1984). For a decision that rejects a civil claim for stalking but holds that the plaintiff was entitled to go to the jury on an intrusion theory, see Troncalli v. Jones, 514 S.E.2d 478 (Ga.Ct.App.1999). The case

Another defendant allegedly intruded on a plaintiff's privacy by taking his discarded body tissue. In that case, the Kansas court approved, at least in principle, a suit against a woman who hired a hospital orderly to get hair from the plaintiff's brush and bandage in an effort to establish, for purposes of litigation, that the plaintiff and her then husband were lovers.[14]

Although law enforcement officers have a broader warrant than private citizens to intrude on people's privacy, there are limits. Illustrative is a holding denying summary judgment to a male parole officer who claimed qualified immunity for his direct observation of a female parolee giving a urine sample. In this constitutional tort case based on a theory of unreasonable search, the court said that there was a fact issue as to whether the defendant's conduct violated the plaintiff's "established constitutional right to bodily privacy." The court invoked a department of corrections regulation saying that "[a]ll unclothed searches will be performed by ... correctional officers of the same sex as the inmate and in a place providing privacy."[15]

---

involves unwanted physical contact—the touching of the plaintiff's breasts at a party—that also could well have qualified as a battery. Following the party, the defendant closely followed the plaintiff's car, for example by speeding when she speeded up and following her through a parking lot. The next night at a meeting he put his mouth on her neck and told her "she had better be careful because someone might be watching her." The appellate court refuses to find a tort of stalking, on which the trial court based an explicit charge on a criminal stalking statute. However, the appellate court concludes that the evidence showed actions by the defendant that "were an unreasonable, offensive intrusion into [the plaintiff's] seclusion and solitude," id. at 482, and it also finds that she stated a claim for intentional infliction of emotional distress, id. at 482–83.

For other discussion of stalking, see supra, ¶ 6.01(C), text accompanying notes 9–10.

14. Froelich v. Adair, 516 P.2d 993 (Kan.1973) (reversing defendant's judg-

ment because trial judge did not make findings of fact).

15. Sepulveda v. Ramirez, 967 F.2d 1413 (9th Cir.1992). The social balancing will change with different facts and legal contexts—for example, outside the realm of tort and tort-type suits when the plaintiff challenges a regulatory safety rule as impinging on privacy. Illustrative is a holding that a state racing board may require jockeys and others who participate closely in horse racing to give urine samples when a representative of the board is "standing by," although "not actually watching the individual urinate." The court identifies as factors supporting the regulation the physical risks that racing creates for persons in the vicinity of the track and the potential harm to state revenues if a belief that races are fixed causes the public to stop betting. Finding that these concerns outweigh "the very limited privacy interest" of the participants, the court concludes that the regulation does not violate the Fourth Amendment prohibition on unreasonable searches. Dimeo v. Griffin, 943 F.2d 679, 683–85 (7th Cir.1991).

¶ 8.03 Policies

A. Interests protected

The intrusion doctrine deals with a fascinating variety of interests, and there are many ways to characterize the basis for plaintiffs' claims. At an abstract level, the tort protects dignity and personhood. More concretely, courts may focus on property interests, although analysts have distinguished from the intrusion tort a separate "appropriation" tort. That theory permits a person to sue when the defendant in effect takes a valuable commercial right, as in the case where the defendant uses the plaintiff's photograph without his or her permission.[16] A New York civil rights statute, originally enacted in 1903, creates a cause of action for "us[ing] for advertising purposes, or for the purposes of trade, the name, portrait or picture of any living person without" obtaining consent.[17] The intrusion tort goes into less concretely definable territory than the appropriation tort, although those who view the world in strictly economic terms may view the cause of action for intrusion as arising principally from the premise that people have property rights in their most intimate secrets and their most private space.

Courts also might apply a utilitarian principle to intrusion claims, asking whether the social benefits of the intrusive conduct outweigh the harm to the plaintiff.

B. Balancing

The utilitarian analysis of the intrusion tort leads to a fundamental generalization that recurs throughout the law of torts. This is that, in deciding whether a tort has been committed, the court must balance various interests, sometimes rating individual interests as paramount but often preferring social interests to individual ones. A rather stark example illustrates where courts will draw the line in favor of individual interests. This is the case of reporters who wiretap or use other means of electronic eavesdropping to acquire information about politically important people. It might provide significant informational benefits to the political process if the law refused to permit tort suits for that type of prying. However, courts are likely to award damages in such cases—even without reference to the statutory prohibitions on such conduct— because they consider the individual interests that are harmed, taking into account the unquantifiable social costs of the invasion,

---

16. See infra, ¶ 69.04.

17. Civ. Rights Law §§ 50, 51 (McKinney 1992). The decision that inspired passage of the statute was Rober-son v. Rochester Folding Box Co., 64 N.E. 442 (N.Y.1902) (denying recovery where defendant placed plaintiff's likeness on advertising material for flour).

to be more important than the social gains that may accrue from the defendant's conduct.

By comparison, courts are likely to be relatively lenient to those who interview others about the personality and activities of a third party in order to get information about his character and points of view, even if the third party would prefer not to have that information publicized.[18] In those cases, courts may at least implicitly reason that the social gains from the acquisition of information by relatively benign investigative techniques justify the losses to the individual, and the attendant social costs.

However one would decide any of these types of cases, it is clear that in such litigation, courts make qualitative judgments. It will often be difficult to fit such assessments within the arithmetic of utilitarianism because of the difficulty of placing quantitative valuations on the interests of the parties in intrusion cases. It is relatively difficult to put a price tag on plaintiffs' privacy, or on the value of public information provided by defendants. One may contrast the more easily monetized interests on both sides in most tort litigation: on the plaintiff's side, such staples of personal injury damages as lost wages and medical bills, and on the defendant's side, the costs of making repairs or changing product designs that liability rules may effectively impose. Thus, whether courts focus on the breadth of the plaintiff's "sphere" of "privacy," or on the offensiveness or impropriety of the defendant's conduct, they are making judgments that are more social than economic when they decide whether conduct is tortiously intrusive.

[Chapter 9 is reserved for supplementary material.]

---

18. *See, e.g.*, Nader, supra note 6, 255 N.E.2d at 770 (refusing to find cause of action on this specific allegation). See also, e.g., Dopp v. Fairfax Consultants, 771 F.Supp. 494, 497 (D.P.R.1990)(complaint that charges no more than that "defendants conducted 'a thorough investigation of [the plaintiff's] business, personal and family affairs' " alleges behavior that is "in and of itself ... not a wrongful act." Cf. Sidis v. F–R Pub. Corp., 113 F.2d 806 (2d Cir.1940) (interview with plaintiff).

Chapter Ten

FALSE IMPRISONMENT

Analysis

The tort of false imprisonment obviously applies to certain acts of public law enforcement officials and to similar acts of private security personnel, but it also may arise in a variety of informal settings, including encounters between people who know each other well. A short working definition of false imprisonment is an (1) intentional, (2) unconsented and unprivileged (3) confinement of another, (4) who either knows of the confinement or is harmed by it.

¶ 10.01   Intended Act

The tort requires an intentional act on the part of the defendant. In line with the intent element of such other intentional torts as battery, the action for false imprisonment requires only that the defendant intended to confine the plaintiff, rather than that he intended to act unlawfully. Thus, one court rejected the argument of a sheriff and a county that their holding of the plaintiff in a detention center for 114 days was not a false imprisonment because the plaintiff had not shown that "they intended to confine [him] wrongfully." The court reasoned that to accept the defendants' argument "would condone wrongful confinement of undetermined length provided that the defendant, while intending to commit the acts that restrain plaintiff's freedom, does not intend *unlawful* confinement."[1]

The same decision indicated that the plaintiff could establish intent by showing the defendants' "deliberate indifference" to his

---

1. Oviatt v. Pearce, 954 F.2d 1470, 1479 (9th Cir.1992).

"right to freedom from prolonged incarceration" because they did not provide procedures to insure a "prompt pretrial court appearance." Rationalizing that conclusion, the court referred to the defendants' maintenance of "a policy that ... did not detect a misarraignment," which it characterized as "tantamount to an intent to confine those individuals who have a right to be released."[2]

¶ 10.02   Lack of Consent and Privilege

As is so with the intentional torts generally, false imprisonment requires a showing that the defendant acted without consent or privilege. Some authorities classify consent under the general heading of privilege,[3] but this text generally views privilege as socially conferred, and consent as a permission personally given.[4] In practice, the privilege issue in false imprisonment typically arises from the question of whether a confinement is an appropriate means of public or private law enforcement. Thus, the element of unlawfulness directly enters false imprisonment cases under the heading of lack of privilege. Indeed, the fact that a detention is in violation of legal rules—for example, those rules prohibiting unlawful arrests—may effectively make it an unprivileged act.

A modern example of lack of police privilege appears in a Missouri case in which security guards at a university arrested and handcuffed a doctor employed at the university hospital who was not carrying identification. When his identity was established, the handcuffs were removed. However, when he asserted that one of the officers had assaulted him, that officer handcuffed him again— explaining later that he wanted to "have a report on the incident." The result was that the doctor was held in jail for 12 hours. Concluding that "the re-arrest amounted to a false and self-serving restraint," the appellate court reversed a judgment n.o.v. for the officers, saying that a jury could have found that the doctor "was subject to confinement without justification when re-handcuffed, arrested and held in jail overnight."[5]

Illustrative of the privilege of private persons to confine is a case in which a psychiatric patient "rant[ed] and rav[ed]" in a confrontation with nurses and was said to "appear[] totally out of control" and to have become "a threat to the safety of herself and others." The court rejected her claim that she was falsely imprisoned when hospital personnel placed her in seclusion. Pointing out

---

2. Id. at 1480.

3. See, e.g., Restatement (Second) of Torts § 10(2)(a) (1965) [hereafter, "Restatement (Second)"] (privilege may be "based upon ... the consent of the other affected by the actor's conduct").

4. See supra, ¶ 7.01(B)-(C).

5. Desai v. SSM Health Care, 865 S.W.2d 833 (Mo.Ct.App.1993).

that the plaintiff had voluntarily signed a form consenting to treatment, the court noted that "[c]onfinement in a secured environment is a common method of treatment in psychiatric wards and Hospitals."[6]

¶ 10.03 Confinement

We may introduce the confinement element of false imprisonment with the story of the sentimental visitor to a prison who told an inmate, "remember, stone walls do not a prison make, nor iron bars a cage." The prisoner's response was, "maybe not, but they sure help." The confinement element requires that the plaintiff be confined completely "within ... boundaries fixed by the actor."[7] The definition is a rather straightforward one, clearly embracing contexts ranging from prisons to locked rooms. It may even include, less obviously, someone throwing another's luggage in his car, thus effectively requiring the other to get in the car and come along in order not to lose the luggage.[8]

Confinement, however, does not include exclusion from a place. Thus, it is not a false imprisonment to bar access to a club, bar, or motel. Of course, that may be a statutory wrong—for example, a violation of a civil rights law—but it simply is not false imprisonment.

¶ 10.04 Methods of Confinement

A confinement that constitutes a false imprisonment may occur through different types of conduct, including threat, force, duress or arrest. Assault-type false imprisonment arises from a threat of physical force of the sort that often is at the heart of the assault tort.[9] In parallel fashion, the use of physical restraint to confine someone would be a battery-type false imprisonment. As is evident from the example above of the defendant putting the plaintiff's luggage in a car,[10] duress represents another means of confining someone in boundaries fixed by the actor.[11] Perhaps most obviously, arrest-type false imprisonment is "taking a person into custody under an asserted legal authority," which includes the authority of a police officer. The Restatement deems the custody to be "complete if the person against whom and in whose presence the authority is asserted believes it to be valid, or is in doubt as to its validity, and submits to it."[12]

6. Morgan v. Greenwaldt, 786 So.2d 1037, 1042–43 (Miss.2001).

7. Restatement (Second) § 36(1) (1965).

8. Griffin v. Clark, 42 P.2d 297, 299 (Idaho 1935).

9. See Restatement (Second) § 40.

10. See supra, ¶ 10.03, text accompanying note 8.

11. Id. § 40A.

12. Id. § 41.

¶ 10.05　Knowledge of Confinement or Harm

Under the modern view, the plaintiff must either know of the confinement or be "harmed by it."[13] The requirement of knowledge of confinement, which under prior law was the sole grounds on which a plaintiff could proceed,[14] is clear enough. The law has now developed to the point that some courts allow false imprisonment actions where the plaintiff suffers harm although he does not know of his confinement, and perhaps even where the confinement creates only a serious risk of physical harm. In a type of case likely to present those issues, police arrest an epileptic, or a diabetic, and put him in jail without legal reason at a time when the confined person is not aware that he is confined. In one such case, involving a diabetic who was having an insulin reaction, the court referred to testimony about the probability that the imprisonment caused brain damage, while emphasizing that the defendant city had a duty to release the plaintiff "because of the extreme danger to [his] health attendant upon lack of immediate care."[15] The result seems eminently reasonable. It would seem equally appropriate to impose liability for false imprisonment when the plaintiff suffered harm after a confinement of which he was unaware by virtue of humiliation from learning of the confinement.[16]

¶ 10.06　Constitutional Dimensions

Beyond common law suits for false imprisonment, the detention of persons against their will now has a constitutional dimension, in cases where that confinement occurs from a violation of due process. An illustration of due process rights that may be violated by confinement appears in a case of a woman who, from the age of 15, was held for 30 years in an institution for care of the mentally retarded. The court concluded that she had "been deprived of her liberty to be free from commitment without procedural due process," because "she was never afforded a hearing before *any* decision maker with authority to resolve her dispute with those who were confining her."[17] The court also affirmed a holding that the plaintiff's confinement, despite "unanimous professional opin-

---

13. Id. § 42.

14. Restatement of Torts §§ 35(1)(b), 42 (1934).

15. Tufte v. City of Tacoma, 431 P.2d 183, 187 (Wash.1967).

16. See, e.g., Donald Cohen, False Imprisonment: A Reexamination of the Necessity for Awareness of Confinement, 43 Tenn. L. Rev. 109, 115–116 (1975) (arguing that confinement, even without awareness or probable present

harm, is an "affront[] to personal security" and the infliction of an indignity). But cf. Restatement (Second) § 42, comment a (a claimant's "mere dignitary interest in being free from an interference with his personal liberty which he has only discovered later is not of sufficient importance to justify the recovery of the nominal damages involved").

17. Clark v. Cohen, 794 F.2d 79, 86 (3d Cir.1986).

ion that she should be placed in a far less restrictive environment," "violated her substantive liberty right to appropriate treatment."[18]

¶ 10.07 Interests and Rationales

The false imprisonment tort protects the interest of persons to go freely through the world, subject to legal restrictions on their entry into particular places. This interest in physical freedom has a corresponding foundation in personal dignity, an interest that receives protection from all of the intentional tort categories.

Further support for the false imprisonment tort appears in the theory of deterrence. Particularly in cases involving defendants like public officers or employees of business establishments, the threat of money damages provides a measure of behavior control. A correlative of this point, which also applies to the other intentional torts, is that the existence of a legal remedy presumably would reduce the inclination to engage in self-help of people who believe their dignity has been offended.

The principal policies at issue in cases involving claims of false imprisonment are rather clear. On the one hand, the law aims to maximize freedom of movement on the part of all citizens. On the other hand, society also needs the stability—"law and order"—that can only be achieved by an appropriate level of law enforcement. Moreover, while seeking to enhance personal freedom of movement, the law protects the freedoms inherent in property rights. Thus, under certain conditions, it may allow merchants to detain persons suspected of theft by means of conduct that otherwise would be deemed false imprisonment. Both of these interests—in social stability and property rights—derive protection from the privileges to arrest and detain that provide defenses against false imprisonment actions. We discuss these privileges below.[19]

18. Id. at 87.

19. See infra, Chapter 11, and ¶ 16.04.

Chapter Eleven

FALSE ARREST

Analysis

¶ 11.01 General Definition

False arrest is a tort category that applies to "an unlawful assertion of police authority over a person resulting in a restraint on his liberty."[1] Actions for false arrest often are twinned with claims for false imprisonment, of which the gist is an unprivileged confinement.[2] Indeed, allegedly false arrests are likely to involve confinements of the plaintiff against his or her will.

There may, however, be a false imprisonment without a false arrest, for example, a merchant may unreasonably detain a customer without asserting police authority. Moreover, one who is legally arrested might claim false imprisonment if he or she is held for an unreasonable period of time without being brought before a magistrate.

¶ 11.02 Specific Rules

The law of false arrest in state courts will vary with specific state rules, typically statutory rules, on the privilege to arrest. The arrest rules depend significantly on the severity of the plaintiff's claimed offense, on whether the arresting officers have a warrant, and on the reasonable beliefs of the officers. Some illustrative examples of state rules are these:

1) Police may arrest a suspected felon without a warrant when a felony actually has occurred and the officer has reasonable cause to believe that the arrestee was the perpetrator.

---

1. Satter & Kalom, False Arrest: Compensation and Deterrence, 43 Conn. B.J. 598, 600 (1969).

2. See generally Chapter 10.

2) An officer may arrest without a warrant for a misdemeanor that was committed in his or her presence. Some states may allow a warrantless arrest when the officer has reason to believe that the arrestee committed a misdemeanor in his or her presence, although the arrestee's conduct did not in fact constitute a misdemeanor.

¶ 11.03 Section 1983

The great body of law developed under 42 U.S.C. section 1983, which allows private persons to sue state and local officials for violations of constitutional rights, is a principal modern source of rules governing suits for alleged police misconduct in making arrests as well as other police misfeasance. The decisions reflect the tensions between the liberty interest of arrestees and society's interest in order.

An especially serious issue under section 1983, analogous to the constitutionalized law of false arrest under that statute, concerns police use of deadly force to stop a fleeing person who allegedly has committed a felony. The Supreme Court's decision under section 1983 in *Tennessee v. Garner*[3] illustrates how constitutional law—in particular the constitutional right against unreasonable search and seizure—provides an extra layer of law upon tort doctrine. A police officer, summoned on a "prowler inside call," fatally shot a teenage boy who was fleeing the scene in a situation in which the officer was "reasonably sure" that the boy was not armed. Under state law, the action would have been legal, for a state statute permitted officers to "use all the necessary means to effect [an] arrest" if the suspect fled after the officer gave notice of his "intention to arrest."

Upholding a suit for the boy's death, Justice White's opinion for a divided Court analyzed the case as one involving a "seizure" of the person under the Fourth Amendment's prohibition of unreasonable searches and seizures. The Court concluded that the state statute was unconstitutional insofar as it permitted the officer to shoot the fleeing suspect. Effectively, the Court enforced a rule that forbade the use of deadly force against an unarmed, fleeing felony suspect concerning whom an officer had no probable cause to believe that he "posed any physical danger to himself or others."[4]

The Court did not simply lay down a hornbook rule; rather, it made a value judgment about the social benefit of the officer's conduct, saying that it was "not convinced that the use of deadly force is a sufficiently productive means" of accomplishing the goal of reducing violence in society "to justify the killing of nonviolent

---

3. 471 U.S. 1 (1985).   **4.** Id. at 21.

suspects."[5] Justice O'Connor's dissent characterized the case much differently, declaring that there was no Fourth Amendment right "allowing a burglary suspect to flee unimpeded from a police officer who has probable cause to arrest."[6] Besides opining that statutes like the Tennessee statute at issue "assist the police in apprehending suspected perpetrators of serious crimes," she adduced statistics indicating that burglaries entailed substantial numbers of crimes against the person.[7]

In its section 1983 setting, *Garner* provides a powerful example of judicial use of competing social rationales that also underlie the common law rules on false arrest. In less emotionally charged contexts, involving misdemeanors as well as felonies, courts also refer, implicitly as well as explicitly, to the same competing values. Illustrative is a section 1983 case in which an officer investigating a hit and run gained admission to an apartment where he had reason to believe the offender might be. Having made known the purpose of his investigation to several people in the apartment, who had been drinking all day and were creating an "antagonistic clamor," he arrested them. One of the arrestees sued, claiming that the arresting officer had violated several of her constitutional rights, including her right to freedom of assembly and her right to be free from unreasonable search and seizure. In dismissing the action, which it labeled in part as a "false arrest claim," a Louisiana federal court approvingly quoted the officer's description of the facts: "[A] drunk in an apartment resenting police is a different drunk to a Mardi Gras drunk."[8] This colorful characterization, effectively justifying a privilege to arrest people whose unruliness threatens the process of law enforcement, indicates how courts sometimes will make rulings of law that reflect an overriding interest in social order.

¶ 11.04 Social Goals, Behavioral Assumptions and Normative Premises

As the discussion above makes clear, the law of false arrest provides a highly focused example of the need for judges to identify the goals of decisionmaking—for example, goals related to individual justice or to encouraging or discouraging particular kinds of conduct—as well as their own behavioral assumptions and philosophical premises.[9] In false arrest cases, most courts will concern themselves, at least in part, with the parallel goals of reducing

5. Id. at 10.

6. Id. at 23 (O'Connor, J., dissenting).

7. Id. at 27–28.

8. Lynn v. City of New Orleans Dep't of Police, 567 F.Supp. 761, 765 (E.D.La.1983).

9. For a brief general discussion of the rationales of tort law, see supra, ¶ 1.04.

crime and reducing lawless police behavior. Judges that focus on these goals may wish to know social statistics concerning the incidence of the crime at issue and the rate of arrest. Besides examining the relevant statutory law and analogous legislation from other jurisdictions, they also may consider custom among law enforcement agencies with respect to the sort of conduct that is challenged. Finally, when goals are in tension and social statistics are in conflict or nonexistent, courts should clarify their policy preferences, taking account of a professional tradition that urges judges to constrain themselves severely in making judgments based on their own biases. Identifying those preferences as they strive for detachment in decisionmaking, they will be conscious that placing higher valuations on "individual liberty" or on "social order" are likely to influence them in one direction or another in close cases of alleged false arrest.

[Chapter 12 is reserved for supplementary material.]

Chapter Thirteen

INTENTIONAL INFLICTION OF EMOTIONAL DISTRESS

Analysis

¶ 13.01 Introduction

The bedrock of tort law protection for human dignity lies in the traditional intentional torts of assault, battery and false imprisonment. The assault tort, in particular, vindicates the emotional interest in being free from apprehension of a harmful or offensive physical conduct. However, increased understanding in the twentieth century of the realities of emotional life, and perhaps a more aspirational attitude on the part of courts, led to a belief at mid-century that the law should give further protection to emotional interests than the traditional theories provided.

The law had in fact been doing this for a generation and more, without placing particular doctrinal labels on results. For example, in various jurisdictions, courts granted recovery for emotional distress caused by extremely culpable conduct on the part of bill collectors. Other courts permitted recovery for anguish caused by the mishandling of dead bodies. With these and other decisions in mind, Dean Prosser ventured a synthesis of case law that would give recovery for a tort defined as "intentional infliction of emotional distress." His initial article on the subject[1] led to a Restate-

---

1. William L. Prosser, Intentional Infliction of Mental Suffering: A New Tort, 37 Mich. L. Rev. 874 (1939).

ment section, discussed just below. The tort has now won almost universal acceptance among American courts.[2]

¶ 13.02   Elements

Section 46 of the Second Restatement of Torts defines the tort of intentional infliction of emotional distress to include three basic elements: (1) extreme and outrageous conduct that (2) intentionally or recklessly (3) causes severe emotional distress.[3]

These elements—particularly the intentionality element and that of outrageous conduct—tend to blend together.[4] However, it is useful to begin analysis by examining them separately, first focusing on the culpability standard of intentional or reckless conduct.

A. *Intentional or reckless*

The Restatement's culpability requirement begins with intentional conduct, but it effectively lowers the barrier of intentionality to the point that a showing of recklessness is also sufficient to make a claim. One court has interpreted the disjunctive use of "intentionally or recklessly" this way: "[t]he interdicted conduct itself must be 'intentional,' that is purposeful, willful, or wanton. What is more, the harm that results must also be 'intentional,' that is, it must have been intended or [at] least recklessly caused."[5] The most sympathetic interpretation of the standard, from the plaintiff's point of view, is that it does not require the plaintiff to show that the defendant knew that severe emotional distress was at least substantially certain to follow from the defendant's act, but rather requires only that the defendant acted with conscious disregard of " 'a high degree of probability that the mental distress will follow.' "[6]

B. *Severe emotional distress*

The requirement that a plaintiff must show severe emotional distress essentially presents a fact question, although courts may decide in some cases that a plaintiff has been so unconvincing on the point that he has not made a case strong enough to go to the jury. One index to a persuasive showing of severe emotional distress is medical testimony, or at least evidence of physician consul-

2. See, e.g., Twyman v. Twyman, 855 S.W.2d 619, 621–22 (Tex.1993) (making Texas "the forty-seventh state to adopt the tort").

3. Restatement (Second) of Torts § 46 (1965) [hereafter, Restatement].

4. See Daniel Givelber, The Right to Minimum Social Decency and the Limits of Evenhandedness: Intentional Infliction of Emotional Distress by Outrageous Conduct, 82 Colum. L. Rev. 42, 46–49 (1982).

5. Russell v. Salve Regina College, 649 F.Supp. 391, 401 (D.R.I.1986).

6. Id. (referring to W. Prosser and W. P. Keeton, The Law of Torts, § 12 at 64 (5th ed. 1984)).

tations. In one decision denying recovery, the court observed that the plaintiff had not sought a physician after the events in question, which stemmed from a termination of employment, and that indeed her only interview with a psychiatrist had occurred in preparation for trial. Moreover, the court noted that the psychiatrist had testified only to "limited distress" that "was temporary at best, for perhaps a period of seven months." Saying that "temporary discomfort cannot be the basis for recovery," and concluding as well that the defendant employer's conduct was not outrageous, the court held that the plaintiff's claim was frivolous.[7]

One should emphasize that even though a defendant may engage in conduct that is plainly outrageous, a lack of evidence of severe distress will defeat an action. In another case, a hotel bartender used a racial epithet to a patron and forcefully escorted him out of the bar. The plaintiff testified that the incident had caused feelings of alienation, and the court said that the use of the epithet was undoubtedly outrageous. However, the court denied the claim, noting that the plaintiff had not received treatment by a doctor or psychologist.[8]

C. *Extreme and outrageous*

The requirement that the defendant's conduct be "extreme and outrageous" lies at the heart of the tort, and it presents significant conceptual difficulties, for outrageousness is in the eye of the beholder. Still, courts and commentators have sought to define the standard in a way that judges can apply it to concrete cases.

If there is a separate conception of "extreme" behavior in the pairing "extreme and outrageous," it appears in comment d to section 46. That comment speaks of conduct that "go[es] beyond all possible bounds of decency, and [is] regarded as atrocious, and utterly intolerable in a civilized community."[9]

The concept of outrageousness appears to be the dominant one of the pair. Comment d explains the outrageousness standard by saying that "[g]enerally, the case is one in which the recitation of the facts to an average member of the community would arouse his resentment against the actor, and lead him to exclaim, 'outrageous!' "[10] This explanation poses a conundrum. Its reference to "the average member of the community" seems to indicate that outrageousness is essentially an issue for the jury. However, the breadth of the concept—and its reliance on a kind of emotional

---

7. Braski v. Ah–Ne–Pee Dimensional Hardwood, Inc., 630 F.Supp. 862, 866 (W.D.Wis.1986).

8. Jones v. City of Boston, 738 F.Supp. 604, 607 (D.Mass.1990).

9. Restatement, § 46, comment d.

10. Id.

judgment—makes it especially important for the court to exercise control over the determination of whether conduct was outrageous.

Thus, as a practical matter, courts will not rely solely on how "average member[s] of the community"—that is, jurors—respond to a recitation of the facts. Instead, courts will make an independent judgment that embodies both social and legal values, deciding whether, in current culture, the lay person's reaction of outrage provides an appropriate basis for judicial intervention.

An interesting difference of opinion as to what is outrageous appears in a case involving an obese nursing student, who claimed that college faculty members humiliated her during her training by, for example, using her to "model hospital procedures incident to the care of obese patients." Denying the college's motion for summary judgment, a federal district judge analyzed the college's acts with emphasis on "the trust implicit in the student's selection of a college, and the peculiar vulnerability of undergraduates." He concluded that the jury could have found the behavior of the defendant's employees to be "so atrocious as to be actionable."[11] However, holding for the college on review, after another district judge granted a directed verdict for the college on the plaintiff's intentional infliction claim, the court of appeals emphasized the "amorphous" character of the "extreme and outrageous" standard. The appellate court said that "[t]he College's conduct may have been unprofessional, but we cannot say that it was so far removed from the bounds of civilization as not to comply with the test set forth in § 46."[12]

Analysis reveals a group of factors that bear on judicial determination of whether "outrage" claims should go to a jury. One of those factors, as suggested by the district judge's opinion in the case of the obese nursing student, is the vulnerability of the plaintiff. Often correlated with that element, and frequently stimulating judicial hospitality to claims of outrage, is the transactional superiority of the defendant in the particular setting. Courts appear to respond to the kind of situation in which the defendant has seriously overreached a plaintiff over whom the defendant exercises power, by engaging in behavior that would be regarded as reprehensible by most persons.

A definable class of conduct that courts recently have become inclined to regard as outrageous, embodying elements of both superiority and vulnerability, is sexual harassment in the employment context. An early version of the elements of such an action under the intentional infliction tort refers to a pattern of conduct

---

11. Russell v. Salve Regina College, 649 F.Supp. 391, 402 (D.R.I.1986).

12. Russell v. Salve Regina College, 890 F.2d 484, 488 (1st Cir.1989), rev'd on other grounds, 499 U.S. 225 (1991).

that includes "a continued course of sexual advances, followed by refusals and ultimately, retaliation."[13]

Courts have now developed two different concepts of sexual harassment under Title VII of the Civil Rights Act of 1964, both of which have analogues in the torts of assault and battery as well as intentional infliction of emotional distress. One of these civil rights theories, represented by the torts decision just quoted, is the "quid pro quo" theory, under which the plaintiff must show that the defendant tried to trade advantages in employment for sexual favors.[14] The other is the "hostile environment" concept, under which the Supreme Court has articulated a test of "severe or pervasive" harassment[15] that creates an environment that would "reasonably be perceived, and is perceived, as hostile and abusive."[16]

The Court later extended the basis for sexual harassment claims by employees to impose vicarious liability on employers for "an actionable hostile environment created by a supervisor." The Court allowed no defense to this form of liability without fault when the harassment led to a "tangible employment action, such as discharge, demotion, or undesirable reassignment." In cases where there was "no tangible employment action" against the employee, the employer could present an affirmative defense. To prove that defense, it would have to show that it had made reasonable efforts "to prevent and correct promptly any sexually harassing behavior" and that the employee "unreasonably failed to take advantage" of the employer's preventive or corrective programs or "to avoid harm otherwise."[17]

Courts are likely to give close scrutiny to common law claims for sexual harassment. A striking illustration is a case that was central to the development of a crisis involving the impeachment of a President: Paula Jones' suit against Bill Clinton, based on an episode that allegedly took place in a hotel room while Mr. Clinton was governor of Arkansas and Ms. Jones was a state employee. The essence of the allegations was that Mr. Clinton had engaged in sexually suggestive touchings and had exposed his penis to the plaintiff and asked her "to 'kiss it.' " He also allegedly invoked his friendship with the plaintiff's boss, who like the plaintiff was the governor's subordinate. However, when the plaintiff rejected his

13. Shaffer v. National Can Corp., 565 F.Supp. 909, 915 (E.D.Pa.1983).

14. See, e.g., Dockter v. Rudolf Wolff Futures, Inc., 913 F.2d 456, 461 (7th Cir.1990).

15. Meritor Savings Bank, FSB v. Vinson, 477 U.S. 57, 67 (1986).

16. Harris v. Forklift Sys., 510 U.S. 17, 22 (1993).

17. This standard, identically worded, appeared in two decisions handed down on the same day: Faragher v. City of Boca Raton, 524 U.S. 775, 806 and Burlington Indus., Inc. v. Ellerth, 524 U.S. 742, 764 (1998).

advances, he said that he did not "want to make you do anything you don't want to do," and told the plaintiff that if she got "in trouble for leaving work," she should have her boss call Mr. Clinton "immediately and I'll take care of it." In concluding that the episode fell "far short" of fulfilling the requirements of the state law tort of "outrage," a federal district court acknowledged that the plaintiff had alleged "odious" conduct. However, the court opined that the allegations "describe[] a mere sexual proposition or encounter ... that was relatively brief in duration, did not involve any coercion or threats of reprisal, and was abandoned as soon as plaintiff made clear that the advance was not welcome."[18]

A particularized question of special difficulty, because of both its implications for society at large and for judicial administration, is whether courts should allow a claim for intentional infliction by one spouse against another. A Wyoming decision that authorizes the claim reflects the tensions in the issue. The court noted the historic rationale for judicial abstention from judging marital behavior: the preservation of domestic harmony. It summarized other arguments against allowing the action, including the fear that it would "open the floodgates to a host of frivolous litigation"; a recognition of the inevitability of emotional distress, "often severe," that will attend the "intensely personal and intimate relationship" of marriage; and the concern that the "inquiry into whether a spouse's conduct is extreme and outrageous constitutes too great an intrusion into the marital relationship." Although acknowledging these concerns, the court observed that "[e]motional distress is as real and tormenting as physical pain," and declared that "psychological well-being deserves as much legal protection as physical well-being." It concluded that "[a]lthough the preservation of marital harmony is a respectable goal, behavior which is truly outrageous and results in severe emotional distress should not be protected in some sort of misguided attempt to promote marital peace." Stressing that trial courts should "be especially cautious when handling such claims," the court said that "[t]he focus of such claims must be on the element of outrageousness" and that "the scrutiny must be stringent enough so that the social good which comes from recognizing the tort in a marital setting will not

---

18. Jones v. Clinton, 990 F.Supp. 657, 677–78 (E.D.Ark.1998). The district judge in the case, although "ethically bound to remain silent" about the litigation, observed in a lecture that "[t]he potential for ambiguities" in sexual harassment cases "is nearly unlimited." She pointed out that, "[f]or example, if a man calls a woman 'honey,' he can either be expressing endearment or condescension," saying that "[t]he inten- tion of the speaker may be different from the listener's interpretation of the speaker's intent." She commented, by contrast, that "[t]his type of ambiguity or misunderstanding is not very likely in a situation of racial harassment," as when "the speaker uses a racial epithet." Susan Webber Wright, Uncertainties in the Law of Sexual Harassment, 33 U. Rich. L. Rev. 11, 30 (1999).

be undermined by an invasive flood of meritless litigation." It quoted the limitation of the tort in comment d to conduct that exceeds "all possible bounds of decency."[19]

Bill collection cases generate an ongoing fund of intentional infliction law. Illustrative of the kind of complaint that may succeed is a case in which the defendant repeatedly mailed bills marked "account referred to law and collection department," and persisted in harassing tactics after the plaintiff had a heart attack, to the point that she suffered a second heart attack.[20] One may contrast a case in which a creditor's agent erroneously sent default notices to the Federal Housing Administration, causing the agency to send foreclosure warnings to a woman whose daughter had recently died. The plaintiff claimed that the aggravation of a "nervous condition" manifested itself in the form of headaches, but the court commented that "the substance and severity of the abuse [was] not set out in the declaration" in concluding that the plaintiff had not alleged outrageous conduct.[21]

It is clear that simple nastiness will not support an intentional infliction claim.[22] Nor will an insensitively angry response to a customer's complaint that a failure to complete work on time was causing serious physical discomfort to her. That was the situation in a Wisconsin case in which a contractor started a renovation project on storm windows as the weather was getting cold and did not reinstall windows, leaving his customer with a frigid house. The plaintiff testified that the defendant had ended one conversation "by telling her that she made him 'sick'" and slammed down the receiver, but the Wisconsin Supreme Court concluded that the contractor's conduct was not "extreme and outrageous." It observed that "[a] person performing a personal service contract carries with him his own feelings of hostility and his own set of emotional pressures."[23]

D. Relationship among the elements of the tort

The applications discussed above indicate the rather complex relationship of the various elements of the tort, a complexity in the background of what has been suggested to be a judicial tendency to blend the elements together and view the tort as an integer. For example, in a case discussed above,[24] the court refused to find that

---

19. McCulloh v. Drake, 24 P.3d 1162, 1169–70 (Wyo.2001).

20. George v. Jordan Marsh Co., 268 N.E.2d 915 (Mass.1971).

21. Medlin v. Allied Investment Co., 398 S.W.2d 270, 272, 275 (Tenn.1966).

22. See, e.g., Slocum v. Food Fair Stores, 100 So.2d 396 (Fla.1958) ("[i]f you want to know the price, you'll have to find out the best way you can . . . you stink to me"; dismissal affirmed).

23. Alsteen v. Gehl, 124 N.W.2d 312, 318–19 (Wis.1963).

24. See discussion of Medlin v. Allied Investment Co., text accompanying note 21 supra.

the defendants acted outrageously in erroneously sending default notices, which triggered foreclosure warnings to which the plaintiff attributed headaches. This holding appears to fuse the requirements of outrage and severe emotional distress. Indeed, more generally, courts are likely to deny recovery in cases where the plaintiff fails to show that he required serious medical intervention—thus putting in question the severity of distress—and the defendant's conduct was a relatively routine, if mean, aspect of an established way of making a legal living, which simultaneously undermines the allegation of outrage. In another combination of elements, the case involving the storm windows[25] demonstrates that a defendant's lack of the requisite intention to cause severe distress, because his anger is a result of his own frustration, may closely overlap a judgment that he did not act outrageously. Professor Givelber argued, along these lines, that the different elements of the tort effectively "collapse" into the outrageousness factor.[26]

E. Effects on third parties

There is some law indicating that persons present when someone inflicts severe emotional distress on a family member may recover for their own severe distress that results from the incident. The Restatement allows the imposition of such liability in favor of third parties.[27] In a case that reflects increased consciousness of the problem of abuse within families, the West Virginia Supreme Court concluded that a child could recover for severe emotional distress caused by witnessing his father's verbal abuse and physical assaults on his mother.[28] In another case involving domestic violence, the Wyoming Supreme Court went so far as to say that a third party claiming intentional infliction "must simply show his 'sensory and contemporaneous observance' of the defendant's acts."[29]

F. Distressing publications

Plaintiffs face a high barrier when they sue for emotional distress caused by scurrilous publications, because of the protection afforded publishers by the First Amendment. One such case reached the Supreme Court,[30] which announced a rigorous standard for judging such actions. The plaintiff was the Reverend Jerry

25. See discussion of Alsteen v. Gehl, text accompanying note 23 supra.

26. Givelber, supra note 4, at 49.

27. Restatement § 46(2).

28. Courtney v. Courtney, 413 S.E.2d 418, 424 (W.Va.1991). See also id., 437 S.E.2d 436 (W.Va.1993) (no statute of limitations bar to mother's claim for distress on witnessing abuse of her son).

29. Bevan v. Fix, 42 P.3d 1013, 1022–24 (Wyo.2002)(child woke up to screaming and shouting attendant on beating of her mother by the defendant and remembered hearing "a bounce" when the defendant "slammed [her mother] against the wall or the floor").

30. Hustler Magazine v. Falwell, 485 U.S. 46, 56 (1988).

Falwell, who complained of a cartoon published by *Hustler* magazine as an advertising parody, which pictured him drunkenly having incestuous relations with his mother in an outhouse. Analyzing the case in light of the complex development of defamation law under the First Amendment,[31] the Court ruled that in order to recover, Falwell would have had to show that the magazine had made a false statement of fact with "actual malice"—that is, reckless disregard of the truth or falsity of the statement.[32] Although the Court opined that the cartoon was "doubtless gross and repugnant in the eyes of most,"[33] it held unanimously for the magazine. It concluded that under the First Amendment, there could be no liability for a satirical caricature that the jury had found could not reasonably be taken to " 'describ[e] actual facts about [the plaintiff] or actual events in which [he] participated.' "[34] Thus, published satire or spoofs, even if they are vicious, will not support an action for intentional infliction if the plaintiff can not identify a false factual statement.

¶ 13.03 Establishing Boundaries for a Developing Tort

A. Balancing

Judges dealing with intentional infliction cases must engage in balancing. On the one hand, they seek to vindicate the integrity of the human personality, and to bring to bear through damage awards the moral disapproval of the community regarding conduct that is judged reprehensible in particular social contexts. On the other hand, they must take into account the countervailing social interests in freedom of action and freedom of speech. In cases like the storm windows case described above,[35] the court may specifically advert to psychological pressures of the defendant's own, for example, tensions generated by his occupation. Another consideration that supports limits on the tort is the concern that a broad interpretation of "outrageousness" will encourage excessive litigation. A definition of the tort that permitted people to claim for slights and insults would burden both society and the judicial system.

B. A problem of principle

Tort law is a relatively flexible kind of law, but courts always seek to ground their decisions in principle. Given that goal, a particular puzzle posed by the intentional infliction tort lies in its

---

31. See infra, ¶ 67.01.

32. Id. at 56–57.

33. Id. at 50.

34. Id. at 57.

35. See discussion of Alsteen v. Gehl, text accompanying note 23 supra.

relative lack of principle. One commentator has sought to rationalize this phenomenon by suggesting that it is essential to the doctrine because it "provide[s] the basis for achieving situational justice."[36]

The very definition of the tort, as summarized in the blackletter language of the Restatement and in the comment that refers to reactions of outrage on the part of an average member of a community, indicates that it is, indeed, a justice-oriented doctrine. However, justice in the sense of consistency requires courts to identify the functional elements of cases that drive their decision-making.

C. Reprise: The role of the judge

These observations underline the importance of the judge's role in intentional infliction cases. The outrageousness standard, as potentially flexible as it is, demands judicial control. It requires that judges measure complaints and evidence against identifiable elements of decision. These may include generally described relations of superiority and vulnerability. They also include specific types of occurrences or patterns of behavior, such as misrepresentations of law by bill collectors, the disposal of dead bodies without consulting relatives, or a combination of sexual advances, refusals, and retaliation in sexual harassment cases.

The legal standard requires judges to employ precedent and reason in putting content into the concept of outrageousness, as well as to estimate what the actual reaction of community members would be to the conduct at issue. It also may give judges some modest leeway to identify aspirations about how a civilized community ought to react to conduct that is notably antisocial, if not criminal. But in the end, the standard demands that courts subject claims to the test of rationality.[37] The law now appropriately recognizes the reality that reprehensible conduct may cause severe emotional distress. At the same time, it must place limits on judicial meddling with the bumpings of mundane existence: the day-to-day encounters that make up the fabric of life in communities filled with persons acting in their own self-interest, responding to their own tensions, and sometimes simply blowing off steam.

---

36. Givelber, supra note 4, at 75.

37. A view of the judicial role that is relatively hospitable to claimants is that "[t]he court's gate-keeping function ... is solely to eliminate those frivolous and meritless clams in which no reasonable jury, composed of a fair cross-section of the community, could find the defendant's conduct sufficiently extreme and outrageous to permit recovery." Bevan v. Fix, 42 P.3d 1013, 1021 (Wyo. 2002).

Chapter Fourteen

FRONTIER THEORIES

Analysis

Like every other branch of law, tort law requires structure. A principal method for providing structure to the law is through the use of doctrine. The principal doctrinal grist for the mill of torts is stored in a few basic theories: frequently used intentional tort categories like assault, battery and false imprisonment; the spacious doctrine of negligence; and theories of strict liability, which subdivide principally into theories covering abnormally dangerous activities and those applied to defective products.

However, in some situations courts have decided that the traditional torts categories are insufficiently responsive to the demands of justice made by claimants. One court referred to "the wise notion that no system of law can completely describe all claims deserving relief."[1] It is for this reason that courts have employed loose classifications—sometimes called non-categorical torts—that provide safety nets for claimants who cannot bring their allegations within the traditional doctrines. This discussion briefly summarizes some of these frontier theories, or quasi-theories.

¶ 14.01 Prima Facie Tort

The category of "prima facie tort" provides one outlet for plaintiffs who cannot fit their cases within established tort categories, such as defamation, fraud, or negligence. One decision described prima facie tort as "a backup concept which, while it may overlap with other sources of tort law, is primarily significant when other sources of law fail to provide guidance to courts in dealing

---

1. National Nutritional Foods Ass'n v. Whelan, 492 F.Supp. 374, 382 (S.D.N.Y.1980).

with a given type of dispute which generates a tort claim."[2] Courts have used varied lists of elements to spell out the requirements of the tort. One decision catalogued the elements of prima facie tort as: "(1) intentional infliction of harm, (2) causing special damages, (3) without excuse or justification, (4) by an act or series of acts that would otherwise be lawful."[3]

As applied by the courts that recognize the doctrine, its requirements are rather rigorous. A leading decision from New York, the jurisdiction that has most fully developed the prima facie tort, requires the plaintiff to show "an intentional infliction of economic damage, without excuse or justification." Using that language, the court applied prima facie tort as an alternative theory of recovery in a case against a teachers' association, which, warring with a school district, subpoenaed 87 teachers for attendance at a single hearing. This action forced the district to hire substitutes for most of the teachers summoned. The court said that when a plaintiff presented evidence that fulfilled its basic definition of the prima facie tort, it would "eschew formalism, and recognize the existence of a cause of action."[4]

One of the most severe restrictions on the action appears in the requirement, often quoted from Justice Holmes, that the defendant act out of "disinterested malevolence."[5] This standard, bordering on a requirement that the plaintiff show that the defendant cited spitefully, makes the prima facie tort category unavailable in suits against parties that have acted in their own perceived economic best interests. For example, a court is not likely to find that there is "disinterested malevolence" on the part of a union that engages in even an illegal strike.[6] Further illustrating the stringency of the standard is a case involving an alleged scheme to deprive owners of tanker ships of their property. In that case, the court denied a prima facie tort claim "because the existence of a business or profit motive appears on the face of the complaint."[7]

¶ 14.02   Section 870 and the "Innominate" Tort

The drafters of the Second Restatement sought to provide a general category of relief for plaintiffs who could not bring their cases into the elements of the traditional categories. In section 870,

2. Cartelli v. Lanier Worldwide, Inc., 872 F.Supp. 1253, 1255 (S.D.N.Y. 1995).

3. Curiano v. Suozzi, 469 N.E.2d 1324, 1327 (N.Y.1984).

4. Board of Education v. Farmingdale Classroom Teachers Ass'n, 343 N.E.2d 278, 284 (N.Y.1975).

5. See, e.g., Burns Jackson Miller Summit & Spitzer v. Lindner, 451

N.E.2d 459, 468 (N.Y.1983), quoting American Bank and Trust Co. v. Federal Reserve Bank, 256 U.S. 350, 358 (1921) (Holmes, J.).

6. See id.

7. Sharma v. Skaarup Ship Mgt. Corp., 699 F.Supp. 440, 446 (S.D.N.Y. 1988).

they described a liability for "[o]ne who intentionally causes injury to another ... if his conduct is generally culpable and not justifiable under the circumstances."[8] Frankly referring to this category as an "innominate tort,"[9] the drafters said that the section did "not attempt to establish precise and inflexible requirements."[10] Rather, the section represented a recognition that courts had been imposing liability for intentionally inflicted harm "in various forms, often incomplete in their expression."[11] The drafters stressed the dual requirements that the conduct "be both culpable (in general) and unjustifiable (under the circumstances)." They emphasized that "[t]he conduct must first be improper or wrongful; it must be blameworthy, not in accord with community standards of right conduct." Moreover, the conduct could not be "excusable or justifiable; a privilege should not be applicable."[12] Various decisions have referred favorably to section 870 as a guideline for decision,[13] sometimes melding it with elements of the prima facie tort.[14]

¶ 14.03 *Morrison v. N.B.C.*

One important judicial opinion, that of Judge Breitel for the New York appellate division in *Morrison v. National Broadcasting Co.*,[15] fashioned another noncategory theory of tort, although one ultimately not adopted by the court of appeals. The occasion for this challenging opinion, one featuring language more charged with ethical overtones than courts usually employ, was a suit by a young university teacher against a television network. The plaintiff alleged that the network had induced his "innocent participation" in a rigged quiz show when he did not know that the game was fixed.

In holding that the plaintiff had stated a cause of action for harm to reputation and deprivation of academic fellowships, Judge Breitel first reviewed and rejected several theories of recovery. He noted that the plaintiff's complaint did not fit into the prima facie tort category, which requires conduct "otherwise ... lawful." Distinguishing that requirement in an almost moralistic vein, he declared that the defendant's "ultimate purpose and the scheme were corrupt, in the sense that no socially useful purpose but only gain by deceit was intended, although perhaps not 'illegal.' "Moreover, he said, the facts did not exhibit "disinterested malevolence," since the defendants were "engaged in the pursuit of economic gain

8. Restatement (Second) of Torts § 870 (1979).

9. Id., comment j.

10. Id., comment a.

11. Id.

12. Id., comment e.

13. See, e.g., Willard v. Caterpillar, Inc., 48 Cal.Rptr.2d 607 (Ct.App.1995)

(factors applied in rejecting claim for spoliation of evidence).

14. See, e.g., Schmitz v. Smentowski, 785 P.2d 726 (N.M.1990); Porter v. Crawford & Co., 611 S.W.2d 265, 271–72 (Mo.Ct.App.1980).

15. 266 N.Y.S.2d 406 (App.Div. 1965), rev'd, 227 N.E.2d 572 (N.Y.1967).

for themselves."[16] Judge Breitel also reviewed other potential causes of action, including defamation, deceit, and negligence, and found that the plaintiff's complaint shared some elements with those torts, but did not fit neatly into their categories.[17]

To solve the problem of justice that he perceived would arise if the court denied recovery, Judge Breitel fashioned a classification that would impose liability "where the conduct is purposively corrupt by conventional standards, intentional as to consequences, or utilizes vicious means." When a plaintiff showed this kind of behavior, he said, "the law will allow general recovery for foreseeable harm to established protected interests," including "reputation in trade or occupation."[18] The court of appeals reversed Judge Breitel's decision for the appellate division, finding that Morrison's case was essentially one for defamation, and thus barred by the short statute of limitations for defamation.[19] The fact that the *Morrison* tort is not established law even in New York, however, should not obscure the effort of Judge Breitel's opinion to create a "non-category tort."[20] The challenge for courts in situations of this kind is to provide "modes of solution ... where the claim rests on elements each of which, considered separately, has been recognized as an operative fact in the law of torts."[21]

¶ 14.04   The Struggle Over Tort Categories and "Formalism"

There is some overlap among these frontier theories of tort law, which share the goal of trying to open a wedge for meritorious injury cases that do not fit within established torts. An element that clearly distinguishes the prima facie tort is its requirement of "disinterested malevolence." One may contrast, in this regard, the non-category theory advanced in *Morrison*, in which the defendant's purpose was to make money for itself, uncaring what the effects were on the plaintiff, rather than intending to spite the plaintiff. The use of judgmental language in *Morrison* like "purposively corrupt" and "vicious means" somewhat distinguishes that theory, in turn, from the relatively cool tone of section 870's reference to conduct "generally culpable and not justifiable under the circumstances."

All the doctrines discussed here represent tensions inherent in the legal system. On the one hand, courts require categories that facilitate judicial administration and insure predictability. On the

---

16. Id. at 409.

17. Id. at 410.

18. Id. at 415.

19. Morrison v. National Broadcasting Co., 227 N.E.2d 572, 574 (N.Y.1967).

20. Cf. 266 N.Y.S.2d at 416 (Breitel, J., referring to the "non-category tort of injurious falsehood").

21. See id. at 417.

other hand, they feel impelled to respond to what they believe are wrongs that should not go uncompensated even though the conduct does not fit into an established legal pigeonhole. Judge Breitel identified the problem of justice when he said that if the law did not allow a remedy in the *Morrison* case, it "would be saying in effect that one is free to lie to another as distinguished from lying about another (which is defamation), for one's private gain, so long as the consequence of the lie is not to take the victim's property (which is deceit), but rather to expose him and his reputation to likely injury."[22] Since, as Judge Breitel put it, "the classical categories of tort were merely classifications, and incomplete ones at that," residual categories of tort would provide a way for courts to avoid a "slavish formalism."[23]

Obviously, courts must be careful and restrained in their application of non-category torts, for the existence of such loosely defined theories provides an opportunity for judges to introduce their own notions of morality into situations where it is difficult to establish objective standards of behavior. However, the Restatement's reference to "community standards of right conduct"[24] indicates that to some extent, judges must interpret community mores, declaring that certain kinds of behavior are simply wrong. This language makes clear both the opportunity that these non-category torts give courts to do justice, and the attendant risk that judges might use such doctrines to further their own ideological agendas.

[Chapter 15 is reserved for supplementary material.]

---

22. Morrison v. National Broadcasting Co., 266 N.Y.S.2d at 411.

23. Id. at 416–17.

24. Restatement § 870, comment e.

Chapter Sixteen

DEFENSE OF PROPERTY

Analysis

Liability for the defense of property is an issue that has produced little appellate litigation, but presents interesting jurisprudential questions. The tension in the subject inheres in the way that it pits individuals' interest in physical integrity against the interest in ownership of property and its associated dignitary interests.

Perhaps the most interesting presentation of the problem lies in the issue of whether one may try to protect one's property with force likely to cause death or serious bodily harm, described generally in this chapter as deadly force. Insofar as courts have addressed the subject, they impose liability against property owners in favor of visitors to the land, including trespassers and even trespassers with criminal intent, who are killed or injured by an owner's deadly protective measures. However, in situations involving an attempt by the plaintiff to commit a property crime in a dwelling place, the defendant will have a chance to defend on the ground that his or her use of deadly force was directed to protection of persons living in the dwelling rather than to protection of property.

¶ 16.01 The Prevailing Rule on Deadly Force: No Privilege

The leading decision on use of deadly force to protect property is the Iowa case of *Katko v. Briney*.[1] The defendant in *Katko* set up a spring gun in a bedroom of an unoccupied farmhouse that was boarded up, a maneuver that followed a series of break-ins and thefts. Seeking to steal items that they considered antiques, such as old bottles and dated fruit jars, the plaintiff and a friend entered

------

1. 183 N.W.2d 657 (Iowa 1971).

the house by taking off a board that covered a window which had no glass. As the plaintiff opened the bedroom door where the defendant had set his spring gun, the weapon went off and caused serious injuries to the plaintiff's leg.

A majority of the Iowa Supreme Court concluded that the defendant was not privileged to set the gun and affirmed a jury verdict for the plaintiff. There was a fairly complex set of jury instructions, which a dissenter insisted left it unclear as to whether the jury had to find that the defendant had acted with "intention to shoot the intruder or cause him great bodily injury."[2]

The majority's affirmance of the plaintiff's judgment relied on a broad principle, announced in the Restatement of Torts, that one is not privileged to use deadly force to defend property "unless the intrusion threatens death or serious bodily harm to ... occupiers or users."[3] This principle forbade the employment of "mechanical device[s]" like spring guns, which would utilize deadly force an owner could not use if he were present; the application in *Katko* was that the defendant could not have used a firearm to protect his bottles and jars if he had been in the farmhouse.

Lining up with *Katko*, the few courts that have addressed the question have dealt severely with death-traps. A Georgia appellate court imposed liability on the owner of a cigarette vending machine, plagued by vandals, who booby-trapped the machine with a dynamite charge that killed a youth. In part, the court rationalized its decision on the basis of the deadly potential that the dynamite carried for innocent bystanders as well as for wrongdoers.[4]

The principal dispute concerning the issue focuses on a proposition advanced by the Restatement: "[t]he value of human life and limb ... so outweighs the interest of a possessor of land in excluding ... those whom he is not willing to admit thereto" that there is no privilege to use deadly force to repel those who would "enter his premises or meddle with his chattel."[5] One's degree of agreement with this comparative valuation will probably determine his or her view of the proper rule to apply.

¶ 16.02   Reasonableness Test

With respect to the issue of deadly force, the prevailing standard essentially creates a per se rule in favor of liability and against the privilege to defend property. One opposing policy argument emphasizes that there are times when property interests are virtually inseparable from dignitary interests. One may picture, for

---

2. Id. at 670 (Larson, J., dissenting).

3. Id. at 660, quoting Restatement of Torts § 85, cmt. a (1934).

4. McKinsey v. Wade, 220 S.E.2d 30, 33 (Ga.App.1975).

5. Restatement of Torts § 85, cmt. a.

example, a case of deadly force used by an owner of a small store who has built up the business over many years and who would say, more than metaphorically, that his life is the store. In this case, the plaintiff is an intending burglar, seriously injured by a deadly device set by the owner after a string of burglaries that threatened the existence of his business. This illustration arguably weakens the case for a per se rule. It suggests, indeed, that it would be appropriate to judge defense of property as many issues in tort law are judged: by a reasonableness test.[6] In the example given, such a test would throw into the balance the weight of the defendant's interest in his property in light of all the circumstances, including the meaning of the property to his life, and the occurrence of repeated burglaries.

Analysis of the proposed application of a reasonableness standard to the use of deadly force to defend property indicates that the characterization of the legal issue may significantly affect results. Thus, for example, if one focuses on whether the defendant's conduct was an intentional tort, then a finding of the requisite intent would make the issue of reasonableness irrelevant. If, by contrast, one fixes on the question of whether the defendant had a privilege, then a reasonableness standard might more plausibly yield a defense.

Of course, an important argument against a reasonableness test and in favor of a per se rule lies precisely in the fact that the per se standard is a clean rule, and thus easy to administer. In that sense, the issue reflects the continuing tension in jurisprudence between the individualization of justice and the promotion of efficiency in judicial administration. Many observers would argue that in this situation, the clean rule is also the just one because of its paramount valuation of life and limb.

¶ 16.03   A Spectrum of Rules

There is a spectrum of possible rules that may be formulated to govern this issue:

1) A rule allowing property owners to use deadly force to repel serious property crimes

2) A rule allowing the use of deadly force with clear notice to intruders (this rule poses particular difficulties with respect to intruders whose language is not that used on the warning sign or who are illiterate)

3) A rule permitting the use of deadly force if there is no reasonable alternative for the protection of property

---

6. For advocacy of a reasonableness standard, see Richard Posner, Killing or Wounding to Protect a Property Interest, 14 J.L. & Econ. 201 (1971).

4) A rule allowing the use of reasonable force when the property owner has a bona fide belief in the reasonableness of his or her actions

5) A reasonableness test using an objective standard, without reference to the defendant's subjective belief

6) A rule that requires the plaintiff to show that the defendant intended great bodily harm to intruders

7) A rule cast in general terms of reasonableness but that specifically deems the use of deadly mechanical devices unreasonable

8) A per se rule against any use of force that threatens death or serious bodily harm.[7]

¶ 16.03A   Statutory Immunities

A particularly interesting refinement of the defense of defense of property—as well as of self-defense—appears in a California statute that immunizes owners of real property for injury or death to those on the premises that occur "during the course or of after the commission of" certain enumerated felonies, when the injured person has been convicted of one of those felonies or a lesser included offense. The statutory immunity does not exonerate "willful, wanton, or criminal conduct." An interesting test of that statute arose in a case in which a store employee shot in the back a man who the employee thought was one of a group of robbers, while that man was fleeing the store. The man who was shot denied that he was a member of the group of robbers, claiming that he had gone into the store only to buy a soda. Despite this denial, he had been convicted of attempted grand theft in connection with his role in the events that led to the shooting. Afterwards he sued the store for the shooting, which left him quadriplegic. Analyzing the statute, the California Supreme Court concluded that a plaintiff who had met the "statutory predicates" could have immunity "not only for negligence . . . but also for the intentional use of deadly or injurious force when such force is justifiable."[8] However, the court refused to grant summary judgment for the defendants, saying that it could not hold as a matter of law that the force they used " 'reasonably appear[ed] necessary, in view of all the circumstances of the case, to prevent [an] impending injury.' "[9] The court focused, in part, on the facts that the employee who did the shooting said he had never seen the plaintiff with a knife that a co-employee had said the

---

7. A leading advocate of this position is Geoffrey Palmer, a law professor who became prime minister of New Zealand. He advocated a legislative ban on spring guns in The Iowa Spring Gun Case: A Study in American Gothic, 56 Iowa L. Rev. 1219 (1971).

8. Calvillo–Silva v. Home Grocery, 19 Cal.4th 714, 968 P.2d 65, 80 (1998).

9. 968 P.2d at 81 (quoting test of a precedent).

plaintiff was wielding, and that the shot was in the back while the plaintiff was running from the store.

¶ 16.04 Merchants' Privilege

A particularized privilege against claims for intentional torts arising from defense of property, principally related to suits brought for false imprisonment or under the label of false arrest, is the privilege to detain those suspected of pilfering goods.

The privilege grows out of a constant, if usually bloodless war. Shoplifting represents a substantial source of property loss inflicted on merchants by crime, and this branch of the law represents a balancing of two strong and well-defined interests. The old common law rule placed almost all of its emphasis on the plaintiff's dignitary interest and little on the defendant's property right. It permitted the imposition of liability for false imprisonment if no theft had been committed, even though a merchant detained a suspected shoplifter on reasonable grounds. The California case of *Collyer v. S.H. Kress Co.*,[10] decided in 1936, modified this rule with its holding that a merchant may use probable cause as a defense to false imprisonment if the detention was reasonable. The court expressly grounded this new principle on the idea that one should balance the merchant's need to provide reasonable protection for his property against the suspect's right to be free from restraint of his person.[11]

This expanded privilege, developed both in common law decisions and statutes as a response to the increasing incidence of shoplifting, still embodies several constraints on merchants. Not only must they have "probable cause," "reasonable cause," or "reasonable grounds" to believe that a suspect has committed an offense, but they may restrain the suspect only in a reasonable manner, in a limited area, and for a limited time.[12]

The issue of "probable cause" has continued to be a focal point of judicial decisions, for it embodies the principal social judgment about the tradeoff between dignitary and property interests. A Maryland case illustrates the legal tensions in cases of detention for shoplifting. An assistant manager of a supermarket, unfamiliar with the exceptionally deliberate shopping habits of one customer, concluded that he had secretly hidden a can of flea and tick spray in his pocket. Confronting the customer, the assistant manager called him a "goddamn thief," frisked him, and forced him to march to the manager's office. A jury awarded $40,000, including $30,000 in punitive damages, on a variety of claims that included false imprisonment. Concerning that issue, the court said that, under existing state law, probable cause was not a defense in cases of arrest by

10. 54 P.2d 20 (Cal.1936).

11. Id. at 23.

12. *See* Note, The Merchant, The Shoplifter, and the Law, 55 Minn. L. Rev. 825 (1971).

private persons. The court defined a "narrow exception to the general rules of arrest," which permitted merchants a privilege to detain suspected thieves "only to prevent theft or to recapture property." As applied to self-service stores, this meant that there is no probable cause for detention until a suspect "actually attempts to leave without paying, unless he manifests control over the property in such a way that his intention to steal is unequivocal." Given the restricted scope of this privilege, the court held that the defendant in the case before it had not shown probable cause, and affirmed the plaintiff's judgment.[13]

State rules vary concerning the purpose for which a merchant may detain. Some jurisdictions at least implicitly allow a merchant to search suspects. Others permit detention "only to investigate ownership or to question and investigate ownership." Another group of states allows detention "for the sole purpose of delivering the suspect to a law enforcement officer."[14]

The merchant who spies a customer behaving in a questionable way must have a sense of both the place where detention is privileged and the amount of time that is reasonable for detention. Some jurisdictions limit the permissible zone of detention to the premises of the store, but others extend it to the immediate vicinity.[15] The law is not digitalized on the time element for detention, but if it does not hold a stopwatch, it provides a general watchman's function. In one case, for example, the court held that it did not constitute detention for "more than a reasonable time" for a security officer to detain for 27 minutes a customer with a large, easily opened handbag, whose activities had been suspicious.[16]

Although the law of merchants' privilege is general, as most tort rules must be, it does communicate a practical set of standards. Advice may begin with the most general and cautious suggestion: "Be certain or risk a false arrest suit is a good rule to follow when catching a shoplifter."[17] It will include other recommendations of varying specificity, such as the suggestion that particularly gentle treatment be given to elderly persons because of the risk of heart attacks.[18] Sometimes advice may run to several pages of suggested do's and don'ts.[19] This range of recommendations reflects the effort of tort law to provide to business persons a spectrum of signals that are relatively clear and understandable, while balancing important customer interests.

13. Great A. & P. Tea Co. v. Paul, 261 A.2d 731, 739–40 (Md.1970).

14. See Note, supra note 12, 55 Minn. L. Rev. at 848–50.

15. See id. at 850–52.

16. Cooke v. J.J. Newberry & Co., 232 A.2d 425, 429 (N.J. Super.1967).

17. A. Kingsbury, Introduction to Security and Crime Prevention Surveys 308 (1973).

18. Id. at 309.

19. See, e.g., Center for Criminal Justice, Case Western University School of Law, Private Police Training Manual 238–46 (5th ed. 1975).

Chapter Seventeen

CONSENT

Analysis

¶ 17.01   Definition

The intentional torts, generally speaking, require that the defendant's behavior be unconsented by the plaintiff. Some courts will view lack of consent as part of the substantive definition of the tort, while others will treat consent as an affirmative defense. This chapter focuses on the issue of how to define consent, whatever the pleading requirement.

Consent is willingness, or assent. It may be communicated by language or manifested by a physical act. An interesting case, involving an immigrant at a port of entry, indicates how one may objectively manifest assent although she has subjective reservations. This plaintiff sued for an "assault," which in current technical tort terminology would be a claim for battery, because she was vaccinated although she protested to the surgeon who was vaccinating people that she already had been vaccinated. The surgeon said there was no vaccination mark on her arm, and the plaintiff, perhaps resignedly, held up her arm to be vaccinated. The court effectively held this act to be consent, barring the action.[1]

Beyond assent manifested by a gesture, one may manifest consent by inaction.[2] A false imprisonment action brought by a telephone company employee illustrates that plaintiffs must articulately protest a confinement to make it actionable. Having admitted that she had an unauthorized telephone in her name, the employee agreed to go with other employees of the company to her home on a trip to recover the phone equipment. She claimed, in part, that she was confined against her will when the driver of the car taking her to her home stopped to pick up security officers. The court rejected

---

1. O'Brien v. Cunard S.S. Co., 28 N.E. 266 (Mass.1891).

2. Restatement (Second) of Torts § 892(1) (1977).

68

her argument that she did not consent to that detour, which she sought to bolster with testimony about her expression of "concern . . . about the unfamiliar route." In essence, the court concluded that since the plaintiff did not object, or indicate that she wanted to get out of the car, she effectively continued her manifested willingness to take the trip.[3]

At least theoretically, a defendant may prove that a plaintiff in fact desired to have the defendant act in a way that would otherwise be tortious, for example, to touch the plaintiff, even though the plaintiff did not communicate that desire. The Restatement gives the example of a patient who goes to a surgeon for the declared reason of having a septum removed, but has been having trouble with his tonsils and actually also wants a tonsillectomy, although he does not communicate that wish to the doctor. The surgeon removes the tonsils as well as the septum. If the doctor can prove that the plaintiff if fact wished to have his tonsils removed, that willingness in fact will constitute consent and defeat a battery action.[4]

Presenting more room for practical applications is a rule giving surgeons discretion to employ "sound surgical procedure in the area of the original incision."[5] The sort of problem to which this rule is typically applied involves a surgeon's decision after an operation has begun to remove an organ that appears diseased, although that organ was not explicitly the subject of a written consent.

Doctrinal characterization becomes important in litigation involving undesired outcomes of medical treatment. If a plaintiff is able to prove a battery, which requires what may be a difficult showing of lack of consent, she may recover for injuries that arise from an unforeseen medical consequence of a procedure, even if the physician was not negligent. This legal result stems from the fact that all that is necessary for a battery is an unconsented contact, meaning that the plaintiff may recover for consequences that were not foreseeably within the risk of that contact. By contrast, a negligence action generally requires a showing of some foreseeable risk of harm; foreseeability is part of the basic definition of the defendant's standard of conduct in negligence.

¶ 17.02   Limitations on Consent

There are various limitations on the validity of even a manifested assent. A threshold point is that the person alleged to have

3. Faniel v. Chesapeake & Potomac Tel. Co., 404 A.2d 147, 153 (D.C.Ct.App. 1979).

4. Restatement (Second) of Torts § 49, comment a, illus. 2 (1965).

5. Kennedy v. Parrott, 90 S.E.2d 754 (N.C.1956).

given consent must have had the capacity to consent. He or she must be of an age at which a meaningful consent was possible, and, presumably, must be endowed with enough mental acuity and stability to render consent a freely made choice.

Fraud or duress may vitiate consent. A modern application of these exceptions appears in cases in which the plaintiff alleges that the defendant engaged in deceit in order to obtain sexual favors. Courts are likely to hold that fraud vitiates consent when the defendant makes an outright misrepresentation of a material fact. Illustrative is a case in which a man knowingly made false representations to a woman to the effect that he was sterile. Their sexual relations produced an ectopic pregnancy and serious medical problems. The court held that the plaintiff had sufficiently pleaded both battery and deceit.[6]

Some courts may not even make a rigorous distinction between outright misrepresentation and nondisclosure. An example is a case in which the defendant did not reveal to the plaintiff that he suffered from a sexually transmissible disease, genital herpes. The court at one point characterized the plaintiff's complaint as alleging that the defendant had "negligently or deliberately fail[ed] to inform her" of his disease.[7] However, in the court's summary of the reasoning that led it to uphold the complaint, it referred to the defendant's "misrepresentation that he was disease-free."[8] It thus appears that in cases involving battery-like torts, courts will not necessarily draw a sharp line between misrepresentation and nondisclosure with respect to fraud as vitiating consent.

An interesting policy dimension of consent appears in the contrasting outcome of another case. In this litigation, the court concluded that a man could not sue a woman who misrepresented that she was taking birth control pills, when intercourse procured by that misrepresentation produced a child the man did not want. The court suggested that to allow the action would work a "radical" "change in the socially accepted ideas and views of sexual conduct, family relationship, parental obligations, and legal and moral responsibility for one's own conduct."[9]

Some other issues that may produce legal difficulty with respect to consent to sexual intimacy, although they have not been the subject of appellate litigation, could arise in situations involving claims of battery for "date rape" or "acquaintance rape." The law would be straightforward in favor of a plaintiff who could prove that the defendant used overwhelming force. Other claimants,

6. Barbara A. v. John G., 193 Cal. Rptr. 422 (Ct.App.1983).

7. Kathleen K. v. Robert B., 198 Cal.Rptr. 273, 276 (Ct.App.1984).

8. Id. at 277.

9. Stephen K. v. Roni L., 164 Cal. Rptr. 618, 620 (Ct.App.1980).

however, would probably be able to recover only by means of arguments that verge on claims of fraud or duress or by proving that the defendant knowingly took advantage of an incapacity, for example, caused by intoxication.

¶ 17.03　Policies Concerning Fraudulently Procured Consent

Conflicting judgments on the question of when fraud will vitiate consent reflect strong, competing policies. On the one hand, the requirement of consent arises from a judicial desire to enhance individual autonomy and personal choice. Cardozo eloquently captured this goal in a 1914 opinion in which he spoke of the right of each person "to determine what shall be done with his own body."[10] Consent requires not only expressed willingness but free choice, which fraud undermines.

On the other hand, public policy sometimes will defeat the argument that fraud vitiates consent. This was the case in a decision, mentioned above, involving a woman's misrepresentation that she was using birth control, which led to the birth of a child. The father of the child sued the mother, citing the support obligations he had incurred and alleging mental suffering. The court referred to moral and cultural considerations in refusing to allow the father to claim that fraud canceled out his manifested willingness to have sexual relations with the mother.[11]

The policy of promoting economy in judicial administration may also override the attempt to argue that fraud vitiates consent. In particular, cases involving intimate relations are likely to involve inquiries of such delicacy and uncertainty that courts may believe themselves ill suited to undertake judgment of such matters.[12] Another argument against judicial intervention is that intimate relations fall within the sphere of constitutional privacy. This contention, however, often will set in motion an escalating series of arguments pitting public policy against privacy rights. Notably, in cases involving the transmission of disease, the state's interest in health will outweigh individual interests in privacy and courts will not defer to consent procured by deception.

---

10. Schloendorff v. Society of New York Hosp., 105 N.E. 92, 93, (N.Y.1914).

11. See Stephen K. v. Roni L., 164 Cal.Rptr. 618 (Ct.App.1980), discussed supra, ¶ 17.02, text accompanying note 9.

12. See id., 164 Cal. Rptr. at 620 (concluding "that as a matter of public policy the practice of birth control, if any, engaged in by two partners in a consensual sexual relationship is best left to the individuals involved, free from any governmental interference"). Cf. Kilduff v. Kilduff, 473 F.Supp. 873 (S.D.N.Y.1979) (refusing to place the "false imprisonment" label on what was essentially a dispute over child custody when the effect would be to confer federal jurisdiction on the basis of the litigants' diverse citizenship).

Section Three

THE STANDARD OF CARE IN NEGLIGENCE

Chapter Eighteen

INTRODUCTION TO NEGLIGENCE

Analysis

Para.

Negligence law seeks to establish standards for conduct, the violation of which will require persons who fall below a standard to pay compensation to parties injured as a result of that violation. Negligence, therefore, includes conduct. However, it may also be an omission to act, and the boundary line between acts and failures to act is sometimes a fuzzy one. Apart from the lack of clarity on that matter, both the student and the practitioner will find that it is difficult to fix on a single definition of negligence, since courts and lawyers refer to several different verbal formulas.[1] Despite this variation in terminology, one can certainly say that the decision on whether an act or omission is negligent requires close attention to the facts of particular cases, and a grounding in basic rules of procedure.

¶ 18.01 Negligence Law and Specific Activities

Courts have tended to use relatively specific standards, when they can, to define the appropriate level of care for particular kinds of activity. One instance of such standards, which we shall discuss in more detail in a later chapter, appears in the specialized categories that courts have developed concerning tort claims of visitors to land against possessors of the land on which the visitor was injured. Many states distinguish among categories of visitors—labeling them invitees, licensees, and trespassers—with the standard of care

---

1. See ¶¶ 19.01–.02 infra.

required of possessors varying according to the classifications.[2]

Medicine is another activity to which the law applies relatively specific standards for testing due care. One source of controversy about these standards resides in geography: a lively debate continues about whether physicians must meet a national standard of care, or whether a plaintiff must show that a doctor fell below a standard defined by local practice.[3]

Transportation activities have generated their own specific rules spelling out the negligence standard. Decisions involving motor vehicle accidents often derive their standard from statutes and regulations that set rules of the road. A rule with long historical antecedents has imposed a particularly high standard of care on common carriers. However, as the New York Court of Appeals said in a 1998 decision, "[t]ime has ... disclosed the inconsistency of the carrier's duty of extraordinary care with the fundamental concept of negligence in tort doctrine"—a single, "objective, reasonable person standard." Although one rationalization for articulating a particularly high standard of care for common carriers was "the perceived ultrahazardous nature of the instrumentalities of public rapid transit," the New York court opined that the single standard "is sufficiently flexible by itself to permit courts and juries to take into account the ultrahazardous nature of a tortfeasor's activity." It should be stressed that as applied to particularly dangerous activities—as to any activities— that standard "necessarily takes into account the circumstances with which the actor was actually confronted when the accident occurred, including the reasonably perceivable risk and gravity of harm to others and any special relationship of dependency between the victim and the actor."[4]

Courts also apply standards of varying degrees of specificity to different kinds of product manufacture. An example of highly fact-specific standards appears in the particularized body of law concerning the time frame during which distributors of blood and blood products knew, or should have known, of the potential for contamination by the HIV virus.[5]

¶ 18.02　Procedural Aspects of Negligence

A continuing procedural challenge for judges is to separate those cases that should not be litigated, because there is no legal

2. See infra, ¶ 20.01.

3. See infra, ¶ 23.04.

4. Bethel v. New York City Transit Auth., 92 N.Y.2d 348, 703 N.E.2d 1214, 1216–17 (1998).

5. See, e.g., Jones v. Miles Laboratories, 887 F.2d 1576, 1581 (11th Cir. 1989) (no negligence in failure to institute policy of questioning high-risk donors during time period when "knowledge about the causes and transmission of AIDS" was in especially rapid period of growth).

support for the plaintiff's allegations, from those that merit consideration by a fact finder, meaning that reasonable persons could differ on whether the defendant could be found negligent under applicable legal rules. For the student, this procedural foundation of negligence law means that it is necessary, while learning the substantive law, to absorb the meaning of the principal procedural motions used for testing complaints and evidence. These include the motion to dismiss, the motion for summary judgment, and the motion for a directed verdict. For the plaintiff's lawyer, it usually requires an emphasis on the flexibility of negligence doctrine to defeat defense motions designed to keep cases from consideration by juries. For the defense lawyer, in most cases it requires stress on rigorous application of those motions. One cannot overestimate the importance of decisions on these motions, because the grant of such a motion means that a jury will never get to give a judgment about the case. Among other effects, this will significantly limit the costs of litigation.

The first line of defense for lawyers opposing negligence complaints is the motion to dismiss, which tests the sufficiency of a legal complaint. When a defendant moves to dismiss a claim, which occurs after the filing of the complaint and before any other stage of the litigation, he concedes for the purposes of argument that the plaintiff can prove what the plaintiff says that she can prove, but he contends that even if the plaintiff can do that, there are no legal rules that would support the claim of liability. An example would be a case in which the plaintiff contended that a restaurant owner was negligent in failing to protect the plaintiff from an assault by another person in the establishment's parking lot, in a state in which there was clear precedent that denied recovery against businesses for crimes committed on their premises by third parties. A trial court would be obliged to dismiss the complaint because the law makes no provision for liability in such a case.

Another tool principally used by defendants is the motion for summary judgment. That motion tests the legal sufficiency of the complaint while allowing the court to consider documents such as affidavits, depositions, or contracts, but does not require the testimony of witnesses at a full-fledged trial. An example is a case in which the plaintiff has signed a document, such as a lease, which contains a clause exculpating the defendant from suits for negligence, a document that the defendant argues indicates that the plaintiff has accepted the risk of the injury at issue. Where state law permits the enforcement of such exculpatory clauses, the court would grant the defendant's motion for summary judgment.

As cases move beyond the stage of preliminary motions to trial, negligence law becomes progressively more focused on facts and the resolution of factual disputes. At trial, the first principal procedural obstacle that one party may raise to another's evidence is the motion for a directed verdict, now called a motion for "judgment as a matter of law" under Rule 50(a) of the Federal Rules of Civil Procedure. This motion may be offered after the plaintiff's evidence or at the close of all the evidence. In negligence cases, the party who typically makes this motion is the defendant, although a plaintiff may also move for a directed verdict.

A party's motion for directed verdict requires the court to decide whether the evidence presented by the other litigant (the "nonmoving party")—or, indeed all the evidence—would entitle the latter to a verdict at all. The question is whether, under the applicable legal rules, reasonable persons could give a judgment for the nonmoving party. For example, when a defendant moves for a directed verdict, the court must determine whether the plaintiff has presented enough evidence to justify a verdict under the law. If the court decides there is not enough evidence, it will grant the motion and dismiss the case. If it decides that the jury could reasonably find for the plaintiff under the governing legal rules, it will give the case to the jury, which will determine whether, under those rules, the evidence supports a verdict for either party.

If a case goes to a jury, which gives a verdict, the party against whom the verdict is rendered may move for what historically has been called the motion for judgment notwithstanding the verdict (judgment n.o.v.), which Rule 50(b) of the Federal Rules also terms a "motion for judgment as a matter of law." Courts employ a similar standard in deciding on that motion as they do concerning a motion for directed verdict. The sum of these sibling motions is that the court must decide whether rational jurors could find for the non-moving party (in the case of a directed verdict motion), or in favor of the party that won the verdict (in connection with a motion for judgment n.o.v.).

The kinds of cases that will win a directed verdict for defendants are those in which there is a relatively well-established rule whose requirements the plaintiff did not meet. For example, if the medical standard of care in a particular jurisdiction requires proof that the defendant violated the rule of a specific "locality," and the plaintiff could only show a violation of a "national" standard of care, proved by out-of-state-experts, the defendant would get a directed verdict. By comparison, in cases involving activities or behavior that do not have such well-defined standards, the court often will be inclined to let the case go to the jury. In making that decision, courts reason that six or twelve ordinary individuals, using their combined experience of life and their collective common sense, are qualified to make the relevant judgment. That judgment is whether, under a general formula of negligence as unreasonable conduct, the defendant's conduct as proved by the plaintiff fell below the standard of reasonable care. An example would be the question of whether a restaurant or a supermarket allowed a slippery condition to persist on a floor for too long.

Typically, controversies over motions for directed verdict in tort cases will involve motions made by defendants. It occasionally happens that a plaintiff successfully moves for a directed verdict, convincing the court that the defendant's conduct was indisputably negligent. However, in most cases, the plaintiff principally seeks to take his or her case to the jury, and the defendant tries by the directed verdict motion to keep the case away from the jury.

Directed verdicts have important implications for the structure of the judicial process as well as the costs of judicial administration. Besides saving some time and expense in trials, since directed verdicts keep cases from going to juries, the giving of a directed verdict underlines the different functions of judge and jury. By directing a verdict, the court has decided that, under the law, there is insufficient evidence to support the non-moving party's case. A central feature of that motion, then, is that it spotlights the role of judge as interpreter of the law, and of the jury as fact-finder.

Chapter Nineteen

DOCTRINE AND TERMINOLOGY
OF NEGLIGENCE

Analysis

¶ 19.01   Doctrinal Definitions

There are several different definitions of negligence, all of them centered on the concept of a defendant's unreasonable acts or omissions. Some of them emphasize the positive, presenting a standard of conduct that actors must meet. Others stress the defendant's failure to meet a standard. A well-accepted general definition that combines both approaches is that "negligence is conduct which falls below the standard established by law for the protection of others against unreasonable risk of harm."[1]

A much cited alternative definition appears in an 1883 opinion by an English judge. Brett, M.R., wrote in *Heaven v. Pender*:

> [W]henever one person is by circumstances placed in such a position with regard to another that every one of ordinary sense who did think would at once recognise that if he did not use ordinary care and skill in his own conduct with regard to

---

1. Restatement (Second) of Torts § 282 (1965) [hereafter, "Restatement (Second)"].

those circumstances he would cause danger of injury to the person or property of the other, a duty arises to use ordinary care and skill to avoid such danger.[2]

We may remark at least two important features of this definition. One is its stress on foresight, or as the term has come to be used routinely in negligence law, foreseeability. Another is that it blends the notion of duty into the concept of negligence, defining duty by the relationship of the defendant to the plaintiff. The present chapter, which emphasizes the standard of care, necessarily incorporates aspects of duty; however, this text principally treats the duty issue under a separate heading.[3]

¶ 19.02   Standard of Care: Concepts and Terminology

The definitions just summarized provide points of departure to examine the basic concepts that courts most frequently use to define the standard of care in negligence cases.

A.   Ordinary prudence

A central idea of negligence law is that people should be judged according to the standards of ordinary persons in the circumstances at issue. The language of "ordinary care and skill" mentioned in *Heaven v. Pender* provides a benchmark for this concept. An important implication of the idea of ordinary care is that the standard for negligence is principally an objective one. At times, the law may hold people to a standard based on knowledge superior to that of the general community, notably, the expert knowledge of professional communities. However, with a few exceptions, the law will not dip below the standard of ordinary prudence; it measures everyone at least by the standard of the average individual.

B.   Knowledge, actual and potential

The defendant's knowledge of risk, or the opportunity to acquire it, are important to the definition of negligence. Courts often use a formula that speaks of what a defendant "knew or should have known." Generally, if the defendant possesses a high degree of knowledge that a certain kind of conduct will cause harm, that conduct may bring her into the categories of intentional tort or reckless behavior. By comparison, if the defendant did not actually know of the risk to others, but should have known about it, the defendant's conduct falls in the domain of negligence. The Restatement's standard for recognition of risks requires people to know "the qualities and habits of human beings and animals and the

---

2. Heaven v. Pender, [1883] 11 Q. B. D. 503, 509.

3. An introductory overview appears in Chapter 55. Other aspects of the problem are treated in Chapters 56–57, 59, 61, 63–64.

qualities, characteristics, and capacities of things and forces, in so far as they are matters of common knowledge at the time and in the community." It also declares that people must know "the common law, legislative enactments, and general customs in so far as they are likely to affect the conduct of" others.[4]

C. Foreseeability; frequency of accidents

Foreseeability, growing out of knowledge or the possibility of knowledge, helps to separate the concept of negligence from that of accident.[5] Holmes identified the ability to foresee risks as central to negligence when he wrote, "relatively to a given human being anything is accident which he could not fairly have been expected to contemplate as possible, and therefore to avoid."[6] Thus, injuries occurring from novel risks will not support liability for negligence.

A colorful example comes from a case in which employees of the defendant express company tried to hammer open a crate that was leaking a substance which seemed to resemble sweet oil. The substance turned out to be nitroglycerin, the explosive properties of which were not well known in 1866, the year of the accident. Because the risk was a novel one, the United States Supreme Court in *The Nitro–Glycerine Case*[7] found the defendants "innocently ignorant of the contents of the case," and affirmed a judgment for them. The Court said that the law did "not charge culpable negligence upon anyone who takes the usual precautions against accident, which careful and prudent men are accustomed to take under similar circumstances."[8]

In another decision that emphasized the "very unusual" nature of the accident at issue, the court rejected a suit against a utility for the electrocution of a worker when a 100–foot boom he was guiding contacted the utility's wires, which were 16 feet above the minimum height specified by safety regulations. Unpersuaded that the defendant had notice of such an occurrence, the court said

---

4. Restatement (Second) § 290.

5. There is some controversy about whether courts should give juries an instruction to the effect that if neither party was negligent, then any harms from the event sued upon "would be the result of an accident." One court that rejects the use of the "accident instruction" points out that "[a]ccident is strictly defined as an occurrence which takes place in the absence of negligence and for which [no] one would be liable." It finds the instruction misleading and confusing because "it implies an accident occurs when the negligence of someone other than the plaintiff or defendant causes the plaintiff's injuries"

and because the definition in the instruction differs from "the commonly understood meaning of the word as an unintended act." Saying that the accident defense amounts to nothing more than an assertion that the defendant did not negligently cause an injury, the court opines that standard negligence instructions are sufficient to define the law for the jury. Tolbert v. Duckworth, 423 S.E.2d 229, 230 (Ga.1992).

6. Holmes, The Common Law 94 (1881).

7. 82 U.S. (15 Wall.) 524 (1872).

8. Id. at 536–37.

that to impose liability on the utility would in effect require that it maintain "constant surveillance" on the land beneath its line.[9]

Decisions like *The Nitro–Glycerine Case*, and the case of the crane boom and the electric wires, exemplify the refusal to impose liability for injuries resulting from risks that are not predictable to the ordinary observer. They also suggest that the low probability, or even novelty, of a particular type of occurrence will affect a court's judgment of whether it was negligence to create the conditions that allegedly led to an accident: to put it colloquially, the law will not find conduct negligent if the risk will cause injury "once in a blue moon."

An important reason that the law focuses on the frequency of injury associated with certain kinds of conduct lies in the value of predictability. The ability to predict the likelihood of a type of event has an obvious relation to fairness concerns. It also relates to the ability of actors to secure insurance against events of that kind, for insurers must be able to calculate the risks of occurrences that cause injury.

Negligence law in effect creates a sliding scale between the frequency and the gravity of injury, factoring in the level of the defendant's knowledge. All things being equal, the law will be less inclined to hold defendants for occurrences that happen very seldom than for those that occur rather often. But even a relatively infrequent occurrence may be grounds for negligence liability if the actor had reason to know of the possibility it could happen and that if it did, it would cause very serious injuries.[10]

D.   The "Learned Hand test" and other economic standards

Seeking to identify these factors in a way that courts could employ them in decisionmaking, Judge Learned Hand fashioned an algebraic formula, the terms of which courts often use in judging negligence cases. In *United States v. Carroll Towing Co.*,[11] in which a barge broke loose from its moorings, he defined the duty of the owner as being "a function of three variables: (1) The probability that she will break away; (2) the gravity of the resulting injury, if she does; (3) the burden of adequate precautions." He then declared that "if the probability be called P; the injury, L; and the

9. Dunnaway v. Duquesne Light Co., 423 F.2d 66, 71 (3d Cir.1970).

10. See Bammerlin v. Navistar Int'l Transp. Corp., 30 F.3d 898, 902 (7th Cir.1994), which involved a jury award of $500,000. The court hypothesizes differing, low probabilities of injury as multipliers for the jury award and compares the injury costs figured on the basis of those probabilities with assumed avoidance costs.

11. 159 F.2d 169, 173 (2d Cir.1947).

burden, B; liability depends upon whether B is less than L multiplied by P: i.e., whether B<PL."

Besides winning adherents among many courts, this "Learned Hand test" has also attracted economists who analyze tort rules, drawn to its implicit premise that the reasonable person is the efficient person. That person is one who will devote resources to avoiding accidents when it is efficient to do so, but only when it is efficient. She compares accident avoidance costs—B in Judge Hand's formula—with accident costs—PL in Judge Hand's terms. So long as the costs of avoiding an injury are less than the costs of the injury, the failure to take the precaution that would avoid the injury is negligence, for the reasonable person will spend the money necessary to avoid the injury. This is so even where the probability of an injury is very low, "if the costs of protecting against it are even lower."[12] When the avoidance costs exceed accident costs, however, the reasonable person will not take the precaution. Because a reasonable person would not spend more to avoid an accident than it would cost to have it, failure to do so is not negligence—that is, it is not a failure to exercise reasonable care.

The Learned Hand test specifies, or implies, a group of considerations that economists analyze in relation to each other in trying to define the efficient level of accidents. These considerations include the frequency of accidents associated with particular types of conduct, the seriousness of the expected injury, and the level of enforcement.[13]

There are other negligence tests that also have a flavor of economic balancing. One of these is risk-utility analysis, exemplified by Restatement (Second) section 291, which says that a "risk is unreasonable" and an "act is negligent if the risk is of such magnitude as to outweigh what the law regards as the utility of the act or of the particular manner in which it is done." Section 292 identifies a principal factor that is "important" in "determining what the law regards as the utility of the actor's conduct" as "the

---

12. See Bammerlin v. Navistar Int'l Transp. Corp., supra note 10, 30 F.3d at 902 (comparing hypothesized low probability of injury from allegedly defective design of seat belt assembly on tractor with hypothesized very low cost of a different method of anchoring the assembly).

13. See, e.g., Louis Kaplow, The Optimal Probability and Magnitude of Fines for Acts That Definitely are Undesirable, 12 Int'l Rev. L. & Econ. 3 (1992). Economic theory identifies many other issues relevant to the definition of negligence, on which we touch only

briefly here. One important theoretical question is whether the populations subject to the law are neutral about risk or averse to risk. See e.g., A. Mitchell Polinsky & Steven Shavell, The Optimal Tradeoff Between the Probability and Magnitude of Fines, 69 Am. Econ. Rev. 880, 883–85. Another issue of particular relevance to tort law concerns the opportunity to secure insurance against potential liability. See, e.g., Fleming James, Jr. & John V. Thornton, The Impact of Insurance on the Law of Torts, 15 Law & Contemp. Prob. 431 (1950).

social value which the law attaches to the interest which is to be advanced or protected by the conduct." It also refers to the chances that that interest "will be advanced or protected" by the defendant's "particular course of conduct," and by alternative courses of conduct that may be less risky. Although the language of "risk-utility" has a quantitative sound, a Restatement comment indicates that its thrust is mainly qualitative, to an extent even political: "[t]he value attached by the law to the great majority of interests is identical with the value which popular opinion attaches to them." However, the comment also notes that sometimes judicial decisions have attached a value to certain interests that is "different from that which the jury would ordinarily attach" to them and declares that in those cases "it is the legal and not the popular valuation which is controlling."[14]

Some courts employee the terminology of "benefits" more or less synonymously with that of "utility." For example, in an important products liability decision, the California Supreme Court stated as one standard for defining a design defect a rule requiring a defendant to show "that, on balance, the benefits of the challenged design outweigh the risk of danger inherent in such design."[15]

Whether one expresses the basic idea in terms of risk-utility, risk-benefit, or cost-benefit, the type of test just described differs from the Learned Hand test. As explained above, the Hand test is essentially a cost/cost test rather than one weighing costs or risks against utility or benefits.

As suggested above, what is common to all of these tests is their at least superficially quantitative approach. However, we should elaborate a point made earlier about the qualitative aspects of negligence. Although courts judging tort cases often refer to efficiency concerns as guidelines, both explicitly and implicitly, they also tend to ask whether a particular decision is fair, either as between the parties or as a social matter. We further note that often the cost or benefit figures that would enable a truly quantitative balancing under economic approaches are simply not available. In particular, it often will be very hard, if not impossible, to put a dollar figure on the benefits that a particular activity confers on society.

Yet even assuming that courts have available precise figures on relevant costs, or costs and benefits, we can spotlight the difficulty of relying on purely quantitative analysis by posing two hypothetical cases. Assume that in a jurisdiction that applies the Learned Hand test, the quantified cost of accidents—the plaintiffs' dam-

---

14. Restatement (Second) of Torts § 292, cmt. b (1965).

15. Barker v. Lull Eng'g Co. , 573 P.2d 443, 456 (Cal.1978).

ages—is $250,000 in both cases. Now assume that in one case, the "B" term in Judge Hand's formula—that is, the cost of avoiding the injury—can be quantified precisely as $249,000. In the second case, assume that the avoidance cost is $251,000. Different judges will view the subject through different lenses, but it is very likely that the $2,000 difference between the cases will not be dispositive for most courts. When the numbers are that close—even when there is a precise balance in favor of the defendant—most judges probably will weigh factors other than the numbers in deciding whether the defendant has met the applicable standard of care. Thus, the economic approaches to negligence wind up in practice simply as convenient ways of expressing the qualitative as well as quantitative balancing that is a central part of judicial application of the standard of care in negligence. They are part of a more broad-gauged effort to determine the justice of individual cases.[16]

E. A Multi–Factored View of Negligence

Although efficiency-focused formulas like the Learned Hand test are academically popular, most courts probably take a broader view of the factors that determine whether conduct is negligent. The decision on what negligence means may refer to a dozen or more different purposes and policy goals of tort law, ranging from a moral conviction that the law should aim to reduce the kinds of risks that arise from conduct like the defendant's to the belief that the principal purpose of law is to achieve an economically efficient level of accidents. These rationales also include the idea that the law should focus on achieving individual fairness between litigants, sometimes termed "corrective justice,"[17] and loss spreading.[18] Professor Kenneth Simons has concisely summarized "two levels" of "value judgments" embodied in "a determination that an actor is negligent." One is "the judgment that the actor should have done something different in light of the foreseeable risks of his conduct." The other is a judgment "about the relative advantages and disadvantages of taking such a precaution."[19] He describes one of the "evaluative standards" for determining negligence as one under which the "decisionmaker properly considers morally relevant features of the situation other than aggregate welfare," including "intentions, motives, rights, consent, social role or responsibility,

---

16. See infra, ¶ 19.02E.

17. See supra, ¶ 1.04.

18. See generally ABA Committee on the Tort Liability System, Towards a Jurisprudence of Injury: The Continuing Creation of a System of Substantive Jus-

tice in American Tort Law, ch. 4 (M. Shapo Rptr. 1984).

19. Kenneth W. Simons, The Hand Formula in the Draft *Restatement (Third) of Torts: Encompassing Fairness as Well as Efficiency Values*, 54 Vand. L. Rev. 901, 935 (2001).

justifiable expectations or reliance of others, and reciprocity and distribution of risk."[20]

¶ 19.03 Guidelines for Deriving the Negligence Standard

Because the negligence standard is such an abstract and flexible one, courts seek to define it as specifically as they can, for example, by reference to rules based in legislative standards or industry practice. Such relatively precise standards provide an opportunity in some cases to determine that there is no liability as a matter of law, and in other cases to guide juries, in part to limit arbitrary impositions of liability.

A. Legislative rules

One relatively precise method of defining the standard of reasonable conduct is to refer to "positive law"—rules passed by legislatures or administrative agencies. Violations of those rules—for example, traffic laws or occupational safety regulations—will usually serve at least as evidence of negligence and in some jurisdictions will deemed to be negligent in themselves.[21]

B. Violation of industry standards

Courts also allow parties to refer to industry standards, both as a sword and as a shield. Plaintiffs may use a defendant's violation of an existing industry standard to show that the defendant was acting below the level of due care. This may be a relatively formal standard, like one set up by a trade association to guide the behavior of its members, for example, how many nails to use per square feet in construction of a building. Claimants may also base allegations of negligence on more informal standards, for example, by offering evidence about industry custom or practice in a particular line of activity.

One very powerful way to establish a standard is to invoke rules of conduct that the defendant itself has written down, or otherwise communicated. Thus, courts will allow juries to consider rules announced in manuals or handbooks that companies or governments use to govern the conduct of their employees.

C. Industry custom as a defense

Defendants may, on their part, use industry custom as a defense. They will argue that the fact that all, or most, actors in that line of activity behave as they did proves that they acted

---

20. Id. at 919.   **21.** See Chapter 22 infra.

reasonably. The notion is that the general level of conduct of a relevant community is, in fact, ordinary and prudent behavior.

A counterargument appears in another famous pronouncement of Judge Learned Hand, who issued an important challenge to industry custom as the standard of care. In the case of *The T.J. Hooper*,[22] which involved the failure of a tug owner to provide radio sets for the vessel, the defendant contended that it should be exonerated because other tug owners did not put radios on their craft. Rejecting this argument, Judge Hand declared, in an often-quoted paragraph:

> [I]n most cases reasonable prudence is in fact common prudence; but strictly it is never its measure; a whole calling may have unduly lagged in the adoption of new and available devices. It never may set its own tests, however persuasive be its usages. Courts must in the end say what is required; there are precautions so imperative that even their universal disregard will not excuse their omission.[23]

An important justification for the point of view embodied in *The T.J. Hooper* is that it may provide some incentive to actors to adopt new and significantly safer ways of doing things. *The T.J. Hooper* thus has "technology-forcing" consequences. However, there exists a strong justice argument on the other side: that it is unfair to impose liability on someone for failing to do something that no one else, or very few others, have done. Yet Judge Hand's pronouncement has attracted many courts, and actors who have access to safer technology or other information about safer ways to do things may ignore possible improvements at the peril of liability.

D. Feasible alternatives

A specific issue, which recently has become especially prominent in products liability cases, involves the question of whether feasible alternatives existed for the defendant's course of action. A threshold question is whether a plaintiff must show that a defendant could have provided a safer way of doing things than the one it employed. A plaintiff unable to show a safer alternative will simply claim that a defendant acted in too hazardous a way, even if it could not have behaved more safely and thus would have had only the option of refraining from the activity altogether. A defendant will argue that it would be unfair, as well as depriving society of useful activities, to hold it liable for doing something in one way that could not practically have been done in any other way.

If the court decides that a plaintiff must prove a feasible alternative, another issue concerns the type of proof the plaintiff

22. 60 F.2d 737 (2d Cir.), cert. de-   **23.** Id. at 740.
nied, 287 U.S. 662 (1932).

must offer. An important practical question is whether the testimony of a single expert about the existence of alternative designs or courses of conduct will be sufficient to bring a plaintiff's case to a jury. In a case that involved the design of a door latch system on an automobile, the plaintiff's expert "faulted almost every car he was asked to consider," and even criticized latch designs that he said were safer than the design in the plaintiff's vehicle. Although this critique arguably was especially quarrelsome, the Seventh Circuit reversed a defendant's judgment when the expert had "clearly testified that other, safer designs were available at the time" that would have avoided the plaintiff's injury.[24] A dissenting judge argued that "something more than a professional witness's conclusion, offered without substantiation, that a whole industry is lagging behind the standard of due care is necessary to create a jury issue."[25]

E. Especially high standards

Some courts say that people who engage in certain kinds of activities must measure up to especially high standards of care. These include, for example, providers of electricity, whose enterprise has very hazardous features. Courts have also said that common carriers and innkeepers must meet particularly high standards, emphasizing that guests entrust their personal safety to such businesses.

By contrast, other courts say that the negligence standard is a general one, and that there is no "especially high" standard for any actor except insofar as the standard varies with the circumstances.[26] Yet, courts taking that position are likely to achieve, in practice, a result very much like that reached by courts who say that actors like providers of electricity or innkeepers must meet an especially high standard. Judges who emphasize the generality of the standard will define the circumstances to include the level of hazard of an activity, the possession of expertise, and the way defendants hold themselves out to the public. This is an example of how what may seem to be significantly different characterizations of a standard come out in the same place.

Whatever position courts take concerning the standard for especially dangerous activities, they generally will hold people with highly specialized training to a standard that comports with that

---

24. Chalk v. Volkswagen of America, Inc., 808 F.2d 639, 642–43 (7th Cir. 1986).

25. Id. at 645 (Posner, J., dissenting).

26. See, e.g., Krull v. Keene Corp., 601 F.Supp. 547, 549 (N.D.Ill.1985) ("the duty is always one of *ordinary*

care, but ordinary care requires a greater exercise of caution where there are greater risks of injury"). See also Bethel v. New York City Transit Auth., 92 N.Y.2d 348, 703 N.E.2d 1214 (1998), summarized supra, ¶ 18.01, text accompanying note 4.

experience. The best known instance is the standard for professionals, for example, physicians.[27] Moreover, defendants in many other lines of work who possess specialized knowledge may find their standard of care defined, at least implicitly, by that level of knowledge.

F. Lay judgments

Some plaintiffs will not be able to show a violation of positive law or industry standards, or to demonstrate that the defendant was subject to a standard of care linked to the special hazardousness of an activity or to his expertise. These claimants may seek to draw on common knowledge. In some cases, courts will conclude that lay jurors are well able to determine what reasonable conduct is, without the benefit of particularized external standards or evidence about special features of the activity.

Thus, for example, in a case in which the plaintiff alleged that a hotel overcrowded the tables it set up for an organization's banquet, the court commented that the case was "not scientifically complicated nor technical." The court said that "[w]hile some training and experience in catering and hotel management may be a necessary prerequisite to the handling of a banquet for 1,200 people . . . such training or background is not a *sine qua non* to the ability to determine what is unreasonable crowding and what is not." From this, the court reasoned that "[t]he lay juror knowing no more than the next man about catering procedures could determine from the evidence . . . whether or not the tables were too close for safety."[28] Risks related to simple spatial relations are just one illustration of the sort of issue on which lay jurors can make informed judgments about whether actors were careless in failing to minimize or eliminate danger.

Juries frequently will be called upon to use their life experience and common understanding to assess situations involving allegedly inadvertent negligence. It will often be difficult in such cases to articulate the relatively crisp sort of principle exemplified by government or industry rules. The motorist who takes his eye off the road just for a second, the worker who spills something because she is in a hurry at the moment—these kinds of cases frequently will present jury issues as to whether someone was negligent in the circumstances.

G. Multiple approaches

The methods of demonstrating the standard of care are not exclusive of one another. Plaintiffs may marshal more than one of

---

27. See Chapter 23 infra.

28. LaPlante v. Radisson Hotel Co., 292 F.Supp. 705, 707 (D.Minn.1968).

the kinds of standards discussed above in order show that a defendant was negligent. For example, a plaintiff might invoke not only the violation of an internal standard in the defendant company's manual, but also a failure of the defendant's employee to utilize superior knowledge derived from specialized training. The same plaintiff might even claim that the conduct of a defendant engaged in specialized activity was so blatantly below par that ordinary people could make that judgment for themselves without reference to expertise.[29]

29. A discussion of this possibility in the medical context appears infra, ¶ 48.01.

Chapter Twenty

POSSESSORS OF LAND: CLASSIFICATIONS

Analysis

Controversy has long raged about the liability of possessors of land to those injured on the land. Advocates have argued about the desirability of a traditional set of categories, which some courts have changed. The argument has centered on the justice of using relatively precise classifications to describe visitors for the purposes of determining possessors' liability. Plaintiffs in these cases range from the business associate who stumbles on a loose brick in the sidewalk to the next door neighbor who comes for coffee and falls on an unsecured throw rug, and to the recreational trespasser who suffers paralysis diving into shallow water in a rural pond.

¶ 20.01 The Traditional Categories

Historically, there was common agreement—although the agreement now has eroded—on three major categories of visitors to land: invitees, licensees, and trespassers. In jurisdictions that retain the categories, the characterization of a visitor as belonging in one classification or another will significantly affect his or her chances for recovery.

A. *Invitees*

The most privileged visitor to land is the invitee, to whom a possessor of land has the highest duty of care. The Restatement defines two sub-categories. One is the "public invitee"—a person "who is invited to enter or remain on land as a member of the

89

public for a purpose for which the land is held open to the public,"[1] for example, a customer in an ordinary restaurant. The other is the "business visitor," one "who is invited to enter or remain on land for a purpose directly or indirectly connected with business dealings with the possessor,"[2] for example, a repairman who has been called to the premises.

The basis for classifying persons as invitees is that their "invitation ... carries with it an implied representation, assurance, or understanding that reasonable care has been used to prepare the premises, and make them safe."[3] Because of this premise, the law imposes an especially high duty of care in favor of invitees. A possessor will be liable to an invitee for failure to exercise reasonable care if he "knows or by the exercise of reasonable care would discover" a danger and realize its risk to invitees and "should expect" that they "will not discover or realize the danger, or will fail to protect themselves against it."[4] The invitee category puts a particular burden on possessors to seek out dangerous conditions and make the premises safe or warn about "latent defects."[5]

These duties do not extend, however, to property off the premises of the landowner. Thus, although it may be "good practice" for a hotel to warn of rip tides on a government-owned beach across the highway, the hotel does not owe guests a duty to warn if it does not exercise any management or supervision over the beach. This is so even if the hotel provides chairs, umbrellas and towels on the beach, as well as a security escort service to convey guests across the highway.[6]

Moreover, the generally high duty of landowners to invitees on the premises is subject to some exceptions. One such exception, which applies to work done by independent contractors that is "inherently dangerous," carries overtones of assumption of risk on the part of the employees of such contractors. An example is a case involving injuries to employees of an independent contractor who were working on a "chiller," a large air conditioning unit on the premises of the defendant. A discharge pipe from the chiller unit discharged a hot chemical solution onto a concrete floor, from which it splashed on the plaintiffs. In concluding that the plaintiffs' work was "inherently dangerous," and therefore that the defendant had no duty to them, the court pointed out that the chiller "utiliz[ed] liquids at high temperatures and pressures" and that the plaintiffs' work "occasionally required them to wear protective equipment and clothing." It declared that the issue of whether a job

---

1. Restatement (Second) of Torts § 332(2) (1965).

2. Id. § 332(3).

3. Id. § 332, comment a.

4. Id. § 343.

5. See id., comment b.

6. Darby v. Compagnie Nat'l Air France, 753 N.E.2d 160 (N.Y.2001).

was "inherently dangerous" was "one of probabilities based upon the nature and circumstances of the work."[7] The philosophy of the exception is evident in the court's quotation of a precedent on the proposition that "[o]ne who engages an independent contractor . . . ordinarily owes no duty to the employees of such contractor . . . who proceeds . . . knowing and appreciating that there is a condition of danger surrounding" the performance of the work.[8]

B. Licensees

The second category of visitor, rather less protected than the invitee, is the licensee—"a person who is privileged to enter or remain on land only by virtue of the possessor's consent."[9] Licensees may be people who play football on a vacant lot with the owner's permission, or door-to-door salespersons before they are invited in to discuss their wares. To licensees, a possessor is liable only if he "knows or has reason to know" of a danger, should realize that it poses an unreasonable risk to licensees, and "should expect that they will not discover or realize the danger." If such a condition exists, liability arises if the possessor "fails to exercise reasonable care to make the condition safe, or to warn the licensees" of the danger and the licensees "do not know or have reason to know of the condition and the risk involved."[10]

There is thus a significant distinction between the duties of possessors of land to invitees and to licensees. The law effectively obliges the possessor not only to know of but to discover dangerous conditions with respect to invitees but imposes liability to licensees only if the possessor "knows or has reason to know of the condition." In practice, this standard will impose duties of inspection and surveillance with respect to invitees, for example, concerning slippery conditions or uneven surfaces, that do not exist with regard to licensees. One premise supporting lesser protection for licensees is that "the licensee takes the premises as he finds them."[11]

Ironically, the courts that adhere to the invitee/licensee distinction tend to classify social guests as licensees despite common connotations of the words that would indicate that a social guest is, in language, if not in law, an invitee. In one decision concerning a weekend social guest, employing the idea of licensees taking premises as they find them, the court rationalized this classification by

7. Tackett v. Columbia Energy Group Service Corp., 2001 WL 1463383, at *4–5 (Ohio Ct.App.2001).

8. Id. at 4, quoting Wellman v. East Ohio Gas Co., 113 N.E.2d 629 (Ohio 1953).

9. Id. § 330.

10. Id. § 342.

11. See, e.g., Mendez v. Knights of Columbus Hall, 431 S.W.2d 29, 32 (Tex. Civ.App.1968).

saying that the plaintiff was "entitled to no greater protection than a member of the owner's household."[12]

Other evidence of judicial inclination to construe the categories severely against visitors appears in a federal appellate case in which the plaintiff was invited to hunt pheasants at a ranch owned by the defendant, a livestock company. The plaintiff, who sued for burns caused by contact with a downed power line, contended that he was an invitee. Conceding that "he was not there for a business purpose," he argued that "his presence was for the mutual purpose and advantage of the owner as well as of himself to participate in the hunt, with major stockholders and a majority of the board of directors of the [defendant] participating ... and that hunting was a normal incident to the maintenance of the ranch." However, the court rejected this argument, and instead classified the plaintiff as a licensee, drawing on the trial court's conclusion that the plaintiff had "entered the ranch for social and recreational purposes," and "that he had no business relationship with [the] defendant."[13]

Even a visitor who pays money to the defendant may not be an invitee. A Washington case[14] that taught this lesson involved a "kegger" party held after a high school commencement at a dairy farm under lease by the family of one of the graduates. That graduate bought 15 kegs of beer for the party, which he financed from tickets that were sold for $4. The plaintiff suffered injuries when an automobile hit her as it drove through an area where partygoers were standing. In holding the plaintiff to be a licensee, the court rejected her argument that she had been invited as a member of the public. It said that "invitee" cases were distinguished by situations in which possessors had arranged the premises to lead visitors to believe that " 'the premises were intended to be used by visitors, as members of the public, ... and that reasonable care was taken to make the place safe for those who enter for that purpose.' "[15]Given that the party occurred on a dairy farm, the court commented that it was "hard to imagine how the [defendants] could have prepared or could have been expected to prepare a dairy farm for a kegger."[16]

C. Trespassers

The least favored visitor to the land, for liability purposes as well as in the common use of the word, is the trespasser. The

---

12. Wilder v. Ayers, 156 N.Y.S.2d 85, 88 (App.Div.1956), aff'd, 143 N.E.2d 514 (N.Y.1957).

13. Madison v. Deseret Livestock Co., 574 F.2d 1027, 1033 (10th Cir.1978) (holding, however, that a jury question existed under the licensee standard).

14. Younce v. Ferguson, 724 P.2d 991 (Wash.1986).

15. Id. at 996, quoting McKinnon v. Washington Fed. Sav. & Loan Ass'n, 414 P.2d 773, 776 (Wash.1966).

16. Id.

general standard absolves possessors of liability to at least adults who come on the land "without a privilege to do so created by the possessor's consent or otherwise,"[17] saying that possessors are not liable to trespassers for a "failure to exercise reasonable care ... to put the land in a condition reasonably safe for their reception, or ... to carry on ... activities so as not to endanger them."[18] However, the law does impose a duty of reasonable care in certain circumstances involving trespassers. These situations include cases where the possessor "maintains ... an artificial condition" with a "risk of death or serious bodily harm," and does not warn trespassers about whom "the possessor knows or has reason to know," when the possessor "has reason to believe that the trespasser will not discover" the condition "or realize the risk involved."[19]

There are special rules, which are much more lenient to plaintiffs, when the claimant is a child trespasser.[20]

D. Trespassers at the boundary

A literal boundary question concerns the duty of landowners to technical trespassers, persons who wander onto the perimeter of the defendant's land and suffer injuries because of conditions there. The general rule, favoring the technical trespasser—for example, someone injured at the edge of a public highway—is that the landowner cannot escape liability if it maintains a "trap."[21] An example of a trap would be an unguarded excavation, which the landowner can make safer with relative ease.

More difficult problems may arise with respect to permanent structures. A New York case resolved the issue against the claimant in a suit for injuries sustained when an auto hit a utility pole owned by the defendant. The pole was on private property just

---

17. Restatement (Second) § 329.

18. Id. § 333.

19. Id. § 337. A trespasser may claim consent or privilege, but will face problems of proof. Illustrative is a case in which the plaintiff claimed she had a "regular and consistent" relationship with the defendants' German Shepherd, which she talked to each morning, "greet[ed]" each afternoon, and which she had fed on occasion. One July 4, she found the dog agitated by fireworks and tried to comfort the animal. Unfortunately, a large firecracker exploded while she was cradling the dog, which "lashed out" at her and bit off the end of her nose. Responding to the affirmative defense of trespass to negligence and strict liability claims, the plaintiff argued that she had "implied consent" to come on the defendants' land because of her prior entries on the property "without objection." However, given testimony by the defendants that they had never consented to the plaintiff coming on their land and unrebutted testimony that with one exception they "had no knowledge of plaintiff ever entering onto their driveway to pet their dog," the court rejected this argument. It also rejected the contention that the plaintiff's trespass was privileged "because she acted out of neighborly concern for the dog." Colmus v. Sergeeva, 175 Or.App. 131, 27 P.3d 166, 168–69 (2001).

20. See id. § 339 ("[a]rtificial conditions highly dangerous to trespassing children").

21. Hayes v. Malkan, 258 N.E.2d 695, 696 (N.Y.1970).

seven inches from the roadway, although before the state widened the road to occupy its entire right of way, the pole had been about five feet from the edge of the roadway. The majority reversed a plaintiff's judgment and dismissed the case, reasoning that the opposite result would impose an "intolerable burden" on landowners, who would have "to remove every tree, fence, post, mailbox or name sign" on their properties.[22] A dissent stressed that it was "clearly foreseeable" that even carefully driven autos might "swerve a few inches from the roadway." Invoking the maxim that one may not use his land in disregard of the rights of others, the dissent argued in favor of a jury finding that the pole "created a dangerous condition to oncoming automobiles."[23]

¶ 20.02   The Categories Disputed

There has been a substantial amount of argument about the fairness, and indeed the utility, of the tripartite categories for visitors to land. The landmark case challenging the distinction is the California decision of *Rowland v. Christian*,[24] in which the state supreme court rejected the traditional categories and applied a general negligence standard to determine the liability of possessors of land. In that case, the court said that "major factors" relevant to the liability of possessors, such as moral blame, deterrence and the ability to get insurance, bore "little, if any, relationship to the classifications." The *Rowland* court took the position that although a "plaintiff's status as a trespasser, licensee, or invitee" might have "some bearing on the question of liability," the appropriate standard of care inhered in the general negligence issue—whether the possessor had "acted as a reasonable man in view of the probability of injury to others."[25] Some other jurisdictions, while not going so far as to eliminate the three-part classification system, have abolished the distinction between licensees and invitees.[26]

---

22.   Id.

23.   Id. at 698–99 (Fuld, J., dissenting).

24.   443 P.2d 561 (Cal.1968).

25.   Id. at 568.

26.   See Younce, supra note 14, 724 P.2d at 993–95, summarizing authorities on the various positions concerning the classifications.

The arbitrariness of the categories as applied in a particular fact situation influences the court's decision to abolish the categories in Heins v. Webster County, 552 N.W.2d 51 (Neb.1996). The plaintiff alleged that he slipped on ice at the entrance of a county hospital, where the county argued he was only "paying a social visit to his daughter[,] ... who was the nursing director." The plaintiff claimed he was not only on a social visit but had come to the hospital "to coordinate plans for him to play Santa Claus for the hospital staff party." The trial judge found that the plaintiff was a licensee and did not fulfill the requirements for imposing liability under that category. In reversing, the supreme court noted that "a patient visitor could have used the same front entrance" where the plaintiff fell and could have sued as an invitee. It pointed out that since the hospital had to exercise an invitee-level of care anyway, it would incur "no additional burden in exercising reasonable care for a social visitor" like the plaintiff. See id. at 56.

Many cases illustrate the difficulty of making distinctions between and among visitors to land under any system that classifies visitors. A classic is Judge Cardozo's opinion in a case in which a teenager was killed as he stood at the end of a makeshift diving board, one end of which was under a rock on the defendant railroad's property, and the other end of which extended over a river. The defendant's high-tension wires struck the youth when they fell from a pole on the defendant's land. The situation was one in which the court could have labeled the youth an authorized visitor to the fringe of the defendant's land, with a possibility of recovery, or a trespasser, to whom recovery would be denied. Judge Cardozo took note that landowners had little obligation to those classified as trespassers but pointed out that "[l]andowners are bound to regulate their conduct in the contemplation of the presence of travelers upon the adjacent public ways." He observed that in "a highly technical and artificial" sense, "the diver at the end of the springboard is an intruder on the adjoining lands," but emphasized that "[i]n another sense . . . he is still on public waters in the exercise of public rights." Judge Cardozo concluded that "considerations of analogy, of convenience, of policy, and of justice, exclude him from the field of the defendant's immunity and exemption, and place him in the field of liability and duty."[27]

¶ 20.03 Competing Considerations of Justice

Courts have disagreed strongly over both the use of the visitor categories, and the application of the categories to particular plaintiffs, because of the strength of the competing policy concerns. Courts that have maintained the categories emphasize the nature of property ownership, suggesting that the level of care owed to visitors relates to whether the possessor derives an economic benefit from an activity. Another set of reasons for preserving the categories relates to stability and predictability in the law. As one court noted, "[t]he traditional classifications were worked out and the exceptions were spelled out with much thought, sweat and even tears."[28] Courts that keep the categories believe that they retain an extra margin of ability to distinguish what they consider meritorious cases from those they find unworthy.

Competing against these considerations is the idea that negligence law operates best as a general formula. The argument in favor of abolishing the categories draws strength from the notion that juries are quite capable of determining what reasonable care is in everyday circumstances, perhaps with instructions that they should take into account the status of the visitor as one factor in

---

27. Hynes v. N.Y. Cent. R.R., 131 N.E. 898, 899–900 (N.Y. 1921).

28. Gerchberg v. Loney, 576 P.2d 593, 597 (Kan. 1978).

determining whether the possessor's conduct has been reasonable. Exerting a strong pull toward loosening or discarding the categories is the fact that many disputed cases in this area embody strong arguments of justice on the visitor's behalf—arguments that are enhanced practically, if not always logically, if the visitor suffers severe injuries. Those who advocate a less structured standard are likely to stress that property ownership is a privilege as well as a right, and imposes high obligations as well as offering substantial benefits.

Debates over the standard of liability for possessors of land are particularly interesting because they pit the law's striving for broad rules that will apply to many factual situations against its need to fashion precise classifications that will produce relative certainty of outcome. These controversies also reflect the tension between our commitments to personal autonomy and property rights and our beliefs about the social responsibilities that ownership confers.

Chapter Twenty–One

LIABILITY OF POSSESSORS OF LAND FOR THIRD PARTY ACTS

Analysis

¶ 21.01   The Functional Problem

Possessors of land owe a general duty of care to persons on their property, enforced in many states through a special set of rules that depend on the status of the visitor as invitee, licensee or social guest, and trespasser.[1] Within the overall duty of due care, and also under the applicable categories of visitor status in particular jurisdictions, a specialized set of standards is developing to govern suits against possessors for injuries to visitors directly caused by others. Liability imposed under these rules has entered a relatively expansive phase, and is particularly worrisome to owners of business property because it involves their oversight of the activities of third parties. Writers have attached such labels as "negligent security" to this branch of torts.

The doctrinal basis for this form of liability yields mixed questions of duty and the standard of care. We will discuss relevant aspects of the duty issue below with specific reference to crimes committed by third parties[2]; in this chapter we concentrate on the standard of care for possessors with respect to injuries directly inflicted by third party acts, including crimes.

---

1. See supra, Chapter 20.   **2.** See Chapter 57 infra.

¶ 21.02 The General Rules

At least two tiers of general rules apply to the liability of possessors for injuries caused by third parties. One relatively general rule applies to business persons who hold their premises open to members of the public. This rule imposes liability for "physical harm caused by the accidental, negligent, or intentionally harmful acts" of third parties where the possessor has been negligent in failing to avoid or minimize the risks.[3] Another set of rules, not limited to possessors of land but including them as potential defendants, imposes liability for crimes or intentional torts by third parties if the defendant negligently "created a situation which afforded an opportunity to the third person to commit such a tort or crime." This liability arises if the possessor knew or should have known "that such a situation might be created and that a third person might avail himself of the opportunity to commit ... a tort or crime."[4]

¶ 21.03 Functional Applications

The exposure of possessors of land to liability for the acts of third parties arises in a broad range of activities in which possessors engage. This section presents some significant functional applications of the rules mentioned above.

A. Public places

Those who open their land to the public for commercial purposes may be liable for injuries caused there by others, who posed risks with which the possessor failed to deal prudently. However, the liability rule hardly sweeps in every act of third parties; rather, courts hold possessors liable only for events that are foreseeable to the defendant or fact patterns presenting policy factors that make it just to require compensation from the defendant.

An interesting comparison appears in two cases involving possessors of land who opened their premises for dancing. A California decision affirmed a judgment for a volunteer hostess at an armed forces canteen for injuries caused by her enthusiastic dance partner, a marine, who spun her around in a series of "wild jitterbug antics." The court said that "the trier of fact could reasonably conclude that those in charge of the dance, in the exercise of due care, should have observed the marine's conduct, realized that it was likely to result in injury, and stopped it."[5]

---

3. Restatement (Second) of Torts § 344 (1965) (focusing on failure to exercise reasonable care by not discovering or warning about risks).

4. Id. § 448.

5. Edwards v. Hollywood Canteen, 167 P.2d 729, 734 (Cal.1946).

A different result appeared in an equally colorful Massachusetts case in which another rampant dancer knocked down the
plaintiff and his partner in a Boston ballroom on the evening of St.
Patrick's Day. The court recognized a general standard of liability
for knowledge or constructive knowledge of "the disorderly or
rowdy actions of third persons which might lead to injury." However, it denied recovery, putting the plaintiff in a legal vise between
his general knowledge of the boisterousness of the occasion and the
defendant's inability to foresee the particular conduct of the third
party. As to the plaintiff, the court observed that he had chosen "on
an evening not noted for restraints on exuberance in the city of
Boston to go ... to a public dance hall where he knew the patrons
were lovers of the cha cha and the jitterbug," dances that involve
"muscular contortions and a degree of abandon not associated with
a minuet." Yet, the court also said that the possibly deliberate
character of the bump that knocked the plaintiff down was "not
such a happening that the defendant was bound to anticipate it,"
for it was "unusual and not reasonably to be apprehended."[6] The
court's emphasis on foreseeability is characteristic of judicial efforts
to set the standard of care with respect to the activities of third
parties, as it is characteristic of standard setting in the law of
negligence generally.

The importance of the often-mentioned factor of foreseeability
may vary, however, with the way courts define the main issue—as
one of standard of care or of duty. Sometimes courts will view
foreseeability as primarily relevant to the standard of care, but at
other times they will discuss it with respect to whether the defendant owed the plaintiff a duty, focusing on the relation between the
parties rather than the criterion for conduct. Courts generally will
employ foreseeability as a principal tool of decision when the
question is whether the standard of conduct has been breached—
the "negligence" issue. Many courts also will refer to foreseeability
with reference to the duty question, but with respect to that issue,
policy factors tend to drive decisionmaking more than does actual
or potential foresight.[7]

B. Multi-family residences: Apartments and condomini-
ums

An increasingly important branch of premises liability for
"negligent security" concerns the standard of care of landlords
with respect to third party assaults on tenants. A landmark decision imposed liability in favor of a tenant in a building with 585
apartment units who was assaulted and robbed in the building. The
main entrance of the building had no doorman, the lobby desk was

---

6. Goggin v. New State Ballroom,
247 N.E.2d 350, 351–52 (Mass.1969).

7. See infra, ¶ ¶ 55.04, 57.04.

left unattended much of the time, one side entrance generally was unguarded because of cutbacks in personnel, and the other side entrance was often left unlocked all night. The court effectively set the standard of care by referring to conditions when the plaintiff first signed her lease. At that time, there were a front doorman and a full-time employee at the desk, there was at least one garage attendant who watched the side entrance that opened into the garage, and the other side entrance was locked after nine o'clock.[8]

The New York Court of Appeals favored tenants under a specialized requirement that confronts plaintiffs assaulted in apartment buildings—that is, the need for those claimants to show that the perpetrators were intruders who came into the buildings through negligently maintained entrances. In one of two companion cases, in which no entrances to the building had functioning locks, two men unknown to the plaintiff beat and robbed her. The building had 25 apartments in which she "claimed to know all the tenants" but the appellate division held for the landlord. That court said that when the landlord disputed the plaintiff's claim that the assailant was an intruder, the plaintiff could not succeed if she had not "allege[d] more than just defective security precautions and a general history of crime" on the premises. In the other case, a man came through a negligently maintained back door and got on an elevator with the 12–year-old plaintiff, without pushing a button. He followed her when she left the elevator, forced her to a roof landing, and raped and sodomized her. Given that the building had more than 150 apartments and "hundreds of residents," the lower court concluded that it was "solely ... speculation" to conclude that the assailant was an intruder, although the plaintiff "knew most of the building residents by sight." The problem for the plaintiffs was that if they could not show that the attackers were intruders they would not be able to connect the assaults to the negligent maintenance of entrances. Had the assaults been committed by residents, there would be no showing of "proximate cause" because attackers who were residents were entitled to be in the building whether the entrances were properly secured or not. However, on the facts of both cases, the court of appeals concluded that reasonable persons could decide that the assailants were intruders who came into the building through negligently maintained doors.[9]

Liability for third party crimes on residential premises is now expanding beyond traditional landlord-tenant relationships. The California Supreme Court, for example, has imposed liability against a condominium association for an assault on the premises.

8. Kline v. 1500 Massachusetts Ave. Apt. Corp., 439 F.2d 477, 485 (D.C.Cir. 1970).

9. Burgos v. Aqueduct Realty Corp., 92 N.Y.2d 544, 706 N.E.2d 1163 (1998).

The occasion was a case in which an unidentified man raped and robbed the plaintiff in her condominium unit, where she had herself installed extra exterior lighting after a burglary, but where the condominium board then forbade her to use the lighting, presumably for aesthetic reasons. There was abundant evidence of criminal activity in the condominium project. In holding that the plaintiff had presented enough facts "to show the existence of a duty," the court concluded that the defendant might "have breached that duty of care by failing to respond in a timely manner to the need for additional lighting and by ordering her to disconnect her additional lights."[10]

The court viewed the condominium association as being "for all practical purposes, the Project's 'landlord' "even though the association argued that it was "a nonprofit association of homeowners" on which it would be unfair to impose "expensive" security burdens.[11] The court made foreseeability a touchstone of its holding that the association could have been found negligent, adducing correspondence from residents about the crime problem, as well as articles in the project newsletter, to show that the defendant "was aware of the link between the lack of lighting and crime."[12]

B–1. Social hosts

There may be some room for the imposition of liability on a "social host" for failure to prevent injury inflicted by a third party on a guest in the host's home. The First Circuit implied the possible existence of such a duty in a case in which three men allegedly forced themselves sexually on a woman who was in the bedroom of one of those men, a room located in a house owned by the defendant. There were insufficient facts concerning the incident for the court directly to apply a rule favoring the plaintiff; for example, it was not clear that the defendant "authorized, acquiesced or even knew" of the plaintiff's presence at the time the assaults were occurring. However, the court suggested that state law might not bar liability if the defendant had known of the assaults and "could have intervened without risk."[13] The case cuts across several legal categories: the duty of landowners to particular classes of persons—here social guests; the existence of that duty with respect to third party crimes; and the question of when affirmative duties exist to protect others.

C. Prisons

A governmental function that may involve liability for the acts of third parties, in a setting involving custody of large numbers of

10. Frances T. v. Village Green Owners Ass'n, 723 P.2d 573, 580 (Cal. 1986).

11. Id. at 576.

12. Id. at 579.

13. Doe v. Walker, 193 F.3d 42 (1st Cir.1999).

people, is the operation of prisons. One decision, for example, imposed liability in a case in which one inmate stabbed another in the back when there was evidence that prison officials had "good reason to think that [the stabber] might act violently toward another inmate." The assailant had come to that prison from another institution. The file that came with him revealed offenses including the murder of an inmate, three assaults on correctional officers, and possession of a dangerous weapon. In an action under the Federal Tort Claims Act, the court concluded that this "prior institutional behavior [had] predictive value for future institutional behavior" and held the government negligent.[14]

Courts also have used civil rights legislation that incorporates constitutional rights to impose liability for injuries caused by prison violence.[15] Indeed, acting under that legislation, they have issued orders that require the restructuring of prison systems on constitutional grounds.[16]

D. Schools

The rise of violence in schools has generated another potential field of tort litigation, targeting the governmental units that administer schools. However, courts have generally not been sympathetic to the claims of students suing for assaults on school premises. In a case involving alleged sexual molestation of students by a teacher, brought under a general civil rights statute, a federal appellate decision distinguished schools from prisons and mental hospitals because the state has custody over the person of mental patients and prisoners. In concluding that the plaintiffs had not made out a claim that the school district and its officials had an affirmative duty arising out of a "special relationship" to students, the court opined that although a "state might require a child to attend school," it did not "assume[] responsibility for [the] entire personal lives" of school children.[17]

---

14. Garrett v. United States, 501 F.Supp. 337, 338–39 (N.D.Ga.1980).

15. See, e.g., Smith v. Wade, 461 U.S. 30 (1983) (affirming award of punitive damages against prison guard for "reckless or callous indifference" to threat to prisoner's security).

16. See, e.g., Holt v. Sarver, 309 F.Supp. 362 (E.D.Ark.1970), aff'd, 442 F.2d 304 (8th Cir.1971).

17. J.O. & P.O. v. Alton Community Unit Sch. Dist. 11, 909 F.2d 267, 271–72 (7th Cir.1990).

In a very specific statutory context, the Supreme Court rejected a sexual harassment claim against a school district based on several acts of sexual intercourse between a teacher and a ninth-grade student. The majority of a closely divided Court turned down an appeal by the student and her mother on a claim based on Title IX of the Education Amendments of 1972. The majority required students suing school districts under that statute for sexual harassment by teachers to show that a district official had "actual notice" of the misconduct and that the official's failure to respond "amount[ed] to deliberate indifference to discrimination." Gebser v. Lago Vista Indep. Sch. Dist., 524 U.S. 274, 285–90 (1998).

Another obstacle to claims for third party assaults in schools is the argument that governmental units that operate schools ought not to be responsible in damages for decisions that allocate limited resources. Illustrative is a suit against the District of Columbia for an injury that occurred in a junior high school printing class, apparently when a student threw a piece of type that hit the plaintiff in the eye. Denying recovery, a majority of the court of appeals rejected the claim that the school was negligent because the printing teacher failed to be present to supervise students when class started, given that the teacher knew about "horseplay" and type-throwing in the room. The court focused on the fact that the school had "deployed" teachers, "in an effort to provide for maximum safety and order," at "various places outside their own classrooms." The court viewed the situation as analogous "to other governmental operations involving the safety or well-being of numbers of people," and found a basis for denying liability in the existence of a plan to allocate faculty resources for security purposes.[18] A dissenter, stressing the dangers of the materials used in printing classes, suggested that the majority had fashioned a "special protection" for the defendant because of its governmental function.[19]

¶ 21.03A Comparative fault

A controversial question in cases involving "negligent security" is whether a negligent landowner can invoke a comparative fault defense against a plaintiff who is the victim of a third party's intentional tort. After controversy over the issue,[20] the Restatement on Apportionment of Liability backed away from the question.[21] A particularly emotive issue is whether a landowner—for example, a hotel proprietor—can claim comparative negligence in a plaintiff's suit for her rape by a third party. Professor Bublick has argued powerfully for a plaintiffs' no-duty rule—that is, that "plaintiffs have no duty to take care to prevent the intentionally inflicted harm of rape."[22] She says this is "the only rule that would establish

18. Butler v. District of Columbia, 417 F.2d 1150, 1152–53 (D.C.Cir.1969).

19. Id. at 1154 (Leventhal, J., dissenting).

20. See Ellen Bublick, Citizen No–Duty Rules: Rape Victims and Comparative Fault, 99 Colum. L. Rev. 1413, 1417 n.19, discussing allowance of the defense by negligent tortfeasors in Restatement (Third) of Torts: Apportionment of Liability § 1 cmt. c, reporters' note (Proposed Final Draft 1998), which said that

"[w]hen several actors cause a single injury, comparative responsibility asks a court to treat the injury as a unit and compare the contributions of the various actors."

21. See Restatement of Torts: Apportionment of Liability § 1, cmt. c (2000) ("[t]his Restatement takes no position" on the issue of whether "a plaintiff's negligence may serve as a comparative defense to an intentional tort").

22. Bublick, supra note 20, at 1478.

the basic tenet that rape is not women's fault, either individually or collectively."

¶ 21.04 Underlying Policies

Several policy factors and rationales compete in cases involving the liability of possessors of land for the acts of third parties. Particularly in the public sector, but in many cases involving private possessors as well, courts must confront problems posed to defendants by limited resources and alternative uses for resources. Naturally, courts will also take into account the potential of damages awards to deter injuries directly caused by third parties through the mechanism of putting pressure on the possessor.

Another consideration that may influence decisionmaking, often implicit rather than explicit, is the possibility of loss spreading. Courts may rationalize liability against the private possessor of land on the basis of its ability to spread the loss through insurance, or against a government on the theory that it can spread losses through taxes.

Yet another potentially important element of decision, which again does not always appear explicitly in the cases, concerns the power relationship between the parties. Courts are likely to be sympathetic to plaintiffs who are relatively vulnerable in situations where possessors of land have more power to prevent the injury than their residents or visitors do. Prisons present an obvious illustration of total power on the part of a governmental custodian. An example in the private sector is the case summarized above in which a condominium association prohibited a resident from maintaining her own exterior lighting.[23]

The problem of "negligent security" is a particularly fascinating one in tort law because it brings to the surface the frequently lurking question of which social account is the most appropriate one to charge for an injury. Any judicial decision in cases of this sort implies a judgment about social accounting procedures. Sometimes courts will base that judgment upon the factor of the parties' relative ability to avoid accidents. In other cases they will rest it on utilitarian concerns, reasoning, for example, that the greater good for a greater number of people will be served if the law does not require possessors of land to compensate a few victims of third party assaults.

One should emphasize that by definition, all of these cases involve situations in which there is a more direct tortfeasor than the possessor—that is, the third party. Usually the possessor becomes a target of suit because it is wealthier, or at least has more insurance, or is easier to find than the third party.

---

23. See supra, text accompanying notes 10–12.

Chapter Twenty–Two

STATUTORY VIOLATIONS

Analysis

Tort law originated as common law and has continued to build on that foundation. However, legislatures have enacted statutes with substantial impact on the domain of tort law, including its safety and compensation goals. Every state has removed a large portion of workplace injuries from the sphere of tort through the mechanism of workers' compensation statutes, and many states have enacted statutes that codify or change the common law in particular areas of torts, for example, products liability.

In this chapter we consider the effect in tort actions of a defendant's violation of a statute that regulates safety. These laws are as diverse as criminal and quasi-criminal statutes for the regulation of traffic, federal and state legislation that regulates occupational safety and health, and federal statutes regulating the design of motor vehicles and the flammability of fabrics.

Safety legislation establishes categories of forbidden conduct in advance of that conduct, whereas courts adjudicate specific cases of injury in light of particular circumstances existing at the time of the injury. Because legislation generally outranks judge-made law, statutes that set precise standards concerning tort liability are superior to common law rules. However, the issues discussed in this chapter often arise because it is unclear whether the legislature intended the statutes at issue to affect the common law, or what effect it intended them to have.

105

¶ 22.01   Creating or Modifying a Cause of Action

Legislatures may create tort causes of action where none had existed before. For example, a safety statute may specifically enable individual citizens to sue for violations of its provisions, in addition to giving power to public agencies to enforce the statute. Legislatures also may modify existing rights under tort law. For example, some state legislatures have redefined theories of liability in products liability cases, and have put dollar maximums, or "caps," on the amount of damages a plaintiff may recover for medical malpractice.

¶ 22.02   Implied Causes of Action

Sometimes courts will infer from a statute a legislative purpose to allow persons to sue for violations of the statute even though it does not specifically create a tort cause of action on behalf of private individuals. A Supreme Court decision set out a four-part test to determine whether courts should imply a private right of action from a federal statute: (1) whether the plaintiff is a member of " 'the class for whose *especial* benefit the statute was enacted' "; (2) whether there was "any indication of legislative intent, explicit or implicit, either to create ... a remedy or to deny one"; (3) whether a judicially implied remedy would be "consistent with the underlying purposes of the legislative scheme"; and (4) whether "the cause of action [is] one traditionally relegated to state law, in an area basically the concern of the States, so that it would be inappropriate to infer a cause of action based solely on federal law."[1] Although it has been argued that the Court has discarded this test,[2] it provides a good summary of the sorts of factors that courts will consider in deciding whether to imply a cause of action from a statute.

Although the implied right of action doctrine permits a court to expand remedies, judges are likely to be rather restrained about implying causes of action. Illustrative is a case involving a claim by two local governments that a railroad had violated the Hazardous Materials Transportation Act when it stored butane on a siding. Dismissing the action, a federal court of appeals said that neither the statute nor its legislative history showed "any intent especially to protect a class that includes the plaintiffs, municipalities, among its members," but rather that "[a]ll residents of the United States are the HMTA's intended beneficiaries."[3] It may seem odd that a

---

1. Cort v. Ash, 422 U.S. 66, 78 (1975).

2. Compare the majority opinion in Thompson v. Thompson, 484 U.S. 174, 178 (1988) ("we have relied on the four factors set out in *Cort v. Ash* ... ," supra) with the concurrence of Justice Scalia, id. at 188–89 (*Cort* as "effectively overruled by our later opinions").

3. Borough of Ridgefield v. New York S. & W. R. R., 810 F.2d 57, 59 (3d Cir.1987).

statute designed to protect everyone should not occasion a cause of action for particular members of a broad class—and indeed in favor of claimants that are as representative as municipalities—but courts insist that to support an implied cause of action, a statute must exhibit a special concern with the protection of the plaintiff.

¶ 22.03 Statutory Purpose

Another set of issues concerning the impact of statutes arises when the plaintiff claims that the defendant's statutory violation caused an injury, but the defendant argues that the injury was not within the purpose of the statute. A simple, antiquarian example is the case in which a defendant injures someone while driving carefully on Sunday in a jurisdiction where Sunday driving is prohibited. The plaintiff would contend that the defendant's violation of the Sunday driving statute conclusively establishes liability for the injuries, since they would not have occurred except for the violation. The defendant would argue that the purpose of the statute is solely a religious one and not to reduce accidents and that therefore the duty created by the statute did not apply to this violation and to an injury associated with safe driving. We discuss this set of problems more fully below.[4]

¶ 22.04 Liability Per Se

Apart from creating and implying of causes of action, courts have fashioned a group of rules governing the efforts of plaintiffs to use a defendant's violation of a statute to establish liability or fault for personal injuries. The most severe liability rule applies only to violations of certain kinds of statutes, like those designed to protect a particular, vulnerable class of individuals for whose special benefit the statute was enacted. The effect of this "liability per se" rule is to require a determination of liability without any defenses. A good example of this sort of situation occurs when an employer employs a child in violation of a child labor law, and the child is injured at work. In the child's tort suit, courts are likely not only to hold that the violation of the statute is dispositive that the defendant breached the standard of care, but also to prohibit the defendant from offering any defenses, for example those based on the plaintiff's conduct.[5] That result follows from the precise policy goal of the statute, to protect a class in special need of protection. Bolstering this judgment would be the interpretation, offered by

---

4. See infra, Chapter 56.

5. See, e.g., Strain v. Christians, 483 N.W.2d 783 (S.D.1992) (refusing to allow defense of contributory negligence in death of 14–year-old boy on tractor).

one court, that the legislature's purpose was *"to protect children from their own negligence."*[6]

Another type of statute that will trigger this stringent form of liability is one that requires school bus drivers to tell students to cross in front of the bus when they leave the vehicle and says that drivers must flash their signal lights until the students have reached the other side of the highway. In holding that a bus driver's violation of such a statute entailed "absolute liability" for fatal injuries to a student, the New York Court of Appeals pointed to the specificity of statutory purpose, calling it "a matter of common knowledge" that "children are often unaware of and disregard dangers which are apparent to adults."[7]

¶ 22.05 Negligence Per Se

The doctrine of "negligence per se" also gives statutes strong effect in private injury litigation, although not as strong as that in the "liability per se" category. Under the negligence per se rule, a statutory violation is dispositive on the question of whether the defendant violated the applicable standard of care, at least if the purpose of the statute covered the accident at issue. The court holds the violation to be negligence as "a matter of law," even if for some reason it may not have been determined to be negligence under common law standards. An illustrative negligence per se holding appears in a case in which the plaintiffs attributed the deaths of their decedents in a fire to the lack of smoke detectors in an apartment building, when a city ordinance required the installation of such devices. Declaring that it was "difficult to envision any apartment dwelling, in which its occupants are expected to sleep, that would not require a smoke alarm in order to minimize fire hazard," the court said that "as a matter of law, the ... failure to install a smoke alarm constituted 'a distinct hazard to life and property' "and ruled that the plaintiffs should get a negligence per se instruction.[8]

Because under negligence per se a statutory violation is conclusive on the issue of the standard of care, that doctrine is a strong weapon in the plaintiff's arsenal. However, by contrast with the limited category of liability per se cases, the defendant in a negligence per se jurisdiction may use the plaintiff's substandard or risk-accepting conduct as a defense.

There is theoretical controversy about the desirability of applying negligence per se. Application of the doctrine may be expected

---

6. Id. at 789.

7. Van Gaasbeck v. Webatuck Central School Dist., 234 N.E.2d 243, 246 (N.Y.1967).

8. Hill v. London, Stetelman, and Kirkwood, Inc., 906 F.2d 204, 209 (5th Cir.1990).

to have significant deterrence consequences, because it provides monetary sanctions beyond those that public enforcement of the regulatory statute would impose. However, an argument against the doctrine inheres in the very fact that the tort damages for personal injury resulting from a statutory violation may be considerably greater than the relatively small fines that statutory breaches often entail. In addition, those who oppose a negligence per se rule argue that when a statute does not specifically declare that it sets a tort standard—as most safety statutes do not—courts should not interpret it to be dispositive on the negligence issue. Courts that refuse to make statutory violations negligence per se draw on the idea that if a statute does not articulate a rule that expands liabilities, one should construe it narrowly.

Similar disagreements arise with respect to the question of whether applying negligence per se to statutory violations will justly fix personal responsibility in a moral sense. Advocates of the doctrine invoke the idea that statutes represent an authoritative community determination of a standard of care, and argue that therefore statutory violations should be conclusive on the issue of whether that standard has been violated. Moreover, a rule that courts must deem a defendant negligent for violation of a statute will give extra predictability to the law. Predictability, indeed, provides several social benefits. Of particular relevance to the moral content of law is the advantage of notifying people what the law is—an important ingredient of procedural fairness. Predictability also contributes to reducing uncertainty about the law for litigants.

By contrast, one may argue that in certain contexts, the concept of moral responsibility is rather attenuated by the nature of the activity. For example, if one believed that the idea of "fault" is an outmoded one in the fast-moving environment of modern traffic, one would assert that the application of the negligence per se rules to cases involving vehicle accidents would sometimes enforce an impossible standard of moral responsibility. Besides being unfair, this would generate disrespect for the law.

¶ 22.06   Presumption of Negligence

Some courts employ the terminology of presumptions to describe the effect of statutory violations in tort actions, saying, for example, that the breach of a statutory rule creates a presumption that the defendant was negligent. A widely accepted technical definition is that a presumption is a rule of law requiring one to draw certain conclusions from certain facts, rather than simply being a rule of evidence—evidence to be weighed along with the other evidence in the case. However, the result of creating a presumption often will overlap the effects produced by other doctrines that we have discussed. Courts do not always distinguish clearly among terms and concepts in this area.

There are two kinds of presumptions that may attach to the violation of a statute. One is a rebuttable presumption of negligence. Although this type of presumption initially favors the plaintiff, it allows the defendant to introduce evidence that the defendant behaved carefully, with the result that the plaintiff cannot argue that the statutory violation necessarily compels an inference of negligence. The use of rebuttable presumptions in this context shares some elements with the negligence per se doctrine. If the defendant fails to rebut the presumption, the defendant will effectively be deemed negligent. However, even if the defendant does not offer a rebuttal on the issue of its care, it may still be able to show that the contributory negligence of the plaintiff was effectively the cause of the accident. In other applications, rebuttable presumptions may simply have the effect of being evidence of negligence that may be rebutted by defensive evidence that there was no negligence.

The other presumption is the irrebuttable presumption, which requires the court to draw the conclusion that the defendant was negligent, and does not permit the defendant to offer evidence that it was not. This will have at least the effect of a finding of "negligence per se," and in some cases it may amount to the imposition of absolute liability, depending on whether the court allows the defendant to offer evidence that the plaintiff's conduct was substandard.

¶ 22.07 Evidence of Negligence

As already has been implied, another possible effect of a statutory violation is that the court simply will regard it as evidence of negligence to be weighed along with the plaintiff's other evidence of the defendant's lack of due care, as well as the defendant's evidence negating negligence. This rule commends itself to many courts. If a court rules that a statutory violation is evidence of negligence, then it does not have to concern itself with the fact that a statute does not specifically mention that its violation should be deemed negligence without the possibility of rebuttal. Moreover, although an evidence of negligence rule is not as chiseled and predictable as a negligence per se rule, many people would argue that in the end it is more just, providing more flexibility in judging than the more rigid standard of negligence per se. Those who believe that tort decisions should principally respond to considerations of economic efficiency may argue in favor of an evidence of negligence standard rather than a negligence per se rule. They would ask why one should allow collectively determined standards, which may often involve moral concerns that cut against efficiency considerations, to be dispositive on the question of negligence.

Even jurisdictions that hold that the violation of statutes is negligence per se are likely to hold that the violation of an agency regulation, as distinguished from a statute, is only evidence of negligence. This reflects the priority that statutes have over administrative rules, which are the creatures of statutorily created agencies as contrasted with elected representative bodies.

The question of even the admissibility of regulations to show negligence has itself been the subject of argument. The Colorado Supreme Court noted that an argument against admitting evidence of violation of a regulation of the Occupational Safety and Health Administration on protective railings was that to allow the evidence would " 'enlarge[]' the defendant's liability." However, in ruling that the evidence should be admitted, the court pointed out that to exclude evidence of the regulation would leave the jury with "fewer tools to determine" the relevant standard of care.[9]

¶ 22.08 Excuse and Justification

An interesting set of questions arises when a defendant who has violated a statute asserts an excuse or justification for the violation. A sympathetic example from the defendant's point of view is a situation in which a technical statutory violation occurs when the defendant has no practical opportunity to avoid the injury at issue. In one case, the defendant was driving a church bus that had a rearend collision when the brakes suddenly failed, an event the defendant attributed to a hole in the brake line that caused a sudden loss of brake fluid. The defendant testified about his efforts to avoid the accident after he realized that the brakes were not working. Although a statute required vehicles to have brakes that were "adequate to control movement," the court derived from precedent the rule that one who "properly maintains brakes . . . will not be liable for damages resulting from unexpected brake failure if he acts as a prudent person after failure occurs."[10]

Other situations in which courts will allow defendants to excuse or justify their accident-causing behavior arise in traffic conditions where the defendant acts in a way that creates a risk to the plaintiff in order to avoid a risk to the defendant that has developed without the defendant's negligence. An example is a situation where a defendant motorist, in order to avoid a dangerous situation ahead of him, tries to pass the plaintiff and moves into the plaintiff's lane in violation of a statute prohibiting such maneuvers until the passing car is "safely clear of the overtaken vehicle."

9. Scott v. Matlack, Inc., 39 P.3d 1160, 1169 (Colo.2002).

10. Gowins v. Merrell, 541 P.2d 857, 860 (Okla.1975).

In a decision holding that it was not error to give an excuse instruction in such a case, the court said that the evidence allowed a finding that the defendants' driver "acted as would a person of ordinary prudence who desired to comply with the law."[11]

The problem of excuse and justification simply highlights the tensions that arise in the area of statutory violations from such competing elements of decision as predictability and fairness. On the one hand, courts are inclined to seek precise and predictable rules, and they give substantial credit to legislative determinations of safety standards because such statutes represent considered community judgments. On the other hand, negligence is a fact-sensitive concept, and courts must take into account compelling considerations of individual justice.

11. Foster   v.   Continental   Can
Corp., 783 F.2d 731, 733 (7th Cir.1986).

Chapter Twenty–Three

MEDICAL STANDARD OF CARE

Analysis

Tort law faces a difficult task in setting standards of care for professionals. There has been particular controversy about the definition of reasonable levels of conduct for physicians. The social and monetary stakes are high in litigation over alleged medical malpractice, and the ferocity of argument about the effects of law on medicine reflects those stakes.

Although some question the efficacy and justice of tort law as a shaper of professional conduct, there is certainly reason to believe that tort standards influence the behavior of doctors, just as they influence the conduct of people in many other forms of activity. The case for legal control of physicians' conduct is evident in statistical estimates that thousands of episodes of negligent medical care occur every year.[1] Another dimension of the problem, however, inheres in the risk that overly stringent standards—or standards too vague to inform practitioners when liability will be imposed—will leave doctors confused and unable to use their best judgment, sometimes even driving them from their practices altogether. It is against this complex background that courts must fashion legal doctrine.

¶ 23.01 Liability Doctrines

A few basic doctrines are the workhorses of medical malpractice litigation. At the most culpable end of the spectrum of physi-

---

1. See, e.g., Troyen Brennan, et al., Incidence of Adverse Events and Negligence in Hospitalized Patients, 324 N. Eng. J. Med. 370 (1991) (estimating that in a one-year period "there were 98,609 adverse events and 27,179 adverse events involving negligence" in New York State alone).

cians' conduct, patients may claim that doctors induced submission to medical care by fraud. In cases that involve a literal laying on of hands—as in surgical procedures—a patient may allege that a procedure was a battery because it was done without consent, or because consent was procured by fraud. The concept of "informed consent," which provides a bridge between battery theory and negligence, receives separate treatment below.[2]

Although informed consent doctrine has developed significantly in the years since its invention in the early 1970s, basic negligence law remains the central theory in medical malpractice litigation. Negligence comprehends a wide range of activities and modes of operation, and it adjusts its standards to those varieties of conduct, including professional activities. A fundamental ingredient of a physician's standard of care is the doctor's level of information, and the legal standard includes a requirement that doctors keep up with developments in their fields, however general or specialized they may be. The negligence standard also applies to diagnosis and to a doctor's selection of a procedure or of a course of treatment. Moreover, negligence law judges the physician's effectiveness in communicating the risks and benefits of treatment to a patient, overlapping substantially with informed consent theory in that regard. Finally, the negligence standard applies to the performance of medical procedures, such as surgical operations.

The world of "managed care," involving complex administrative structures, has generated a new set of issues about standard of care and duty. Illustrative of issues that overlap those topics is a Kansas case in which a pregnant woman was tested and treated during her pregnancy by a succession of doctors. Early in the pregnancy she tested positive for hepatitis B. After the plaintiff child was born, she was not given the gamma globulin injection and hepatitis B vaccine that were medically indicated, and she later proved to be hepatitis B antigen positive and was identified as a chronic carrier of the disease. The court concluded that "a physician who has a doctor-patient relationship with a pregnant woman ... also has a doctor-patient relationship with the fetus."[3] However, it also said that a doctor who transfers a patient to another physician can argue that a "different standard of care" applies to a transferring doctor. Specifically, it said that it was up to the jury to decide "whether a patient's primary care physician continues to be responsible for the well-being of the expectant patient and the ... fetus, even when the patient is referred to an obstetrical specialist."[4]

---

2. See Chapter 27 infra.

3. Nold v. Binyon, 31 P.3d 274, 289 (Kan.2001).

4. Id. at 287.

¶ 23.02   Judge and Jury

The doctrines summarized above do their work within a procedural frame in which a crucial question is whether the court should send a case to the jury. In the medical malpractice area, because practically all jurors are at some times patients and few jurors are doctors, courts must concern themselves with the possibility that juries will be unduly empathetic to injured patients. They must fashion standards in the context of the fact that much medical treatment involves specialized forms of knowledge that are not part of the everyday experience of jurors. For that reason, courts have developed a number of particularized rules that bear on the question of whether juries should be allowed to determine what is reasonable care in medical malpractice cases. Some of the most important of these rules relate to the specialization of medical care, the use of expert testimony, and the geographical environment in which care is delivered.

¶ 23.03   Specialization and Expert Witnesses

Important issues in medical malpractice arise from the plaintiff's burden to show the breach of the standard of care at issue, particularly the standard of a medical specialty. In some cases, courts may hold that alleged malpractice is so clearly within the sphere of common knowledge that lay jurors may decide for themselves that the standard has been violated.[5] However, in most instances, courts will require that claimants use experts to prove the standard. Within a specialty, of course, experts may testify about the performance of other experts. Moreover, as we explain further in the next section,[6] a physician with a high degree of expertise may testify, with adequate preparation by the examining lawyer, about the standard of care of someone who has less expertise or fewer resources. In cases of this sort, the examining lawyer must familiarize the witness "with the facilities, resources, services and options available" to the defendant.[7]

The other side of the problem appears when a plaintiff offers as an expert a physician who has no training or experience in a specialized field. In some cases, courts will simply hold that the proffered witness has insufficient expertise to testify. However, they may also decide that the witness's status as a physician gives him the ability to speak to the standard of care, and leave it to the defense to point out his lack of specialization and the weakness that implies for his testimony.[8]

---

5. See Chapter 48 infra.

6. See infra, ¶ 23.04.

7. See, e.g., Hall v. Hilbun, 466 So.2d 856, 875 (Miss.1985).

8. See, e.g., Ouellette v. Subak, 391 N.W.2d 810, 816–17 (Minn.1986) (allowing testimony of pediatric neurologist on issue of obstetrics).

An important practical problem concerning expert testimony arises from a group of competing concerns. On the one hand, particularly in small communities, the pool of available experts may be tiny and as a practical matter closed to the plaintiff, because of a reluctance of physicians to opine that other doctors have erred. Even in the wider world, specialists may be unwilling to testify against colleagues who they encounter at professional conferences and whose good will they particularly value, for example, for the purpose of securing referrals. For these reasons, courts are likely to give latitude to witnesses who do not possess a particularized kind of expertise, so long as they are licensed physicians. On the other hand, one must consider the potential unfairness of judging a specialist by a different standard of care than that which her training has bred into her as the standard of her specialty. It is a cardinal principle of jurisprudence, which carries over into medical malpractice law, that a person should be able to know the standards by which he or she will be judged in the future.

¶ 23.04 The Factor of Geography

Geography is an important factor in determining the standard of care in malpractice cases. This is not surprising in a vast and diverse country, one with a judicial system in which 50 states make their own negligence rules, and federal courts as well as state courts must interpret those rules.

The main battleground lies in the question of whether the standard of care is essentially a "national" or "local" one. The idea of a national standard of care for professional malpractice continues to attract support. Courts that have adopted one version or another of the national standard concept have aligned themselves with the declaration of the Mississippi Supreme Court that "[w]e would have to put our heads in the sand to ignore the 'nationalization' of medical education and training." The court made that observation in a decision that reversed the exclusion of testimony of two physicians from Cleveland, Ohio, in a case involving alleged malpractice in Pascagoula, Mississippi. It pointed out that physicians were "far more mobile than they once were," and that throughout their careers, doctors have "ready access to professional and scientific journals and seminars for continuing medical education from across the country."[9] Specifically with respect to an element of the case before it, the court commented that "[a] pulse rate of 140 per minute provides a danger signal in Pascagoula, Mississippi, the same as it does in Cleveland, Ohio."[10]

9. Hall, supra note 7, 466 So. 2d at 870.

10. Id.

Yet, courts also feel compelled to take into account the variation in resources available to physicians. As the Arkansas Supreme Court said, although an ideal standard might require that small town physicians send patients to larger centers, "when this is not practicable, the small town doctor should not be penalized for not using means or facilities not reasonably available to him."[11] One way to harmonize these positions, insofar as it can be done, appears in a statement by the Mississippi court in the decision mentioned above. That court observed that a physician could not be expected to use the most up-to-date facilities and equipment if he or she does not have ready access to them. However, it opined that the "objectively reasonable expectations regarding the physician's knowledge, skill, capacity for sound medical judgment and general competence are, consistent with his field of practice and the facts and circumstances in which the patient may be found, *the same everywhere.*"[12]

A related harmonizing principle in this area is that while physicians with access only to limited resources cannot be expected to utilize the most sophisticated equipment, doctors also must know their own limitations. This principle also suggests that when a rural physician, for example, is in a position to refer a patient to a more sophisticated facility, he or she should do so. However, given realities of geography and poverty, as a practical matter courts must sometimes bend the principle to allow a physician with relatively limited skills or resources to do his or her best in the setting of a particular case.

Thus, courts have developed a spectrum of standards that include "national standards of care," "locality rules," and "modified locality rules." What courts struggle for is a way to encourage the provision of care as good as possible in medical communities with limited resources, while holding specialists to standards matched to their training and their advertised expertise.

Some states have effectively introduced a "locality" feature in their rules concerning expert testimony by requiring that medical experts must be licensed to practice in the jurisdiction. A Tennessee statute sets forth this general rule, with exceptions that allow a plaintiff to offer a witness from a "contiguous bordering state," and that permit the trial court to allow out-of-state witnesses "when it determines that the appropriate witnesses otherwise would not be available."[13] The Tennessee Supreme Court upheld this statute against a constitutional challenge, saying that it provided a " 'safe-

---

11. Gambill v. Stroud, 531 S.W.2d 945, 950 (Ark.1976).

12. Hall, supra note 7, 466 So.2d at 872.

13. Tenn. Code Ann. § 29–26–115(b) (1997).

ty valve' for those situations in which a party is unable to locate a qualified expert within this state or one of our bordering states."[14]

Important policy considerations bear on geography-centered issues related to the medical standard of care. In a time of advancing knowledge and technology, courts naturally seek to enforce advanced "states of the art" in order to assure the best care for patients. At the same time, they must be cognizant of the disincentives that rigid enforcement of uniform standards would provide concerning practice in relatively isolated or impoverished places. If the application of sophisticated standards causes doctors to leave or shun such locales, depriving entire communities of the services of a licensed physician, it would be counterproductive.

¶ 23.05   Honest Error in Judgment

An issue whose resolution will sometimes prove crucial is whether courts should tell juries that doctors are "not responsible for an honest error in judgment in choosing between accepted methods of treatment." The Minnesota Supreme Court subtly balanced the competing considerations on this question in a case involving alleged negligence in the management of a pregnancy and the delivery of a baby who turned out to be seriously brain-impaired. The court agreed with the plaintiffs that words like "honest" or "good faith" were too "subjective," but also said that it was important to preserve a sense of "the limitations of professional liability" that would "serve to caution the jury that liability should not be imposed merely because of a bad result or the 'wrong' choice of an accepted method of professional care." The court stressed that "[t]he fact a doctor may have chosen a method of treatment that later proves to be unsuccessful is not negligence if the treatment chosen was an accepted treatment on the basis of the information available to the doctor at the time a choice had to be made." However, having noted that "[p]rofessionals are hired for their judgment and skill," the court declared that "a doctor must . . . use reasonable care to obtain the information needed to exercise his or her professional judgment, and an unsuccessful method of treatment chosen because of a failure to use such reasonable care would be negligence."[15]

¶ 23.06   Custom

The influence of custom on the medical standard of care generates interesting issues from both practical and academic points of view. The rules discussed above on specialization[16] and

14. Sutphin v. Platt, 720 S.W.2d 455, 458 (Tenn.1986).

15. Ouellette, supra note 8, 391 N.W.2d at 815–16.

16. See ¶ 23.03 supra.

geography[17] often will effectively decide the question of whether a physician may use her adherence to professional custom as a defense. In jurisdictions that incline to a locality-based rule, community custom is likely to provide a defense as a practical matter. Where state rules allow specialists from other jurisdictions to prove the standard of care, courts are more likely to view observance of local custom that falls below a developing national standard as grounds for a negligence claim.

Perhaps the most-discussed challenge to the defense that a physician employed a widespread mode of medical practice appeared in *Helling v. Carey*,[18] which fell at the intersection of two much-cited standards developed by Learned Hand. In that case, the defendant ophthalmologist did not give a "simple" and "relatively inexpensive" test for glaucoma to a thirty-two-year-old woman, when the test was not routinely given to people under forty. Explaining a decision that in effect allowed a jury to find that eye specialists generally were acting negligently in failing to give the test to members of the younger age group, the court declared that it was "the duty of the courts to say what is required to protect patients under 40 from the damaging results of glaucoma." The court quoted Learned Hand's declarations in *The T.J. Hooper* that "a whole calling may have unduly lagged in the adoption of new and available devices," that "[c]ourts must in the end say what is required," and that "there are precautions so imperative that even their universal disregard will not excuse their omission."[19]

It may seem extraordinary that courts should set a new standard for medical practice where the existing one is virtually universal. However, scholars have rationalized the decision in *Helling* by arguing that its invocation of *The T.J. Hooper* actually provided a cost-effective and therefore efficient rule, in keeping with the "Learned Hand test" in the *Carroll Towing Company* case that compares the burden of the costs of accident avoidance with the probable cost of injuries.[20]

¶ 23.07 Competing Approaches to the Medical Standard of Care

From a theoretical point of view, one can identify several judicial approaches that may significantly influence the standard of

---

17. See ¶ 23.04 supra.

18. 519 P.2d 981 (Wash.1974).

19. Id. at 983, quoting The T.J. Hooper, 60 F.2d 737, 740 (2d Cir.1932). For discussion of The T.J. Hooper, see supra, ¶ 19.03(C).

20. See William Schwartz and Neil Komesar, Doctors, Damages and Deter-

rence: An Economic View of Medical Malpractice, 298 New Eng. J. Med. 1282 (1978), discussing this hypothesis in the context of the "Learned Hand rule" in United States v. Carroll Towing Co., 159 F.2d 169 (2d Cir.1947), which is discussed supra, ¶ 19.02(D).

care in cases of medical malpractice. An instrumental, public policy-oriented approach would specifically center on the consequences of judicial decisions. On the one hand, for example, a higher standard of care is likely to inspire improvements in the overall care that physicians provide. On the other hand, a relatively high standard of care may drive up malpractice insurance premiums and generate unnecessary diagnostic tests for the purposes of avoiding liability ("defensive medicine"), thus increasing patients' bills. Moreover, as we have suggested, the practical effects of those costs may be to push some physicians out of medical practice, especially physicians in small towns whose skills are not at the highest level but who may provide generally adequate levels of care. Economic models would fix on the relative costs of imposing liability or not imposing it, taking into account the cost of securing advanced equipment or information about improvements in techniques.

Advocates of an approach focused on individualized justice would emphasize the vulnerability of patients and their relative lack of information, but would also consider the unfairness of imposing standards that are not easily knowable upon physicians who act in good faith. Finally, a contract-oriented model would view doctors and patients as arms-length economic actors and bargainers. It would raise, among other issues, such questions as how effectively a physician has communicated to a patient the risks and benefits of a course of treatment, as well as whether the doctor has informed the patient of the limitations of the physician's own abilities or access to facilities.

Courts may not always identify this competition among approaches, or indeed their own major premises, but the choices they make among these ideas will have an impact on their decisions.

[Chapters 24–25 are reserved for supplementary material.]

Section Four

DEFENSES TO NEGLIGENCE CLAIMS

Chapter Twenty–Six

EXPRESS ASSUMPTION OF RISK

Analysis

The most direct way for potential tort defendants to avoid liability for negligence is to have prospective plaintiffs explicitly assume the risk of injury, by agreeing in advance that they will not sue for injuries, even those that occur because of the defendant's culpable conduct. A procedural result of enforceable agreements of this sort—often called exculpatory clauses—is that they may make possible a summary judgment for defendants, obviating the need to conduct a trial in order to determine the culpability of either party. Variations on exculpatory clauses appear in disclaimers and limitations of liability in contracts for goods and services.

¶ 26.01   Clarity and Conspicuousness

An initial set of issues related to defendants' attempts to "contract out" of tort liability for injuries concerns notice of the terms of the agreement. Because courts are likely to look critically at efforts to bar a liability that otherwise would exist under the general law, they will require defendants seeking to enforce exculpatory agreements to show that the agreement is clear and conspicuous.

As to clarity of meaning, a product seller that wishes to disclaim liability for harms caused by negligence is well advised to name that theory of liability in the disclaimer clause of the sales contract. In a case involving industrial machine components that did not work properly, the seller's printed form had a provision headed "Warranty" that limited its liability "to the purchase price

121

of the defective item" and said that "in no event are we to be liable for any loss of profits or special or consequential damages." In the buyer's suit for losses attributed to performance failures of the components, the court refused to enforce the exculpatory language with respect to tort damages based on allegations of negligence.[1]

Among other factors that influenced the decision was a state law standard that required "clear and explicit language" or an expression in "unequivocal terms" of the parties' intent to exculpate themselves from liability. The court referred specifically to the form's lack of explicit reference to the theory of negligence. It viewed this as "one factor to be weighed" in deciding whether the defendant had clearly exculpated itself from liability for negligence.[2]

Besides making clear what legal theories are covered by exculpatory clauses, those who deal in goods and services must be sure that their efforts to absolve themselves of liability through documents are conspicuous. This is an explicit requirement of the Uniform Commercial Code's disclaimer provisions concerning implied warranties,[3] a form of liability that closely parallels tort liability for defective products.[4] Sometimes this may resolve itself into a matter of typography. Courts frequently hold disclaimers invalid on grounds of inconspicuousness because the paragraphs that contain them do not catch the reader's attention in documents which include many other provisions. And courts may especially be inclined to deny legal force to a disclaimer buried within a document featuring language that "extols the virtues and the effectiveness" of a product. In a case involving defective cattle vaccine that focused on a breach of warranty theory, in which language about the benefits of the product dominated a disclaimer, the court expressed "doubt that a busy rancher would pour over the last few lines of [a paragraph] after earlier being assured of the safety and effectiveness of the vaccine."[5]

There are some cases in which the requirements of clarity of meaning and conspicuousness run together. Illustrative is a case where a seller positioned a disclaimer under the bold print heading "TERMS OF WARRANTY." The court refused to enforce the clause, saying that the presentation suggested "a grant of warranty rather than a disclaimer."[6]

1. Berwind Corp. v. Litton Indus., 532 F.2d 1 (7th Cir.1976).

2. See id. at 4 n.6, 7.

3. See U.C.C. § 2–316(2) ("to exclude or modify the implied warranty of merchantability ... the language must mention merchantability and in case of a writing must be conspicuous, and to exclude or modify any implied warranty of fitness the exclusion must be by a writing and conspicuous").

4. See infra, ¶ 38.01.

5. Pearson v. Franklin Labs., 254 N.W.2d 133, 142 (S.D.1977).

6. Hartman v. Jensen's, Inc., 289 S.E.2d 648, 649 (S.C.1982).

Some subtle problems lie behind the simple requirements of clarity and conspicuousness. They concern, among other things, the question of whether the plaintiff in fact understood that exculpatory language negated the opportunity to bring a tort suit for culpable conduct or a defective product. This obviously ties into the matters of clarity and conspicuousness, but it also raises the issue of how to judge exculpatory clauses in cases where the plaintiff has relatively limited knowledge or expertise. Although courts may only occasionally invalidate disclaimers in agreements between business firms, they are more likely to be hostile to such clauses in consumer contracts.

¶ 26.02   "Public Policy" and Competing Rationales

The question of the ability of consumers and others to understand exculpatory language leads into an important and controversial issue: whether courts ought to invalidate some exculpatory clauses as being against "public policy." That abstract phrase alone does not justify denying effectiveness to an exculpatory agreement; one always must ask which policy, in particular, provides support for the invalidation of such a clause.

The answer depends in part on the nature of the activity that caused the injury and its place in the social and economic scheme of things. Frequently it also depends on the necessity of the activity to the plaintiff and on the plaintiff's relative vulnerability in the circumstances of the transaction.

One type of agreement concerning which courts have been prone to overturn exculpatory clauses is apartment leases. A policy umbrella for holdings of this sort appears in the idea that exculpatory clauses in leases, even for private housing, are a matter of public interest. Making that point, the Washington Supreme Court referred to the rental of multi-family housing as having "developed into a major commercial enterprise directly touching the lives of hundreds of thousands of people who depend upon it."[7]

Some courts have reserved special condemnation for attempts to enforce exculpatory agreements against low-income tenants, reasoning that such tenants have no meaningful choices to secure shelter. An illustrative case involved an infant who was scalded by very hot water in the bathroom of a public housing unit. She sued the housing authority for providing an apartment in which water could be as hot as 200 degrees. An exculpatory clause in the lease purported to absolve the defendant from all liability for injury on the premises. The Washington court, referring to the statute that enabled the construction of the public housing, concluded that the legislature had determined to build the housing on behalf of people

7. McCutcheon v. United Homes Corp., 486 P.2d 1093, 1097 (Wash.1971).

who were "unable to obtain safe and sanitary housing elsewhere." Employing language of a sort frequently used to invalidate exculpatory clauses, the court said that the situation "presents a classic example of unequal bargaining power" and declared that to uphold the exculpatory provision would be to "put[] the tenants at the mercy of the defendant housing authority's negligence."[8]

In another case, which involved a tenant in low income housing who received a rent subsidy from a county, the court focused on several factors that it used to test exculpatory clauses. A principal factor applicable to the case at issue was that "[h]ousing in general, and residential leases in particular, are increasingly the subject of governmental regulation." Referring to other factors in its standard, the court spoke of housing as "a basic necessity of life," and noted that there was no indication that the defendant had made provisions that would have allowed the plaintiff to pay for the opportunity to sue for negligence.[9]

The basic nature of shelter, no matter how fancy, is a principal reason that even lessors who provide relatively expensive housing may not be able to enforce exculpatory agreements. For example, in one case, the defendant tried to require tenants to sign an exculpatory clause in order to use a swimming pool. The court gave summary judgment for the plaintiffs, invalidating the clause, saying that it would have "insulate[d] defendants civilly from the consequences of violations of their duties to the public under the common law" and the local building code.[10]

The policy considerations we have discussed may favor defendants in cases in which the plaintiff is not as driven by necessity as in the case of housing. Particularly where the plaintiff is a pleasure-seeker, courts will be much more inclined to uphold agreements in which the plaintiff accepts risks and releases the defendant from liability. A graphic example is the case of parachute jumping. In a decision that enforced an exculpatory clause against a chutist, the court contrasted parachuting with, for example, the provision of medical care. It declared that "[p]arachute jumping ... is not an activity of great importance to the public and is a matter of necessity to no one."[11]

8. Thomas v. Housing Auth. of Bremerton, 426 P.2d 836, 842 (Wash. 1967).

9. Henrioulle v. Marin Ventures, Inc., 573 P.2d 465, 469 (Cal.1978).

10. Tenants Council of Tiber Island–Carrollsburg Square v. DeFranceaux, 305 F.Supp. 560, 562–63 (D.D.C. 1969).

11. Hulsey v. Elsinore Parachute Ctr., 214 Cal.Rptr. 194, 199 (Ct.App. 1985). The same point of view informs a decision holding that an exculpatory clause barred a claim against a fitness club for injuries sustained on an exercise machine. Besides concluding that the services of a fitness center were not "essential" in nature, the court focused on the competitiveness of the industry, pointing out that the metropolitan area

This court, noting the conspicuousness of the exculpatory language at issue, also rejected the plaintiff's argument that the agreement was "unconscionable." Pointing to the capitalized bold-faced words, "AGREEMENT & RELEASE OF LIABILITY," the court said it was "hard to imagine that plaintiff, after having initialed the agreement in three places and signed it in one, could have harbored any *reasonable* expectations other than what was unambiguously recited in the title and text of the agreement."[12]

The controversy over whether courts should refuse to enforce exculpatory clauses because of "public policy" features a particularly vigorous set of arguments involving competing rationales. A crucial aspect of the dispute has to do with what is meant by individualized justice in the tort context. Courts dealing with this issue must define for themselves the ethical bases of tort law in order to determine whether a decision achieves a just result.

Defendants relying on exculpatory clauses will emphasize that the plaintiff freely chose the risk by signing the agreement. To the argument that choice is hardly free in environments like low-income housing, defendants will stress that all human beings face significant constraints on their lives and that freedom is a very relative concept. They will insist, moreover, that a refusal to enforce exculpatory clauses will undercut the workings of a free market. This argument theorizes that tenants in low-income housing have "elected" to take a chance on scalding hot water, as a trade-off for rent levels that would increase if exculpatory clauses were not enforced. The argument continues that such tenants would be better off than if they lived as squatters in a shack without water at all.

The argument in favor of invalidating such agreements reaches beyond the scarcity-based concepts of microeconomic theory. In particular cases, it may emphasize that within the relationship of the parties, it is the defendant who holds all the significant power and who has control over the environment and the perils that confront the plaintiff. This line of argument emphasizes that to be held to an agreement, one should have sufficient autonomy to make the agreement with a meaningful degree of freedom.

Judicial use of "public policy" as a rationale for holdings that invalidate exculpatory clauses sometimes seems to inject considerations of social justice into a process that focuses on individual disputes. Legislatures are generally considered the proper arm of government for achieving redistributive justice, and courts are unable, for example, to undertake to provide decent housing for

---

where the plaintiff lived was "home to many exercise and fitness clubs." Seigneur v. National Fitness Inst., Inc., 132   Md.App. 271, 285, 752 A.2d 631, 639 (2000).

12. Id. at 201.

large numbers of people. Cognizant of these realities, judges are likely to base the articulated reasons for refusing to enforce such clauses on the idea that agreements that eliminate liability for clearly unsafe conditions do not effectively represent the "will" of the plaintiff. Thus, even when a court is motivated by a sense of social justice, the stated rationale may well be one that focuses on the autonomy of an individual litigant.

Chapter Twenty–Seven

INFORMED CONSENT

Analysis

A focal point of the legal tensions surrounding medical practice is the question of how much information, and what kinds of information, physicians must provide patients in order to avoid liability. The idea of informed consent provides an important conceptual basis for legal arguments in this area.

¶ 27.01 General Doctrines

The "informed consent" idea is important for medical tort cases brought under both battery and negligence theories. As we have indicated,[1] the basic concept of a battery is a very powerful tool in the law of torts. The heart of the definition of a battery is an unconsented touching, and as applied in medicine, this definition means that a physician who does a procedure on a patient without fully explaining the potential consequences may be liable for a battery because the physician has not elicited the patient's informed consent.[2] Another doctrinal way to describe this result is to say that the physician obtained consent to the touching by fraud.

---

1. See supra, introduction to Chapter 7.

2. See, e.g., Blanchard v. Kellum, 975 S.W.2d 522 (Tenn.1998)(extraction of 16 teeth by dentist who was on the way to extracting all 32 of the plaintiff's teeth until pain became unbearable; under state code, "[l]ack of informed consent in a medical malpractice action ... operates to negate a patient's authorization for a procedure thereby giving rise to a cause of action for battery; plaintiff does not need expert testimony, since "[t]here is no prior authorization or con-

sent ... to be negated by expert testimony"; "the primary consideration in a medical battery case is simply whether the patient knew of and authorized a procedure").

Among other things, the principle may be applied to the choice of the physician who will do a procedure. See, e.g., Grabowski v. Quigley, 684 A.2d 610 (Pa.Super.1996), appeal dismissed as improvidently granted, 717 A.2d 1024 (Pa. 1998). In that case, Doctor A performed the major portion of a surgical proce-

Although battery might seem to be the foundational theory of informed consent, courts have tended to invoke the concept more under a negligence heading than that of battery. As is so throughout the law of negligence generally, the test for informed consent is whether the defendant has behaved with reasonable care in the circumstances. In the medical realm, the circumstances always include the physician's professional training and expertise, and the issue is whether, given the standards associated with that background, the physician gave the plaintiff sufficient information to assure a proper consent. One should note that, besides applying to procedures or courses of treatment to which a patient agrees, the informed consent doctrine also may apply to omissions, like the failure to inform a patient adequately of the need for a procedure that the patient rejects.[3]

Several jurisdictions that have adopted the doctrine of informed consent in effect have opted for a " 'lay' standard of disclosure," which requires the doctor to provide information that a reasonable patient would find material to the decision of whether to undergo a course of treatment.[4] This test contrasts with the "professional standard," which requires disclosure "of what a reasonable medical practitioner would have disclosed under the same or similar circumstances."[5] One court declared that the "incongruity" of the professional standard is that it makes "the medical profession the sole arbiter of what information [is] necessary for an informed decision to be made by a patient concerning his own physical well-being."[6]

In jurisdictions where the professional standard is the rule, courts presumably will have to resolve the tension between a national standard of care and one that relies at least partly on local standards, perhaps even including custom.[7] Plaintiffs in those jurisdictions usually will have to produce expert testimony to prove the standard of disclosure for physicians, either a national one or a local one. This is in line with general medical malpractice law, at

---

dure on the plaintiff, who believed that Doctor B, with whom he initially consulted, would do the surgery. The plaintiff claimed he would not have had the surgery if he had known that Doctor B would not do the entire operation. Finding a fact issue raised under battery theory, the court says that the plaintiff did not have to provide expert testimony because "[t]he dispositive issue is ... the nature and scope of [the plaintiff's] consent," 684 A.2d at 614–15.

For other material on battery as a theory of recovery in medical cases, see ¶ 17.01 supra.

3. See, e.g., Truman v. Thomas, 611 P.2d 902, 907–08 (Cal.1980) (negligence in failure to disclose danger of failing to have a pap smear).

4. See, e.g., Logan v. Greenwich Hosp. Ass'n, 465 A.2d 294, 299–300 (Conn.1983).

5. See, e.g., Aiken v. Clary, 396 S.W.2d 668, 675 (Mo.1965).

6. Logan, supra, 465 A.2d at 299.

7. See supra, ¶ 23.04.

least when negligence is not so obvious that ordinary lay persons could make an independent judgment about it.

¶ 27.02　Elements of the Doctrine

The principal elements of informed consent doctrine, whether classified under a heading of negligence or battery law, require disclosure to patients of 1) the nature of a procedure or course of treatment, 2) the possible alternatives, 3) the material risks of the treatment, and 4) the anticipated benefits of the proposed course of conduct.

Within these broad elements, there is much room for disagreement. For example, some courts take the position that a physician must disclose competition among schools of thought on alternative procedures.[8] A related issue is whether a physician must tell a patient about alternatives that are more dangerous than the one the doctor proposes. In one case, the medical judgment was that the plaintiff needed a kidney biopsy. A physician told the plaintiff about the serious risks of a needle biopsy that would be done under a local anesthetic, which was the procedure he wanted to perform, but did not mention the alternative of an open biopsy, which would require an incision and general anesthesia. The court concluded that it was error to instruct the jury that a physician could withhold information about a more hazardous alternative, because this would "relieve[] physicians of any obligation to discuss alternatives with their patients and substitute[] merely a duty to recommend the safest procedure." The court therefore found the instruction "incompatible ... with the view ... that the patient must be provided with sufficient information to allow him to make an intelligent choice."[9]

Another specific question concerning disclosure is a byproduct of medical and technological progress: whether a physician must tell a patient that a treatment is experimental. Courts are certainly likely to require that disclosure on the ground that such an obligation follows easily from a "duty to inform of *known* risks for *established* procedures."[10]

Some commentary, at least, would place the burden on physicians who do not disclose "all known material risks" to "prove the reasonableness of any lesser disclosure or the immateriality of the

8. See, e.g., Marino v. Ballestas, 749 F.2d 162, 168 (3d Cir.1984) (although a doctor "may, and indeed should, express his opinion regarding preferable methods of treatment," the defendant should have fairly presented an alternative to that preference).

9. Logan v. Greenwich Hosp. Ass'n, supra note 4, 465 A.2d at 301.

10. Estrada v. Jaques, 321 S.E.2d 240, 254 (N.C.App.1984).

undisclosed risk."[11] The kinds of treatments about which doctors inform patients often have complex features, and physicians necessarily must make selections among many kinds of information that are in some sense relevant to a patient's decision. An example concerns the risks in administration of anesthesia for surgery, not counting the risks of the surgery itself. Information that conceivably would be deemed material to anesthesia risks would include the insertion of a needle for administration of pentothal, insertion and removal of a tube in the windpipe, different types of anesthetic agents and their effects, the length of the procedure, the amount of blood and fluids that may have to be administered, and the use of anti-nausea drugs after the operation. An anesthesiologist who catalogued all these aspects of his job added, "I have not told [the patient] of the risk of each drug, the danger of air embolism from the needle stick, the possibility of death from vomiting and aspiration, [or] the danger from explosion from the anesthesia that I am using." He concluded, "So I have not really informed her. Literally, I could go on for hours without [explaining] all the possible complications she may have."[12]

The question of whether a risk is material requires sharp focus on the facts, normally including the relative frequency and the severity of a risk. In one case, the D.C. Circuit decided that, with respect to a patient's decision about whether to have impacted wisdom teeth removed, it was not material that the operation entailed a .001 percent risk of paresthesia—a permanent loss of feeling—in a small part of the face.[13] By comparison, the same court found that a risk of one to three out of one thousand that a sterilization operation would fail was material, at least to a woman who had suffered significant medical problems from prior pregnancies and evinced great emotional distress about the pregnancy that prompted the operation.[14] That decision teaches that physicians sometimes may have an obligation to disclose rather slight statistical risks, in cases where the risk at issue is particularly grave.

11. Comment, Informed Consent in Medical Malpractice, 55 Calif. L. Rev. 1396, 1407 (1967).

12. How Informed Must Consent Be?, Am. Med. News, Feb. 3, 1969 (quoting Maryland anesthesiologist).

13. Henderson v. Milobsky, 595 F.2d 654, 659 (D.C.Cir.1978). Cf. Lauro v. Knowles, 785 A.2d 1140 (R.I.2001), in which the plaintiff suffered a corneal abrasion from the taping of her eyes during an operation on her wrist. There was testimony that the risk of corneal abrasions in such procedures ranged from 0.17 per cent to .029 per cent, and one expert for the defendant testified that "most corneal abrasions heal within twenty-four hours of the injury." Although the plaintiff alleged that her abrasion was "not trivial" because she continued to suffer from its effects, the court affirmed summary judgment for the defendants on the ground that there was uncontradicted evidence that the risk was "minimal and of relatively trivial impact." Thus, if the risk of both occurrence and impact is very small, the fact that the actual injury is serious may not save a plaintiff's case.

14. Hartke v. McKelway, 707 F.2d 1544 (D.C.Cir.1983).

Causation is an important component of the materiality issue. If a particular piece of information is extraneous to the injury being sued upon, a physician's failure to disclose that information will not be actionable. An example is a case in which the plaintiff said he would not have consented to an operation if he had known of the defendant's use of cocaine. Where there was no evidence that the defendant's drug use caused the plaintiff's injury, the court concluded that the drug use was "too attenuated from the subject matter of the professional relationship to support a battery claim." The court distinguished cases where physicians obtain consent to treatment "by an artifice that is directly related to the subject matter of the professional relationship—i.e.: diagnoses, treatments, procedures."[15]

Another significant issue is whether a claim based on informed consent requires evidence on the subjective reaction of the plaintiff, as reflected in hindsight testimony. In a case described above, the court said that while "it might be helpful" to have a statement from the patient that she would not have undergone a procedure if the risks had been explained, it was not necessary to present testimony from her to take an informed consent case to the jury.[16] Rather, the court stressed that the standard is an objective one, depending on " 'what a prudent person in the patient's position would have decided if suitably informed of all perils bearing significance.' "[17]

Since many medical procedures continue over an appreciable period of time, some interesting questions arise about the physician's obligation to have a fresh discussion of consent when a patient expressly withdraws her consent to a procedure. Dealing with a case involving a woman in childbirth, the Wisconsin Supreme Court opined that when there occurs a "substantial change in circumstances, be it medical or legal," the physician owes the patient a "new informed consent discussion." The plaintiff in this case previously had delivered two children by caesarean section, but chose to have her third child by vaginal birth. However, as her labor progressed, producing "excruciating" pains, she told her obstetrician that she wanted to have a caesarean delivery. She said she was "upset and intimidated" by his answer, which was to the effect that if did a caesarean on "every woman who wanted one . . . all deliveries would be by caesarean section." Overturning a trial court ruling that it described as "only consider[ing] medical changes in circumstances"—that is, "a new risk or benefit previously unforeseen"—the court described a "legal change[ ] of cir-

15. Albany Urology Clinic v. Cleveland, 528 S.E.2d 777, 781 (Ga.2000).

16. Hartke, supra, 707 F.2d at 1551.

17. Id. at 1550, quoting Canterbury v. Spence, 464 F.2d 772, 791 (D.C.Cir. 1972).

cumstances" as one where "the alteration is a withdrawal of an option previously foreseen," in a situation where "there exist alternative viable modes of medical treatment." The court "decline[d] to view the [original] informed discussion as a solitary and blanketing event, a point on a timeline after which such discussions are no longer needed because they are 'covered' by some articulable occurrences in the past." The basic model it sketched was one where the patient's withdrawal placed her and her doctor "in their original position—a physician, a patient, and a series of options for treatment," creating "a blank slate on which the parties must again diagram their plan."[18]

Because of the trust that patients place in their doctors, a difficult issue is whether physicians may employ the defense of contributory negligence in an action based on failure of informed consent. The Wisconsin court said that they may but limited the use of the defense, primarily to cases involving patients' failure to use "ordinary care in providing complete and accurate information" to doctors about their family and medical histories. The court generally opposed use of the defense with respect to patients' obligations to "ask questions" of their physicians or "undertake independent research," and in situations where the plaintiff chooses a "viable medical mode of treatment presented by a doctor." With respect to such matters, though, the court said it might allow the defense in "extraordinary fact situation[s]."[19]

¶ 27.03   Philosophical Premises

The informed consent problem forces courts to identify several tiers of premises, concerning philosophy as well as human behavior and economics. An important philosophical font for informed consent law is a 1914 opinion by Cardozo, premising that "[e]very human being of adult years and sound mind has a right to determine what shall be done with his own body," and concluding that "a surgeon who performs an operation without his patient's consent commits an assault, for which he is liable in damages."[20] In its landmark decision on the subject, the D.C. Circuit asserted that "the test for determining whether a particular peril must be divulged is its materiality to the patient's decision: all risks potentially affecting the decision must be unmasked."[21] The heart of the matter in these formulations is self determination, resting on ideas of individual autonomy and free choice. Those premises, in turn, require sufficient information to enable a meaningful choice.

18. Schreiber v. Physicians Ins. Co., 223 Wis.2d 417, 588 N.W.2d 26, 31–33 (1999).

19. Brown v. Dibbell, 595 N.W.2d 358, 368–70 (Wis.1999).

20. Schloendorff v. Society of New York Hosp., 105 N.E. 92, 93 (N.Y.1914).

21. Canterbury v. Spence, 464 F.2d at 786–87.

Given those premises, however, one may consent to unconventional medical treatment that worsens a desperate condition, even fatally, so long as the facts of the case fulfill the elements of informed consent. A poignant illustration is a decision involving a 65–year-old woman who had received a diagnosis of cancer. Instead of choosing surgery that physicians said "would have given her a very good chance of recovery," she allegedly opted for a set of treatments that "consist[ed] of urine monitoring, urinalyses and the ingestion of various mineral compounds." The 96–year-old physician who administered these treatments claimed that he had told the patient that although "he thought that he could cure her," his treatments "were not FDA approved and . . . he could offer no guarantees." The patient's condition "deteriorated greatly" within a year and she died. The trial court refused an instruction on "express assumption of risk" that would have totally barred recovery for the patient's administrator. After a substantial jury verdict for the plaintiff, reduced only by a few percentage points for contributory negligence, the Second Circuit reversed. It said that the jury should have been asked to assess the credibility of the defendant's evidence that the decedent "had expressly assumed a risk in opting for the unconventional cancer treatment."[22]

¶ 27.04　Behavioral Assumptions

The question of what constitutes an informed choice turns on some rather complex elements of human behavior. At the threshold is the question of whether the plaintiff is acting voluntarily, a difficult concept to apply in the emotionally charged situations in which a patient must make decisions like whether to undergo surgery. Running parallel to the question of voluntariness are issues related to the intelligence and understanding of the individual plaintiff, as well as the ability of patients to retain crucial information. There is evidence that within a day of signing consent forms for major medical procedures, "[o]nly 60 per cent of all patients correctly described what their treatment would involve, 59 per cent could describe the essential purpose of the treatment, only 55 per cent were able to list even a single major risk or complication, and only 27 per cent could name one alternative treatment."[23] Data like this may seem to cast doubt on the general enterprise of requiring informed consent, but they have not deterred courts from fashioning and enforcing standards about disclosure of risks that are likely to affect patient decisionmaking.

22.　Boyle v. Revici, 961 F.2d 1060 (2d Cir.1992).

23.　Barrie Cassileth, et al., Informed Consent—Why Are Its Goals Im-
perfectly Realized?, 302 New Eng. J. Med. 896, 897 (1980).

Social research offers a concept applicable to how patients make decisions that is known as "[t]he framing effect." This phrase refers to data indicating that people's reactions to choices depend significantly on the way alternatives are "framed," for example, how risks are numerically described. Illustratively, it has been shown that one kind of treatment will appear "much less attractive" than another when the person who presents the alternatives describes the first treatment in terms of how many people will die rather than how many people will survive.[24]

The concept of "framing" may help courts to judge the effectiveness of the presentation of alternatives. For example, a court persuaded that physicians should have a relatively substantial burden of disclosure might fashion a rule that effectively required the presentation of information to tilt toward a relatively gloomy forecast rather than an optimistic one. Yet, one must remember that one requirement of informed consent is a fair presentation of benefits as well as risks.

¶ 27.05   Economic Premises

It is useful to link these observations about the philosophical basis for informed consent and judicial assumptions concerning behavior to the assumed economic foundation of the doctrine. Courts that choose what is in form an objective informed consent standard appear to rely on an abstract conception of rationality. However, often their application of informed concept doctrine must take into account subjective features of cases that may place their decisions at odds with the economically efficient result. Illustrative of potential difficulties for economic theory is the case in which the statistics would indicate to a physician that a "rational" patient could choose only one of two or more alternatives. An economist might argue that it is inefficient to provide information on the other alternatives, reasoning that the physician must incur some cost in providing information—although it may be a slight cost— and that a patient might make an "irrational" choice if she is provided with information that the physician believes is essentially irrelevant.

In such cases, particular circumstances may provide a mediating force between objectivity and subjectivity. For example, the fact that a patient's medical history makes it desperately important that a sterilization procedure be successful may provide a way to particularize the principle to the individual, while retaining the "objectivity" of decisionmaking. In a case discussed above presenting that

---

24. See, e.g., Donald Redelmeier, et al., Understanding Patients' Decisions: Cognitive and Emotional Perspectives, 270 JAMA 72, 73 (1993) (summarizing literature).

problem,[25] the court noted that judicial opposition to "a subjective standard of causation" arose from distrust of the "hindsight" assertion by a patient about what she would have done if certain information had been provided to her. At the same time, the court declared that a jury did "not need the patient's testimony to decide what a reasonable person" in the circumstances facing that patient would have done.[26]

A related point concerns rationality and attitudes toward risk. Patient "self-determination" may entail a wide range of rationalities, depending in part on the patient's level of preference for or aversion to risk.

One decisionmaking approach that would resolve these issues very simply would employ a thoroughgoing contract model. The most simplified solution would permit physicians and patients to contract for an exculpatory clause that essentially allows the physician to select whatever treatment she chooses, on the basis of her reasoned medical judgment, without having to offer particularized explanations to the patient of risks and benefits. Although an approach of this sort is theoretically interesting,[27] most courts would refuse to enforce a general exculpatory clause in medical cases.

One should note, however, that extreme situations may make a case for a true bargain-oriented approach. Illustrative are cases in which a physician proposes to use a procedure or device that has not been approved by a regulatory agency—a novel cancer treatment as in a case described above,[28] or a new device implanted by surgery that might relieve a chronic condition. Considerations of self-determination and autonomy would suggest that this is a bargain that patients should be able to strike with their doctors. Yet, one should emphasize that this is precisely the kind of situation in which the patient needs—and the physician owes—the fullest information.[29] Thus, a well-informed bargain becomes the antithesis of a general exculpatory clause.

The rise of health maintenance organizations (HMOs) has produced a range of disputes in the realm of public policy that have spilled over into tort law. Under the lens of informed consent, a particularly important issue arises when cost-saving regimens insti-

---

25. See the discussion of *Hartke v. McKelway*, text accompanying note 14 supra.

26. *Hartke*, 707 F.2d at 1549–51.

27. See Richard Epstein, Medical Malpractice: The Case for Contract, 1976 Am. B. Found. Res. J. 87.

28. See text accompanying note 22 supra.

29. Cf. Karp v. Cooley, 493 F.2d 408, 421–22 (5th Cir.1974) (in case involving experimental use of mechanical heart, plaintiffs did not show lack of informed consent when patient signed document that set out "each step of the three-stage operation," in the context of at least two conversations with the surgeon).

tuted by HMOs create conflicts with the professional judgment of physicians about proper treatment. One commentator has suggested that if a doctor's "clinical judgment of medically appropriate treatment differs from the HMO's judgment of medically necessary treatment, the physician should inform the patient of this discrepancy."[30] Disclosure of that situation would allow the patient to "decide whether to forego the physician-recommended treatment and accept only the insurer reimbursable treatment, or to contest the insurer's decision, or to pay for [the] additional treatment himself or herself." Justification for this standard focuses on the materiality of the disclosure.[31]

[Chapters 28–29 are reserved for supplementary material.]

30. Grant Morris, Dissing Disclosure: Just What the Doctor Ordered, 44 Ariz. L. Rev. 313, 363 (2002).

31. See id. at 364 ("[t]he physician's clinical judgment is pertinent medical information that may well affect the patient's decision").

Chapter Thirty

IMPLIED ASSUMPTION OF RISK: GENERALLY

Analysis

¶ 30.01   The Basic Concept and Variations

A.   Basic Definition

Courts use the term implied assumption of risk to describe their responses to situations where a plaintiff's voluntary confrontation with a risk, about which he knows, will prevent his right to

137

recover against the party who created the risk. Implied assumption of risk, therefore, is conduct, and generally distinguishable from cases where the plaintiff expressly assumes a risk in writing, for example, by signing a document with an exculpatory clause.[1] As traditionally applied, the doctrine of implied assumption of risk provides a complete defense, and courts have often used it in cases based on strict liability as well as cases based on negligence.

The doctrine has several variations, including descriptions of the plaintiff's conduct as "primary" or "secondary" assumption of risk. Among other variants, the courts employ the ideas that the defendant owed no duty to the plaintiff, and that the obviousness of the risk bars the plaintiff from recovery. Sometimes the courts simply conclude that the defendant was not negligent. Moreover, it is important to some courts whether the plaintiff behaved reasonably, or unreasonably, in confronting the risk.[2]

The concept itself is somewhat controversial, with some commentators arguing that there should be no separate defense of implied assumption of risk.[3] In states that have adopted comparative negligence, a doctrine that requires the fact finder to compare the fault of the parties,[4] some courts have said that assumption of risk will only partly reduce the plaintiff's recovery instead of barring it entirely. However, the doctrine, and the terminology, remain in use.

1. *Voluntariness*

Products liability law provides a rich set of examples concerning the requirement that a plaintiff voluntarily encounter a risk. A blunt explanation of the basic doctrine appears in a case in which the plaintiff attributed injuries in a lawnmower accident to the absence of safety devices on the mower. In denying recovery, the court said that the fact that the machine lacked the devices "was apparent at the time of purchase, and in a free market, [the plaintiff] had the choice of buying a mower equipped with them, of buying the mower which he did, or of buying no mower at all."[5]

The main lines of battle have formed on the issue of what constitutes choice in a world in which people generally face many constraints on their freedom. A straightforward presentation of the problem appears in products liability cases involving workplace

---

1. See Chapter 26 supra.

2. We discuss how courts use these concepts throughout the chapter, most particularly at ¶¶ 30.01(B)-(D) and ¶ 30.04.

3. Restatement drafters engaged in a spirited argument on the issue in the so-called "Battle of the Wilderness,"

chronicled at Restatement (Second) of Torts, Tent. Draft No. 9 at 70–87 (1963).

4. See Chapter 33 infra.

5. Myers v. Montgomery Ward & Co., 252 A.2d 855, 864 (Md.Ct.App. 1969).

injuries in which the plaintiff's only practical alternative to working with dangerous machinery is to quit her job.[6] In one case, the plaintiff was injured when she was working on an allegedly defective press. Rejecting defense arguments based on the plaintiff's use of the press when she knew of the dangers inherent in its design, the court observed that the "option of quitting ... was no doubt available" to the plaintiff, but emphasized that this alternative was "effectively foreclosed, or at least circumscribed." The trial judge commented that the plaintiff "lacked a trade or college degree and had to help support a family," and said that "[f]or a woman in her constrained position, commanded to follow a questionable practice but needing her job, the facts strongly rebut voluntariness in the ordinary sense of the word."[7]

2. *Knowledge of risk*

Another element of the assumption of risk doctrine is the requirement that the plaintiff know of the risk. Courts often require defendants to show that plaintiffs had highly specific knowledge of a hazard, as is evident in a Seventh Circuit case in which two men were splitting logs. After the plaintiff's maul stuck in a log, he and his friend tried to free it. When the friend administered "a whack with the flat surface" of his maul to the plaintiff's maul, the impact produced a chip from the friend's maul that blinded the plaintiff in one eye. The court reversed a verdict for the manufacturer of the friend's maul, observing that there was "little or no evidence" that the plaintiff knew that that tool was defective. Judge Posner commented that the plaintiff "probably knew that striking a maul against another maul can cause one of the mauls to chip," but he emphasized that "to assume the risk of an eye injury from a flying maul chip is not the same thing as assuming the risk of an eye injury caused by a chip from a *defective* maul." He pointed out that "[t]hese could be risks of different orders of magnitude."[8]

In another case, a worker knew, from past experience, that pipes would slide off a ramp. However, he did not know at the time of the accident "that the hook of the air hoist line, which secured the pipe, had come loose," with the result that "the pipe was no longer being held in place by the air hoist, and was free to roll off of the ramp." In this situation, the court refused to bar the plaintiff,

6. For a particular focus on application of the doctrine of assumption of risk in workplace cases, see infra, ¶ 30.03.

7. Downs v. Gulf & W. Mfg. Co., 677 F.Supp. 661, 665 (D.Mass.1987).

8. Traylor v. Husqvarna Motor, 988 F.2d 729, 732 (7th Cir.1993).

saying that his prior knowledge of pipes falling off the ramp "establish[ed] only general knowledge."[9]

Courts have extended the requirement that the plaintiff specifically know of a risk to kinds of injury as well as types of accident. In a case in which a worker suffered an amputation at the elbow when he was using an industrial machine, the defendant emphasized that the plaintiff said that he had known that he risked "serious injury to his hand" from the way he was using the machine. However, upholding a plaintiff's judgment, the court focused on the plaintiff's testimony that he interpreted "serious injury" to include the possibility that he "could have badly bruised" himself or "could have even lost a finger." The plaintiff said he had not at all considered that he could "lose an entire arm," declaring that he "never dreamed" of that possibility.[10]

Although the fact-specific aspects of the knowledge issue frequently turn it to the advantage of plaintiffs, the facts of some cases convince courts that plaintiffs were fully aware of particular dangers. In an illustrative products liability case, an electrician pointed a screwdriver into a capacitor box, causing an explosive electrical flash. The Pennsylvania Supreme Court focused on a written warning, "designed for electricians," that indicated that "the capacitor stored electricity and could not be handled safely even after the electricity was shut off until the necessary steps were taken to drain it of its charge."[11] Where there was testimony that the electrical arcing that apparently produced the explosion could not occur unless an object came within forty/one thousandths of an inch of the capacitor, the supreme court stressed that the relevant danger was not "arcing itself," but rather the "live, exposed electricity." It declared that "[a]rcing is a principle of electricity and a propensity of exposed high voltage electrical power" that should be "known by a skilled electrician."[12]

While in practice, the question of knowledge tends to focus on whether the plaintiff knew of the potential severity of the risk, it necessarily also includes the frequency of the plaintiff's exposure to that risk. Illustrative is a case in which a plaintiff complained that the headlamp on his motorcycle was too dim. Given that he had operated the cycle for several years, the court found it "inescapable that by his continuing use of the motorcycle even after he believed

---

9. Hobbs v. Armco, Inc., 413 So.2d 118, 121 (Fla.Dist.Ct.App.1982).

10. Goulet v. Whitin Machine Works, Inc., 568 N.E.2d 1158, 1160–61 (Mass.App.Ct.1991).

11. This was the characterization of the intermediate appellate court in Mackowick v. Westinghouse Elec. Corp., 541 A.2d 749, 751 (Pa.Super.Ct.1988).

12. Mackowick v. Westinghouse Elec. Corp., 575 A.2d 100, 103 (Pa.1990).

that the light was insufficient," he "assumed any risk attendant to continued operation."[13]

3. *Unreasonable*

The implied assumption of risk doctrine, at least in its so-called secondary sense, also requires that the plaintiff acted unreasonably in choosing to confront the risk, an element that this defense shares with ordinary contributory negligence. The unreasonableness element also overlaps with the other requirements of the assumption of risk doctrine itself, namely, that the plaintiff know of the specific risk and that he or she voluntarily encounter it.

Opinions of the Queen's Bench in an 1848 case indicate how these various elements come together. The occasion was a suit for the death of a horse that the plaintiff tried to lead over construction work that occupied the passage from his stable to the street. The horse was strangled when it fell into piled-up earth that gave way. One judge said that the verdict should have been for the defendant "[i]f the danger was so great that no sensible man would have incurred it." However, linking the elements of the plaintiff's knowledge and the reasonableness of his conduct, he upheld a verdict for the plaintiff when the jury apparently had decided that the danger was not "so obvious that the plaintiff could not with common prudence make the attempt."[14] Further implying that the defendant's activities had constrained the plaintiff's choice, another judge commented that "[t]he plaintiff was not bound to abstain from pursuing his livelihood because there was some danger," and that it was "necessary for the defendants to shew a clear danger and a precise warning."[15]

B. *Open and obvious*

A concept that closely parallels the idea of implied assumption of risk goes under the name of "obviousness" or "open and obvious danger." Courts employ this label to deny recovery to plaintiffs in a variety of doctrinal settings, sometimes using it by itself and sometimes joining it with the language of assumption of risk and with such doctrines as misuse in products liability cases. The spectrum of incidents in which judges invoke the concept ranges from accidents involving industrial machines to catastrophic injuries suffered by people who dive into shallow parts of swimming pools.

In a case involving an above-ground pool, a majority of the Michigan Supreme Court declared that "[s]ince the dangers associ-

---

13. Barnes v. Harley–Davidson Motor Co., 357 S.E.2d 127, 130 (Ga.Ct.App. 1987).

14. Clayards v. Dethick, 116 Eng. Rep. 932, 935 (Q.B. 1848).

15. Id.

ated with diving into visibly shallow water in an above-ground pool are open and obvious to the reasonably prudent user, plaintiff . . . must, as a matter of law be held to the knowledge and appreciation of the risk likely to be encountered in his headfirst dive.''[16] As this language implies, frequently the terminology of "obviousness" is virtually synonymous with a conclusion that the plaintiff has behaved unreasonably. Sometimes, however, the obviousness label may principally stand for a conclusion that in the circumstances the defendant had no duty to the plaintiff.[17] When that is the underlying meaning of obviousness, the plaintiff's reasonableness would be technically irrelevant. This is because if there is no duty, the court would not reach the question of whether the defendant was negligent or, therefore, the question of whether the plaintiff assumed the risk because of the plaintiff's substandard conduct.

When courts apply the obviousness defense, it generally will have the effect of holding that a plaintiff's claims do not merit consideration by the jury, whether because the plaintiff was unreasonable as a matter of law or the defendant had no duty. By contrast, a refusal to recognize that defense usually means that a jury will consider the reasonableness of the plaintiff's conduct as well as of the defendant's conduct or of the level of safety of its product.

In a case in which the court rejected the defense that a risk was "open and obvious," the plaintiff's decedent died after spending an hour and a half trying to work on a feeder machine that generated hot flue dust. Given that there were no warnings of the hazards of the dust, the court favorably quoted the plaintiff's argument that none of the employees who did the work "would have been bent on suicide." Reversing a summary judgment for the maker of the feeder machine, the court concluded that there was evidence from which a jury could infer that the danger was not "open and obvious."[18]

C. "No duty"

Another concept that parallels implied assumption of risk, sometimes incorporating the idea of obviousness, lies in the idea that the defendant had "no duty" to the plaintiff to act more safely. A much quoted New York decision that involved alleged negligence in the design of an onion-topping machine, since overruled, stated the proposition simply. The court said a manufacturer was "under no duty to render a machine or other article 'more' safe—as long as

---

16. Glittenberg v. Doughboy Recreational Indus., Inc., 462 N.W.2d 348, 359 (Mich.1990) (plurality).

17. See infra, ¶ 30.01(C), for illustrations of the "no duty" defense.

18. Ruther v. Robins Eng'g and Constructors, 802 F.2d 276, 279 (7th Cir.1986).

the danger ... is obvious and patent to all."[19] Rulings that there is no duty sometimes cancel out plaintiffs' arguments that there is a duty to warn. On a rehearing of the Michigan swimming pool case cited above, the majority in denying recovery said that "the obvious nature of the danger serves the exact function as a warning that the risk is present."[20]

A Texas decision, denying liability despite particularly sympathetic facts, combined no-duty phraseology with other defensive concepts. The case involved injuries to a woman who slipped on the icy steps to a hospital emergency room, to which she was trying to gain entrance in order to get treatment for a severed fingertip. Although the plaintiff argued that she did not encounter the risk of the icy steps "as a result of an intelligent choice," the court insisted that the situation did "not impose a duty on defendant." It held that the plaintiff could not recover, "since the danger encountered was open and obvious," and she knew and appreciated the risk.[21]

D. No negligence

The ideas of implied assumption of risk, "open and obvious danger," and "no duty" run together as cousins, if not siblings, and provide potent defensive tools. Beyond those concepts, there is an alternative argument to consider in cases where an injury was in some way attributable to the defendant's activity, but the plaintiff's conduct also comes into play. This is simply that the defendant was not negligent. Consider, for example, a case in which a worker is injured using an industrial machine. A court may deny recovery to the worker on the ground that he voluntarily and foolishly encountered a known hazard—the classic doctrine of implied assumption of risk. Or it may use the relatively non-doctrinal phrasing that denies liability for injuries caused by "open and obvious" dangers. Yet, what the court may really be thinking is that given the kind of work the machine was designed to do, the manufacturer's balance of risks and benefits was not an unreasonable one. Thus, it may be that in many decisions that exonerate defendants on the basis of defenses like assumption of risk, the underlying explanation for the outcome is a judgment that there was no negligence on the defendant's part or that a product was not unreasonably dangerous.

In an illustrative case, a longshoreman sued a shipowner for injuries suffered when he slipped on an oil slick in a cargo hatch. The plaintiff admitted that the oil slick "was obvious to all," but the court focused on the question of whether the stevedoring

---

19. Campo v. Scofield, 95 N.E.2d 802, 804 (N.Y.1950).

20. Glittenberg v. Doughboy Recreational Indus., Inc., 491 N.W.2d 208, 215 (Mich.1992) (on rehearing).

21. Gulfway Gen'l Hosp., Inc. v. Pursley, 397 S.W.2d 93, 94 (Tex.Civ. App.1965).

company's work crew that included the plaintiff could have practically avoided the danger. Noting that there was sawdust available to treat oil spills, and that there was no evidence that there was "such a time schedule that it would have been impractical for [the stevedore] to eliminate the hazard," the court held for the shipowner. It focused not so much on the conduct of the plaintiff and his employer, the stevedore, but on the issue of whether the shipowner had been unreasonable in assuming that the longshoremen on the job would have avoided the danger caused by the spill. Concluding that the plaintiff had not shown that the shipowner "should not have assumed that [the stevedore] and its employees would avoid the obvious danger," the court held that the shipowner was not negligent.[22]

¶ 30.02   Underlying Ideas and Competing Philosophies

The elements of knowledge and choice, central to assumption of risk and related defenses, present difficult questions of fact and law, which in turn require courts to articulate underlying philosophies and policies. By comparison with the objective standard of the defense of contributory negligence, which bars or reduces recovery for plaintiffs who should have known of a hazard,[23] the assumption of risk doctrine requires that plaintiffs actually know of a danger, and with some specificity. It also requires a relatively subjective finding that the plaintiff chose to confront the known risk, by contrast with the relatively objective requirement of the contributory negligence doctrine that the plaintiff did not behave as a reasonable person under the circumstances.

When one applies the implied assumption of risk doctrine, one should be clear about the behavioral assumptions and ethical premises that underlie the particular application. In a wide range of settings—from the workplace to the backyard swimming pool—some of the crucial behavioral questions concern the image of risk that actually imprinted itself on the plaintiff's mind. Perhaps application of a doctrine this subjective requires identification of one's assumptions, not only about how people in general act, but how the plaintiff understood and approached the danger at issue.

Underlying these behavioral considerations are issues concerning the ethical bases of decision. Although courts do not always identify those premises explicitly, some decisions that deny recovery on the basis of implied assumption of risk articulately rely on the concept of freedom of action. The notion is that even in a world of

22. Kirsch v. Plovidba, 971 F.2d   **23.** See ¶ 31.01 infra.
1026, 1033–34 (3d Cir.1992).

constrained choices, plaintiffs as well as defendants should be held accountable for the consequences of their own conduct.

By contrast, other decisions stress constraints on the plaintiff's freedom rather than his freedom to choose a risk. For example, the New Jersey Supreme Court refused to apply an assumption of risk-type contributory negligence defense in products liability cases in the industrial setting. The court said that as a "matter of policy" it would not allow the defense, "[i]rrespective of the rationale that the employee may have unreasonably and voluntarily encountered a known risk." The court reasoned that a manufacturer "should not be permitted to escape from the breach of its duty to an employee while carrying out his assigned task ... when observance of that duty would have prevented the very accident which occurred."[24] Such decisions appear to embody a judgment that some actors, such as employees under pressure from employers to work at a particular pace, are so relatively unfree with respect to some dangers that it is inappropriate to apply a defense that assumes freedom of action and choice. The argument over implied assumption of risk thus may frequently resolve itself into an issue of how the law should deal with imbalances of power between parties.

¶ 30.03   The Workplace

Having provided a general overview of the doctrine of implied assumption of risk, we proceed to two specific applications, one in traditional employment contexts, and one in the arena of sports and games, some of which also involve employment.

One of the most important functional battlegrounds of the assumption of risk defense is the workplace, which has provided several examples in our general definition of the doctrine above. This section presents some particularized applications of the elements and policies of assumption of risk where workers are the claimants. It is natural that that setting should generate many issues of this kind, because many work environments feature several situations a day that workers as well as employers recognize as "accidents waiting to happen." The spectrum of risk that is known by workers at some level of consciousness runs from dangerous industrial machinery to hazards related to explosions, falls, and heavy vehicles.

The financial toll of workplace accidents, a convenient index to the level of risk in a wide range of employment settings, is enormous. A standard source reports that the total costs of workplace accidents for 1992 were $115.9 billion, including "wage and produc-

---

24. Suter v. San Angelo Foundry and Mach. Co., 406 A.2d 140, 148 (N.J. 1979).

tivity losses of $62.5 billion, medical costs of $22.0 billion, and administrative expenses of $14.5 billion." Included in the overall figure are "employer costs of $10.2 billion such as the money value of time lost by workers other than those with disabling injuries, who are directly or indirectly involved in accidents," and the "cost of time required to investigate accidents [and] write up accident reports."[25]

A. Voluntariness as crucial element

The voluntariness requirement of the assumption of risk defense is particularly crucial to worker plaintiffs. Courts tend to be dubious about whether the doctrine is consistent with the pressures faced by employees ordered to do hazardous things or face the loss of their jobs. Illustrative is a Fifth Circuit case that arose on an offshore drilling platform. The claimant was a worker who, acting under orders of a supervisor, continued working with a hose on which bubbles were forming in an operation designed to clean out a clogged oil well. The plaintiff and a fellow employee kept working although "apprehensive or even frightened by the bubbles" and concerned that "the hose might rupture and bring about a fire or an explosion." The hose in fact burst, and an explosion and fire did occur, injuring the plaintiff.

Although the jury could have found that the plaintiff "both knew and appreciated the risk"—indeed that he might have "appreciated it much better" than the supervisor—the court concluded that his "actions were not voluntary." The court noted that the plaintiff considered the assignment dangerous in light of his "limited experience" with the job. However, it pointed out that the supervisor had told the plaintiff that "there was no danger," ordered him to discontinue corrective measures he had already started, and required him to start working again. The court rejected the argument that the plaintiff "should have refused the work and shut down the job," saying that this was "not a reasonable alternative."[26]

Other decisions echo the idea that voluntariness requires a meaningful choice. An example is a case in which a worker fell to his death while he was working alone on planking over an open elevator shaft, which was ordinarily a two-man job. The court found that his act of "continuing to remove the planking alone" occurred "under the economic duress of the possible loss of his job." Melding the element of unreasonableness with the requirement of voluntariness, the court concluded that in "working alone," the worker "did

25. Accident Facts, 1993 ed., at 35.   26. Arnold v. Union Oil Co., 608 F.2d 575, 579 (5th Cir.1979).

not act voluntarily or unreasonably."[27] Such decisions reflect a policy orientation concerning the fairness of allocation of risks in the workplace.

B.   The fireman's rule and related bars to recovery

A contrasting viewpoint is that certain employees assume risks inherent in their employment as part of their jobs. A specialized version of this principle is the "fireman's rule," which bars suits by firefighters, for example, against building owners whose negligence caused a fire. Illustrative of the reach of the rule is a decision announcing the broad principle that a firefighter "assume[s] all ... inherent risks" of fighting fires.[28] The court applied this principle to bar recovery to a part-time fireman who jumped off the roof of a burning building after an explosion, and attributed his injuries to a defective product that allegedly caused the fire. Under this view that taking a firefighter's job constitutes the acceptance of a risk package, voluntariness accompanies the plaintiff from his job application right into the burning building. Courts have applied analogous rules against police officers who sue for injuries arising out of the negligence of third parties.

Those who undertake exceptionally dangerous public employment are not alone in their plight in tort litigation. An example of hurdles that face other workers is the case in which a mentally ill patient assaults a caretaker. A California appellate decision concluded that a certified nurse's aide could not recover against the estate of a patient with Alzheimer's disease who became combative when she was being moved by another nurse's aide from a chair to a bed. The court pointed out that the plaintiff knew she was working among Alzheimer's patients, in whom violence was a "common trait." It said that she had "placed herself in a position where she assumed the duty to take care of patients who were potentially violent and to protect such patients from committing acts which might injure others." From a broader policy perspective, the court said that in such situations it was "the health care provider, not the patient, who is in the best position to protect against the risks to the provider rooted in the very reasons for the treatment." Employing a somewhat stretched analogy, the court said that it if were to rule for the plaintiff, "nurses working in an infectious disease unit could sue a patient for giving them tuberculosis."[29]

27. DiSalvatore v. United States, 499 F.Supp. 338, 339 (E.D.Pa.1980).

28. Brown v. General Elec. Corp., 648 F.Supp. 470, 472 (M.D.Ga.1986).

29. Herrle v. Estate of Marshall, 45 Cal.App.4th 1761, 53 Cal.Rptr.2d 713, 716, 719 (1996).

C. Theory and policy

The application of assumption of risk in the workplace is so controversial because the cases embody sharp disputes about policy. One argument, based on economic theory, insists that employees should not be able to sue for workplace hazards because the wage rates for dangerous jobs provide a premium to workers, who in effect accept extra money in payment for the risks that they confront.

Related to that theory are disputes about whether the employer or the worker is in the better position to avoid a hazard. These issues frequently have complex dimensions. Initially, an employer typically has superior information about hazards, and often the ability to avoid them by making the workplace safer. However, not only may the worker have a general sense of the risks of the job when he takes it, but at the point of the injuring event, it often is the worker who possesses the information that is crucial to the risk of the accident that happens. One also may pose the issue in terms of which party was in the position to avoid the accident at the least cost, but statements of the issue in terms of economic policy may eventually have to give way to arguments about moral principles.

It is, indeed, the moral question that hangs over many arguments about the use of the assumption of risk doctrine in cases of workplace injuries. A simple hypothetical illustrates that courts sometimes must resort to moral principles in this area of the law. In a time of job scarcity, an employer tells a steeplejack to fix a church steeple using a frayed rope. The steeplejack complies, being without alternative opportunities for employment, and suffers serious injuries when the rope breaks. Assuming that the steeplejack was working for an established wage, an open-and-shut way to rationalize a defendant's judgment would be to say that the wage rate represented a payment for the risk level of the job. However, the plaintiff will point out, this bargain-oriented argument does not take into account the conditions of necessity that drove him to go up on the frayed rope. The defendant will respond that we all must live with various forms of scarcity and that an employer's responsibility in a tight job market does not extend to compensating employees who choose to take risks that they would not choose in more affluent circumstances.

This set of arguments simply focuses the philosophical confrontation over the issue of whether "necessity" or "duress" will cancel the assumption of risk defense. In the end, the legal question resolves itself into one of oughts, and judges must make decisions with moral content. For some judges, manifested choice is sovereign, even in marketplaces of extremely constrained choice. For others, a moral approach requiring meaningful choice will dictate rejection of implied assumption of risk in situations where the doctrine fits poorly with the conditions of employment.

D. Simplifying doctrine

The implied assumption of risk doctrine adds a layer of complexity to defenses based on the conduct of worker plaintiffs. One way to reduce that complexity would be to judge employees' conduct only under a general reasonableness standard. This solution would in effect do away with the assumption of risk defense and related doctrines.[30] It would have the doctrinal advantage, in states that have adopted comparative negligence,[31] of facilitating an across-the-board comparison of the unreasonableness of a defendant's conduct and the unreasonableness of a plaintiff's conduct in the circumstances. This simplification of doctrine is somewhat defense-oriented, because it does away with the requirement that a defendant establish that the plaintiff knew of a particular risk. However, plaintiffs might still contend that specificity of knowledge of a risk is one aspect of whether the plaintiff reasonably confronted that risk. They might also argue that courts should judge the reasonableness of their acceptance of a risk in light of the realities of the workplace, including duress stemming from fear of losing a job.[32]

¶ 30.04 Sports and Recreation

Another specialized area in which the doctrine of assumption of risk and related theories operate is that of sports and recreation. Both types of activity, deeply embedded in American culture, provide interesting comparisons with the everyday workplace. Of particular note is the parallel nature of the terminology that courts use across a spectrum of activities including conventional work, professional sports and recreational athletics.

The use of the terms sports and recreation conjunctively in this section suggests that there is not a clear line between the two. Obviously, there will be many activities where both professionals and amateurs suffer the same kind of injury. For example, both professionals and weekend athletes engage in such diverse activities as baseball, automobile racing and skiing. Sometimes, however, courts have drawn distinctions based on whether the plaintiff is a professional: they may view professional athletes as behaving more

---

30. See, e.g., Farley v. M M Cattle Co., 529 S.W.2d 751, 758 (Tex.1975).

31. For a discussion of the relationship of comparative negligence to assumption of risk, see infra, ¶ 33.03.

32. For a functional classification system, designed to simplify analysis of defenses based on the plaintiff's conduct, spanning such categories as assumption of risk, contributory negligence, no duty, no negligence, and "obviousness," see infra, ¶ 32.02.

voluntarily, and perhaps more knowledgeably, than people who engage in risky activities simply for recreation.

This section reviews the application of different assumption of risk doctrines and related concepts to play-for-pay and to games for fun. Although some of the terminology discussed here duplicates that analyzed earlier, other categories break down assumption of risk into even more detailed compartments than those previously mentioned, and sometimes use different combinations of terms to describe the same concept. This summary may be useful, even with some necessary repetition, as a description of the varied terms that courts use when defendants argue that plaintiffs have voluntarily chosen to confront a risk.

Recurrent themes with respect to both professional and amateur sports are that the knowledge of the plaintiff about a risk, or the obviousness of a risk, effectively cancel the defendant's duty. Additionally, the unreasonableness of the plaintiff will always bar or reduce recovery, but courts will differ about whether recovery should be denied or reduced when plaintiffs have behaved reasonably in the face of negligent conduct by the defendant. Sometimes courts use assumption of risk terminology when they appear to mean that the defendant simply was not negligent. And some state statutes impose risks of injury encountered in recreational activities on those who engage in them.

A. *Professional sports*

Professional sports provides an interesting menu of doctrines tied in with the assumption of risk idea. The decisions are relatively few, but they are particularly instructive, perhaps because of the intensity of the competition they reflect. Manifesting the level of violence in professional football in particular is a 1992 statistic for the National Football League. By early December of that season, 482 players suffered injuries serious enough to to miss at least one game: an average of 17 players per team. One star player said that "one of the first things you notice in this league is how steadily people step in and out of the lineup because of injuries. After a while you hardly notice it any more. You just go on." As a college trainer who had studied NFL injuries summarized it, "[t]he game is one of collision, and people get hurt."[33]

The cases analyzed here span sports from horse racing to football to tennis and baseball. The doctrines employed by the courts range from concepts of implied consent and no duty to notions of "primary" assumption of risk and "secondary" assump-

---

33. Peter King, The Unfortunate 500, 77 Sports Illus. No. 24, 20 at 23 (Dec. 7, 1992).

tion of risk—both reasonable and unreasonable—and also include obviousness. This overlapping use of concepts suggests the limits of language in the area, and, as a practical matter, the need for attorneys to tailor their arguments to the specific terminology that appeals to particular courts. For example, although many people may believe that "consent" and "assumption of risk" are rather different ideas, some courts discern a functional equivalence among "implied consent," "implied primary assumption of risk" and "no duty."

An interesting pair of decisions that illustrates this collection of doctrines involves serious injuries to jockeys. In *Turcotte v. Fell*,[34] the New York Court of Appeals used implied consent and no duty doctrines in rejecting a suit by a noted jockey against another jockey and a race track. The plaintiff suffered paralyzing injuries when he was thrown to the ground after his horse clipped the heels of another horse, tripped and fell.

In *Rini v. Oaklawn Jockey Club*,[35] the plaintiff attributed serious injuries to the traffic pattern near the starting gate, which he said had a "great potential to 'spook' horses coming out of the . . . gate." A federal trial court and appellate court, which disagreed in *Rini*, discussed a number of defensive theories. These included several varieties of assumption of risk terminology, with the appellate court ultimately holding that assumption of risk defenses must either give way to, or be subject to, comparative fault. The doctrines discussed in *Turcotte* and *Rini*, taken together, comprise an instructive catalog of terminology.

1. *Implied consent*

In *Turcotte*, the court denied recovery, rejecting the plaintiff's claims that the other jockey had committed a tort by "foul riding," and that the race track owner was negligent in its watering and grooming of the track. The court spoke of an athlete's implied "consent" to certain dangerous aspects of his sport, specifically to dangers that "are inherent in the sport" and "are recognized as such" by the athlete. Focusing on the plaintiff's status as a professional, the court said that a professional athlete is "more aware of the dangers of the activity, and presumably more willing to accept them in exchange for a salary, than is an amateur."[36]

With specific reference to the situation at issue, the court pictured the peril of "[j]ockeys weighing between 100 and 120 pounds" trying to control horses that weigh a half ton and some-

34. 502 N.E.2d 964 (N.Y.1986).

35. 662 F.Supp. 569 (W.D.Ark. 1987), rev'd, 861 F.2d 502 (8th Cir. 1988).

36. Turcotte, 502 N.E.2d at 969.

times run up to 40 miles an hour. The court also referred to "bumping and jostling" as being "normal incidents of the sport." The court viewed actors like the defendants before it as effectively being immunized against suit unless they acted recklessly or intentionally.[37]

2. No duty

The *Turcotte* court in effect employed a "no duty" concept while also drawing on the locution of obviousness. It spoke of the defendant's duty as being "to exercise care to make the conditions as safe as they appear to be," and commented that "[i]f the risks of activity are fully comprehended or perfectly obvious, plaintiff has consented to them and defendant has performed its duty."[38]

3. Implied primary assumption of risk/no duty

In *Rini*, the trial court held for the defendant race track, overlapping a no duty defense based on a notion of consent with that of "implied assumption of risk." The trial judge said that if a jury found "that the plaintiff consented to defendant's negligence," he could not recover, but "not ... because he caused his own injury"; rather, he would lose "because the defendant owed him no duty."[39] The issue on appeal concerned the effects on the assumption of risk defense of Arkansas' adoption of comparative fault. The Eighth Circuit ultimately reversed the trial court on the grounds that comparative fault had supplanted any defenses based on the defendant race track's conduct. However, the appellate court listed a "no duty" theory, to which it referred as "implied primary assumption of risk"—in a summary of assumption of risk defenses. It identified that category as applying to cases where the plaintiff "assumed known risks *inherent* in a particular activity or situation."[40]

4. Implied secondary unreasonable assumption of risk

Distinguishing other forms of implied assumption of risk, the Eighth Circuit in *Rini* used the phrase "implied secondary unreasonable assumption of risk" to describe the situation "where the plaintiff voluntarily encounters a known risk created by the defendant but the plaintiff's conduct in doing so is unreasonable."[41] The court said that under comparative fault, this type of conduct would "no longer be a complete bar to recovery, but rather one element to

---

37. Id.

38. Id. at 968. Cf. id. at 969 (plaintiff "consented to relieve" the other jockey of "the legal duty to use reasonable care").

39. Rini v. Oaklawn Jockey Club, 662 F.Supp. 569, 572 (W.D.Ark.1987).

40. 861 F.2d at 506.

41. Id.

be factored into the comparative fault analysis."[42] Unreasonable conduct by the plaintiff, of course, is most simply described as contributory negligence, and, as a practical matter, the application of comparative fault to knowledgeably careless conduct by a plaintiff merges unreasonable assumption of risk with contributory negligence.

5. Implied secondary reasonable assumption of risk

Finally, the Eighth Circuit in *Rini* used the term "implied secondary reasonable assumption of risk" to describe the case where the plaintiff was "aware of a risk created by the negligence of the defendant" and voluntarily encountered it in a reasonable way. Drawing on a precedent, the court illustrated this category by a hypothetical case where a landlord's negligence exposed an infant to a fire on a tenant's premises and the tenant was injured when he rushed into the dwelling to rescue the trapped infant.[43] It concluded that, with the advent of comparative fault, this type of conduct should neither bar nor reduce the plaintiff's recovery because to allow a defense would "inequitably punish[] reasonable conduct."[44]

Applying its classification scheme to the facts, the court pointed out that the case clearly did not involve express assumption of risk or "assumption of risk in its primary form." Therefore, whichever form of secondary assumption of risk was involved—either reasonable or unreasonable—the court concluded that the case exhibited no form of assumption of risk that "survive[d] the adoption of comparative fault."[45] The court thus held it error for the trial court to have given instructions on assumption of risk.

6. Obviousness

Decisions on professional sports injuries have also employed the terminology of obviousness, sometimes linking it with assumption of risk. In a tennis case involving Wightman Cup matches, the court reversed a verdict for a competitor who suffered severe knee injuries when she fell on an indoor court surface marketed by the defendant. There was testimony from several athletes, including the plaintiff, that they were aware of bubbles and gaps in the seams of the court surface when they practiced on it. Under a state assumption of risk standard that required either that the plaintiff have actual knowledge of a danger or that it was patently obvious, the appellate court concluded that it was error for the trial court not to instruct on assumption of risk.[46]

---

42. Id. at 508.

43. Id. at 506, referring to Blackburn v. Dorta, 348 So.2d 287, 291 (Fla. 1977).

44. Id. at 509.

45. Id.

46. Heldman v. Uniroyal, Inc., 371 N.E.2d 557, 567 (Ohio Ct.App.1977).

In another case, a center fielder for the New York Yankees was unsuccessful in a suit for injuries that occurred when he slipped on wet grass in the outfield. Observing that "the danger of falling on the wet playing field was obvious," the court referred to "playing on an open wet field" as being "part of the game of baseball."[47]

7. *Beyond civilization?: Hackbart*

Perhaps the farthest extension of assumption of risk thinking—philosophically a very challenging one—appears in a trial court decision, later reversed, in the one officially reported tort case that has emerged from professional football. In *Hackbart v. Cincinnati Bengals*,[48] the defendant committed a palpable foul on his opponent after a sudden reversal of a play that went in favor of the plaintiff's team. In frustration concerning this event, the defendant delivered a powerful blow with his forearm to the back of the plaintiff's head, causing what later appeared as a career-ending injury.

The trial judge in *Hackbart* referred to evidence, including testimony by the plaintiff's own coach, that aggressiveness was the prime consideration in selecting players for professional football teams, and that coaching "did not include any training with respect to a responsibility or even any regard for the safety of opposing players."[49] Although recognizing that there was a conflict in witnesses' opinions about whether the defendant's act could "be considered 'part of the game,' "the trial judge pointed out that the incident did not excite special comment during a review of films of the game by players and coaches of the plaintiff's team. He concluded that "the level of violence and the frequency of emotional outbursts in NFL football games are such that [the plaintiff] must have recognized and accepted the risk that he would be injured by such an act" as the defendant's.[50]

The court's summary of the law as applied was that "the plaintiff must be held to have assumed the risk of such an occurrence," even if the defendant had breached a duty to the plaintiff.[51] However, the court went much further, punctuating this holding on legal theory with the comment that "[t]he NFL has substituted the morality of the battlefield for that of the playing field, and the 'restraints of civilization' have been left on the sidelines."[52]

---

47. Maddox v. City of New York, 487 N.Y.S.2d 354, 357 (App.Div.), aff'd, 487 N.E.2d 553, 557 (N.Y.1985) (applying "assumption of risk," court noted that the risk from the muddy field "was evident to plaintiff").

48. 435 F.Supp. 352 (D.Colo.1977), rev'd, 601 F.2d 516 (10th Cir.1979).

49. 435 F. Supp. at 355–56.

50. Id. at 356.

51. Id.

52. Id. at 358.

The court of appeals reversed the trial court, saying that the appropriate legal standard was one of "reckless misconduct."[53] The appellate court specifically disagreed with what it characterized as the trial judge's position that "there are no principles of law which allow a court to rule out certain tortious conduct by reason of general roughness of the game or difficulty of administering it."[54] It quoted a league rule that explicitly prohibited the defendant's act, as well as citing disapproval by "general customs of football" of the "intentional punching or striking of others."[55]

Of particular relevance to assumption of risk and related doctrines was the appellate court's conclusion that it was "highly questionable whether a professional football player consents or submits to injuries caused by conduct not within the rules" and its statement that it had seen no evidence to prove that this was so.[56] The disagreement between the trial and appellate courts on that point is symbolic of the arguments concerning the range of doctrines discussed in this chapter, including various formulations of assumption of risk, implied consent, and no duty. The trial court sets out a particularly interesting challenge: what, if any, are the human activities where "the 'restraints of civilization' have been left on the sidelines"?

B. Recreation

1. Common law

Courts have applied to cases involving recreational activity a set of common law defenses, including assumption of risk and no duty, that parallel those used concerning professional athletes. The ski slopes are an important venue for cases that employ these doctrines, with a Third Circuit skiing case illustrating the close overlap of the theory labeled primary assumption of risk with the notion that the defendant had no duty to the plaintiff. In this case, the court noted that the slope on which the plaintiff was injured was "marked with the international symbol designating it one of the most difficult slopes" at a ski resort. The court pointed out that skiers ahead of the plaintiff "were having trouble negotiating [the] steep icy slope," and observed that "unprotected telephone-like poles that were part of the resort's snowmaking apparatus lined the center of the headwall." Stressing that the plaintiff had not gone back to "a gentler slope" or "side-step[ped] down the slope to safety," the court concluded that he therefore "took his chances" on the ice, on which he fell and slid into one of the poles. Because the plaintiff had extensive skiing experience, the court said that his

53. 601 F.2d at 524.

54. Id. at 520.

55. Id. at 521.

56. Id. at 520.

maneuver was "probably quite reasonable" but that it also "absolved defendant of any obligation to exercise care for his protection."[57] The court distinguished the defense of assumption of risk "in its primary sense" from "its secondary sense," in which it "overlaps with the defense of contributory negligence."[58]

2. Spectators

The problem of spectators injured from fast-flying objects projected off baseball bats and hockey sticks presents an interesting set of doctrinal overlaps. A facile defense is that the spectator injured by a foul ball or a hockey puck has "assumed the risk," providing a complete defense to owners of sports facilities. Defendants in such cases may also offer the argument that they had no duty to the plaintiff. Another defensive tactic, arguably more direct but also not obvious at first glance, is to contend that the defendant was not negligent—that is, it did not act below the standard of care of those conducting such sports events with reference to spectator protection. A New Jersey appellate opinion captures some of these conceptual wrinkles in holding that a hockey rink has a limited duty to spectators. It makes a bow to the no duty/assumed risk set of arguments in saying that "[t]he critical circumstance that determines the scope of the duty of a baseball field or hockey rink is that most spectators prefer to sit where they can have an unobstructed view of the game and are willing to expose themselves to the risks posed by flying balls or pucks to obtain that view." However, the court also declares that the facility operator must "provide[] sufficient screened seats for those spectators who may be reasonably expected to request protected seats" and also to "screen[] any seats that pose an unduly high risk of injury from flying balls or pucks."[59]

3. Statutory assumption of risk defenses

State legislatures have enacted statutes that provide a form of "primary assumption of risk" with respect to sports activities. The Vermont statute, for example, declares that "a person who takes part in any sport accepts as a matter of law the dangers that inhere therein insofar as they are obvious and necessary."[60] Not surprisingly, skiing presents a focal point for application of this legislation,

---

57. Smith v. Seven Springs Farm, Inc., 716 F.2d 1002, 1009 (3d Cir.1983).

58. Id. at 1006.

59. Schneider v. American Hockey & Ice Skating Ctr., Inc., 342 N.J.Super. 527, 777 A.2d 380, 384 (2001). On the facts of the case before it, in which the plaintiff was hit between the eyes by a puck, the court grants summary judgment to the defendant. It notes that the facility "did not contain any seating directly behind the goals, which generally is considered to be the most dangerous spectator area in a hockey rink," and that the plaintiff "did not offer any evidence that the unprotected seats in the side area of the rink pose an unduly high risk of injury from flying pucks." 777 A.2d at 385.

60. Vermont Sports Injury Statute, Vt. Stat. Ann. Title 12 § 1037 (1991).

the interpretation of which features ideas borrowed from the common law doctrines. In a case involving a collision between skiers, a court that affirmed a defendant's judgment said that a jury could decide "that skiers who lose control even while exercising due care—that is, have breached no duty owed to other skiers—may pose a danger which is inherent, obvious and necessary to participants in the sport of skiing." The court held that it was not error "to instruct the jury to decide whether plaintiff had assumed the risks inherent in skiing before it considered defendant's negligence."[61]

In another case, in which a plaintiff slipped on a "shiny glaze" on a ski trail, the court noted that "[n]o improvements in grooming technique have been able to eliminate ice from the New England ski slopes." Commenting that ice was "an obvious and necessary danger in the sport of skiing," the court said that a resort operator had "no duty to warn . . . of the icy conditions of the trail, or take any steps to attempt to eliminate the ice."[62]

Statutes of this sort clearly represent a legislative response to resort owners who find liability to be bad for business. In one case, the court chronicled a political "groundswell . . . to restore" the immunity of ski area owners, noting that "the two primary ski area insurers threatened to withdraw from Vermont . . . effectively putting in jeopardy one of the state's major industries."[63] Yet such statutes do not simply reflect political pressure from narrow interest groups. They codify social attitudes about recreational activities that carry high quotients of danger—the social norms that have been embedded in what some courts call "primary assumption of risk."[64]

4. No negligence

To round out this survey of defensive doctrines in sport and recreation cases, we reiterate that one of the most straightforward defensive maneuvers is to assert that the defendant simply was not negligent. One may apply this idea, for example, in the case of skiing dangers. Where ice is a fact of life on ski slopes, perhaps the most elegant explanation of results for defendants is to say that it is not a lack of due care to maintain ski slopes that are icy. This may be an even more direct way of presenting the case against liability than focusing on a hypothesized consent to "inherent

61. Dillworth v. Gambardella, 970 F.2d 1113, 1122–23 (2d Cir.1992).

62. Nelson v. Snowridge, Inc., 818 F.Supp. 80, 83–84 (D.Vt.1993).

63. Dillworth, supra note 57, at 1117.

64. See id. at 1121 (referring to affidavit of state judiciary committee member that Sports Injury Statute "affirm[ed] the doctrine of primary assumption of risk").

danger" and a resulting lack of duty on the part of the defendant. Certainly, it provides an alternative way of looking at the subject and of rationalizing many decisions that refuse to impose liability in the context of sports and games, as well as of explaining many other cases across the range of tort law where plaintiffs encounter risk at some level of knowledge and choice.

Chapter Thirty–One

CONTRIBUTORY NEGLIGENCE

¶ 31.01 Definition: An Objective Standard

Contributory negligence, simply defined, is "conduct on the part of the plaintiff which falls below the standard to which he should conform for his own protection."[1] Although this language of the Restatement Second may seem to imply subjective moral content, the defense is, in its classic form, an objective one. It thus contrasts, at least theoretically, with the traditional definition of assumption of risk, which depends on subjective features of the plaintiff's knowledge.[2]

Originally, any contributory negligence, no matter how slight, was a complete bar to a plaintiff's claim of negligence. Today, however, in the many states that have adopted the theory of comparative negligence, the contributory fault of the plaintiff—whether or not of the assumption of risk variety—will often operate to reduce the plaintiff's recovery rather than to bar it, although under some versions of comparative negligence rules, any contributory negligence will still defeat the plaintiff completely.[3]

Illustrative of the objective character of the test for contributory negligence is a products liability case in which the plaintiff's hand was struck by a cylinder in a machine used in a yarn mill. The plaintiff insisted that he did not know that there were moving parts inside the machine when he put his hand in it. However, the court concluded that the jury could have found contributory negligence because the plaintiff was aware of circumstances that would have caused an ordinary prudent person to be alert to the possibility that the cylinder would continue to move through the machine.[4] The court stressed that under the contributory negligence doctrine, it was "not necessary that plaintiff be *actually aware* of the unreason-

---

1. Restatement (Second) of Torts § 463 (1965).

2. See supra, ¶ 30.01[A][2].

3. See ¶ 33.01 infra.

4. Smith v. Fiber Controls Corp., 268 S.E.2d 504, 508–09 (N.C.1980).

able danger of injury" but only that he unreasonably ignore risks that "would have been apparent to a prudent person exercising ordinary care for his own safety."[5]

¶ 31.02   Questions of Fact and Questions of Law

The contributory negligence issue generates many interesting problems concerning the distinction between fact and law, presenting the question of whether judge or jury is the better decisionmaker. Courts often refuse to rule as a matter of law that a plaintiff was contributorily negligent, reasoning that the jury should decide whether the plaintiff exercised reasonable care under the circumstances. Illustrative of the type of situation in which courts give the issue to the jury is a case in which the maker of a forage harvester argued that a farm worker was "negligent as a matter of law" because he did not comply with a safety caution in the operating manual. The court disagreed, saying that it would not hold an operating manual dispositive on the question of the plaintiff's conduct. The court said that both "[t]he existence and appropriateness of the warning, as well as [the plaintiff's] knowledge of the warning and his conduct," presented jury questions.[6]

There are, however, some situations in which courts will take the contributory negligence question from juries. More often than not, these decisions weigh in favor of defendants. In one case in which the court held that a reasonable jury could not find that a plaintiff had behaved carefully, the claimant crossed a street "somewhere in the middle of the block at two in the morning wearing dark clothing in a dark area," although he saw a car approaching about one-third of a city block away. When he "proceeded to cross anyway, in an unhurried, casual manner without looking around to see" if the oncoming car had stopped, the court decided that his inattentiveness was "so unreasonable that no jury could properly conclude that he was not contributorily negligent."[7]

5. Id. at 507.

6. Bauer v. Piper Indus., Inc., 454 N.W.2d 28, 30 (Wis.Ct.App.1990).

7. Garcia v. Bynum, 635 F.Supp. 745, 747–48 (D.D.C.1986), aff'd without opin., 816 F.2d 791 (D.C.Cir.1987). Cf. Dang v. New Hampshire Ins. Co., 798 So.2d 1204 (La.Ct.App.2001), writ denied, 811 So.2d 939 (La.2002), in which the plaintiff started to cross a street while the light was green. Walking in a marked pedestrian crosswalk, she continued past the median. About halfway between the median and the other side of the street, the light went yellow to her. She hesitated and then kept going to the other side. The defendant, driving a truck, proceeded into the intersection even though his view on one side was blocked by a van. His vehicle struck the plaintiff. The trial court set aside a jury verdict assessing 60 percent comparative fault to the plaintiff and apportioned 100 percent comparative fault to the truck driver. The appellate court ruled that the trial court had not abused its discretion. Referring to evidence that the plaintiff had not "place[d] herself at any greater risk whether she continued across the street or decided to return to the median," the appellate court declared that "no reasonable juror could have reached the conclusion that [the plaintiff] was 60% at fault." Id. at 1208.

In such decisions, courts exercise their independent judgment about the practical obligations of persons for their own safety.

Another case that makes the point even more strongly involved a suit against the United States for its alleged negligent failure to confine a mentally disturbed patient. The plaintiff's decedent saw the escaped patient carrying a rifle, which he pointed at the window of the decedent's car. After driving around for a little while, the decedent returned to where the patient was walking, got out of his car and shouted a vulgar comment at him. The patient fatally shot the decedent. Saying that the facts known to the decedent when he approached the patient "were sufficient to apprise him of the danger and risk of injury," and noting that he had not informed the police of the situation and had used "extremely inflammatory language ... to a man holding a rifle," the court decided that the decedent "was contributorily negligent."[8] Decisions involving such blatant hazards may verge on applications of traditional assumption of risk, but even without reaching for the sort of subjective assessment courts make under that doctrine, holdings of this kind reflect a judicial conviction that objectively, there was no reasonable aspect to the plaintiff's conduct. One should note that in some cases, the defense may apply as rigorously to children as to adults.[9]

By comparison, courts occasionally hold that, as a matter of law, a plaintiff's conduct may not be said to be contributorily negligent. For example, one decision concluded that it was not careless of a lender to fail to conduct an independent search for liens on farm machinery that was offered as security for a loan, when a lawyer represented that he had conducted such a search. Suggesting that it would encourage economic waste to hold otherwise, the court said that "[t]he law normally does not require duplicative precautions unless one is likely to fail or the consequences of failure (slight though the likelihood may be) would be catastrophic." The court concluded that "[o]ne UCC search is enough to disclose prior liens, and [the lender] acted reasonably in relying" on a lawyer to conduct the search.[10]

---

8. Voss v. United States, 423 F.Supp. 751, 753–54 (E.D.Mo.1976).

9. See, e.g., Mangold v. Indiana Dep't of Natural Resources, 756 N.E.2d 970 (Ind.2001), in which the 12–year-old plaintiff attended a hunter education class at his school in which the instructor said that when the firing pin on a shotgun strikes the primer, "the primer 'sparks' setting fire to the powder." The instructor "warned the students that they should never handle ammunition unless accompanied by an adult." Af- firming summary judgment for the defendants, a majority of the supreme court incorporated the relevant facts of an after-school incident that cost the plaintiff an eye in its declaration that "the trial court need only have been satisfied that a twelve-year-old who smashed live ammunition with a hammer and chisel in the face of his recent firearm safety instruction was minimally negligent as a matter of law." Id. at 977.

10. Greycas, Inc. v. Proud, 826 F.2d 1560, 1566 (7th Cir.1987), cert. denied, 484 U.S. 1043 (1988).

One should also note that contributory negligence may not provide a defense when the plaintiff's conduct has a particularly close link to the reason that the defendant is held negligent. An illustration is a case in which a psychiatric patient suffered injuries when she jumped out of a hospital window. In her suit against doctors, nurses, and the hospital, two levels of New Jersey appeals courts affirmed the trial judge's refusal to instruct on contributory negligence. The trial court having summarized evidence of a suicide attempt by the plaintiff that was the event that sent her to the hospital,[11] the appellate division pointed out that the plaintiff had "committed the very act that defendants were under a duty to prevent."[12] In its affirmance, the supreme court said that the contributory negligence issue did "not present itself ... because the plaintiff's inability to exercise self-care attributable to her mental disability was itself subsumed within the duty of care defendants owed to her."[13]

There is, however, considerable room for dispute on this fascinating question. The Wisconsin Supreme Court, for example, held a mental patient contributorily negligent as a matter of law when he executed a complicated, furtive plan for escape from his room in a county psychiatric hospital. Among other facts on which the court focused was the plaintiff's selection of his escape route after he had used a toothbrush to pry off a device that had been used to keep a window secure. The court noted that the plaintiff chose a relatively safe route because, as he testified, another route "would be definitely suicide." This rational core of his behavior led the court to conclude that he must be held to an objective standard, even in the face of the fact of his protective institutionalization.[14]

In an analogous decision, an Illinois court allowed the use of the defense when the mother of a college student sued a physician at her late daughter's university health clinic. The decedent was hospitalized for more than two weeks after the defendant became concerned that she "might be having suicidal thoughts," but was released and a few days later appeared to be "smiling and upbeat." After the decedent subsequently expressed concern about running out of her antidepressant medication and "the cost of filling small prescriptions frequently," the defendant gave her a prescription for a large number of pills. Two weeks later, an episode of severe depression followed the theft of her backpack with her school notes. Two days after that, she registered under a fictitious name at a hotel, where she took an enormous fatal dose of the antidepressant pills. Noting the decedent's apparent improvement at the time she

---

11. Cowan v. Doering, 522 A.2d 444, 447–48 (N.J.Super.App.Div.1987), aff'd, 545 A.2d 159 (N.J.1988).

12. 522 A.2d at 450.

13. 545 A.2d at 163.

14. Jankee v. Clark County, 235 Wis.2d 700, 612 N.W.2d 297 (2000).

requested the prescription for a larger number of pills, the Illinois Supreme Court said that the defendant and another treating physician who testified on the subject had considered the request "to be both natural and rational." Given the "premeditated and deliberate" nature of the decedent's actions just before her suicide, the supreme court said that the trial court had correctly held that the issue of her contributory negligence should have been given to the jury.[15]

Perhaps the most dramatic and instructive confrontation on the fact/law, judge/jury question with respect to contributory negligence occurred between two of the greatest American jurists. In *Baltimore and Ohio Railroad v. Goodman,*[16] Justice Holmes dealt harshly with a suit by a survivor of a motorist killed by a train at a grade crossing. Referring to the need for a clear standard, Justice Holmes said that "[w]hen a man goes upon a railroad track he knows that he goes to a place where he will be killed if a train comes upon him before he is clear of the track." Underlining the point, Holmes said that "[i]f at the last moment Goodman found himself in an emergency it was his own fault that he did not reduce his speed earlier or come to a stop."[17]

Only seven years later, Justice Cardozo presented a more flexible approach to the problem in another case involving a motorist injured by a train. Cardozo focused on facts indicating that the plaintiff had to make choices between potentially dangerous alternatives as he approached the crossing. In reversing a judgment for the defendant given on grounds of contributory negligence, Cardozo spoke of "the need for caution in framing standards of behavior that amount to rules of law," especially in situations where there was "no background of experience out of which the standards have emerged."[18]

¶ 31.03　Rationales

There are several rationales for the doctrine for contributory negligence, which are often implicit rather than explicit in the decisions. Courts presumably reason that over time, the message that careless behavior by accident victims will be penalized in tort litigation will tend to make people more careful for their own safety. Beyond that, there are intuitive reasons of fairness that motivate courts to bar or reduce the recovery of plaintiffs whose conduct falls below objective standards. When they employ the defense, courts simply are applying against careless plaintiffs the

---

15. Hobart v. Shin, 185 Ill.2d 283, 705 N.E.2d 907 (1998).

16. 275 U.S. 66 (1927).

17. Id. at 69–70.

18. Pokora v. Wabash Ry. Co., 292 U.S. 98, 105 (1934).

notions of corrective justice inherent in the imposition of liability on defendants for negligence.

Another justification for applying the doctrine is that some contributory negligence, besides putting the plaintiff at risk, imperils other persons. One scholar uses the example of "[t]he motorist who drives at night without lights" as one who "creates an unreasonable risk to himself and to others at the same time."[19] We note that the application of contributory negligence on this basis may not only be fair but deter undesirable conduct as well.

A somewhat different concern inheres in the idea that when a contributorily negligent plaintiff sues a negligent defendant, "the harm involved in the plaintiff's original conduct 'reaches' the defendant, another person." The plaintiff's conduct thus contributes to make the defendant potentially responsible for an injury that, although the defendant helped to cause it, "would never have occurred had the plaintiff himself not behaved in a foolish way." Thus, "it would be basically unfair ... to ignore entirely the plaintiff's conduct by imposing full liability on the negligent defendant."[20]

19. Gary Schwartz, Contributory and Comparative Negligence: A Reappraisal, 87 Yale L. J. 697, 723 (1978).

20. Id. at 724–25.

Chapter Thirty–Two

CLASSIFYING DEFENSES BASED ON PLAINTIFF'S CONDUCT

Analysis

This chapter provides a functional overview of the theories of defense based on the plaintiff's conduct surveyed in the immediately preceding chapters.[1] Sometimes more than one of these doctrinal labels, including contributory negligence, various forms of implied assumption of risk, and no duty, may be applied to the same behavior. Therefore, both advocates and judges should look to the functional purpose of defenses involving the plaintiff's conduct in order to determine how best to characterize that behavior. On occasion, characterization will have important consequences for litigation. For example, if one decided that the reason to bar a plaintiff's suit was that the defendant had no duty to the plaintiff, it would not be necessary to consider the question of whether the plaintiff was at fault.

¶ 32.01 Contributory Negligence and Assumption of Risk: Overlaps and Contrasts

The principal categories that courts use to describe conduct by claimants that will bar recovery or reduce damages are contributory negligence and assumption of risk. The general definition of contributory negligence is conduct by a plaintiff that falls below a reasonable standard of care for his own safety, judged on a relatively objective basis.[2] By contrast, the more subjectively oriented defense of assumption of risk requires the defendant to show that the plaintiff not only behaved unreasonably, but voluntarily confronted a known risk.[3]

---

1. Chapters 30–31.
2. See supra, ¶ 31.01.

3. See supra, ¶ 30.01(A).

Some analysts believe it would be wise to chalk up most "assumption of risk" defenses under the contributory negligence rubric. This solution would have the advantage of simplifying the law, making the only question whether the plaintiff's conduct was unreasonable under the circumstances. This formulation of a single defense would override the view that there are certain kinds of plaintiff conduct that should be regarded as careless only when the plaintiff knowledgeably and voluntarily confronts danger—the traditional formula for assumption of risk. Those advocating retention of a separate assumption of risk defense might focus on such cases as those involving employee injuries in hazardous workplaces. With respect to those cases specifically, they would contend that because of the nature of such employment, the only plaintiff carelessness that deserves the label of contributory negligence is a voluntary and unreasonable confrontation with a particular danger.

A decision under the Federal Employers' Liability Act (FELA) illustrates another, somewhat unusual, angle of distinction between contributory negligence and assumption of risk. The FELA, which provides railroad workers a negligence action against their employers, bars the use of the assumption of risk defense, although it permits defenses based on contributory negligence. In this case, the plaintiff claimed that he became a paranoid schizophrenic because of his foreman's harassment. The railroad defendant argued that the plaintiff was contributorily negligent because he had not "bid off" the foreman's section gang when he felt the harassment become severe. The court, though conceding there was "some overlap" between the defenses, articulated a distinction. Defining assumption of risk as requiring "an employee's voluntary, knowledgeable acceptance of a dangerous condition," it contrasted contributory negligence as "a careless act or omission on the plaintiff's part tending to add new dangers to conditions that the employer negligently created or permitted to exist." The court characterized "[r]eporting to work or facing the risks inherent in one's job" as "the essence of assumption of risk." It said that employees who entered "the workplace for a routine assignment in compliance with the orders and directions of [an] employer or its supervising agents," thereby "incur[ring] risks not extraordinary in scope," were "not contributorily negligent," but rather "engaging in an assumption of risk."[4]

---

4. Taylor v. Burlington N. R.R., 787 F.2d 1309, 1316–17 (9th Cir.1986) (holding that it was not error to refuse to allow the jury to decide whether the plaintiff's failure to "bid off" his foreman's gang was assumption of risk or contributory negligence, although finding that it was error for the trial court not to give a comparative negligence instruction with reference to the possibility that the plaintiff's "heated verbal exchanges" with a foreman and his fighting with co-workers contributed to his stress, id. at 1314).

This opinion simply illustrates the varied concepts that potentially fall under the label "assumption of risk"—concepts describing behaviors that may either be reasonable or unreasonable under particular circumstances. It is true that courts continue to distinguish between contributory negligence and assumption of risk, and lawyers must try to conform their arguments to the distinction where it is made. A critical analysis suggests, however, that the potential for confusion in this terminology makes it advisable to fashion the most simplified possible classification system for cases in which the plaintiff's conduct is at issue.

The desirability of a spare classification system becomes the more evident when one considers that in products liability cases, courts sometimes apply yet another classification of plaintiffs' conduct, that of "misuse." Some decisions use this as a separate category in cases in which the plaintiff employs a product for a purpose for which the manufacturer clearly did not intend it. Illustrative is a case in which a woman placed her almost 2–year-old great-granddaughter in a homemade, open wooden box attached to the fender of a rider mower. Rejecting a suit by the child for injuries caused when she was thrown from the mower, which then ran over her foot, the court said that the maker and seller of the vehicle could not "have reasonably anticipated" its use "as a motorized baby buggy."[5]

However, the decisions also speak of "foreseeable misuse," a use of a product that the seller did not intend for which courts will not bar a plaintiff if the defendant at least should have known of the likelihood of that type of use. The legal tension inherent in that phrase is apparent in a case in which two painters anchored their scaffold to a guardrail on an offshore oil platform. The rail collapsed, and the painters died when they fell into the sea. The trial court directed a verdict for the defendant, saying that the guardrail was not intended to support scaffolds. However, the appellate court reversed, concluding that a jury could have found "that the guardrail ... offered a convenient and commonly-used support for hanging a painting scaffold," a use that was foreseeable. The appeals court indicated that the trial court should not have "restricted its vision to intended uses" and should not have viewed "the guardrail only as a handrail."[6]

¶ 32.02　A Basic Classification System

Courts probably will continue to employ a variety of doctrinal labels to describe defenses that refer to plaintiffs' conduct. It therefore may be useful for judges, advocates and students to

5. Erkson v. Sears, Roebuck & Co., 841 S.W.2d 207, 210 (Mo.Ct.App.1992).

6. Branch v. Chevron Int'l Oil Co., 681 F.2d 426, 429–30 (5th Cir.1982).

outline a set of classifications that combine a functional orientation with a doctrinal one:

1) *The defendant does not fall below the standard of care in the activity—that is, the defendant is not negligent.* This may be an efficient way to account for denials of recovery in such situations as the case in which a baseball fan suffers injury from a foul ball when he is sitting in an area unprotected by a screen, a location that no ball park has ever covered with a screen. Sometimes courts will speak of "assumption of risk" to rationalize rejection of such claims. But it seems more elegant, and more helpful in explaining such results, simply to say that the ball club has not fallen below the appropriate standard of care, given the costs of screening all fans in the ball park from any contact with a foul ball.

2) *The defendant falls below the standard of care and is therefore negligent, but the plaintiff acts unreasonably.* Using a term familiar to lawyers and lay persons alike, the law calls the plaintiff's unreasonable conduct "contributory negligence." Ordinary contributory negligence, as it is sometimes described by contrast with assumption of risk, straightforwardly rationalizes cases like one described above, in which the plaintiff alleged that the federal government was negligent in not confining a mental patient but the plaintiff's decedent used extremely provocative language to the patient, who was wielding a firearm.[7]

3) *The defendant falls below the standard of care—and is therefore negligent—and the plaintiff subjectively knows of the danger but acts reasonably in the circumstances.* There is controversy about whether liability should be imposed in cases of this kind, like one discussed above in which an intending emergency room patient slipped and fell on ice in front of the hospital entrance.[8] A court that focused on the fact that the plaintiff chose to encounter a risk about which she well knew might call this a "no duty" case, as the court did in that case,[9] or one of "primary assumption of risk." A court that disallowed the defense would fix on the idea that it is negligence for a hospital with an emergency room to fail to remove ice from its entrance, and on the fact that although the plaintiff knew and understood the danger, she acted reasonably in the circumstances in trying to proceed over the ice. A label sometimes given to this type of case, that of "implied secondary reasonable assumption of risk," is not a solving phrase. Rather, it simply identifies the problem and highlights the choice that courts must make in judging the issue.

---

7. See discussion of Voss v. United States, 423 F.Supp. 751 (E.D.Mo.1976), supra at ¶ 31.02, text accompanying note 8.

8. See discussion of Gulfway Gen'l Hosp., Inc. v. Pursley, 397 S.W.2d 93 (Tex.Civ.App.1965), supra at ¶ 30.01(C), text accompanying note 21.

9. See 397 S.W.2d at 94.

4) *The defendant falls below the standard of care in the activity at issue and the plaintiff acts knowing of a hazard in a way that is objectively unreasonable in the circumstances, but because of the nature of an environment like an industrial workplace, the plaintiff arguably did not act voluntarily.* Some courts might deny recovery to a plaintiff in this situation for "assuming the risk," because he knew about the danger and he acted unreasonably in an abstract sense. They would emphasize that people at large are often constrained in their choices and would conclude that it is wrong to say that a confrontation with a well-known risk is not volitional. Other judges would argue that the only kind of contributory negligence that ought to be a defense to an employer's careless maintenance of a dangerous workplace is "assumption of risk"-type contributory negligence, which emphatically requires a voluntary choice by the plaintiff to confront the risk. Those taking this position would contend that it is unrealistic to label an employee's decision to carry on with an extremely dangerous task as "voluntary" when the alternative is to be fired.

5) *The defendant falls below the general standard of care in the activity at issue, but arguably behaves reasonably towards the plaintiff.* In a particularly interesting hypothetical presenting this challenging problem, Laurence Eldredge pictured a plaintiff who knows that his family is trapped in a burning building down the highway. The plaintiff flags down the first driver who comes along, who happens to be very drunk. Smelling the alcohol on the driver's breath and clearly on notice that the driver's perceptions are dulled, the plaintiff still elects to accept a ride so that he can try to rescue his family, and the driver has an accident that injures the plaintiff.[10]

For those who believe the defendant should not be liable, the hypothetical may provide an example of a true "assumption of the risk." Alternatively, it may represent a case of situational non-negligence on the part of both parties. In the particular circumstances that confronted the plaintiff, he behaved quite reasonably in accepting the ride with the drunk, and the drunk arguably behaved reasonably toward the plaintiff—although not to the rest of the world. Yet others favoring a judgment for the defendant would say that although drunk driving is substandard conduct, the defendant had no duty to this particular plaintiff. Analysts more oriented to the plaintiff's claim would view the case as falling in the third category described above, a category they would say is one that should yield liability. This response would entail the following reasoning, tracking that classification: the defendant behaved below

---

10. Laurence Eldredge, in Restatement (Second) of Torts, Tent. Draft No. 9, at 73–74 (1963).

the standard of care, the plaintiff knew of the peril but acted reasonably, and because the plaintiff acted reasonably, he should not be barred from recovery.

* * *

This set of classifications simply highlights the kinds of considerations that a court must take into account in dealing with conduct traditionally described—sometimes without sufficient analysis—as "contributory negligence" or "assumption of risk." Under the approach advocated here, the first question the court should ask is whether the defendant fell below the standard of care the law prescribes for the activity at issue. Only if the answer to that question is yes, for if the defendant was not negligent the action will proceed no further, the court will ask whether the plaintiff fell below the standard prescribed for the plaintiff's activity. Ordinarily, if she did not, she will win outright. If she did, then her action will be barred or her recovery will be reduced under comparative negligence.[11]

Questions that may be relevant to whether the plaintiff fell below the standard of care, sometimes implicating the nature of the defendant's conduct, concern the particularity of the plaintiff's knowledge of the danger and the meaning of "voluntary" acceptance of risk, an issue that forces judges to identify their behavioral and philosophical preconceptions about the nature of choice. In making decisions on these questions, judges may have to lay bare their premises about the reality of bargaining in conditions of relative scarcity, and about the morality of one party offering another a perilous bargain that the other feels constrained by economic circumstances to accept.

11. See Chapter 33 infra for a discussion of comparative negligence.

Chapter Thirty–Three
COMPARATIVE FAULT

Analysis

¶ 33.01 Basic Principles and Models

Comparative fault, now adopted in one form or another in most states, has replaced contributory negligence[1] and some forms of assumption of risk[2] in those jurisdictions. As its name implies, comparative fault requires the court or jury to compare each party's negligence or fault and to reduce a plaintiff's damages based on that comparison. It represents a response to the perceived injustice of the common law rules that dictated that a plaintiff's contributory negligence or assumption of risk is a complete bar to an action against a negligent defendant. The rules that fully barred negligent plaintiffs arose in the nineteenth century, when courts were particularly concerned about protecting developing industries.[3] In the twentieth century, however, comparative fault attracted courts and legislatures repelled by the harshness of these rules—for example, in situations where they allowed no recovery at all to a person who was only slightly negligent and was suing a very negligent injurer.

As courts and legislatures came to the conclusion that in at least some situations it would be more sensible and just to reduce the recovery of negligent plaintiffs than to cut them off entirely, they developed several different forms of comparative fault:

- The so-called "pure" comparative negligence model requires a reduction of the plaintiff's damages in proportion to his negligence, no matter what ratio that negligence bears to the defen-

---

1. See Chapter 31 infra.

2. See Chapter 30 infra.

3. See, e.g., Alvis v. Ribar, 421 N.E.2d 886, 887 (Ill.1981) (citing authorities).

dant's fault. This means that a plaintiff's negligence could have been ninety percent of the combined negligence of the parties, with the defendant being only ten percent at fault, and the plaintiff would still recover ten percent of the damages that a jury assessed as representing the plaintiff's total loss.

Three other comparative negligence rules, however, retain the potential to bar a plaintiff entirely from recovery:

● One of these rules allows the plaintiff a proportional recovery only if the plaintiff's negligence is not greater than that of the defendant. One result of this rule is that if a jury decides that the negligence of the parties is exactly equal, the plaintiff will still recover 50 percent of the assessed damages, but another is that a plaintiff who is 51 per cent at fault recovers nothing.

● Another rule, numerically close to the one just described, cuts more strongly against plaintiffs. It allows proportional recovery only if the plaintiff's negligence is not as great as the defendant's. Application of this rule means that, for the plaintiff to recover anything, a jury must find that the defendant was at least 51 percent comparatively at fault, with the result that a plaintiff whose negligence is only equal to the defendant's can recover nothing.

● A fourth model, which has been adopted in only a few states, allows the plaintiff to escape the complete-bar rule when his or her contributory negligence is "slight" and the defendant's negligence is "gross by comparison." This formula thus mitigates the perceived harshness of the old rule only in cases in which the plaintiff was just slightly at fault and the defendant clearly the more culpable party.

¶ 33.02   Policy Considerations

The arguments for and against comparative negligence are rooted in differing views of policy. The elements of these disputes, both about whether comparative negligence is a good idea generally and concerning which model is preferable, include competing definitions of fairness, differing assumptions about the effects of law on primary conduct, and disagreements about the impact of comparative fault on the litigation process.

A. *Fairness*

A powerful set of arguments in favor of comparative fault doctrines draws on notions of equity and justice. The idea of proportioning recovery to the fault of the parties has commended itself to courts on grounds of "fairness." A philosophical basis for this position lies in the idea of corrective justice, which can be interpreted in a case of negligence on the part of both parties to mean that damages should strictly follow fault as the fact finder apportions it between the parties.[4] Courts have not often plumbed the jurisprudential depths of the subject; rather, they tend to encapsulate their views in phrases like "[t]he basic logic and fairness of such apportionment," which the Illinois Supreme Court called "difficult to dispute."[5]

A broader view of fairness, one that goes beyond achieving justice between the parties, suggests that comparative negligence will promote the most just social distribution of the costs of injuries. Those who see tort law through a corrective justice lens, focused on the moral claims of the individual litigants upon one another, may take issue with this position. However, some decisions indicate that, in addition to achieving individualized justice, the goal of fairly distributing accident costs among classes of litigants is also attractive to courts.[6]

B. Deterrence

There is disagreement about the effects of comparative fault on conduct. Some observers will suggest that in at least certain settings, it is often unrealistic to expect negligence rules to significantly affect the behavior of either potential plaintiffs or potential defendants. They will contend that in fast-moving activities like motoring, it is much less likely that reducing plaintiff recoveries will provide meaningful deterrence than in other activities where there is more opportunity for deliberation on the part of potential plaintiffs as well as potential defendants.

Others argue that liability rules have significant marginal effects on conduct even where injury-causing events occur swiftly, as in motor vehicle accidents. Indeed, some studies have reported that the adoption of no-fault legislation for vehicle accidents, which partly or completely eliminates tort litigation based on fault, is associated with a rise in fatal accident rates.[7] These studies provide a sobering reminder of the economic axiom that as a form of activity (like careless driving) becomes more expensive, people will engage in it less. That theory suggests that contributory and comparative negligence rules, as well as negligence rules, will deter carelessness to an extent that would not happen without those rules.

---

4. See, e.g., Richard Wright, Allocating Liability Among Multiple Responsible Causes: A Principled Defense of Joint and Several Liability for Actual Harm and Risk Exposure, 21 U.C. Davis L. Rev. 1141, 1189 (1988).

5. Alvis, supra note 3, 421 N.E.2d at 892.

6. See, e.g., id. at 893 ("comparative negligence ... produces a more just and socially desirable distribution of loss").

7. For a critical summary of this literature, see Don Dewees, David Duff & Michael Trebilcock, Exploring the Domain of Accident Law 22–26 (1996).

Another interesting set of arguments concerning the effects of comparative negligence on conduct arises in litigation over product design, where the issue is whether contributory or comparative fault affects the care levels of product users. In an illustrative case, which involved a tractor that had a blade in front, a foreman stepped on the blade as he tried to dismount from the hood with the result that "[t]he blade rode up and pinned his foot." The court thought it appropriate to use comparative fault to reduce the foreman's recovery, saying that the application of the doctrine "will promote user care." Also setting out its premises concerning the effects of comparative fault on the conduct of manufacturers, the court added that the application of comparative fault would not "drastically reduce" incentives to make products safe. It endorsed the idea that " 'the presence of realistic incentives for careful product use prevents the manufacturer from reasonably relying on careless use by future users' " to decrease its liability.[8]

Economic analysis, paralleling common sense, suggests that there is a sliding scale of incentives to care for both potential plaintiffs and defendants that follows the various comparative negligence models. Thus, pure comparative negligence provides the strongest incentive for potential injurers to take care, because defendants will never be able to invoke plaintiffs' fault as a complete bar to recovery. The intermediate forms of comparative negligence—those requiring plaintiffs to show that the defendant was at least fifty or fifty-one percent negligent—provide less incentive for the injurer to be careful. And the rule that requires plaintiffs to show that their own negligence was only slight and that the defendant's negligence was gross will be the least demanding of care on the part of defendants. These rules present a mirror image with respect to the potential victim's incentive to take care. At the extremes, the slight/gross rule theoretically will spur plaintiffs to be most careful, and the pure comparative negligence rule will provide them the least incentive for care.[9]

C. Effects on the legal process

An important set of systemic issues concerns the actual workings of the comparative rules in a legal process that relies on jury determinations of fault. One question is whether juries are capable of the precision in assessing percentages of negligence that is required by comparative rules generally, and especially by standards like the rule that allows recovery to plaintiffs only if their

8. Employers National Ins. Co. v. Chaddrick, 826 F.2d 381, 385 (5th Cir. 1987) (quoting Winston v. International Harvester Corp., 791 F.2d 430, 434 (5th Cir.1986)).

9. Robert Cooter and Thomas Ulen, An Economic Case for Comparative Negligence, 61 N.Y.U. L. Rev. 1067, 1090–91 (1986).

negligence is less than that of the defendant. The difference between plaintiff negligence of 49 per cent and 50 per cent under that rule will be the difference between recovery of half the damages and no recovery at all. Critics of comparative fault say that juries who report percentages so exquisite are being almost as arbitrary as the traditional rule that entirely barred recovery by contributorily negligent claimants. Even in verdicts well outside of the 49 to 51 per cent battleground, juries may reduce comparative fault to percentages that seem impossibly precise—for example, finding that a plaintiff "assumed the risk to the extent of 96%."[10]

However, those who view such calculations as arbitrary must consider that jurors probably have routinely made comparative judgments even in jurisdictions where theoretically the all-or-nothing rule is the technically governing law, those assessments being reflected in awards of reduced damages. A strong argument in favor of a comparative approach, then, is that jurors are implementing such a regime anyway and that it is more candid, as well as more productive of justice, to have a comparative fault rule that juries follow than an all-or-nothing rule that is ignored.

Another important empirical issue is how comparative negligence may influence the rate of litigation. An early study of comparative negligence in Arkansas suggested that the rule "increased potential litigation," which is not surprising since it would encourage plaintiffs to sue who otherwise would not do so because of an assumption that they would be barred for being partly at fault for their own injuries. The study also found that the comparative negligence rule "promoted before-trial settlements." This also seems plausible since the rule may give lawyers a more precise idea of the range of probable jury verdicts while, especially in the case of pure comparative negligence, making it more likely that the plaintiff will win some kind of award. Other survey results that seem plausible were that plaintiffs "won a higher proportion of the verdicts," but did not win larger ones, and that "injury claims were valued higher for compromise purposes."[11]

It is certainly possible to visualize cases in which the application of comparative fault rules will produce outcomes that initially might appear perverse in terms of ordinary conceptions of justice. Consider, for example, a situation in which drivers A and B collide. Driver A sustains $5,000 of damage and is only 20 per cent comparatively negligent and driver B suffers $100,000 in losses but is 80 per cent comparatively negligent. Under at least pure comparative negligence, this case would yield a result in which A recovers

---

10. Erickson v. Muskin Corp., 535 N.E.2d 475, 477 (Ill.Ct.App.1989).

11. Maurice Rosenberg, Comparative Negligence in Arkansas: A "Before and After" Survey, 13 Ark. L. Rev. 89, 108 (1959).

$4,000—80 per cent of his losses—but B recovers the $20,000 that is 20 per cent of his losses. Critics might question the justice of allowing B any recovery, let alone an award significantly greater than A's, when B was primarily responsible for the injury. A response to this line of argument is that this seemingly odd set of results is not so odd—that A in having to pay B $20,000 is doing no more than paying for the injury that he actually caused, just as B is doing with his $4,000 payment.

One should note, in connection which the hypothetical just explored, that the presence or absence of liability insurance will have important practical results in a system where compensation is based on fault. If both parties had liability insurance, each would receive from the other party's liability insurer the full amounts— $4,000 for A and $20,000 for B—to which they were entitled under the comparative negligence rules. If there were no insurance and the parties had to rely only on the results of their direct suits against each other, the result would be a setoff in which B emerged with a net of $16,000 and A with nothing.

The way that one frames the problem will affect one's view of the justice of either answer. If one focuses on the compensation goal, with a corresponding emphasis on causation, one will tend to prefer a regime with liability insurance in which there is no setoff. If one focuses on deterrence, one might prefer a setoff, which would be the natural result if there were no liability insurance. Since a setoff would mean less money in the pocket of both parties, thus bringing home to each more of the consequences of his fault, that outcome would provide an extra measure of deterrence. People who viewed themselves as both potential injurers and victims—a typical perspective for motorists, especially—would theoretically be more careful if there were a setoff rule than if they believed they would recover, in pocket, their damages reduced only by their comparative fault. Of course, the traditional rule, which would bar both parties if both were at all contributorily negligent, presumably would achieve the strongest deterrent effects.

¶ 33.03 Doctrinal Issues

Comparative negligence presents some interesting issues concerning its application to particular defensive doctrines based on the plaintiff's conduct. It is clear enough that ordinary contributory negligence and unreasonable assumption of risk are types of conduct that will reduce a plaintiff's recovery under comparative doctrines. There is, however, an interesting range of argument concerning the defense that some courts call "reasonable implied assumption of the risk" (RIAR).

Some California history is instructive. A pair of appellate decisions, both involving athletic activity, disagreed on whether RIAR should only reduce a plaintiff's recovery or should bar it outright.[12] The California Supreme Court then weighed in with a declaration that its precedents did not bar the claims of plaintiffs who act reasonably in encountering a known risk "caused by the defendant's breach" of a duty of care to the plaintiff. The supreme court interpreted its precedents as saying that although comparative negligence would not apply in cases of "primary assumption of risk," "cases involving 'secondary assumption of risk' properly are merged into the comparative fault system." However, confronted with an injury in a touch football game, the court said that in cases involving active sports, the only breach of duty on a defendant participant's part would be intentional or reckless conduct. Finding no behavior of that sort, if granted summary judgment to the defendant.[13]

A difficult set of doctrinal problems concerning comparative fault arises in the products liability area, especially when the chosen theory is strict liability. The core problem is apparent in the view that strict liability for products is an "independent tort species" that is "wholly distinct" from negligence and warranty.[14] Those taking this position have contended that the attempt to compare negligence with strict liability is to compare "apples and oranges,"[15] or to put it more formally, to "reduce . . . two noncomparables"—that is, the plaintiff's negligent conduct and a defective product—"to a common denominator."[16] An underlying policy argument against comparative fault in cases based on strict liability is that the conduct of those injured by products used in a contemplated or foreseeable manner is irrelevant to strict liability theory, given the complexities of marketing and the vulnerability of consumers injured by product defects that inspired that doctrine.[17]

The response to these criticisms, by courts that have found it appropriate to apply comparative fault to strict products liability, has been practical and non-doctrinal. As a majority opinion for the

12. Segoviano v. Housing Auth., 191 Cal.Rptr. 578, 579 (Ct.App.1983)(in flag football case, RIAR not even "a partial defense justifying allocation of a portion of the fault for the accident to the plaintiff"); Ordway v. Superior Court, 243 Cal.Rptr. 536, 539 (Ct.App. 1988)(in case involving injury to a jockey in a race track accident, court reasons that "[w]here no duty of care is owed with respect to a particular mishap, there can be no breach" of duty).

13. Knight v. Jewett, 834 P.2d 696, 703, 711 (Cal.1992).

14. Daly v. General Motors Corp., 575 P.2d 1162, 1182 (Cal.1978), (Mosk, J., dissenting).

15. For opposed references to the metaphor, see the majority opinion in Daly, supra, 575 P.2d at 1167, and the dissent of Justice Mosk, id. at 1184.

16. Id. at 1180 (Jefferson, J., concurring and dissenting).

17. See id. at 1181–85 (Mosk, J., dissenting).

California Supreme Court put it, "[f]ixed semantic consistency ... is less important than the attainment of a just and equitable result."[18] Besides pointing out that a comparative fault regime avoids the great difference between no recovery at all and a significant recovery, advocates of the use of comparative fault in strict liability cases stress that this will result in "uniformity of defenses between negligence and strict liability."[19] It also has been argued that by decreasing recoveries by careless plaintiffs, comparative fault "will reduce the amount consumers are forced to spend on product insurance through higher prices."[20]

¶ 33.04 Summary: Justice, Doctrine and Terminology

The main lines of the arguments about justice with reference to comparative doctrines are clear, although there are potential traps in terminology. At the level of policy, courts must decide how well comparative doctrines advance sometimes conflicting goals like fairness and deterrence, and must judge whether the extra quotient of justice achieved by comparative doctrines outweighs the value of doctrinal purity. Moreover, at the level of concept and associated terminology, it is important for courts to decide what it is they are comparing. To speak of "comparative liability" or "comparative responsibility" seems conclusory, for those terms announce a result rather than describing the things that are to be compared. To speak of "comparative negligence" raises the problem of how to compare negligence with strict liability. With respect to that difficulty, "comparative fault" is somewhat less objectionable from a linguistic standpoint. Particularly in cases where the theory of liability is strict, the practical point of comparison often is causation rather than fault, and thus "comparative causation" may be the most descriptive concept. In choosing among these concepts, courts need to clarify their own views about the subjects of comparison when they adopt a "comparative" method to allocate damages in tort cases.

[Chapter 34 is reserved for supplementary material.]

18. Id. at 1168.
19. Note, 67 Cal. L. Rev. 936, 961–64 (1979).

20. See id. at 965.

Section Five

STRICT LIABILITY AND ANALOGUES FOR ENVIRONMENTAL DAMAGE

Chapter Thirty–Five

STRICT LIABILITY FOR ACTIVITIES

Analysis

¶ 35.01 Strict Liability and Fault: Disputes About History

Lawyers are accustomed to thinking of fault as the principal basis for tort liability.[1] However, there is a long-standing argument about what the basis of liability was at the dawn of the common law. The question is whether fault or strict liability—liability without fault—was the main foundation then for shifting injured parties' losses to injury-causing actors.

There has been considerable dispute about the meaning of cases extending as far back as the fifteenth century. A noted decision is the Thorns Case, in which thorns cut by the defendant on his property fell onto the plaintiff's land and the defendant went on the plaintiff's land to retrieve them. The court held that the defendant was liable for a trespass, indicating that it was an inadequate defense to plead that the defendant did not want the thorns to fall on the plaintiff's land.[2] Holmes read this case, in light

---

1. A bold challenge to the idea appears in Richard Epstein, A Theory of Strict Liability, 2 J. Legal Studies 151 (1973).

2. Chief Justice Choke declared that "when the principal thing is not lawful, then the thing which depends upon it is not lawful," and reasoned that

179

of later precedents, as indicating "that liability in general ... was founded on the opinion of the tribunal that the defendant ought to have acted otherwise, or, in other words, that he was to blame."[3]

There have been conflicting interpretations. Professor Arnold, for example, argued that the absence of pleas by defendants of a lack of negligence "when a plaintiff had made no mention of negligence" supported an inference that liability was strict in the late medieval period. He concluded that it was "for a later age to invent the proposition that some showing of fault was ordinarily necessary in order to impose on an actor the duty to compensate."[4] Holmes, however, pursued the fault theme of liability into the seventeenth century in England[5] and traced it up to the landmark 1850 decision in *Brown v. Kendall*. In that case, Chief Justice Shaw of Massachusetts articulated a liability standard of "ordinary care"—"that kind and degree of care, which prudent and cautious men would use, such as is required by the exigency of the case, and such as is necessary to guard against probable danger."[6]

¶ 35.02   *Rylands v. Fletcher*

It is perhaps ironic that just as fault became broadly accepted as the basic ground for tort liability in the nineteenth century, the most famous judicial beacon of strict liability for activities issued from that patrician body, the House of Lords. This was the 1868 decision in *Rylands v. Fletcher*,[7] in which a mine owner sued owners of a mill who had a reservoir constructed on their land, from which water poured into the workings of the plaintiff's mine. Apparently there was no way for the plaintiffs to show that the defendant mill owners had themselves been negligent, although there was evidence that an engineer and a contractor employed by the defendants may have been careless.

when the defendant "cut the thorns and they fell on my land, this falling was not lawful, and then this coming to take them away was not lawful." He concluded that "[a]s to what has been said that they fell *ipso invito* [that is, without willingness], this is not a good plea; but [the defendant] should have said that he could not do it in any other manner or that he did all that was in his power to keep them out." The Thorns Case, Y.B. Mich. 6 Ed. 4, f. 7, pl. 18 (1466), translated in C.H.S. Fifoot, History and Sources of the Common Law 195–97 (1949, reprint 1970). Holmes' somewhat different translation appears in Oliver Wendell Holmes Jr., The Common Law 103 (1881).

3. See Holmes, supra, at 102–03.

4. Professor Arnold's analysis of the pleas in the Year Books suggested to him that defense lawyers logically would have pleaded a lack of fault if they had been inclined to present evidence on the point. Morris Arnold, Accident, Mistake, and Rules of Liability in the 14th-Century Law of Torts, 128 U. Pa. L. Rev. 361, 368, 378 (1979).

5. See discussion of Weaver v. Ward, Hobart 134 (K.B.1616), in Holmes, supra note 3, at 104.

6. Brown v. Kendall, 60 Mass. (6 Cush.) 292, 296 (1850), discussed in Holmes, supra note 3, at 105–06.

7. L.R. 3 H.L. 330 (1868).

The Law Lords confronted directly the question of whether it was necessary to show fault to impose liability on the mill owners, and decided that it was not. They built on the declaration of Justice Blackburn in the lower court that a person who knows that something that escapes from his property will "be mischievous if it gets on his neighbour's, should be obliged to make good the damage which ensues if he does not succeed in confining it to his own property."[8]

Favorably citing these remarks, Lord Cairns upheld a judgment for the plaintiff, saying that when the defendants made "a non-natural use" of their land resulting in the escape of water onto the plaintiff's property, the defendants acted "at their own peril."[9] Lord Cranworth generalized that "[i]f a person brings, or accumulates, on his land anything which, if it should escape, may cause damage to his neighbour, he does so at his peril." Sharply articulating the practical meaning of this concept of strict liability, he said that if the substance "does escape, and cause damage, he is responsible, however careful he may have been, and whatever precautions he may have taken to prevent the damage."[10]

¶ 35.03   The Restatement Formula

The rule of *Rylands v. Fletcher* gradually found its way into American law, particularly with reference to activities on the land that had explosive or polluting results. The general concept won a place in the Restatement of Torts in 1938 under the label of "ultrahazardous activity."[11] Sections 519 and 520 of the Restatement Second, published in 1977, articulated the principle under the heading of "abnormally dangerous activities."[12]

Section 520 of the Restatement Second defined "abnormally dangerous activities" by presenting a catalog of "factors ... to be considered." These factors included a "high degree of risk," the likelihood that resulting harm would be "great," and the "inability to eliminate the risk by the exercise of reasonable care."[13] On the latter point, the comments declared that "when safety cannot be attained by the exercise of due care there is reason to regard the danger as an abnormal one."[14] Another factor that the Restatement suggests should be considered is the "extent to which [the activi-

8. Fletcher v. Rylands, (1866) L.R. 1 Ex. 265, 280.

9. Rylands v. Fletcher, L.R. 3 H.L. at 339–40.

10. Id. at 340.

11. Restatement of Torts § 519–520 (1938).

12. Restatement (Second) of Torts §§ 519–520 (1977).

13. Id., § 520(a)-(c).

14. Id., comment h.

ty's] value to the community is outweighed by its dangerous attributes."[15]

The Restatement also identifies as potential grounds for holding an activity "abnormally dangerous" the "extent to which the activity is not a matter of common usage" and the "inappropriateness of the activity to the place where it is carried on."[16] Thus, under the Restatement definition, the fact that an activity is relatively unusual or is in some way "out of place" will tilt decisions toward strict liability. The storage of explosives in a densely populated area is a good example of an "abnormally dangerous activity." By contrast, the Restatement views the operation of motor vehicles as an activity not fitting the definition; the motor vehicle is a very dangerous instrumentality, but one that has "come into such general use that [its] operation is a matter of common usage."[17]

We note that in cases involving environmental harms, a staple theory for imposing liability or justifying injunctions has been the complex doctrine of nuisance. The Restatement's summary of nuisance law, analyzed below,[18] includes language that covers liability for "abnormally dangerous ... activities."[19] Thus, strict liability as a subclassification of nuisance, as well as an independent theory of tort liability, is part of the framework of legal doctrine for "environmental torts."

¶ 35.04 Applications and Controversies

Over several decades, various American courts have considered whether to adopt the *Rylands* concept and the Restatement formulas. Those that have accepted the general principle in one form or another have further struggled to define the boundaries of strict liability for activities. Since 1960, courts have developed one other important zone of strict liability, liability for defective products, which is discussed below.[20] But it is clear that the basic standard for judging human conduct that unintentionally causes injury is still that of negligence. Where courts have moved to apply strict liability to activities, they have done so cautiously, designating only specific activities for that classification on the basis of special factors of risk.

A 1931 decision by Judge Augustus Hand illustrates some of the factors that motivate holdings of liability without fault for activities. This decision applied what Judge Hand called "absolute liability" against a utility company for storing dynamite that ex-

---

15. Id., § 520(f).

16. Id., § 520(d)-(e).

17. Id., section 520, comment i.

18. See generally infra, Chapter 36.

19. See infra, ¶ 36.02(C).

20. See infra, Chapter 38.

ploded. Speaking of "an act connected with a business conducted for profit and fraught with substantial risk and possibility of the gravest consequences," he concluded that "[w]hen a person engages in such a dangerous activity, useful though it be, he becomes an insurer."[21] Over the succeeding two generations, courts have extended strict liability to such diverse activities as "oil drilling, fumigation, crop dusting, commercial fuel hauling, [and] agricultural field burning."[22]

An interesting example of competing arguments over application of the doctrine appears in federal trial and appellate decisions in a suit against a chemical firm that shipped acrylonitrile, a toxic chemical, which spilled from a tank car into a freight yard located in a Chicago suburb. In a suit for cleanup costs, the district judge applied strict liability against the shipper, tracking the factors mentioned in Restatement Second 520. He opined that "perhaps the single most important factor in determining whether or not an activity is abnormally dangerous" is the "inappropriateness" of the activity. Noting that 3,000 people had to evacuate their homes and that the spill had contaminated their water supply, he declared that "[s]ending thousands of gallons of this toxic chemical" through the freight yards seemed "singularly 'inappropriate' in the *Restatement* sense of the word, given the character of the area surrounding that yard." With respect to the element of common usage, he observed that "[v]ery few persons ship 20,000 gallons of acrylonitrile by tank car."[23]

Disagreeing, the Seventh Circuit refused to impose strict liability against the shipper. Judge Posner pointed out that to apply strict liability might actually generate more risk. Even though he thought it "unlikely" that shippers would reroute shipments of hazardous chemicals "around all the metropolitan areas in the country," he noted that even rerouting would be "no panacea," because it would "[o]ften ... increase the length of the journey, or compel the use of poorer track, or both." This, he said, would actually increase the probability of accidents, "even if the consequences of an accident if one occurs are reduced."[24]

Judge Posner directly confronted the implications of his position for the allocation of resources. "Brutal though it may seem to say it," he remarked, "the inappropriate use to which land is being

21. Exner v. Sherman Power Constr. Co., 54 F.2d 510, 514 (2d Cir. 1931).

22. Virginia Nolan & Edmund Ursin, The Revitalization of Hazardous Activity Strict Liability, 65 N.C. L. Rev. 257, 290 (1987) (summarizing "applications of the hazardous activity doctrine").

23. Indiana Harbor Belt R.R. Co. v. American Cyanamid Co., 662 F.Supp. 635, 641–43 (N.D.Ill.1987).

24. Indiana Harbor Belt R.R. Co. v. American Cyanamid Co., 916 F.2d 1174, 1180 (7th Cir.1990).

put in the Blue Island yard and neighborhood may be, not the transportation of hazardous chemicals, but residential living."[25] This pronouncement presents the challenge of an analysis that focuses on the highest and best use of land from a technical efficiency point of view, without taking into account the moral concerns that appear to motivate many impositions of strict liability.

¶ 35.05   Rationales

The dispute over whether strict liability should be applied to particular activities is symbolic of broader arguments about the role of tort law in modern life. These arguments often pit rationales of individual fairness and broader notions of loss-spreading against economic analyses hinged on efficiency.

Efficiency analysis frequently will cut against the imposition of strict liability for activities. It is useful in exposing the economic implications of proposed applications of strict liability, for it requires the decisionmaker at least initially to strip moral considerations away from the examination of cases. However, it may involve courts in complex and uncertain inquiries into cost factors, including "transaction costs." For example, in a case like the litigation about the chemical spill summarized above,[26] a court using efficiency analysis might have to speculate on the outcome of bargaining between the shipper and the 3,000 affected neighbors of the railroad yard concerning the shipper's use of that route to transport its chemical.

When courts do apply strict liability to activities, their reasoning is likely to draw more on moral considerations and related social policy rationales than on efficiency-based concepts. Robert Keeton frankly spoke of loss spreading as an important reason for imposing liability on those who blast with high explosives. He said that the imposition in such cases of what courts call strict liability—which he described as "conditional fault"—would "effect[] distribution according to the principle of unjust enrichment, among those who realize benefits from the blasting." He suggested that "those who benefit by receiving the products of blasting activities . . . should pay, as part of the price of construction, the equivalent of an insurance premium or contribution to a fund to cover risks from blasting accidents."[27]

Professor Fletcher suggested the creation of "nonreciprocal risks" as a rationalization for strict liability, and indeed for a

---

25. Id. at 1181.

26. See text accompanying notes 23–25 supra.

27. Robert   Keeton,   Conditional Fault in the Law of Torts, 72 Harv. L. Rev. 401, 441 (1959).

spectrum of liability that included negligence and intentional torts as well as strict liability.[28] He viewed this broad category of liability as applicable to defendants who "generate[] a disproportionate, excessive risk of harm, relative to the victim's risk-creating activity."[29] In Fletcher's view, no one could demand compensation for harm from "background risks," but people should not have to "suffer harm from additional risks without recourse for damages against the risk-creator."[30]

Under Fletcher's "paradigm of reciprocity," liability should be imposed "whenever . . . disproportionate distribution of risk injures someone subject to more than his fair share of risk."[31] A pair of hypothetical cases illustrates the "paradigm." Presenting a case for nonliability is the case of "two airplanes flying in the same vicinity [that] subject each other to reciprocal risks of a mid-air collision"; by contrast, typifying the case for liability is the situation where "a pilot or an airplane owner subjects those beneath the path of flight to nonreciprocal risks of harm" if the plane should fall.[32]

The dispute over whether and when strict liability should be applied to activity-caused injury is likely to rage on. As we have noted, historical scholarship features disagreement on the topic even as to the medieval roots of tort law. The controversy exists today because of the power of competing philosophical positions. There is a strong moral attraction in the notion that liability should rest only on fault, but there also is a powerful moral pull in the idea that those who engage in risky activities should not be able to impose risks of injury on others, particularly persons in a vulnerable position, without compensating them for resulting losses.

The arguments over strict liability exert conflicting pulls on courts because they duplicate the competing moralities that frequently are at war in human minds, including the minds of judges. Although some decisions for strict liability may be rationalized as applications of particularly high standards of care—or as ways to facilitate the imposition of liability for negligence that cannot easily be proved—the fundamental dispute about strict liability for activities is one over the fairness of particular risk allocations.

28. George Fletcher, Fairness and Utility in Tort Theory, 85 Harv. L. Rev. 537 (1972).

29. Id. at 542.

30. Id. at 550.

31. Id. at 550–51.

32. Id. at 542.

Chapter Thirty-Six

PRIVATE NUISANCE

Analysis

¶ 36.01   The Social Problem and an Overview of Doctrine

A.   Nuisance

Nuisance is a legal theory that may be used by any persons who believe that another's conduct is harming their interests as possessors of land. In its simplest definition, nuisance is a party's unreasonable interference with an interest in the use and enjoy-

186

ment of land; a fleshed-out definition appears below.[1]

Today an important theory in suits for "environmental torts," nuisance is only one of the law's responses to the general problem of environmental injuries to which tort law has addressed itself for many years. From a societal point of view, the problem is a large and complex one, featuring intense rivalries between classes of parties. Plaintiffs typically are persons who have an ongoing attachment to land and the surrounding ambient air and to flowing streams or coastal waters, an attachment that sometimes is difficult to capture entirely in money valuations. Defendants frequently are producers of useful goods with high social value whose productive activities create negative consequences, such as air and water pollution, to surrounding parcels of land.

A preponderance of the rules that govern environmental damage appear in statutes and regulations, which reflect legislative compromises on what often are many-sided political questions. Yet, tort doctrine, of which nuisance is a significant element, continues to play an important supporting role in sorting out and assessing competing interests.[2] In deciding cases where those interests come in conflict, courts find themselves torn. On the one hand, they confront the desire for hard-edged rules and the goal of promoting production; on the other hand, they face demands for flexible legal doctrines hospitable to equity and to compensation for relatively intangible social values.

The doctrine of nuisance, literally a law unto itself, emerged from a background described by a master of common law history as "very obscure."[3] As history has been transmitted through judicial opinions, there developed in England a tribunal called the "assize of nuisance" that "provided redress . . . where the injury was not a disseisin"—literally, a dispossession—"but rather an indirect dam-

---

1. See ¶ 36.02 infra.

2. For an analysis of the advantages of nuisance law over public enforcement in certain situations, see Keith Hylton, When Should We Prefer Tort Law to Environmental Regulation?, 41 Washburn L.J. 515 (2002). Professor Hylton identifies one strong argument for private enforcement under nuisance doctrine as the possibility of a mismatch of the interests of public regulators and those of victims of environmental harm. He says that, by contrast with plaintiffs' lawyers, regulators have "no strong connection between their interests and those of the potential victims they are supposed to protect." Id. at 520. He also suggests that a system

of private litigation will not tend to foster the "overzealous enforcement" that may be associated with public regulation—that is, spending large amounts to prevent relatively small harms. See id. at 521–22. He identifies as another advantage of private law the way that it provides incentives to the parties to bring forth information about relevant costs and benefits. See id. at 525–26.

3. Theodore F.T. Plucknett, A Concise History of the Common Law 469 n.2 (5th ed. 1956)(describing the history of the apparent derivation of the action on the case "for damage to realty which did not amount to an entry" from "the twelfth-century assize of nuisance").

age to the land or an interference with its use and enjoyment."[4]

According to another judicial reading of history, "the English concept of nuisance" as a property concept became transmuted by American courts into something that was "not merely an infringement of property rights, but a wrong against both person and property—a tort."[5] The struggle over nuisance law continued as commercial development brought increasing conflict with residential uses—and sometimes even as commercial uses clashed.[6] To be sure, the emergence of nuisance as a tort did not swing the door wide to litigation in America, for the courts began to tighten the sphere of cases in which they would grant injunctions against nuisances, or, alternatively, the cases in which they would find nuisances at all.[7] Yet, there also developed a body of doctrine that associated nuisances with the full spectrum of tort culpability, ranging from "intentional" conduct to strict liability.[8] We now briefly summarize the common law counterparts of these concepts.

B. Trespass

Persons seeking to bring tort actions for environmental damage may select from a battery of other legal theories, which exist as independent causes of action as well as being conceptually tied in with nuisance. The simplest of these doctrines is the theory of trespass, a tort that involves an invasion of another's exclusive possessory interests in land.[9] Most typically, courts apply this doctrine when the defendant has made a physical entry on the land, or has pushed or hurled a tangible object there. Even invisible particulates associated with the emission of gases may constitute a trespass.[10] Trespass is an absolute liability doctrine, against which the defendant cannot offer a defense of reasonable care.

---

4. Copart Indus., Inc. v. Consolidated Edison Co., 362 N.E.2d 968, 970 (N.Y.1977).

5. Carpenter v. Double R Cattle Co., 669 P.2d 643, 647 (Idaho Ct.App. 1983), vacated, 701 P.2d 222 (Idaho 1985).

6. An old English case, fully rendered a classic in a much-cited article, is Sturges v. Bridgman, 11 Ch. D. 852 (1879). In that case, a doctor won an injunction against a confectioner when noise from the latter's machinery made it difficult for the doctor to use a consulting room he had constructed near the confectioner's kitchen. The most famous discussion is in Ronald Coase, The Problem of Social Cost, 3 J. L. & Econ. 1, 8–10 (1960). A modern version is Page County Appliance Ctr., Inc. v. Honeywell, Inc., 347 N.W.2d 171, 182

(1984)((travel agent's computer caused electronic interference with appliance store's display televisions; judgment for appliance store reversed for determination of whether it "was devoting its premises to an unusually sensitive use").

7. Carpenter, supra note 5, 669 P.2d at 647–48.

8. See infra, ¶ 36.02(B).

9. See, e.g., Restatement (Second) of Torts § 158, comment c (1965).

10. See Martin v. Reynolds Metals Co., 342 P.2d 790, 794 (Or.1959) (defining trespass "as any intrusion which invades the possessor's protected interest in exclusive possession, whether that intrusion is by visible or invisible pieces of matter or by energy which can be

C. The Rylands doctrine

An independent strict liability doctrine for environmental damage as well as personal injury traces back to the famous case of *Rylands v. Fletcher*.[11] In that case, Lord Cairns declared that one who introduces onto his land something that escapes in the course of a "non-natural use" does so "at [his] own peril."[12] Lord Cranworth underlined the principle, saying that if someone brought something on his land that escaped and caused damage, he would be liable, "however careful he may have been."[13]

In modern American law, the general principle of *Rylands* has largely become transmuted into the concept of "an abnormally dangerous activity" described in the Second Restatement of Torts,[14] discussed in an earlier chapter.[15]

D. Negligence

Another doctrine that plaintiffs may utilize in environmental harm cases is that of negligence, a general concept focusing on the failure to meet the standard of care that a reasonable person would observe in the activity at issue.[16]

¶ 36.02 Nuisance Defined

Prosser provided a memorable caution to those seeking to define nuisance: "[t]here is perhaps no more impenetrable jungle in the entire law than that which surrounds the word 'nuisance.' "[17] With this warning in mind, we proceed to examine some of the main elements of nuisance doctrine. Insofar as possible, to facilitate analysis, this section seeks to separate discussion of the substantive

---

measured only by the mathematical language of the physicist"). But cf. Adams v. Cleveland–Cliffs Iron Co., 602 N.W.2d 215 (Mich.Ct.App.1999), in which the plaintiffs sued for tremors resulting from year-round blasting in mining operations, and for constant invasions of their homes by dust generated by the processing of iron ore. The court criticizes the "redirection of trespass law toward nuisance law," inter alia, by the elimination of "the requirements of a direct invasion by a tangible object," id. at 221, and concludes that "[b]ecause noise or vibrations are clearly not tangible objects, ... they cannot give rise to an action in trespass." The court also says that "dust must generally be considered intangible and ... not actionable in trespass," but adds that "[i]f the quantity and character of ... dust are such as to disturb the ambiance in ways that substantially interfere with the

plaintiff's use and enjoyment of ... land, then recovery in nuisance is possible." Id. at 223.

11. L.R. 3 H. L. 330 (1868), discussed supra, ¶ 35.02.

12. Id. at 339.

13. Id. at 340.

14. Restatement (Second) of Torts §§ 519–520 (1965) (providing a catalog of several factors, including the degree of risk of the defendant's activity, the "extent to which the activity is not a matter of common usage," and its "inappropriateness ... to the place where it is carried on").

15. See ¶ 35.03 supra.

16. See generally Chapter 19 supra.

17. W. Prosser & W. Keeton, The Law of Torts, § 86, at 571 (5th ed. 1984).

tort from remedies, which are discussed below;[18] however, it will appear that the "tort" and the "remedies" are difficult to separate in practice.

A. Interference with use and enjoyment

A distinguishing feature of the law of private nuisance is that the defendant must have interfered with the plaintiff's interest in the use and enjoyment of land. Courts have applied this definition to a broad spectrum of activity on the part of defendants, for example, industrial pollution of water and air, the maintenance of odor-causing animal feedlots, and activities that cause electronic interference with the plaintiff's business.

B. The spectrum of culpability standards

The chameleon nature of nuisance doctrine is apparent in the fact that a modern definition of the "elements of liability" for private nuisance[19] spans the traditional tort theories of liability from intentional torts to negligence to strict liability. According to the Restatement, a plaintiff seeking to establish a private nuisance must show an invasion that "is either

(a) intentional and unreasonable, or

(b) unintentional and otherwise actionable under the rules controlling liability for negligent or reckless conduct, or for abnormally dangerous conditions or activities.[20]

Similarly to the potential difficulties in defining what "unreasonableness" means in nuisance, discussed just below,[21] this formulation may lead to confusion as to what courts are about, or should be about, in applying the doctrine of nuisance. One jurist has opined that "[w]ords such as 'intent', 'negligence' and 'absolute liability' refer not to the result of the conduct of a defendant who intrudes unreasonably on the use and enjoyment of another's property, but rather to the method of bringing it about."[22] By comparison, the Iowa Supreme Court has said that "nuisance ordinarily is considered as a condition, and not as an act or failure to act on the part of the responsible party."[23]

C. Unreasonableness

The general definition of a nuisance as an intentional interference with use and enjoyment of land—there being separate cat-

---

18. See ¶ 36.03 infra.

19. 4 Restatement (Second) of Torts 108 (topic heading).

20. Id. § 822.

21. See ¶ 36.02(C) infra.

22. Copart Indus., supra note 3, 362 N.E.2d at 973 (Fuchsberg, J., dissenting).

23. Page County Appliance Ctr., supra note 6, 347 N.W.2d at 176.

egories of nuisance based on negligent or reckless conduct or abnormally dangerous activities[24]—requires that the interference be unreasonable. Courts do not define "unreasonableness" in a uniform manner. For example, some decisions focus on the character of the activity in context and others on various comparisons of costs and benefits.

One court has said that "[a] fair test of whether the operation of a lawful trade or industry constitutes a nuisance is the reasonableness of conducting it in the manner, at the place, and under the circumstances shown by the evidence."[25] By comparison, the Restatement Second declares that "[a]n intentional invasion of another's interest in the use and the enjoyment of land is unreasonable if

(a) the gravity of the harm outweighs the utility of the actor's conduct, or

(b) the harm caused by the conduct is serious and the financial burden of compensating for this and similar harm to others would not make the continuation of the conduct not feasible.[26]

The latter part of this definition overlaps into the remedies question, since it indicates that the issue of whether an activity is unreasonable may turn on the feasibility of the defendant continuing the activity if it is required to compensate.

D. *Factors in the determination of nuisance*

Whatever doctrinal banner that courts raise in nuisance decisions, the application of nuisance principles tends to fall into a catalog of factors that arise in the context of particular cases. We offer here a list of those factors, noting that many courts will use different labels to identify the same considerations, that courts usually engage in various forms of balancing whatever terminology they use, and that the list is not exhaustive.

1. *The nature of the activity*

Courts undoubtedly will make social judgments about the nature of the defendant's activity, for example, being more sympathetic to backyard tennis courts[27] than to houses of prostitution.[28]

---

24. See Restatement (Second) of Torts, § 822(b), quoted text accompanying note 20 infra.

25. Page County Appliance Ctr., supra note 6, 347 N.W.2d at 175.

26. Restatement (Second) of Torts § 826 (1977).

27. See Hardy v. Calhoun, 383 S.W.2d 652 (Tex.Civ.App.1964).

28. See, e.g., Restatement (Second) of Torts § 821B, comment h (1979).

2.   The gravity of harm to the plaintiff

The gravity of harm frequently is part of the balancing tests that courts generally use in applying nuisance doctrine. The likelihood of a serious impact on the plaintiff's health, or even property values, will increase the probability that courts will find a nuisance.

3.   Frequency of occurrence

It makes a difference how often an offending activity takes place. Bringing a band to one's yard for a family celebration on one occasion is less likely to be a nuisance than operating a fraternity house that plays rock music on loudspeakers every night.

4.   Comparative economic interests

Courts routinely consider the utility of the defendant's conduct, balancing against that the plaintiff's economic interests insofar as they can be quantified. If the defendant's activity makes a very substantial economic contribution to the community, some courts may decide it is not a nuisance even if it causes significant interference to the interests of some possessors, if the legally valued injury to those interests is relatively slight compared to the value of the activity. Even where courts find that a highly valued activity is a nuisance, they may provide only a limited remedy.[29]

5.   The environmental context

Nuisance law embraces a notion of normalcy of use in particular neighborhoods. To take an obvious example, when a farmer keeps hogs, it is not, ordinarily, a nuisance; when your urban neighbor does, it may be.

6.   Priority in time

Courts will take into account the fact that one party was on the land before the other. For example, they are more likely to hold that there is a nuisance created by a polluting industry that has moved into an established residential neighborhood than when the plaintiffs buy their homes after the polluter has located its business on the site—in nuisance parlance, plaintiffs who "move to the nuisance."

¶ 36.03   Remedies

An operative definition of the tort of private nuisance requires reference to the remedies courts use to enforce plaintiffs' rights. The following discussion of remedies draws on some functional

---

29.   See infra, ¶ 36.03(A).

classification schemes that scholars have fashioned in analyzing nuisance-like activities.[30]

A. Damages

A straightforward remedy for environmental harms and associated physical injuries is to require the defendant to pay money damages. An obvious situation for the application of the damages remedy alone is the case where the defendant's activity has social or economic value so high that it would not be sensible to force it to move or shut down. In the much-cited New York case of *Boomer v. Atlantic Cement Co.*,[31] the court found that pollution from the defendant's cement plant, which represented a $45 million investment, caused losses to the plaintiffs valued at $185,000. The court rejected the plaintiffs' demand to enjoin operation of the plant and instead awarded damages on the theory that the defendant had imposed a "servitude" on the plaintiffs' land.[32] A comparison of the plaintiffs' losses with the costs of closing the plant—which would have included rendering 300 people unemployed and the effective ruination of the investors' stake[33]—indicates why the court employed only a damages remedy.

In this connection, we note that one of the more difficult problems in nuisance law is the valuation of interests and costs on which it is hard to put a dollar figure. Plaintiffs will refer to such intangible factors as the relatively settled character of communities and the trauma of tearing up roots and moving, although in a quantitatively definable economic sense a nuisance-creating enterprise may be more socially "valuable" than a residential neighborhood. It is because of such clashes between tangibles and intangibles that, while subjective valuations may support the application of nuisance as a tort doctrine, courts will be inclined to focus on objective economic realities when they fashion remedies.

B. Full injunction

A powerful remedy for nuisance-type harms is that of an unqualified injunction against the defendant's activity. A premise for this remedy lies in the idea that a plaintiff possesses a property right in her land and its amenities, and that if she does not wish to sell that right, she may invoke it to completely prevent the defendant from interfering with her use and enjoyment of the land. Generally, courts are reluctant to adopt the absolutist view of legal, or economic, life that injunctions tend to represent. Thus, as in the

---

30. A pioneering analysis drawing on economics as well as law is Guido Calabresi & A. Douglas Melamed, Property Rules, Liability Rules, and Inalienability: One View of the Cathedral, 85 Harv. L. Rev. 1089 (1972).

31. 257 N.E.2d 870 (N.Y.1970).

32. Id. at 875.

33. See id. at 873 & n.*.

Boomer case,[34] courts are likely to favor a one-time award of damages to compensate plaintiffs for loss of property values while preserving a going business.

Just as damages suits always allow the possibility of paying money to settle the case, injunction actions involve the opportunity for the defendant to buy off the plaintiff. In economic parlance, a polluting defendant might "bribe" neighboring landowners to tolerate its activity in exchange for their agreement to forego a lawsuit. This solution, while theoretically appealing, entails practical problems, like that posed by the "opting out" plaintiff who will not go along with other landowners at an economically rational buy-off figure.

C. *Injunction with plaintiffs paying off defendants*

An interesting variation is to allow an injunction to plaintiffs, but require them to pay off the defendant for the cost of having its operation shut down. There are cases in which courts have formulated this precise solution,[35] although its feasibility will diminish when the defendant is highly profitable and the plaintiffs possess few resources. In any event, the theoretical possibility provides a useful tool for analysis.

D. *No nuisance*

The other alternative—no remedy—is effectively a determination of substantive law: the court may hold that there is no nuisance. Courts have reached this conclusion when they believe that the utility of the defendant's conduct far outweighs the plaintiff's economic interest, or when the plaintiff "came to the nuisance." In one decision concluding that the defendant's activity had overriding value, the Idaho Supreme Court held that a feedlot was not a nuisance despite the discomfort it caused to neighboring landowners. In justifying its decision, the court referred to the state's dependence "upon the benefits of agriculture, lumber, mining and industrial development."[36] Given such a holding, the only way that plaintiffs could stop an activity would be to pay the defendant to desist from it—the economic "bribe." In cases where the economic benefits of the defendant's activity are relatively great, this is not likely to be a practical alternative for plaintiffs.

¶ 36.04 Policies at Issue

As the prior discussion makes clear, a principal line of policy clash in nuisance law occurs between economic and moral argu-

---

34. See supra, text accompanying notes 31–33.

35. The leading example is Spur Indus., Inc. v. Del E. Webb Dev. Co., 494 P.2d 700 (Ariz.1972) (plaintiff developer to "indemnify" defendant "for a reasonable amount of the cost of moving or shutting down" cattle feedlot).

36. Carpenter v. Double R Cattle Co., 701 P.2d 222, 228 (Idaho 1985).

ments. Frequently, the persuasiveness of competing arguments may depend on how tightly one focuses on individual parties, or how broadly one expands the lens to include the economy as a whole.

A. *Economics and the law*

As we have noted, courts often strike rough economic balances in nuisance cases, taking into account the relative contributions of the litigants to the economy. In some cases they do this at the threshold point of deciding whether an activity is a nuisance,[37] while in others, they do their balancing when fashioning remedies.[38]

The theoretical bases of the economic analysis of nuisance have at least two facets of legal interest. One lies in the concept of putting resources to their "highest and best use," and another in the notion of externalities. One who adopts the "best use" point of view is likely to be relatively unsympathetic to nuisance complaints. The premise requires the decisionmaker to focus on what will produce the most efficient result from an economic point of view. Consider, for example, the case where a polluter's productive activity elevates the net value of its land and its neighbors' land taken together, even allowing for reduction in value of the neighbors' property because of the pollution. In that case, courts focusing on efficiency would be relatively restrained in granting compensation, even if they found a nuisance, and ordinarily would not impose injunctive relief.

The second idea, the concept of "externalities," casts the issue in a light typically more favorable to the plaintiff. The argument, in brief, is that one whose activities impose negative consequences on others must compensate for them, because only by being required to pay compensation will the defendant be forced to internalize the social costs of its activities. Sometimes this idea will clash with the notion that the principal relevant question is what the most efficient use of land is, and with the resulting view that the law should encourage entrepreneurs to put land to its highest and best use. An alternative presentation of the issue is to ask which party would be in the position to avoid the injury sued upon at lower cost. Analyzing the problem that way, one could determine the most efficient legal solution only if one could accurately calculate what it would cost both parties to avoid the costs the plaintiff sues to recover, as well as what the relevant costs are.

B. *Strategic behavior*

Allied to efficiency/resource allocation analysis is the interplay between legal rules and "strategic behavior," the calculated actions

---

37.　See, e.g., Carpenter, supra.

38.　See, e.g., Boomer v. Atlantic Cement Co., discussed text accompanying notes 31–33 supra.

of parties who try to use the law to extract gains for themselves beyond the gains that a well-functioning market would yield. A commentator offers, as one illustration of strategic behavior, the situation that may occur when a court "has imperfect information and is likely to understate the plaintiff's damages." He points out, in this example, that "since the defendant's output will initially exceed the efficient output when damages are understated, the plaintiff will have an incentive to bribe the defendant to reduce output." He notes further that "the defendant can hold out for more than his lost profits, thereby extorting the plaintiff," and can even "threaten to increase output beyond his profit maximizing output, thereby extorting the plaintiff in a different way."[39] Arguing to courts that try to align nuisance decisions with economic efficiency, claimants' lawyers may use this analysis to contend that strategic behavior creates inefficient outcomes that should trigger findings of nuisance and should entail relatively severe remedies.

C. Moral considerations

Courts and commentators have referred to various moral considerations in discussing the application of substantive nuisance principles and remedy rules. An argument insistently advanced for plaintiffs is that they are relatively powerless in the face of defendants, typically firms that conduct polluting activities. In their extreme form, arguments of this sort may have an absolutist character, implying that everyone is entitled to pure and noise-free air in his own environment. Although that idea may seem unsophisticated in a crowded society, it probably is a partial core of the law of nuisance, given the very existence of nuisance as a tort to remedy interference with "use and enjoyment" of land.

One may also cast the moral question in the terms of "justice as fairness" elaborated by the philosopher John Rawls. In the nuisance setting, the question would be what legal rule would commend itself to one who, in advance of a dispute, does not know whether he will be the industrial polluter or the aggrieved homeowner. Rawls would suggest that the law should fashion rules that work to the benefit of the least advantaged party.[40]

It is important to note, in discussing moral considerations, that a form of analysis that focuses on achieving economic efficiency has a morality of its own, rooted in the utilitarian idea that society should strive to achieve the greatest good for the greatest number. This view might be used, for example, to rationalize a refusal to order remedies for environmental damage—especially injunctive

---

39. A. Mitchell Polinsky, Resolving Nuisance Disputes: The Simple Economics of Injunctive and Damage Remedies, 32 Stan. L. Rev. 1075, 1110 (1980).

40. See generally John Rawls, A Theory of Justice (1971).

remedies—so long as the ultimate social balance produced by the defendant's activity is a positive one. However, in particular cases this position would not necessarily cut against requiring compensation through a damages remedy.

D. *Wealth distribution*

A related consideration in applying nuisance doctrines and choosing remedies concerns their effects on the distribution of wealth. In the kinds of situations that most people typically associate with nuisance cases—like residential landowners suing smokestack companies for pollution—courts may favor plaintiffs on the ground that allowing environmentally harmful conduct without a remedy would place an unfair burden on those who suffer identifiable harms. There are, however, certain situations in which nuisance questions may present a different image than the conventional one of a wealthy defendant getting richer by unilaterally reducing the value of a poor person's property. An illustrative case of this kind involves a plant causing air pollution that affects surrounding homes, which include the dwellings of workers at the plant and also a cluster of vacation residences. To the vacationers, who sue to stop or reduce the pollution, the plant would seem a nuisance with no redeeming value. However, to the workers who rely on the plant for jobs, it may be simply a necessary evil in their lives as wage earners.[41]

---

41. See Calabresi & Melamed, supra note 30, 85 Harv. L. Rev. at 1124 & n.36 (citing description of actual case in which resort developers and environmental groups opposed unemployed town residents who supported proposal to build chemical factory, in Frady, The View From Hilton Head, Harper's, May 1970, at 103).

Chapter Thirty–Seven

PUBLIC NUISANCE

Analysis

¶ 37.01 Public Nuisance as a Substantive Tort

As is already evident, the very term nuisance signifies a legal thicket—one might almost say itself something of a nuisance to lawyers—full of difficult definitional issues. The doctrine of private nuisance, discussed just above,[1] occupies only part of the thicket. The term also applies to the very different concept of "public nuisance," which originated in a "common law criminal offense" that "involved an interference with a right common to the general public,"[2] such as the obstruction of a public highway, the keeping of diseased animals, or the storage of high explosives in an urban area.[3] "[T]he use of the single word 'nuisance' to describe both the public and the private nuisance" led to a public nuisance analysis that was "substantially similar to that employed for the tort action for private nuisance."[4] However, there remain significant differences between the two theories. This chapter summarizes the doctrine of public nuisance.

A. General Definition

The Restatement Second defines a public nuisance as "an unreasonable interference with a right common to the general public."[5] One circumstance that may make an activity unreasonable

---

1. See Chapter 36 supra.

2. Restatement (Second) of Torts § 821B, comment e (1977).

3. See id., comment b (listing these among several examples).

4. Id., comment e.

5. Id. § 821B(1).

under this definition is the fact that it significantly interferes "with the public health, the public safety, the public peace, the public comfort or the public convenience." Other factors tending toward a finding of public nuisance include the fact that the defendant's conduct violated a statute or regulation, or that it "is of a continuing nature" or has permanent effects and the defendant at least has reason to know that it "has a significant effect upon the public right."[6] Moreover, courts may be inclined to find a public nuisance when the defendant significantly interferes "with recognized aesthetic values or established principles of conservation of natural resources."[7]

B.   Public right; private nuisance distinguished

It is clear that an activity becomes a public nuisance only when it "interfere[s] with a public right." This means that the right must be "common to all members of the general public," for example, the right to use a public highway or to fish in a navigable stream. Interference with private enjoyment is not the key to public nuisance: thus, "[t]he obstruction of a public highway is a public nuisance, although no one is traveling upon the highway or wishes to travel on it at the time."[8] By comparison, "[c]onduct does not become a public nuisance merely because it interferes with the use and enjoyment of land by large numbers of persons."[9] For example, it is not necessarily a public nuisance when an industry causes air pollution that affects a substantial number of scattered homesites or water pollution that deprives dozens of homeowners of the use of a stream. Yet, it is true that most cases of private nuisance that involve effects to "a large number of persons in their use and enjoyment of land" will usually involve "some interference with the rights of the public as well." Illustrative is "the spread of smoke, dust, or fumes over a considerable area filled with private residences" that "interfere[s] also with the use of the public streets or affect[s] the health of so many persons as to involve the interest of the public at large."[10]

The line between public nuisance and private nuisance may well be uncertain and subject to interpretation, but the key to public nuisance is the violation of rights—be they in air, water, or streets—that are open to all. Moreover, courts confronted with public nuisance issues will take into account policy considerations that may go beyond the efficiency concerns on which many analysts of private nuisance have focused. For example, a nude dancing cabaret might turn a profit that outweighed the devaluation it

---

6. Id. § 821B(2).

7. See id., § 821(B), comment e.

8. Id. comment g.

9. Id.

10. Id.

caused to neighboring properties, but many courts would find that its adverse effects on public sensibilities created a public nuisance. Analogously, the fact that some courts take conservation principles into account indicates that there is more political content to this doctrine than one might ordinarily find in the private law of torts.

¶ 37.02 Remedies

A. Damages

The payoff in public nuisance litigation—as in private nuisance law—lies in the remedies: damages and injunctions. The law imposees stringent requirements on litigants seeking either kind of remedy. With respect to damages, even though an activity is called a public nuisance, not every member of the public can recover money compensation for it. Rather, one must show that he "suffered harm of a kind different from that suffered by other members of the public exercising the right common to the general public that was the subject of interference."[11] Under this standard, anyone who suffers personal injury from a public nuisance can recover damages for it.

Plaintiffs may also sue for serious interferences with use of property when they can distinguish their injuries from those of the public at large. Illustrative is a suit against petroleum companies for the contamination of well water by a chemical used to increase the oxygen content of gasoline. The plaintiffs alleged a "serious interference with the use, benefit and/or enjoyment of their properties." The court ruled that the plaintiffs had met the "special injury" requirement by alleging that "[m]uch of the population" of the states where they lived was "served by surface water that is not susceptible to the problems caused" by the chemical in groundwater. The court also noted that "public water supplies that rely on groundwater are monitored for safety, unlike plaintiffs' private wells."[12]

By contrast, someone who sustains only inconvenience of a sort experienced by many other members of a community—for example, travel detours or delays caused by the obstruction of a highway— cannot recover damages.[13] In enforcing this distinction, the law seeks to avoid the burden on the courts of a "multiplicity of actions," concerning matters that might better be "left to be remedied by action by public officials."[14]

---

11. Restatement (Second) of Torts § 821C(1).

12. In re Methyl Tertiary Butyl Ether ("MTBE") Prod. Liab. Litig., 175 F. Supp.2d 593, 629 (S.D.N.Y.2001).

13. See Restatement (Second) § 821C, comment c.

14. Id. comment b.

There are alternative concepts that courts may employ to achieve the same limiting result as the requirement that the plaintiff suffer harm that is different in kind from other members of the public. For example, courts may use the following characterizations to refuse damages to private plaintiffs suing for a public nuisance:

1.   That the plaintiff's suit is for "economic loss," to which tort law is not generally sympathetic.

2.   That the defendant's activity does not interfere with a definable "property right."

3.   That the defendant's conduct is not the cause in fact of the plaintiff's harm.

4.   That damages are too uncertain to calculate.

B. Injunctions

There are several routes to getting an injunction for a public nuisance. One group of persons who can do so consists of plaintiffs who may recover damages; they must show, as explained above, a harm different from that "suffered by other members of the public." In the Restatement's summary of the topic, others who may sue for injunctions are governmental bodies or officials, and persons who "have standing to sue as a representative of the general public, as a citizen in a citizen's action or as a member of a class in a class action."[15]

¶ 37.03 Standing

Because litigation over alleged public nuisances frequently will involve large numbers of potential plaintiffs, the rules concerning both damages and injunctions for public nuisance seek to establish administrative limits on the ability to sue. The courts must balance the rights of people who have in fact suffered injuries[16] against the potential burdens to defendants and systemic inefficiencies posed when scores or even thousands of litigants sue for essentially the same injury, attributed to the same source.[17] The doctrine of standing to sue plays a gatekeeping role in this process of balancing.

Since private citizens may sue for public nuisance if they can recover damages for harms different in kind than those generally suffered, and governments may also bring public nuisance actions, the most difficult problems of standing have to do with who may

---

15. Id. § 821C(2).

16. See Osborne Reynolds, Public Nuisance: A Crime in Tort Law, 31 Okla. L. R. 318, 337 (1978).

17. See, e.g., Restatement (Second) § 821C, comment b.

sue, in the words of the Restatement's classification system, "as a representative of the general public" or "as a citizen in a citizen's action."[18] The answer will depend largely on the breadth of the standing concept in particular jurisdictions.

An Arizona decision illustrates how courts may seek to achieve both the reality and the perception of fairness for persons who are suffering significant injuries while also trying to protect defendants from extortionate litigation and from being overwhelmed by large numbers of individual suits. Residents of a Tucson neighborhood sued a community center because transients who came to take advantage of a meal program "frequently trespassed onto residents' yards, sometimes urinating, defecating, drinking and littering on the residents' property." The court found both that "the residents of the neighborhood" had standing to sue, and that a nonprofit neighborhood association could "bring the action as the representative of its members." It characterized the damage to the "residents' use and enjoyment of their real property" as being "special in nature and different in kind from that experienced by the residents of the city in general." The court referred to the purpose of the neighborhood association as being "to promote and preserve the use and enjoyment of the neighborhood by its residents." In allowing the association standing, the court declared that it would advance the "[p]rinciples of judicial economy" to allow "the issues to be settled in a single action rather than a multitude of individual actions because the relief sought is universal to all of its members and requires no individual quantification by the court."[19]

The case exhibits some of the important policy concerns to which courts refer in litigation over public nuisances—notably, administrative economy—and also the policy tensions that arise in such disputes. It presents the problem in an especially poignant context, since the defendant was a nonprofit organization that was doing charitable deeds. One implication of the approach to standing represented by the decision is that it allows groups to act as private attorneys general in situations where public regulation is nonexistent or is not fully operative, or political factors reduce its effectiveness.[20]

18. See text accompanying note 15 supra.

19. Armory Park Neighborhood Ass'n v. Episcopal Community Services in Arizona, 712 P.2d 914, 918–19 (Ariz. 1985).

20. An exhaustive study of public nuisance doctrine concludes with a proposal for a standard of "actual community injury" as a test for recovery of damages or entitlement to injunctive relief. The author would require a showing of "an actual or threatened injury in common with the community that was the subject of the nuisance." She defines "injury" to include "environmental and aesthetic injury," suggesting that a court could draw on "administrative law principles of the jurisdiction" that might recognize "aesthetic, conservational, and

¶ 37.04   Choices in the Characterization of Issues

Sometimes different ways of characterizing litigation brought under the public nuisance label may affect the outcomes of cases. Illustrative of the importance of characterization is the question of whether one who discharges hazardous substances into the environment should be liable for emotional distress suffered by members of the public, especially in situations involving threats of serious and widespread physical harm. Consider, for example, a case in which a utility's nuclear reactor is threatened by a meltdown, which the utility attempts to avert by venting radioactive gas. In a situation like this, it is plausible that many residents of nearby communities will suffer significant emotional consequences from fear of radiation.

That intuition about factual causation does not settle the issue, however. The issue of whether an activity is a public nuisance and the procedural question of who may sue for a public nuisance exist side by side with the substantive issue of whether there is a duty to protect people from negligent infliction of emotional distress.[21] Yet another way to state the question is whether, as a matter of "damages" law, fear of illness is an appropriate item of compensation, analogous to pain and suffering.[22] Thus, a court's decision about whether to put a case in one category or another of legal issues will affect its decision. For example, if a jurisdiction is hospitable to claims for negligently caused emotional distress, classifying the case under that heading will favor plaintiffs. But if the state law is relatively strict about its substantive definition of a public nuisance, categorizing the case as presenting that problem will favor defendants. It is likely that a court's view of both substantive justice and judicial administration will affect its characterization of such issues.

cultural losses." Denise Antolini, Modernizing Public Nuisance: Solving the Paradox of the Special Injury Rule, 28 Ecology L. Q. 755, 862–63 (2001). Proposals for such a broadened standard would obviously generate controversy over the substantial costs they might shift from community plaintiffs to industry. An argument for such proposals is that they could "provide important supplemental paths for community and environmental justice" "[w]hen political winds shift at the federal level to disfavor statutory avenues of access such as environmental citizen suits." Id. at 893.

21.   See generally Chapter 59 infra.

22.   See infra, ¶ ¶ 49.06(B), 72.01(C).

Section Six

PRODUCTS LIABILITY

Chapter Thirty–Eight

STRICT LIABILITY FOR PRODUCTS

Analysis

American courts have developed a separate strict liability category for defective and dangerous products that parallels the version of strict liability for abnormally dangerous activities that evolved from *Rylands v. Fletcher*.[1] In the 1960s, courts began articulately to recognize injuries from products as a special classification, under which consumers could sue in tort without having to show fault. Questions persist as to the strictness of strict products liability in some applications of the doctrine, but the terminology and the general concept have captured a great majority of the courts.

1. See generally Chapter 35.

¶ 38.01   Historical Background

As the twentieth century opened, people injured by product defects faced insuperable barriers to suing manufacturers, or any firm except the seller from whom they bought a product, if indeed they were product buyers at all. The law applied in the nineteenth century permitted actions for negligence only against the party with whom an injured person had a contractual relation—a requirement of contractual "privity." The great 1916 decision in *MacPherson v. Buick Motor Co.*[2] was thus revolutionary when it created a cause of action in negligence for injured consumers suing product sellers with whom they did not have contractual privity. Other American courts followed this holding one by one in negligence cases. In the same decade, the courts also began to use a non-fault theory, the contract-based doctrine of implied warranty, to impose a strict form of liability against non-privity sellers for products injuries.[3]

Implied warranty presented a substantial advantage for persons suing for product injuries because it did not require a showing of negligence. However, it had certain limitations for claimants, including the fact that sellers could disclaim liability in advance in the contract. After some decades of judicial development of liability without a privity requirement under implied warranty, there appeared in 1944 a judicial harbinger of strict liability for products under an explicit tort label. This was Judge Traynor's separate opinion in *Escola v. Coca Cola Bottling Co.*,[4] arguing for what he then called "absolute" liability for product defects.

After more development of the warranty theory, a much-cited scholarly synthesis, published by Dean Prosser in 1960, identified the strict liability underlying implied warranty as a separate legal phenomenon and advocated the reclassification of that form of liability into the tort category.[5] In the same year there came a landmark in the decisional history, which fashioned warranty theory into a solid foundation for the doctrine that came to be called

---

2. 111 N.E. 1050 (N.Y.1916).

3. A landmark case is Mazetti v. Armour & Co., 135 P. 633 (Wash.1913), which permitted suit by a restaurant owner against a manufacturer of a "foul and poisonous" tongue for loss of reputation and profits that resulted when customers became sick. The complaint both invoked the defendant's representations that its products were pure and fit for consumption and alleged negligence in manufacture of the product. The court based its reversal of a demurrer on the theory that "a manufacturer of food products ... impliedly warrants

his goods when dispensed in original packages ... to all who may be damaged by reason of their use in the legitimate channels of trade." Especially noteworthy was the fact that the court allowed a cause of action for the plaintiff restaurant owner's economic loss, apart from any direct claim for personal injuries caused by the contaminated food.

4. 150 P.2d 436, 440–41 (1944) (Traynor, J., concurring and dissenting).

5. William Prosser, The Assault upon the Citadel (Strict Liability to the Consumer), 69 Yale L. J. 1099 (1960).

strict liability in tort. This was *Henningsen v. Bloomfield Motors*,[6] in which the New Jersey Supreme Court, using the then traditional contract terminology of "implied warranty of merchantability," granted recovery against the non-privity manufacturer of a car that ran off the road, causing personal injuries.

Henningsen with its warranty terminology generally is taken to have launched the strict liability revolution, but it was only in 1963 that the California Supreme Court, speaking through Judge Traynor, first defined a purely tort version of strict liability for products. In *Greenman v. Yuba Power Products*, Judge Traynor set out a theory of strict liability in tort applicable to a manufacturer that places a product "on the market, knowing that it is to be used without inspection for defects, [which] proves to have a defect that causes injury to a human being."[7] Judge Traynor indicated that the doctrine would apply only to products used as they were intended to be used and to plaintiffs who were not aware of the defect that made the product unsafe for the use in question.[8]

¶ 38.02 Section 402A

The central formulation of the strict liability theory for products appeared in section 402A of the Restatement (Second) of Torts, published in 1965. In full text, this section declares that

> (1) one who sells any product in a defective condition unreasonably dangerous to the user or consumer or to his property is subject to liability for physical harm thereby caused to the ultimate user or consumer, or to his property, if
>
> (a) the seller is engaged in the business of selling a product and
>
> (b) it is expected to and does reach the user or consumer without substantial change in the condition in which it is sold.
>
> (2) The rule stated in Subsection (1) applies although
>
> (a) the seller has exercised all possible care in the preparation and sale of his product, and
>
> (b) the user or consumer has not bought the product from or entered into any contractual relation with the seller.[9]

This formula not only applied a tort version of strict liability to products, but did so without requiring that the plaintiff show privity of contract with the seller. The practical effect of this was

6. 161 A.2d 69 (N.J.1960).

7. 377 P.2d 897, 901 (Cal.1963).

8. Id.

9. Restatement (Second) of Torts § 402A (1965).

that plaintiffs who previously had to show that sellers remote in the distributional chain were negligent could now sue such sellers—typically manufacturers—without having to prove that the defendant was at fault.

Over the course of the 1960s and 1970s, most states adopted some version of this strict liability, although some did so under different labels. New York, for example, made a rather tortuous journey from warranty to strict liability in a series of decisions.[10] For several years, Ohio employed a doctrine called "implied warranty in tort" until it concluded that the section 402A theory was virtually identical and that the adoption of that formula would "greatly facilitate[] analysis."[11] Alabama adopted its own version of strict liability for products under its label of the "extended manufacturer's liability doctrine."[12] By contrast, Massachusetts has persisted in its retention of implied warranty as its theory of choice for nonfault liability against sellers not in contractual privity with consumer plaintiffs.[13]

¶ 38.03   Products as a Special Category

A.   Goods to which definition applies

The definition of product for strict liability purposes includes a very wide range of goods, running from automobiles to prescription drugs, and including such diverse products as food and earthmoving machines. The decision of whether a good fits into the "product" category for purposes of strict liability depends largely on the policies underlying the doctrine, many of which are summarized below.[14]

One limitation on the product category is that the good must be inanimate. This requirement excludes from strict liability animals such as dogs, because their character is "shaped by the purchaser rather than the seller,"[15] and swine, because they are "by their nature in a constant process of internal development and growth and they are also participants in a constant interaction with the environment around them as part of their development."[16]

---

10. See, e.g., Goldberg v. Kollsman Instr. Corp., 191 N.E.2d 81 (N.Y.1963) (using implied warranty as its theory but saying that " 'strict tort liability' "was "surely a more accurate phrase"); Victorson v. Bock Laundry Mach. Co., 335 N.E.2d 275 (N.Y.1975) (confirming strict liability as preferred theory).

11. Temple v. Wean United, Inc., 364 N.E.2d 267, 271 (Ohio 1977).

12. Casrell v. Altec Indus., 335 So.2d 128 (Ala.1976).

13. Swartz v. General Motors Corp., 378 N.E.2d 61, 62 (Mass.1978) ("there is no 'strict liability in tort' apart from liability for breach of warranty under the Uniform Commercial Code").

14. See ¶ 38.05 infra.

15. Whitmer v. Schneble, 331 N.E.2d 115, 119 (Ill.Ct.App.1975).

16. Anderson v. Farmers Hybrid Cos., 408 N.E.2d 1194, 1199 (Ill.Ct.App. 1980).

Several jurisdictions have gone so far as to apply strict liability to homes.[17] However, one court firmly drew the line to exclude a municipal parking garage from strict liability, distinguishing the building itself from defects in products installed in homes.[18]

Symbolizing the fine distinctions that may be made about whether to classify something as a "product" are the fact that the Illinois Supreme Court implicitly accepted that an exit sign on a highway is a "product" under strict liability,[19] but an Illinois appellate court denied that a highway guardrail is a product.[20]

A principal battleground on the definition of "product" involves the question of whether the classification includes electricity. Some courts have firmly rejected calling electricity a product on the grounds that "at least until the electricity reaches a point where it is made available for consumer use," it has not been " 'sold' or otherwise 'placed in the stream of commerce.' "[21] However, other courts have concluded that the classification of electricity as a product is "warranted, indeed mandated, by the social policies which underlie and justify the imposition of strict liability on sellers who place dangerously defective products into the stream of commerce." One such decision emphasized that "[c]onsumer self-protection from . . . electricity of an excessively high voltage . . . is not feasible in the case of the ordinary consumer," and that the seller "is in a better position to anticipate, protect against and eliminate possible dangerous electricity overloads of this type."[22]

B. Comparison with Rylands-type doctrines

Courts have maintained a rather sharp separation between strict liability for products, the subject of this chapter, and the strict liability for activities that has been applied on the model of *Rylands v. Fletcher*[23] and under the "abnormally dangerous activities" category of the Restatement Second.[24] The Oregon Supreme Court, for example, declared that the *Rylands* rule applies "when an *activity* creates an abnormally dangerous condition, or by its nature presents extraordinary risk of harm to person or property," but that the doctrine "has no applicability in a products case." Underlining the distinction, the court said that "[t]he fact that a

---

17. A landmark decision, relating to mass-built homes, is Schipper v. Levitt & Sons, Inc., 207 A.2d 314 (N.J.1965).

18. Lowrie v. City of Evanston, 365 N.E.2d 923 (Ill.Ct.App.1977).

19. Hunt v. Blasius, 384 N.E.2d 368 (Ill.1978) (rejecting liability on grounds that there was no proof of defect).

20. Maddan v. R.A. Cullinan & Son, Inc., 411 N.E.2d 139, 141 (Ill.Ct.App. 1980).

21. Smith v. Home Light and Power Co., 734 P.2d 1051, 1055 (Colo.1987).

22. Ransome v. Wisconsin Elec. Power Co., 275 N.W.2d 641, 647–48 (Wis.1979).

23. L.R. 3 H.L. 330 (1868), discussed supra at ¶ 35.02.

24. See Restatement (Second) of Torts §§ 519–520 (1977), discussed supra at ¶ 35.03.

product may create an 'ultrahazardous condition' by virtue of defective design or manufacture is ... of no moment under our present law."[25]

Given the pragmatic nature of tort law as it has developed, it is not surprising to find that it has created these parallel tracks of strict liability, making a separate category for products on the basis of a particular concern with such factors as deficiencies in consumer information and the promotional activities of sellers.

¶ 38.04 Categories of Strict Products Liability

Courts and scholars have divided products liability cases, and often the application of strict liability, into three rough categories: manufacturing defects, design defects, and failures to warn. The new Restatement of Products Liability employs the tripartite classification system.[26] There is a consensus that strict liability applies to manufacturing defects, but there are disputes over whether it should be applied to design defects and failures to warn.

A. Manufacturing defects

The general agreement on strict liability for manufacturing defects embraces cases in which "the product departs from its intended design even though all possible care was exercised in the preparation and marketing of the product."[27] In terms accessible to laymen as well as to lawyers, a manufacturing defect is a flaw, a deficiency that the manufacturer of the product did not intend to exist and would have eliminated if it were possible to do so. Courts justify strict liability for manufacturing defects on the basis that it is usually impossible for consumers to detect such flaws, for example a piece of wire in a cookie, reasoning that as between a seller who profits from the sale of such a product and an entirely innocent consumer, it is appropriate that the seller should have to pay for the consumer's injury.

B. Design defects

The issue of strict liability for design defect has excited much controversy. One's answer to the question of whether there should be such liability will depend significantly on one's views of policy. In assessing competing policies, one should keep in mind that the very nature of a design defect lies in the fact that the disputed feature of the product is one that the manufacturer intended it to

25. Cavan v. General Motors Corp., 571 P.2d 1249, 1251–52 (Or.1977).

26. Restatement (Third) of Torts: Products Liability § 2 (1998)(hereafter, "Products Restatement"), citing various authorities for this classification system, see id. § 1, reporters' note comment a.

27. See id. § 2(a).

have, often choosing the design after balancing such considerations as utility, style and price.

A principal practical concern about imposing liability without fault for a design defect is that such a liability presumably will apply to every product of that line that causes injury because of the hazard at issue. This could create a potentially ruinous liability for many manufacturers, especially manufacturers of mass-produced products, rendered vulnerable to suits by anyone injured by the feature of a product that allegedly makes it defective. Opponents of this type of strict liability emphasize the disincentives to innovation it may cause, arguing that manufacturers may become unduly fearful about marketing new types of products.

Those who argue that strict liability should apply to design defects contend that there is no reason in principle to distinguish between products that are unreasonably dangerous because of manufacturing flaws and those that are unreasonably dangerous because of design choices. They say that the same considerations that support strict liability for manufacturing defects—among them deterrence, the vindication of consumer expectations, and fairness[28] —militate in favor of strict liability for design defects.

In rebuttal, those who believe that courts should impose design liability only where the manufacturer has been at fault emphasize that "[m]any product-related accident costs can be eliminated only by excessively sacrificing product features that make the products useful and desirable."[29] Some commentators suggest that the only fair way to judge liability for product design is to employ the sort of analysis required for determinations of negligence.[30] A specific liability-limiting principle, adopted by the Restatement of Products Liability, is that plaintiffs claiming design defects must show that "the foreseeable risks of harm posed by the product could have been reduced or avoided by the adoption of a reasonable alternative design," the omission of which "renders the product not reasonably safe."[31]

A final response, from those who support strict liability in design cases, stresses that it is not unfair to make manufacturers of entire product lines internalize the costs of injuries caused by the unreasonably dangerous features of those products. These observers declare that even the lack of an alternative design should not save a model of product from strict liability if it is so dangerous

---

28. See ¶ 38.05 infra.

29. Products Restatement, supra note 26, § 2, comment a, at 16.

30. See, e.g., Sheila Birnbaum, Unmasking the Test for Design Defect: From Negligence (to Warranty) to Strict

Liability to Negligence, 33 Vand. L. Rev. 539 (1980).

31. Products Restatement, supra note 26, § 2(b).

that it would otherwise be labeled defective under the standards of the strict liability doctrine.[32]

C. Failure to warn

There is also considerable argument about whether the strict liability concept applies to claims that consumers were not adequately warned about the dangers of a product. Some courts have insisted that claims for failure to warn under section 402A are practically determined under "negligence theory," since a manufacturer "can only be required to warn of risks known during the time in which the plaintiff was using the product in question."[33]

A few courts have found conceptual room for a pure strict liability theory in warnings cases, emphasizing that the very nature of strict liability makes it applicable even if the seller could not have known of the dangers on which the plaintiff bases a claim for failure to warn. In particular, a controversial New Jersey decision held it proper to impose strict liability for failure to warn of the dangers of asbestos products that were "undiscoverable at the time of manufacture." Saying that the "defendants' products were not reasonably safe because they did not have a warning," the court stressed that it was not imposing liability because the defendants behaved unreasonably—which was a matter of "negligence principles"—but because the users were "unaware of [the products'] hazards and could not protect themselves from injury."[34]

The Restatement of Products Liability has articulated a separate defect classification for claims based on lack of adequate instructions or warnings. Section 2(c) says that a product may be "defective because of inadequate instructions or warnings" when the "provision of adequate instructions or warnings" could have reduced or avoided its "foreseeable risks of harm."[35] The Restatement comments say that this section "adopts a reasonableness test for judging the adequacy of product instructions and warnings."[36]

¶ 38.05 Rationales

The rationales for strict liability are a subject of much discussion in judicial opinions and scholarly commentary. We summarize here some of the most-discussed policy goals and rationalizations for the application of strict liability in products cases.

---

32. For a more detailed discussion of the controversy about standards for design defects, see ¶ 39.03 infra.

33. Ortho Pharmaceutical Corp. v. Chapman, 388 N.E.2d 541, 552–53 (Ind. Ct.App.1979).

34. Beshada v. Johns–Manville Prods. Corp., 447 A.2d 539, 546–49 (N.J. 1982).

35. For further discussion of this section, see infra, ¶ 39.05(B).

36. Products Restatement, supra note 26, cmt. i.

A. Controlling behavior

All courts would agree, to some extent, that a rationale of strict liability is to influence the conduct of sellers in order to make products safer. Commentators who view the subject from an economic point of view will emphasize the optimization of product risks, that is, bringing risk levels to an efficient point so that consumers buy a package of benefits and risks that is acceptable to them at the price they pay. By contrast, many courts that speak of "deterrence" as a rationale for products liability appear to reason moralistically. They seem to emphasize accident reduction as a goal of the law even when that might mean that the level of injuries would fall below the market-dictated point. This approach may embody a view that life and limb have values that cannot be fully captured on demand curves.

B. Redressing imbalances in information

Closely related to the deterrence rationale, particularly under the lens of economic analysis, is the goal of redressing imbalances in information between the parties. Many plaintiffs in products cases rely, implicitly if not explicitly, on the theory that the manufacturer had superior knowledge about the hazards of the product sued upon. One result of the application of strict liability when a manufacturer has such an informational advantage is to correct that imbalance after the fact. It is at least implicit in applications of strict liability on this premise that if the consumer had adequate information about the risk, either she would not have bought or encountered the product, or if she had done so, she would in effect have been declaring herself satisfied with the package of risks and benefits the product represented.

C. Fairness

Many courts impose strict liability because they believe that fairness requires it. There are some different meanings of fairness in the environment of products injuries. An individualistic, party-centered view is that of corrective justice, which seeks to achieve, after the injury, a moral balancing between the plaintiff's losses and the assumed gains of the defendant.

A much more instrumental and societal view of fairness appears in the rationale of loss spreading. In its simplest form, loss spreading entails distribution of the financial cost of an injury, which occurs to one unfortunate user of a product, among the many satisfied users. The cost of the injury finds its way into the liability insurance premiums paid by the manufacturer, and then is reflected in the price all consumers pay. Critics of the spreading rationale will contend that such spreading of costs is a social justice function that is the business of the legislature, to be achieved through taxation, but several courts have found the idea congenial as a basis for tort decisions.

D. Avoiding problems of proof

A practical circumstance that has motivated courts to impose strict liability is the difficulty that plaintiffs often have in proving a defect or showing how it came to exist. Frequently, one senses that when courts impose strict liability, they are doing so because they cannot verify that the defendant was negligent although they suspect it was. Some have rationalized the application of strict liability, particularly in cases involving the classic manufacturing defect, as a way of avoiding the artificiality, if not lack of candor, associated with holdings that the plaintiff has proven negligence by circumstantial evidence. By employing strict liability, the court may sometimes avoid the intellectual difficulties of ascribing an event to negligence, for example, through application of the doctrine of res ipsa loquitur,[37] when the proof is derived from no more than the malfunction of a product. Beyond that, strict liability may reduce the expense associated with proving negligence, and in some cases will overcome insuperable difficulties of even circumstantial proof. All this vaulting of technical legal obstacles represents a judicial policy choice in favor of injured consumers.

E. Response to product portrayals

Strict liability also responds to the marketing of products by a complex and sophisticated system of product promotion. Sometimes, the defendant's specific representations in a promotional campaign may be grounds for findings of liability on such theories as fraud,[38] negligent misrepresentation[39] and express warranty.[40] However, strict liability represents a broader judicial response to the allure of product portrayals that do not fit easily into representational theories of liability.[41]

---

37. See Chapter 45 infra.

38. See, e.g., Miller's Bottled Gas, Inc. v. Borg–Warner Corp., 955 F.2d 1043 (6th Cir.1992) (brochure claiming that carburetor had been "thoroughly tested" when in fact it had been tested "only spottily and hastily").

39. See, e.g., Hanberry v. Hearst, 81 Cal.Rptr. 519 (Ct.App.1969) (Good Housekeeping Consumers' Guaranty Seal conferred on a slippery pair of shoes).

40. See, e.g., McCarty v. E.J. Korvette, Inc., 347 A.2d 253 (Md.App.1975) ("Lifetime Guarantee" for auto transmission).

41. See, e.g., Leichtamer v. American Motors Corp., 424 N.E.2d 568, 578 (Ohio 1981) ("the commercial advertising of a product will be the guiding force upon the expectations of consumers with regard to the safety of a product, and is highly relevant to a formulation of what those expectations might be" under a consumer expectations test for unreasonable dangerousness).

A broad analysis of the representational basis of products liability appears in Marshall Shapo, A Representational Theory of Consumer Protection, 60 Va. L. Rev. 1109 (1974).

F.   Consumer expectations

An important basis for products liability generally is consumer expectations. A comment to section 402A declared that "the public has the right to and does expect, in the case of products which it needs and for which it is forced to rely upon the seller, that reputable sellers will stand behind their goods."[42] The idea that the public "does expect" certain qualities and performance standards from products is an empirical assertion, as a formal matter. The question of what consumers do expect thus might depend on public opinion surveys, or even on the subjective testimony of a plaintiff. But the comment's reference to what the public has "the right to ... expect" appears to draw on more socially oriented premises, and to require from courts a judgment about the policy foundations of that right.

G.   Redressing deficiencies of warranty law

Several courts have referred to the hurdles that warranty law presents to injured consumers as reasons for the adoption of strict liability. These features of warranty law include the requirement that consumers must give relatively prompt notice to sellers of their injuries, as well as the fact that in many cases, the application of statutes of limitations for warranty will favor sellers more than tort statutes of limitations. Moreover, often devastatingly from the consumer point of view, warranty law allows sellers to use disclaimers[43] and limitations of remedies,[44] although the Uniform Commercial Code makes limitations of damages "for injury to the person in the case of consumer goods ... prima facie unconscionable."[45] In many cases, strict liability sweeps away these obstacles to consumer recovery.

¶ 38.06   Summary

Judicial acceptance of strict liability for products has been one of the most remarkable developments in the history of the common law. Arguments over the propriety of this theory, like the arguments over products liability in general, reflect tensions in society about many potential elements of decision. These include the value that we place on the products we buy, our views about the responsibility of sellers, and our beliefs about the burden of choice that rests on consumers. Strict liability represents judicial recognition of such things as the complexity of the distribution scheme for products, the sophistication of the process of promoting consumer goods,

---

42. Restatement (Second) of Torts § 402A, comment c (1965).

43. U.C.C. § 2–316.

44. U.C.C. § 2–719(1).

45. U.C.C. § 2–719(3).

the relative lack of consumer information about some products, and the ability of sellers to distribute loss. At the same time, products liability law seeks to weigh the consumer interest in access to a wide variety of products as well as the differing tastes of consumers, including the wide spectrum of consumer preferences for or aversion to the risk of injury.

Chapter Thirty–Nine

DEFECT IN PRODUCTS LIABILITY

Analysis

———————

The plaintiff in a products liability case must show that the product was defective. This is an explicit requirement of the strict liability theory, but there also is effectively a defect requirement if the plaintiff sues under implied warranty of merchantability—itself a form of strict liability—or under a negligence theory. The concept of defect is central to products liability, because it embodies the social views, policy considerations, and legal intuitions that underlie the decision on whether a seller must pay a consumer for a product injury. The analysis of defect in this chapter focuses at first on two of the three major categories of products cases, those involving manufacturing and design defects, not always distinguishing them but frequently concentrating on controversial issues related to design defects. A discussion of the third major category, decisions concerning failure to warn about hazards, concludes the chapter.[1]

¶ 39.01 Rationales

The rationales on which courts draw in determining whether a product is defective overlap closely with those discussed in our

---

1. See ¶ 39.05 infra.

analysis of the strict liability concept above.[2] Courts concern themselves in significant measure with reducing the danger level of products, a rationale closely linked with the sometimes overwhelming cost to consumers of personal injuries. Relevant background factors are the ways that the promotion of products can condition consumers to purchase or otherwise encounter products. A related, important aspect of the defect formulation lies in the balance of information concerning product hazards. In determining whether a product is defective, courts will take into account the information available to the seller concerning the risks of the product and the seller's ability to anticipate the way those risks arise in particular uses. At the same time, courts will consider the level of consumer information about product hazards, and will be less inclined to find a defect as that level goes up. Another significant factor in the judgment of whether there is a defect is the difficulty that sometimes faces injured litigants, and courts themselves, in securing information about the process of design and manufacture. Courts will be relatively inclined to find a defect when there are grounds to suspect negligence in design or manufacture and also reason to believe that information pertinent to that issue is not likely to be fairly available to the claimant.

¶ 39.02   Tests for Defect

Courts and commentators have developed several verbal tests in their efforts to formulate a standard for defect. This section discusses a number of these competing and complementary formulas.

A. *The stark definition*

The starkest definition of defect is one that defines the concept by reference to itself, requiring only that the court and jury find that a product was "defective."[3] The generality of this spare definition is attractive, because of its broad applicability to the vast number of situations in which the defect concept is at issue. However, that generality is also a vice, for in its self-referential character, the definition lacks an explanation of what a defect is. For that reason, practically all courts have insisted on putting more flesh on the bare bones of the concept.

B. *Unreasonably dangerous*

The definition that has attracted most courts is the one presented in section 402A of the Restatement Second, which requires the plaintiff to show that a product was in "a defective condition

---

2. See ¶ 38.05 supra.

3. See, e.g., Cronin v. J.B.E. Olson Corp., 501 P.2d 1153, 1155 (Cal.1972).

unreasonably dangerous."[4] This definition parallels the requirement of the basic negligence formula that the defendant's conduct
be unreasonable. However, a principal theoretical distinction between strict liability and negligence is that the concept of defect in
strict liability focuses on the product, rather than on the behavior
of the seller. In any event, courts have found it desirable to
elaborate the "unreasonably dangerous" concept beyond the general language of section 402A.

C. Dean Wade's catalog

Many courts have drawn on a list of factors, devised by Dean
John Wade, that "seem ... of significance in applying the [unrea-
sonably dangerous] standard." Dean Wade's catalog of factors included:

(1) the usefulness and desirability of the product—its utility to the user and to the public as a whole.

(2) The safety aspects of the product—the likelihood that
it will cause injury, and the probable seriousness of the injury.

(3) The availability of a substitute product which would
meet the same need and not be as unsafe.

(4) The manufacturer's ability to eliminate the unsafe
character of the product without impairing its usefulness or
making it too expensive to maintain its utility.

(5) The user's ability to avoid danger by the exercise of
care in the use of the product.

(6) The user's anticipated awareness of the dangers inherent in the product and their avoidability, because of general
public knowledge of the obvious condition of the product, or of
the existence of suitable warnings or instructions.

(7) The feasibility, on the part of the manufacturer, of
spreading the loss by setting the price of the product or
carrying liability insurance.[5]

Many courts have quoted and paraphrased this diverse catalog as
the basis for their analysis of the defect question. Others have
drawn on one or more of these factors, plus others, in formulating
their own standards.

D. The Barker test

An important illustration of the varied tests that courts have
fashioned for defect appears in the California Supreme Court's

4. Restatement (Second) of Torts
§ 402A(1) (1965).

5. John Wade, On the Nature of
Strict Tort Liability for Products, 44
Miss. L. J. 825, 837–38 (1973).

decision in *Barker v. Lull Engineering Co.*[6] The *Barker* test included two principal factors that have commended themselves to other courts, each of which provided the plaintiff an independent opportunity to prove a defect. The first "prong" of the *Barker* formula was a consumer expectations test, under which the plaintiff could demonstrate that the product failed to perform "as safely as an ordinary consumer would expect when used in an intended or reasonably foreseeable manner."[7] Alternatively, if the consumer could show that the "product's design proximately caused his injury," the product could be found defective if the defendant did not "establish, in light of the relevant factors, that, on balance, the benefits of the challenged design outweigh the risk of danger inherent in such design."[8]

¶ 39.03   The Products Restatement and Criticisms

The Restatement of Products Liability, the first project in the Restatement (Third) of Torts, has offered a three-part definition of defect, divided into categories of manufacturing defects, design defects, and products "defective because of inadequate instructions or warnings."[9] Its definition of a manufacturing defect, which captures a consensus, describes a product that "departs from its intended design even though all possible care was exercised in the preparation and marketing of the product."[10]

The Restatement's more controversial definition of design defect rests in part on two ideas that have generated argument, one of which is explicit in the blackletter, and the other explicated in the comments. Section 2(b) of the Restatement says that a product

> is defective in design when the foreseeable risks of harm posed by the product could have been reduced or avoided by the adoption of a reasonable alternative design ... and the omission of the alternative design renders the product not reasonably safe.[11]

One much debated component of this definition is its requirement that the plaintiff show a reasonable alternative design. Comment d to section 2 emphasizes that this requirement "applies in most instances even though the plaintiff alleges that the category of product sold by the defendant is so dangerous that it should not have been marketed at all." It declares that the requirement applies to "[c]ommon and widely distributed products such as

---

6. 573 P.2d 443 (Cal.1978).

7. Id. at 454.

8. Id. at 456.

9. Restatement (Third) of Torts: Products Liability § 2 (1998) (hereafter, Products Restatement). For a discussion

of the concept of defects based on inadequate warnings, see infra, ¶ 39.05(B).

10. For a brief discussion of this concept, see supra, ¶ 38.04(A).

11. Products Restatement, supra note 9, § 2(b).

alcoholic beverages, tobacco, firearms, and above-ground swimming pools," saying that "courts have not imposed liability for categories of products that are generally available and widely used and consumed, even if they pose substantial risk of harm." The comment explains that courts consider the "desirability of commercial distribution" of such products to be more appropriately a subject for "legislatures and administrative agencies."

The comments do leave open an avenue for avoidance of the requirement of proof of a reasonable alternative design.[12] Comment e observes that "[s]everal courts" have indicated that the requirement does not apply to products whose designs are "manifestly unreasonable, in that they have low social utility and high degree of danger." It provides as an example a "toy gun that shoots hard rubber pellets with sufficient velocity to cause injury to children."

Comment f identifies "[a] broad range of factors" for consideration "in determining whether an alternative design is reasonable and whether its omission renders the product not reasonably safe." These include "the magnitude and probability of the foreseeable risks of harm, the instructions and warnings accompanying the product, and the nature and strength of consumer expectations regarding the product, including expectations arising from product portrayal and marketing."

This catalog of factors is quite diverse, but a second disputed aspect of the Restatement formulation appears in a comment declaring that the design defect section "adopts a reasonableness ('risk-utility' balancing) test as the standard for judging the defectiveness of product designs."[13] Although a major competing standard in the case law and the commentary has been a consumer expectations test,[14] the Restatement comments insist that "consumer expectations do not constitute an independent standard for judging the defectiveness of product designs." While observing that "[c]ourts frequently rely, in part, on consumer expectations when discussing liability based on other theories of liability," comment g explains that "[c]onsumer expectations, standing alone, do not take into account whether the proposed alternative design could be implemented at reasonable cost, or whether an alternative design would provide greater overall safety."[15]

---

12. Comment b notes that "[s]ome courts, while recognizing that in most cases involving defective design the plaintiff must prove the availability of a reasonable alternative design, also observe that such proof is not necessary in every case involving design defects." Products Restatement, § 2, cmt. b.

13. Id., cmt. d.

14. See, e.g., Barker v. Lull Eng'g Co., quoted supra ¶ 39.02(D), text accompanying note 7.

15. Products Restatement, supra note 9, § 2, cmt. g.

There has been significant argument over the Products Restatement's reading of the case law on these points. Some studies have directly disagreed with the claim that the Restatement definition of design defect reflects a consensus.[16]

There is also contemporaneous judicial authority that rejects the new Restatement standard. A Connecticut decision, for example, found in its "independent review of the prevailing common law ... that the majority of jurisdictions *do not* impose upon plaintiffs an absolute requirement to prove a feasible alternative design."[17] In the same decision, the court "continue[d] to adhere to our long-standing rule that a product's defectiveness is to be determined by the expectations of an ordinary consumer," but modified this test because of a recognition "that there may be instances involving complex product designs in which an ordinary consumer may not be able to form expectations of safety." The court said that "under this modified formulation, the consumer expectation test would establish the product's risks and utility, and the inquiry would then be whether a reasonable consumer would consider the product design unreasonably dangerous."[18]

The lines are thus drawn over two important propositions advanced by the Restatement: that plaintiffs in design defect cases ordinarily must show a reasonable alternative design, and that the risk-utility test is the principal standard for determining a design defect. As to the first point, critics would say that courts should be able to make an independent determination of whether a product is so dangerous that it should be called defective, unhampered by a general requirement that the consumer show the existence of a reasonable alternative design. As to the second, they would argue that to subordinate the consumer expectations test to risk-utility analysis gives insufficient consideration to the crucial role that product promotion plays in the decisions of consumers to use or encounter products. In general, critics would advocate allowing courts to use a more supple and varied standard than that of the Restatement.

¶ 39.04   Challenging Issues in Defect Jurisprudence

The literature on product defect is voluminous. This section analyzes a few important issues that, taken together, reveal some of the richest aspects of the problem by identifying major strains and

---

16. See, e.g., John Vargo, The Emperor's New Clothes: The American Law Institute Adorns a "New Cloth" for Section 402A Product Liability Design Defects—a Survey of the States Reveals a Different Weave, 26 U. Mem. L. Rev. 493 (1996).

17. Potter v. Chicago Pneumatic Tool Co., 694 A.2d 1319, 1331 (Conn. 1997).

18. Id. at 1333.

tensions that bear on the definition of defect. These issues principally arise from claims that a product's intended characteristics
make it unreasonably dangerous—that is, that its design is defective.

A. *The unavoidably unsafe product*

An important limitation on the defect idea appears in the
concept of the "unavoidably unsafe" product, a formulation offered
in comment k to section 402A. This label covers products that carry
high levels of danger but are extremely useful, and, "in the present
state of human knowledge, are quite incapable of being made safe
for their intended and ordinary use." Referring to prescription
drugs and vaccines as examples, the comment declares that if such
a product is "properly prepared, and accompanied by proper directions and warning," it "is not defective, nor is it *unreasonably*
dangerous."[19] An important interpretation of comment k appeared
in a California Supreme Court decision that applied the comment's
test to prescription drugs, emphasizing the need "to vindicate the
public's interest in the availability and affordability of prescription
drugs."[20]

The tensions in this area are evident in a Nevada decision that
criticized comment k. In a case involving serious injuries to an
infant caused by a vaccine, the court said that it saw "no public
policy need for … shifting from the drug manufacturers to the
consumer/victim the responsibility for all of the 'unfortunate consequences' " that vaccines could cause. The court ruled in the context
of a nationwide inoculation program, which it said gave "little or no
choice" about whether to take the vaccine at issue. Confronting the
argument that comment k was necessary to preserve the incentives
to produce useful drugs, the court said that it was up to the
legislature to decide "whether we should leave 'unfortunate' victims of drug injury to their own resources and free drug manufacturers from tort liability, on the unsubstantiated pretext that such
a drastic measure is necessary in order to encourage drug research
and development."[21]

B. *Common "good" products*

Another ongoing controversy in products law relates to products that are in common use, and made according to their manufacturers' designs, but present substantial risks. A comment to the
Restatement Second suggested that such products as "[g]ood whis-
key," "[g]ood tobacco," and "[g]ood butter," although they carried

19. Restatement (Second) of Torts
§ 402A, comment k.

20. Brown v. Superior Court, 751
P.2d 470, 482 (Cal.1988).

21. Allison v. Merck & Co., 878
P.2d 948, 956 (Nev.1994).

dangers, were not "unreasonably dangerous" and therefore not defective despite their inherent hazards.[22] The Restatement of Products Liability parallels this idea with the statement that "[c]ommon and widely distributed products such as alcoholic beverages, firearms, and above-ground swimming pools" may be held defective only if they meet the general tests of the blackletter— essentially, that they were sold "without reasonable warnings as to their danger ... or if reasonable alternative designs could have been adopted." The drafters referred to judicial reasoning "that legislatures and administrative agencies" are the more appropriate institutions to "consider the desirability of commercial distribution of some categories of widely used and consumed, but nevertheless dangerous products."[23]

The fact that products are in common use undoubtedly is a factor in judicial reluctance to call them defective. However, the argument against immunizing certain categories of products from liability for injuries caused by their inherent dangers is simply that all products should be judged according to the same general standards, regardless of long-time market acceptance. Indeed, the American Law Institute eliminated tobacco from a draft of the Restatement of Products Liability as a subject of so-called categorical immunity.[24]

C. Product continuums

An important concept that courts have not really given a name is that of the product continuum, a spectrum of goods serving the same purpose, which have different levels of safety from which a variety of consumers may choose to meet their own specific desires and needs. Recognition of this idea is at least implicit in many decisions on the defect issue. A tragic example is a case in which a state trooper was killed by shots fired by a driver he stopped for questioning.[25] His survivors sued the maker of his contour style protective vest, which the highway patrol had selected as standard issue for troopers. This vest was one of several models on the market, at least some of which covered more areas of the body. The decedent's vest successfully stopped the bullets that hit it; however, the fatal shots hit him in parts of his body that the vest did not cover but would have been covered by another model.

In denying recovery, the court noted that there were "trade-offs to be made" in choosing among protective vests, with some

---

22. Restatement (Second) of Torts § 402A, comment i.

23. Products Restatement, supra note 9, § 2, comment d.

24. The proposed inclusion of tobacco in that list appears in Restatement (Third) of Torts § 2, comment d (Proposed Final Draft April 1, 1997).

25. Linegar v. Armour of Am., Inc., 909 F.2d 1150 (8th Cir.1990).

purchasers selecting the kind of vest that the decedent was wearing because it was less confining than vests that provided protection for more of the body. The court pointed out that the product "was designed to prevent the penetration of bullets where there was coverage, and it did so," with "the amount of coverage" being "the buyer's choice." The court declared that "[a] manufacturer is not obliged to market only one version of a product, that being the very safest design possible." It remarked that if the law were otherwise, "automobile makers could not offer consumers sports cars, convertibles, jeeps, or compact cars," and that "[a]ll boaters would have to buy full life vests instead of choosing a ski belt or even a flotation cushion."[26]

This decision captures a potentially broad lesson about products liability. It indicates that even though most individual consumers do not directly bargain with manufacturers who design products, there is a kind of massed bargaining process that takes place when consumers choose among the packages of risks and benefits that are associated with a range of products.

D. Judge and jury

As is often so in tort law generally, a crucial question with respect to the determination of defect concerns the allocation of decisionmaking between court and jury. Dean Wade argued that ordinarily juries should not participate in decisions concerning policy matters, unless one of the factors he summarized as relevant to the defect decision had "especial significance."[27] An interesting Oregon decision on this issue dealt with the separation of the rim of a truck wheel from its interior portion when the wheel hit a rock in the highway. The majority distinguished the question of "what reasonable consumers do expect from the product," which it termed a "basically factual question" for the jury, from the question of "how strong products *should* be," which the court said that *courts* had decided was "strong enough to perform as the ordinary consumer expects." The court ruled against the plaintiff because of a lack of proof as to what consumers did expect, saying that to let the case go to the jury on that record would be to allow jurors to give their opinion of "how strong the product *should* be."[28]

Other decisions have given more leeway to juries. A federal judge's instructions to the jury in a case involving automobile design referred to factors including the likelihood and seriousness of injury, and the defendant's ability to eliminate unsafe product characteristics, as well as whether the product was dangerous

---

26. Id. at 1154.

27. Wade, supra note 5, at 840, referring to list of factors quoted, text accompanying note 5.

28. Heaton v. Ford Motor Co., 435 P.2d 806, 809 (Or.1967).

beyond the expectations of an ordinary user. The instructions also told the jury that the manufacturer did not have to design a "crashproof" car "or to provide absolute safety against all risks of the road, but to provide reasonable safety against the foreseeable risks of the road."[29]

Another decision that gave broad room for jury decisionmaking involved the placement of the bell cord on a bus that was used to request a stop, and related design features on the vehicle. As the elderly plaintiff reached for the bell cord above the windows, she was thrown to the floor when the bus braked sharply and she found no pole to grasp. The court concluded that the issues of both design negligence and contributory negligence were for the jury.[30]

The Products Restatement's requirement that plaintiffs show a reasonable alternative design is a good example of a rule of law that narrows the ability of juries to decide a crucial issue, in this case the defect issue. This rule has the advantage of certainty and the disadvantage of inflexibility. Opposing it is the argument that a variety of factors go into the determination of whether there is a defect. In one decision identifying such factors, which refused to require the plaintiff to prove an alternative design, the court pointed to a state products liability statute that listed kinds of evidence that *"may be considered"* by the trier of fact. These included "[e]vidence of custom in the products seller's industry," "technological feasibility," and the product's compliance with legislative, administrative, or non-governmental standards.[31]

¶ 39.05   Relation of Defect to Defenses and Warnings

There are significant interfaces between claims of defect and defenses based on the plaintiff's conduct and knowledge—such as assumption of risk or the argument that a danger was obvious—and also between claims of defect and claims for failure to warn.

A.   Defenses based on plaintiff's conduct and knowledge

The relationship between defect and defenses based on the plaintiff's conduct and knowledge reflects the reciprocity between the design and appearance of products and their use in a context conditioned by the consumer's information. Illustrative is a case involving a hockey helmet that was designed in three sections, in which the puck penetrated the helmet in a gap where the three sections joined. Citing the obviousness of the gaps in the helmet,

29. Bowman v. General Motors Corp., 427 F.Supp. 234, 242–44 (E.D.Pa. 1977).

30. Turner v. American Motors Gen'l Corp., 392 A.2d 1005 (D.C.1978).

31. Couch v. Mine Safety Appliances Co., 728 P.2d 585, 589 (Wash. 1986) (court's emphasis of statutory language).

the trial court gave judgment n.o.v. for the defendant on negligence counts on the grounds that the plaintiff had "assumed the risk of his injury."[32]

Overturning this judgment, the appellate court said that "it was the function of the jury to balance the obviousness of the helmet design against the plaintiff's testimony and the circumstances in which he received the helmet in order to arrive at a conclusion as to what the plaintiff knew at the time of the injury."[33] The effect of this decision is to limit the effectiveness of a combination of potential defense arguments—not only that the plaintiff assumed the risk, but that the design of the product was not negligent, and, additionally, that there was no duty to warn.

Another case illustrates how the linkage of defect and defenses may lead to a different conclusion. This case involved the design of a bar countertop, on which the plaintiff bartender bumped her head as she walked under it, a route she had taken "thousands of times." A majority of the court concluded that there was no defect because there was no disappointment of consumer expectations.[34] A concurring judge opined that the countertop "was in a 'defective condition' when it left the designer's drawing board," because users had to "assum[e] [an] unnatural stooping posture" to get to their work stations. Moreover, he pointed out that state law did not allow an "open and obvious" defense, and also said that because the plaintiff could not be said to have "*unreasonably* use[d] the bar," she had not technically assumed the risk. Despite these interpretations of doctrine favoring the plaintiff, the concurring judge viewed the plaintiff's awareness of the danger as an element of the ultimate conclusion that the countertop was not unreasonably dangerous: "[a]lthough the product may be considered somewhat dangerous in view of a particular defect, that defect may not be *unreasonably* dangerous if the user has full awareness of the defect and the likelihood of injury."[35]

The concepts of defect and misuse are also reciprocal. A finding of defect necessarily will deny the defense of misuse, whereas a holding that there was misuse often is equivalent to a finding of no defect. Illustrative of this relationship is a case in which the plaintiff sued an automobile lessor for injuries caused by a brake failure. The defendant claimed that the plaintiff had caused the failure because she drove with the emergency brake on, causing

---

32. Everett v. Bucky Warren, Inc., 380 N.E.2d 653 (Mass.1978).

33. Id. at 659 (separately upholding trial court judgment for plaintiff on strict liability, without reaching question of whether assumption of risk was defense under that theory).

34. Hamilton v. Roger Sherman Architects Group, Inc., 565 N.E.2d 1136, 1139 (Ind.Ct.App.1991).

35. Id. at 1140–41 (Sullivan, J., concurring).

heat to build up abnormally in the braking system. In upholding a plaintiff's verdict on the ground that the braking system was unreasonably dangerous, the court rejected a misuse defense. It said that even if the plaintiff had driven with the emergency brake partly on, the feasibility of providing a warning lamp at low cost showed that "such a 'use' was objectively foreseeable by the defendant."[36]

B.   Defect and failure to warn

Yet another instance of reciprocity exists between defect and failure to warn, where the essence of a finding of no duty to warn may be a conclusion that a product was not defective. Illustrative is a case involving an exercise device that was simply an elastic rubber rope, which snapped back and hit the plaintiff in the eye. Rejecting the plaintiff's suit, a majority of the D.C. Circuit observed that "every adult knows" that when an elastic band is stretched and slips, it will snap back. Arguably, the court's holding that there "was no duty to ... warn of that simple fact"[37] was at base a finding of no defect.

The other side of the idea that no failure to warn equals no defect appears in decisions that closely meld actionable failure to warn with the concept of defect. The New Hampshire Supreme Court did this in a case in which a car "went out of control." The plaintiff contended that the manufacturer of the vehicle should have warned about its handling characteristics and the court found it error to refuse a jury instruction on "failure to warn," although the jury had answered a special issue that the vehicle's design was not unreasonably dangerous. The court pointed out that because of the refusal of the instruction on failure to warn, the jury had not been able to consider "whether warnings were necessary and whether the absence of warnings may have made the car defective and unreasonably dangerous." The court premised that "[i]f the design of a product makes a warning necessary to avoid an unreasonable risk of harm from a foreseeable use, the lack of warning or an ineffective warning causes the product to be defective and unreasonably dangerous."[38]

The Restatement of Products Liability has defined a separate category for products "defective because of inadequate instructions or warnings when the foreseeable risks of harm posed by the product could have been reduced or avoided by the provision of reasonable instructions or warnings ... and the omission of the instructions or warnings renders the product not reasonably

---

36. Knapp v. Hertz Corp., 375 N.E.2d 1349, 1354–55 (Ill.Ct.App.1978).

37. Jamieson v. Woodward & Lothrop, 247 F.2d 23, 28 (D.C.Cir.1957).

38. Chellman v. Saab–Scania AB, 637 A.2d 148, 150–51 (N.H.1993).

safe."[39] Rather than aligning failure to warn with the "unreasonably dangerous" language of section 402A, the Products Restatement explicitly associated this category with a "reasonableness test."[40]

Whether those who equate the lack of a warning to a defect do so under a negligence theory or one of strict liability, the writer notes his skepticism of the concept of a "defect" based on lack of warning. Though the notion has attracted some courts, it seems useful to keep separate the concept of defect from the idea that adequate warnings did not accompany a product. The concept of defect would seem to connote physical or chemical properties inherent in a product, whereas warnings claims involve the informational structure that accompanies the product to market. If that informational structure misleads the consumer about the properties of the product, seller liability should be based on the inadequacy of the informational structure. To call a lack of warning a defect is to confuse the information that surrounds a product with its physical and chemical properties.

Whatever one's preferences about terminology, it may be helpful to underline both a distinction and an overlap. First, the recognition of a separate category for warnings cases is in line with the fact that, in the main, courts treat warnings issues separately from design defect questions. The second point, however, is that the issues of design defect and warnings often closely overlap because of the theme of information that runs through the defect concept as well as the law on warnings.

It is well to emphasize that several concepts and terms come together when the issue in a products case concerns pertinent information about hazards. In cases presenting that question, a court might draw on such diverse ideas as defect, duty to warn, obviousness of danger, and assumption of risk. The most apt choice of concept and terminology will determine the success of advocates and the persuasiveness of judicial decisions.

[Chapters 40–41 are reserved for supplementary material.]

---

39. Products Restatement, supra note 9, § 2(c).

40. See id., § 2, comment i.

Section Seven

THE BOUNDARIES OF FAULT

Chapter Forty–Two

PRIVATE NECESSITY

Analysis

¶ 42.01   The Problem Defined

Special problems for tort doctrine appear in fact situations where the defendant acts by choice in the protection of his own interests, but not negligently, and his conduct harms an innocent plaintiff. A particularly interesting group of cases of this kind sometimes are labeled cases of "necessity." The defendant knows that his choice—often made under the pressure of events, but sometimes with opportunity to deliberate—both defends his interests and creates a high degree of risk to the plaintiff. An important part of the legal conundrum is that the defendant's choice is a reasonable one under the circumstances.

¶ 42.02   A Classic Case: *Vincent v. Lake Erie Transportation Company*

A.   *The case*

The 1910 decision of the Minnesota Supreme Court in *Vincent v. Lake Erie Transportation Co.*[1] is a classic in this category of cases. The defendant in *Vincent* owned a steamship that was moored to the plaintiff's dock to unload cargo. While that task proceeded, an exceptionally violent storm arose, one so extraordinary that navigation in the area stopped for more than 24 hours. As the storm raged, and the cables that bound the ship to the dock parted, the master of the ship continued to replace the cables in order to keep the vessel moored to the dock. The result was that the force of the storm caused the ship to hammer the dock for many hours, damaging the dock, but saving the ship from possible destruction by wind and water.

A majority of the Minnesota court affirmed an award for the dock owner, although it made it clear that the ship's master had not acted negligently. Indeed, it is crucial to the doctrinal problem the case poses that the master acted prudently. Although he might have pursued other alternatives—for example, trying to haul the vessel onto a ramp—the court applied the standard of care for emergencies and found that in that setting, the master had "exercised good judgment and prudent seamanship."[2]

B. Tort doctrine

Confronted with a problem of justice—an injury inflicted by conduct that was deliberate but not negligent, the *Vincent* court in effect created a doctrine of private necessity. In analyzing that legal feat, it is useful to ask how the court might have tried to rationalize the outcome for the plaintiff in terms of traditional tort doctrines other than negligence.

Since the majority held the defendant liable for conduct that was not below the relevant standard of care, one might try to characterize its theory as one of strict liability. However, there was no basis in the facts for applying strict liability doctrine, which at the time of *Vincent* was limited to the theory embodied in *Rylands v. Fletcher*.[3] Today that form of liability is principally classified as "strict liability" for "abnormally dangerous activities," a designation that would hardly apply to the facts of *Vincent*.

Another possible characterization of the case would be as a species of intentional tort, analogizing the defendant's conduct to a trespass to real property. But even if one could characterize the actions of the ship's master as a trespass, a principal difficulty for the dock owner in utilizing such a theory would be the defense of privilege. Since the defendant was saving its vessel from a storm of exceptional violence, arguably it had a privilege to continue tying

---

1. 124 N.W. 221 (Minn.1910).   **3.** See supra, ¶ 35.02.

2. Id. at 221.

onto the dock in order to preserve its property so long as it did not endanger lives.

A further alternative would be to analogize the case to conversion, the intentional tort to personal property that requires a deliberate appropriation by the defendant of the plaintiff's property for the defendant's use. The theory would be analogical only, because the dock presumably was real property. In any event, since the defendant's conduct did not ruin the dock entirely, the element of the conversion tort that requires a complete appropriation of the property or of its value would presumably defeat a claim based on such a theory. A weak cousin of conversion, the less demanding tort of trespass to chattels, might also serve as an analogy. However, the damage to the dock was substantial enough to make that analogy a pallid one, since trespass to chattels usually applies to relatively trivial interferences with property.

One other way to view the case would be as one of "an inevitable accident,"[4] a concept used by the dissenter in *Vincent* in opposing liability. The majority, however, insisted that the case was not one of "unavoidable accident," nor one resulting from an "act of God."[5]

Two interesting decisions appeared prominently in the body of then recent case law to which the *Vincent* court referred. In these cases, each of which presented a reverse image of *Vincent*, courts awarded damages to people whom the defendants had turned away from their premises in circumstances where the plaintiffs could not shift for themselves. *Depue v. Flateau*[6] imposed liability on the owners of a home who, when a business visitor became ill after staying for dinner, refused him permission to stay over on a Minnesota night in January. In *Depue*, which it decided just three years before *Vincent*, the Minnesota court made clear that the visitor "was not a trespasser." Yet, the majority in *Vincent* posed a hypothetical question based on *Depue*: whether, if the defendant homeowner "had furnished the traveler with proper accommodations and medical attendance," the guest could have "defeat[ed] an action brought against him for their reasonable worth?"[7]

In the Vermont case of *Ploof v. Putnam*,[8] the court affirmed the overruling of a demurrer when the defendant dock owner unmoored the plaintiff's sloop after the plaintiff had tied onto the dock in a storm. The result of the vessel being cast loose was that it was driven onto the shore, causing its destruction as well as injuries to the plaintiff and his family. The *Vincent* court's characterization of *Ploof* demonstrated the difficulty that a claimant like

---

4. Id. at 222 (Lewis, J., dissenting).
5. Id. at 222 (majority opinion).
6. 111 N.W. 1, 3 (Minn.1907).

7. 124 N.W. at 222.
8. 71 A. 188 (Vt.1908).

the *Vincent* plaintiff would face in employing an intentional tort-type theory, for the *Vincent* court stressed that the *Ploof* plaintiff "was not guilty of trespass."[9]

Vincent thus presented a situation of high-risk conduct that could not be characterized as negligent and could not be labeled an intentional tort. Even in the face of those legal hurdles, however, the court held that the dock owner should get compensation from the shipowner. It did not cast this result in terms of defined doctrine, but it used a vivid analogy. It observed "that a starving man may, without moral guilt, take what is necessary to sustain life," but it stressed that one could hardly say "that the obligation would not be upon such person to pay the value of the property so taken when he became able to do so." The court further noted that "public necessity . . . may require the taking of private property for public purposes" but only if the taker makes compensation. Using these analogies to rationalize a plaintiff's judgment, essentially on the basis of private necessity, the court concluded that "where the defendant prudently and advisedly availed itself of the plaintiffs' property for the purpose of preserving its own more valuable property," the defendant must pay compensation.[10]

¶ 42.03 Explanations and Rationales

A. *Economic consequences*

It is clear that if one views tort law through a deterrence lens, imposing liability on the defendant in *Vincent* would not affect its incentives in a way that would change its conduct. In fact, the shipowner in *Vincent* acted in a cost-effective way. Because the damage to the dock was significantly less than the cost of losing the ship, it chose the path of least cost avoidance. Thus, to make the shipowner in *Vincent* liable would not achieve a deterrent effect, for even if a court held for the plaintiff—as the Minnesota court did—the defendant presumably would not act differently if the same situation occurred again.[11] A useful perspective is that of a vertically integrated enterprise which owned both the ship and the dock. Such a firm would undoubtedly have chosen to do what the ship's master did, which was to injure the dock, incurring the costs of repairing it, in order to save the ship.[12] It simply would have had to absorb the cost to the dock of its undoubtedly rational choice.

---

9. 124 N.W. at 222.

10. Vincent, 124 N.W. at 222.

11. See, e.g., Richard Epstein, A Theory of Strict Liability, 2 J. Legal Studies 151, 188 (1973) (commenting, with respect to another precedent, that "it will be cheaper for the defendant to pay the damages than to take the precautions, so the precautions will not be taken").

12. See id. at 158.

B.　Fairness

Some persuasive rationales for liability in *Vincent* are based on notions of fairness. One commentator, George Fletcher, suggested that a good explanation for *Vincent*-type cases focuses on the creation of a "nonreciprocal risk," one in which "the defendant creates a disproportionate, excessive risk of harm, relative to the victim's risk-creating activity."[13] An alternative way to view the decision is as one requiring compensation for "unjust enrichment." However, noting the overly broad expansion of that doctrine that its application in *Vincent* might permit,[14] Robert Keeton suggested that a persuasive rationalization for liability depends on a reading of the moral sense of the community. Developing that theme, Keeton wrote that the case was one of "conditional privilege," under which one could "use the property of another in circumstances of private necessity" if one "compensate[d] for any harm done."[15] By contrast, Professor Christie has argued that *Vincent* "is not an instance of the exercise of a privilege at all." Rather, he says, "[i]t is simply a case of intentionally damaging the property of another in the civil sense of 'intention,' that is, of engaging in conduct that one knows, with substantial certainty, will lead to that result." This, he says, would be "[a]t the very least, ... negligent or reckless behavior" and he concludes that it is not at all surprising that the defendant must pay compensation.[16]

C.　General private law doctrine

The three broad storehouses of private law—torts, property, and contracts—provide different angles of potentially useful analysis on the subject of private necessity. We have reviewed various tort theories that plaintiffs might use to justify liability in a *Vincent*-type case. If one examines the problem from the point of view of property law, a threshold question is to whom to assign the dominant property right concerning use of the dock. If it is the dock owner, he presumably should be able to get compensation. If the shipowner has the dominant right, it should not have to pay for the damage, a result bolstered by the fact that the ship is worth more than the dock.

One also might view the case through the lens of a property analogy that the majority employed. This analogy was one in which the defendant "appropriated a valuable cable lying upon the dock"

---

13. George Fletcher, Fairness and Utility in Tort Theory, 85 Harv. L. Rev. 537, 542 (1972), further summarized supra, ¶ 35.05, text accompanying notes 28–32.

14. See Robert Keeton, Conditional Fault in the Law of Torts, 72 Harv. L. Rev. 401, 410–18 (1959).

15. Id. at 428–29.

16. George Christie, The Defense of Necessity Considered from the Legal and Moral Points of View, 48 Duke L.J. 975, 1002–03 (1999).

in order to secure its vessel,[17] a taking of property for which no one would claim the ship would not have to pay.

Finally, one might analyze the issue from the point of view of contract, which basically was the perspective of the dissenting judge in *Vincent*. Emphasizing that the defendant was "lawfully in position" at the dock, he argued that "one who constructs a dock to the navigable line of waters and enters into contractual relations with the owner of a vessel to moor at the same, takes the risk of damage to his dock by a boat caught there by a storm" if the damage "could not have been avoided in the exercise of due care."[18]

¶ 42.04   Implications for Policy and Doctrine

A. *Corrective justice and instrumental effects*

Is *Vincent* primarily an instance of party-centered corrective justice, or does it have broader, instrumental implications, for example, concerning effects on future behavior? It should be emphasized that from one point of view, the decision represents only a determination of wealth distribution between the parties, a decision about what is fair. However, if the holding in *Vincent* had gone for the defendant shipowner, it might have had a significant effect on primary conduct, with dock owners demanding that shipowners promise in advance to pay for damages arising in such situations, or raising their rates to offset those sorts of costs.

B. *Cutting across doctrines*

Commentators have viewed *Vincent* as a stimulant to synthesis of a wide variety of cases in which courts impose liability without negligence. One scholar saw the decision as paralleling strict liability for products and *Rylands*-type liability for certain kinds of activity-caused accidents.[19] Under another theory previously mentioned, the appropriate classification is one that emphasizes the creation of nonreciprocal risk. Embracing a range of cases traditionally categorized under negligence, intentional tort, and strict liability categories, this theory rationalizes liability on fairness grounds "for injuries caused by a risk greater in degree and different in order from those created by the victim and imposed on the defendant."[20] This analysis also lines up *Vincent* with *Rylands*-type cases.[21]

For another commentator, *Vincent* is an example of an appropriate application of "strict liability," one that "reduce[s] the

---

17. 124 N.W. at 222 (majority opinion).

18. Id. (Lewis, J., dissenting).

19. See Keeton, supra note 14.

20. See Fletcher, supra note 13, at 542–44.

21. See id.

administrative costs of decision" by relieving the court of the necessity to use cost-benefit analysis, leaving that analysis "in private hands where it belongs."[22] The present author has viewed the decision as creating a noncategory tort, grounded in social mores, which requires compensation from a party that used its temporal power to protect its interests, with substantial certainty of injury to another, in a situation about which the parties had not engaged in prior bargaining.[23]

C. Broad issues of loss distribution

Beyond these efforts to make sense of tort doctrine are broader policy questions about when it is appropriate to impose liability without a showing of fault. It may be useful here to refer to two types of legislative no-fault solutions to significant social problems of injuries caused by activities. One of these, worker's compensation, is a universally adopted, comprehensive system that eliminates fault from the compensation inquiry. The other is no-fault legislation in the area of vehicle accidents, enacted in many states, which at least partially eliminates the tort liability action for injuries caused by vehicles, and substitutes insurance payments principally from the insurer of the person injured rather than the insurer of the injuring party.

Both of these systems of compensation emphasize fairness as a basis for distributing losses from injury. To be sure, legislative no-fault compensation schemes aim to reduce administrative costs and hope to achieve efficient levels of accidents as at least a desired byproduct. At their core, however, these approaches to non-fault allocation of accident risks embody community judgments about the morally preferable distribution of losses resulting from injuries. Those policy judgments tie together these large-scale statutory schemes with the singular tort created in *Vincent v. Lake Erie Transportation Co.*

22. Epstein, supra note 11, at 188.

23. See Marshall Shapo, A Social Contract Tort, 75 Tex. L. Rev. 1835 (1997).

*

Part Three

PROBLEMS IN CAUSATION AND LIMITATION OF LIABILITY

Section Eight

PROOF AND CAUSATION

Chapter Forty–Three

PROOF: AN OVERVIEW

Analysis

¶ 43.01 Introduction: Facts and Truth; Law and Policy

The issues that courts generally classify under the heading of "proof" are complex and their labeling may sometimes deceive. This chapter and those immediately following[1] seek to penetrate the labels and to simplify analysis. It is well to point out that although the terminology of "evidence" and "proof" may seem to connote only a "scientific" search for "facts" and the "truth," issues under those headings often require analysis of policy considerations.

An examination of problems of proof in tort law also involves an often-mentioned distinction, that between the roles of judge and jury. It is accepted among lawyers, in a very general sense, that juries find the facts and courts apply the law. However, that distinction sometimes becomes blurred. Courts not only reserve the power to make some screening judgments about the facts, they may sometimes turn over to juries mixed questions of fact and law. Of course, in a trial without a jury, the judge is the fact finder as well as the exclusive arbiter of the law.

¶ 43.02 Sufficiency of the Evidence

The plaintiff in an injury case has the burden of proof, that is, the plaintiff must establish, among other things, that it was more

---

1. See infra, Chapters 44–45, 48–49.

probable than not that the defendant was negligent, or made a defective product, and that the culpability or defect caused the plaintiff's injury. The focus in this chapter is on proof of negligence, but the analysis may be applied by analogy to proof of product defects.

A. Negligence

In order to prove negligence, the plaintiff must present evidence from which a fact-finder may reasonably infer that the defendant fell below the proper standard of care in the activity at issue. To sustain this burden, the plaintiff may present evidence of behavior as a violation of industry standards, of a statutory violation, or of conduct from which ordinary persons could infer on the basis of their own experience that the defendant did not act prudently.

A simple case involving an athletic conditioning exercise illustrates the kind of facts on which a court may allow a jury to find negligence in an everyday situation. A girl sued her school for injuries that occurred when she fell during the exercise, which required her to keep stepping on and off a bench. There was evidence from which a jury could have found that the bench had been placed on uneven ground. The plaintiff had been rowing for one to two-and-one-half hours before she participated in this exercise, her coach did not see her fall, and there were no "spotters" for the exercise. The plaintiff simply testified that she "fell off the bench." Given this evidence, the trial court directed a verdict for the school, but the appellate court reversed. The appellate court concluded that the jury could have found negligence in the positioning of the bench for young, fatigued athletes, or negligence in the supervision of the exercise.[2]

The step exercise case provides just one example of the kinds of mixed questions of fact and law that courts will sometimes give to juries. In such cases, the jury must abstract certain features of a situation as "facts" at the same time that it must make a judgment about the propriety of conduct. While it informally measures the level of danger posed by the positioning of the bench and the way the exercise was conducted, the jury also assesses the occurrence

---

2. Hornyak v. Pomfret School, 783 F.2d 284, 284–85 (1st Cir.1986). Cf. Ortega v. Kmart Corp., 36 P.3d 11 (Cal. 2001), in which the plaintiff slipped on a puddle of milk in a pantry aisle next to a refrigerator. A former manager of the defendant testified that employees usually walked that aisle every 15 to 30 minutes and that employees were trained to clean up spills, but admitted that "the milk could have been on the floor for as long as two hours." Affirming a plaintiff's judgment, the court concluded that the jury could have inferred from the circumstantial evidence that the defendant had "constructive notice" of the hazard for a long enough period that the condition "would have been discovered and remedied ... in the exercise of reasonable care." Id. at 18–19.

from a social perspective. It in effect creates a very precise rule concerning the reasonableness of the behavior at issue. This rule may be a rather complicated sentence, for example, "the placement of a bench on uneven ground for a step exercise, and the failure to have 'spotters' or persons to support fatigued athletes who fall during the exercise [a descriptive measurement to this point], is substandard conduct in the circumstances [the legal rule]." When courts permit a jury to give a verdict in situations of this kind, they are making certain positive assumptions concerning the possibilities of human knowledge about both the actual events and sequences of occurrences in an episode, as well as permitting laymen to make a judgment about the standards of behavior that one can expect of reasonable persons.

More complex cases involving sufficiency of evidence arise in a great variety of technological contexts. Illustrative is a decision concerning a claim that there were defects in the suspension system on a truck that was involved in an accident which killed its owner and a co-driver. The plaintiff, the widow of the owner, presented evidence that the defendant manufacturer had received more than fifty warranty claims for the failure of that type suspension system over a two-year period, as well as testimony from "several local truckers who had experienced spring failure." Other evidence included the truck's relatively short period of use by industry standards; with 190,000 miles on the road, it was "considered practically new." Moreover, the plaintiff gave evidence that her husband had been a trucker for many years and "carefully maintained his equipment." The jury found for the plaintiff on a negligence count. On appeal, the defendant contended that there was insufficient evidence of a design defect in the truck, or that the defect caused the accident. The appellate court affirmed the verdict for the plaintiff, concluding that the evidence was sufficient to support jury findings of defect and causation.[3]

This decision demonstrates how, in a relatively complicated situation, factual findings concerning the occurrence of several events may become fused with an inference that the defendant's conduct was substandard. Moreover, because of the several different proofs introduced by the plaintiff, the case implies how delicate the balance may be on a question of sufficiency of the evidence. To subtract any one or two pieces of evidence from the plaintiff's case—for example, the prior warranty claims or the relatively short period of use by industry standards—would reduce the chance that the court would conclude there was enough evidence to support a finding of negligence.

3. Farner v. Paccar, Inc., 562 F.2d 518, 523–24 (8th Cir.1977).

The rules concerning sufficiency of the evidence in negligence cases thus intersect with the substantive law of negligence in various ways. At one level, those rules provide a method to assess the competing arguments of parties about the legal effect of past events described by the evidence. But those rules perform other functions that are important to the system of conducting trials. They enable judges to define boundaries between themselves and jurors with respect to the application of "rules of law" and the determination of "questions of fact," with an understanding that there are some zones around those boundaries where both judges and juries may participate in decisionmaking.

B. Causation

In addition to illustrating sufficiency of evidence on the negligence issue, the step exercise case[4] demonstrates how a simple piece of circumstantial evidence that supports an inference of negligence may also support a jury finding of causation. It also shows that plaintiffs in cases based on circumstantial evidence must try to eliminate explanations for an accident that are alternative to the ones they advance. Although there was "no direct evidence of the cause of plaintiff's fall," the court noted that there was no proof of causative factors other than the placement of the bench, "such as ice, snow, wind, or dizziness on the part of the plaintiff." In this context, the court thought, "it would not be unreasonable" for jurors to infer that the unstable condition of the bench caused the fall.[5]

Even beyond demonstrating how evidence tending to show negligence also may be used to show causation, the step exercise case exhibits the practical overlap between determinations of negligence and causation. Formally, the law seeks to separate these questions, requiring the plaintiff to show more than a 50 per cent probability of both negligence (or product defect) and causation, rather than allowing a high probability of one to suffice even if there was less than a 50 per cent probability of the other. However, many juries probably tend to meld the issues in some fashion. A pragmatic explanation for this tendency is that a finding that a defendant has violated a standard of care often necessarily implies a view of the high potential of that conduct for causing an accident.

¶ 43.03 Judge and Jury; Proof Rules and Policy

The traditional classification of trial functions, which allocates questions of "law" to the judge and issues of "fact" to the jury,

4. See supra, text accompanying note 2.

5. Hornyak, supra note 2, 783 F.2d at 285.

For further discussion of the need for plaintiffs to negate alternative hypotheses, see infra, ¶ ¶ 44.03, 45.01(C).

initially awards to the judge the decision of whether there is a sufficient factual question for jury determination. In making that determination about whether there is a triable issue, courts are making a judgment of legal policy. For example, when a court directs a verdict in a tort case, it is saying that as a matter of judicial administration, it would be inefficient to allow the case to go to a "fact"-finder because the chances are unacceptably slim, if not nonexistent, that the fact finder could find probable negligence and probable causation. The proof rules thereby enable judges to exercise some control over their workloads, and make it possible to avoid the expense of trials by cutting off claims that very probably would not succeed.

The court may also be enforcing a rule of justice based on a conclusion—often implicit—that it would violate due process to let a jury find negligence. The court might believe that any finding of negligence in the case would be arbitrary—a decision based on whim and on no more than a roll of the dice—or, just as bad in terms of outcome, an inaccurate reading of the numbers on the dice. When courts decide defendants' directed verdict motions, which typically present the appellate tort issues on this subject, they will seek to avoid arbitrary judgments by requiring that the nonmoving party, the plaintiff, present a plausible reason for his assertions of negligence and causation in order to advance to the jury.

Decisions on sufficiency of the evidence also require consideration of the underlying rationales and goals of substantive tort law, including compensation and deterrence. Courts confronted with close evidentiary questions may give plaintiffs relatively broad leeway to prove a case in order to further the compensatory purposes of tort law. A special case of this sort of judicial approach appears in the liberal evidentiary standards that courts apply to the Federal Employers Liability Act (FELA), which governs claims for negligence by railroad workers. That legislation exhibited a definite plaintiffs' tilt, for example eliminating the defense of assumption of risk and substituting a comparative fault standard for the rule that contributory negligence was a complete defense.

The judicial history of the last half century has increased that tilt. In a controversial series of decisions, the Supreme Court set as the test of when to send a case to jury "whether the proofs justify with reason the conclusion that employer negligence played any part, even the slightest, in producing the injury or death for which damages are sought."[6] The Court noted the argument that it would have been preferable to achieve the social goals sought by Congress with legislation like workers' compensation, which does not require

---

6. Rogers v. Missouri Pac. R.R., 352 U.S. 500, 509 (1957).

claimants to show fault. However, the Court said that given the policies underlying the FELA, it had an obligation to prevent the "erosion" of that statute "by narrow and niggardly construction."[7]

With respect to the deterrence rationale, if one views the principal purpose of negligence law as setting a permissible level of risky conduct, that perspective will affect the character of proof rules. For example, in the case of the school athlete summarized above,[8] a court might semi-consciously reason this way: There were several factors in the case that indicated that the school's coach was behaving below the standard that reasonable persons would think were appropriate in those circumstances. A jury finding that the standard had been breached would imply, among other things, a rough quantitative definition of a degree of instability that is unacceptable in positioning a bench for a step exercise.

To allow a jury to find negligence in the case, at least by defining what is unacceptable, would provide a signal that would influence conduct toward a safer level of bench stability. It might also more generally encourage the adoption of safety measures in school sports exercises. Thus, in deciding whether there were factual questions for the jury concerning both negligence and causation, the court would be making a particularized judgment about the substantive negligence standards that govern supervision of school athletes by coaches.

The law of products liability provides some good examples of substantive judgments embedded in proof rules. When a court finds that the presence of an insect in a soda bottle implies negligence on the part of a bottler, or that a fire that occurs in a new vehicle provides proof that the vehicle was defective, the court is at least implicitly making a judgment about the way that products ought to perform. Sometimes, indeed, that judgment is explicit. The Nebraska Supreme Court summarized both facts and law concisely in a way that makes the point: "[A] haystacking machine which will only stack hay for half a day before consuming itself in flames is not suitable for the ordinary purposes for which haystacking machines are sold."[9]

In sum, the proof rules help to define the ambit of the substantive law by providing relatively liberal or restrictive gateways to enforcement of liability rules. Thus, at the same time that they help courts to review "facts," the proof rules also shape "the law."

---

7. Id. at 509.

8. See Hornyak v. Pomfret School, discussed supra, ¶ 43.02, text accompanying notes 2, 4–5.

9. Nerud v. Haybuster Mfg., Inc., 340 N.W.2d 369, 376 (Neb.1983).

Chapter Forty–Four

CIRCUMSTANTIAL EVIDENCE GENERALLY

Analysis

A principal dichotomy in the law of evidence is between direct evidence—typically involving eyewitness testimony—and circumstantial evidence, which requires the fact finder to draw inferences from facts adduced by the parties. It is not unusual to have conflicts in eyewitness testimony, which will frequently present jury questions. The knottier legal issues, however, typically will arise with respect to circumstantial evidence.

¶ 44.01   Proving Probabilities

Like any plaintiff in negligence litigation, a claimant seeking to establish a circumstantial case must convince the court that it is more likely than not that the defendant was at fault and that the defendant's negligence caused the plaintiff's harm. We discussed above the practical overlap between proof of negligence and proof of causation.[1] The key to the plaintiff's case is the establishment of probabilities—both that the defendant was negligent and that the negligence is the most probable explanation for the injury. A plaintiff's reliance on circumstantial evidence adds a step to the reasoning process that the jury brings to bear on direct evidence. The jury must make inferences from the circumstances alone, rather than being able to rely on the reported sensory perceptions of witnesses.

¶ 44.02   Experts

In situations involving everyday kinds of accidents, the plaintiff may be able to appeal to the fact finder's ordinary sense of

---

1. See ¶ 43.02(B) supra.

probabilities. However, in cases involving relatively technical questions about the meaning of reported facts, plaintiffs often must combine expert testimony with their circumstantial evidence. For example, in a case in which a truck bed fell during normal use, the plaintiff established a prima facie case of a design defect by combining that circumstantial fact with expert testimony that the bed fell because the hoisting pins were not strong enough. The expert did not make a metallurgical analysis of the pins, but he did consult reports on the plaintiff's accident as well as reports on two prior accidents involving similar trucks whose beds had collapsed.[2]

In some cases, courts will accept the testimony of experts based on personal observations. An example is a case in which a farmer attributed illness in his cows to the defendant's feed. He offered evidence that the feed was discolored and had "an off-odor and an off-taste," and proof that the cattle "appeared gaunt, acted nervous and refused to eat" after they had eaten the feed for two or three days. The plaintiff's veterinarian opined, on the basis of his examination and treatment of the animals, that the feed had caused a decrease in milk production as well as in the percentage of conceptions in the herd. The court found "substantial evidence" of "a causal connection between defendant's feed and plaintiff's loss."[3]

¶ 44.03 Alternative Hypotheses

It is often necessary for the plaintiff to negate explanations—"alternative hypotheses"—for an accident other than the one he offers. One may consider, for example, cases in which the plaintiff's decedent is found drowned, whether in the sea[4] or in a creek.[5] In one such case, an engineer on an oil tanker that was docked was found floating in the sea, having left his wrist watch and wallet on the ship. His widow, who sued the shipowner and others for negligence, testified that her husband usually wore his watch at work. There was general testimony about unsafe conditions on the pier and on the crane barge to which the ship was moored. The district court rejected the case on the basis that only "speculation and conjecture" would support the plaintiff's claim that negligence on the part of the shipowner caused the decedent to fall into the water.[6] The court of appeals affirmed, concluding that there was no evidence of causation.[7]

2. Martin v. Unit Rig & Equip. Co., 715 F.2d 1434 (10th Cir.1983).

3. Kircher v. Purina Mills, Inc., 775 S.W.2d 115 (Mo.1989).

4. See Quam v. Mobil Oil Corp., 496 F.Supp. 986 (S.D.N.Y.1978), aff'd, 599 F.2d 42 (2d Cir.1979), cert. denied, 444 U.S. 950 (1979).

5. See Baker v. City of Festus, 418 S.W.2d 957 (Mo.1967), discussed infra, text accompanying note 8.

6. Quam, supra note 4, 496 F. Supp. at 989.

7. 599 F.2d at 43.

If such a case could go to a jury at all, it probably would be on the basis of the jury's ability to explain the event on the basis of its own experience and knowledge. But it is here that alternative hypotheses become pertinent. One might adduce, as possible competing explanations for the engineer's death, the hypotheses of contributory negligence and suicide, as well as the possibility of foul play. Given the lack of experience with how events of that kind occur in such particular circumstances—on the part of jurors, and presumably of anyone—it would be difficult to negate those hypotheses enough to conclude that the defendant's negligence probably caused the engineer's death.

A Missouri case[8] teaches a similar lesson. The plaintiff's decedent walked on a family errand on a route that took her on a bridge over a creek. A sidewalk ran along the bridge over the creek, paralleled by a bannister that ended at the end of the bridge. There was a gap between the end of the bannister and a fence that then ran adjacent to the sidewalk. The decedent was found floating face down in the creek. Except for a single undefined mark on the embankment that sloped down to the creek, there was no indication that she had fallen through the gap and rolled down to her death.

The plaintiff attributed his wife's death to the negligence of the city in maintaining an unsafe condition in the vicinity of the bridge. Saying that for the jury to accept that theory would require "guesswork, speculation and conjecture," the court denied recovery. Even conceding negligence for the sake of argument, the court was unable to discern a case on causation. Notably, the court mentioned that the decedent had been subject to epileptic seizures, suggesting as one explanation of her death that she might have fallen over the bannister during such an episode.[9]

Terms like "speculation and conjecture" make up a standard formula in decisions denying recovery in circumstantial cases. What this language means, in practical terms, is that the plaintiff has not provided a reason to hold in his favor. A decision based on conjecture, from the point of view of the judicial process, is one that is no better than throwing dice.

8. Baker v. City of Festus, supra note 5.

9. 418 S.W.2d at 958–59. Cf. Fedorczyk v. Caribbean Cruise Lines, Ltd., 82 F.3d 69 (3d Cir.1996), in which the plaintiff suffered injuries from a slip in a bathtub on a cruise ship. There were several abrasive strips in the tub, but the plaintiff did not recall whether her feet were on the strips when she fell. Her expert opined that "if there had been more stripping, it would be more likely than not" that the plaintiff "would not have fallen," but he also said that a person could "fall in a bathtub under ordinary circumstances" and that bath oil and soap were " 'great variables' that could have caused the fall." The court concluded that without evidence on whether the plaintiff was standing on or off the strips when she fell, the jury would be "left to speculate" whether the cruise line's failure to have more stripping in the tub "was the cause in fact of her injury." Id. at 75.

¶ 44.04   Circumstantial Proof and Tort Rationales

The general rules of circumstantial evidence exhibit an important linkage of standards for proof of negligence with the rationales for tort law. For example, proof rules tie in with the goals of achieving fairness in injury disputes and of providing realistic signals for controlling behavior. To take two abstract hypotheticals, the proof rules teach us that it would be insufficient grounds to impose tort liability on A for B's injury only because A was B's employer at the time he died, or on X for no more reason than the fact that X's machine was in the vicinity of Y at the time of an injury.

A case described above,[10] in which a woman's body was found floating in a creek, specifically illustrates the connection between evidentiary rules and tort rationales. The court's denial of recovery suggests a judgment that it would be unfair, in the name of compensation, to conclude that only because of the proximity of an accident victim to a defendant's property or activities, negligence probably occurred and that negligence probably caused the injury. Because there is no probable connection between the defendant's conduct and the accident, it would be arbitrary to construct such a connection.

Another lesson of the case relates to the behavior-influencing aspect of tort law. If there was no evidence that the fall of the plaintiff's decedent was attributable to the defendant's construction or maintenance of its bridge and sidewalk, then any safety measure the defendant might take in response to a liability judgment would not save lives lost in the way that the decedent lost hers. The proof rules thus embody a deterrence-based logic as well as a fairness-based view of compensation, demanding a reason that links conduct to an injury, even if the conduct is arguably substandard in the abstract.

---

10.   See supra, ¶ 44.03, text accompanying notes 8–9.

Chapter Forty–Five

RES IPSA LOQUITUR

Analysis

A specialized form of circumstantial evidence takes the name res ipsa loquitur, literally, "the thing speaks for itself." As is the case with circumstantial evidence generally, the fact finder in res ipsa cases can only draw secondary inferences about probabilities because the plaintiff has presented no direct evidence about the event. The res ipsa doctrine imposes some particular requirements on the drawing of inferences about negligence and causation in circumstances of unexplained, often mysterious occurrences.

¶ 45.01　The Substantive Rule

The contents of the res ipsa doctrine differ somewhat among jurisdictions. In its most detailed form, the doctrine has the following elements:

• The accident must be one that ordinarily does not occur in the absence of negligence, a particular hallmark of res ipsa

• The instrumentality alleged to have caused the plaintiff's injury was in the exclusive control of the defendant

• The plaintiff has negated other possible explanations for the event

• The explanation for the event is more readily accessible to the defendant than to the plaintiff.

This catalog represents the maximum number of elements in the doctrine; some jurisdictions have trimmed down the list, omitting one requirement or another.

A.　*"Ordinarily does not occur"*

An element that is common to every rendition of the doctrine of res ipsa requires that the plaintiff show that the event is one that ordinarily would not occur unless someone, other than the plaintiff, was negligent. This element requires that the fact finder possess sufficient knowledge about the activity in question to be able to make a judgment on probabilities. That knowledge may be derived from everyday experience. A setting illustrative of the kind of facts from which some courts will allow juries to draw an inference of negligence is the occurrence of an escalator accident. In one such case, Judge Starr invoked the generalization "that the circumstance of being injured while standing on a moving escalator provides evidence that the escalator was the cause of the injury."[1]

B.　*Exclusive control*

Many courts have adhered to the requirement that the plaintiff show that the defendant had exclusive control of the "instrumentality" that caused the injury. However, the Restatement Second does not impose this requirement.[2] A more sensible formulation, indeed, may be to say that the degree of a defendant's control of the instrumentality is simply one factor from which a jury could infer that the circumstances do or do not point to negligence on the part of that defendant.

---

1. Londono v. Washington Metrop. Area Transit Auth., 766 F.2d 569, 574 (D.C.Cir.1985). In this case, the court found res ipsa a viable theory when a two and one-half year old girl "suddenly screamed in pain" while riding an escalator and was found to have a "significant laceration" on one leg.

2. See Restatement (Second) of Torts § 328D (1965).

C. Elimination of other causes

Another element of the doctrine, which in one form or another is common to the law of many jurisdictions, requires that "other responsible causes, including the conduct of the plaintiff and third persons, are sufficiently eliminated by the evidence."[3] For some courts, this means, among other things, that the plaintiff must negate contributory fault on her part. More generally, this element provides a challenge to plaintiffs because in cases pleaded under res ipsa, creative defendants usually will present a variety of hypothetical explanations for the accident other than the defendant's negligence.

In an illustrative case, a loaner battery exploded when the borrower pulled up the latch on his car's hood. Refusing to approve res ipsa instructions, a Florida appellate court referred to possible alternative explanations, including both external and internal ignition sources.[4] In another kind of situation where alternative explanations may undermine a res ipsa claim, prior events could explain the accident. In one such case, a car unexpectedly surged out of control after a history that included two prior accidents. Rejecting the plaintiff's attempt to use the doctrine to impose liability on the auto maker, the court referred to the possibilities that repairs by the dealer or another person had damaged the accelerator or that the prior accidents had "caused some mechanism or part to jar loose or some process to begin which eventually caused the alleged defect."[5]

An interesting comparison appears in a Wisconsin decision holding that disputed evidence that a motorist had a heart attack did not prevent the application of res ipsa to his collision with three vehicles "on a straight, dry road under good weather conditions." There was opposing expert testimony concerning the time that the heart attack occurred, with the defendant's medical witness opining "to a reasonable degree of medical certainty" that it happened before the first collision. By contrast, the plaintiff's expert said he could not say "with certainty" which event occurred first. The court concluded that "the inference of negligence arising from the doctrine of res ipsa loquitur survives alongside evidence" that the defendant's decedent had a heart attack "sometime before, during, or after the collision."[6]

---

3. Id., § 328D(1)(b).

4. Bardy v. Sears Roebuck and Co., 443 So.2d 212, 215 (Fla.Dist.Ct.App. 1983) (a "possibility" of negligence, as contrasted with a showing that it was "more likely than not that the probable cause is negligence on the defendant's part," is not enough to justify a res ipsa instruction).

5. Chambers v. General Motors Corp., 333 N.W.2d 9, 11 (Mich.Ct.App. 1982).

6. Lambrecht v. Estate of Kaczmarczyk, 623 N.W.2d 751, 769 (Wis. 2001).

D.　Accessibility of explanation to defendant

Another element that courts sometimes employ in res ipsa analysis requires that the explanation of an event be more readily accessible to the defendant than to the plaintiff. This element tends to merge with the other elements of the doctrine, including the "ordinarily does not occur" requirement and the requirement that the plaintiff negate other responsible causes, and even with the "exclusive control" element. In form, it may appear to place a burden on the plaintiff. However, tactically, it may put pressure on the defendant to offer an explanation that shows that the accident probably occurred in a way other than the plaintiff suggests, that a cause other than the defendant's substandard conduct produced the event, and that the defendant was not in exclusive control of the instrumentality alleged to have caused the accident.

¶ 45.02　Procedural Effects

The procedural effect of the doctrine is to give the court an important filtering, or gatekeeping, role. The court must decide, on the basis of precedent and policy as well as its independent assessment of probabilities, whether the jury could rationally find negligence and causation based on the accident profile presented by the plaintiff's evidence. If it does not believe that reasonable persons could derive that explanation, it must direct a verdict for the defendant. If the court does believe one could rationally draw the inference, then it should submit the case to the jury, defining the jury's room for decision in terms of the jurisdiction's res ipsa elements.[7] If it concludes that the inference is mandatory, it will submit the case in a way that requires the defendant to respond.

Within these generalizations concerning judge and jury, there are several competing procedural formulations of the res ipsa rule. These include the following:

(1) The classic exposition of the doctrine, tied in with the idea that it is basically a rule of circumstantial evidence, declares that res ipsa evidence is only evidence, to be considered by the jury along with the other evidence in the case.

(2) A version of the doctrine that strongly favors plaintiffs requires the defendant to carry the burden of proof that it was more likely than not that the injury did not result from the defendant's negligence.

---

7. See Restatement (Second) of Torts § 328D(2), (3) (1965) (the court must "determine whether the inference may reasonably be drawn by the jury or whether it must necessarily be drawn," and it is "the function of the jury to determine whether the inference is to be drawn in any case where different conclusions may reasonably be reached").

(3) Another severe version from the defendant's point of view is that the defendant must explain the accident or suffer a directed verdict in the plaintiff's favor. This appears to have the same functional effect as creating a rebuttable presumption that the defendant was negligent.

¶ 45.03 Multiple Defendants

A specialized problem in res ipsa applications arises when several defendants may have been engaged in activities in the vicinity of the accident. If a court holds that res ipsa evidence may be presented against more than one defendant, it is effectively concluding that if there is a better explanation than the negligence of at least one defendant for the injury-causing event, the defendants are best able to give that explanation, singly or in combination.

In an illustrative multiple-defendant case, a piece of lumber fell from "an undetermined source at least ten stories above ground level" on a construction site for a high-rise building. In approving res ipsa instructions against the owner-general contractor and two subcontractors on the construction site, including the plaintiff's employer, the Second Circuit said that New York law "permits a 'thing to speak for itself' as a matter of inference even when plaintiff has not shown that the instrument was in the defendant's *exclusive* control." The inference, the court said, "may be equally applicable to several persons if 'they shared a common duty and there was no indication that any one of them in particular had actually caused the injury.' "[8]

¶ 45.04 Practical Limits on Res Ipsa

There are important practical limits on the application of res ipsa. As noted above, the doctrine requires that the fact finder must be capable of knowledge of a sort that would allow it to draw an inference of negligence. This requirement puts a premium on the kind of "common experience" that is associated with such occurrences as objects falling from buildings on pedestrians or workers.

Courts faced with issues of scientific causation are likely to be wary of applying the doctrine. In one case in which the court rejected application of res ipsa, the plaintiff sued the maker of a cosmetic product used to mend and extend fingernails. Some weeks after the plaintiff used the product, she experienced pain in her fingers and her nails rose from their beds, which contained blood and pus. Concluding that there was no "showing that ... a com-

---

8. Dullard v. Berkeley Assocs., 606 F.2d 890, 894 (2d Cir.1979), quoting, in part, De Witt Properties, Inc. v. City of New York, 377 N.E.2d 461, 466 (N.Y. 1978).

mon experience exists" with reference to such an occurrence, the court denied the claim.[9]

The problem of failures in vehicles and automotive equipment also illustrates limits on attempted uses of res ipsa. A recurring type of case involves blowouts of tires after some use. Denying recovery in a pair of blowout cases, in which the tires had been used for 4,000 and 9,500 miles respectively, the Florida Supreme Court asked rhetorically—and incredulously—whether it could "realistically be concluded on the basis of previous human experience, that this 'happening' does not ordinarily occur in the absence of negligence by the manufacturer?"[10]

¶ 45.05   Res Ipsa, the Substantive Standard of Care, and the Policies of Tort Law

We summarize here some important connections between res ipsa—in form a proof rule—and substantive legal standards as well as the policies underlying tort law.

A. *Substantive implications*

The application of res ipsa may have important substantive implications, at least negatively establishing standards of conduct and product quality. A decision for a plaintiff under res ipsa in effect signifies that when certain events occur, particular levels of conduct or performance are substandard. Illustrative is a New Jersey case, in which a six-month-old Lincoln Continental that had been driven 11,000 miles skidded off the road and hit a tree after the plaintiff heard a "gink" in the front of the car. The court opined that "[a] new Lincoln Continental properly operated and maintained should not in normal experience develop a critical malfunction in the steering mechanism in six months and after being driven about 11,000 miles." The court therefore concluded that a jury could "reasonably infer that the malfunction was due to some manufacturing defect."[11]

When a court announces, as part of its application of res ipsa doctrine, what a new car "should not" do "in normal experience," it is saying at least that the minimum substantive standard for product quality is somewhere above a level that permits that event to happen. A court makes an analogous judgment about the quality and maintenance of facilities on a cruise ship when it allows application of the doctrine to the collapse of a bunk bed.[12]

9. Bohnsak v. C.E.B. Prods., Inc., [1975–1977 Transfer Binder] Prod. Liab. Rep. (CCH) ¶ 7797, at 15,405 (Tenn. Ct. App. 1976).

10. Goodyear Tire & Rubber Co. v. Hughes Supply, Inc., 358 So.2d 1339, 1342 (Fla.1978).

11. Moraca v. Ford Motor Co., 332 A.2d 599, 602 (N.J.1975).

12. See O'Connor v. Chandris Lines, Inc., 566 F.Supp. 1275 (D.Mass. 1983).

B. Justice in explaining unexplained accidents

It is important to stress that the res ipsa doctrine evolved in an effort to allow fact finders to explain the unexplained, when injured persons are disadvantaged by their ignorance of the cause of an event. The fact that an accident has happened in a situation in which the defendant may possess superior information about its probable genesis provides a justice rationale for permitting the inference.

C. The still-unexplained accident

Some accidents must simply remain unexplained. In one case, a "loud explosive noise came through [a] telephone" and knocked a phone user off his feet. Denying recovery, the Delaware Supreme Court emphasized that the happening of an unexplained event "permits, but does not require" an inference of negligence. The court agreed with the trial judge that "despite modern technical knowledge, some events occur which no one can explain, and ... this was such an unfortunate occurrence."[13] The delicate balance for courts, therefore, is to keep the path of justice open to plaintiffs in suspicious circumstances while recognizing that some misfortunes do not have human authors.

D. Policy arguments

An important jurisprudential question is how much judges should take into account the wider ramifications of their decisions. In academic parlance, the question is how "instrumentalist" courts deciding tort cases should be, referring to considerations of public policy when deciding disputes between private individuals. Certainly the tradition followed by American judges, and largely endorsed by American legal educators, has been that courts should give significant consideration to policy.[14]

A variety of policies militate against easy application of the res ipsa rule. As we noted in our general discussion of circumstantial evidence, courts will be concerned about the potential of the doctrine to impose liability without a reason—the very essence of arbitrariness.[15] Moreover, a liberal application of res ipsa may produce widely varying inferences on the part of different juries, and therefore a profile of unlike results in like cases.

Courts also are likely to be wary of a sympathetic tendency to stretch tort law into a compensation system for heart-rending injuries, even in the absence of fault. A type of language that often

---

13. Scott v. Diamond State Telephone Co., 239 A.2d 703, 705 (Del.1968).

14. For a powerful argument that they should not, see, e.g., Ernest J.

Weinrib, Corrective Justice, 77 Iowa L. Rev. 403 (1992).

15. See ¶¶ 44.03–.04 supra.

commends itself to courts rejecting res ipsa in such situations is that the defendant's liability should not be that of an "insurer."

A helpful way to test res ipsa applications is to ask whether, given the circumstances, the imposition of liability on the defendant is likely to create desirable incentives for actors to use more care. If a defendant would not try to do any better, simply because it could not effectively take more care to avoid the type of injury at issue, then the use of res ipsa would impose an insurance form of liability rather than one based on negligence.

In this regard, one should note the potential distinction between using res ipsa to prove negligence and using it to prove a causal linkage. In certain situations where there is evidence from which a defendant may be found negligent, the application of res ipsa would provide an incentive for actors situated like the defendant to increase their level of care with respect to the act or omission that arguably was substandard. However, in some cases of that kind, the particular negligence might not be the cause in fact of the plaintiff's accident. For example, a person injured in an auto accident when a car "grabbed to one side" and skidded off the road might show that there were bolts missing on a fender of his car. But a court might conclude that even if the missing bolts showed negligence in manufacture, they did not exhibit a link to the event of the car going off the road.[16]

Thus, while imposing liability against a defendant who has behaved carelessly may signal that the defendant should be more careful, it would not be just to impose that liability if the defendant's carelessness did not in fact cause the injury at issue. One suspects that courts do not always confront this problem rigorously when they apply res ipsa to situations in which there may be more than one explanation for an accident. What they appear to do is to try to achieve a rough matching between one possible explanation and one or more things that the defendant has contributed to a product or an activity, ranging from tangible components to physical acts to planning and design.

Undoubtedly res ipsa lacks the precision and certainty of more finely chiseled theories, and will leave some defendants vexed and some readers frustrated. We conclude this general survey only by emphasizing that res ipsa by its nature deals with mysteries and the efforts of imperfect legal processes to unravel them. One can say with some assurance that if the doctrine of res ipsa did not exist, the courts would have to invent it in order to do justice when injuries occur in connection with unexplained events.

16. See Segler v. Ford Motor Co., 438 So.2d 297, 299 (Ala.1983).

¶ 45.06 Medical Res Ipsa

At least one application of res ipsa has developed a rather particularized set of rules. This is the case of unexplained injuries that occur in the process of medical care, where the courts have tuned the res ipsa rules and their policy applications to the special problems involved in delivering health care services.

A. *Elements of medical res ipsa*

1. *Substantive*

The elements of medical res ipsa track those of the general doctrine, set out above,[17] and the areas of controversy roughly parallel those arising under the general doctrine. An often compelling aspect of the case for res ipsa in the medical setting, whether it is formally an element of the doctrine or not, lies in the availability of information about the happening of the accident. The expertise of medical defendants contributes to making this a critical feature. It is particularly a prime consideration in cases involving anesthetized patients undergoing surgery, because the patient is unconscious and thus entirely unable to give any direct evidence herself.

2. *Procedural effects*

Some courts have added to the possible procedural effects of general res ipsa doctrine discussed above—that is, a plain evidentiary rule, a rule shifting the burden of proof, and a rule requiring explanation by the defendant[18]—a rule that compels medical defendants to show that they were "free from negligence by evidence which cannot be rationally disbelieved."[19] This probably represents the strongest effect of the doctrine—a true shifting of the burden of proof from the plaintiff to the defendant on the issue of breach of the standard of care.

B. *Collateral legal rules*

1. *Malpractice doctrine*

Several limiting rules associated with medical malpractice law tie in closely with res ipsa. Some of these rules, which courts articulate in varying ways, are reflected in instructions to the jury that there are inherent risks in medical treatment quite apart from the hazards of substandard care.[20] In some versions, this point appears in language that points out that physicians do not guarantee results, or that a maloccurrence is insufficient by itself to

---

17. See supra, ¶ 45.01.

18. See supra, ¶ 45.02.

19. Clark v. Gibbons, 426 P.2d 525, 533 (Cal.1967).

20. See, e.g., Siverson v. Weber, 372 P.2d 97, 99 (Cal.1962).

provide a basis to infer negligence.[21] Other judges stress that just the rarity of an accident is not enough to support a res ipsa case.[22] Rulings within a single decision may reflect the tension between the tendency of general res ipsa doctrine to favor plaintiffs and the constraints of some malpractice rules.[23]

2. The role of experts

An important practical consideration in medical res ipsa cases is the use of expert testimony. We elaborate below on issues pertaining to expert testimony in cases of professional malpractice.[24] We simply underline here that most medical treatment involves the use of specialized knowledge. Lay fact finders may not be able to determine probabilities without some evidence from a physician about the likelihood of a breach of professional standards as well as the likelihood that the breach caused the plaintiff's injury.

3. Circumstantial evidence plus specific acts of negligence

One special avenue for plaintiffs trying to establish medical negligence from the circumstances is to combine evidence of a specific act of negligence with proof of an allegedly unusual outcome. This approach often requires the use of experts. An illustrative case arose from the performance of a hysterectomy for the purpose of alleviating pelvic inflammatory disease. The plaintiff, who sued because of the unusual occurrence of a vaginal fecal fistula following the hysterectomy, presented the testimony of a physician that it was inadvisable to perform an operation for pelvic inflammatory disease when that illness was in an acute stage. A majority of the Illinois Supreme Court opined that "a reasonable person would conclude that plaintiffs' expert believed that [the] fistula, more probably than not, resulted from defendant's negligence" and declared that this testimony, if found credible, would provide "evidence of more than a mere unusual occurrence ... , from which the jury could have inferred negligence under *res ipsa loquitur*."[25] A dissenter argued, inter alia, that the plaintiff had not shown "that the defendant committed a specific act of negligence of a type which could have caused the injury."[26]

21. See, e.g., Miller v. Kennedy, 588 P.2d 734, 737 (Wash.1978).

22. Clark, supra note 19, 426 P.2d at 540–41 (Tobriner and Traynor, JJ., separate opinions).

23. See, e.g., Jones v. Porretta, 405 N.W.2d 863, 869, 875 (Mich.1987), which supports the "no guarantor" idea but finds error in an instruction that the occurrence of an "adverse result ... is not in itself evidence of negligence."

24. See Chapter 48 infra.

25. Spidle v. Steward, 402 N.E.2d 216, 219–20 (Ill.1980).

26. Id. at 226 (Ryan, J. dissenting).

C. *Special policy considerations in medical res ipsa*

Medical res ipsa is one branch from the trunk of a general doctrine. However, there are several features of medical care that present special aspects of the application of the theory to that activity.

1. *Statistical probabilities*

The highly specialized nature of medical and surgical treatment underlies some statistical traps in the use of res ipsa. The complexity of the human body, and large areas of medical ignorance about its workings, often may make it practically unknowable whether a particular outcome is most rationally explained by negligence or by another hypothesis. Consider, for example, the question of whether members of a surgical team are negligent if anesthesia wears off prematurely. There may be a certain number of cases where that occurrence is due to negligence, but it may also be that there are more cases when it happens for reasons that are unforeseeable to and uncontrollable by the surgical team.[27] The application of res ipsa in such cases would work an injustice, because it would permit the inference that it was more likely than not that a particular occurrence was the result of negligence when, as a matter of statistical probability, it was not.

2. *Policy concerns about health care delivery*

The question of how much weight judges should give to the social impact of their decisions is a challenging one with respect to issues concerning proof of medical negligence. Important concerns include costs and effects on behavior. One question is whether, in deciding to adopt a relatively lenient or demanding rule of proof, courts should take into account the potential impact of that rule on the price and availability of malpractice insurance. The problem is particularly relevant in medical malpractice because of the high degree of public concern about the costs of medical care generally and the negative impact of adverse judgments on physicians, as well as about statistics on the frequent occurrence of medical malpractice.

With respect to deterrence, one useful test of the application of res ipsa in medical cases—as with the use of the doctrine generally—is to ask whether it would have a salutary effect on conduct. In a case where res ipsa is incorrectly applied, presumably a physician would not change his or her conduct, reasoning that the court has effectively imposed strict liability and that there is nothing that can be done to do the job better. By contrast, when the doctrine

---

27. For a statistical illustration of this type of problem, see Clark, supra note 19, 426 P.2d at 537 n.2 (Tobriner, J., concurring).

uncovers fault in otherwise unexplained events, it is likely that it will lead to a better way of doing things. The proper application of res ipsa provides a proxy for information about the causes of accidents. If a judicial estimate of probabilities is correct in a medical res ipsa case, it theoretically would enhance the efficiency of the market for medical services. The problem for courts is to administer medical res ipsa in a way that identifies probable cases of fault, rather than one that in effect creates a no-fault compensation system for unfortunate accidents.

A different set of concerns, featuring a different set of tensions, arises under the heading of fairness. On the one hand, there is the fact that the patient is usually unknowledgeable and sometimes literally unconscious at the time of the alleged negligence. It may be argued that the resulting inability of the plaintiff to establish the facts makes it especially unfair to apply a doctrine of circumstantial evidence narrowly. On the other hand, physicians contend that an unjustified finding of negligence is peculiarly stigmatizing to them. An associated fairness concern lies in the possibility that, as suggested above, there may be a significant number of cases in which the application of res ipsa to medical situations involves a statistical error. It is difficult to know whether this occurs more in medical applications of res ipsa than in other uses of the doctrine.

[Chapters 46–47 are reserved for supplementary material.]

Chapter Forty–Eight

EXPERT EVIDENCE AND PROFESSIONAL NEGLIGENCE

Analysis

Litigation about alleged professional negligence presents difficult issues concerning proof of the standard of care and causation. A closely related question is when a plaintiff must present expert testimony to show that a professional has been causally negligent. Focusing on that question, this chapter refers to issues, previously discussed, that relate to the qualifications of expert witnesses[1] and to inferences that can be drawn from unexplained events.[2]

In the background of the expert testimony issue is the question of how wide the gulf is between the specialized knowledge of professionals and that of other workers. Airline pilots, painting contractors, and grocery owners may ask whether there is a sufficient difference between their work and that of doctors and lawyers to justify a special requirement for proving professional negligence. The recurring issue in professional negligence litigation is whether, in given fact situations, lay persons are capable of knowing what due care is, and whether that standard has been met, without the explanation of an expert. That leads back to the questions of whether lay persons possess sufficient relevant knowledge—which includes the learning associated with the possession of a mental data base—and whether they can conceptualize the kinds of judgments fostered by sophisticated professional training.

¶ 48.01   The Rule, the Principal Exception, and Rationales

Generally, courts require plaintiffs in professional malpractice litigation to establish their cases by expert testimony. The major

---

1. See ¶ 23.03 supra.   2. See ¶ 45.06 supra.

qualification to this principle is generally labeled the "common knowledge" exception. As one court put it, "[t]he only exception ... is in cases where the matter under investigation is *so simple,* and the lack of skill or want of care *so obvious,* as to be within the range of the ordinary experience and comprehension of even non-professional persons." The court presented several examples of this kind of occurrence, including cases "where a gauze pad is left in the body of a patient following an operation," or a surgeon's knife slips in an effort to cut off a scalp tumor and "cut[s] off his patient's ear."[3]

The basic idea behind the general rule is that the activities of professionals involve matters so complex, and so demanding of expertise, that usually lay persons would not be able to determine whether, in fact, a defendant fell below the standard of care. No doubt also supporting the application of this rule is judicial concern that juror hostility to highly paid professionals, and sympathy for persons who allege that they suffered harm at the hands of such defendants, will translate into unjust verdicts.

In one decision that applied the rule requiring expert testimony,[4] the court affirmed a dismissal in a case involving a laminectomy, surgery designed to remove bulging material between spinal disks. The defendant, an orthopedic surgeon, took out the material at the wrong site—that is, between the first two sacral vertebrae and not between the last lumbar vertebra and the first sacral

---

3. Demchuk v. Bralow, 170 A.2d 868, 870 (Pa.1961).

An extension of the exception for objects left in a surgical patient's body is the case where a doctor attempts to remove such an object, deliberately left in the body to aid the healing process, but leaves behind a fragment of it. See Miller v. Jacoby, 33 P.3d 68 (Wash.2001), in which the plaintiff's surgeon placed a drain in her incision to facilitate healing of the wound. A nurse "felt resistance" as she tried to remove the drain in response to the orders of another physician. That doctor then pulled out the drain, remarking, "I hope I got it all." However, she left a piece of the drain in the plaintiff's body. The Washington Supreme Court concluded that the plaintiff did not have to present expert testimony in those circumstances. The supreme court quoted a characterization of a dissenter in the intermediate court who described the "incomplete removal of the drain" as "result[ing] in a foreign object that was placed in the body intentionally and temporarily during sur-

gery," which then became "a foreign object inadvertently and permanently left in the patient at the completion of surgery." Id. at 73–74, quoting 6 P.3d 1204 (Wash.Ct.App.2000)(Appelwick, J., dissenting).

There is a slightly different emphasis, but the same result, in Boyd v. Chakraborty, 550 N.W.2d 44 (Neb.1996), in which there was evidence that a fragment of a catheter tube was left in the patient's body after surgery following the collapse of a lung. Distinguishing a precedent, the court stressed that the issue was not "whether a physician was negligent in fracturing a catheter" and that "the only skill required" with respect to "the alleged negligent conduct" of the surgeon defendants was "to inspect the equipment used in the surgical procedure to make certain everything is intact and has not been left in the patient's body." This, the court said, was "within the knowledge of laypersons." Id. at 49.

4. Sitts v. United States, 811 F.2d 736 (2d Cir.1987).

vertebra. There was evidence that it was not usual that the sacral vertebrae could be moved, by contrast with the fact that lumbar vertebrae can be manipulated. The plaintiff apparently had the unusual condition called "lumbarization"—that is, movability between the sacral vertebrae. The defendant, who found "bulging and soft disk material between the lowest movable vertebra and the highest immobile vertebra," decided "that he had located the ... interspace" between the lowest lumbar vertebra and the first sacral vertebra. He proceeded to remove the disk material in that space. Deposition testimony from orthopedic surgeons, offered by the defendant, indicated that the defendant followed "accepted medical practice."

The plaintiff, who did not offer expert testimony on negligence or causation, argued that he did not have to do so because the issues were "within the ordinary experience and knowledge of lay persons." However, although concededly the surgeon operated in the wrong place, the court concluded that the plaintiff had to present expert testimony "to establish a prima facie case of medical malpractice." It declared that the procedure for locating the vertebrae was "not visual or simple" and that neither the "procedures [nor] the normal anatomical considerations that underlie them are within the common knowledge of ordinary lay persons." The court also opined that jurors could not determine without expert evidence the degree to which the plaintiff had lumbarization between the sacral vertebrae, or "the degree to which lumbarization complicates the surgical procedure, or to know whether preoperative procedures should have revealed such lumbarization to the ... surgeons."[5]

Beyond that, the court said that it did not think that lay persons could "judge, without expert assistance," whether the plaintiff would have avoided his pain and suffering if the operation in question had been performed at the right place, or whether he would have required further surgery to remove the bulging material that was in fact taken out during that operation. In this connection, the court noted that there was evidence that "back patients often are required to undergo spinal surgery more than once."[6] This rather extended catalog of technical matters provides a good illustration of the kinds of events about which courts will require experts.

The main lines of the legal rules are pretty well laid out concerning the decision of when to require expert testimony in cases of professional negligence. But there will always be cases in the middle, between the obviously negligent amputation of the

5. Id. at 741.   6. Id.

wrong limb and the subtle problem of identifying the correct spinal disk.

¶ 48.02   Linkage With Circumstantial Evidence

There is an interesting relationship between the circumstantial evidence doctrine known as res ipsa loquitur and the requirement of expert testimony in cases of alleged professional negligence.[7] The res ipsa doctrine allows jurors to infer both negligence and causation from circumstances. Yet, the requirement of expert testimony may prevent plaintiffs from ever asking jurors to make those inferences from only the happening of an unusual event. A good example is a case in which a patient asserted that her dentist had injected a needle that " 'he stuck in too far.' " She claimed that after this incident, she suffered "constant pain" and her "entire face swelled up," with the eventual result that "all of her teeth subsequently had to be removed." The plaintiff presented no expert testimony to support her claim of negligence. In affirming a nonsuit, the court commented that "[t]he treatment of teeth is not a simple matter."[8] Such decisions indicate that sometimes the thing speaks for itself only when an expert says it does.

¶ 48.03   Policies in Conflict

The question of when expert testimony should be required in cases of alleged professional malpractice features difficult issues involving fairness, the effects of various rules on conduct, and the knowledge of which lay persons are capable.

On one side of the arguments about behavior and policy, advocates emphasize that there are certain kinds of knowledge that are peculiarly within the province of professionals. From this they argue that it is unfair, indeed arbitrary, to allow those who do not possess that knowledge, and have not been informed about it by experts, to judge how it was used in the disputed circumstances.

Those who support a rigorous requirement of expert testimony also express the concern that failure to enforce such a standard would permit claimants to succeed on no more than a showing that an injury occurred during the rendition of professional services. This, they argue, could turn a tort system that requires a showing of fault into a compensation system that disregards culpability.

On the other side is what might be called the sanctum sanctorum argument. Plaintiffs using this line of attack will contend that defendants who are professionals place a self-serving overemphasis on the mysterious, guild-like aspects of their knowledge. Plaintiffs

---

7. See ¶ 45.06 supra.   8. Lambert v. Soltis, 221 A.2d 173, 177 (Pa.1966).

also assert that they are disadvantaged by a "conspiracy of silence," in which professionals refuse to testify against other professionals because they fear reprisals.[9] With the professions becoming less monolithic, this has become less of a problem. However, particularly in smaller communities, the closed profession is likely to continue to present obstacles for plaintiffs required to present expert testimony, fencing them out of presenting a basis of knowledge from which jurors could infer negligence and causation.

Courts approaching this question from a policy point of view are likely to take into account the presumed effect of their decisions on the cost of professional services, particularly medical services. In close cases, courts probably will tilt toward requiring expert testimony on the grounds that to allow litigation to go forward without it would impose unwarranted costs not only on physicians, but on the community.

As is so concerning proof rules generally, one useful way to put the expert testimony issue is to ask whether judgments for plaintiffs in cases where expert testimony is not required would be likely to have a desirable influence on professional practices. Defendants naturally will argue that if jurors may infer negligence without the testimony of a professional, except in the most blatantly obvious cases of errant behavior, there will be no meaningful signal to members of the profession about what practices they should improve. Plaintiffs will respond that a refusal to permit jurors to make judgments about medical maloccurrences without expert testimony will permit an unacceptable number of cases of negligence to go uncompensated and thus decrease incentives for appropriate levels of care. As arbiters of these arguments, court must ask whether tilting the proof rules towards plaintiffs is, on balance, likely to produce net gains in consumer welfare as well as to produce individual justice.

9.   See also supra, ¶ 23.03.

Chapter Forty–Nine

PROOF OF CAUSATION AND SCIENTIFIC EVIDENCE

Analysis

Plaintiffs in tort cases must prove not only that the defendant was negligent or sold an unreasonably dangerous product but that the negligence or the defect caused the harm at issue. This chapter more fully discusses issues touched on in prior chapters, involving proof and circumstantial evidence,[1] focusing principally on questions involving scientific evidence of causation.

¶ 49.01   What Must Be Proved

Generally, the standard for proof of causation aligns itself with the standard for proof of negligence. The plaintiff must show that it is more probable than not that the defendant's conduct or product was a cause in fact of the alleged harm, and must demonstrate this by a preponderance of the evidence.[2]

Theoretically this inquiry is, as the formulation above indicates, entirely a "factual" one. At its most pristine, the model is

---

1. See Chapters 43–45, 48.

2. See, e.g., David Rosenberg, Damage Scheduling in Mass Exposure Cases,

1 Courts, Health Science & the Law, 335, 335 (1991).

one of a scientist who makes a retrospective inquiry into the probability of a causal relationship between an event—for example, the negligence of an alleged tortfeasor—and a subsequent occurrence—for example, the illness of a plaintiff.

¶ 49.02   Proof and Substantive Rules

Although some analysts rigorously isolate this conception of "cause in fact" from other matters, others believe that in the real world of litigation there is a reciprocity between the "proof rules" and the substantive rules and policies of tort law. Continuing a theme developed in earlier chapters, we note that the relative rigor or leniency of proof rules may affect the tendency of the substantive law to restrict or expand the possibility of recovery. The remarks of two distinguished lawyers provide an interesting contrast. Thomas Henderson, a plaintiffs' advocate, has insisted that "policy considerations" may support liability judgments "even where scientific inquiry and knowledge are not certain or not complete."[3] By contrast, the defense lawyer Bert Black has argued that once one has framed a causation question, "the analysis becomes a policy-free factual inquiry."[4]

¶ 49.03   Exposure

A class of cases that generates many modern causation issues has featured problems involving so-called "toxics"—chemicals and fibers to which plaintiffs attribute illness. A major set of issues with respect to such substances—whether claims are brought under functional labels of "products liability," "environmental torts," or "toxic torts," or more traditional theories of negligence, nuisance, or strict liability—relates to the plaintiff's exposure to the substance. Courts examine a variety of proofs and factors to try to separate valid claims from those based on inadequate science. This evidence includes physical evidence such as X-rays, testimony about the duration and intensity of exposure, and expert opinions about the statistical association of certain kinds of overt pathology and particular levels of exposure.

Issues concerning exposure will usually call forth expert testimony. As is so with respect to other questions involving scientific evidence, experts must establish a factual basis for their opinions. In a Fifth Circuit case, the plaintiff's expert opined that dioxin had caused the plaintiff's illness, pointing out that the plaintiff had worked at a site where dioxin had been found and saying that therefore he " 'definitely could have come into contact with it.' "

---

3. See Thomas Henderson, Causation in Toxic Litigation, Courts, Health Science & the Law, 331, 333 (1991).

4. Bert Black, A Complete Picture of Causation, Courts, Health Science & the Law, 327, 327 (1991).

However, in reversing a plaintiff's verdict, the court noted that the expert had no "knowledge about the amount or duration of [the plaintiff's] exposure" and concluded that there was thus "an insufficient factual basis for his opinion."[5]

A related causation issue concerns the toxicity and disease-causing propensities of substances. In some cases, there is highly reliable knowledge concerning the relationship of certain illnesses to exposures to particular substances—for example, the malignant disease mesothelioma is very closely linked to asbestos exposure. Because of that association, courts deciding cases in which a worker has been exposed to asbestos and develops mesothelioma will usually regard the relationship as highly probable. At the other pole, that of relative uncertainty, are cases involving so-called "toxic soups," where several chemicals run at large in bodies of water or waste dumps,[6] and where it may be difficult to link a particular substance to a claimant's disease as well as to establish the degree of exposure to a specific substance. Cases of this kind often pose difficult problems for plaintiffs, and also contribute to the controversy about whether to impose joint and several liability in litigation where the tortious conduct of more than one party has contributed to an injury.[7]

¶ 49.04 Expert Testimony

A. General requirement and exceptions

In cases where scientific causation is an issue, courts generally will require plaintiffs to use experts to prove a relationship between the defendant's conduct and the harm. This requirement, as applied in such cases as litigation over toxic substances, is similar to one discussed above concerning disputes about claimed linkages between the conduct of physicians and unfortunate outcomes.[8] For the same kinds of reasons that they require experts in malpractice cases, courts usually rule that causal relationships between such occurrences as exposures to chemicals and alleged results like illnesses are so technical that lay jurors cannot on their own make rational judgments about causal connections.

However, on occasion, courts will utilize an idea akin to the "common knowledge" exception used in some medical malpractice cases[9] to permit the use of lay testimony on causation. In one such

---

5. Thompson v. Southern Pac. Transp. Co., 809 F.2d 1167, 1169 (5th Cir.1987), cert. denied, 484 U.S. 819 (1987).

6. Henderson, supra note 3, at 331–32.

7. See generally Chapter 50 infra.

8. See supra, ¶ 45.06(B)(2); see generally Chapter 48.

9. See supra, ¶ 48.01.

case,[10] the court affirmed a plaintiff's jury verdict against a polluter, partly on the basis of the testimony of several homeowners that they could see a "cloud" of particles coming out of the defendant's stack. These witnesses testified that when the particles descended, they would "eat up clothes hanging on the line [and] make brown spots where they land on buildings," and that the material could not be "washed off the house or cars because it smears in water and a residue remains." Moreover, the homeowners testified that the particulates caused "burning of the eyes," and, in the case of one plaintiff, caused a burning of the throat, nosebleeds and chest congestion. The court said that expert testimony was "not as a matter of law required ... where six lay witnesses graphically described the pollutants and resulting damage."[11]

B. Some relevant sciences

Several scientific disciplines provide knowledge that may be useful in solving tort causation problems, but conflicting testimony of scientists often generates factual disputes as well as arguments about the qualifications of witnesses and about the validity of the science itself.

The branch of science called toxicology uses animals, and sometimes cell cultures, to test the effects of chemicals and fibers on biological tissue, seeking data that may be extrapolated to human beings.[12] Expert opinion concerning the application to human beings of the results of animal testing may thus present disputed issues in tort litigation. Particularly important in pollution cases is the sub-science of environmental toxicology, which studies the "incidental exposure" of human beings to chemical contaminants in the environment, food, and water.[13]

The science of epidemiology studies the way that diseases and injuries are caused and distributed among populations.[14] The findings of epidemiologists are likely to be a subject of argument with respect to the manner in which they devise their hypotheses, their statistical methods, and their choice of prospective or retrospective studies. The latter decision often reflects how costs influence the

10. Alton Box Board Co. v. Pantya, 236 So.2d 452 (Fla.Dist.Ct.App.1970).

11. Id. at 454–55. The Alaska court extends the principle to "a rear-end automobile collision causing relatively common injuries" in Choi v. Anvil, 32 P.3d 1, 3–4 (Alaska 2001). Where the plaintiffs' symptoms included "pain, stiffness, and loss of strength," the court says that "[a]lthough a medical expert might have more precisely described the relationship between the impact and the effects described by the plaintiffs, the

jury, using everyday experience, could readily find a causal relationship without this expert assistance."

12. See Ted A. Loomis, Essentials of Toxicology 2, 157–58 (1978). Strictly controlled toxicity studies use human beings as subjects for clinical investigation of new drugs.

13. Id. at 7.

14. J. Mausner and S. Cramer, Epidemiology: An Introductory Text 1 (1985).

search for truth in science as well as law. Prospective studies follow populations over a period of years to test hypotheses devised before the fact about the possible linkage of a "factor and a disease," whereas retrospective studies compare people who already have a disease with control subjects.[15] Retrospective studies are typically less expensive than prospective ones.

C. Qualifications of experts

A recurrent area of legal dispute concerns the qualifications of experts to speak about the issues on which their testimony is offered. A decision dealing with children's illnesses attributed to ground water contamination illustrates how courts may compartmentalize expertise with respect to specific types of issues. The plaintiffs offered the affidavit of a chemist who had been employed by a state environmental protection agency. The affidavit said that the plaintiffs' medical problems "might or could have been caused by the drinking of the water from the wells in question" and that "[o]ne of the probable causes" for those problems "would be the disposing of hazardous wastes." Although finding the case a close one, the court permitted the evidence, distinguishing the expert's ability to "opine on the health effects of water contaminated by phenols" from his ability to make medical judgments. The court said that the witness was "incompetent to diagnose a case of rheumatoid arthritis" but that if he were shown a medical report diagnosing a child as suffering from rheumatoid arthritis, he might be "competent to give an opinion on the cause of that disease"— "indeed ... more competent to give such an opinion than the doctor who examined the child."[16]

D. Verbal formulas

A principal battleground in this area involves sometimes delicate decisions concerning the exact language that expert witnesses use in testifying about causation. A medical malpractice case illustrates the importance to outcomes of decisions about whether a witness must use particular verbal formulas, such as "reasonable medical probability." In this case, the plaintiff claimed that a physician had missed a diagnosis of a blood clot in her neck, which traveled to her skull, where it caused paralysis and partial blindness. The plaintiff alleged that because the doctor did not use diagnostic tests in time, she lost the opportunity to have an operation that would have prevented her injuries. On direct and cross examination, the plaintiff's expert testified that "[s]he may

---

15. Bert Black and David Lilienfeld, Epidemiologic Proof in Toxic Tort Litigation, 52 Fordham L. Rev. 732, 756–59 (1984).

16. Backes v. Valspar Corp., 783 F.2d 77, 78–79 (7th Cir.1986).

have had development of a clot in the neck," but answered "no" to the question of whether he could say where the clot was located "with a reasonable degree of medical probability?" The witness also testified, with respect to what arteriograms would have shown if the defendant had taken them earlier than he did, "I believe that they would have shown a developing thrombosis." The court concluded that there was enough in this testimony to justify a reversal of a directed verdict for the defendant. The court said that "[l]ike any other physical fact that must be established by expert medical opinion in a negligence case, testimony concerning where the clot formed may rest upon a 'medical probability,' 'more likely-than-not' standard based upon the doctor's experience." The court further commented that "[a]dding the words 'reasonable' and 'to a reasonable degree' merely confuses the issue."[17]

Courts must perform something of a balancing act when they review the verbal formulas used by experts concerning scientific causation. On the one hand, the standard for such testimony must be sufficiently rigorous to ensure that a jury may reasonably infer causation. On the other hand, courts should fashion standards that are flexible enough that they do not create a disincentive to candor on the part of conscientious experts, who otherwise may feel that they must fit testimony into a predetermined box of language.

E. Standards for admissibility of expert testimony: Daubert

The landmark case of *Daubert v. Merrell Dow Pharmaceuticals, Inc.*,[18] formulates authoritative federal guidelines concerning standards of admissibility for expert testimony about scientific causation. *Daubert* rejected the previously accepted rule of *Frye v. United States*,[19] which required that scientific evidence be generally accepted in the relevant field,[20] and adopted a more liberal standard that asks whether an expert's testimony will aid understanding of the evidence. The scientific issue in *Daubert* was whether prenatal ingestion of a prescription drug that women took while pregnant could cause birth defects in children. The plaintiffs sought to use animal studies, "in vitro" studies of animal cells, "pharmacological studies of the chemical structure" of the product, and "the 'reanalysis' of previously published" human epidemiological studies. Invoking the *Frye* rule, the defendants insisted that there was no issue for a jury because "more than 30 [epidemiological] ... studies involving more than 130,000 patients" had yielded no evidence of a causal relation between the product and birth defects.

17. Poertner v. Swearingen, 695 F.2d 435, 438 (10th Cir.1982).

18. 509 U.S. 579 (1993).

19. 293 F. 1013 (D.C.Cir.1923).

20. Id. at 1014.

However, the Court disagreed and found that Frye had been "superseded"[21] by Rule 702 of the Federal Rules of Evidence as the governing standard. That rule provides that

if scientific, technical, or other specialized knowledge will assist the trier of fact to understand the evidence or to determine a fact in issue, a witness qualified as an expert by knowledge, skill, experience, training, or education, may testify thereto in the form of an opinion or otherwise.[22]

Although it rejected the *Frye* rule's "austere" standard of "general acceptance" as "the exclusive test for admitting expert scientific testimony," the Court sought to articulate limits on the admission of such evidence in litigation. The Court stressed that Rule 702's " 'helpfulness' standard requires a valid scientific connection to the pertinent inquiry as a precondition to admissibility." The Court also indicated that an expert's opinion must "have a reliable basis in the knowledge and experience of his discipline."[23] Cataloguing factors that would "bear on the inquiry," the Court included the questions of whether the theory advanced by the expert "can be (and has been) tested," and whether "the theory or technique has been subjected to peer review and publication."[24] The Court also referred to the limitation that Rule 703 imposes on expert opinion based on otherwise inadmissible hearsay, namely, that it is admissible only if the underlying data are "of a type reasonably relied upon by experts in the particular field in forming opinions or inferences upon the subject."[25]

In a later decision, *General Electric v. Joiner*,[26] the Court stressed the need for experts to connect data to their opinions. This case involved the application of the Court's "abuse of discretion" standard by a federal appellate court's review of a trial court ruling on expert testimony. The trial court had excluded testimony on the question of whether the substances called PCBs had "promoted" the development of a cancer but the appellate court reversed, applying a "particularly stringent" standard of review because it viewed the Federal Rules as "display[ing] a preference for admissibility."[27] Reversing the appellate court decision as having applied "an overly 'stringent' review" to the trial court ruling, the Supreme Court emphasized that its abuse of discretion standard made the trial court a "gatekeeper" in screening expert testimony.[28] The Court concluded, inter alia, that animal studies on which the

21. See 509 U.S. at 586.

22. Fed. R. Evid. 702.

23. 509 U.S. at 589, 591–92.

24. Id. at 593.

25. Fed. R. Evid. 703, quoted in Daubert, 509 U.S. at 595.

26. 522 U.S. 136 (1997).

27. 78 F.3d 524, 529 (11th Cir. 1996).

28. 522 U.S. at 142.

plaintiffs' experts relied were so "dissimilar" to the facts of the case before it that the trial court had not abused its discretion in rejecting the experts' reliance on those studies. Also saying that it was within the trial judge's discretion to find that four epidemiological studies did not support the experts' opinions that PCBs had contributed to the plaintiff's illness, the Court declared that neither *Daubert* nor the Federal Rules of Evidence required a trial judge "to admit opinion evidence which is connected to existing data only by the *ipse dixit* of the expert."[29]

It is clear that in the realm of expert testimony, utterances by experts in the form of either fact or opinion may be the subject of dispute. The *Joiner* decision highlights the point that, while conflicting data presented by competing studies present questions of fact, legal arguments about causation are likely to focus on the conflicting opinions of experts about what data mean.

¶ 49.05 Tort and Compensation Systems Compared

The requirements for proving scientific causation are likely to be more lenient in workers' compensation cases than in tort litigation, with courts responding to the nature of workers' compensation law. That legislation aims to provide compensation to workers injured in the scope of their employment without proof of fault on the part of the employer.

A good example of judicial flexibility on "industrial causation" in workers' compensation, linked to a refusal to require that expert testimony fit a single verbal formula,[30] appears in a case involving the claim of a fireman's widow for his death from lung cancer.[31] At issue was whether the cancer had been caused by smoke inhalation while the decedent was fighting fires. The evidence included an expert's opinion "that it was 'probable' that the smoke inhaled [by the decedent] contained carcinogens," as well as his statement that "smoke from burning tar or creosote 'may well' contain the same type of carcinogen found in cigarette smoke." There was also undisputed testimony by a fireman who had worked with the decedent that tar or creosote were in "most buildings."[32]

The workers compensation appeals board annulled a referee's award for the claimant, ruling that she had not proved that her decedent's cancer arose out of his employment, but the California Supreme Court annulled the decision of the appeals board. The court said it could not find "a plausible reason to believe the degree of likelihood intended by 'probable' and 'may well' is less than that

29. Id. at 145–46.

30. See supra, ¶ 49.04(D).

31. McAllister v. Workmen's Compensation App. Bd., 445 P.2d 313 (Cal.

1968) ("industrial causation" phrase at 315).

32. Id. at 315–16.

in the requirement of 'reasonable probability.' "[33] Reflecting the relative liberality of proof standards in workers' compensation cases, the court said it was "bound to uphold a claim in which the proof of industrial causation is reasonably probable, although not certain or 'convincing.' "The court declared, indeed, that it would have to uphold such an award "even though the exact causal mechanism is unclear or even unknown."[34]

¶ 49.06   The Problem of Future Harm

An important set of issues related to the problem of scientific proof of causation concerns the remedies, if any, that courts should provide in response to proof of probable future harm from exposure to dangerous conditions. Three kinds of issues have generated case law and commentary. This discussion begins with the most theoretical claim, that for increased risk of illness. That analysis provides a basis for comparison of two other types of claims that have been somewhat more attractive to courts, claims for present fear of illness and for medical surveillance or "monitoring"—periodic examinations to check for the development of disease.

A.   Compensation for increased probability of illness

One particularly interesting question, although at the moment the principal interest is theoretical, is whether courts should impose liability for the probability that a person exposed to a risk, like that associated with a toxic substance, will suffer illness in the future. The argument for requiring compensation for increased risk of disease includes the thesis that this is simply one example of situations in which courts engage in "averaging" with respect to the probability of future harm. Justifying such awards, one commentator has pointed out that courts routinely undertake "averaging" with respect to many aspects of future loss, such as life expectancy, an injury victim's potential rehabilitation and the time value of money.[35]

If courts do permit such recovery, they will be likely to emphasize that the prospect of future illness must be a "reasonable medical probability" rather than a "possibility."[36] However, courts are likely to be conservative about imposing probabilistic damages in toxic tort cases.[37] One reason lies in the simple fact that no

33. Id. at 316.

34. Id. at 319.

35. David Rosenberg, Damage Scheduling and Mass Exposure Cases, 1 Courts, Health Science & the Law 335, 339–40 (1991).

36. See Herber v. Johns–Manville Corp., 785 F.2d 79, 81–82 (3d Cir.1986) (dictum).

37. For a summary of authorities reflecting this tendency concerning claims for "unquantified enhanced risk," see Ayers v. Township of Jackson, 525 A.2d 287, 305–08 (N.J.1987).

specific injury has occurred at the time of suit.[38] A practical consideration is that particularly in the situation of so-called "mass torts," courts may feel that they are doing well enough to compensate people who show actual evidence of illness. When there is only a limited pool of funds available, courts will find it more just to use scarce funds to compensate people who have actually gotten sick than to exhaust available funds by compensating those who face only increased risk.

B. Fear of illness

Some courts have been more sympathetic to plaintiffs' claims for fear of illness than to suits for increased risk. Although suits for fear of illness obviously deal with an intangible kind of damage, these courts appear to rationalize liability on the ground that present fear is an existing emotional harm. In an illustrative case, an asbestos worker sued for "fear of developing cancer" even though he could give no evidence of "substantial bodily illness or sickness resulting from the fear." The New Jersey courts upheld this claim, with the appellate court declaring that it was appropriate to submit the fear-of-cancer issue to the jury when there was evidence from which the jury could find "serious emotional distress and that the distress was reasonable."[39]

In approving claims both for the cost of medical surveillance and for emotional distress, at least in cases where exposure to toxic chemicals caused physical injury, the New Jersey Supreme Court emphasized the distinction between such claims and actions for increased risk for disease that did not meet the "reasonable medical probability" standard. The court said that its rules allowing claims for present emotional distress and the costs of medical surveillance "realistically address[] significant aspects of the present injuries sustained by toxic-tort plaintiffs, and serve[] as an added deterrent to polluters and others responsible for the wrongful use of toxic chemicals."[40]

C. Medical Monitoring

Even for those concerned about the relatively amorphous nature of mental anguish or fear of disease, the cause of action for medical monitoring would appear to strike a measured balance. It recognizes the enhanced probability—though not the certainty—of future illness. It takes into account the reasonable belief of persons

38. See, e.g., Sorenson v. Raymark Indus., Inc., 756 P.2d 740, 742 (Wash.Ct. App.1988) (in asbestos case, it was improper to admit evidence on risk of contracting cancer, because the plaintiff was seeking "redress for a merely speculative harm, the onset of cancer").

39. Mauro v. Owens–Corning Fiberglas Corp., 542 A.2d 16, 24 (N.J.Super.1988), aff'd, Mauro v. Raymark Indus., 561 A.2d 257 (N.J.1989).

40. 561 A.2d at 267 (N.J.1989).

who have been exposed to toxic substances that a sword of disease is hanging over their heads. Moreover, its cost is relatively quantifiable. All these factors combine to make the case for medical monitoring perhaps the strongest of the claims that may be brought for what are essentially concerns about future harm resulting from past exposure.

Section Nine
MULTIPLE TORTFEASORS
Chapter Fifty
JOINT AND MULTIPLE LIABILITIES

Analysis

¶ 50.01   Definitions and Mechanisms

Some difficult problems of justice in tort law arise when more than one party has been negligent or sold a defective product, and the plaintiff seeks to fix responsibility in tort on each of these multiple parties. In many of these cases, the plaintiff's theory is that each defendant contributed to the specific injury. In some cases, particularly in the area of products liability, the plaintiff argues that each defendant should be liable because its product was probabilistically involved in the plaintiff's injury on account of its involvement in many similar injuries.

There are various ways in which multiple defendants may be brought under the umbrella of the same litigation for the sake of administrative convenience. The plaintiff may join multiple defendants in her initial pleading, or if the plaintiff sues more than one defendant individually, the court could consolidate the actions. Moreover, if the plaintiff sues a single defendant, who believes that other parties are entirely or partially responsible for the injury, that initial defendant may bring others into the litigation by means of third party complaints.

276

With respect to the plaintiff's claim, a principal issue in cases of this kind is whether the court should impose what is commonly termed "joint" liability—that is, liability for the entire injury—on each of the defendants. (The frequently used term "joint and several liability" may have more than one connotation, depending on the jurisdiction, but usually it at least denotes that multiple defendants may be sued separately as well as joined together in one action.) Generally speaking, a plaintiff seeking to impose joint liability must show that she sustained an indivisible injury, by contrast with separable injuries that easily can be ascribed to individual defendants.

When several defendants are brought together in one lawsuit, the practical significance of a holding of joint liability is that the plaintiff may collect the total damages for her injury from any one of the defendants held to be "joint tortfeasors." To be sure, any joint tortfeasor may then seek to collect a portion—or even all—of the assessed damages from other tortfeasors.[1] But the burden to track down and force other parties to pay is that of the defendant against whom the plaintiff seeks to execute judgment, who otherwise is subject to paying the whole amount of the damages. That party may wind up being saddled with the entire loss—for example, if other joint tortfeasors are insolvent or cannot be brought before the court.

¶ 50.02   Theories of Joint and Multiple Liability

Courts have imposed liability on multiple defendants on the basis of several theories, which vary in their requirements and according to the situations to which courts apply them. In addition to discussing joint liability theories—those under which a joint tortfeasor is subject to paying the total amount of the plaintiff's damages, unless he can legally apportion part or all of the liability to others—we shall summarize other forms of liability against multiple defendants. Under some of those theories, courts may hold each defendant only for part, rather than all, of the damages.

A.   Joint venture and joint enterprise

One relatively rigorous set of theories usable against multiple defendants, all of whom have acted tortiously, includes the doctrines of joint venture and joint enterprise. The more rigorous test is that of the joint venture doctrine, which requires the plaintiff to show that the defendants combined for a business purpose for profit; by comparison, the joint enterprise theory requires a show-

---

1. For analysis of issues regarding apportionment of liability among defendants, see infra, Chapter 51.

ing that the defendants joined in a common activity.[2] Illustrative of judicial conservatism in applying even the joint enterprise theory is a case in which the plaintiff sought to impose joint liability on a driver and passengers who were "actively engaged" in providing alcohol and marijuana to the driver. Although conceding that "the passengers and the driver embarked on a common purpose," the court denied application of the joint enterprise theory, defining the missing "critical element" as a showing of "the common right to control the vehicle on the part of its occupants."[3]

B.　Concert of action

Another theory, employing such labels as "concert of action" and "joint concerted tortious activity," imposes liability on a defendant for harm caused by the tortious act of another person if the defendant did "a tortious act in concert with the other or pursuant to a common design with him." Alternatively, the defendant may be liable if he knows "that the other's conduct constitutes a breach of duty and gives substantial assistance or encouragement to the other so to conduct himself," or if he gives "substantial assistance to the other in accomplishing a tortious result and his own conduct, separately considered, constitutes a breach of duty to the [plaintiff]."[4]

The court in the drunk driving case described above imposed joint liability under this rule, even though it refused to do so under joint venture and joint enterprise theories. The court referred, in particular, to allegations that the passengers had "directly participated and ... encouraged the driver to continue to drink and smoke marijuana when he was already visibly intoxicated." The court found a policy basis for its decision in the need to curb the toll from alcohol or drug-influenced driving.[5]

C.　Alternative liability

Another form of joint liability takes the label "alternative liability." The seminal decision for this theory is the California case of *Summers v. Tice*,[6] in which the court imposed joint liability on two hunters for two birdshot wounds sustained by a plaintiff in whose direction the defendants both negligently fired. There was no way to know which defendant's shot had caused either wound, so that shot from the gun of one might have caused both wounds or each hunter could have caused one wound. The case is a landmark

---

2. See Price v. Halstead, 355 S.E.2d 380, 383–84 (W.Va.1987).

3. Id. at 384–85 (cataloguing precedents).

4. Restatement (Second) of Torts § 876 (1977).

5. See Price, supra note 2, 355 S.E.2d at 387.

6. 199 P.2d 1 (Cal.1948).

because it avoids the traditional requirement that the plaintiff show more than a 50 percent probability that the defendant was negligent and that the negligence caused the plaintiff's harm. In this case, where it was clear that both defendants were negligent, the probabilities were exactly balanced as to whose negligence caused the injury. However, the court said that in order to escape liability, each defendant would have to "absolve himself if he can," declaring that the defendants had put the plaintiff "in the unfair position of pointing to which defendant caused the harm."[7]

Any justification for the result in *Summers* must draw on the fact that both defendants were negligent. The case presented the problem of either imposing liability on two culpable persons for an injury which by hypothesis one of them may not have caused, or of letting both go entirely free and thus denying any recovery to the plaintiff.

D.   Products liability

The most controversial modern applications of theories of multiple liability, some of which are not technically joint liability theories, have appeared in the area of products injuries. Courts have fashioned a small set of doctrines to impose liability on groups of producers for injuries to individuals, when each member of a group of defendants has made products that are essentially the same and the plaintiff cannot prove which defendant's product caused the harm. One court has aptly characterized these theories as "non-identification theories" of liability, since typically the plaintiff in such cases asserts that he or she was not in a position to identify which of several companies sold the product at issue.[8]

A pioneering theory of this kind, one of relatively limited direct applicability, appeared in *Hall v. E.I. DuPont De Nemours & Co.*[9] That case involved suits against six manufacturers of blasting caps and their trade association by children who had been hurt in eighteen separate accidents attributed to blasting caps. In its preliminary analysis of the litigation, the court fashioned a joint liability theory that it termed "enterprise liability."[10] In rationalizing this theory, the court spoke of placing liability on "the most strategically placed participants in a risk-creating process."[11] Under the court's analysis and as the case has been interpreted, a crucial fact is that the industry was a relatively concentrated one.[12]

---

7. Id. at 4.

8. See Tidler v. Eli Lilly & Co., 851 F.2d 418, 421 (D.C.Cir.1988).

9. 345 F.Supp. 353 (E.D.N.Y.1972).

10. See id. at 376–78.

11. Id. at 376.

12. See id. at 378 ("special application" of theory to "industries comprised of a small number of units"); Vigiolto v. Johns–Manville Corp., 643 F.Supp. 1454, 1460 (W.D.Pa.1986) (*Hall* theory "wholly dependent upon either the informed exercise of control over the

Several decisions have applied the controversial theory of "market share liability," mostly in a specific product context. *Sindell v. Abbott Laboratories*[13] presented the initial, and most discussed, version of this theory. The plaintiffs in *Sindell* attributed cancers that they suffered to the administration of the hormone DES to their mothers in an attempt to stave off miscarriages. They sued a few firms out of the 200 companies that had made DES. After reviewing and rejecting several of the theories described above, the California Supreme Court created a "market share" theory, under which "[e]ach defendant will be held liable for the proportion of the judgment represented by its share of [the] market unless it demonstrates that it could not have made the product which caused plaintiff's injuries." The court framed the theory with a requirement that a plaintiff show that the defendants before the court represented a "substantial percentage" of the market.[14] A dissenter argued that the majority had excised from the law the requirement that plaintiffs must prove causation in order to succeed in a tort action, and suggested that application of the market share theory would treat plaintiffs "far more favorably than ... plaintiffs in routine tort actions."[15]

The *Sindell* theory has flowered in several varieties, mostly targeted to the specific problem of "DES daughters." Courts have not widely applied the theory outside of that particular situation.[16]

¶ 50.03   Competing Arguments

The issue of whether to impose joint liability, or to apply analogous theories like the "market share" theory, has featured some of the most contentious arguments in tort law, because of the stark contrast between the competing claims of justice offered by both parties.

A.   *The justice of joint and multiple liabilities*

The simplest, and perhaps most powerful, argument in favor of joint and multiple liability theories is that without them, many plaintiffs would be seriously undercompensated, if not go uncompensated, in cases in which several defendants have engaged in substandard conduct. Advocates of joint liability also argue that the doctrine minimizes litigation expense and ameliorates the problem

uniform practices of a given industry by a small number of manufacturers or the delegation by them of safety functions to a trade association").

13.   607 P.2d 924 (Cal.1980).

14.   Id. at 937.

15.   Id. at 940–41 (Richardson, J., dissenting).

16.   For a summary of decisions on efforts to apply the theory in cases involving such products as asbestos, vaccines, and lead paint, see 1 Marshall Shapo, The Law of Products Liability ¶ 12.21[4]–4[b], [6] (4th ed. 2001 & integrated Supplements).

of delay for plaintiffs desperate to secure compensation. The doctrine provides extra incentives for tortfeasors to settle.[17]

A rather theoretical argument in favor of the general principle of "group causation" represented by some of these theories is that it "would require an individual producer ... to attend to the safety practices of fellow producers making similar products and to expect them to attend to his safety practices, because each stands to be affected by what the others do or fail to do." This argument posits that "by inducing dialogue and positive interaction among all the members of an injurer group, group responsibility encourages injurer community."[18] It has been contended, moreover, that use of *Sindell*-type liability would make it easier for plaintiffs to bring class actions, thus contributing to systemic efficiency through the consolidation of dockets and the reduction of litigation costs to individual plaintiffs.[19]

B. *The injustice of joint and multiple liabilities*

The arguments against various forms of joint and multiple liabilities stem from the justice-centered concern that these doctrines enable a plaintiff to impose liability on a defendant for an injury, or a portion of an injury, that that defendant has not caused. Opponents of joint liability contend that the remedy departs from a most basic principle of tort law: the plaintiff has the burden of proof to show that the defendant's culpable conduct caused the injury. They argue that it is especially unjust that under true joint liability, a defendant might well be held for an entire loss if its joint tortfeasors were insolvent or unreachable. Critics have also complained that *Sindell*-type liability, in particular, is "the first products liability doctrine to base liability on wealth rather than responsibility."[20]

Opponents focusing on the economic effects of market share-type liability argue that it will unfairly and inefficiently drive up insurance premiums, creating disincentives to the development and sale of useful products. Moreover, they contend that the imposition of what they view as a virtual insurer form of liability will not

---

17. See, e.g., Richard Wright, Allocating Liability Among Multiple Responsible Causes: A Principled Defense of Joint and Several Liability for Actual Harm and Risk Exposure, 21 U.C. Davis L. Rev. 1141 (1988).

18. Robert A. Baruch Bush, Between Two Worlds: The Shift From Individual to Group Responsibility in the Law of Causation of Injury, 33 U.C.L.A. L. Rev. 1473, 1546 (1986).

19. Note, Market Share Liability: An Answer to the DES Causation Problem, 94 Harv. L. Rev. 668, 674–75 (1981).

20. Comment, Market Share Liability for Defective Products: An Ill-Advised Remedy for the Problem of Identification, 76 Nw. U. L. Rev. 300, 328 (1981).

create any useful incentives to manufacturers to take appropriate precautions.[21]

Finally, in rebuttal to the assertion that market share liability will reduce plaintiffs' costs, critics have argued that the threat of such liability is inefficient for multiple defendants. They point out that each defendant would have to hire its own lawyer in order to battle litigation over an injury that it may not have caused and, in the case of many defendants in the sort of cases brought under the market share theory, more likely than not did not cause.[22] A partial response to this argument is that market share liability, at least, is not joint: it requires the defendant to pay only the "proportion of the judgment represented by its share of that market."[23]

21. Note, Industry–Wide Liability, 13 Suffolk U. L. Rev. 980, 1003–04 (1979).

22. See David A. Fischer, Products Liability—An Analysis of Market Share Liability, 34 Vand L. Rev. 1623, 1657 (1981).

23. See Sindell, supra note 13, 607 P.2d at 937.

Chapter Fifty–One

APPORTIONMENT AMONG
MULTIPLE DEFENDANTS

Analysis

There are several ways in which issues arise concerning apportionment of liability among multiple defendants. In one typical situation, the plaintiff sues A, who believes that B (and perhaps others) are partly or completely responsible for the plaintiff's injury, and A then brings B and any others into the litigation by third-party practice. In other cases, the plaintiff originally joins more than one defendant in the action.

Once there is more than one defendant in the litigation, the court may impose joint liability on the multiple defendants—an outcome that means that any defendant held as a joint tortfeasor is subject to paying the total amount of the damages if it cannot find another solvent defendant to pay all or part of the award.[1] Whether courts initially make a finding of joint liability, or proceed directly to assess multiple defendants' relative contribution to an injury, they often must determine how to apportion the final burden of the injury between or among the defendants. There are at least three major techniques for doing so: indemnity, contribution, and comparative apportionment or responsibility.

¶ 51.01 Indemnity

Indemnity is a complete shifting of the loss from one party (the indemnitee) to another (the indemnitor). Courts have employed two

---

1. See supra, ¶ 50.01.

principal concepts in utilizing the indemnity remedy: the "active-passive" distinction and the "primary-secondary" dichotomy.

A. Active-passive

The "active-passive" distinction relies on the intuitively plausible notion that in some situations involving multiple defendants, one has participated in causing injury so much more directly—that is, actively—than the other, and with so much more control, that it is appropriate both from a standpoint of fairness and of economic incentives to impose the entire liability on that party. One case that drew on this distinction involved injuries suffered by spectators at a state fair when part of a catwalk on a grandstand collapsed during a performance by an Army Special Forces unit called the Green Berets. The plaintiffs sued the United States under the Federal Tort Claims Act, claiming that the Green Berets had been negligent. However, the plaintiffs' only proof of that negligence was that, in relying on representations by agents of the state about the construction of the grandstand roof, the soldiers failed to inspect in a way that would have revealed the manner in which the catwalk was attached to the roof. In a third party action by the federal government against the state, the court held that the state was actively negligent and must indemnify the federal government.[2]

The more directly a party acts, by comparison with acquiescence in a representation or act of another, the more difficult it will be for that party to get indemnity. Wrestling with factual questions about its contribution to the occurrence, the indemnitee must contend with a judicial bias against a complete shifting of responsibility as between parties that have had some operative role in causing an injury. In the terms of the active-passive dichotomy, any culpable activity by an indemnitee beyond acquiescence is likely to propel it into the category of active negligence and thus defeat its effort to shift the loss entirely to the other defendant.[3]

B. Primary-secondary

Although there is overlap between the categories of active-passive and primary-secondary, the latter stands theoretically separate. A situation in which courts are likely to consider a defendant to be a secondary tortfeasor, thus justifying a transfer of the entire loss to another defendant as a primary tortfeasor, is the accident where the liability of the defendant seeking to shift the loss arises

---

2. United States v. State of Illinois, 454 F.2d 297, 302 (7th Cir.1971).

3. Cf. C & O Ry. Co. v. Illinois Cent. Gulf R. Co., 564 F.2d 222 (7th Cir.1977) (in prior action, injured ICG employee successfully sued C & O for misalignment of switch; C & O then sought indemnity from ICG on theory that ICG's control tower employees were "actively" negligent in failing to prevent collision of trains; held, judgment in ICG employee's suit against C & O estopped C & O from denying that its own negligence was "active").

only by operation of law. A prime illustration is the case of vicarious liability, as in a case in which an employer is held liable for the negligence of an employee on grounds of respondeat superior. Although because of economic realities, employers would seldom sue employees to recover the cost of a tort judgment, this kind of situation would present a clear case for indemnity. The employee is the only party who was in fact negligent and the employer's liability is vicarious, existing only because of its agency relationship with the employee. Theoretically, therefore, the law would require the party who was in fact at fault, the employee, to reimburse the party that was not at fault, the employer.

An interesting comparison appears in certain cases involving independent contractors. By contrast with the vicarious liability of employers for the torts of their employees, those who employ independent contractors, as a general rule, are not liable for the torts of their contractors. One exception to this rule of non-liability, an exception under which employers of independent contractors are initially liable for the contractor's negligence, has motivated courts to apply a primary-secondary distinction in order to allow the employer to get indemnity from the contractor. This is the case where the non-negligent employer of a culpable independent contractor has a non-delegable duty to the plaintiff and is therefore initially liable to the plaintiff. In a New York case, a statute imposed such a duty on the owner of an apartment house to maintain the building safely. However, in a case involving an elevator accident, the court permitted the apartment owner to sue an elevator maintenance company for indemnity when the maintenance company, an independent contractor, had breached a contractual obligation to keep the elevator safe. The court characterized the liability of the apartment owner as being only vicarious, with the result that as between the apartment owner and the elevator maintenance company, the latter should bear the full responsibility.[4]

¶ 51.02   Contribution

Unlike indemnity, which mandates a complete shifting of loss from one defendant to another, the contribution remedy apportions damages between or among tortfeasors. The basic principle is a pro rata division of damages, with equal shares of liability being enforced upon multiple defendants. Thus, even if the facts indicate that one defendant is more responsible for an injury than another, the contribution rules apportion the liability equally.

A case involving an injury on a store escalator illustrates the appeal of contribution as a rough-and-ready equitable remedy. The

---

4. Rogers v. Dorchester Assocs., 300 N.E.2d 403, 408–09 (N.Y.1973).

plaintiff, a boy who suffered injuries when his tennis shoe was caught in the escalator mechanism, initially sued the owner of the store, which brought a third party action against the escalator manufacturer. The court drew on policy considerations, focusing on incentives for safety, in holding that the manufacturer and its insurer must pay contribution to the store owner and its insurer. The court said that because neither the manufacturer or the store "undertook to warn those using the escalator, and both were aware of the risk, both are equally at fault. While Otis might theoretically manufacture a safer product, Maison Blanche could purchase a better escalator, switch to stairs or use elevators." The court observed that the manufacturer was "in a better position to improve the design of the machine than" the store owner, but declared that the store owner "should not be allowed to keep a defective escalator and pass all liability to the manufacturer."[5] This language captures a sense of equity as well as a desire to focus tort remedies toward the prevention of accidents.

Some interesting variations on contribution appear when it is possible to view groups of defendants as classes. In one case, the plaintiff claimed injuries when a flower pot fell from a party wall, one part of which was owned by one person and the other jointly owned by two. Instead of dividing the liability three ways among all of the owners of the wall, the court viewed the two joint owners as a group that was liable for only a single share of the judgment. The court said that "to saddle the owners of one house with two-thirds of the judgment and allow the owner of the other house to escape with payment of only one-third" would be "inequitable."[6]

A case involving the collapse of a volleyball net standard provides another set of variations. The New Mexico court of appeals theorized, as an initial matter, that the damages should be divided equally among the manufacturer of the standard, its retailer, and the city that purchased it, with the manufacturer then paying two-thirds of the judgment because of an unchallenged trial court determination that the manufacturer must indemnify the retailer.[7] The state supreme court, however, insisted that there were "two different torts, and two active tortfeasors," which "support[ed] a fifty-fifty split of the judgment" between the city and the manufacturer. The supreme court stressed how inequitable it would be if, for example, there were eight intermediate distributors between the manufacturer and the city, which under the court of appeals' approach would mean that the manufacturer would wind up paying

5. Hunt v. City Stores, Inc., 387 So.2d 585, 590 (La.1980).

6. Wold v. Grozalsky, 14 N.E.2d 437, 439 (N.Y.1938).

7. Sanchez v. City of Espanola, 615 P.2d 993, 994–96 (N.M.Ct.App.1980).

90 per cent of the judgment and the city only 10 per cent.[8] These different approaches indicate that the concept of equity is a supple one, and may flexibly be applied to justify a variety of results in contribution cases.

¶ 51.03 Immunity Rules: Workers' Compensation

An important pocket of immunity against suits for apportionment, which bars third party suits against employers, arises from the exclusivity provisions of workers' compensation statutes. The root of the legal problem is that workers' compensation legislation prohibits employees, who receive compensation payments from their employers under the statute, from bringing tort actions against their employers. The exclusivity of this remedy was part of the legislative bargain that facilitated the passage of workers' compensation laws; in that pragmatic political deal, employees in effect traded for a relatively assured recovery of compensation benefits by sacrificing their opportunity to sue for the less certain but sometimes more lucrative recoveries that are possible in tort.

Although clearly employees covered by workers' compensation cannot sue their employers in tort, third parties who have had to defend tort actions by employees of other firms have tried to sue those employers for indemnity or contribution, alleging that those employers' conduct was a sole, or active cause of the injury. However, most courts have not been hospitable to these suits by tortious third parties against workers' compensation employers. These courts stress both the language of the exclusivity provisions of the compensation statutes, and the idea that employers' duties run only to their employees and not to the third party plaintiffs. Courts denying third party actions against employers have also stressed the sharp distinction between workers' compensation and negligence law,[9] bluntly observing that workers' compensation "has nothing to do with the concepts of negligence."[10]

This immunity rule cuts broadly in favor of employers in cases originating with products liability claims. The almost universal application of the rule means that a product manufacturer—for example, the maker of a dangerous workplace machine—is vulnerable to tort suits by employees of an employer that uses the machine in its business, but cannot sue that employer for its contribution to the injury by requiring use of an unsafe machine. Courts have used various conceptual formulas to justify this result. One court, for example, offered a no-duty explanation for the immunity, reasoning

8. Aalco Mfg. Co. v. City of Espanola, 618 P.2d 1230, 1232 (N.M.1980).

9. See generally 1 M. Shapo, The Law of Products Liability § 15.03[2]–[3]

(4th ed. 2001 and integrated Supplements).

10. Williams v. Weiler & Co., 498 F.Supp. 917, 920 (S.D.Iowa 1979).

that, while an employer's "obligations run to its employee," it does not have a "separate duty ... to the manufacturer ... which allegedly caused the injury itself."[11] Under an analogous rationale, a manufacturer cannot get contribution from a workers' compensation employer because the employer is not "liable" in tort. Starting with that premise, another court concluded, "Where there is no joint and several liability, there is no right of contribution."[12]

There is, however, contrary authority. A Supreme Court case yielded an unusual decision in favor of a third party suing the federal government, which was the employer of the decedent of the original tort plaintiff. A civilian employee of the government died in the crash of an airplane while she was on a mission to evacuate orphans from Vietnam just before the fall of Saigon. Her administrator sued Lockheed on the grounds that the craft was defective. After settling the administrator's claim, Lockheed brought a third party action against the government. Although it did not dispute that it was "primarily responsible for the fatal crash," the government defended on the basis that it had already paid death benefits to the employee's survivors under the Federal Employees Compensation Act, the workers' compensation legislation for federal employees. It invoked that statute's declaration that the government's liability "is exclusive and instead of all other liability ... to the employee, his legal representative ... [or] any other person otherwise entitled to recover damages from the United States ... because of the [employee's] injury or death." The government argued that Lockheed was an "other person otherwise entitled to recover damages from the United States."[13]

However, a majority of the Supreme Court permitted Lockheed to bring a third party action for indemnity, quoting a much-cited statement by Professor Larson that the issue of whether third parties could sue employers for indemnity was "[p]erhaps the most evenly-balanced controversy in all of workers' compensation law."[14] The Court drew on a precedent for the proposition that there was " 'no evidence ... that Congress was concerned with the rights of unrelated third parties, much less of any purpose to disturb settled doctrines of [tort] law affecting the mutual rights and liabilities of private [parties] in [indemnity] cases.' "[15] A dissent lamented that the decision would "greatly expand[] the liability to which the

---

11. Langley v. Harris Corp., 321 N.W.2d 662, 667 (Mich.1982).

12. Glass v. Stahl Specialty Co., 652 P.2d 948, 952 (Wash.1982).

13. Lockheed Aircraft Corp. v. United States, 460 U.S. 190 (1983).

14. Id. at 193, quoting Larson, Third–Party Action Over Against Work-

ers' Compensation Employer, 1982 Duke L. J. 483, 484. Many courts quote the same assessment from 2 Larson, Workmen's Compensation Law ¶ 76.20 (1983).

15. Lockheed, supra note 13, 460 U.S. at 195, quoting Weyerhaeuser S.S. Co. v. United States, 372 U.S. 597, 601 (1963).

government may be subjected on account of injuries to its employees."[16] The dissent stressed the particular burden that indemnity, by contrast with contribution-type remedies, would impose on the government.[17] In any event, despite the majority's decision, the "evenly-balanced" nature of this issue is more intellectual than quantitative, since the clear weight of state decisions immunizes the employer against third-party tort actions.

The results of litigation in this area will turn in part on the exact language of the exclusivity provision at issue, but an important ground of decision will be the policy considerations involved in the delicate balance between workers' compensation and tort law. On the one hand, courts that deny third-party claims concern themselves with maintenance of the so-called "quid pro quo" in the hypothesized bargain between employers and employees that underlay workers' compensation legislation. On the other hand, there may be some situations in which allowing third party tort actions will produce a more desirable level of deterrence to culpable behavior.

¶ 51.04   Comparative Responsibility

A.   Concepts and language

The other major technique for allocating losses among defendants, in addition to indemnity and contribution, is a set of doctrines that permit percentage apportionments of liability among defendants. The terminology of these doctrines reflects the underlying concepts that courts have in mind in trying to achieve precise apportionments. When the several defendants have all been found to be negligent, courts have found it congenial to speak of principles of "comparative fault."[18] Particularly when the theory of liability for one defendant is negligence but that for another defendant is strict liability, courts or legislatures may talk in terms of "comparative degrees of responsibility,"[19] "relative responsibility,"[20] or even "comparative liability."[21] Interesting, if disconcertingly hybrid, are the mixtures of terminology that appear in the phrases "comparative contribution"[22] and even "comparative indemnity"[23] and "pro-

---

16. Id. at 203 (Rehnquist, J., dissenting).

17. Id. at 202.

18. See Safeway Stores v. Nest–Kart, 579 P.2d 441, 442 (Cal.1978) (characterizing findings of jury).

19. Kennedy v. City of Sawyer, 618 P.2d 788, 804 (Kan.1980).

20. Dole v. Dow Chem. Co., 282 N.E.2d 288, 295 (N.Y.1972).

21. Kennedy, supra note 19, 618 P.2d at 790, 795, 796–97.

22. McMeekin v. Harry M. Stevens, Inc., 530 A.2d 462, 466 (Pa.Super.1987). Cf. Tolbert v. Gerber Indus., Inc., 255 N.W.2d 362, 367 (Minn.1977) ("contribution based upon relative fault").

23. Safeway Stores, supra note 18, 579 P.2d at 445.

portional indemnification."[24] A rather different approach is evident in the term "comparative cause."[25]

B. *Rationales*

A principal justification for a comparative method of apportionment, even as compared with pro rata shares of contribution, is precisely that it is more measured than the other apportionment remedies and gives the fact finder more of an opportunity to refine an equitable division of losses. Certainly, a comparative approach permits courts to harmonize the method of apportionment among defendants with comparative fault regimes that use percentage methods to divide the financial burden of accidents between plaintiffs and defendants. Opponents of comparative apportionment contend it will itself lead to arbitrary results, and, with respect to claims involving strict liability, will undermine the purposes of that doctrine.

An intramural argument in the California Supreme Court displayed both advantages and disadvantages of a comparative regime in situations where the liability of multiple parties is grounded on both negligence and strict liability. The contrasting opinions appeared in a case in which a jury had found a supermarket 80 percent responsible under "both negligence and strict liability principles" and the manufacturer of a shopping cart to be 20 percent responsible, "grounded solely on strict liability principles." The majority opinion, employing the hybrid concept of "common law comparative indemnity," justified its choice on grounds of fairness and "basic equitable considerations."[26] It referred to the precision that form of apportionment made possible by contrast with "an inflexible pro rata apportionment pursuant to ... contribution statutes." The majority declared that the differences between negligence and strict liability were "more theoretical than practical." Specifically referring to cases involving manufacturers and other tortfeasors, it pointed out that if courts did not apply a comparative doctrine, strictly liable defendants might not be able to get apportionment whereas "actually negligent" manufacturers would be in a better position because they would be able to shift liability to "more negligent cotortfeasors."[27]

A concurring judge argued that it would be better to have an equal division of liability. Interestingly, he contended that the majority approach reflected an "arbitrary" apportionment in the

---

24. In re Consolidated Vista Hills Retaining Wall Litig., 893 P.2d 438, 448–49 (N.M.1995).

25. Busch v. Busch Constr., Inc., 262 N.W.2d 377, 394 (1977) (quoting Jensvold, A Modern Approach to Loss Allocation Among Tortfeasors in Products Liability Cases, 58 Minn. L. Rev. 723, 725 (1974)).

26. Safeway Stores, supra note 18, 579 P.2d at 444 (1978).

27. Id. at 445–46.

case at issue, opining that "[b]lind inquiry into relative fault is no better than the flip of a coin."[28] A polar position appeared in a dissenting opinion, which complained of "the total infusion of negligence theories into the previously independent doctrine of products liability." Emphasizing the burdens that strict liability imposes on manufacturers, he declared that to allow such firms "to place in issue the conduct of other defendants" would wrongly provide strictly liable manufacturers a way to dilute their responsibility.[29]

Another instructive disagreement in a products liability setting appeared in a case in which a majority of the Minnesota Supreme Court rejected an indemnity action by an installer of defective equipment against the manufacturer. The installer had claimed that its negligence consisted only of its failure to discover and prevent the manufacturer's misconduct. The majority opted for "reallocation of loss between joint tortfeasors" limited to "contribution based upon relative fault." Opposing the application of the "blunt instrument" of indemnity to cases where both parties were partly at fault, the court rationalized its rule on the basis that "the more culpable tortfeasor will continue to bear a greater share of the loss, but . . . his joint tortfeasor will not . . . escape all liability" as was the case under an indemnity regime.[30] A dissenter, stressing that the installer's negligence lay only in its failure to discover a defect not obvious in the process of installation, argued that "fundamental fairness and sound economic principles of loss allocation" supported indemnity.[31] Another dissenter expressed doubt that "an intelligible rule or jury instruction could be fashioned which would permit a jury to apply equitable principles necessarily required to justly apportion liability."[32]

A substantial amount of the argument on the subject of apportionment among defendants resolves itself into the question of how refined are the judgments that juries can realistically make on percentage allocations of liability. There is a certain irony in the fact that with many observers viewing doctrinal progress as being measured in terms of the degree of calibration that the law allows, others insist that the mind—or at least the lay juror's mind—is best suited to make rather gross determinations of the sort represented by the contribution and indemnity remedies.

[Chapters 52–53 are reserved for supplementary material.]

28. Id. at 448 (Clark, J., concurring).

29. Id. (Mosk, J., dissenting).

30. Tolbert v. Gerber Indus., Inc., 255 N.W.2d 362, 367 (Minn.1977).

31. Id. at 368 (Kelly, J., dissenting).

32. Id. at 372 (Rogosheske, J., dissenting).

Chapter Fifty–Four

SETTLEMENT

Analysis

An important group of problems related to apportionment of damages arises when one member of a set of defendants settles with the plaintiff but another—or others—go to trial. If the plaintiff prevails against a defendant who chose to go to a verdict, the principal questions concern whether that defendant can get credit on the verdict for all or part of the settlement. Although the principles courts have applied to these issues are not part of the substantive law of torts, they illuminate the workings of the litigation system that develops that law.

We will analyze a few recurrent situations of this kind, and then discuss the legal policies that courts apply to the question of what rights settling and non-settling defendants have with respect to plaintiffs, and to each other. The very factually oriented nature of the categories analyzed here implies the difficulty of formulating abstract principles. In all of the situations discussed below, which are functionally defined and sometimes overlap, one defendant,

D–1, has settled, and one defendant, D–2, has not. In all of these cases, the settling defendant is no longer a party in the litigation because of the settlement. Although the judge must know of any settlement and how much it is for, practice varies on whether the jury knows about a settlement, a matter the cases do not always reveal.

The general problem that confronts courts in deciding settlement issues includes several elements of policy, including concerns about equity, considerations of individualized justice and efficient judicial administration. Courts sometimes favor rules designed to assure that the plaintiff is fully compensated for his injuries through a combination of the jury award plus any settlement, but does not get a "windfall." On other occasions, they will allow the plaintiff a sum from the jury award and the settlement together that totals more than the assessed injury costs, reasoning in part that the money paid in settlement is theoretically gratuitous, and that the officially sanctioned award is the only legally compelled payment. Faced with the difficulty of putting cases into neat boxes of principle, courts will try to figure out what result provides the most equitable solution. They will also pay attention to whether a rule seems likely to promote settlement, thus taking pressure off the judicial system.

¶ 54.01 Classes of Settlement Situations

A. Verdict against non-settling defendant for more than settlement multiplied by the number of defendants, but jury views settling defendant as also culpable

One situation finds D–1 settling for a particular amount, with the jury giving a verdict against D–2 for an amount that is more than the settlement figure multiplied by the number of parties, but indicating that it thinks that D–1 was also culpable. An interesting solution appears in a case of this kind in which D–1 settled for $700. The jury, aware of the settlement, found for the plaintiff against D–2 for $2,000, but "in favor of [D–2] against [D–1] 'for contribution,' " with the parties stipulating that the court should set "the amount of contribution." The appellate court allowed D–2 a credit on the award against him that was pro-rated by the number of parties—that is, a $1,000 reduction. The court's theory was that the jury award had fixed the total amount of damages, and that the plaintiff, by settling, had "sold one-half of his claim for damages."[1] It will be noted that, whatever incentives this approach will create for defendants, each under uncertainty about winning or losing and about the amount a plaintiff's verdict would award, it

1. Martello v. Hawley, 300 F.2d 721, 724 (D.C.Cir.1962).

leaves the plaintiff a sum that is less than what the jury set as the total amount of damages. It would thus seem to present less incentive for plaintiffs to settle than rules allowing less credit to non-settling defendants.

Obviously, another technique would be simply to reduce the judgment by the amount of the settlement. This result appears in a case with some doctrinal complexity, arising from the overlap of tort and contract theories, in which a university administrator sued for events associated with a failure to renew his contract.[2] He claimed against a department chairman for libel and interference with contract and also sued the university for breach of contract as well as libel and interference with contract. The plaintiff settled with the university on the breach of contract action for $5,000. In a subsequent trial, the court gave directed verdicts for the university on the claims for libel and interference with contract and for the department chairman on the libel claim. A jury then rendered a verdict for the plaintiff against the chairman on the interference claim for $15,000.

The court decided to credit the judgment against the chairman for the amount the university paid for its settlement. It reasoned that with the libel claim out of the picture, the gist of both the contract claim that the university and the plaintiff had settled, and of the interference claim, on which the plaintiff won a judgment against the chairman, was the same. Thus, essentially, there had been one loss from the nonrenewal of the plaintiff's contract, a loss for which the compensation sources were the university's settlement on the breach claim and the jury verdict against the chairman on the interference claim. The court reasoned that if it were not to credit the settlement on the judgment, the effect would be to make the plaintiff "more than whole" for the injury he suffered.[3]

For the sake of theoretical completeness, we should consider a third alternative: not permitting D–2 any credit on the judgment for the settlement. The result of this would be that, relative to the damages as fixed by the jury, the plaintiff would be overcompensated.[4] We discuss below the rationales for this result.[5]

---

2. Kassman v. American Univ., 546 F.2d 1029 (D.C.Cir.1976).

3. Id. at 1035.

4. A fact-specific variation appears in the intermediate appeals court's decision in *Martello*, supra note 1, which "directed entry of judgment on the original judgment of $2,000." That court reasoned that because the jury was aware of the settlement, it "must have award-

ed the $2,000 as additional damages necessary to fully compensate [the plaintiff]." See 300 F.2d at 723. Disapproving this outcome, the court of appeals said that to allow jurors to know the "fact or the amount of any settlement" would "only tend[] to mislead them in their deliberations concerning a just compensatory verdict." Id. at 724.

5. See infra, ¶ 54.02(B).

B. Settling defendant "absolved" at trial of non-settling defendant; judgment for more than settlement multiplied by number of defendants

A somewhat different problem arises when, in the trial in which D–2 has chosen to litigate, the jury or the court in some way declares D–1 not to have been at fault, and renders a verdict that exceeds the settlement times the number of defendants. This absolution of D–1 is artificial in the sense that D–1's defense had not been exposed to the adversary test of a full trial, but some courts allow the jury to make such a determination. In one case in which this occurred, the bus on which the plaintiff was riding collided with a car. D–1, the driver of the car, settled for $5,000, although this was not announced to the jury. The jury proceeded to "exonerate[]" D–1 but to give a verdict against D–2, the bus company, for $12,500. Despite the jury's view that D–1 was not at fault, the appellate court decided to give D–2 credit on the plaintiff's judgment against it for the amount of the settlement by D–1.[6] This solution assures that the plaintiff will not recover more than the figure at which the jury assessed her damages. However, it shares the disadvantages naturally associated with any rules that allow credit to D–2 for D–1's settlement. In particular, it takes away some incentive for D–2 to settle because it knows that if the plaintiff wins a judgment against it, it will be able to escape the full brunt of the injury costs by getting credit for the settlement.

C. Jury exonerates defendant who settled for a comparatively large amount and holds non-settling defendant completely responsible, or significantly at fault, for a sum compared with which the settlement figure is close in amount, if not more

Another kind of case raises the twin problems of avoiding a situation where a D–2 judged culpable pays little or nothing and also avoiding substantial overcompensation to the plaintiff by the combined total of settlements and the jury award. In one case of this type, after a settlement with D–1 for a substantial amount, the plaintiff goes to verdict against D–2. The jury holds D–2 to be completely responsible, giving its opinion that the settling defendant was not at fault. It awards against D–2 a sum that presumably represents the total cost of the plaintiff's injury, a sum compared with which the settlement is close in amount, if not more. That was the situation in a case where the settlement by two plaintiffs with

---

6. Snowden v. D.C. Transit System, Inc., 454 F.2d 1047 (D.C.Cir.1971), distinguishing *Martello*, supra note 1, on the basis that in that case "the jury determined that both defendants were liable," and "therefore a formula requiring [D–2] to pay more than half the verdict would have deprived him of his right to contribution from the other defendant," but that in the case before the court, D–1 was "exonerated." Id. at 1049 n.6.

two D–1's—a surgeon and a partnership of anesthesiologists—was for $270,000 and the verdict against D–2, a hospital, was for $294,777.[7] D–2, the hospital, sought to credit the entire settlement on the verdict, the effect of which would have been that although the jury had said that D–2 was completely responsible, it would have paid only $24,777 on an injury that the jury found to be worth $294,777. The other part of the legal puzzle was that if the plaintiffs collected the $294,777 award and retained the entire $270,000 settlement, they would emerge with $564,777 in payments for an injury that had been found to be worth only a little more than half that figure.

Confronted with the equitable difficulties inherent in this situation, the court of appeals concluded that D–2, as one of three initial defendants, must pay its pro rata share of the judgment, or about $98,000; the two D–1's, the surgeon and the partnership of anesthesiologists, were treated as separate defendants for the purpose of figuring shares. To put it another way, the hospital could credit on the judgment only a figure that did not exceed two-thirds of the verdict.[8] This result certainly has the advantage of at least bringing home against D–2 a significant amount of the burden of the injury, relative to what D–2 would pay if the entire settlement were credited against the verdict, thus fostering deterrence. It is less clear how much effect it has with respect to putting pressure on D–2 to settle when the other parties settle.

In a variation on this problem, there is a settlement by one or more defendants for a large amount. Then the jury calculates damages of a somewhat greater figure than the settlement to represent the plaintiff's total loss, attributing a significant percentage of fault to the nonsettling defendant. If the nonsettling defendant must then pay the dollar share of his causal percentage of the total loss established by the jury, when that amount is added to the settlement the result may be to boost the plaintiff's overall recovery significantly above the total loss figure.

An Arizona decision in a medical malpractice case explains why this may be a just outcome. Two defendants, a physician and a hospital, settled for $700,000 each. At the trial of D–2, a surgeon, the jury fixed the plaintiff's loss at $1,965,000 and decided that D–2 was 47 per cent at fault, assessing the rest of the causal fault to the settling defendants. The trial court subtracted the total settlements from the total loss figure established by the verdict to give the plaintiff a recovery against D–2 for the difference—$565,000.[9]

---

7. Rose v. Hakim, 501 F.2d 806 (D.C.Cir.1974).

8. See id. at 808.

9. Roland v. Bernstein, 828 P.2d 1237 (Ariz.Ct.App.1991), review denied (1992).

The court of appeals reversed, concluding that D–2 should have to pay $923,550—that is, 47 per cent of the total loss of $1,965,000. The outcome of this was that the plaintiff would recover $2,323,-550—the total of the settlements plus the nonsettling defendant's causal percentage of the verdict amount. But although this total was well over $300,000 above the verdict, the appellate court pointed out that if the plaintiff had "made a disadvantageous settlement, she would have borne that consequence because her recovery against [the nonsettling defendant] would have been limited to $923,550." It then declared that "[a]t a minimum, symmetry requires that if the disadvantage of settlement is hers so should the advantage be." Moreover, the court said that a contrary rule "might well discourage settlement by the last tortfeasor on the reasoning that his exposure is limited to his degree of fault and even that might be reduced by reason of pre-existing settlements."[10]

D.   Settling defendant seeks reimbursement from non-settling defendant

Quite distinct from problems of credit against the plaintiff's verdict are the intra-defendant issues that come up when D–1 seeks reimbursement from D–2, who has been found completely responsible for the plaintiff's injuries. A standard response by D–2 is that D–1 deserves no reimbursement at all because D–1's payment as a settling defendant was "voluntary." Perhaps a more persuasive rationale for denying reimbursement to D–1 is that the idea of a settlement is precisely to fix, at a relatively early stage of litigation, a figure that the plaintiff and the settling defendant think is fair between them. In terms of the logic of the litigation process, the settling defendant has completely resolved its legal relationship with the plaintiff by the settlement itself; thus, to allow any reimbursement to D–1 from D–2 would in a sense be allowing D–1 to have his cake and eat it too. The Uniform Contribution Among Tortfeasors Act opposes contribution in favor of settling tortfeasors against other tortfeasors.[11]

E.   When to calculate plaintiffs' fault: "Fault first" vs. "settlement first"

An interesting issue that combines facets of both equity and incentives to settle appears in the case in which a negligent plaintiff settles with D–1 and wins at trial against D–2, although the jury finds the plaintiff to have a substantial amount of comparative fault. In the "fault first" method, the court discounts the jury verdict by the assessed fault of the plaintiff and only then subtracts

---

10. Id. at 1239.

11. Uniform Contribution Among Tortfeasors Act § 1(d) (1955), 12 Unif. Laws Ann. 195 (West 1996).

the amount of the plaintiff's settlement with D–1. Under the "settlement first" solution, the court reduces the jury verdict by the amount of the settlement and then subtracts an amount corresponding to the plaintiff's assessed fault from the remainder. The New York Court of Appeals chose the "settlement first method," the effect of which was to favor a plaintiff in a situation in which the "fault-first" method would have left a negative balance against D–2, who would not have had to pay anything.[12] The court rationalized its choice of "settlement first" partly on the ground that it would "result in a more precise allocation of loss," premising that the settlement with D–1 "approximate[d] the parties' intuitive assessment of [D–1's] fault and damages." It also reasoned that "the settlement-first approach offers incentive for defendants to settle, because nonsettling defendants will tend to risk increasing their liability as other defendants settle, and the remaining defendants are more likely to be assessed increasing shares of the comparative fault."[13]

¶ 54.02 Policies Associated With Credits for Settlements

There are several policies that enter into judicial consideration of whether to allow non-settling defendants to credit verdicts for the amount of settlements made before the verdict. Some of the principal policies invoked by courts involve notions of "equity" and "fairness," the theory that a settling defendant is a "volunteer," and the related idea that the settlement simply represents a private contract between the plaintiff and the settling defendant.

A. Policies in favor of allowing credit to non-settling defendants

The arguments in favor of allowing credit to non-settling defendants tend to resolve themselves into the idea that the law frowns on "windfalls" to plaintiffs. Thus, courts may speak in

---

12. Whalen v. Kawasaki Motors Corp., U.S.A., 703 N.E.2d 246 (N.Y. 1998). The plaintiff had settled with D–1 for $1,600,000. The nonsettling defendant, D–2, went to trial and the jury gave a verdict of $2,415,000 against it, but found the plaintiff 92 per cent comparatively negligent and D–2 only 8 per cent at fault. Under the "fault first" method, the jury verdict against D–2 of $2,415,000 would be discounted initially by the plaintiff's 92 per cent negligence, leaving $193,200. Subtracting the $1,600,000 settlement would produce a negative balance against D–2, relieving him of any responsibility to pay damages. Under the "settlement first" method, the court would reduce the verdict against D–2 by the amount of D–1's settlement and only then discount the remainder by the percentage of the plaintiff's comparative fault. This would yield a positive sum for the plaintiff—in this case, the verdict for $2,415,000 minus the settlement of $1,600,000, or $815,000, which would then be multiplied by 8 per cent to give the plaintiff a recovery against D–2 of $65,200. See id. at 249.

13. 703 N.E.2d at 250–51.

terms of awarding to plaintiffs compensation that is "full but only full." Allowing credits to nonsettling defendants assures that plaintiffs will not emerge from litigation, including the process of settlement, with more money than a sum that represents their total damages as assessed by a fact finder.

B. Policies opposing credits to non-settling defendants

A number of policies oppose allowing credits to non-settling defendants, even if the result is to overcompensate the plaintiff. One of these policies is, simply, the promotion of settlement: if a defendant knows that it will not get credit for the value of settlements arrived at by other defendants, it will be more inclined to settle expeditiously.[14] This has the side effect of discouraging nonsettling defendants from dilatory tactics that squeeze meritorious, but desperate, plaintiffs into selling their claims too cheaply. Another argument against allowing credits to non-settling defendants draws on the rule, known as the collateral source rule, which prohibits defendants from reducing damage awards by the amount of other payments made to plaintiffs on account of an injury, ranging from insurance payments to gifts from others who wish to make up the plaintiff's losses. Many courts, however, reject this analogy as applied to settlements. One decision, pointing out that the collateral source rule only keeps defendants from getting credit for payments made to plaintiffs "gratuitously," or made under prior contract—like payments by insurers—observed that "[a] settlement made by one liable potentially, but not in fact, is made under Damoclean pressure, not gratuitously."[15]

One of the strongest arguments against allowing credits to non-settling defendants, or at least for placing limitations on those credits, is that to the extent that a credit is allowed, the non-settling defendant escapes the effects of its culpable conduct. Since the true social costs of that defendant's negligence would not be imposed on it, forcing it to internalize those costs, the allowing of credit would undermine the law's efforts to achieve appropriate levels of deterrence.

14. This is one ground for the court's decision in Alexander v. Director, Office of Workers' Compensation Programs, 297 F.3d 805 (9th Cir.2002), refusing credit to an employer found liable under the Longshore and Harbor Workers' Compensation Act, who sought credit for the plaintiff's prior settlements with three other employers. The court says that to interpret a credit provision in the statute to allow the defendant to get credit for the prior settlements would have "the perverse effect of discouraging settlements." Id. at 809. The court also says that the opposite holding would make the plaintiff "risk a settlement in which his last employer would get all the benefit," quoting a precedent on the idea that "[t]he employee's 'good fortune in striking a favorable bargain' is not to be treated as a boon to the other defendants." Id. at 808.

15. See Snowden, supra note 6, 454 F.2d at 1049.

Moreover, the effect of allowing a complete credit for the settlement may be unfair as among defendants, although fairness may have two edges. Consider, for example, a case like one involving physicians and a hospital, described above, where the jury exonerates a party that settled for a large figure, and holds the non-settling defendant entirely responsible for a sum to which the settlement is at least close in amount.[16] In such a situation, there is an obvious unfairness in allowing the non-settling defendant a full credit that permits it to pay very little for a severe injury. At the same time, one may argue that it is unfair not to allow at least some credit, since the plaintiff opted to accept a large settlement from the settling defendants. Courts must struggle to balance the equities in cases of this sort.

C. *Incentives summarized*

It is useful to summarize some of the competing incentives that will influence courts in their consideration of the issue of whether to credit settlements against plaintiffs' verdicts. With an eye to judicial administration, courts have an institutional incentive to promote settlement, aiming at a reduction of their workloads and of systemic costs generally. Yet, courts also must take into account that providing incentives for settlements may sometimes limit the information that society gets about the causes of injuries. This is because a settlement means that evidence that would be introduced against a defendant if there were a trial will not be presented. Legal rules that promote settlement also tend to minimize the involvement of the community as a whole, primarily through juries, in the resolution of disputes in a way that conveys public messages about appropriate standards of conduct. The difficulty of the issue of whether to allow credits reflects these varied policy concerns. Moreover, beyond the social and economic effects of the settlement rules, the law exhibits the differing views of equity and individual justice represented by diverse combinations of verdicts and settlement amounts.

---

16. See supra, ¶ 54.01(C), text accompanying notes 7–8.

Section Ten

DUTY AND PROXIMATE CAUSE

Chapter Fifty–Five

DUTY AND PROXIMATE CAUSE: AN INTRODUCTION

Analysis

¶ 55.01 Some Basic Terms and Concepts

A substantial and particularly fascinating set of cases presents an equally fascinating set of legal issues that courts discuss under such headings as "duty" and "proximate cause." These cases typically exhibit a profile of this kind: The defendant acts, or fails to act, in a way that a court would abstractly find negligent, in the sense that the defendant violated a standard of care derived from such sources as industry practice, custom or statute. The plaintiff suffers injury that certainly would not have happened if the defendant had not been negligent, but occurs in a way that people might not ordinarily think is envisioned by the standard that defines due care.

Examples of this sort of result are cases where forces unleashed by the defendant's negligence cause injuries beyond the time or place that might ordinarily be predicted, cases where the manner in which the injury occurs is unusual, and cases in which the harm to the plaintiff or the plaintiff's interests is indirect or of a kind that is difficult to calculate. The question always presented is whether an initially negligent defendant should be liable for these injuries.

Courts use a wide range of terms in their effort to conceptualize and to resolve these problems. When they reject the claims of

301

plaintiffs seeking to recover in such situations, they may use one or more of the following explanatory concepts:

(1) the defendant did not have a duty to the plaintiff

(2) the defendant's negligence was not the "proximate cause" of the plaintiff's harm

(3) an "intervening cause," such as the act of a third party, "broke the chain of causation" between the negligence and the injury

(4) there should be no recovery for "unforeseeable" harms

(5) the plaintiff's injury was "too remote" from the defendant's negligence to justify recovery

(6) the defendant's conduct was not negligent as to the plaintiff

(7) the injury was not the "natural and probable consequence" of the defendant's negligence

(8) the result was not "within the risk" of the defendant's conduct.

Each of these locutions—and the list is not exhaustive—represents a judicial effort to come to terms with cases like those involving extended chains of consequences or unpredictable, even freakish, outcomes. In this introductory chapter, we illustrate how courts use diverse terminology in their efforts to solve the puzzle. In subsequent chapters,[1] we discuss some important areas in which the courts adapt their chosen concepts to particular, functionally defined fact patterns. An important caution is that it is a mistake to think of the problem discussed here as primarily one of causation, at least in the sense of causation in fact. In the typical case in these categories, the plaintiff would not have suffered the injury at issue except for the allegedly negligent act or omission of the defendant, and thus factual causation is a given.

¶ 55.02   The *Palsgraf* Case

The most noteworthy case concerning chains of odd consequences—perhaps the most famous of all tort cases—is *Palsgraf v. Long Island Railroad Co.*[2] There are various disagreements about the facts in this case,[3] but it is probably best to analyze it on the basis of Judge Cardozo's summary for a majority of the New York Court of Appeals. The plaintiff, who had paid for a ticket on the defendant's railroad, was standing on the platform waiting for a train. A different train came along, and a man carrying a package

---

1. See infra, chapters 56–57, 59, 61, 63–65.

2. 162 N.E. 99 (N.Y.1928).

3. See, e.g., Richard Posner, Cardozo: A Study in Reputation 33–43 (1990).

tried to board it as it began to move out of the station. The defendant's guards tried to help the man get on the car, presumably extending their aid in a negligent way. In this process, the man lost control of his package, which fell to the rails. The seemingly innocuous package, which contained fireworks, exploded. As Cardozo summarized it, "[t]he shock of the explosion threw down some scales at the other end of the platform many feet away. The scales struck the plaintiff, causing injuries."[4]

This strange set of events inspired two famous judicial essays that presented very different ways of looking at the subject, one focusing on duty and foreseeability and the other on proximate cause. Judge Cardozo, whose majority opinion overturned a jury verdict for the plaintiff, viewed the crucial issue as one of duty. Even if the defendant were negligent in some abstract sense—that is, if its guards had not lived up to the proper standard of care in helping the man carrying the fireworks get onto the train—this carelessness could not be actionable if the defendant had no duty to Mrs. Palsgraf. The duty question is whether there is a legally recognized relation between the defendant and the plaintiff, and here there was not: "The conduct of the defendant's guard, if a wrong in its relation to the holder of the package, was not a wrong in its relation to the plaintiff, standing far away. Relatively to her it was not negligence at all."[5] For Cardozo, although not for all analysts of the problem, a touchstone of duty was foreseeability: "The risk reasonably to be perceived defines the duty to be obeyed."[6]

Judge Andrews' dissent, which supported the plaintiff's verdict, cast the question as one of proximate cause rather than one of duty. For him, the legal question was at which point a lack of proximate cause would cut off liability for negligent acts: "[t]he damages must be so connected with the negligence that the latter may be said to be a proximate cause of the former."[7] And "proximate," in this sense, represents a variety of pragmatic considerations. It means, said Judge Andrews, that, "because of convenience, of public policy, of a rough sense of justice, the law arbitrarily declines to trace a series of events beyond a certain point. This is not logic. It is practical politics."[8] The question, as Judge Andrews summarized it, is one of "fair judgment, always keeping in mind the fact that we endeavor to make a rule in each case that will be practical and in keeping with the general understanding of mankind."[9]

---

4. 162 N.E. at 99.

5. Id.

6. Id. at 100.

7. Id. at 103 (Andrews, J., dissenting).

8. Id.

9. Id. at 104.

The Cardozo and Andrews opinions present two very different perspectives on the problem, as well as the different terminologies of duty and proximate cause. Interestingly, however, many of the considerations that Judge Andrews mentioned in his discussion of proximate cause have found their way into discussions of duty by courts and commentators.

¶ 55.03 Concepts Illustrated

Two less heralded decisions of a later generation serve to illustrate further dimensions of the problem, adding some other terms to the concepts of duty and proximate cause. In one of these cases,[10] a police officer sued a savings bank and the mother of a young child. At issue were injuries the plaintiff sustained in responding to a robbery alarm that had been activated by the child, whose mother was a customer at the bank. The alarm button was located on a bank employee's desk, in a corner of the knee-space. There was evidence that six false alarms had emanated from the bank in a period of less than five months, and that the child had activated the alarm in question within the week before he set off the alarm that led to the accident. In responding to the alarm, the plaintiff had to swerve to avoid a car driven by another defendant, resulting in the plaintiff's collision with a telephone pole.

The trial judge granted the bank's motion to dismiss because he thought the "intervening acts" of the mother's failure to control her child and of the driving maneuvers of the plaintiff and the motorist defendant placed the case "just too far out from foreseeability as well as violating the concept of proximate cause."[11]

The appellate court reversed. It opined that foreseeability was not the " 'make or break' factor" regarding duty that the defendant bank had insisted that it was, but rather was only one consideration among several. Instead, the court viewed the crucial duty issue as "heavily based upon public policy considerations," including "the magnitude of the risk," the burden on the defendant to avoid the risk, "and the consequences of placing that burden upon the defendant." The court insisted that "foreseeability" would be "determinative" only if the accident was "so extreme, that as a policy decision, it would be unwise to require the defendant to guard against it."[12]

With analogous reasoning, the appellate court also denied the mother's motion to dismiss on the duty issue. It declared that the "likelihood of injury to the plaintiff was ... not so 'freakish' as to be an unforeseeable consequence" of the mother's negligence. It

---

10. Duncan v. Rzonca, 478 N.E.2d 603 (Ill.Ct.App.1985).

11. See id. at 606.

12. Id. at 610.

stressed the ease with which the mother could have avoided the accident by controlling her son, and declared that there was "no social need" for the risk created by her negligence.[13]

Further rejecting a defense of "no proximate cause," the court reasoned in a way analogous to its position on the duty question. It referred to the metaphor of "forces set in operation" by the defendants "com[ing] to rest."[14] Spinning out that metaphor, the court viewed the "negligent activation of a false alarm" as the creation of "forces," and commented that "those forces would 'come to rest' ... only when the risk of harm to the plaintiff created by the defendants' alleged negligence had passed; i.e., when plaintiff arrived safely at the bank."[15]

In this view, the negligence of the bank and the mother created the risk that a "responding emergency vehicle would be involved in a collision." In consequence, when the defendant driver's car "caused the plaintiff to swerve to avoid that very risk," the negligence of the bank and the mother could "be viewed as having done quite as much to bring about the harm to the plaintiff" as the defendant driver.[16]

One may compare a case in which the alleged negligence of a ship and a tug caused a collision on the Mississippi River, leading to an oil spill from a tank of the ship.[17] Oil from that spill moved downriver on a one-knot current over a two-day period and slopped onto a barge on which the plaintiff was working. He suffered injuries when he slipped as he was cleaning up the mess.

Granting summary judgment to the owner of the colliding ship, a federal court said that to impose liability would be "to stretch the concept of legal cause too far."[18] The court's opinion carried some echoes of Cardozo's definition of the problem in *Palsgraf*,[19] saying that the case "turn[ed] upon whether a limitation should be placed on defendant's duty." It also sounded some echoes of Andrews' characterization of the issue,[20] declaring that "at some point common sense must take over and dictate as to how far the defendant's responsibility should extend." The court concluded that the plaintiff's accident was "at best, a fortuitous event for which defendant's conduct was not a legal cause"—an event "too remote from the collision, both in time and space" to justify liability.[21]

---

13. Id. at 613.

14. Id. at 615, quoting Prosser, Torts 248 (4th ed. 1971).

15. Id. at 616.

16. Id.

17. Brown v. Channel Fueling Service, Inc., 574 F.Supp. 666 (E.D.La. 1983).

18. Id. at 668.

19. See supra, ¶ 55.02, text accompanying notes 5–6.

20. See supra, ¶ 55.02, text accompanying notes 7–9.

21. Brown, supra, 574 F.Supp. at 668.

The decisions in the false alarm case and the oil spill case—one holding for the plaintiff and one for the defendant—present a picture of courts struggling to solve a legal problem in which elements of fairness, economic rationality and common sense contend for recognition. It is not difficult to conclude that turning in a false alarm will "naturally" and "probably" trigger a quick response by an emergency vehicle, creating a relatively high risk of accidents on the route to the scene. But is it not also "natural" and "probable" that oil from a spill on a river will wash up on the deck of some other ship and that someone will slip on it—even two days later?

Given that both injuries were "caused" "in fact" by the defendants' negligence, one could resort to notions of "proximate cause" to try to solve the problem. In both cases there were multiple "causes." With respect to the bank's involvement in the false alarm case, one could identify as "causal" the negligence of the mother in controlling the child, the action of the child, the failure of the bank to position the alarm button more safely or to control the child, and the culpable conduct of the colliding driver. In the oil spill case, one could point to the negligence of the pilot of the colliding ship, the negligence of the pilot of the tug, the negligence of the plaintiff's employer in providing unsafe working conditions (the original ground of the plaintiff's suit), the action of the river current, the force of the winds, and perhaps even the course taken by the barge on which the plaintiff worked.

In both cases, several "causes"—including more than one defendant—metaphorically launched some "forces" into the environment that in some way led to the plaintiff's injury. The language of causation, and proximate causation, has a superficially strong attractiveness for judges who have to solve such problems. However, a satisfactory solution requires an analysis that digs deeper, seeking the reasons for granting or denying recovery. What courts must try to do in such cases is persuasively to allocate the risk from multiple causes in situations where many observers will have competing intuitions within themselves about the justice of the case.

The oil spill case illustrates the power of competing arguments from which courts often must choose in cases of this sort, and makes clear that a persuasive solution requires more than a reference to causation concepts as magic words. In that case, the "fairness" instincts of some observers might lead them to conclude that the causal contribution to the plaintiff's injury of the negligence of the colliding ship's pilot would justify imposing liability on the shipowner. Those supporting liability would stress the culpability of the defendant and the fact that the injury would not have occurred except for that fault, as well as arguing that the defendant should absorb and perhaps could spread a cost it inflicted on the plaintiff.

Others, opposing liability, would fix on the relatively long time and the geographical distance between the initial accident and the injury. They also would offer the argument—embedded in the notion of "a fortuitous event"—that there are some injuries we simply must accept, without compensation, as part of the risk of living. Opponents of liability would add that those unhappy with that result from perspectives of justice or compassion must look to legislative alternatives, including activity-based compensation systems like workers compensation or broader social security programs for income maintenance.

The factual contexts that generate duty issues are diverse. One such context illustrates the corresponding diversity of rationales that courts employ in solving duty questions, and their attempts to generalize concerning certain fact patterns. It features the question of what obligations landowners have to those on adjacent highways who are injured as a result of activities that distract travelers on those roads. Searching for an administrable rule, an Illinois appellate court focused on the "licensed and authorized" status of a defendant that operated a bungee-jumping business alongside an interstate highway in the Chicago area. The plaintiff, a motorist, alleged that the driver of another car who was looking up at a bungee jumper cut her off and forced her in a median wall. She attributed her injuries to the distraction that the bungee operation created to the driver who cut her off. In refusing recovery, the court relied on a duty analysis, bolstered by a comparison of other distractions on public roads and a reference to opportunities for cost avoidance. It identified a number of potential distractions to Chicago area motorists, including low-flying planes at airports, kite-flying in parks, "a constant barrage of colorful and creative advertisements," and even fireworks on a baseball park scoreboard located near an expressway "when a member of the Chicago White Sox hits a home run (however a rare this occurrence may be)." The court's cost avoidance analysis took into account the "considerable undertaking" it would require to put up a "wall or curtain" that would block the bungee operation from view, given that the "jumping platform was approximately 180 feet in the air." It concluded that drivers on the highway "were in the best position to avoid accidents by operating their vehicles with care." Its formulation of a general rule was that "businesses that operate a licensed and authorized business near a street, road or highway do not have a duty to passing motorists who might become distracted by the activities of the business."[22]

¶ 55.04 Duty, Justice and Judgment

For courts as well as for advocates and students, the beginning of comprehension of the problem discussed here lies in a recognition that ultimately we are not speaking of "cause." Rather, the issue is one of duty[23]—of whether there is a sufficient legal relation between the parties to justify the imposition of liability on the defendant. This question inevitably will involve some resort to intuition. But at the threshold of analysis it requires logic, and thus an identification of the major premises of the law.

Some of these premises of duty come from the same root as the factors that determine the "negligence" issue, which is also referred to as the "standard of care" or "breach of duty" issue. A principal set of considerations shared between the duty and negligence issues is the comparison of accident costs and avoidance costs or of accident risks and the utility of defendants' conduct that caused those risks. And foreseeability, emphasized by Cardozo as a test of duty, is a primary ingredient in the determination of whether the defendant has fallen below the standard of care.

Other premises of duty, embedded in the relatively amorphous idea of fairness, are often associated with the need to set limitations on a liability—liability for negligence—otherwise without rational boundaries. Fairness-oriented elements of duty—some of which may work to the advantage of plaintiffs as well as defendants—include the ability to calculate risks in advance, the potentially ruinous impact of judgments, and the ability to insure or otherwise to spread risk. These considerations are likely to come more heavily in play on the duty issue than will the cost comparisons that are a significant focus of the negligence/breach of duty question.

It is in this connection that terms like "remoteness" enter the conversation. Many people, visualizing a lag of two days and a span of several miles of river between a negligently caused oil spill and a cleanup accident, will react intuitively that there was literally too much distance between the events to justify liability against the party that caused the spill. That reaction arises from a sense of fairness that does not necessarily partake of economic concerns. In a case that involved a much more bizarre shipping accident than the oil spill case, Judge Kaufman said, simply, that "[t]he connection between the defendants' negligence and the claimants' dam-

22. Largosa v. Ford Motor Co., 303 Ill.App.3d 751, 708 N.E.2d 1219, 1222–23 (1999).

23. The classic is Leon Green, The Duty Problem in Negligence Cases: I, 28 Colum. L. Rev. 1014 (1928); II, 29 Colum. L. Rev. 255 (1929).

ages is too tenuous and remote to permit recovery."[24] As vague as it is, language like this captures the way that judges, like ordinary people, resist accepting claims of liability involving unusual chains of consequences.

We must stress that language of the sort just quoted represents a judgment—one typically involving a balance among competing factors—that utilizes tools ranging from statistical data to the sort of metaphor for which both lawyers and laymen reach when statistics prove unavailing. What is important is precisely that it is a *judgment:* it requires a process of rationalization that arrays both facts and precedents on a legal grid for analysis, and a weighing of policy considerations. We emphasize that in the end, this process defines not a causal connection but a legal relation. That is why a duty analysis is the best starting point for cases involving extended or unusual causal consequences. And, as we shall explain, it is why—since the crucial issue is not one of factual causation—the duty question tends to be one for the judge.[25]

¶ 55.05   Diverse theories

The duty/proximate cause problem has inspired reams of commentary. This section will summarize just a few approaches to the problem in recent literature.

♦ An English commentator suggests that a "risk theory," employing the concept of reasonable foreseeability, is viable if one focuses on the "causal set that gave rise to" the plaintiff's harm rather than the harm itself.[26] He instances a famous English case in which, as he summarizes it, a child "suffered injury after a paraffin lamp, which he knocked into an open manhole[,] unexpectedly exploded."[27] The rationalization for liability stems from the fact that the defendant "faultily supplied both ... causal conditions"— that is, the lamp and the manhole.[28] This writer concedes that "policy" considerations sometimes influence findings on the liability issue,[29] but views these as "forming a limited group of exceptions" to the "risk theory,"[30] which he finds to be the most powerful general theory.

♦ Another commentary identifies several different concepts of duty:

---

24. Petitions of Kinsman Transit Co., 388 F.2d 821, 825 (2d Cir.1968), discussed further infra, ¶ 64.04(C).

25. See, e.g., infra, ¶¶ 57.04, 61.02.

26. Marc Stauch, Risk and Remoteness of Damage in Negligence, 64 Mod. L. Rev. 191, 214 (2001).

27. Id. at 205, summarizing Hughes v. Lord Advocate, [1963] AC 837.

28. See id. at 206.

29. See generally id. at 207–14.

30. Id. at 214.

• An "obligation" theory, centering on whether the defendant "was under a *duty* or *obligation* to act with vigilance of the plaintiff's interests."[31]

• A requirement that "there must be a certain 'nexus' between the breach and the duty," with a negative example being the case in which there was "not a breach of a duty of care owed to the plaintiff, but, at most, a breach of a duty owed to someone else."[32]

• A category labeled "breach-as-a-matter-of-law," in which the issue is whether "the evidence is such that a reasonable juror could resolve the breach question only one way." This approach "asks courts to set general and relatively stable guidelines for how one must conduct oneself, while leaving to juries more fact-intensive issues of whether those guidelines are met or breached in a given case."[33]

• A category in which courts exempt defendants "from the operation of negligence law," typified by cases in which the court effectively immunizes the defendant on policy grounds— for example, cases in which liability would place an overwhelming burden on a defendant or in which the court is not the appropriate institution to allocate costs for the type of injury at issue.[34]

♦ A critic of the analysis just summarized suggests that its categories are "hyper-refined."[35] Cataloging a wide range of considerations that courts take into account in deciding "duty" questions—"foreseeability, fairness, compensation, and deterrence," as well as the problem of opening the "floodgates to litigation"—he comments that "[t]raditionally, courts have addressed all of these considerations under the guise of duty, often in tandem, without resort to categorical refinements reflecting a fixed hierarchy of interests." This, he insists, is "the reality of duty jurisprudence."[36]

---

31. John C.P. Goldberg and Benjamin C. Zipursky, The *Restatement (Third)* and the Place of Duty in Negligence Law, 54 Vand. L. Rev. 657, 705 (2001).

32. Id. at 709.

33. See id. at 712–17.

34. See id. at 717–23.

35. Robert Rabin, The Duty Concept in Negligence Law: A Comment, 54 Vand. L. Rev. 787, 798 (2001).

36. Id. at 801–02.

Chapter Fifty–Six

STATUTORY VIOLATIONS AND "CAUSE"

Analysis

¶ 56.01 The Problem

An interesting set of problems concerning limitations on liability arises in connection with the violation of statutes. Analogously to the main body of cases involving problems of duty and proximate cause,[1] the typical cases posing these issues arise when a defendant falls below an abstract standard of care—in these cases defined by a statute. As with the duty/proximate cause cases, the plaintiff always can persuasively argue that the defendant's statutory violation was a "but for" cause of the injury—that is, if the defendant had not violated the statute, the plaintiff would not have been injured. However, the legal problem exists because the defendant contends that the plaintiff's injury was not the kind of event the statute was designed to prevent, and the statute does not specifically speak to the issue of civil liability. Courts employ a range of terminology, some of it rather confusing, in dealing with this question.

¶ 56.02 The Rules

A good starting point is a pair of sections of the Restatement Second, which frame the issue as when courts may use the requirements of a statute or administrative regulation as the tort standard of care.[2] These sections focus on four major factors for resolving that issue. Those factors pose the questions of whether the enactment is designed "to protect a class of persons which includes the one whose interest is invaded," whether the purpose of the statute

---

1. See supra, ¶ 55.01.

2. Restatement (Second) of Torts §§ 286, 288 (1965).

311

is "to protect the particular interest which is invaded" and "to protect that interest against the kind of harm which has resulted," and finally, whether the statutory purpose is "to protect that interest against the particular hazard from which the harm results."[3]

Under this formula, if the plaintiff is in the protected class and can show that the statute was designed to protect a particular interest against a particular kind of harm and the specific hazard at issue, the court "may adopt" the statutory or regulatory standard.[4] However, the court will not adopt the statute as the applicable standard of conduct when the purpose of the legislation is only to protect a class of persons other than the plaintiff, or the interest sought to be protected by the statute or the harm or hazard at which it is directed is one other than those in the case at issue.[5] The Restatement specifically declares that courts should not adopt the standard of the statute if its "purpose is found to be exclusively ... to protect the interests of the state," or to protect individuals "only as members of the public."[6]

The idea of statutory purpose has a strong hold on courts. A decision favoring a plaintiff is illustrative of judicial commitment to the idea that a plaintiff must show that his or her injury fell within the ambit of protection that the legislature visualized. In this Montana federal case,[7] in which a motorcyclist claimed that he was injured because the defendant's goats were on the highway, a state statute made it "unlawful for any owner or person in control of swine, sheep, or goats to willfully permit the same to run at large." The first version of this legislation, enacted in 1895, applied only to swine. A 1945 enactment not only included swine in the prohibited category, but also removed goats and sheep from the category of open range animals. The defendant contended that the law, having originally been passed in 1895, was designed "for the protection of the property of landowners" against marauding stock and that "since there were no motor vehicles in common use at that time," the statute could "not have been enacted for the protection of motorists."

While denying the defendant's motion for summary judgment, the court evinced its commitment to the idea of statutory purpose in its statement that "[e]ven if in 1895, the Legislature intended to protect only landowners against damage caused by swine, it is difficult to believe that in 1945 a legislature fully aware of paved roads, automobiles, and accidents did not, by changing the status of

---

3. Id. § 286.

4. See id.

5. See id., comments f-i.

6. Id. § 288.

7. Read v. Buckner, 514 F.Supp. 281 (D.Mont.1981).

sheep and goats, intend that the protection of the law should extend to all who are injured by violations of it."[8]

¶ 56.03 Language and Doctrine

Courts employ a variety of concepts and terms to solve cases in which defendants contend that their statutory violations do not merit tort judgments because plaintiffs' injuries did not fall within the purpose of the statute. Often, courts use the terminology of causation, although that idea is frequently not well-suited to solution of the problem.

In one case of historical interest,[9] the plaintiff was a volunteer air raid warden during World War II. He and two other wardens sought to extinguish lights in the defendant's apartment house, which were burning in violation of a state statute designed to enforce blackouts for national security purposes. The perceived risk, one fortunately beyond the experience of later generations, was that lights would target urban areas for enemy bombers.

The plaintiff's co-wardens hoisted him so that he could unscrew a light bulb, the unavoidable result of which was to plunge the room where they were into darkness. When the plaintiff missed his step and fell, he broke an ankle. In concluding that "defendant's negligence was not the proximate cause of plaintiff's injury," the court used such terminology as "[p]laintiff's injury was not the natural and probable consequence of a violation of the statute"; "[i]t resulted from a cause independent of defendant's negligence in violating the statute"; "[i]t happened because of an intermedial accident which no one in the position of the defendant could reasonably have anticipated."[10]

Language of this sort demonstrates the linkage that this issue has in judicial minds to causation as well as to culpability. Some courts are comfortable in casting the issue in terms of causation, particularly "proximate causation." An alternative formulation of the reason for denying liability would be to say that even if a defendant was shown to be negligent—or "negligent per se"—for violating a statute, he was not negligent as to a particular plaintiff.

Since courts often use the locutions of causation in these situations, one must report this phraseology as descriptions of the law as judges view it. However, as applied in cases of statutory violation where the harm inflicted is different from the one that the legislature apparently targeted, the language of causation would appear to be more a label than an analytically probing concept.

---

8. Id. at 283.

9. Klein v. Herlim Realty Corp., 54 N.Y.S.2d 144 *aff'd mem.*, 58 N.Y.S.2d 344 (1945).

10. Id. at 147.

¶ 56.04   The Uses and Limits of Statutory Purpose

When a defendant's statutory violation is a but-for cause of a plaintiff's injury, it will usually be desirable for courts to focus on policy in order to exercise their judgment about the range of statutory purpose. For example, in a case like that of the air raid warden,[11] the compelling public need to extinguish lights could well be construed to imply tort protection for a person injured while figuratively cleaning up after another's statute-violating omission. By contrast, one might argue, as the court in that case did, that the statute "was not enacted for the direct benefit or protection of air raid wardens, but to promote the defense and safety of our population generally." Each of these views of the case has the virtue of being oriented to the policy sought to be implemented by the statute, which courts often use as a principal measure of duty for a statutory violation. As is so concerning the broad range of cases that present questions of duty, a policy focus usually offers a more persuasive way to solve the problem than relying on concepts of causation when, after all, the plaintiff's injury would not have occurred except for the defendant's violation of the statute.

There are cases in which the imposition of liability for statutory violations has at least a tinge of strict liability. One may consider, for example, a case in which a person who is carefully driving an unregistered motor vehicle skids on an unexpected slick spot in the road and unavoidably hits a pedestrian. If there were no automobile registration statute, the case clearly would be considered one of "unavoidable accident." But with such a statute on the books, the plaintiff could argue that she would not have been hurt if the defendant had not been driving—and thus necessarily violating the statute—and that therefore the defendant should be liable. Literal "but-for" causation is clear in such a case, and in a certain general sense, the statute is designed to minimize accident rates by preventing people who do not have the providence and good sense to register a vehicle from engaging in the activity of motoring.

However, such statutes do not explicitly impose tort liability against statutory violators who are behaving carefully in fact, and indeed do not even refer to that possibility. Therefore, it might be argued to be an unjust application of strict liability to impose a tort judgment on someone who was in fact driving carefully, because the legislative intention was to create a census of motor vehicles for various administrative and revenue-raising purposes, with perhaps only an incidental goal of enhancing highway safety. A rebuttal argument would draw on the idea that the driving of unregistered vehicles is likely to be statistically associated with careless driving. The plaintiff would contend that it is appropriate to impose liability

---

11. See supra, ¶ 56.03, text accompanying notes 9–10.

even in a case lacking specific evidence of negligence or a focused statutory purpose because of the strong social interest in safety that is effectively promoted by the statutory rule.

In determining statutory purpose, courts often look to history—both legislative history and the apparent function of the statute in the historical environment in which it was enacted. They also may take into account the kinds of sanctions that the statute imposes, viewing them as a reflection of legislative purpose. Consider, for example, the provision of relatively minimal penalties for the breach of a statute, in a case in which the plaintiff sued for a physical injury he attributed to a statutory violation. The light penalties might be taken as evidence that the legislature did not concern itself with the protection of persons against that kind of harm.

In some cases, courts may be disinclined to build walls of purpose around a statute. A vigorous controversy arose in a Supreme Court case in which a Coast Guard navigation rule required scows to "carry a white light at each end ... not less than 8 feet above the surface of the water," and "to show an unbroken light all around the horizon." A scow on which the plaintiff's decedent served as a seaman carried an open flame kerosene lamp no more than three feet above the water. This lamp ignited vapors on oil slicks on the river, and caused a fire that resulted in the decedent's death. In a case brought under the Jones Act, a specialized negligence statute for seamen, the courts below held for the defendant, with the trial court pointing out that the purpose of the Coast Guard rule was only to prevent collisions. The Supreme Court reversed, rejecting the defendant's attempt to restrict liability to the assumed purpose of the statute.[12] The majority referred to "liberal" principles developed under the Federal Employers Liability Act that also governed claims under the Jones Act, and stressed that the Court's precedents had "repeatedly refused" to limit FELA-based liability for violations of safety statutes to injuries that a "statute was designed to prevent."[13] Justice Harlan, dissenting, stressed that the purpose of the regulation "was simply to prevent collisions rather to guard against such unforeseeable occurrences as the explosion in this case."[14]

A much discussed nineteenth century case presents a different view of the problem, metaphorically fencing the plaintiff's case outside the statutory purpose. In *Gorris v. Scott*,[15] the plaintiff shipped cattle on a vessel that lacked livestock pens, which the shipowner should have supplied in observance of a statute designed

12. Kernan v. American Dredging Co., 355 U.S. 426 (1958).

13. Id. at 432.

14. Id. at 448–49 (Harlan, J., dissenting).

15. L.R. 9 Ex. 125 (1874).

to prevent the spread of disease among animals. A storm washed the cattle overboard; by hypothesis, this would not have happened if the cattle had been in pens. The court denied liability, with one judge invoking the principle that there could be no liability for negligence when "the damage is of such a nature as was not contemplated at all by the statute."[16] Another judge concurred on the ground that even if the statutory "precautions . . . [were] useful and advantageous for preventing animals from being washed overboard, yet they were never intended for that purpose."[17]

Commentators using economic analysis have said that to hold the defendant liable in *Gorris*, "adding in effect to the penalties of the statute by making the defendant liable for an unrelated harm[,] could result in overdeterrence." These commentators say that adding what they describe as a "causal" limitation to "the legal analysis of negligence" will achieve the economically optimal result—denying recovery in *Gorris*.[18] One response to this argument is that despite the single-focus purpose of the statute, the cattle owner could reasonably expect that it would be obeyed, protecting his animals from their watery fate as well as from disease.[19]

¶ 56.05 General Policies

Undoubtedly both the concept of statutory purpose, and that of causation, proximate or otherwise, have a strong hold on many judges who deal with these cases. However, in close cases it is often useful to turn to general policy considerations. Thus, for example, one might ask whether the overall social interest in achieving desirable levels of protection from accidents would be furthered by imposing liability for a statutory violation even if an injury did not fit neatly into a perceived legislative purpose. A related question would be how the expense of complying with the statute compares with the cost of injuries caused by its violation, or perhaps even the benefits of violating the statute.[20]

Courts considering cases of this sort are also likely to think about fairness. Under that heading, they will consider such factors as the relatively bizarre nature of an occurrence, since, for better or worse, the concept of "foreseeability" has a powerful attraction. A different consideration is the fact that statutes represent general societal commands, implying a lack of sympathy for those who violate such mandates even if an injury was not within the evident scope of the statutory "purpose."

---

16. Id. at 128 (Kelly, C.B.).

17. Id. at 131 (Pollock, B.).

18. William Landes & Richard Posner, Causation in Tort Law: An Economic Approach, 12 J. Legal Studies 109, 131 (1983).

19. I am grateful to Cris Carmody for a suggestion on this point.

20. See Landes & Posner, supra note 18, at 130–32.

The subject is an especially fascinating one, because it requires consideration of the public policies inherent in the statutes that are violated, and of other public policies that are often employed in torts decisions, as well as traditional concepts of negligence and of "causation." What is important, in the end, is that courts keep in mind not only the "purpose" of a particular statute, but the purposes of the law of torts.

Chapter Fifty–Seven

INTERVENING CRIMINAL ACTS

Analysis

A specialized problem in extended causation/duty cases involves intervening criminal acts. In these cases, the plaintiff sues A for an injury that B criminally inflicted on the plaintiff. The class of defendants in cases of this sort is quite varied, including people who legally possess firearms, psychotherapists whose patients assault others, and landlords on whose premises attacks take place. The plaintiff claims that the defendant contributed to the risk of the crime that B committed, or failed to minimize a risk about which the defendant knew or should have known.

¶ 57.01   Doctrine and Phraseology

One may characterize these cases in different ways. In one sense, they present issues of causation by multiple parties, since the plaintiff's complaint necessarily attributes causation to the person who committed the criminal act as well as to the named defendant, who allegedly failed to prevent it. Some courts will focus the inquiry on what they call "proximate causation," but it is well to remember that one should not confuse that concept with causation in fact. As to causation in fact, we note that by the very terms of the plaintiff's complaint in these cases, the defendant's conduct or failure to act is always alleged to be a "but-for" cause of the plaintiff's harm.

Other courts will talk in terms of duty, a concept that has the decided virtue of not invoking the idea of causation. Many decisions focus on foreseeability, and courts may stress the difference between general and specific foreseeability of particular kinds of crimes and injuries. All of these terms represent judicial attempts to solve the problem of justice inherent in a situation where an injury allegedly would not have occurred if the defendant had not been negligent but the direct cause of the harm was a third party, and a criminal to boot.

Although this chapter focuses on duty/proximate cause analysis, the inclination of courts to use the language of foreseeability is indicative of the overlap of that analysis with a definition of the problem as whether the defendant was negligent. That issue is sometimes described as one of whether there was a breach of duty, or a violation of the standard of care. A discussion of the problem defined in those terms appears above.[1]

¶ 57.02   Application of Doctrines Illustrated

We may analyze the application of these concepts by examining some illustrative decisions in diverse factual contexts. In a D.C. Circuit case, the plaintiff's decedent was killed with a handgun owned by an employee of the National Rifle Association, who had left the weapon and its ammunition locked in a closet in the annex of the NRA's national headquarters. The key was hidden in the owner's desk. Burglars broke into the building and found the key, stole the weapon and the ammunition, and committed several robberies with the gun. Four days later, one of the burglars and an accomplice robbed the plaintiff's decedent and the accomplice shot him when he resisted. The plaintiff sued the NRA as well as the gun owner.

Judge Scalia concluded that "the NRA was entitled to the benefit of the general rule of nonliability at common law for harm resulting from the criminal acts of third parties." In part, he fixed on the "extraordinary and unforeseeable" nature of the "chain of events" in the case, which he summarized as including the employee's "storage of the weapon, a burglary of the annex, a search of [the employee's] desk, discovery of his hidden closet key, a search of the closet, discovery of the gun and ammunition, use of the gun in a robbery, [the decedent's] resistance to the robbery, and the ultimate murder of the [the decedent] by someone not a party to the original burglary."[2] This summary presents a graphic illustration of extended chains of consequences of the sort that inspire judicial findings of unforeseeability and refusals to impose liability.

One may compare a case in which the Eleventh Circuit affirmed a jury verdict for more than four million dollars in favor of the sons of a man killed by a confederate of a hired assassin, who ran an advertisement in Soldier of Fortune Magazine headed **"GUN FOR HIRE."** The decedent's business partner and another associate, wishing to have the decedent murdered, responded to the

---

1. See Chapter 21 infra, focusing on such claims as actions for "negligent security."

2. Romero v. National Rifle Ass'n of America, Inc., 749 F.2d 77, 80–81 (D.C.Cir.1984).

ad, which included the language "37–year-old professional merce-
nary desires jobs" and "[a]ll jobs considered."

In upholding the plaintiffs' judgment against the magazine, the
court of appeals took note of jury instructions that set as a
requirement for liability a finding that "a reasonable reading" of
the ad "would have conveyed to a magazine publisher" a "clear and
present danger of ... serious harm to the public from violent
criminal activity" and that "the ad ... contained a clearly identifiable unreasonable risk." The court said that this language "properly conveyed to the jury that it could not impose liability on SOF if
[the assassin's] ad posed only an unclear or insubstantial risk of
harm to the public and if SOF would bear a disproportionately
heavy burden in avoiding this risk."[3]

In an opinion in which the court's anger rose to the surface,
the Fourth Circuit concluded that a claim could be stated against
the publisher of a book titled *Hit Man* for "aiding and abetting"
the murders of three people killed by a man who followed many of
the instructions in the book. In rejecting a First Amendment
defense, the court referred to the publisher's "astonishing stipula-
tions" that in marketing the book it intended to "attract and
assist" would-be murderers for hire and that the book in fact
"assisted" the killer "in the perpetration of the very murders" at
issue.[4] The court also wrote of the

> extraordinary comprehensiveness, detail, and clarity of *Hit
> Man's* instructions for criminal activity and murder in particu-
> lar, the boldness of its palpable exhortation to murder, the
> alarming power and effectiveness of its peculiar form of in-
> struction ... and the book's evident lack of any even arguably
> legitimate purpose beyond the promotion and teaching of mur-
> der.[5]

Some courts have imposed liability on those who control premises—for example, landlords—for assaults committed on their property. In a landmark case, discussed above, the court held that an
apartment corporation owed a duty of protection to a tenant who
was assaulted in a 585–unit building. That decision found a duty in
the relationship of landlord and tenant, analogizing it to such
relationships as innkeeper-guest and carrier-passenger.[6] Many
courts have since required landlords to compensate tenants for
injuries caused by the crimes of others. Demonstrating the vigor of
this liability rule, a Louisiana decision refused to allow an apart-

3. Braun v. Soldier of Fortune Magazine, Inc., 968 F.2d 1110, 1113, 1116
(11th Cir.1992), cert. denied, 506 U.S.
1071 (1993).

4. Rice v. Paladin Enters., 128 F.3d
233, 241 (4th Cir.1997), cert. denied, 523
U.S. 1074 (1998).

5. Id. at 267.

6. Kline v. 1500 Massachusetts Ave.
Apt. Corp., 439 F.2d 477, 482–85
(D.C.Cir.1970), discussed supra,
¶ 21.03(B).

ment management firm to allocate fault to an unknown person who raped a tenant.[7] Another court found a landlord liable for an assault by a casual worker who had access to a key to a tenant's cottage, emphasizing the landlord's "nondelegable duty with regards to safety of her tenants' premises."[8]

Schools have now begun to face lawsuits over failures to protect students on their premises. An example of judicial emphasis on factual circumstances that tends toward allowing plaintiffs to reach juries is an Oregon case in which a high school student was "attacked on the schoolhouse steps," dragged into nearby bushes and raped. The plaintiff's mother had dropped her off more than an hour before classes, but there was evidence custodians "routinely opened the building before that time." There also was evidence that a woman had been "sexually assaulted on the school grounds 15 days before the attack on the plaintiff" and the plaintiff tried to offer "evidence of various other kinds of attacks." Overturning a directed verdict for the defendant, the court spoke of the "special duty" that schools owe to students, practically all of whom are minors, and who are "entrusted to a school" under the mandate of a compulsory attendance law. Saying that there were factual issues concerning whether the school should have taken precautions against such an attack, including the giving of warnings, the court sought abstractly to define the parameters of foreseeability. It declared that "foresight does not demand the precise and mechanical imagination of a Rube Goldberg nor a paranoid view of the universe," summarizing a precedent on the idea that "the concept of foreseeability refers to generalized risks of the type of incident and injuries that occurred rather than predictability of the actual sequence of events."[9]

Among other enterprises, fast food restaurants have now become vulnerable to suits for "premises security." In one case, the court reversed a summary judgment for a restaurant in an action brought for the death of a woman shot in the establishment's drive-through line by men trying to steal her car. The court referred to the history of crime in the area in finding triable issues of fact as to whether the restaurant should have provided more protection for its patrons, for example, by stationing a uniformed security guard.[10]

Cases like those summarized teach that although courts are generally reluctant to impose liability for injuries from the criminal acts of third parties, courts will impose a duty in some circumstances. These include situations where the defendant's alleged

7. Veazey v. Elmwood Plantation Assocs., 650 So.2d 712 (La.1994).

8. Hickman v. Allen, 458 S.E.2d 883, 885 (Ga.Ct.App.1995).

9. Fazzolari v. Portland Sch. Dist. No. 1J, 734 P.2d 1326, 1338 (Or.1987).

10. Midkiff v. Hines, 866 S.W.2d 328 (Tex.Ct.App.1993) (issues of duty and proximate cause, both related to foreseeability, as well as of cause in fact).

carelessness relates to a very specific risk, as in the case of the "gun for hire" advertisement, or where a special relationship exists between the defendant and the plaintiff, for example, the relationship between landlord and tenant.

¶ 57.03 Caretakers of Potentially Violent Persons

A definable category of defendant includes persons or institutions alleged to occupy some kind of caretaker role for people who may be inclined to violent acts. One of the most interesting fact patterns involves psychotherapists who fail to report or otherwise control allegedly violent tendencies of their patients. The most famous case—one relatively unusual for its imposition of liability— is *Tarasoff v. Regents of University of California.*[11] In this case, a patient named Poddar told a therapist at the university hospital that he was going to kill an unnamed person, who the court characterized as being "readily identifiable" as the plaintiffs' decedent. After the therapist sent a letter to the campus police chief, asking help in confining Poddar so he could be committed for observation, officers took Poddar into custody. However, they satisfied themselves that he was rational and released him on a promise to stay away from the decedent, who was then out of the country. The director of the department of psychiatry of the university hospital asked the police to return the letter the therapist had written to the police chief, and ordered that all copies of the letter and the therapist's notes be destroyed. He also ordered that "no action" be taken to put Poddar in an evaluation facility. When the decedent returned from abroad, Poddar killed her. The plaintiffs, the parents of the decedent, sued a group of defendants including therapists, police officers and university officials, alleging causal negligence in the failure of the defendants to warn the decedent or the plaintiffs about the threat to the decedent.

Although recognizing the social interest in maintaining the confidentiality of the therapeutic relationship, the court concluded that the plaintiffs could state a claim "for breach of a duty to exercise reasonable care to protect" the decedent. Against the need for confidentiality, the court weighed "the public interest in safety from violent assault," and it focused in significant part on the fact that in this case there was a threat to a "foreseeable victim."[12] Epitomizing its view of the law, the court declared that "[t]he protective privilege ends where the public peril begins."[13]

The criminal's literal targeting to the defendants of a particular individual was a significant element in *Tarasoff.* One may compare the holding of the Tenth Circuit in the dramatic circumstances of a suit against a psychiatrist who treated John Hinckley

---

11.   551 P.2d 334 (Cal.1976).   **13.**   Id. at 347.

12.   Id. at 345–48.

Jr., the man who shot President Reagan in an attempted assassination. The plaintiffs included Press Secretary James Brady and Secret Service officers wounded in the attack. Focusing on the fact that there were no allegations "that Hinckley made any threats regarding President Reagan, or indeed that he ever threatened anyone," the court affirmed a dismissal. Even assuming that a competent psychiatrist "would have learned that Hinckley suffered from delusions and severe mental illness," the court said, the plaintiffs' allegations were "insufficient to create a legal duty on the part" of the psychiatrist to protect the plaintiffs.[14]

¶ 57.04 Policy Considerations

The issue of liability for third party criminal acts presents some interesting doctrinal questions involving the relationship of negligence and duty. There is significant overlap between those concepts in such cases as those involving a therapist's alleged duty to report the violent tendencies of a patient. Courts frequently weigh the same kinds of risk-utility considerations that are put to juries with respect to the standard of care when they determine whether the defendant owes a duty to the plaintiff.

Yet, the duty issue provides a principal lens for focusing an important battle in this type of litigation, a battle that concerns the allocation of decisionmaking functions between judge and jury. The judge must determine whether the often sympathetic facts of these cases present situations in which the jury should have the opportunity to decide if the defendant fell below the standard of care—that is, the judge must initially rule whether there is a duty before letting the jury decide whether the defendant was negligent.

Judgments on that issue, involving such things as the need to balance the confidentiality of therapeutic communication against the right of individuals to security from declaredly murderous patients, do not fit neatly on a quantitative scale. They call for courts to make the kinds of interstitial policy choices that feed into the decision of whether there is a duty—that is, a legal relationship between the parties that would justify the imposition of liability on the defendant if the defendant was negligent. Whether one expresses these choices in terms of "duty" or "proximate cause," this is the sort of question on which judges must make an initial policy decision before allowing juries to do "fact-finding" on such matters as risk and foreseeability. It is true that the role of juries inevitably will include a certain amount of policy formulation. However, the court must be careful to keep the principal wedge of the policy decision in its own hands.

In making this judgment, some courts will focus on providing incentives to desirable conduct on the part of persons situated like

14. Brady v. Hopper, 751 F.2d 329, 331 (10th Cir.1984).

the defendant. The court declared in the *Tarasoff* case, for example, that "[i]n this risk-infested society we can hardly tolerate the further exposure to danger that would result from a concealed knowledge of the therapist that his patient was lethal."[15] One may compare the conclusion of the New York Court of Appeals that a college was not liable for its failure to restrict the activities of a convicted felon, treated for various mental disorders during his stay in prison, who had been admitted to the college under an established state program for disadvantaged high school graduates. In ordering the dismissal of a claim based on the ex-convict's murder of one of his fellow students, the court said that the "release and return to society" of the murderer "were mandated by law as well as by public policy," including the policies of rehabilitating ex-convicts and "reintegrating" them into productive social roles.[16]

The court also concluded that it was improper to impose liability on the state of New York for a prison physician's failure to disclose the murderer's history of mental illness or the fact that he had been a heroin addict. With reference to the claim against the state, the court characterized its precedents as having "limited the universe of permissible plaintiffs because a failure to do so would impose a duty of reasonable care enforceable by any member of an indeterminate class of persons, present and prospective, known and unknown, directly or indirectly injured by any negligence."[17]

Fueling judicial opposition to the extension of liability in cases like these are such factors as the relative unforeseeability to the defendant of a criminal assault by the third party, and the temporal remoteness of the attack from the defendant's alleged negligence. Also coloring these decisions is a belief that the economic burden on defendants from liability for incidents involving such extended chains of causation would be intolerable. Judges might chalk up these considerations under headings of either economic pragmatism or fairness.

Courts considering the duty question in these cases find themselves required to make such social assessments as balancing the policy of rehabilitating criminals against the danger that ex-felons pose to persons in the environments that they enter after prison. Where courts do open the door to liability for crimes by third parties, the components of duty, when it is distinguishable from negligence, include the existence of a "special relationship" between the defendant and the plaintiff.

[Chapter 58 is reserved for supplementary material.]

15. Tarasoff, supra note 11, 551 P.2d at 347.

16. Eiseman v. State, 511 N.E.2d 1128, 1137 (N.Y.1987).

17. Id. at 1135.

Chapter Fifty–Nine

NEGLIGENTLY INFLICTED EMOTIONAL DISTRESS

Analysis

An important problem that involves the duty question is whether plaintiffs suing for negligence should be able to recover for emotional distress. Almost all states have adopted the tort of intentional infliction of emotional distress, but only a minority of courts have been willing to recognize an independent cause of action for emotional distress alone against defendants who are no more than negligent. In struggling with this issue, the courts have fashioned a rather complicated body of law.

¶ 59.01   Impact on the Plaintiff's Body

A.   *General parasitic damages*

It is generally accepted, even in states that refuse to recognize a general cause of action for negligently caused emotional distress, that when the defendant's negligence causes an impact to the plaintiff's body, the plaintiff may recover for emotional distress on a so-called parasitic basis. In this metaphor, the emotional distress damages become figuratively attached to any damages the jury may assess for physical injury resulting from the contact. Critics of restrictive rules on liability for emotional distress argue that it is not logical to deny recovery for what may be serious emotional harm that the defendant causes, although he does so without impact, when a slight impact allows the plaintiff to recover emotional distress damages even if the quantified loss for physical injury from the impact is trivial.

B.   *Odd chains of psychological consequences*

There is some controversy about whether to allow recovery, even when there is an impact, if the alleged psychological consequences are relatively odd. Two Wisconsin cases a generation apart, each of which involved an unusual chain of events, indicate the difficulties of fashioning meaningful categories in this area. Although one theoretically might differentiate the injuries involved between mental and physical harms, both cases involved an initial trauma that led to a chain of psychological consequences. In the earlier of these cases, decided in 1928, there was at least an indirect impact on the plaintiff: she was riding in an auto that the defendant's street car hit from the rear. She did not sustain a physical injury but did become hysterical for a brief period. Two months later in another city, a street car approached the plaintiff, clanking its bell. On this occasion, she again became hysterical, fainted and then became paralyzed. The court permitted recovery against the owner of the first street car, mentioning medical testimony that the paralysis "could be referred back" to "the nervous shock" "at the time of the collision."[1] One can plausibly justify this result on the grounds that there was ultimately a serious physical consequence to the plaintiff. But given the dichotomy between mind and body that many courts have employed, the decision is remarkable because the initial consequence to the plaintiff appears only to have been "mental," and the later "physical" injury stemmed from a "mental" reaction to the second incident.

In the other Wisconsin case, decided in 1960,[2] the defendant ran a red light and hit the plaintiff's car, which continued on for 90 feet from the intersection where the collision occurred. Before the plaintiff's vehicle stopped, he fell or was thrown from his car, and when he became conscious was aware that he was standing next to the car. The unusual aspect of this case inhered in the scene that then confronted the plaintiff. He saw the defendant "lying on the ground, apparently dead, and bleeding," and the defendant's wife "standing there rather helpless, confused and no one helping her." Both the defendant and his wife were elderly. This tableau apparently evoked in the plaintiff the image of his parents, related to repressed conflicts growing out of his family history, including specifically an incident in which he threw his father down when his father was abusing his mother. Bringing to the surface these conflicts, this image triggered an ongoing and serious psychological reaction that included episodes during which the plaintiff did not "have his normal mental faculties," and as his psychiatrist testified, "[a] hysterical reaction result[ed] with ... crying and shaking."

Given medical testimony that the plaintiff's neurotic reaction "did not have its origin in the brain concussion" that he sustained in the accident, "but was due to the plaintiff having seen [the

1. Sundquist v. Madison Ry., 221   **2.** McMahon v. Bergeson, 101
N.W. 392 (Wis.1928).   N.W.2d 63 (Wis.1960).

defendant] immediately after the accident lying on the pavement with his wife standing alongside," the court denied recovery for that reaction. It invoked a rule rejecting liability for "negligence for emotional distress which is due to a pre-existing susceptibility to emotional disturbance not present in a normal individual, unless the actor had prior knowledge of such susceptibility."[3]

It seems difficult to harmonize these two cases as a practical matter. One might rationalize the later decision's holding for the defendant on the basis that, although the initial event involved a physical trauma, the harm sued upon was only emotional distress— a factor that often impels courts to draw the line against liability. One might distinguish the earlier case as one in which the ultimate harm sued upon was the physical effect of paralysis, even though an underlying factor was the mental conditioning of a prior impact on a vehicle in which the plaintiff was a passenger. Yet, given the liberality of the earlier decision, which involved an occurrence two months after the one in which the defendant's vehicle was involved, it is hard to rationalize the denial of liability in the later one. The later case involved an impact that threw the plaintiff out of his car, and was decided in an era presumably more sensitized to the life of the mind. This apparent disharmony simply illustrates the special problems that bizarre chains of psychological consequences pose for courts, even when there is a negligent impact on the body or vehicle of the plaintiff.

¶ 59.02 Physical Effects of Shock or Fright Without Impact

The obstacles to recovery are high, but not always insuperable, when the plaintiff suffers physical consequences from shock or fright although there is no direct impact by the defendant or its instrumentality on the plaintiff's body. Some courts have been receptive to the plaintiff who suffers a shock from an immediate threat of injury, when that shock produces palpable physical harm. One leading case, the 1941 decision in *Orlo v. Connecticut Co.*,[4] arose when a power line fell on the car in which the plaintiff was a passenger. The terrified plaintiff had to sit in the car as the wires hissed and flashed around him, although they did not touch his person. Given proof that the incident aggravated the plaintiff's pre-existing diabetes and arteriosclerosis, the court reversed a judgment for the power company. It fashioned a liability rule for "fright or shock" negligently caused to "one who is within the range of ordinary physical danger from that negligence," when the fright or

---

3. Id. at 71.   4. 21 A.2d 402 (Conn.1941).

shock caused "injuries such as would be elements of damage had a bodily injury been suffered."[5]

Despite decisions like *Orlo*, controversy continued even on liability for physical consequences when there is no impact. A recurrent fact situation has been the case in which a charging animal or an oncoming vehicle stops short of the plaintiff. Decisions stretching back to the nineteenth century, but reaching into the mid-twentieth century, denied recovery in this situation for a miscarriage[6] and for the aggravation of a preexisting medical condition.[7] However, courts that had rejected claims in that situation later began to allow recovery, sometimes reversing themselves after a relatively short period of time.[8]

A special category of plaintiffs who attribute emotional distress to a defendant's negligence consists of people often called "bystanders" or "bystander witnesses." These claimants sue for the consequences—often emotional but sometimes physical—from the shock of seeing accidents that inflict physical injuries on others, particularly members of their families. A separate chapter discusses the case of the bystander plaintiff.[9]

¶ 59.03   Mental Consequences of Distressing Events

When there is no impact on the plaintiff's person, and negligence suits move beyond definable physical effects to claims for only "mental" consequences, claimants face increased barriers to success. In that situation—the unadorned case of negligent infliction of emotional distress—the majority of courts have drawn the line against claimants,[10] although the cause of action for intentional infliction of mental distress is well established.[11]

In a group of cases that presents particular difficulties for plaintiffs, the defendant's words or conduct initially disconcert or embarrass the plaintiff, but the practical core of the claim lies in

---

5. Id. at 405.

6. A standard precedent is Mitchell v. Rochester Ry. Co., 45 N.E. 354 (N.Y. 1896) (horse car).

7. Bosley v. Andrews, 142 A.2d 263 (Pa.1958) (charging bull; collapse associated with coronary insufficiency ascribed to arteriosclerosis).

8. See, e.g., Niederman v. Brodsky, 261 A.2d 84, 90 (Pa.1970) (allowing recovery where plaintiff was in personal danger of impact from car that skidded into sidewalk and in fact struck plaintiff's son, and plaintiff did fear physical impact), *overruling Bosley*, supra note 7. Cf. Battalla v. State, 176 N.E.2d 729 (1961)(defendant's employee failed to

lock plaintiff into chair on ski lift and she "became frightened and hysterical upon the descent, with consequential injuries"; reversing dismissal, court opines that *Mitchell*, supra note 6, "should be overruled," id. at 730.

9. See Chapter 61 infra.

10. The majority rule is summed up in Restatement (Second) of Torts § 436A (1965) (no recovery for "emotional disturbance alone" when defendant's conduct "is negligent as creating an unreasonable risk of causing either bodily harm or emotional disturbance").

11. For analysis of that tort, see Chapter 13 supra.

the long-term effects of that utterance or behavior on the plaintiff's emotions. Two Texas decisions within six years produced a sharp intra-court confrontation on this problem. A majority of the state supreme court first allowed recovery for negligently inflicted "mental anguish" despite the lack of a showing of physical injury, but a later decision explicitly overruled the earlier one.

In the first case, the parents of a stillborn child brought negligence claims against a hospital and physician for the failure to perform an autopsy on the infant, and for the delivery of the body to a mortuary and its disposal "in an unmarked, common grave without the knowledge or consent of either parent." Responding to this sympathetic fact situation, the court rejected the contention that plaintiffs should have to show a "physical manifestation" in order to "guarantee the genuineness of claims for mental injury." The court pointed out that the enhanced information provided by modern medicine on "the interaction between mind and body" had led to a recognition that "certain psychological injuries can be just as severe and debilitating as physical injuries." The court found "[t]he distinction between physical injury and emotional distress" to be "no longer defensible." It said that "[t]he problem is one of proof," and that jurors were "best suited to determine whether and to what extent the defendant's conduct caused compensable mental anguish by referring to their own experience."[12]

Only six years later, a new majority of the Texas court held that there was "no general duty ... not to negligently inflict emotional distress."[13] The occasion was a case with sensational aspects. The plaintiff was a 19–year-old woman. She sued a 17–year-old man, with whom she had had sexual intercourse, for his participation in a videotaping of the occasion and his showing of the tape to as many as ten people, with resultant gossip among many friends of both litigants. The plaintiff claimed that the tape had "stigmatized" her "with the reputation of 'porno queen,' " and alleged that "the embarrassment and notoriety affected her academic performance."

The majority characterized the rule announced in the case of the infant's body as "an anomaly," a decision outside the mainstream of American jurisprudence. The majority pointed out that "[m]ost other jurisdictions do not recognize a general duty not to negligently inflict emotional distress," and that "[m]any limit recovery by requiring proof of a physical manifestation."[14] A dissent stressed that there was adequate protection against fraudulent

12. St. Elizabeth Hosp. v. Garrard, 730 S.W.2d 649, 652–54 (Tex.1987).

13. Boyles v. Kerr, 855 S.W.2d 593, 594 (Tex.1993).

14. Id. at 597–98.

claims for emotional distress in the ability of juries to screen them out, and opined that the plaintiff's claim should be accepted as an "ordinary negligence action" if not under the separate label of negligently inflicted emotional distress.[15]

The language of liability insurance policies may critically affect the strategy of pleading in cases where the plaintiff alleges only emotional distress. In the Texas videotape case, for example, the plaintiff's lawyers may have chosen to plead only negligent infliction of emotional distress, rather than to invoke the intentional infliction tort, because they believed that the principal source from which the defendant would be able to pay a judgment would be his family's homeowners' liability policy. As a concurring judge in that case noted, such policies in Texas "cover[] only accidents and careless conduct and exclude[] intentional acts."[16]

Stress by itself has not been a sympathetic ground of suit for most courts, even when the plaintiff pleads resultant physical injury. Illustrative is a case in which a railroad employee who had been a brakeman was assigned for a few days to work as a conductor without a pilot. The assignment was over his objection, because he did not consider himself qualified as a conductor. During that period, he "frequently threw the wrong switches" and once "was almost crushed during a switching operation." The stress of these few days led to both mental problems—"anxiety and depression"—and "physical consequences attributable to this emotional state," including heart palpitations, a spastic colon and "involuntary rectal discharge." He also suffered "sleep disorder including nightmares of train wrecks." Concluding that the plaintiff could not succeed under the Federal Employers Liability Act, which required a showing of an "injury," the court said that "the fact that on one occasion [the plaintiff] was in physical danger" was not enough to fulfill that statutory requirement. Saying that there was no cause of action under the FELA for "plaintiffs ... who allegedly suffer from stress-related physical or purely emotional injuries or illnesses caused by their general working conditions," the court viewed the case as one "involv[ing] nothing more than a situation in which the stresses of the job over a very short period were too much for him."[17]

Although there is compelling logic in the argument that it is odd to deny recovery for serious emotional distress without physical

---

15. See id. at 613–14 (Doggett, J., dissenting).

16. See id. at 604 (Gonzalez, J., concurring). For a critical analysis of the strategic "underlitigation" of tort claims because of insurance exclusions, see Ellen S. Pryor, The Stories We Tell: Intentional Harm and the Quest for Insurance Funding, 75 Tex. L. Rev. 1721 (1997).

17. Holliday v. Consolidated Rail Corp., 914 F.2d 421, 422, 424–25 (3d Cir.1990).

injury when liability may be imposed for any mental anguish that is attendant to a slight physical impact, a majority of courts resist the extension. Their refusal to adopt a general liability rule for negligent infliction of emotional distress appears to stem from a concern that a broad rule permitting recovery would lead to fraudulent and otherwise ill-founded litigation. Despite the much-cited advances in medical science and the erosion of the mind-body distinction, these courts seem skeptical of the quality of proof on "purely emotional" injuries. Even when plaintiffs present medical testimony about psychological harm, there is a deep distrust of such evidence because of a judicial perception that a slippery slope descends sharply from meritorious cases to faked and insubstantial claims.[18] In cases involving mental anguish consequent on economic loss, some courts have reasoned that "the plaintiff can be fully recompensed by the recovery of any economic loss."[19]

An important battleground on the general question of recovery for negligently inflicted emotional distress has been California. In one much-noted case where opposing opinions illustrate the controversy, the court allowed recovery in a galling fact situation. A staff physician in a woman's health care organization erroneously told her that she had an infectious type of syphilis and that she should advise her husband of the diagnosis. Tests showed that the husband did not have the disease, but the erroneous diagnosis created hostility and suspicion between the couple, leading to a breakup of their marriage. In overturning a dismissal of the husband's claim against the health care organization and its physician for emotional distress arising from the incident, the court focused on "foreseeability of the risk." It said that it was "easily predictable" that the wrong diagnosis, and its implication that the husband was the source of the disease, would cause "marital discord" with "resultant emotional distress" to the husband.[20]

The court found the "unqualified requirement of physical injury" to create a classification that was both "overinclusive and

---

18. An evocative phrase is "phantom medical understandings," see the concurring and dissenting opinion of Spears, J., in St. Elizabeth Hosp. v. Garrard, 730 S.W.2d 649, 655 (Tex.1987).

19. See, e.g., Douglas v. Delp, 987 S.W.2d 879, 885 (Tex.1999). This decision refuses recovery for mental anguish resulting from economic losses attributable to an attorney's malpractice. The court distinguishes cases involving mental anguish consequent on the negligence of physicians, quoting a decision in which it had said that "most physicians' negligence also causes bodily injury." Id., quoting City of Tyler v. Likes,

962 S.W.2d 489, 496 (Tex.1997). By contrast, the court in *Douglas* says, "[t]he foreseeable result of an attorney's negligence ... typically extends only to economic loss." The distinction with medical cases does not seem persuasive, but the result in *Douglas* simply underlines the general reluctance of courts to give damages for mental anguish when the plaintiff has not proved physical contact or injury.

20. Molien v. Kaiser Foundation Hospitals, 616 P.2d 813, 816–17 (Cal. 1980).

underinclusive when viewed in the light of its purported purpose of screening false claims." It was "overinclusive" because of the rule that allowed recovery for emotional distress where there was "any physical injury whatever, no matter how trivial." At the same time, the court criticized the rule as "underinclusive because it mechanically denies court access to claims that may well be valid and could be proved" at trial. The court added that the requirement of physical injury "encourages extravagant pleading and distorted testimony."[21]

A dissenter argued that it would be unwise to create such a cause of action "[b]ecause such disturbances are commonplace in our complex society, because they cannot be objectively observed or measured," and because of the danger of "open[ing] ... the door to damage claims fraught with potential abuse." This judge argued that the issue was not one of "foreseeing (by unguided hindsight) the consequences of unintended conduct, but rather realistically limiting liability for those consequences." He contended that to impose liability for emotional distress caused by negligence was "far disproportionate to the degree of culpability."[22]

[Chapter 60 is reserved for supplementary material.]

21. Id. at 820.

22. Id. at 823, 825 (Clark, J., dissenting).

Chapter Sixty–One

BYSTANDERS

Analysis

¶ 61.01   The Problem

The question of whether so-called "bystanders" should be able to recover from negligent persons is effectively a sub-set of the duty/proximate cause problem.[1] In significant part, it is also a sub-set of the more limited category of the law concerning liability for negligent infliction of emotional distress.[2] The bystander issue reflects competition among several policy goals and rationales, which are summarized below.[3] Many of these policies are pertinent to other topics that comprise the duty problem, so in many ways the bystander issue presents a nice microcosm of that more general subject.

The factual situation that generates the legal issues occurs when a defendant negligently causes physical injury to A, and B sues for injuries that resulted from witnessing or hearing about the incident. One class of case, essentially a straightforward example of negligent infliction of emotional distress and apt to be labeled that way, arises when a witness to a physical injury to another was himself physically endangered by the defendant's conduct and suffers emotional consequences from the incident. This type of plaintiff is at the boundary between direct victim and bystander,

---

1.   See generally Chapter 55 supra.

2.   See generally Chapter 59 supra.

3.   See infra, ¶ 61.03.

being in a position where he could easily be assumed to fear for himself as well as for the other person. In this sort of case, courts are likely to extend liability in favor of the plaintiff.[4]

Beyond that are the true bystander cases. They exhibit the same basic matrix as the general problem discussed in immediately preceding chapters:[5] the defendant is negligent, the plaintiff would not have suffered her injuries except for that negligence, and the law must establish limits to what might otherwise be an uncontrollably long chain of causal events.

¶ 61.02 The Limits

It took some time for American courts to begin to fashion rules that would permit bystanders to recover for the consequences of witnessing accidents that cause direct physical injuries to others but not themselves. An illustration of the early reluctance of courts to impose liability in such cases appears in a leading 1935 decision that denied a claim when a mother's death was ascribed to the consequences of shock from witnessing the death of her child, who was hit by a negligently driven car. In this case, the Wisconsin Supreme Court limited recovery to persons who were "actually put in peril of physical impact" by the "defendant's negligence." It said that injuries from shock to those "out of the range of ordinary physical peril" were "so unusual or extraordinary" that a careless motorist could not be said "to subject others to an unreasonable risk" of such injuries and that to impose liability would be "wholly out of proportion to the culpability of the negligent tort-feasor."[6] Although the decision has effectively been overruled, it is symbolic of the difficulty courts perceive in these cases that it took 59 years for the Wisconsin court to "formally forsake" its prior decision.[7]

---

4. See, e.g., Rickey v. Chicago Transit Auth., 457 N.E.2d 1, 5 (Ill.1983), in which a child watched his brother choke when the brother's clothing became entangled in an escalator mechanism. The court defined the protected class as one where there was "a high risk to [the plaintiff] of physical impact" and a resultant "reasonable fear for his own safety." Since it was not clear whether the plaintiff was on the escalator at the time of the accident, or was himself endangered by the alleged hazards of the machine, the court allowed him to replead under a "zone-of-physical-danger" standard.

Cf. Bowman v. Williams, 165 A. 182 (Md.1933), in which a father was in the dining room of his house when a truck crashed into a basement where his two children were. The court said there "was no basis to differentiate the fear caused the plaintiff for himself and for his children, because there is no possibility of division of an emotion which was instantly evoked by the common and simultaneous danger of the three." It concluded that "under the circumstances . . . , the father could have recovered whether his fright was for the safety of his children or of both himself and his children." Id. at 184–85.

5. See Chapters 55–57, 59 supra.

6. Waube v. Warrington, 258 N.W. 497, 501 (Wis.1935).

7. See Bowen v. Lumbermens Mut. Cas. Co., 517 N.W.2d 432, 436 (Wis. 1994).

Now some courts permit bystander recovery, fashioning a catalog of elements to define its limits. Judges are generally inclined to keep a close policy rein on recovery, rather than giving juries a significant amount of room to decide what makes for justice. This approach is in line with the general idea that duty is principally a question for the court.[8]

The limiting elements that courts have articulated include a close relationship between the plaintiff and the direct victim, a requirement that the plaintiff witness the accident, and a requirement that the plaintiff's distress be severe. The relationship limitation requires that the plaintiff be a relative—generally speaking, a close relative—of the person who was directly injured by the defendant's negligence. Most decisions have drawn this line for reasons of perceived justice and administrative convenience, although there certainly will be cases in which persons who are rather distantly related to the victim, or not related at all, suffer seriously from witnessing a violent accident.

To be sure, some courts have fashioned relatively relaxed categories. Notably, the Hawaii Supreme Court permitted bystander recovery to a step-grandmother, pointing out that in extended Hawaiian families, that relationship was a relatively close one.[9] One California decision, although rejecting a "close relationship" characterization, extended liability in favor of friends of the directly injured victim, a water skier, in a case involving an alleged defect in a motorboat. The initial victim was a close friend of the boat owner's daughter, and there was evidence that she was treated "as a 'filial member of the ... family.' "[10] Affirming one demurrer on a theory of negligent infliction of emotional distress that invoked that relationship, the court reversed dismissals under defective product theories as to both the boat owner and her daughter, who suffered great emotional distress from the incident.[11]

Paralleling arguments that appear throughout the area of duty and proximate cause, disputes about the relationship limitation exhibit the tension between the appealing nature of individual cases and the search by courts for a workable rule that draws relatively bright lines.

Further illustrating that tension, there has been some controversy about a second limitation, requiring that the "bystander" must directly observe the injury to the initial victim. Courts searching for ways to restrict liability will seize upon this requirement to

---

8. See generally ¶ 55.04 supra.

9. Leong v. Takasaki, 520 P.2d 758, 766 (Haw.1974).

10. Kately v. Wilkinson, 195 Cal. Rptr. 902 (Ct.App.1983).

11. Id. at 909–10.

deny recovery to plaintiffs who were not present at an accident scene.

The California court drew a rather firm line against a mother who "neither saw nor heard" an accident in which her son was injured but "rushed to the scene where she saw her bloody and unconscious child, whom she believed was dead, lying in the road- way." A majority held that it was appropriate to give summary judgment to the defendant although the mother alleged "great emotional disturbance, shock, and injury to her nervous system." Saying that it was "unavoidable" to "draw[] arbitrary lines" in order to "limit liability" and necessary to "establish meaningful rules" to guide "litigants and lower courts," the court required that the bystander plaintiff be "present at the scene of the injury producing event at the time it occurs and ... aware that it is causing injury to the victim." The majority expressed concern that if it allowed recovery beyond that class, it would be inviting the imposition of an "unlimited liability for emotional distress on a defendant whose conduct is simply negligent."[12]

A dissenter, saying that the majority's formula was rigid and arbitrary, contended that "reasonable foreseeability is the basis for determining liability." He argued that some relevant policy fac- tors—for example, "moral blame" and deterrence—favored the plaintiff, and that others, related to the costs of judgments and insurance, could not be shown to militate in favor of defendants.[13]

The rule requiring presence and direct observation has the advantage of defining parameters for recovery. However, it neces- sarily ignores the likelihood that the witness who arrives shortly at a bloody scene may well suffer a direct emotional impact as pro- found as the effect on an on-the-scene witness. If the focus of the inquiry is "shock" to the plaintiff, it is hard to distinguish cases involving immediate witnesses and those who appear within mo- ments. The Indiana Supreme Court softened the requirement of immediate observation in a case in which an eight-year-old girl heard the impact of a vehicle on her six-year-old brother, and turned to see the boy's body roll off the highway. Employing a standard of "direct involvement," the court held that the plaintiff sister could take her claim of "mental trauma" to the jury.[14]

Of course, courts inclined sympathetically to such cases must keep in mind the specter of drawn-out extensions of liability, for example, for injuries consequent on shock by long-distance notifica- tion. In one such case, a man died in a plane crash near Chicago,

12. Thing v. La Chusa, 771 P.2d 814, 828–29 (Cal.1989).

13. See id. at 839, 841–43 (Brous- sard, J., dissenting).

14. Groves v. Taylor, 729 N.E.2d 569 (Ind.2000).

and his mother, in Massachusetts, learned of the event by phone seven hours later. The mother almost immediately suffered a series of angina attacks, and died of a heart attack two days later. Although it assumed on a summary judgment notion that the mother's death was a "direct result" of hearing this news, the court denied recovery. It cited the element of "substantial distance from the scene of the accident," as well as the fact that the plaintiff "did not observe either the scene or the injuries inflicted on the victim."[15]

Another pragmatic limitation appears in the requirement that the plaintiff have suffered serious or severe emotional distress, an element that lines up the negligence-to-bystander cases with a requirement of the test for intentional infliction of emotional distress. This standard helps to guarantee the substantiality of a claim in an area where there is some incentive for plaintiffs to inflate their injuries. The California court synthesized this idea in its requirement that the bystander must "suffer[] serious emotional distress ... beyond that which would be anticipated in a disinterested witness."[16]

A major competing formulation to categories pivoting on particular relationships and proximity to the accident focuses on the concept of foreseeability. In a decision that held sway in California for some years, the court fixed partly on this factor, saying that liability should turn on "the neutral principles of foreseeability, proximate cause and consequential injury that generally govern tort law."[17] A later decision, summarized above, found this test "amorphous," declaring that "the only thing that was foreseeable" from the earlier precedent was "uncertainty" in the law.[18]

¶ 61.03　Governing Policies

A. Fairness and justice

A considerable amount of the argument on the problem of bystander suits has to do with competing conceptions of fairness and justice. Some courts, emphasizing the idea that like cases should be treated alike, will reason that it is difficult to achieve that goal unless rules are quite firm. Comparatively flexible rules, for example, those that turn on concepts like "foreseeability," will probably produce more variation in results than more chiseled standards, like those that limit recovery to persons who are on the scene when accidents occur.

---

15. Cohen v. McDonnell Douglas Corp., 450 N.E.2d 581, 589 (Mass.1983).

16. Thing, supra note 12, 771 P.2d at 830.

17. Dillon v. Legg, 441 P.2d 912, 918 (Cal.1968).

18. *Thing*, discussed supra, text accompanying note 12, 771 P.2d at 819, 821.

Courts relatively favorable to bystander recovery are likely to emphasize that the defendant has, in fact, caused an injury to the plaintiff that would not have occurred had the defendant not been negligent. A rather unqualified general argument from this point of view is that given culpability and causation, it is unfair to deny recovery to an innocent injured party. But it is the function of doctrines like duty and proximate cause to place limits on the otherwise unlimited liability that would flow from that argument.

One reason offered to support restrictions on liability is that witnesses to accidents who suffer injuries would not reasonably expect a tort recovery. However, there is likely to be little data on the relevant expectations. Thus, the question turns back to intuitive notions of fairness, on which there will be differences of opinion among courts as there will be among lay persons. It would appear that the concepts of justice and fairness are often rooted in more specific concerns like those discussed below.

B. Insurance factors

One factor that enters into any case involving extended chains of consequences is insurance. To be insurable, risks should be calculable, requiring a reasonable level of statistical certainty about the kinds of claims likely to be made. Perhaps, over time, insurers could establish actuarial tables that would take into account bystander recoveries. Yet, there is another factor that may generate issues concerning the presence of insurance in this kind of litigation. This is that insurance premiums are a medium for passing on the costs of injuries to the general public, which in effect pays those costs through the prices charged by insured sellers of goods and services that create accident risks. The question of whether it is appropriate to justify tort liability on that basis is a question of justice.

C. Certainty as a general jurisprudential concern

Our references to calculability with respect to insurance, as well as to the desirability of uniform application of the law, find an echo in the role of certainty as a prime concern of jurisprudence. Relatively precise legal rules serve as guides for potential litigants, with respect to such questions as whether to sue and whether to settle, and for courts, as legal standards for decision. Moreover, it is fair, as well as helpful to the efficient administration of justice, that people engaging in risky activities have notice about their probable exposure to liability.

D. Concern about proof of injury

In limiting liability in bystander cases, courts are at least indirectly responding to concerns about loose standards of proof, especially concerning emotional injuries. Here, one discerns an interface of causation in fact and "proximate cause"—the latter a concept that is roughly equal to the existence of a duty between the defendant and the plaintiff. The need for doctrines of proximate cause and duty—of which the rules limiting bystander recovery are in effect examples—exists because causation in fact does not by itself embody sufficient limitations to prevent the imposition of potentially unlimited liability. An argument in favor of relatively structured categories to restrict bystander recovery, for example, the limitation of recovery to those in a close family relationship with the direct victim, is that the existence of such a relation tends to guarantee the genuineness of the injury.

It is reasonable to assume that a lurking hostility to allowing recovery for mental injuries often underlies decisions that draw relatively tight lines on bystander recovery. Those opposing this bias, where it is apparent, will point out that medical science has shown that the mind/body distinction is a rather unsophisticated one. Although courts must guard their processes against fraud and manufactured evidence, it is now a commonplace idea that the possibility of fraud should not prevent a plaintiff's chance at recovery in a meritorious case.

E. The vicissitudes of life

A homespun argument in favor of relatively restrictive rules on bystander recovery may be summarized in the expression "[t]hat's life." The California Supreme Court put the idea more formally in denying recovery to a mother who arrived at the scene of her son's accident after it happened:

> [c]lose relatives suffer serious, even debilitating, emotional reactions to the injury, death, serious illness, and evident suffering of loved ones. These reactions occur regardless of the cause of the loved one's illness, injury, or death. That relatives will have severe emotional distress is an unavoidable aspect of the "human condition."

The court declared that "[t]he overwhelming majority of 'emotional distress' which we endure . . . is not compensable."[19] Carried to an extreme, this argument might erase a substantial amount of well-established tort law. However, there is a nucleus of common sense in the observation that courts cannot extend the category of tort "victim" indefinitely in a world filled with sadness and suffering.

F. Moral proportionality and degrees of culpability

Another argument opposing recovery against negligent defendants by a wide range of bystanders—or indeed by any bystanders

---

19. *Thing*, supra, 771 P.2d at 829.

at all—inheres in the fact that the tortfeasor is, after all, only negligent. Advocates of this position might accept, by contrast, the cause of action for intentional infliction of emotional distress. However, they would argue that, in justice, courts should rather tightly restrict the range of liability for carelessness. Although the character of intentional or reckless conduct ethically justifies liability for long chains of consequences, they would say, proportionality requires that the ambit of responsibility for negligence be relatively limited.

G.　Economic incentives

The bystander case forces courts to deal with various economic concerns in addition to those linked with the insurance considerations discussed above. Courts viewing accidents from an economic perspective will seek, insofar as it is practical, to force defendants to internalize costs they have inflicted on others. Besides itself embodying some justice features, internalization at least theoretically will generate some deterrence effects, and frequently does so in practice in many areas of activity. However, an empirical question arises with respect to the issue of liability to bystanders: will people who tend to act carelessly, made more prudent by the prospect of liability to those who their conduct directly injures, be further deterred from culpable conduct by the knowledge that they will also have to compensate bystander witnesses? If the answer is not clear, that would indicate that deterrence may be a suspect rationale for liberalizing bystander recovery.

H.　Arguments over a single recovery rule

A challenging argument that opposes bystander recovery entirely is a very simple one. It arises from the fact that most bystanders who have won recoveries are relatives, and usually close relatives, of the initial victim. Defendants will argue that awards of compensation to family bystanders, at least those based on emotional distress, are likely to have a significant component of payment for injuries to kin relationships. Stressing the difficulty of valuing those interests, they will contend that in the case of an injury directly caused to only one person, justice ordinarily should require no recovery for emotional injury to family members beyond that in favor of the direct victim.

There are counterarguments, to be sure, linked to the obvious point that each family member is an individual as well as part of a unit. The emotional interests that bystanders often seek to vindicate are interests quite distinct from the interests in bodily and emotional integrity for which tort law routinely awards compensation to directly injured persons, and quite as meritorious. Responding themselves, defendants will point out that both justice and economic common sense require courts to draw lines that cut off liability in long chains of events, even where those events would not have occurred were it not for the defendant's negligence. One practical, if arguably harsh, place to draw the line is at the person who is the direct victim of an accident. Opposing that entirely restrictive rule, the refinements explored in this chapter—factors of relationship, geography and time, and severity of distress—represent judicial efforts to capture the nuances of justice.

[Chapter 62 is reserved for supplementary material.]

Chapter Sixty–Three

RESCUERS

Analysis

¶ 63.01   The Problem

An intrinsically interesting favorite of courts and commentators is the problem of a negligent party's liability to rescuers, a category under which the law chalks up a variety of fact situations. A common element in the rescue cases is the same general situation that has fueled our discussions above of issues arising from extended chains of causal consequences, including "intervening cause" problems.[1] The rescue problem fits neatly within the pattern of a defendant's negligence followed by an injury that is indirect or unusual, which would not have occurred except for a series of events set in motion by the defendant's conduct.

The special fact that sets rescue cases apart is that the defendant's negligence places A in peril, and B, the plaintiff, suffers injuries in an attempt to come to the aid of A. Generally speaking, the primary obstacle to recovery is that the defendant did not directly injure B, but directly harmed or imperilled only A, the party that B tried to aid.

¶ 63.02   The *Wagner* Case

One case, vintage 1921, stands out in practically all judicial discussion of the rescue doctrine. This is *Wagner v. International*

---

   1. Various types of these situations
are analyzed in Chapters 55–57, 59, and
61 supra.

Ry. Co.,[2] in which Judge Cardozo wrote one of his most memorable opinions for the New York Court of Appeals. In that case, the plaintiff and his cousin were riding on the defendant's overcrowded electric railway car between Buffalo and Niagara Falls. A "violent lurch" threw the cousin out of the car. The driver stopped the vehicle, and the plaintiff went back on the trestle to search for his cousin. He found his cousin's hat but then missed his footing, fell, and was injured. The trial judge told the jury that it could find for the plaintiff only if the conductor had invited him to go out on the bridge and the conductor had followed with a light. The jury gave a verdict for the defendant, but the court of appeals reversed.

Judge Cardozo's opinion featured a string of verbal gems:

▶ "Danger invites rescue."

▶ "The cry of distress is the summons to relief."

▶ "The wrong that imperils life is a wrong to the imperiled victim; it is a wrong also to his rescuer."

▶ "The risk of rescue, if only it be not wanton, is born of the occasion. The emergency begets the man."

▶ "It is enough that the act, whether impulsive or deliberate, is the child of the occasion."[3]

In addition to delivering these rhetorical pearls, Judge Cardozo described the mental reactions of potential rescuers as being "within the range of the natural and probable."[4] He concluded that it was a question for the jury as to "whether plaintiff in going to the rescue . . . was foolhardy or reasonable in the light of the emergency confronting him."[5]

¶ 63.03   General Concepts and Terminology

Many general legal concepts surrounding Cardozo's biblical language concerning rescuers are ones that courts traditionally apply to the spectrum of cases involving chains of consequences. Courts may speak of "an independent duty of care as between the negligent party and the rescuer."[6] Or they may cast the question as one of "proximate causation."[7] As with many other situations that courts classify under headings like duty and proximate cause, judges also find themselves attracted to the concept of foreseeability.[8]

2. 133 N.E. 437 (N.Y.1921).

3. Id. at 437–38.

4. Id. at 437.

5. Id. at 438.

6. See Day v. Waffle House, Inc., 743 P.2d 1111, 1113 (Okla.Ct.App.1987).

7. Esposito v. Christopher, 443 P.2d 731, 732 (Colo.1968).

8. See, e.g., Day, supra note 6, 743 P.2d at 1114 (rescue attempt as a "foreseeable consequence of [the defendant's] breach of duty").

There is a particularly strong human interest element in another case, in which the court rejected the use of the rescue doctrine as a metaphor. In that case, the defendants negligently removed a man's kidneys. His mother, who donated one of her kidneys for a transplant to her son, sued for adverse consequences to her health that resulted from the loss of that organ. The trial judge wrote an opinion rejecting the plaintiff's claim, saying that the negligence of the defendants had "[come] to rest on the body of [the son]."[9] The opinion takes on ironic poignancy because the trial judge who wrote it was the plaintiff's attorney in the *Wagner* case. Judging this situation, however, he distinguished *Wagner* as a case in which "the rescuer acted without knowing his fate." Contrasting the suit before him, he said that the plaintiff mother, in surrendering her kidney, had engaged in an act that was "wilful, intentional, voluntary, free from accident and with full knowledge of its consequence."[10]

¶ 63.04   Fact Patterns

A. *Diversity of situations*

Cases successfully pleaded under the "rescue" label feature a wide diversity of facts. They range from a claim by the rescuer of a victim of contaminated restaurant food[11] to a case in which a negligent driver was sued for the death of a passenger who tried to help the driver with his disabled car,[12] and include a products liability case in which the plaintiff attempted to aid a person endangered by a runaway earthmoving machine.[13]

B. *Professionals as rescuers*

An interesting small cluster of cases involves professionals who serve as rescuers, for example, doctors. There is a split of authority concerning physicians who perform heroic deeds. In one case, a physician aggravated his own heart condition when he performed an operation in cramped quarters on a diver, who was eviscerated when the toilet on which he was sitting was "unaccountably

---

9. Sirianni v. Anna, 285 N.Y.S.2d 709, 712 (N.Y.Sup.1967).

10. Id.

11. See, e.g., Day v. Waffle House, supra note 6 (restaurant patron discovered broken glass in food and began spitting out food, broken glass and blood; companion injured while taking him to hospital; defendant's summary judgment reversed). But cf. Crankshaw v. Piedmont Driving Club, Inc., 156 S.E.2d 208 (Ga.Ct.App.1967) (plaintiff's friend became nauseous from unwholesome shrimp dish; plaintiff injured as

she rushed to restroom to aid friend and slipped on friend's vomit; demurrer sustained).

12. Rossman v. LaGrega, 270 N.E.2d 313 (N.Y.1971) (reversing dismissal based on finding that plaintiff's decedent was contributorily negligent as a matter of law).

13. Fedorchick v. Massey–Ferguson, Inc., 438 F.Supp. 60 (E.D.Pa.1977), aff'd without opin., 577 F.2d 725 (3d Cir.1978).

flushed from the outside" in a pressurized chamber. Denying recovery in the doctor's suit against the diver's employer, the court fixed, in part, on the fact that the plaintiff charged substantial rates for his services.[14] In another case, however, the court permitted recovery for a doctor against a building contractor for injuries that occurred when the plaintiff tried to reach employees trapped by a negligently caused landslide at a construction site. The court referred to uncontradicted evidence that the employees "were in peril of their lives" and that "immediate . . . action was required to save or assist them."[15]

A specific doctrine denying recovery in a functionally defined group of rescue-type cases, discussed earlier,[16] is the "fireman's rule," rationalized on the basis that firefighters accept the inherent risks of their hazardous job.

C. *Odd consequences*

There comes a point at which rescue cases merge into the general class of cases involving bizarre consequences, although the freakish nature of an injury may not keep courts from imposing liability on originally negligent parties. In a Louisiana case, an employee of defendant A parked his truck negligently and defendant B ran into the truck. B's car caught fire and the plaintiff, a bystander, tried to rescue B and his seriously injured wife from the vehicle. As the plaintiff engaged in this effort, he found a firearm on the floor of B's car and handed it to B. The delirious B shot the plaintiff. In successive opinions, the Louisiana appellate court first reversed judgments for both defendants and then affirmed a judgment against A but reversed a judgment against B, who in the later decision it absolved of "contributory negligence."[17]

D. *Rescued person as defendant*

The rescue doctrine applies against the person being rescued if the initiating negligence that created the need for rescue was his or her own. Illustrative is a case in which a man removed the sides of a swamp cooler, negligently exposing its moving parts. After he tripped on an electrical cord, the machine fell over him. The plaintiff, fearing the consequences to a person in the defendant's poor medical condition, suffered severe hand injuries from a moving part when she tried to lift the machine off the defendant. Concluding that the defendant owed his rescuer a duty, the court asked rhetorically, "[w]hy should the rescuer recover after helping a third

14. Carter v. Taylor Diving & Salvage Co., 341 F.Supp. 628 (E.D.La.1972).

15. Solgaard v. Guy F. Atkinson Co., 491 P.2d 821, 825 (Cal.1971).

16. See supra, ¶ 30.03(B).

17. Lynch v. Fisher, 34 So.2d 513 (La.Ct.App.1947), on rehearing, 34 So.2d 513 (La.Ct.App.1948); 41 So.2d 692 (La. Ct.App.1949).

party victim of negligence, but not recover for helping the negligent actor?"[18]

¶ 63.05 Applicable Policies

As they do across the spectrum of decisions involving chains of consequences, courts and commentators have invoked a variety of rationales for allowing or denying recovery in rescue cases. Economic analysis has produced the idea that permitting recovery to rescuers will have desirable results from the point of view of resource allocation. Two leading commentators have said that "to the extent that rescue efforts are undertaken" and that rules favoring rescuer recovery "encourage[] such undertakings," then "the number of accident victims, and hence the number of lawsuits, will be fewer than if recovery is not allowed."[19] We observe, however, that it is not clear that imposing liability in favor of rescuers will generate an appreciably greater amount of deterrence to negligent activity than simply imposing liability in favor of persons directly injured by culpable conduct.

We note also that, as is so throughout the general area of extended consequences cases, the concept of foreseeability does not seem consistently to aid decision in rescuer suits. Illustrative is a case discussed above, involving a mother's donation of a kidney to her son.[20] The court denied recovery in that case, even though it would seem entirely foreseeable to a surgeon who negligently removed a person's kidneys that the patient's relatives, particularly parents, would seek to donate their own organs as substitutes.

It would appear that a more convincing rationalization for the liability rules concerning rescuers lies elsewhere. Where courts impose liability, the explanation may inhere in a belief that as between the negligent party and the rescuer, fairness requires an extra toll from one who has acted below the social norm; it may also reside in a view that heroism in emergencies created by others

---

18. Sears v. Morrison, 76 Cal. App.4th 577, 589, 90 Cal.Rptr.2d 528, 536 (1999). See also Saltsman v. Corazo, 317 N.J.Super. 237, 721 A.2d 1000 (1998), in which the defendant Verdi was the manager of an entertainment complex who had ejected patrons for bringing beer on the premises. After an alleged battery on Verdi by one of the ejected patrons, Verdi followed them to a parking lot. There followed a scuffle in which the plaintiff, a "social acquaintance" of Verdi and an invitee on the premises, was seriously injured when he tried to help Verdi. There was a factual question about whether Verdi "negligently instigated" the scuffle by throw-

ing the first punch at one of the ejected patrons or insulting that man's female companions. The court concluded that if Verdi had been negligent in that regard, the jury would have to determine whether he "could have reasonably anticipated that plaintiff . . . might intervene to rescue him from the assaults which his negligence at least partially created." 721 A.2d at 1006–07.

19. William M. Landes and Richard A. Posner, Causation in Tort Law: An Economic Approach, 12 J. Legal Studies 109, 133 (1983).

20. See text accompanying notes 9–10 supra.

merits compensation, if not a bonus. An alternative explanation is that courts are responding to a sense that the genes of human beings are biologically coded by evolution for lifesaving responses to crises, indicating that nature values rescue as a means of perpetuating the species.

Finally, both the rhetoric and the reasoning of Cardozo carry a distinctively persuasive appeal. In saying that "danger invites rescue," Cardozo may intuitively have captured a rationale rooted in the wiring of human genes for altruistic responses. But whether or not that was even a subconscious reading of human biology, when Cardozo said that the original negligence is "a wrong ... to [the] rescuer" as well as to the initial victim, he was making a legal statement of duty. Finally, when he wrote that although "[t]he wrongdoer may not have foreseen the coming of a deliverer," "[h]e is as accountable as if he had,"[21] he was teaching that foreseeability is not always the controlling element in the rescue cases. What is dispositive, it would seem, is a moral judgment about the appropriate allocation of loss between negligent persons and heroes.

21. Wagner, supra note 2, 133 N.E. at 438.

Chapter Sixty–Four

ECONOMIC LOSS

Analysis

¶ 64.01 The Problem

An important set of issues arises under the general question of whether there should be tort liability for "economic loss." What courts refer to as the "economic loss rule" has denied liability, with the decisions drawing a sharp distinction between "personal injury" and "property damage," both of which are compensable, and "economic loss," which is not. Economic loss, in this sense, includes damages like the loss of business opportunities or profits resulting from tortious conduct, rather than the quantifiable costs of personal injuries or the replacement cost of property that has been damaged or destroyed.

As we shall explain, the courts use the classification of economic loss to deny recovery in two different types of cases, employing two rather different, although not mutually exclusive, sets of rationales. In cases where the litigants are in a contractual relationship—for example, a contract for the sale of an allegedly defective product—the courts emphasize that contract law is the only proper basis for deciding a claim for economic loss. They reason that the process of contract bargaining is the most efficient way to allocate essentially commercial risk. In cases where the parties had no contractual relation, courts reject claims for what they call economic loss on policy grounds, for example, emphasizing the plaintiff's superior ability to calculate in advance and insure that type of loss.

The distinction between personal injury and economic loss is important because plaintiffs who suffer personal injury can recover tort damages for a variety of losses stemming from that injury. The

348

most common pecuniary consequences of personal injury for which tort damages are given include such items as medical bills, lost earnings, and the cost of household services.[1] These are, truly, economic losses, but the fact that they result from personal injury makes them compensable in tort. Courts also routinely uphold tort awards for such intangible harms related to personal injury as pain and suffering.[2]

Courts also give tort awards for physical damage to property. An obvious example is damage to a vehicle caused by a collision. The decisions do draw various distinctions concerning the type of property damage for which they will allow tort recovery. As explained below, products liability is a field where these distinctions become particularly subtle.[3] However, most courts refuse to give tort recovery where the injury consists of no more than internal damage to or a devaluation of a product purchased by the plaintiff.

Although all courts give recovery for the quantifiable consequences of personal injury and for damage to property other than an allegedly defective product itself, courts are generally reluctant to allow tort suits for what they call "purely economic loss." A typical example of economic loss for which courts will not impose tort liability is the sort of damages usually associated with breach of contract. Thus, courts are likely to reject tort suits against sellers of goods that do not perform well, when buyers claim for "expectation loss," like loss of profits, or other consequential damages like repair costs or losses associated with the idling of plant machinery.

Plaintiffs who are contracting parties have a particularly difficult time convincing courts that such claims are properly brought under any heading but contract. Courts view such suits as essentially claims for "loss of bargain," the bargain being defined by the contract between the parties, which may include disclaimers and limitations of warranties. In those kinds of cases, the plaintiff theoretically could protect himself by contracting for a better deal— for example, paying for a higher level of quality in the product he purchases from the defendant or paying for a better warranty.

There is, however, a very different type of case in which courts also sometimes apply the economic loss rule. This is the case in which there is no contractual relationship between the parties, express or implied. These cases range from an explosion, caused by the defendant's negligence, which cripples a business with which the plaintiff has commercial dealings,[4] to an oil spill caused by the defendant that kills marine life on which commercial fishermen

---

1. See ¶ 71.01 infra.

2. See ¶ 72.01 infra.

3. See ¶ 64.04(A) infra.

4. See, e.g., Stevenson v. East Ohio Gas Co., 73 N.E.2d 200 (Ohio Ct.App. 1946), discussed infra, ¶ 64.03, text accompanying note 11.

depend for their livelihood.[5] When the court uses the economic loss rule to reject a claim in that kind of case, it is employing a form of duty or proximate cause analysis to limit liability for policy reasons.[6] Thus two kinds of cases—involving both contracting parties and strangers—become commingled in discussion of the economic loss rule.

Because of sometimes unappealing results associated with certain applications of the rule denying tort recovery for economic loss, courts have fashioned various exceptions to the rule. They also have liberally construed the category of property damage in ways that favor plaintiffs. For example, the fact that the defendant's negligence or product created a safety hazard will occasionally motivate courts to hold that the deprivation to the plaintiff of the use of goods, premises or services falls within the category of "property damage," even though there has been no destruction of a physical object belonging to the plaintiff other than the thing purchased.

In the case of goods sold to the plaintiff, these exceptions and interpretations often represent a reaction against the defendant's ability to disclaim or limit liability under warranty or contract theories. In other cases, they manifest judicial reluctance to absolve defendants whose negligence has caused real harms that otherwise could not be sued upon.

¶ 64.02   Concepts and Language

Viewed in a broad tort law perspective, the economic loss question is a sub-set of the questions discussed in previous chapters under the labels of "duty" and "proximate cause."[7] Some courts, indeed, have analyzed the issue within those linguistic classifica-

---

5. See the discussion of contrasting decisions on this question, infra, ¶ 64.04(B), text accompanying notes 22–24.

6. See, e.g., Aikens v. Debow, 208 W.Va. 486, 541 S.E.2d 576, 589–89 (2000), in which the defendant trucker caused "substantial damage" to an overpass bridge when he tried to force under it a load that was too high for the clearance. Repairs required 19 days, during which the bridge was closed. The plaintiff, owner of a motel and restaurant, sued for decreased revenues that he attributed to a diminution in traffic that otherwise would have used the bridge. The court rejected his claim, saying that "[t]he common thread which permeates the analysis of potential economic recovery in the absence of physical harm is the recognition of the

underlying concept of duty." The court defines a general rule of nonrecovery for "purely economic loss from an interruption in commerce caused by another's negligence" where there is no "physical harm to [the plaintiff's] person or property," and no "contractual relationship with the alleged tortfeasor, or some other special relationship between the alleged tortfeasor" and the plaintiff that would "compel the conclusion that the tortfeasor had a duty to the particular plaintiff and that the injury complained of was clearly foreseeable to the tortfeasor." The court says that "[t]he existence of a special relationship will be determined largely by the extent to which the particular plaintiff is affected differently from society in general."

7. See, e.g., chapters 55, 57, 61, 63 supra.

tions.[8] The question does fit within that matrix, because it involves a situation in which the defendant's negligence or unreasonably dangerous product has been a but-for cause of a certain kind of harm to the plaintiff. Categorized that way, the economic loss question presents the familiar general problem of the need to fashion a limitation on liability. However, although not necessarily suggesting that it does not fall under that general inquiry, many courts have tended to view the economic loss issue as a separate realm unto itself without tying it to concepts of duty and proximate cause.

Whatever label courts pin on the problem, discussion often tends to proceed under concepts and terminology that courts employ in cases involving extended chains of consequences or unusual results. Some courts have used the concept of "foreseeability," attempting to construct limitations on liability by such requirements as that of "an identifiable class of plaintiffs."[9] The decisions have also emphasized policy concerns of the sort discussed just below.

¶ 64.03 Policy Arguments

Many of the fundamental arguments on the issue of economic loss flow from the market nature of our society. On the one hand, particularly in certain products liability cases, where the parties at least could have contracted on the allocation of the loss at issue, defendants contend that loss of bargain is only the province of contract and not of tort. The argument, simply, is that parties should be held to their bargains. On the other hand, plaintiffs may argue that a society that so closely equates wealth and success, even tending to define one's personal value by wealth, has effectively meshed the elements of personality with those of the purse. They will thus contend that there is no meaningful distinction between purely pocketbook losses due to negligence and the pecuniary losses associated with personal injury caused by negligence.

In cases involving accidents not subject to pre-bargaining allocation of loss, courts have invoked a number of reasons for limiting or denying liability for economic loss. These reasons often replicate the rationales for finding that there is no duty with respect to a particular type of injury, or that the injury was not "proximately caused" by the defendant's negligence. Courts fear fraudulent claims and they oppose the imposition of a "liability out of proportion to the defendant's fault."[10] Judicial reluctance to award dam-

---

8. See, e.g., People Express Airlines, Inc. v. Consolidated Rail Corp., 495 A.2d 107, 110 (N.J.1985).

9. See id. at 115–16.

10. See, e.g., id. at 110.

ages for economic loss has often focused on concerns about virtually limitless liabilities.

An Ohio decision, frequently cited, presented a parade of hypothetical horribles while denying recovery to an employee who lost wages for several days because of a fire attributable to the defendant's storage of explosive materials near the plaintiff's place of work. The court said that if it allowed recovery beyond "personal injuries or physical property damage ... to every one who has suffered an economic loss, ... we might well be appalled by the results that would follow." The court gave, among other examples, these instances:

> the power company with a contract to supply a factory with electricity would be deprived of the profit which it would have made if the operation of the factory had not been interrupted by reason of fire damage; a man who had a contract to paint a building may not be able to proceed with his work; a salesman who would have sold the products of the factory may be deprived of his commission; the neighborhood restaurant which relies on the trade of the factory employees may suffer a substantial loss.[11]

Insurance is an important factor in application of the economic loss rule, both in cases subject to contract and those where the parties were not in a bargaining relationship. A significant concern is one that is familiar throughout the duty/proximate cause area: the inability of insurers to calculate risks with reasonable confidence in order to underwrite those risks. In some cases, an argument against liability is that the plaintiff is in the better comparative position to insure the risk at issue. An illustration would be a case in which a power company's negligence leads to a blackout that causes spoilage of all the meat in a freezer owned by a frozen food storage firm. One assumption of the argument is that the food storage firm can more efficiently calculate the potential loss from this rather specialized risk than can the power company. The argument would also apply to losses incurred by a firm that did business with the food storage company. A firm in that position could assess the potential losses to it of an interruption in that commercial relationship and insure against those losses.

By contrast, a foundational argument in favor of tort recovery for economic loss replicates a basic plaintiffs' contention in any case where there has been negligence and cause in fact. This is, quite simply, that "wronged persons should be compensated for their injuries and that those responsible for the wrong should bear the

---

11. Stevenson v. East Ohio Gas Co., 73 N.E.2d 200, 203–04 (Ohio Ct.App. 1946).

cost of their tortious conduct."[12] However, even courts that are relatively sympathetic to such claims feel impelled to consider potential limiting factors—for example, the identifiability of a foreseeable class of plaintiffs, "the certainty or predictability of their presence, the approximate numbers of those in the class, [and] the type of economic expectations disrupted."[13]

¶ 64.04   Functional Applications

It is useful to examine how competing analyses of the economic loss issue play out in situations that are defined by the nature of the defendant's activity or by the nature of the accident. The areas of products liability and environmental accidents are important functional battlegrounds for efforts to apply the economic loss rule, and incidents involving unusual chains of events provide another interesting set of applications.

A.   Products liability

Products liability cases feature significant disagreement about how to distinguish economic loss from property damage. A recurrent issue arises in cases where a product defect causes damage to the purchased product itself and the plaintiff is the buyer of the product. Many courts have insisted that because the product itself was subject to contractual bargaining, its loss—even through physical destruction—is only economic loss. However, when the defect actually causes the destruction of the purchased product, some courts have allowed recovery in tort, as in a case where fire attributable to a defect destroyed a new motor home.[14]

The case for the defendant becomes much stronger when an alleged defect causes only internal malfunctions in the purchased product that deprive the plaintiff of its use and, therefore, of expected profits. The United States Supreme Court denied recovery in such a case, in which defective components on supertanker turbines allegedly caused malfunctions and damage to the turbines themselves.[15] The charterers of the ships claimed for repair costs and loss of income for the time the ships were out of service. In rejecting the suit, Justice Blackmun defined the plaintiffs' loss as "purely economic," saying that damage to the product itself "means simply that the product has not met the consumer's

12. People Express Airlines, Inc., supra note 8, 495 A.2d at 111.

13. Id. at 116.

14. Rocky Mountain Fire & Casualty Co. v. Biddulph Oldsmobile, 640 P.2d 851 (Ariz.1982).

15. East River S.S. Corp. v. Transamerica Delaval, Inc., 476 U.S. 858 (1986).

expectations, or, in other words that the customer has received 'insufficient product value.' "[16]

However, some courts have even granted tort recovery against sellers when a product has defects that seriously reduce its value below what the consumer expected, without causing traumatic physical harm. One illustration is a case involving a mobile home where the roof shingles blew off, the living room ceiling sagged, and the walls became bowed. Reversing a dismissal, the court held that the plaintiff could sue under strict liability in tort.[17] The court referred to a variety of rationales for strict liability, including the "unfair bargaining position" of consumers relative to manufacturers and the difficulty of proving negligence. Notably, it mentioned the problem faced by consumers who do not have "large damages" in securing the services of lawyers working on contingency fees.

Another issue that has generated judicial disagreement in products cases has to do with situations in which the plaintiff suffers only "economic loss," but where the defendant's conduct created significant physical hazards. A classic decision, denying liability, is a New York case in which an airline fortunately discovered defects in airplane engines before they caused an accident, and sued the engine manufacturer on a negligence theory for repair or replacement costs. The court effectively concluded that there could be no tort recovery for such a commercial loss unless there had been an injury to person or property.[18]

Some courts have not found that view appealing. In a contrasting decision, the Eighth Circuit read Arkansas law to allow strict liability recovery in a case involving the sale of a used aircraft, which during the year after its purchase required major repairs and ultimately was found to be "so corroded as to be 'economically unfeasible' to repair." In upholding a tort claim for what was described as the losses the plaintiff incurred "as a result of the plane's failing to perform as expected," the court focused on evidence "that the plane was in a defective condition and unreasonably dangerous."[19]

An interesting intra-court confrontation on this type of issue occurred in a case in which chicken feed sold by the defendant allegedly caused eggs produced by the plaintiff's chickens to taste

---

16. Id. at 872 (quoting James J. White & Robert Summers, Uniform Commercial Code 406 (2d ed. 1980).

17. Thompson v. Nebraska Mobile Homes Corp., 647 P.2d 334, 337 (Mont. 1982).

18. Trans World Airlines, Inc. v. Curtiss–Wright Corp., 148 N.Y.S.2d 284, 290 (Sup.Ct.1955) ("[u]ntil there is an accident, there can be no loss arising from breach of [a] duty" grounded in negligence law; under those circumstances, the plaintiff's sole remedy was "for breach of warranty"), aff'd without opinion, 153 N.Y.S.2d 546 (App.Div. 1956).

19. Alaskan Oil, Inc. v. Central Flying Service, Inc., 975 F.2d 553, 555 (8th Cir.1992).

bad, essentially rendering them valueless. A majority of the Oregon Supreme Court denied recovery on a strict liability claim on the grounds that an action under that theory would exist "only when the defective goods are 'unreasonably dangerous to the user or consumer or to his property.' "[20]A dissenter argued that since there presumably would have been grounds for a strict liability suit if the feed had killed the chickens, the doctrine should apply as well if the feed disabled the fowl from "properly performing the function that give chickens their value as property." This dissenter said that the definition of "unreasonably dangerous" as "dangerous to an extent beyond that which would be contemplated by the ordinary purchaser" clearly applied to "the danger of damaging property as well as injuring the user or consumer."[21]

B. Environmental incidents

There has been fierce argument about how far liability should extend for various losses attributed to the escape of dangerous products or hazardous emissions into the environment. Some interesting decisions have involved oil and chemical spills that send toxic products in destructive paths through bodies of water. In a frequently cited case arising in California waters, commercial fishermen sued an oil company for fish kills they attributed to a spill in the Santa Barbara channel. In upholding a cause of action for the plaintiffs, the Ninth Circuit fixed on the foreseeability of the loss to the fishermen, declaring that "[t]he dangers of pollution were and are known even by school children." The court opined that "[t]o assert that the defendants were unable to foresee that negligent conduct resulting in a substantial oil spill could diminish aquatic life and thus injure the plaintiffs is to suppose a degree of general ignorance of the effects of oil pollution not in accord with good sense."[22]

One may compare a case in which a Fifth Circuit majority rejected the claims of a number of plaintiffs who sued for losses resulting from injuries to marine life caused by a chemical spill. These claimants included marina and boat rental operators and seafood restaurants as well as recreational fishermen. Inter alia, the court focused on the comparative availability of loss insurance to many of the plaintiffs. Noting that defendants might not be able to get liability insurance for the kinds of losses for which the plaintiffs claimed, the court said that by contrast, "[e]ach businessman who might be affected by a disruption of river traffic or by a halt in fishing activities can protect against that eventuality at a

---

20. Brown v. Western Farmers Ass'n., 521 P.2d 537, 540–41 (Or.1974).

21. Id. at 543 (O'Connell, C.J., dissenting).

22. Union Oil Co. v. Oppen, 501 F.2d 558, 569 (9th Cir.1974).

relatively low cost since his own potential losses are finite and readily discernible."[23]

One might be able to distinguish among and within classes of plaintiffs in such a case. For example, a court might find the losses to fishermen to be more "direct" than those to owners of seafood restaurants, and indeed might also distinguish between classes of fishermen.[24] In any event, cases like marine spills demonstrate how the economic loss problem taxes the ingenuity of courts and counsel, particularly when the chains of events are relatively long.

An illustration of the definitional issues about what constitutes "property damage" rather than economic loss in the case of environmental hazards appears in a case brought by townships against the owners of the Three Mile Island nuclear plant in Pennsylvania. In this case, in which safety hazards created by the defendants' conduct clearly influenced the appellate court's decision, the governmental plaintiffs sought reimbursement for various costs they attributed to a much-publicized accident in the plant's reactor. The claimed damages included the temporary reduction in use of municipal buildings, overtime pay for personnel responding to the incident, and lost work time of employees. The district court denied recovery for all these costs, viewing them as "all purely economic losses,"[25] but the Third Circuit reversed.[26]

Referring to the plaintiffs' contention that radioactivity had made "public buildings unsafe for a temporary period of time," the appellate court concluded that the plaintiffs had stated a claim for "temporary loss of use of property and 'damage to property' as a result of the intrusion of radioactive materials upon plaintiffs' properties ... , irrespective of any causally-related permanent physical harm to property."[27] Even as to overtime payments for employees who worked to replace employees who did not show up for work during the crisis, the appellate court said that the plaintiffs should have an opportunity to clarify the factual basis for their claim.[28]

C. Bizarre chains of consequences

A certain group of decisions involving economic loss may best be classified in the category of cases involving bizarre chains of

---

23. Louisiana ex rel. Guste v. M/V Testbank, 752 F.2d 1019, 1029 (5th Cir. 1985), cert. denied sub. nom. White v. M/V Testbank, 477 U.S. 903 (1986).

24. Although the trial court granted summary judgment to the defendants on the claims of recreational fishermen as well as other plaintiffs, it denied summary judgment on claims by commercial fishermen, see 524 F.Supp. 1170, 1173–74 (E.D.La.1981), and the commercial fishermen's claims were not before the

appellate court. See 752 F.2d at 1021 & n.2.

25. In re TMI Litigation Governmental Entities Claims, 544 F.Supp. 853, 856 (M.D.Pa.1982).

26. Pennsylvania v. General Pub. Utils. Corp., 710 F.2d 117 (3d Cir.1983).

27. Id. at 123.

28. Id. at 122.

consequences, like those in the famous *Palsgraf* case.[29]

From the artistic perspective of the lawyer, one of the most factually wonderful of these cases arose when a ship moored on the Buffalo River broke loose and "careened" down the channel, striking another vessel that also broke loose and drifted downstream with the first ship until it crashed into a bridge. As the court summarized the resulting events, "[t]he bridge collapsed and its wreckage, together with [the two ships], formed a dam which caused extensive flooding and an ice jam reaching almost 3 miles upstream." This occurrence disrupted river transportation for about two months. The defendants included companies whose negligence contributed to the breaking loose of the first ship. Among the plaintiffs who sued for their economic losses was a company that had contracted to deliver wheat stored aboard a ship moored in the harbor below the bridge. The accident kept the firm from moving the ship to its grain elevators above the bridge so it could unload the wheat. Inter alia, the trial court rejected a commissioner's award to the firm for its expenses in securing replacement wheat, including extra transportation costs and "increased 'storage costs.' "[30]

In the Second Circuit's first review of cases arising from the incident, which involved a complex allocation of damages for harms to the property of several plaintiffs, Judge Friendly posited that "[s]omewhere a point will be reached when courts will agree that the link has become too tenuous—that what is claimed to be consequence is only fortuity."[31] In a later opinion that focused on the economic losses incurred by grain shippers, Judge Kaufman declared that the plaintiffs' damages were "too ... remote" from the defendants' negligence to justify recovery. He quoted a much-cited statement of Holmes: " 'The law does not spread its protection so far.' "[32] Such language illustrates the point at which courts are driven to intuitions concerning fairness and propriety in cases where long chains of occurrences eventuate in "purely economic loss," or "unforeseeable consequences," or, indeed, any results that judges' legal common sense deems too far-fetched to impose liability.

29. Palsgraf v. L. I. R. R., 162 N.E. 99 (N.Y.1928), discussed supra, ¶ 55.02.

30. See Petitions of Kinsman Transit Co., 388 F.2d 821, 823 (2d Cir.1968) ("Kinsman II").

31. Petitions of Kinsman Transit Co., 338 F.2d 708, 725 (2d Cir.1964).

32. Kinsman II, supra note 30, 388 F.2d at 825, quoting Robins Dry Dock & Repair Co. v. Flint, 275 U.S. 303, 309 (1927).

Chapter Sixty–Five
DUTY TO ACT

Analysis

An intriguing set of controversies in tort law arises with respect to liability for failure to act. Courts have classified the cases in several categories, with the most challenging theoretical issue being whether there should be a duty to rescue someone in peril when the defendant has no prior relationship with that person and has not undertaken to aid him. With a few exceptions, current law imposes no duty in that situation.

¶ 65.01   Elements of the Rules Where Duty Imposed

A. *Relationships*

A rather well-established category of cases in which courts will impose a duty to act involves litigants who were in a pre-existing relationship before the occasion at issue. A straightforward example of such a relationship is that of employer and employee. In an illustrative case, the court imposed liability on a railroad under the Federal Employers' Liability Act for failing to give medical care to a track laborer who died after collapsing from heat prostration. The court declared that when an employee "receives injuries, whether or not due to the negligence of the master, rendering him helpless to provide for his own care," the employer must provide "such medical care and other assistance as the emergency ... may in reason require." The court found the rationale for this obligation in "dictates of humanity, duty and fair dealing."[1]

---

1. Szabo v. Pennsylvania R.R., 40 A.2d 562, 563 (N.J.L.1945).

Undoubtedly, the nature of the relationship will affect decisions on whether there is a duty. It is pretty clear that when a patient collapses in his or her doctor's office, the doctor has a legal obligation to give medical aid. It also seems reasonable to impose a duty on a doctor to tell a patient about another physician's negligent treatment of the patient about which the current doctor knows.[2] Moreover, one decision imposed liability on a corporation whose physician did not inform a job applicant of test data that would have led to a cancer diagnosis.[3]

By comparison, courts are not likely to impose a duty on a physician to render medical aid to a stranger who collapses on the sidewalk as the doctor is taking a stroll. A different aspect of community thinking on the subject, exhibiting legal leniency to the person who does give aid, appears in the so-called Good Samaritan legislation enacted in many states. These statutes exempt people from tort liability for injuries occurring during the rendition of emergency care, except where their conduct is more culpable than ordinary negligence.

Decisions rejecting claims for failure to act often represent a denial of plaintiffs' attempts to construct legally meaningful relationships with defendants. Illustrative is a case in which a county crime laboratory allegedly did not do blood and semen-typing that it could have done, leading to the result that the plaintiff was wrongfully charged with several rapes. In denying liability against the laboratory, the court said, inter alia, that "a crime lab's undertaking to render services to the police simply cannot be regarded as necessary for the protection of a particular suspect or class of suspects."[4] The court noted, among other things, that the discretion exercised by police and the district attorney about whether to prosecute a criminal suspect meant that the lab had "no control over, or ability to foresee, the disposition of criminal suspects."[5]

B. *Undertakings*

In another class of cases in which courts will be relatively sympathetic to plaintiffs, the defendant in some way undertakes to aid the plaintiff and then does so negligently. In certain circumstances, courts may even impose liability when the undertaking is to another person but the defendant has reason to know that the activity is necessary to protect the plaintiff. According to the Second Restatement, this liability arises if the defendant's negli-

2. Lopez v. Swyer, 279 A.2d 116, 124 (N.J.Super.1971), modified on other issues, 300 A.2d 563 (N.J.1973).

3. Coffee v. McDonnell–Douglas Corp., 503 P.2d 1366, 1372–73 (Cal. 1972).

4. Cantwell v. Allegheny County, 483 A.2d 1350, 1355 (Pa.1984).

5. Id. at 1354.

gence "increases the risk of ... harm," or "he has undertaken to perform a duty owed by the other to the [plaintiff]," or "the harm is suffered because of the reliance of the other or the [plaintiff] upon the undertaking."[6]

Within the varied kinds of activity embraced by this heading, an interesting set of issues focuses on the conduct of insurers that conduct inspections as part of their safety programs. In one case, the court imposed liability against an insurer whose engineer neglected to make a detailed inspection of the components of a construction hoist that later failed, causing fatal injuries. Concluding that the insurer's "gratuitous" inspection had created "an enforceable duty" to workers who rode the hoist,[7] the court pointed out that the engineer was experienced in testing machines of that kind and that the insured company's employees were not.[8] A distinction appears in a decision that denied liability when an insurer did not undertake to inspect an area in a plant where an accident occurred, having inspected only parts of the plant that management asked it to inspect or concerning which it received accident reports.[9]

¶ 65.02 The Pure Duty to Act Problem

The most interesting jurisprudential question in this area is whether courts should impose tort liability on someone who fails to aid another person with whom the defendant has no pre-existing relationship and to whom the defendant has not undertaken to furnish aid, when the effort to help would not imperil the defendant himself. The common law rule is simple: there is no duty to provide aid for a stranger, no matter how emergent that person's peril. There would be unanimity that one should not be liable in tort for not giving money to a starving stranger, although there might be sharp disagreement about one's moral duty in such a situation. The sorts of hypotheticals often used to illustrate the common law rule are similarly heartrending. For example, courts presumably would not impose tort liability, although they might indulge in strong moral condemnation, against a person who does not aid a baby as the baby crawls toward a cliff and falls off.

The reasons usually given for this rule reside in notions of individualism fixed in Anglo–American jurisprudence. Some commentators have argued that to impose a duty would be a violation of the defendant's right to personal freedom, and some have even suggested that the imposition of liability would violate the Thir-

---

6. Restatement (Second) of Torts § 324A (1965).

7. See Nelson v. Union Wire Rope Corp., 199 N.E.2d 769, 774–78 (Ill.1964).

8. Id. at 783–84.

9. Stacy v. Aetna Casualty and Surety Co., 484 F.2d 289, 293–95 (5th Cir.1973).

teenth Amendment's prohibition against slavery or involuntary servitude.[10] In any event, under common law a plaintiff who is not able to show a legally recognized relationship or an undertaking generally cannot succeed in a tort action for failure to act.

¶ 65.03　Arguments in Favor of a Duty

The persistence of the common law rule is matched by persistent discontent with a message that many people consider immoral. Criticism of the rule begins with such sources as John Donne's ringing declaration that "no man is an Iland, intire of it selfe; every man is a peece of the *Continent*, a part of the *maine*; . . . any mans *death* diminishes *me*, because I am involved in Mankinde; And therefore never send to know for whom the *bell* tolls; It tolls for *thee*."[11]

Such language is, of course, too poetic and unfocused a foundation on which to build a tort duty. A somewhat less abstract formulation appears in the case of the railroad employee summarized above in which the court referred to "dictates of humanity, duty and fair dealing."[12] Those words make clear that judges do think in moral terms, rather than—as some economists would insist they do and even should—pinning tort doctrine primarily or even solely to a test of economic efficiency.

Justice Cardozo emphasized factors of power and control in a suit brought by the administrator of a seaman who died from pneumonia in a hospital at his home port. The plaintiff claimed that better care on board ship would have saved the seaman's life. In concluding that a duty existed that could be breached by "negligent omission to furnish cure or care,"[13] Cardozo focused on the "despotic" authority that masters have over seamen. On that premise, he built the idea that "[o]ut of this relation of dependence and submission there emerges for the stronger party a corresponding standard or obligation of fostering protection."[14] Although Cardozo employed these concepts in a dispute involving a well-established relationship, courts might apply them by analogy to cases of life-threatening emergencies where there was no pre-existing relationship. In those situations, a bystander, by force of circumstances, may have a short-term power over life or death for another individual.

Professor Weinrib has sought to make the "duty of beneficence" philosophically precise. Observing that courts cannot en-

10. U.S. Const. amend. XIII.

11. John Donne, Complete Poetry and Selected Prose 441 (Charles Coffin, ed., Modern Library Random House 1952).

12. See *Szabo*, text accompanying note 1 supra.

13. Cortes v. Baltimore Insular Line, 287 U.S. 367, 372 (1932).

14. Id. at 377.

force a "general duty of beneficence" but that Western democracies provide "programs for social assistance" through "primarily legislative and administrative" institutions, Weinrib points out that "[a]n imminent peril cannot await assistance from the appropriate social institutions." In that situation, he comments, the provision of aid to the victim "does not deplete the social resources committed to the alleviation of more routine threats to physical integrity."[15]

Perhaps more controversially, Weinrib contends that to require individuals to provide aid in that circumstance "presents no unfairness problems in singling out a particular person to receive the aid," nor of "unfairly singl[ing] out one of a class of routinely advantaged persons" as the aid-giver: "the rescuer just happens to find himself for a short period in a position, which few if any others share, to render a service to some specific person." In this situation, Weinrib argues, "the general duty of beneficence that is suspended over society like a floating charge is temporarily revealed to identify a particular obligor and obligee, and to define obligations that are specific enough for judicial enforcement."[16]

¶ 65.04 Legislation

In the absence of judicial inclination to change the common law rule, the legal solution to its perceived moral injustices must be a legislative one. On the civil law side, several European nations have enacted code provisions that impose duties to act. The French penal code, for example, makes it a crime for one "to voluntarily abstain[] from giving assistance to a person which he could, without risk either to himself or to third persons, give either by his personal action or by securing assistance,"[17] and it has been suggested that violations of this provision are civilly actionable.[18]

There has been a little legislative activity in America on the subject, but what legislation there is provides only for light criminal penalties and, in some cases, the immunization of rescuers from tort suits, rather than creating a civil cause of action for the endangered person. The first statute imposing any sort of duty of "convenient rescue," as it is sometimes called, was Vermont's "Duty to Aid the Endangered Act." That statute makes it an offense, entailing a small fine, to fail to render aid to another who is "exposed to grave physical harm" so long as the defendant can provide the aid "without danger or peril to himself or without interference with important duties owed to others."[19] At least two

---

15. Ernest Weinrib, The Case for a Duty to Rescue, 90 Yale L. J. 247, 291–92 (1980).

16. Id. at 292.

17. French Penal Code art. 63.

18. See McClure v. United States Lines Co., 368 F.2d 197, 199 (4th Cir. 1966) (citing expert testimony).

19. 12 Vt. Stat. Ann. § 519 (1973).

other states have passed similar statutes.[20]

A very different kind of legislation, one that immunizes from liability those who give aid to imperiled persons, is known as "Good Samaritan" legislation. Each state has such a statute, and some of these laws have complex categories defining the classes of persons and situations that will trigger the immunity.[21] Only illustrative of the kinds of questions that can arise under such statutes is a decision holding that a Good Samaritan law does not bar suits against physicians rendering service in hospitals. The case arose in New Jersey, one of the 29 states whose statutes did not specifically address the issue of care given in hospitals. The court rationalized its refusal to immunize hospital physicians for alleged negligence in the delivery of a baby on the basis of what it viewed as the purpose of the legislation. That purpose, it said, was to encourage "the rendering of medical care to those who need it but otherwise might not receive it (ordinarily roadside accident victims), by persons who come upon such victims by chance, without the accoutrements provided in a medical facility, including expertise, assistance, sanitation or equipment."[22] The court concluded that "[a] hospital or medical center does not qualify under the terms of" the legislation.[23]

¶ 65.05   Conceptual Overlaps

One should note the overlap between the "duty to act" issue as it is defined here and certain kinds of duty issues discussed elsewhere. In this area of overlap we find suits against A for failure to protect the plaintiff against direct injury by B, even if B's act was a crime. That category of cases includes issues like psychotherapists' duties to protect the public, or specific persons, from the violent acts of patients, as well as questions about the obligation of

20. Minn. Stat. Ann.§ 604A.01 (duty to give "reasonable assistance" "to the extent that the person can do so without danger or peril to self or others"); R.I. Gen. Laws § 11–56–1 (similar language).

21. See, e.g., Stewart Reuter, Physicians as Good Samaritans, 20 J. Legal Med. 157, 157 (1999), quoting Mason, Good Samaritan Laws—Legal Disarray: An Update, 38 Mercer L. Rev. 1439, 1442 (1987), as reporting that "117 statutes provide varying degrees of immunity to different classes of rescuers under a multitude of settings," with California protecting "eleven specified classes of individuals at more than six types of

emergencies acting under five standards of conduct as provided in fifteen statutes located in six state codes."

22. Velazquez v. Jiminez, 798 A.2d 51, 57 (N.J.2002).

23. Id. at 65. But cf., e.g., Roberts v. Myers, 569 N.E.2d 135 (Ill.App.Ct. 1991) (granting summary judgment to doctor, who was at hospital caring for own obstetrical patients, and who was summoned from doctors' lounge to aid in delivery of baby of other doctors' patients; defendant fulfilled requirement of statute that "Good Samaritan" have no "prior notice" of emergency to which he responded).

educational institutions to protect their students against the acts of others who pose a danger on the campus or in its environs.[24]

Sometimes issues concerning affirmative duties arise in the context of an asserted obligation to protect members of the public from the tortious or otherwise risky, but not criminal, acts of a third party. The New York Court of Appeals denied recovery to a person struck by a speeding car, driven by a voluntary resident of a health-related facility who had suffered a stroke that left her susceptible to blackouts.[25] The plaintiff sued the institution and its medical director, a physician who had taken a medical history from the driver but had not questioned her about whether she owned a car or intended to drive while she was a resident.

In refusing to impose liability, the court focused on the driver's status as a voluntary resident "with no medical reason . . . impeding her ability to leave [the facility] unaccompanied," which meant that she "could come and go as she pleased." Pointing out that "[a] physician's duty of care is ordinarily one owed to his or her patient" and noting that the defendant doctor was not the driver's treating physician, the court declared that the doctor "therefore was under no legal obligation to warn her of possible dangers involved in activities in which she chose to engage off the premises of the facility." In this context, the court was unpersuaded that the defendants "owed a duty to plaintiff to prevent [the driver] from driving off the premises of their facility."[26]

---

24. See ¶ ¶ 57.03–.04 supra.

25. Purdy v. Public Adm'r of County of Westchester, 526 N.E.2d 4 (N.Y.), reconsideration denied, 529 N.E.2d 428 (N.Y.1988).

26. Id. at 7–8.

Part Four

THE TORT LIABILITY
OF PUBLISHERS

Section Eleven

DEFAMATION AND INVASION OF PRIVACY

Chapter Sixty–Six

DEFAMATION: THE BASIC LAW

Analysis

¶ 66.01 Defamation Defined

A. *Overview*

The tort of defamation provides remedies for publications that injure reputation—called libel in the case of written publication or broadcast communication, and slander for spoken words. This chapter focuses principally on the law of libel, although it refers to some specific requirements of slander doctrine.

The tort has a long and complicated history, and its modern rules are themselves complex. This chapter establishes a basic framework of definitions and discusses principal areas of controversy. It is helpful, at the outset, to summarize the fundamental requirements of the tort:

- The defendant must publish

- Material that sufficiently identifies the plaintiff,

- Which injures the plaintiff's reputation,
- By false statements, purportedly of fact, or of opinion implying the existence of facts, and
- Is unprivileged.

B.   The core concept

A threshold requirement for defamation actions is that the communication at issue must be false. Some true statements about people—for example, dredging up unsavory material from their pasts—may lower their esteem in the community. However, although such publications may be actionable under another heading—principally the "public disclosure of private facts" branch of the tort of invasion of privacy[1]—they are, by definition, not defamation because they are true. We also note that, although damages for defamation may include mental suffering, the underlying interest protected by the tort is one of reputation, rather than emotional integrity.

The traditional definition of defamation, using language that may sound antique today, required the plaintiff to show that the defendant's false statements had held the plaintiff up to "hatred, contempt and ridicule." The more modern version of the Second Restatement says that a communication is "defamatory" if "it tends so to harm the reputation of another as to lower him in the estimation of the community or to deter third persons from associating or dealing with him."[2] It is under these abstract standards that courts begin their analysis of whether publications are injurious to reputation. The basic defamation issue overlaps with the often difficult question of whether a statement represents "fact" or "opinion."[3] A category usually distinguished from defamation is that of insult, which in most states does not create a cause of action.

A couple of examples will provide some flavor of the types of cases that present the question of whether statements are defamatory. In one case, the court concluded that a statement that a county highway superintendent did not "have the guts to fire" people had "cast aspersions" on that official's professional abilities and that an assertion that he was a "liar" "suggest[ed] a lack of integrity" in the way he performed his job. It thus denied a motion to dismiss a defamation action based on those statements. However, in the same case the court held that there was no cause of action for the phrases "gutless bastard" and "black son of a bitch," which

---

1. See infra, ¶ 69.01.

2. Restatement (Second) of Torts § 559 (1977) (hereafter, Restatement (Second)).

3. See generally Chapter 68 infra.

it said did not implicate the plaintiff's "professional abilities" although the language was "abusive, offensive and indecent."[4]

Also indicative of judicial insistence on injury to reputation, as contrasted with insulting or snide remarks, is a holding that there was no defamation in a book that spoke of the plaintiff as having a "disappearing fringe of hair at the crown [that] resembled a hard boiled egg," and that said that "[a] few more pounds and he would be roly-poly, like a rubber beach toy that bounces up every time it is knocked to the sand." The plaintiff argued that this language was defamatory because it was "a publication of his 'natural defects'" that "exposed him to public ridicule," but the court gave summary judgment for the defendant, saying that baldness and pudginess do not qualify as a "natural defect."[5]

C. The "libel proof" plaintiff

A specialized category under the issue of whether communications are defamatory is that of the "libel proof" plaintiff, a classification whose very creation may reflect modern mores. A libel proof plaintiff is a person whose reputation on the matter at issue is already so low that realistically there can be no impairment of reputation. In one case that used that test, *Hustler* magazine printed an article about the publisher of *Penthouse* magazine, Robert Guiccioni, which showed him with his arm around an unclothed model sitting on his knee. The article said, "[c]onsidering he is married and also has a live-in girlfriend, Kathy Keeton ... we wonder if he would let either of them pose nude with a man." Guiccioni sued on the basis that this language falsely accused him of committing adultery in 1983, the date of the article. He and his wife had married in 1956 and separated in 1964, but had been divorced in 1979, and he had not remarried. It was undisputed that Guiccioni had cohabited with Ms. Keeton since 1966. In holding for the defendant, the court premised "that a plaintiff's reputation with respect to a specific subject may be so badly tarnished that he cannot be further injured by allegedly false statements on that subject." Referring to Guiccioni's testimony that "his relatives, friends, and business associates knew that he was living with Keeton while still legally married," the court concluded that his "reputation regarding adultery rendered him libel-proof on this subject."[6]

¶ 66.02 Publication

Once a plaintiff has shown that matter is defamatory, she must prove that the defendant published it, meaning that the defendant

---

4. Fleming v. Kane County, 636 F.Supp. 742, 747 (N.D.Ill.1986).

5. Raymer v. Doubleday & Co., 615 F.2d 241, 243 (5th Cir.1980).

6. Guccione v. Hustler Magazine, Inc., 800 F.2d 298, 303–04 (2d Cir.1986).

communicated it to a third party. Thus, saying something to the plaintiff that would injure her reputation if someone else heard it is insufficient for defamation if the remark was not in fact communicated to another, although it may be a grave insult to the plaintiff. Illustrative of the issues that may arise in this connection is whether sending a defamatory letter only to the plaintiff constitutes publication when there is reason to believe that the plaintiff's secretary will open her mail. The Restatement opines that if the secretary opens the letter and reads it, the defendant "has published a libel."[7]

An important technical question concerning the medium of communication is whether to characterize broadcast material as libel, a term usually used to refer to printed matter, or as slander, which historically has referred to spoken remarks. The Restatement flatly labels broadcast defamation "libel, whether or not it is read from a manuscript."[8] This seems appropriate, because broadcast material typically will be much more widely disseminated than ordinary spoken language, and thus is much more analogous to print.

Congress has generally decided that internet service providers (ISPs) may not be held liable for defamatory remarks by users of their services. Before Congress legislated on the subject, a New York trial court had concluded that an ISP could be considered a publisher of defamatory material because it "held itself out to the public and its members as controlling the content of its computer bulletin boards."[9] Effectively overruling that holding, section 230 of the Communications Decency Act says that "[n]o provider or user of an interactive computer service shall be treated as the publisher or speaker of any information provided by another information content provider."[10] This legislative immunity has drawn criticism, with one author saying that Congress "should have imposed liability" on what she calls "cyberspace intermediaries," which she defines as "those online entities who have some ability to prevent or at least stem serious online defamation injury." She says Congress could then have permitted intermediaries to contract with users for different rules in a way that would "reasonably allocate[] the costs of reducing injury between" the intermediaries and users.[11]

---

7. Restatement (Second) § 577, comment k, illus. 6, at 205.

8. Restatement (Second) § 568A.

9. Stratton Oakmont, Inc. v. Prodigy Servs. Co., 1995 WL 323710 (N.Y.Sup.Ct.1995).

10. 47 U.S.C. § 230(c)(1). Identifying a possible gap in this immunity is a

dictum in Blumenthal v. Drudge, 992 F.Supp. 44, 50 (D.D.C.1998)(opining that statute "does not preclude joint liability for the joint development of content").

11. See Susan Freiwald, Comparative Institutional Analysis in Cyberspace: The Case of Intermediary Liability

It should be noted that any part of a communication—for example, a newspaper headline—maybe be defamatory. The *National Examiner* stumbled on this rule when it published a story about Kato Kaelin, a house guest at O.J. Simpson's estate who had testified in a criminal trial about events associated with the murder of Simpson's wife and another man. The headline read,

COPS THINK KATO DID IT!

    ... he fears they want him for perjury, say pals

Given that the story did not indicate that police thought that Kaelin had been guilty of the murders, the court reversed summary judgment for the publisher. It specifically rejected the *Examiner's* argument that "a headline by itself cannot be the basis of a libel action." The court said that state law made it clear that "headlines are not irrelevant, extraneous, or libel-free zones," but rather "are essential elements of a publication."[12]

¶ 66.03   Identification

An interesting set of issues, although these questions are not frequently litigated, concerns whether defamatory remarks that focus on groups of people, without specifically naming particular individuals, have sufficiently identified persons in those groups to libel them. In one case, the plaintiffs worked on a newspaper, which the defendant characterized as "probably the worst newspaper in America" in an op-ed column that said that the publisher "runs a newspaper by paranoids for paranoids." The court rejected a complaint by 24 office boys, reporters, and assistant editors, saying that they were insufficiently identified by the publication. It even turned down a claim by three of the paper's eight editors, saying that the text did not "provide[] a reasonable basis to focus on these three men," and that "as to these three editors no 'special application' or 'particular reference' " could "be reasonably inferred" from the column.[13]

One may compare, and to an extent contrast, a case in which the writers of a book attributed sexual misconduct, or what was then viewed as deviation, to three groups of employees at the Neiman–Marcus store in Dallas in the early 1950s.[14] At the pleading stage, these classes of plaintiffs fared differently:

(1) *The store's nine female models*: The defendants did not move to dismiss a claim on the statement, "some Neiman models are call girls."[15]

for Defamation, 14 Harv. J. L. & Technol. 569, 585, 636–37 (2001).

12. Kaelin v. Globe Communications Corp., 162 F.3d 1036, 1040 (9th Cir.1998).

13. Loeb v. Globe Newspaper Co., 489 F.Supp. 481, 484 (D.Mass.1980).

14. Neiman–Marcus v. Lait, 13 F.R.D. 311 (S.D.N.Y.1952).

15. See id. at 313 (noting that these plaintiffs were the store's "entire group

(2) *The salesmen in the men's store*: The court denied a motion to dismiss concerning a statement that attributed homosexuality to "most of the sales staff" in the men's store, a group of 25, saying that "an imputation of gross immorality to some of a small group casts suspicion upon all, where no attempt is made to exclude the innocent."[16]

(3) *The store's saleswomen*: By contrast, the court granted a motion to dismiss on a claim by members of a group of 382 saleswomen with respect to the assertion "[t]he salesgirls are good, too ... twenty bucks on the average." The court invoked the principle that when the "group or class disparaged is a large one, absent circumstances pointing to a particular plaintiff as the person defamed, no individual member ... has a cause of action."[17]

¶ 66.04   Fact vs. Opinion

The law of defamation effectively requires plaintiffs to show that the statement at issue was made as if it had a factual basis. It may, of course, be made as "a statement of fact."[18] If it is "a statement in the form of an opinion," it is "actionable only if it implies the allegation of undisclosed defamatory facts as the basis for the opinion."[19] A detailed discussion of the difficult questions arising from the "fact/opinion" distinction appears below.[20]

¶ 66.05   Culpability

The traditional rule for defamation allowed recovery for defamatory communications published without fault, but the constitutionalization of this area of the law has implanted a set of culpability requirements in American jurisprudence. The heart of these standards lies in the rules that a private individual suing publishers or broadcasters for libel must prove that the defendant was at least negligent, and that public officials or public figures who are libel plaintiffs must show that the defendant published the material at least recklessly of its truth or falsity. We discuss some details of these rules below in our examination of the constitutionalization of libel law.[21]

of models at the time of the publication"), 316 n.1.

16. Id. at 315–16.

17. Id. at 316.

18. Restatement (Second) § 565.

19. Id. § 566.

20. See infra, Chapter 68.

21. See infra, ¶¶ 67.01–67.03.

¶ 66.06 Libel Per Se, Slander Per Se and Special Damages

A complicated and mischievous doctrine is that of libel per se. The basic idea is that a statement is libel per se if it is "defamatory on its face—that is if extrinsic circumstances are not necessary to reveal its defamatory character."[22]

A clearcut example of libel per se would be the statement, "X stole Y's wallet," which is unambiguous as to its allegation that X committed a crime. By comparison, an assertion that someone has engaged in "blackmail" may not be libel per se when it is in the context of a document indicating that the plaintiff is taking an unfair negotiating position on a commercial matter.[23]

The practical importance of fitting a publication into the libel per se category in states that use it is that the plaintiff who is able to do so may recover without pleading and proving special damages. For these purposes, special damages means rather specifically quantifiable harms, for example, the kind of pecuniary loss that would be associated with a provable drop in business receipts. Thus, in a libel per se jurisdiction, the sort of injury that many people would intuitively associate with defamation—harm to one's "good name" alone—would not be recoverable without proof of special damages unless a plaintiff could show that the defamatory meaning of the statement at issue was apparent without a showing of extrinsic circumstances. Often, if a plaintiff cannot bring herself within the libel per se category, and also cannot prove special damages, she will have little chance of establishing the kind of case that will make litigation financially worthwhile.

There has been something of a tendency to equate the category of libel per se to the traditional classifications under the heading of slander per se. The slander per se rules require a plaintiff to plead and prove special damages unless she can place the defendant's publication in one of four categories: the imputation of a crime, the imputation of unchastity to a woman, the assertion that the plaintiff suffers from a loathsome disease, and statements that would injure the plaintiff in her business, trade or profession. Although it has been pointed out that to engraft the slander per se categories onto "libel per se" is a misreading of history, this is the way that some courts have fashioned their libel per se doctrine. There thus

---

22. Charles E. Carpenter, Libel Per Se in California and Some Other States, 17 So. Calif. L. Rev. 347, 347 (1944).

23. See, e.g., Garber–Pierre Food Prods., Inc. v. Crooks, 397 N.E.2d 211 (Ill.Ct.App.1979) (statement that refusal to deliver goods on credit was blackmail was not libel per se). Cf. Greenbelt Cooperative Publ. Ass'n v. Bresler, 398 U.S. 6 (1970) (defendant labeled developer's negotiating position in seeking zoning variances as blackmail because of his efforts to use price of parcel of his land for bargaining leverage with city; held, in context, statement "was no more than rhetorical hyperbole").

exist two overlapping categories of libel per se: (1) publications that fall into the slander per se categories, and (2) publications susceptible of a defamatory meaning without a showing of extrinsic circumstances.

Particular cases test the limits of the libel per se category, forcing courts to struggle with the question of whether remarks are defamatory as opposed to being merely insults or expressions of opinion. Two cases involving very different subjects illustrate the kinds of situations that fall into a zone of uncertainty where parties will insist on litigating.

In one case, a defendant who was "an influential member of her community" distributed publications in which she described a younger woman of apparently quite different political views, who held an academic appointment and worked on a family newspaper, as being a "Narcissus." The defendant told readers to "hunt up your psychology textbooks for that one." The publications also contained various sexual innuendos. Focusing on the term "Narcissus," the court referred to expert testimony that "the word 'Narcissus' has a special meaning to a psychologist in the field of abnormal psychology," referring to "abnormal self-love," and that it was a term that "would only be used to refer to psychopathic or abnormal behavior." The court concluded that the publication was "libelous on its face," saying "[t]o ascribe to any individual the sexual deviation described in psychology textbooks as constituting narcissism ... is to expose that person to hatred, contempt, ridicule, obloquy, and to cause him to be shunned or avoided."[24]

The fact that the court referred to extrinsic material that was explanatory of the target word "Narcissus" demonstrates that the libel per se category is somewhat flexible. Yet, it probably would be desirable, as a general matter, if courts could concentrate on the overall tenor of a publication, and the general question of whether it injures reputation,[25] rather than having to deal with the strictures of the libel per se category. In any event, what courts eventually must do is to determine the bedrock question of harm to reputation.

Another case, focusing directly on alleged harm to the plaintiff's business, exhibits an overlap between libel per se and the slander per se categories. In this case, a television commentator, referring to cigarette advertising, said,

> That's the strategy of the cigarette slicksters, the cigarette business which is insisting in public, "we are not selling cigarettes to children."

---

24. Menefee v. Codman, 317 P.2d 1032, 1036 (Cal.Ct.App.1957).

25. See the definition offered in the Restatement (Second), text accompanying note 2 supra.

They're not slicksters, they're liars.

Providing context was the commentator's prior statement:

> Go for the youth of America, go get 'em guys.... Hook 'em
> while they are young, make 'em start now—just think how
> many cigarettes they'll be smoking when they grow up.

The court found this language to fit the slander per se-type
category of material injurious to a business. Although noting the
"anachronistic" and in some cases even "quaint" flavor of the
slander per se categories, the court said it "doubt[ed] that a
cigarette company could survive in the short run and thus be
around to enjoy the long run if it flouted the strong public policy
against encouraging children to smoke." Moreover, the court concluded that the broadcast was "libelous per se" under state law,
because "[a]ccusing a cigarette company of what many people
consider the immoral strategy of enticing children to smoke ... is
likely to harm the company." The court noted that "[t]hese harms
cannot easily be measured," but said that "so long as some harm is
highly likely the difficulty of measurement is an additional reason,
under the modern functional approach ... for finding libel per se
rather than insisting on proof of special damage."[26] Some of this
application of defamation law to cigarette marketing, in particular,
may strike the present reader as rather archaic, but its legal
premises are formally logical.

¶ 66.07   Privilege

Publishers of alleged defamatory material may invoke several
privileges, which we briefly summarize under the headings of
absolute and qualified privilege.

A. *Absolute privileges*

There are a few classes of persons who may defame others with
impunity—that is, under the cloak of absolute privilege. These
include persons speaking in judicial proceedings—not only judges
and lawyers, but witnesses and jurors. Legislators uttering defamatory material in the course of legislative proceedings may also claim
an absolute privilege. The federal model for this extraordinary
protection is the provision in the Constitution that legislators may
not be questioned "in any other Place" for what they say in
Congress.[27] Some ranks of executive branch officials also have
absolute privileges to publish defamatory material, at least when it

---

26. Brown and Williamson Tobacco
Corp. v. Jacobson, 713 F.2d 262, 267–69
(7th Cir.1983).

27. U.S. Const. art. 1, sec. 6.

concerns matters within the "outer perimeter" of their "line of duty."[28]

B. Qualified privileges

Quite a number of people may claim qualified privileges, which may be characterized in ordinary terms as allowing defendants to escape liability for defamation if they act reasonably and decently. An important example of a qualified privilege is the situation, common in the business world, in which either or both the publisher and the recipient of a defamatory communication has an important interest that would justify protection if the defendant has at least spoken or written in good faith. Common examples are a statement derogating someone's competence to a prospective employer[29] or communications among themselves by members of nonprofit associations concerning the "alleged misconduct of some other member."[30] Despite the existence of these privileges, there appears to be an increase in lawsuits over matter arguably covered by qualified privilege, particularly in the employment context.

The Supreme Court has developed a specialized set of constitutional qualified privileges, which protect publishers and broadcasters concerning defamatory statements about public officials and "public figures" so long as those statements are not made knowingly or recklessly of their falsity. These privileges are discussed separately below.[31] Litigation over qualified privileges, both those rooted in general defamation law and constitutional privileges, reflects the increased tension over the conflicting goals of defamation law, to which we now turn.

¶ 66.08 Goals in Conflict

Defamation law has become a battleground involving some of our most cherished ideas. On one side stands the avowed belief in the sanctity of reputation and the related interest in personal dignity that defamation suits help to vindicate. Those claiming defamation also invoke the idea that words can cut just as much as knives, even if the wounds are metaphorical.

---

28. This language appears in the leading case on the absolute immunity of federal officials, Barr v. Matteo, 360 U.S. 564, 575 (1959), which has been qualified as applying only to "discretionary" functions, see Westfall v. Erwin, 484 U.S. 292, 297–98 & n. 4 (1988). Congress subsequently reinstated the immunity of federal employees for "negligent or wrongful act[s] or omission[s] ... within the scope of his office or employment," at the same time providing an action against the Government under the Federal Tort Claims Act for such torts. 26 U.S.C.A. § 2679(d)(1).

29. See, e.g., Weir v. Equifax Servs., 620 N.Y.S.2d 675 (App.Div.1994) (qualified privilege for former employer of plaintiff, as well as credit investigating firm, concerning information reported to prospective employer).

30. Restatement (Second) § 596, comment e.

31. See infra, ¶ 67.01.

On the other side is the great social interest in freedom of the press, especially with respect to statements that may bear on the conduct of public affairs. A significant part of the argument over the constitutionalizing of defamation has concerned the kinds of material that may fairly be said to affect discussion of public matters, and indeed the definition of what a public matter is. The prospect that defamation suits will "chill" such discussion has been a motivating factor in judicial inclination to sacrifice some interest in reputation in exchange for an added measure of protection for speech, as part of a process of public discourse that may advance the overall interest of society.

The conflicting concerns we have described bear on all of the categories of legal issues that arise from allegations that publications have injured reputation: the definition of defamation itself, the distinction between fact and opinion, the level of culpability that plaintiffs must prove, and the breadth of the privileges to defame. The chapters that follow, dealing with several of these categories, exhibit these policy tensions.[32]

32. See infra, Chapter 67 (generally describing the constitutionalization of defamation law); Chapter 68 (fact/opinion distinction in defamation). See also ¶¶ 69.01–03, 69.06 (discussion of the same policy conflicts with respect to "privacy" torts).

Chapter Sixty–Seven

CONSTITUTIONAL DEFAMATION LAW

Analysis

The Supreme Court has constitutionalized the law of defamation under the First Amendment, initially embedding in it a group of privileges to defame persons who are in the public eye and then refashioning the boundaries of culpability standards concerning allowable damages for private individuals. We begin with some history, and then describe the classifications that the Court's developing jurisprudence has imposed on the law.

¶ 67.01 Constitutional Development

Before 1964, many jurisdictions imposed liability for defamation without fault. Thus, anyone who published material that injured another's reputation, even without actual or constructive knowledge of its falsity, could be held for libel, at least if the defamatory meaning of the communication were "actionable per se.''[1] Plaintiffs also could receive punitive damages on a showing of "common law malice"—"ill will or fraud or reckless indifference to consequences."[2] The privileges to defame consisted essentially of the absolute privileges for legislators, participants in judicial proceedings and some governmental executives, and the common law qualified privileges that resided in such factors as the publisher's interest or the recipient's interest in the defamatory material, or the interests of both in the matter to which the defamatory communication pertains.[3]

A.   The New York Times case

The landmark case of *New York Times v. Sullivan*[4] initially used the First Amendment to establish a federal constitutional privilege in defamation law. In that 1964 decision, the Supreme Court said that one who defamed a public official in the performance of his or her official duties would be liable only if the publication was made with "actual malice," which the Court defined to mean either knowledge of the falsity of the publication or "reckless disregard of whether it was false or not."[5] The Court justified the *New York Times* rule, as a matter of constitutional protection of free expression, on the basis that it would promote "uninhibited" and "robust" discussion of public matters.[6]

B.   Butts and Walker

Three years later, the Court extended the *New York Times* privilege to those who defame "public figures,"[7] rather than only public officials. The plaintiffs in the two companion cases that yielded that rule were Wally Butts, a well-known football coach at the University of Georgia who sued on a publication reporting that he had conspired to fix a football game, and Edwin Walker, a former major general who alleged that he had been falsely accused of participation in a campus riot over a racial integration issue. Chief Justice Warren wrote a concurring opinion that effectively captured a majority of the Court. In it, he "adhere[d] to the *New York Times* standard in the case of 'public figures' as well as 'public officials,' "[8] thus applying the requirement of *New York Times* that plaintiffs prove "actual malice" to Butts and Walker, who were classified as public figures. Four other members of the Court

---

1. See, e.g., Gertz v. Robert Welch, Inc., 418 U.S. 323, 371–76 (White, J., dissenting). For a discussion of libel per se and slander per se, see ¶ 66.06 supra.

2. See 418 U.S. at 395–96.

3. See ¶ 66.07 supra.

4. 376 U.S. 254 (1964).

5. Id. at 279–80.

6. Id. at 270.

7. Curtis Publ'g Co. v. Butts and Associated Press v. Walker, 388 U.S. 130 (1967).

8. Id. at 164 (Warren, C.J., concurring).

supported that standard in two separate opinions.[9] An opinion by Justice Harlan, joined by three other justices, advocated a less demanding standard that required plaintiffs to prove "highly unreasonable conduct constituting an extreme departure from the standards of investigation and reporting ordinarily adhered to by responsible publishers."[10]

C. Gertz: Private individuals

The Court considerably elaborated its constitutional analysis of defamation law in *Gertz v. Robert Welch, Inc.*[11] Justice Powell's opinion for the majority in that case defined the boundaries of liability, at least for defendants that are "publisher[s] or broadcaster[s]," for defamations of "private individuals"—those who are "neither a public official nor a public figure." Continuing its expression of a concern originally highlighted in the *New York Times* case, the Court stressed that "punishment of error runs the risk of inducing a cautious and restrictive exercise of the constitutionally guaranteed freedoms of speech and press."[12] In its quest to strike a balance between preventing the chilling of media and compensating for the real harms caused by defamation to private individuals, the Court proceeded on several fronts:

1) *Fault requirement.* It required that private individuals claiming defamation must prove at least some fault—negligence, if not reckless or intentional conduct.[13]

2) *Damages for "actual injury."* The Court allowed recovery "for actual injury" on a showing of at least negligence, but declared that states could not constitutionally allow recovery of "presumed" damages unless the plaintiff could prove that the defendant had "knowledge of falsity or reckless disregard for the truth"[14]—the test known as *"New York Times* malice." Justifying this limitation, the majority referred to "the largely uncontrolled discretion of juries to award damages where there is no loss," which it said "unnecessarily compound[ed]" the chilling effect of defamation law on "the vigorous exercise of First Amendment freedoms."[15] However, the Court did offer a relatively expansive definition of "actual harm" to include such injuries as "impairment of reputation and standing in the community, personal humiliation, and mental anguish and suffering."[16]

---

9. See id. at 170 (Black, J., joined by Douglas, J., concurring in the result in one case and dissenting in the other); 172 (Brennan, J., joined by White, J., concurring in the result in one case and dissenting in the other).

10. Id. at 155 (Harlan, J., announcing the judgments of the Court).

11. 418 U.S. 323 (1974).

12. *Id.* at 340.

13. *See id.* at 347.

14. *Id.* at 349.

15. Id.

16. Id. at 350.

3) *Punitive damages.* The Court also required plaintiffs seeking punitive damages to show malice under the *New York Times* standard.[17]

D. Gertz: Limited purpose public figures

In a tantalizingly brief passage, the *Gertz* decision identified a special category of qualified immunity, which protects a publisher who defames what has become known as a "limited purpose public figure," a category that has spawned considerable case law.[18] The Court noted that a person "may achieve such pervasive fame or notoriety that he becomes a public figure for all purposes and in all contexts." However, it also fashioned a category for the plaintiff who "voluntarily injects himself or is drawn into a particular controversy and thereby becomes a public figure for a limited range of issues."[19]

The plaintiff in *Gertz* was a lawyer who represented the family of a youth killed by a Chicago policeman in a civil suit for the youth's death. Although the case was a newsworthy one, the Court concluded that even under its expanded category of public figures, it was "plain that [the plaintiff] was not a public figure." It noted that *Gertz* had not "thrust himself into the vortex of this public issue, nor did he engage the public's attention in an attempt to influence its outcome."[20]

E. The Greenmoss case

Subsequently, focusing on the subject of the communication rather than on the type of plaintiff, the Court appeared to limit its *Gertz* holding in *Dun & Bradstreet, Inc. v. Greenmoss Builders, Inc.*[21] That case involved a credit report that seriously misrepresented the assets and liabilities of the plaintiff, but was communicated only to five confidential subscribers of the defendant. In *Greenmoss*, taking note that "*Gertz* involved expression on a matter of undoubted public concern,"[22] the Court said that "when . . . defamatory statements do not involve matters of public concern," it would allow "recovery of presumed and punitive damages . . . absent a showing of 'actual malice.' "[23]

F. The complete immunity position

Justices Black and Douglas adopted a polar position during the Court's fashioning of constitutional libel law. They contended, in the strongest version of this argument, that because of the potentially destructive effects of libel law on the media, members of the

17. *Id.*
18. See infra, ¶ 67.02(A).
19. Id. at 351.
20. *Id.* at 352.

21. 472 U.S. 749 (1985).
22. Id. at 756.
23. Id. at 763.

press and broadcasters should have complete immunity from defamation suits.[24] The Court has not adopted this view.

¶ 67.02   Applying the Constitutional Rules

The case law that has grown from the seeds of *New York Times* and *Gertz* presents several principal compartments of analysis. The initial question concerns the status of the plaintiff as a public or private person. If the plaintiff is a public official, or a public figure at least for purposes of the defamatory material, then the defendant publisher may take advantage of the *New York Times* test. If the plaintiff is a private individual, then he must bring his case within the culpability test as well as the damage rules of *Gertz*.

A.   *The type of plaintiff: Defining the limited purpose public figure*

Courts dealing with defamation cases under constitutional standards must decide the category into which the plaintiffs fit, for the type of plaintiff determines the standard of conduct to which the defendant will be held. Often there will be a battle about whether the plaintiff is a "public figure"—including a "limited purpose public figure"—or a "private individual." We have noted that the court in *Gertz* held that its plaintiff, although a lawyer engaged in a case that was in the public eye, was not a "public figure."[25]

In another colorful case in which the Court rejected the public figure designation, *Time, Inc. v. Firestone*,[26] the plaintiff claiming defamation was a woman who had been involved in a divorce from an heir to the Firestone fortune. Although the trial was well publicized, the court noted that the plaintiff had not "freely [chosen] to publicize issues as to the propriety of her married life," but rather was "compelled to go to court by the State in order to obtain legal release from the bonds of matrimony."[27] The Court added that it did not think that the fact that the plaintiff had "held a few press conferences during the divorce proceedings in an attempt to satisfy inquiring reporters" had "convert[ed] her into a 'public figure.' "[28]

In still another case featuring a plaintiff involved in the legal process, the alleged defamation appeared in a book on Soviet

---

24. *See, e.g.,* Curtis Publ. Co. v. Butts, 388 U.S. 130, 170–72 (1967) (Black, J., concurring and dissenting).

25. See supra, ¶ 67.01(D).

26. 424 U.S. 448 (1976).

27. Id. at 454.

28. Id. at 454–55 n.3. See also, *e.g.,* Bell v. National Republican Congressional Comm., 187 F.Supp.2d 605, 611, 613 (S.D.W.Va.2002)(plaintiff made one-line statement in television advertisement for Congressional candidate who was a former neighbor, and posed with candidate for campaign photo that appeared in four campaign pamphlets and on candidate's web site; such "peripheral[] involve[ment]" and "minimal engagement in a political campaign" does not make plaintiff a limited-purpose public figure; to hold otherwise "would serve to chill citizen participation in the

espionage written and published by the defendants. The Court held that the claimant was not a limited purpose public figure because he had received a "mere citation for contempt," which arose from his failure to respond to a grand jury subpoena related to an espionage investigation.[29]

Federal appellate courts have sought further to shape the category of the "limited purpose public figure." The D.C. Circuit identified a three-step process of analysis. First, the court "must isolate the public controversy," assuring itself that the issue involved in the defamatory material "is not simply a matter of interest to the public," but is "a real dispute, the outcome of which affects the general public or some segment of it in an appreciable way."[30] Second, the plaintiff "either must have been purposely trying to influence the outcome" of the public controversy "or could realistically have been expected, because of his position in the controversy, to have an impact on its resolution."[31] Finally, the defendant must show that the defamatory material was "germane to the plaintiff's participation in the controversy," a standard under which the plaintiff's "talents, education, experience, and motives could have been relevant to the public's decision whether to listen to him."[32]

In a decision elaborating that standard, the same court found that the president of Mobil Corporation was a limited purpose public figure with respect to the allegedly defamatory statement that he had used the influence of his position to "set up" his son as a partner in a company that had a lucrative contract with Mobil.[33] The court noted that there had been significant public controversy about whether the "management and structure" of the American oil industry required reform. In that context, the court found influential the plaintiff's "substantial role[]," along with his company, "in spearheading a public counterattack on the movement for reform of the oil industry."[34] Finally, the court concluded that the publication was germane to the "credibility and integrity of representatives of the oil industry."[35]

B. Standards governing actions by private individuals

1. Culpability requirements

A defamation plaintiff classified as a private individual is not subject to as demanding a basic culpability standard as is a claim-

---

political process and further the lamentable trend toward public passivity").

29. Wolston v. Reader's Digest Ass'n, 443 U.S. 157, 167 (1979).

30. Waldbaum v. Fairchild Publications, Inc., 627 F.2d 1287, 1296 (D.C.Cir. 1980).

31. Id. at 1297.

32. Id. at 1298.

33. Tavoulareas v. Piro, 817 F.2d 762 (D.C.Cir.1987).

34. Id. at 773.

35. Id. at 774.

ant who is a public official or a public figure. Under *Gertz*, a private individual may recover damages for "actual injury" on a showing of negligence. But the sum of *Gertz* and later cases is that in order to recover "presumed" damages—and also punitive damages—a private individual must meet the *New York Times* malice test. One illustration of how a plaintiff may do this appears in the remand from the Supreme Court's decision in *Gertz*, in which the court of appeals found that the plaintiff had shown "actual malice." Inter alia, the appellate court pointed out that the defendant publication had "shortcut" "[t]he usual editing time of several weeks or more," and that indeed its managing editor had "submitted the article for typesetting only three to four hours after it was received." The court's summary of the case included the observation that the defendant had "made virtually no effort to check the validity of statements that were defamatory per se of Gertz."[36]

2. *The type of defamation*

The Supreme Court's constitutionalized rules appear to have affected the definition of actionable defamation, tending to reduce whatever advantages private individuals may receive from "libel per se" doctrines. Under the constitutional rules, even a showing that material is defamatory without reference to extrinsic circumstances apparently will not entitle private individuals to "presumed" damages—those not based on "actual injury"—without a showing of *New York Times* malice. Moreover, a state presumably might still enforce the limitations of the libel per se rule against private individuals, requiring them to plead and prove "special damages" if they did not fit themselves into the jurisdiction's libel per se requirement.

3. *Kinds of damages*

A closely related set of issues concerns the kinds of damages for which plaintiffs may recover. Crucial here is the definition of "actual injury," for which the *Gertz* court said it would allow recovery if the plaintiff proved negligence, since private individuals cannot recover for "presumed" damages unless they show *New York Times* malice. As the Supreme Court in *Firestone*[37] amplified its requirement of "actual injury," the concept is relatively broad. In *Firestone*, the Court effectively approved a finding that that test was met by the plaintiff's "anxiety and concern" over inaccurate reports "that she had been found guilty of adultery" and "her fears," revealed in her testimony, "that her young son would be adversely affected by this falsehood when he grew older."[38] The

---

36. Gertz v. Robert Welch, Inc., 680 F.2d 527, 538–39 (7th Cir.1982).

37. See text accompanying notes 26–28 supra.

38. See Time, Inc. v. Firestone, 424 U.S. at 460–61.

practical effect of this holding is to define a relatively broad field of damages that plaintiffs may recover if they show a degree of fault that is negligence, though not "actual malice."

Although this interpretation is rather favorable to plaintiffs, some have contended that the Court's requirement that plaintiffs show negligence to recover for "actual injury" is too favorable to defendants. Viewing that requirement as unduly restrictive in his dissenting opinion in *Gertz*, Justice White criticized both the culpability requirement of the decision and its damages rules. He contended that it was appropriate to impose strict liability in favor of private individuals who sue for defamation, noting that especially in cases of material defamatory on its face, "the publisher is no doubt aware from the nature of the material that it would be inherently damaging to reputation." Justice White argued that when someone knows this and "publishes notwithstanding, knowing that he will inflict injury," it is torturing words to claim that the defendant is "faultless." Even if the publisher's mistake is "in good faith," Justice White stressed, "it is he who launched the publication knowing that it could ruin a reputation."[39]

¶ 67.03 Specialized Constitutional Libel Rules

We briefly summarize here a few other notable holdings by the Supreme Court in its development of constitutional defamation law.

A. Burden of proof: Philadelphia Newspapers v. Hepps

In *Philadelphia Newspapers, Inc. v. Hepps*,[40] the Court effectively placed the burden of proof on "private-figure plaintiff[s]" in cases involving matters of "public concern," saying that such claimants "cannot recover damages without also showing that the statements at issue are false."[41] The *Hepps* decision found unconstitutional a state statute which adopted the common law rule that put the burden on the defendant to prove the truth of defamatory statements.

B. "Clear and convincing" standard for actual malice: Anderson

In *Anderson v. Liberty Lobby, Inc.*,[42] the Court held that a standard of "clear and convincing" evidence applied to the question of whether there was "a genuine issue of actual malice." The Court required that the evidence be "such that a reasonable jury might find that actual malice had been shown with convincing clarity," although it emphasized that in order to survive a summary judg-

---

39. Gertz, 418 U.S. at 389–90 (White, J., dissenting).

40. 475 U.S. 767 (1986).

41. Id. at 769.

42. 477 U.S. 242 (1986).

ment motion, the plaintiff "need only present evidence from which a jury might return a verdict in his favor."[43]

C. Attributed quotations: Masson

In *Masson v. New Yorker Magazine, Inc.,*[44] the Court indicated that altered quotations could provide grounds for a finding of defamation, although they would not necessarily have that result. In that case, celebrated in the literary community, the plaintiff, a well known psychoanalyst, sued the writer Janet Malcolm and the *New Yorker* magazine. At issue was an article Malcolm contributed to the publication that was based, in part, on a series of interviews with the plaintiff. The plaintiff alleged, among other things, that the article "used quotation marks to attribute to [the plaintiff] comments he had not made."

The Court posited that "a deliberate alteration of the words uttered by a plaintiff does not equate with knowledge of falsity" under the *New York Times* and *Gertz* rules "unless the alteration results in a material change in the meaning conveyed by the statement." However, declaring that "[m]eaning is the life of language," the Court observed that "quotations may be a devastating instrument for conveying false meaning." In reversing a defendants' summary judgment, the Court noted that Malcolm's portrait of the plaintiff might have been found "especially damning" by readers "because so much of it appeared to be a self-portrait, told by [the plaintiff] in his own words." The Court said that "if the alterations of [the plaintiff's] words gave a different meaning to the statements, bearing upon their defamatory character, then the device of quotations might well be critical in finding the words actionable."[45]

¶ 67.04 Rationales and Public Policies

The policy tensions that surround the law of defamation generally are at an especially high point in the arguments over the application of First Amendment principles to the tort. On one side is concern over the "chilling" effect of a defamation law that is relatively liberal to plaintiffs; on the other are complaints about the tendency of restrictive liability rules not only to permit irresponsible media persons to tarnish reputations, but to reduce the inclination of able but sensitive people to engage in public life.

Several important underlying questions relate to behavioral effects of law, and the incentives it creates, which are not easy to pin down. The evidence on "chilling effects" in both directions tends to be anecdotal and subject to argument. On the one hand,

43. Id. at 257.   **45.** Id. at 517–18.
44. 501 U.S. 496 (1991).

for example, is the general expression of concern that "punishment of error runs the risk of inducing a cautious and restrictive exercise" of press freedom.[46] On the other hand, it has been called "incredible" that the press would be made less robust by a return to defamation standards that prevailed before the *Gertz* decision.[47] Moreover, it seems difficult to square rules that are relatively liberal to defamers with the power of an increasingly concentrated press.[48] Some important empirical issues include whether there is a factual basis for the maxim that "the truth never catches up with the libel," and the related question of whether it is possible in practice to make an effective reply to a libel, which is an assumption underlying the relatively stringent liability standards concerning defamation of public figures.[49]

Certainly, the rules of libel law reflect the pushes and pulls of conflicting opinions about the balance to be struck between the reputation of individuals and freedom for the media in a democratic society. Although the nursery rhyme has it that "sticks and stones may break my bones but names will never hurt me," everyone is aware that some "names" can sting and even lacerate, and may be financially costly to boot. Bumping against that understanding, derived from common experience, is an almost religiously held conviction about the dependence of the democratic process on a broad range of speech and publication. That belief assumes that for a democracy to work, it not only must tolerate damaging opinions and insults but must provide a certain amount of elbow room to make statements that may turn out to be false in fact. It is an index to the degree of emotion that surrounds libel litigation that an experimental project that sought to attract the parties in 128 libel cases into a program of alternative dispute resolution was able to bring only five of those cases into the program.[50]

46. Gertz, 418 U.S. at 340 (majority opinion).

47. See id. at 390 (White, J., dissenting).

48. See id. at 390–91.

49. See, e.g., Butts, supra note 7, 388 U.S. at 155 (premise of "sufficient access" by public figure plaintiffs "to the means of counterargument to be able 'to expose through discussion the falsehood and fallacies' of . . . defamatory statements").

50. Little Interest in Libel ADR, 78 A.B.A.J. 22 (Jan. 1992).

Chapter Sixty–Eight

FACT AND OPINION

Analysis

¶ 68.01 Defining the Problem

Some of the most slippery issues in libel law involve the question of whether an allegedly defamatory communication was one of fact or opinion. Statements of opinion are not subject to suits for defamation. Given the requirement that a defamatory statement be one that is false, a principal reason for immunizing statements of opinion is that one cannot prove that an opinion is true or false. Especially given the constitutionalization of libel law,[1] the topic is important both philosophically and practically, implicating prized values on both sides. The value of reputation is clear; equally obvious is the importance of free discussion on public issues. The "fact/opinion" controversy replicates concerns of both publishers and plaintiffs that we have discussed under more general headings of defamation law.

In the landmark *Gertz* case, discussed above,[2] Justice Powell's opinion for the Court presented a majestic ideal, saying that "under the First Amendment there is no such thing as a false idea." He elaborated that even "pernicious" opinions depend "for . . . correction not on the conscience of judges and juries but on the competition of other ideas." By contrast, Justice Powell declared, there is "no constitutional value in false statements of fact," for "[n]either the intentional lie nor the careless error materially advances society's interest in 'uninhibited, robust, and wide-open debate on public issues.' "[3]

1. See generally Chapter 67.

2. See ¶ 67.01(C) supra.

3. Gertz v. Robert Welch Inc., 418 U.S. 323, 339–40 (1974) (quoting N.Y. Times Co. v. Sullivan, 376 U.S. 254, 270 (1964), on "robust . . . debate")).

¶ 68.02   Summarizing the Law: Leading Cases

The case law reveals the difficulty of crafting blackletter principles on whether a publication is fact or opinion. The problem of fashioning standards is inherent in the prismatic quality of language itself, as well as the diversity of contexts in which language appears. A crucial, if abstract, set of concepts lies in the notions of core meaning and verifiability[4]: if a statement has a relatively definable common meaning and is capable of some kind of empirical verification, it will be deemed fact. By contrast, if what it communicates in context is that it is an expression of the personal views of the writer, and it does not imply an underlying set of verifiable data, then courts will hold that it is opinion.

The phrase "rhetorical hyperbole" has found its way into the decisions as a linguistic cousin to the defense that a statement is "opinion" rather than "fact." A vividly illustrative use of the phrase arose from a "well-known piece of trade union literature," a definition of the term "scab" as used in the context of labor-management controversies. A union local published this definition, attributed to Jack London, in a newsletter:

> The scab sells his birthright, country, his wife, his children and his fellowmen for an unfilled promise from his employer.

> Esau was a traitor to himself; Judas was a traitor to his God; Benedict Arnold was a traitor to his country; a SCAB is a traitor to his God, his country, his family and his class.

The Supreme Court found it " . . . impossible to believe that any reader" of the newsletter would have understood it to "charg[e] the [defendants] with committing the criminal offense of treason." Invoking precedent on the proposition that "such exaggerated rhetoric was commonplace in labor disputes," the Court said that "Jack London's 'definition of a scab' is merely rhetorical hyperbole, a lusty and imaginative expression of the contempt felt by union members to those who refuse to join."[5]

---

4. See, e.g., Ollman v. Evans, 750 F.2d 970 (D.C.Cir.1984), cert. denied, 471 U.S. 1127 (1985), discussed infra, text accompanying notes 13–19, 26–28.

5. Old Dominion Branch No. 496, Nat'l Ass'n of Letter Carriers v. Austin, 418 U.S. 264, 284–86 (1974). George Harrison, the former Beatle, successfully used this defense in a case that arose from his remarks to a reporter about a controversy concerning an easement over Harrison's property on the island of Maui. Harrison was quoted as saying, "Have you ever been raped? I'm being raped by all these people . . . . My privacy is being violated." In rejecting a defamation claim against Harrison, the reporter and the publisher, the Hawai'i Supreme Court said "[e]ven the most casual reader would understand that 'these people'—whether neighbors of Harrison or persistent journalists—were not actually raping Harrison." It concluded that the statement was "rhetorical hyperbole and protected by the first amendment." In the course of the opinion, the court made a distinction between rhetorical hyperbole and opinion. It said that "[a]lthough Harrison's [s]tatement reflected his opinion, it could not be construed as a statement that Harrison believed the

Decisions involving two very different arenas of educational life—high school athletics and political science scholarship—present instructive examples of judicial thinking on the fact/opinion distinction. In one case,[6] the Supreme Court discerned facts, rather than opinions, in a newspaper columnist's language that allegedly libeled a high school wrestling coach. The subject matter of the column was testimony by the plaintiff coach and a school superintendent at a judicial hearing, which focused on responsibility for an altercation at a wrestling meet in which several people were injured. Headlines over the column, referring to the testimony, used the phrase "the 'big lie' " and the word "lie." Among other statements sued upon was the columnist's assertion that a lesson that would be learned by high school students and others who attended the meet was, "If you get in a jam, lie your way out." The columnist also wrote that anyone who was at the wrestling meet "knows in his heart that [the plaintiff coach and the superintendent] lied at the hearing after each having given his solemn oath to tell the truth."

Chief Justice Rehnquist, in his opinion for the majority, used illustrative hypotheticals to support the conclusion that a jury could have found the defendant's publication to be a defamatory assertion about a "fact" rather than "opinion." He emphasized that "[e]ven if [a] speaker states the facts upon which he bases his opinion, if those facts are either incorrect or incomplete, or if his assessment of them is erroneous, the statement may still imply a false assertion of fact." He stressed that "[s]imply couching such statements in terms of opinion does not dispel these implications," and observed that "the statement, 'In my opinion Jones is a liar,' can cause as much damage to reputation as the statement, 'Jones is a liar.' "[7] Referring to the "proposition that a statement on matters of public concern must be provable as false"[8] to justify "liability under state defamation law," the Chief Justice contrasted two other hypothetical statements. He viewed one—"[i]n my opinion Mayor Jones is a liar"—as potential grounds for liability. By contrast, he said that it "would not be actionable" to say, "In my opinion Mayor Jones shows his abysmal ignorance by accepting the teachings of Marx and Lenin."[9]

The Chief Justice declared that, given the culpability requirements of the Court's decisions in cases like *New York Times*, *Butts*, and *Gertz*,[10] he did not think that "an additional separate constitu-

---

Plaintiffs were, in fact, rapists, but was clearly rhetorical hyperbole expressing Harrison's feelings about the [e]asement [a]ction." Gold v. Harrison, 88 Haw. 94, 962 P.2d 353, 361–62 (1998).

6. Milkovich v. Lorain Journal Co., 497 U.S. 1 (1990).

7. Id. at 18–19.

8. Id. at 19, referring to Philadelphia Newspapers v. Hepps, 475 U.S. 767 (1986).

9. Id. at 20.

10. See supra ¶ 67.01(A)-(D).

tional privilege for 'opinion' " was "required to ensure the freedom of expression guaranteed by the First Amendment." Specifically referring to the defendant columnist's language, he said it was "not the sort of loose, figurative or hyperbolic language which would negate the impression that the writer was seriously maintaining that [the plaintiff] committed the crime of perjury."[11] The Chief Justice's general emphasis, rather than being on "breathing space" for publishers, was on society's "pervasive and strong interest in preventing and redressing attacks upon reputation."[12]

A fierce and revealing clash appeared in the D.C. Circuit's intramural argument on *Ollman v. Evans*.[13] That case presented a dramatic confrontation on the constitutionality of imposing defamation liability on writers of an op-ed column, which criticized a University of Maryland political science professor who had been nominated to head his department. Among the statements at issue were the authors' claim that the plaintiff was "widely viewed in his profession as a political activist" and their quotation of an assertion by an unnamed political scientist that the plaintiff had "no status within the profession, but is a pure and simple activist."

Concluding that the statements in the column were opinion, the court of appeals affirmed a summary judgment for the defendants. Writing for a plurality of the court, Judge Starr set out four criteria for drawing the line between fact and opinion:

> 1.   The "common usage or meaning" of the defendant's language, because "[r]eaders are ... considerably less likely to infer facts from an indefinite or ambiguous statement than one with a commonly understood meaning."

> 2.   The "verifiability" of the statement—whether it was "capable of being objectively characterized as true or false?"

> 3.   "The full context of the statement," for example, the "entire article or column" in which it appeared.

> 4.   "[T]he broader context or setting in which the statement appears."[14]

The *Ollman* opinions featured considerable disagreement about the application of these criteria. For example, the plurality opinion said that the statement that the plaintiff had "no status" in his profession was, in the words of a precedent, "rhetorical hyperbole" and thus opinion. The plurality also focused on the fact that the language at issue appeared in an op-ed column, as to which "the average reader [would] be influenced by the general understanding

---

11.   497 U.S. at 21.

12.   Id. at 22, quoting Rosenblatt v. Baer, 383 U.S. 75, 86 (1966).

13.   750 F.2d 970 (D.C.Cir.1984), cert. denied, 471 U.S. 1127 (1985).

14.   Id. at 979.

of the functions of such columns and read the remark to be opinion." The policy basis for the plurality's conclusion in favor of the defendants was that to impose liability on such language would reduce " 'breathing space,' " inhibiting "the scope of public discussion on matters of general interest and concern."[15]

Judge Bork's concurring opinion noted that in twice seeking election to the council of the American Political Science Association, the plaintiff said that he would "use every means at my disposal to promote the study of Marxism and Marxist approaches to politics throughout the profession." For Judge Bork, such statements indicated that the plaintiff had "placed himself in an arena where he should expect to be jostled and bumped in a way that a private person need not expect,"[16] and that the remarks in the column were "the kind of hyperbole that must be accepted in the rough and tumble of political argument."[17]

Judge Wald's separate opinion, partly dissenting, argued that "[t]he statement that Ollman has no status within his profession undoubtedly admits of a sufficiently ascertainable and stable core of meaning: a decisive plurality of his fellow political scientists do not regard him as a good scholar."[18] In another partial dissent, Judge Scalia made the parallel argument that the defendants did not say that the plaintiff was incompetent; rather, "[t]hey said that his *professional peers* regarded him as incompetent." There was "no way," said Judge Scalia, that "*that* conclusion can be understood to be a product of [the defendants'] econo-political opinions."[19]

---

15. Id. at 990–91.

16. Id. at 1002–03 (Bork, J., concurring).

17. Id. at 998. A Michigan court makes a very broad argument, embodying a similar point of view, in ruling against Jack Kevorkian in a case involving language that on its face imputes criminal conduct. Kevorkian, who the court described as "possibly the best known and most controversial proponent of assisted suicide," sued on statements by officials of the American Medical Association. The defendants had asserted that Kevorkian "serve[d] merely as a reckless instrument of death" and engaged in "criminal practices," attributed "continued killings" to him, and called him "a killer." The court opined that "with respect to the issue of assisted suicide, plaintiff is virtually 'libel proof.'" Beyond that, it said that even if the statements were defamatory, they were "either nonactionable rhetorical hyperbole or must be accorded the special solicitude re-

served for protected opinion." The court observed that the plaintiff's "very celebrity (or notoriety, if you will) derives exclusively from his participation in a national debate over the propriety of assisted suicide." It opined that since he had "exercised his leadership on behalf of one side of this debate," and had "contributed substantially to the awareness of the American people of this debate," it was "more than a little disingenuous" for him "to accuse those on the opposite side of this debate of defamation." The court suggested that to allow a tort action would "chill legitimate public debate." Kevorkian v. Am. Med. Ass'n, 602 N.W.2d 233, 239–40 (Mich.Ct.App.1999), appeal denied, 613 N.W.2d 720 (Mich.2000).

18. Id. at 1033 (Wald, J., dissenting in part).

19. Id. at 1037 (Scalia, J., dissenting in part).

¶ 68.03   Functional Analysis

A central consideration in the effort to develop a functional definition of the line between fact and opinion is the nature of the sting to reputation that grows out of the alleged libel. That is important because the defamatory character of a communication depends significantly on its tendency to injure the plaintiff's standing in the community. A salient factor in this regard will be the relative concreteness of the defendant's statements about the plaintiff. Judge Starr's plurality opinion for the *Ollman* court touched on this point when he asked "whether the statement has a precise core of meaning for which a consensus of understanding exists or, conversely, whether the statement is indefinite and ambiguous."[20] Exactness of meaning is thus an important marker for the issue of whether to characterize language as fact or opinion, just as it is likely to be a significant indicator of the degree of harm on which the damages issue focuses.

Another often crucial feature of fact/opinion issues has to do with whether the character of the allegedly defamatory statement is primarily that of argument. There clearly is a difference between asserting the fact, which may be verified or disproved from court records, that someone has been convicted of a crime and, for example, making a statement that an act "was a criminal thing for her to do." The former statement rests, without need for inference, on data. The latter represents an attempt to persuade the reader about the speaker's characterization of an event. Either the datum or the argument may leave an image with the reader about the plaintiff; but the second statement relies only on the power of characterization rather than on an assumed underlying fact. Faced with making choices within the fact/opinion dichotomy, courts are likely to view statements that are in essence argument as opinion.

¶ 68.04   Fair Comment

The privilege sometimes labeled "fair comment" runs closely parallel to the characterization of a statement as opinion rather than fact. Courts apply this category to publications like criticisms of artistic performance. Still a landmark is a 1901 decision, involving a stage act, which defined the privilege as allowing critics to hold performers "up to ridicule" when they "exhibit [themselves] to the public, or . . . give[] any kind of a performance to which the public is invited." The court set limitations on the defense of fair comment that included requirements of "truth, or . . . what in good faith and upon probable cause is believed to be true." Moreover, it

---

20.   Ollman, supra note 13, 750 F.2d at 979.

said, "the matter must be pertinent to the conduct that is made the subject of criticism."[21]

The case of restaurant reviews provides an example of where concepts of opinion, hyperbole, and fair comment may run closely together. In a review of a Chinese restaurant, the author wrote, inter alia, that it is "impossible to have the basic condiments ... on the table," that "[t]he sweet and sour pork contained more dough than meat," and the pancakes with the Peking Duck were "the thickness of a finger." The appellate court reversed a verdict that had found the review libelous and had awarded $20,000 compensatory damages and $5 million punitive damages. The court said that it was clear that the review would not have been actionable if it had said, "I found it difficult to get the basic seasonings on my table. The sweet and sour pork was too doughy for my tastes.... And the pancakes served with the Peking Duck were too thick."[22] The court concluded that "the writer's use of metaphors and hyperbole" did not make his "comments into factual statements,"[23] saying that "the average reader would understand the statements ... to be opinion."[24] The court also noted the similarity of the law on fair comment to the rules concerning hyperbole and opinion.[25]

¶ 68.05   The Policies at Issue

The policy debates over the fact/opinion distinction replay and elaborate those concerns at the heart of the arguments over defamation generally, as well as those central to the constitutionalization of defamation. Accompanying the "eleva[tion] to constitutional principle" of "the distinction between fact and opinion"[26] is judicial warfare over the societal values represented by the distinction. On the one hand, courts must take into account the potential "chilling" of public speech threatened by the ability of plaintiffs to sue on vague or hyperbolic language or criticism. On the other hand, they must consider the risk to reputation that lies in the ability of publishers to employ innuendo that implies reputation-damaging facts.

The underlying question remains how to operate a democracy, which premises great respect for the individual, while permitting a certain latitude to statements that may injure individual reputations in the name of the democratic process. Increases in the amount of libel judgments over the last generation, and corresponding rises in libel insurance premiums, have stimulated concern about the effects of relatively broad liability rules on the media.

21. Cherry v. Des Moines Leader, 86 N.W. 323, 325 (Iowa 1901).

22. Mr. Chow of New York v. Ste. Jour Azur S.A., 759 F.2d 219, 228 (2d Cir.1985).

23. Id.

24. Id. at 229.

25. Id. at 228 n.8.

26. Ollman, supra note 13, 750 F.2d at 975 (plurality opinion by Starr, J., characterizing Gertz).

However, the generally rich variety of media would indicate that publishers and broadcasters have not suffered significant disincentives to disseminating potentially sensitive material. With respect to the argument that libel law gives too much power to potential plaintiffs, the concentration of media in such markets as daily newspapers would seem to indicate that the question of who is in the superior power position is empirically an open one.

The fact/opinion distinction focuses the policy issue on the latitude that the definition of opinion gives to publishers. The problem exists, in significant measure, because a relatively broad definition of opinion—with the salutary freedom it provides for publishers—creates a correspondingly broad warrant for damaging insinuation. Judge Scalia captured a vexing aspect of the problem in his dissent in the *Ollman* case,[27] in which he described the defendants' op-ed essay as "a classic and cooly crafted libel." Accenting his dispute with the plurality's characterization of the column as "hyperbole" was his attack on what he called the view "that hyperbole excuses not merely the exaggeration but *the fact sought to be vividly conveyed by the exaggeration.*" To take this position, Judge Scalia said, was "to mistake a freedom to enliven discourse for a freedom to destroy reputation." His illustrative hypothetical was pungent: "[t]he libel that 'Smith is an incompetent carpenter' is not converted into harmless and nonactionable word-play by merely embellishing it into the statement that 'Smith is the worst carpenter this side of the Mississippi.' "[28]

The fact/opinion cases place in the spotlight an important theoretical problem associated with the law of defamation, namely, defining the social product of communication. Consider, for example, the obstacles that would confront an effort to do a thoroughgoing economic analysis of that question, which would require the analyst to value the social loss in the communications foregone because of a libel law that was relatively favorable to plaintiffs. A threshold problem is that it would be practically impossible to estimate how many, or what kind of, stories did not get written or broadcast because of the threat of liability. Beyond that, it is not likely that economists, or courts, would be able to place a dollar value on those opportunity costs; rather, the social benefit derived from communication relatively free from the threat of litigation tends to be an article of faith and not of numbers. This reality provides an interesting parallel between tort law and the constitutional law that has stamped itself on the tort called defamation: in both branches of jurisprudence, the ultimate decisions on many important issues rest on judgments that are relatively unquantifiable.

27. See supra, ¶ 68.02, text accompanying notes 13–19, for a summary of the facts and opinions in *Ollman*.

28. Id. at 1036 (Scalia, J., dissenting).

Chapter Sixty–Nine

MEDIA AND PRIVACY

Analysis

The branch of tort law labeled "privacy" includes several different, if sometimes overlapping, types of cases, some of which parallel traditional defamation jurisprudence. The privacy categories include publications of embarrassing facts that people generally would agree are private; fictionalized publications that use true events as points of departure; the publication of material, technically accurate, in a way that gives a false impression; the commercial appropriation of people's identities or images for which they have given no permission; and physical intrusions on personal affairs by such means as electronic eavesdropping.

A sharp contrast with defamation appears in "privacy" cases in which the defendant has published material about the plaintiff that is true; the contrast inheres in the fact that in order to succeed on a defamation count, a plaintiff must show that the defendant's publication was false. As will appear, however, there is some overlap between the concepts, as when technically truthful material conveys a false image. Noting these distinctions and crossovers, we analyze the categories that figure most prominently in "privacy" complaints, principally against publishers of material that in some way proves upsetting or demeaning to complainants or impinges on their economic interests.

¶ 69.01   Public Disclosure of Private Facts

A theoretically important category, although one that has not yielded high returns to plaintiffs, is the publication of truthful material that the plaintiff considers private, matter that usually places the plaintiff in an embarrassing light. Prosser, who set out most of the principal classifications of the "privacy" cluster of torts discussed here in a much-cited article, labeled this group of cases "public disclosure of private facts."[1]

The Restatement Second attempted to capture the elements of the action for "publicity given to private life" in this language:

One who gives publicity to a matter concerning the private life of another is subject to liability to the other for the invasion of his privacy, if the matter publicized is of a kind that

(a) would be highly offensive to a reasonable person, and

(b) is not of legitimate concern to the public.[2]

A classic pairing of cases on this subject came into the literature more than a half century ago. In *Melvin v. Reid*,[3] the plaintiff complained that a motion picture used her correct name in portraying "unsavory" events that had occurred several years before. At the time the film appeared, she was living a quiet and reformed life. The court imposed liability, invoking theories of "rehabilitation of the fallen" and saying that the dredging of events from the plaintiff's past life and the use of her true name "was not justified by any standard of morals or ethics known to us."[4]

In the somewhat contrasting case of *Sidis v. F–R Publishing Corp.*,[5] the plaintiff had been a child math prodigy who suffered several nervous breakdowns and retreated into a rather reclusive existence in which he generally shunned publicity. The New Yorker magazine published a mercilessly accurate portrait of him, based in part on an interview with him. The court denied recovery, saying that "truthful comments upon dress, speech, habits, and the ordinary aspects of personality will usually not transgress [the] line" of "the community's notions of decency."[6]

One might rationalize *Sidis* on the basis that the plaintiff had allowed himself to be interviewed. *Melvin* presents the starkest presentation of the issue of whether courts should ever impose liability for publication of the truth, including truth shoveled up from the distant past. A publisher-oriented characterization of the problem would ask whether it is possible to harmonize with the First Amendment a judgment that makes the publication of history a tort. This statement of the issue, defendants would say, virtually answers itself in favor of them. Yet, there is also case law imposing liability for truthful publications about recent events, when the

1. William L. Prosser, Privacy, 48 Calif. L. Rev. 383, 392–98 (1960).

2. Restatement (Second) of Torts § 652D (1977).

3. 297 P. 91 (Cal.Ct.App.1931).

4. Id. at 93 ("[e]ven the thief on the cross was permitted to repent during the hours of his final agony").

5. 113 F.2d 806 (2d Cir.), cert. denied 311 U.S. 711 (1940).

6. Id. at 809.

plaintiff had a reasonable expectation of confidentiality in matters that most persons would consider private. These few decisions suggest that at some point, the dignity and autonomy of individuals must be held to have primacy over the social benefits conferred by publication of truthful material.

In an especially appealing case in which the court supported a cause of action based on the public disclosure tort, although reversing a plaintiff's judgment on other grounds, the plaintiff was the student body president at a California community college who had undergone gender corrective surgery. After the plaintiff alleged that college administrators had misused student funds, a newspaper columnist published an item saying that students at the college would "be surprised to learn their student body president, Toni Diaz, is no lady, but is in fact a man whose real name is Antonio." Although the newspaper argued that the plaintiff's "original gender was a matter of public record," the court was unsympathetic to the publisher on this point. It noted, inter alia, that the plaintiff had taken "affirmative steps to conceal this fact by changing her driver's license, social security, and high school records and by lawfully changing her name."[7]

A particularized problem involves the privacy of rape victims. On two occasions, the Supreme Court has held that the First Amendment protects the publication of the names of rape victims, despite state statutes making it unlawful to publish the names of victims of sexual assault. In both of these cases, a factual basis for the Court's holding was that the identity of the plaintiff was in some way publicly available. In the later case,[8] a sheriff's department prepared a report that identified by name the plaintiff, a victim of robbery and sexual assault by an unknown assailant. The department placed the report in its press room, to which it did not restrict access. On these facts, although a statute forbade identification of the victim of a sexual offense in "any instrument of mass communication," the Court reversed a judgment for the plaintiff against a newspaper that published her name.

In his opinion for the Court, Justice Marshall observed that "where the government has made certain information publicly available, it is highly anomalous to sanction persons other than the source of its release."[9] The Court drew on an earlier decision in which it had invalidated a tort award against a television station. That defendant had broadcast the name of a victim of rape and murder whose father sued on the basis of a state law that made it a

---

7. Diaz v. Oakland Tribune, Inc., 188 Cal.Rptr. 762, 771 (Ct.App.1983).

8. Florida Star v. B.J.F., 491 U.S. 524 (1989).

9. Id. at 535.

misdemeanor to publish the name or identity of rape victims. In that case, the Court focused on the fact that the information had been available in official court records.[10]

¶ 69.02 Fictionalization

Another category of cases involves the publication of "fictionalized" matter about the plaintiff. In some of these cases, the plaintiff appears to complain not that the publication ridicules or even embarrasses him, but that its fictional nature puts alleged facts before the public that, even if they had been true, the plaintiff would consider confidential.

The leading case, *Time, Inc. v. Hill*,[11] dealt with a complex mixture of facts and law. The trial court had imposed damages on the publisher of *Life* magazine because of an article that implied that a Broadway play was a truthful reenactment of events during which the plaintiff's family had been taken hostage by escaped convicts. The play presented a situation in which hostage takers maltreated the family, whose members bravely resisted. In the real life episode, the plaintiff emphasized, the hostage takers treated the family quite courteously. The judgment for the plaintiff in the lower courts rested on sections 50 and 51 of the New York Civil Rights Law, which permit damages actions for persons whose "name, portrait or picture" is used "for the purposes of trade without . . . written consent."[12]

A Supreme Court majority overturned the plaintiff's judgment, which had been affirmed on the liability issue throughout the New York state court system. In an opinion by Justice Brennan, the author of the majority opinion in *New York Times v. Sullivan*,[13] the Court applied the *New York Times* "actual malice" test to require plaintiffs to show "knowledge of . . . falsity or . . . reckless disregard of the truth" in cases involving "false reports of matters of public interest."[14] The Court justified this holding on the basis that it protected the "breathing space"—a concept stressed in the *New York Times* case—that was necessary for a "free press in a free society."[15] Going beyond the focus of *New York Times* on the protection of discussion concerning "government and public officials,"[16] and speaking of freedom of the press as "assur[ing] the maintenance of our political system and an open society," the Court in *Hill* opined that "[t]he guarantees for speech and press are not

---

10. Cox Broadcasting Corp. v. Cohn, 420 U.S. 469, 494–97 (1975).

11. 385 U.S. 374 (1967).

12. New York Civil Rights Law §§ 50–51.

13. 376 U.S. 254 (1964), summarized supra, ¶ 67.01(A).

14. Hill, supra, 385 U.S. at 387–88.

15. Id. at 388–89.

16. See *New York Times*, 376 U.S. at 270.

the preserve of political expression or comment upon public affairs.''[17]

The Court pointed out that the press featured a "vast range of published matter which exposes persons to public view, both private citizens and public officials," and declared that "[e]xposure of the self to others in varying degrees is a concomitant of life in a civilized community."[18] The Court's holding on the technical profile of the case fixed on jury instructions on a punitive damages issue, which indicated that the jury could find for the plaintiff if the defendant had falsely connected him to the play "knowingly or through failure to make a reasonable investigation." In the view of the majority, this instruction erroneously would have allowed the jury to find for the plaintiff on proof of negligence, by contrast with the *New York Times* standard of knowledge of falsity or reckless disregard.[19]

Justice Fortas's dissent in *Hill* stressed, in part, that the jury instructions had made it clear that the law required the plaintiff to show that the defendant's article had fictionalized the family's role in the hostage episode in its relationship to the play. Words in the jury instructions like "altered or changed the true facts," "fictionalization," and "fiction" seemed to Justice Fortas to support a finding of "knowing or reckless falsity," because they connoted a departure "from fact and reality" that was "*deliberately* divorced from the fact—not merely in detail but in general and pervasive impact."[20]

¶ 69.03 The "False Light" Tort

Closely related to "fictionalization" is the so-called "false light" tort, which has features of both traditional defamation and privacy. A plaintiff establishes a case under this category by showing that the defendant's publication conveys something that is untruthful and thus damaging to reputation, even if it is not technically defamatory.[21] Some jurisdictions have rejected the false light doctrine, citing the substantial "overlapping" of the tort with defamation and expressing concern about the added pressure that allowing false light claims would place on First Amendment rights of publishers.[22] Those permitting actions for "false light" have emphasized the distinction between that tort—"a cause of action

---

17. Hill, supra, 385 U.S. at 388–89.
18. Id. at 388.
19. Id. at 394–96.
20. Id. at 419 (Fortas, J., dissenting).
21. See Restatement (Second) of Torts § 652E & comment b (1977) (not-

ing that in many cases to which this category applies, the material will be defamatory as well, and thus actionable as libel or slander).
22. See, e.g., Renwick v. News & Observer Pub. Co., 312 S.E.2d 405, 412 (N.C.1984).

based upon injury to plaintiff's emotions and his mental suffering"—and defamation, "a remedy for injury to plaintiff's reputation."[23]

A leading case recognizing the doctrine is *Cantrell v. Forest City Publishing Co.*,[24] in which the Supreme Court affirmed a jury verdict on a false light claim advanced by plaintiffs who lost their husband and father in a collapse of a bridge. The defendant newspaper published a Sunday magazine feature that used the plaintiffs' family to illustrate how the bridge collapse had affected people in the area. The plaintiffs alleged that the article made knowingly false statements about their appearance and living conditions in their home that subjected them to shame and humiliation. The Court found its way through a thicket of argument on the definition of "actual malice" under the test of *New York Times*[25] and *Time, Inc. v. Hill*, discussed just above,[26] to find that there was adequate evidence to support a compensatory award, if not one for punitive damages.[27]

A literally illustrative decision on the false light theory involved the publication of nude photographs of Robyn Douglass, an actress and model, who had consented to have the photos taken on the assumption that they were intended for use in *Playboy* magazine. The pictures wound up in a photo spread in *Hustler* magazine. The court, contrasting the "vulgar and offensive" character of *Hustler* with what it viewed as the relatively tasteful aspects of *Playboy*, concluded that "to portray Robyn Douglass as voluntarily posing nude for *Hustler* could be thought to place her in a false light even though she had voluntarily posed nude for *Playboy*."[28] The court thus concluded that Douglass had a cause of action for the false light tort, although it reversed a judgment for her, in part on the grounds that the trial court had erred in failing to require her to prove *New York Times* malice by clear and convincing evidence. It was necessary for her to meet that test, the appellate court said, because she was "a public figure in a literal sense."[29]

It is interesting to compare this case with *Cantrell*, the Supreme Court decision just summarized concerning the article on the bridge collapse,[30] as well as with *Time, Inc. v. Hill*.[31] In all of these

---

23. See, e.g., Rinsley v. Brandt, 446 F.Supp. 850, 858 (D.Kan.1977), quoting Froelich v. Adair, 516 P.2d 993, 996 (Kan.1973).

24. 419 U.S. 245 (1974).

25. See supra, ¶ 67.01(A).

26. See supra, ¶ 69.02, text accompanying notes 11–20.

27. See 419 U.S. at 251–53.

28. Douglass v. Hustler Magazine, Inc., 769 F.2d 1128, 1135–37 (7th Cir. 1985).

29. Id. at 1141.

30. See supra, text accompanying notes 24–27.

31. See supra, ¶ 69.02, text accompanying notes 11–20.

cases, the defendant's publication had an effect on the plaintiff's image that was at variance with the facts. In *Douglass*, the plaintiff complained that the "false light" was the placement of her image before the public in a way that was degrading, relative to her own conception of herself and her own expressed will about the venue of publication. The court there accepted the plaintiff's false light theory although reversing the judgment for her on other grounds. In *Cantrell*, where the Court upheld an award for the plaintiffs, they alleged that the defendants' article had presented a humiliatingly false image of them. By contrast, in *Hill*, where the Court set aside the plaintiffs' judgment, the play and the story about the play arguably presented the plaintiffs in a light more heroic than the historical facts warranted.

¶ 69.04   Appropriation

Another category of cases that courts have slotted under the "privacy" label employs the concept of "appropriation." The theory behind this classification is that the plaintiff has a property right in matters that are confidential to himself, and in public appearances for which he may charge admission or require payment for their reproduction. Thus, a communication medium cannot appropriate that information or those images for its commercial use unless it buys the right to do so from the plaintiff.

In one spectacular case, the plaintiff was a traveling entertainer who performed a "human cannonball" act that lasted about 15 seconds. A television news show used a video tape of the entire act. Despite the obviously newsworthy aspect of the performance, a closely divided Supreme Court reversed a judgment for the broadcaster that the Ohio Supreme Court had justified on First Amendment grounds.[32] Inter alia, the Court distinguished *Time, Inc. v. Hill*[33] as not "involv[ing] a performer, a person with a name having commercial value, or any claim to a 'right of publicity.' "[34] The majority declared that it was "quite sure that the First and Fourteenth Amendments do not immunize the media when they broadcast a performer's entire act without his consent."[35]

The state cause of action in this case was based on a "right of publicity," a concept quite similar to the Restatement's separate "privacy" category that imposes liability against "[o]ne who appropriates to his own use or benefit the name or likeness of another."[36] Although recognizing that "the protection of [a plaintiff's] personal feelings against mental distress is an important factor leading to a

---

32. Zacchini v. Scripps–Howard Broadcasting Co., 433 U.S. 562 (1977).

33. See supra, ¶ 69.02, text accompanying notes 11–20.

34. 433 U.S. at 572.

35. Id. at 575.

36. Restatement (Second) of Torts § 652C (1977).

recognition of" this liability rule, the Restatement drafters said that "the right created by it is in the nature of a property right, for the exercise of which an exclusive license may be given to a third person."[37]

The mixed ancestry of the "appropriation" tort—that is, its foundations in both property notions and ideas of dignity—is evident in the background of the New York civil rights statute that was at issue in the *Hill* case.[38] The historical basis for that statute was public outrage about a decision by the New York Court of Appeals, which rejected a suit for the use of a young woman's likeness in advertising material for flour that included the phrase "Flour of the Family."[39] The legislation, which provides a cause of action for unauthorized commercial use of a person's "name, portrait or picture," represented a response to the court's denial of recovery on a common law claim. One can understand how some observers would discern the theoretical basis of such a statute in "property rights," while also recognizing that the public reaction that principally fueled the legislation was probably anger at a violation of personal dignity.

Where the asserted "appropriation" of a plaintiff's name or likeness is essentially a published disclosure of embarrassing facts that are on the public record, courts are likely to provide First Amendment protection to defendants. Illustrative is a case involving an article in a newsletter that the defendant, a private investigator, distributed free to law enforcement agencies, financial institutions and others. The article summarized five cases in which the defendant's firm helped to recover stolen assets. In particular, it reported the defendant's role in investigating the plaintiff, who was convicted for stealing bearer bonds belonging to a customer of her employer and cashing them for her own use. The court found the article constitutionally protected, saying that it was "primarily noncommercial because it related to a matter of public concern, namely the facts of the plaintiff's crime and felony conviction."[40]

¶ 69.05 Intrusion and Other Privacy–related Doctrines

One other category of "privacy" torts deserves separate mention here, as does the privacy-related potential in some doctrines not classified under that heading. The other "privacy" category, analyzed in a separate chapter above,[41] has been labeled "intrusion

---

37. Id. comment a.

38. See supra, ¶ 69.02, text accompanying note 12.

39. Roberson v. Rochester Folding Box Co., 64 N.E. 442 (N.Y.1902).

40. Joe Dickerson & Assocs., LLC v. Dittmar, 34 P.3d 995, 1004 (Colo.2001).

41. Chapter 8 supra.

upon seclusion."[42] Perhaps the most straightforward cases in this category focus only on the technological process of gathering information, as by wiretapping and eavesdropping. However, the intrusion category may also provide an independent ground for suit in cases related to the publication of confidential information. Thus, for example, the taking of a picture of someone in intimate circumstances might constitute an intrusion by itself, as well as generating an action for publication of that picture under the heading of "public disclosure of private facts."

The California Supreme Court employed an intrusion theory to allow a suit against a network for its reporter's covert videotaping of conversations with coworkers by a "telepsychic" who gave "readings" to customers who called a phone number on which they were charged by the minute. The reporter, who got a job as a telepsychic at the firm where the plaintiff worked, did the videotaping with a small camera hidden in her hat and a microphone in an undergarment. The court's definition of the factual basis for the cause of action was quite specific. It said that "a person who lacks a reasonable expectation of complete privacy in a conversation, because it could be seen and overheard by co-workers (but not the general public) may nevertheless have a claim for invasion of privacy by intrusion based on a television reporter's covert videotaping of that conversation."[43]

Some litigants have sought to vindicate privacy-type interests through other doctrines, including theories that are quite traditional. Illustrative is another case involving covert TV taping, in which a grocery chain sued a TV network for the use of a hidden camera in the deli and meat departments of one of its stores. The network employees had secured jobs in those departments on the basis of falsified applications that did not reveal their investigative purposes. The plaintiff sued on the time-honored theories of fraud and trespass, basing its fraud claim on misrepresentations by the network investigators in securing employment with the store and its trespass claim on the theory that the network's agents exceeded the scope of the store's consent to their entry on its premises. The court denied the network's motion for summary judgment on both counts.[44]

---

42. Restatement (Second) of Torts § 652B (1977).

43. Sanders v. American Broadcasting Cos., 20 Cal.4th 907, 978 P.2d 67, 77 (1999) (distinguishing situations where "the workplace is regularly open to entry or observation by the public or press, or the interaction that was the subject of the alleged intrusion was between proprietor (or employee) and customer").

44. Food Lion, Inc. v. Capital Cities/ABC, 951 F.Supp. 1217 (M.D.N.C. 1996). The court of appeals later upheld a jury verdict for trespass, 194 F.3d 505, 519 (4th Cir.1999). However, although finding that the network's reporters had "knowingly made misrepresentations with the aim that Food Lion rely on them," the court concluded that the plaintiff had not shown injurious reliance. Id. at 512–14.

¶ 69.06   The Policies at Issue

It is useful to summarize the conflicting policies in the area of media and related activities alleged to invade various privacy interests. The most fundamental interest on the defense side is enwrapped in the First Amendment; the argument is that reports on society in general, as well as on public affairs more narrowly defined, advance the interests of the community. In this regard, one may refer to the *Sidis* case, previously mentioned.[45] One theoretical, if arguable, justification for immunizing the merciless sketch at issue in that case was that it might warn parents of prodigies about the dangers of pushing their children too fast.[46]

Beyond that, publishers will invoke the social interest in the publication of history, and the difficulties in drawing a line between history and news. Moreover, when plaintiffs point out that media publications represent profitmaking activities, and often overlap into the area of entertainment, defendants will respond that it is not feasible for courts to try to distinguish between news and entertainment.

Plaintiffs will themselves stress policy considerations that range from the quantitatively commercial to the personally intangible. One touchstone lies in the "property right" idea. A strategic advantage of claiming under an appropriation-type theory is its identification of a commercially-founded right in a commercially-minded society.

However, one cannot ignore the roots of even property-related privacy claims in dignitary interests that increasingly have been protected by tort law. Moreover, with respect to cases arising from news stories and features, where defendants argue that the news value of a publication outweighs dignitary concerns, it is worth noting that the psychological conditioning of judges may produce reactions of outrage at offensive and embarrassing publications about confidential features of personal life. This reaction may be especially strong in cases involving dignitary privacy interests where media defendants work with long lead times from initial reporting to publication. In this sense, law establishes some boundaries to both art and judgments of newsworthiness.

[Chapter 70 is reserved for supplementary material.]

45. See supra, ¶ 69.01, text accompanying note 5.

46. This was the view of James Thurber, who did the rewrite on the Sidis article for the New Yorker. See James Thurber, The Years With Ross 210–12 (1959).

Part Five

VALUING THE INTERESTS

Section Twelve

DAMAGES IN TORT LAW

Chapter Seventy–One

QUANTIFYING ECONOMIC LOSSES FOR PERSONAL INJURY

Analysis

The subject of damages is the business end of tort law. It is a topic of fierce debate, in part because of the difficulty of establishing coherent principles, both philosophical and practical, for the award and review of damages.[1] This chapter and the next one

---

    1. See generally Am. Bar Ass'n, Spec. Comm. on the Tort Liability Sys-tem, *Towards a Jurisprudence of Injury* 5–163—5–186 (M. Shapo Rptr. 1984).

analyze theories of compensatory damages for personal injury in two major categories. The one discussed in this chapter, "economic loss," represents the pecuniary consequences of personal injury that have direct marketplace equivalents. These include medical bills, lost earnings and household services.

It is important to note that tort literature includes a rather different use of the term "economic loss" than the one on which the present chapter focuses. That other meaning distinguishes harms like lost profits and business interruption expenses caused by tortious acts from the direct economic consequences of personal injury or property damage.[2]

The category of "noneconomic loss" for personal injury, discussed in the next chapter,[3] includes damages for items that cannot be quantified through exchange values. The quantitatively most significant type of "noneconomic loss" for personal injury is pain and suffering.

In addition to losses already incurred at the time of trial, the categories of both economic and noneconomic damages include anticipated future harm—losses that will occur after trial because of a personal injury. The law has uncontroversially recognized categories like loss of earnings, medical bills, and pain and suffering as proper items of compensation for future losses. More of a subject of dispute have been claims for other types of future injuries. Those headings of loss, discussed above,[4] include enhanced risk of illness resulting from the defendant's conduct or product—entirely a risk rather than a present injury; reasonable fear of illness, which some courts have viewed as a present injury because it afflicts the plaintiff at the time of trial; and the cost of medical surveillance to keep an eye on the potential development of illness about which there is reason to be concerned.

¶ 71.01   Categories of Economic Loss

A. *Medical expenses; the collateral source rule*

In most personal injury cases, a principal category of economic special damages is medical losses. Here the issue is relatively uncomplicated, with a premise of compensation based on restoration to the plaintiff of his or her expenditures for hospital bills, the costs of medical care, surgery and drugs, and other aids to recovery or rehabilitation.

An important practical issue that arises in this connection concerns the so-called collateral source rule, under which American

2. See supra, Chapter 64.
3. See supra, Chapter 72.
4. See ¶ 49.06 supra.

courts have refused to permit a defendant to subtract from a damages award payments that a plaintiff receives from third parties. These "collateral source" funds might include payments from such sources as disability insurance and pensions, but the rule is especially significant in the area of medical expenses because a substantial amount of collateral sources comes from medical insurance that pays for physician and hospital costs. Several state statutes have nullified the collateral source rule—some doing so only for particular types of cases like medical malpractice litigation—thus permitting defendants to deduct from tort judgments such payments as insurance reimbursements received by plaintiffs.

B. Earnings

Another principal category of economic special damages is that of lost earnings. This subject, which on the surface may appear quite simple, features many factual issues and problems of legal theory. Issues may arise, for example, with respect to whether a plaintiff reasonably might have expected continued employment in a particular occupation or, in the case of a suit for fatal injuries, whether the representative of the dead person can plausibly claim that the decedent would have continued working at particular wage rates. Illustrating the difficulties often inherent in this sort of problem is a commentator's observation that injured persons with degenerative conditions are likely to retire early or change jobs.[5]

Another interesting set of issues concerns life expectancy. Where damages are awarded on a lump sum basis, the payment of a lump sum to a particular individual based on a certain life expectancy necessarily represents a probability judgment, since almost all people will diverge from the average with respect to when they actually die. Although the law generally does employ this kind of statistical averaging, it might be argued that parties should be able to challenge those averages in certain situations. For example, a defendant might argue against damages based on statistical life expectancy where a plaintiff is suffering from a terminal illness at the time of injury.

A further illustration of uncertainty associated with calculating damages, specifically with respect to the prediction of earnings, appears in the case of disabling or fatal injuries to a student who had plausible ambitions for high paying jobs but had not yet established a career. Indeed, people with established occupations may present analogous uncertainties. An example would be a lawyer whose attainments qualify her for highly paid legal positions, who elected to do public interest work at a relatively low

5. J. Michael Veron, Evaluating the Economic Impact of Personal Injuries, 31 Loyola L. Rev. 825, 839 (1986).

salary but, before she was injured, fully intended to move within a year to a much more lucrative job. In these types of cases, the expectancies on which plaintiffs would base damage claims are significantly greater than those associated with present employment. These examples simply highlight the difficulties in establishing a fully coherent theory of even economic damages.

C. Household Services

Courts have begun to quantify the value of household services. For example, they will award damages to a married person representing the economic contributions to the household, such as cooking, laundering and house cleaning, made by an injured spouse who has been primarily a homemaker. They may also take into account the dollar value of household services rendered by a family member who works in the labor force but who also performs, for example, "handy person" tasks around the home. A separate item of damages, often labeled consortium, attempts to put a price tag on family relationships of society and affection.[6]

¶ 71.02   Theories of Personal Injury Damages

A. General concepts

There are several general theories of personal injury damages, which relate to both quantifiable economic loss and intangible losses without direct marketplace yardsticks. One classification of the subject treats the plaintiff's life, faculties, and capacity for enjoying life as personal assets, each with "an objective 'value.' "[7] A somewhat different approach emphasizes "functional compensation," asking about "the use to which the money can be put."[8] A traditional concept focuses on restoration of the plaintiff to his position before the injury, but this compensatory premise is quite unrealistic in many situations, and entirely irrelevant in the case of actions for death, at least with respect to the loss to the decedent of his life. Another theory holds that "[m]easurement can only be made in terms of human happiness," requiring assessment in "monetary terms" of "past, present and future loss of pleasure and happiness."[9]

B. Economic approaches

1. Capital

A major issue of damages philosophy turns on whether one views damages as representing a return of capital or as "rent."

---

6. See infra, ¶ 72.01(E).

7. See A.I. Ogus, Damages for Lost Amenities: For a Foot, a Feeling, or a Function?, 35 Mod. L. Rev. 1, 2 (1972).

8. See Beverley McLachlin, What Price Disability? A Perspective on the Law of Damages for Personal Injury, 59 Canad. Bar Rev. 1, 8–12 (1981).

9. See Ogus, supra note 7, at 3.

Some advocates of the "human capital" approach view the economic premise for compensatory tort damages as one that analogizes human beings to tangible goods. The theory is that damages should represent a reparation by an injurer for loss of capability akin to that which would occur with a damaged machine. One treatise has referred to the "important similarities between human beings and physical assets" when the subject is "economic evaluation."[10] In this perspective, to view injury victims as capital assets presents the best practical way to return them to the position they occupied before an accident.

2. Rent

The major competing position is that instead of representing a reparation of capital to be awarded in a lump sum, tort damages should be viewed as representing "rent" in the economic sense. Under this approach, the defendant would make periodic payments to replace losses only as they actually occur over time, for example, as medical payments or lost earnings. This method prevents the overcompensation that would occur, for example, with a substantial award of damages to someone who, after the litigation, happens to get a very good job despite an injury that was considered to be disabling at the time of trial, or, indeed, to someone who dies well short of his or her predicted life expectancy.

Crucial to the choice between these approaches is the question of what we mean by restoring someone to his or her original position, a goal sometimes summed up in the phrase "making whole." Generally, one's views of what it is to be a functioning human being will affect one's choice of the "capital" or "rent" solution, as those views will influence one's assessment of the rationales for compensatory damages. We turn now to the latter subject.

¶ 71.03   Rationales for Compensatory Damages

A.   Corrective justice

One set of rationalizations for compensatory damages focuses on fairness between individuals. Like fairness rationales that support substantive rules of tort law, these ideas often partake of notions of corrective justice. A fundamental concept of corrective justice, which traces to Aristotle,[11] is that when someone has lost something because another has injured him, the other should give up the gain that resulted from the conduct that caused the injury,

---

10. Stuart Speiser & John Maher, *Recovery for Wrongful Death: Economic Handbook* 2–14 (4th ed. 1995).

11. See 2 Complete Works of Aristotle 1786–87 (Jonathan Barnes ed. 1984).

in order to compensate for the victim's loss. Unfortunately, because often the gain is not coextensive with the loss, this theoretical image frequently does not advance practical analysis very far.[12]

B. Reparation

A related idea that helps to explain why society compels tortious actors to pay for personal injuries is that of reparations. Suggesting that an injurer must make amends for harm he has caused in order to balance the moral scales in favor of one to whom he owed a duty, the concept of reparations connotes expiation of a wrong to the victim. American courts do not typically articulate this concept in common law tort decisions. However, the idea probably is part of the implicit intellectual framework for personal injury damages.

C. Restoration

Another approach to compensation focuses on restoring the plaintiff, as much as possible, to his or her situation before the injury. As applied in many cases where the loss cannot easily be monetized, this rationalization may have an unrealistic and rather bitter sound. We have noted that in a death case, it is quite irrelevant to the decedent's own loss of life. Bitterness enters the picture when one tries to calculate the affective value to surviving family members of the life of a decedent.

When the plaintiff is an injured person who is alive, an example of unresponsiveness to reality appears in the inconvenience and frustration associated with loss of a limb. One might speak of a prosthetic device as restorational; yet, one is reduced to trying to translate into money a loss that it is difficult to quantify. It is, however, relatively practical to speak of a dollar equivalent with respect to economic deprivations caused by injuries, as when the loss of a limb has produced a significant diminution in earning capacity. The law frequently does achieve that much realism in restorational compensation.

D. Disappointment of expectations

One might also justify compensatory damages on the ground that the defendant's tortious conduct has violated the plaintiff's

---

12. An interesting comparison to the basic theory of corrective justice appears in the suggestion that in some cases, the traditional measure of compensatory damages should be reduced to take into account situations where a defendant has been no more than negligent and "harm appears greatly to exceed culpability." Neal R. Feigenson, Merciful Damages: Some Remarks on Forgiveness, Mercy and Tort Law, 27 Fordham Urb. L. J. 1633, e.g., at 1645–46 (2000)(reasoning, inter alia, that such an option would empower decisionmakers "to relieve defendants who have merely been careless of some of the overwhelming consequences of their behavior—behavior in which any of us could easily imagine ourselves engaging").

reasonable expectations of physical security or emotional integrity. The expectations rationale is more fundamentally associated with contract remedies than tort. As applied to tort, it would require at least proof that the hazard presented by the defendant's conduct raised the profile of risk beyond that ordinarily expectable in daily existence.

E.   Deterrence

A familiar rationale for tort damages is that of deterrence. Those with a bent toward economic theory will ground their ideas of deterrence on achieving marketplace efficiency. Their premise concerning the desired effect of tort awards on conduct is that the injurer should pay the true social costs of its risky activities because this will provide incentives to make its behavior efficient. Others will justify tort damages as deterring accidents in a more general way, without reference to nicely calculated concepts of economically optimal behavior.

A fundamental theoretical dispute concerns the validity of deterrence as a rationale for compensatory damages. One view is that it is inappropriate to argue to a jury that deterrence is an objective of compensatory damages, because of the "punitive" overtones of deterrence.[13] Others, however, contend that "the purpose of ordinary tort damages, as distinguished from 'punitive' damages, is both to compensate and to deter."[14] In practice, the latter view is probably congenial to most courts.

F.   Supply and Demand for Danger

Related to efficiency-oriented deterrence is an approach that asks what sum a potential injury victim would pay to avoid an injury risk. The underlying idea is that when one engages in a dangerous activity in response to a specific economic incentive, one is in effect selling, in a probabilistic way, part of his right to physical security. A specific example of this mode of analysis is to ask how much of a decrease in pay a worker would take to reduce to zero the probability of death connected with a job. For economists, this is a routine way of putting the question, but it is not without difficulties in making the relevant calculation. Illustrative of the range of economic opinion on the subject are two articles published two years apart. The authors of one study estimated the value of a life saved at $176,000[15] and the author of the other

---

13. See Vanskike v. ACF Industries Inc., 665 F.2d 188, 209–210 (8th Cir. 1981), cert. denied sub nom. St. Louis–San Francisco Ry. Co. v. Vanskike, 455 U.S. 1000 (1982).

14. Kalavity v. United States, 584 F.2d 809, 811 (6th Cir.1978).

15. See Richard Thaler & Sherwin Rosen, The Value of Saving a Life: Evidence from the Labor Market, in *Household Production and Consumption*, vol.

article put the figure above one million dollars.[16] This sort of analysis may be off-putting to ordinary sensibilities, but it does provide a way to focus the question of what is economically efficient, if not fair, compensation.

G. Self-Assessment

Another way to rationalize tort damages would derive the valuation of an injury from the plaintiff's own assessment, before the fact, of the worth of the interest injured. One commentator has indeed suggested a "self-assessment" based on the plaintiff's first-party insurance coverage, reasoning that the amount of that coverage will assure the accuracy of a tort victim's "valuation of damages in the event of a tort" because of his outlay of "premium dollars to provide for that amount of recovery in the event of a nontortious accident."[17]

H. Dignitary Valuations

In a policy perspective very different from that of economic analysis, the question of what appropriate compensation is for personal injury resolves itself into an issue of human dignity. When one views the subject from this perspective, the substantive basis for tort may overlap with the rationales for damages. For example, a medieval Jewish text indicates that the same injury arguably could support different levels of compensation depending on how the injury was inflicted. One rabbi indicated in a commentary that if someone slapped another person, he would have to pay him 200 zuz, but that if he hit him with the back of his hand he would have to pay 400 zuz. That authority, Rabbi Judah, declared: "This is the general principle: it all depends on a person's dignity."[18] This difference in the level of damages suggests that it is as if two rather similar offensive acts were two different torts because of their differing impact on dignitary interests. The rabbinical commentary illustrates how the dignitary rationale provides a bridge from economic damages for personal injury to noneconomic damages, on which the next chapter focuses.[19]

I. Policy critiques

Among the many policy critiques that cut across the topic of compensatory damages, we note two of special interest. One of

40 of Studies in Income & Wealth, at 265, 292 (Nestor Terleckyj ed. 1976).

16. See Kip Viscusi, Labor Market Evaluations of Life and Limb: Empirical and Policy Implications, 26 Public Policy 359, 372–85 (1978).

17. Saul Levmore, Self–Assessed Valuation Systems for Tort and Other Law, 68 Va. L. Rev. 771, 811 (1982).

18. The Mishnah on Damages, Mishnayath, Vol. 4, at 66, Order Nezikin, Tractate Baba Kamma, chapter 8:6 (Philip Blackman, Judaica Press, 1983).

19. See generally Chapter 72 infra.

these arguments, associated particularly with socialist scholars, focuses on the anti-egalitarian features of the present system of awarding compensatory damages for economic loss. This criticism finds injustice in the fact that compensation based on earnings levels necessarily will provide higher awards to those with high paying jobs than to those with relatively low earnings.[20]

A double-edged critique of tort law, offered by the influential scholar Fleming James, criticized fault as a requirement for compensation for economic loss, but also attacked damages for intangibles. James suggested that "accident law" should move towards a general system of liability without fault, recognizing that "some classes of accidents are the inevitable by-product of enterprises" that could efficiently distribute accident losses which "fall initially on those who are ill-equipped to meet them." He reasoned that, so based, this strict enterprise liability would justify awards that "provide assurance that accident victims will be rehabilitated, and that they and their dependents will be cared for during the period of disability without imposing on the victims or their families a crushing burden." However, he suggested that this system should exclude damages for "many speculative nonpecuniary items,"[21] a subject discussed in the next chapter.[22] Pointing out that "accidents bring a net pecuniary loss to society as a whole—the social wealth and income is thereby diminished," James argued that "if the victim is made entirely whole, he will fare better than society and will not himself share the economic burden he is asking society to distribute."[23]

¶ 71.04   Damages for Death

A problem that merits separate treatment is that of assessing compensatory damages in death cases. In more than one sense, it may seem impossible to place a valuation on human life when the loss is precisely that of life itself. The pragmatic solution that the law offers is to calculate the value of a life in dollars, to be paid to those who had a stake in the continued life of the dead person that can be translated into money. With respect to economic loss, this at least has the logic of quantifying potential future earnings or other contributions to the household and awarding them to people who would have counted on those resources as dependents of the decedent. If it seems crass to view life as a commodity in this way, it is still a solution that helps to meet the practical needs that tort-

---

20. *See, e.g.*, Richard Abel, A Critique of Torts, 37 U.C.L.A. L. Rev. 785 (1990).

21. Fleming James, Damages in Accident Cases, 41 Cornell L.Q. 582, 584 (1956).

22. See generally Chapter 72 infra.

23. James, supra note 20, at 584.

caused deaths—or any deaths—create. Moreover, a moral basis for awarding death damages against tortfeasors resides in the culpability, or the creation of hazards, that give rise to the substantive cause of action.

Here, we discuss the two kinds of legislation that provide ways to compensate for tortiously caused death: wrongful death legislation and survival statutes.

A. Wrongful death statutes

Wrongful death statutes vary from state to state. Typically they provide that certain categories of claimants defined in the statute, usually persons related to a decedent, may recover for deaths caused by "wrongful act, neglect or default of another."[24] The stimulus for these statutes was a peculiar strand of law that led nineteenth century American courts to the conclusion that there was no common law cause of action for the consequences of tortiously caused deaths, by contrast with injuries that left their victims alive.[25]

The principal purpose of wrongful death statutes is to provide a cause of action for family members who naturally would be expected to rely on the deceased person for income or other benefits that can be translated into money. The statutes vary as to the elements of damages for which compensation may be awarded. Explicitly or by interpretation, death statutes provide for recovery in well-established categories of pecuniary loss, including loss of earning capacity and deprivation of household services that would have been performed by the decedent.[26] Some statutes use broad language that enables juries to award "such damages . . . as they shall deem fair and just."[27]

A typical death statute will list categories of beneficiaries, giving a priority ranking of who may receive damages. For example, spouses and children would be the first eligible category, followed by parents or siblings if there is no surviving spouse or child. Courts are likely to construe these categories strictly, on the grounds that like any legislation, wrongful death statutes are "in derogation of the common law." For example, "children" will not include grandchildren, even if they are the children of deceased children of the person who was tortiously killed.[28] However, there

---

24. See, e.g., N.M. Stat. Ann. § 41–2–1 (1996 Repl.).

25. For a historical description and critique of these developments, see Stuart M. Speiser, et al., Recovery for Wrongful Death & Injury § 1.1–1.7 (3d ed. 1992).

26. For a discussion of non-economic damages in death cases, see infra ¶ ¶ 72.01(E)–(G), 72.03(B)(2).

27. See, e.g., N.M. Stat. Ann. § 41–2–3 (1996 Repl.).

28. Babb v. Matlock, 9 S.W.3d 508, 509 (Ark.2000).

are at least dicta indicating that a personal representative of a decedent may recover wrongful death damages even if there are no classes of family beneficiaries in existence. One opinion, referring to statutory language, viewed the personal representative as "a trustee for the state and for estate creditors where none of the named kin were left."[29]

B. Survival statutes compared

The classic distinction between wrongful death statutes and survival statutes lies in the fact that under survival statutes, the court awards damages for the cause of action that theoretically would have existed in favor of the decedent himself for losses occurring between the time of injury and death. An important practical aspect of survival statutes is that they have been construed to provide a claim for the pain and suffering of the deceased between the tortious injury and death.

The plaintiff under a survival statute usually must be the personal representative of the decedent, who may or may not be a family member, and who will distribute any tort award under the decedent's will or according to the laws of intestacy that govern estates of persons who die without a will. As a practical matter, those who get money under survival statutes will usually be the same family members who recover under wrongful death statutes. But by contrast with the theory that survival actions are the property of the decedent through his representative, the principal purpose of wrongful death statutes is directly to compensate the statutory beneficiaries, usually members of the decedent's family. In its pure form, "wrongful death" recovery represents only the financial worth of the decedent to those persons. Some statutes blur the distinction between wrongful death and survival concepts, but the analysis in this text preserves it.

C. Technical issues and policy controversies in wrongful death and survival

An interesting set of technical questions concerns the effect that should be given to the contributory negligence of the decedent and of plaintiffs under both wrongful death and survival statutes.[30] One might readily argue that at least with respect to survival statutes, the decedent's contributory negligence should bar or reduce recovery, since the action is theoretically only that of the dead person. A more difficult question may arise with respect to the impact of the decedent's contributory negligence on a wrongful death claim. Some courts insist that the decedent's conduct will bar

---

29. See, e.g., Henkel v. Hood, 156 P.2d 790, 794 (N.M.1945).

30. For a concise discussion of these issues, see Mitchell v. Akers, 401 S.W.2d 907, 909–12 (Tex.Civ.App.1966).

the action.[31] However, it may be argued that since, in theory, the wrongful death cause of action is for the direct benefit of the decedent's statutory beneficiary, the decedent's fault should be no bar to the beneficiary's claim.

A parallel set of questions arises with respect to the contributory negligence of survivors. It would appear that the fault of statutory beneficiaries should bar or reduce recovery under wrongful death legislation, since the cause of action is theoretically theirs. However, one at least may raise the question of whether the contributory negligence of living family members should bar a survival claim, precisely because the survival action in theory belongs to the estate of the deceased person.[32]

This discussion of the technical effects of the contributory negligence of both deceased persons and living plaintiffs in tort actions involving death leads us to focus on the basic purposes of tort law. The theory that a survival action is the property of the decedent, transferred to his or her personal representative, is appealing. If a person suffers terribly for a time but then lives to sue, all courts would agree that a jury should be able to value that suffering in that person's own tort action. It would seem that the fortuitous fact that a person has died after a period of suffering should not deprive his representative of the opportunity to sue for that suffering, an opportunity that would have been the decedent's if he had lived.

This reasoning, however, takes us only so far when we consider the question of why we award damages for tortiously caused death. Beyond the obvious wrongful death rationale of providing a replacement for a lost stream of income, one may suggest that as a practical matter, awards for the consequences of death depend, or in large measure should depend, on injuries to relationships. For example, if a young child dies of drowning because of the negligence of a third party,[33] the practical effect of awarding damages under a survival statute for the pain and suffering of the child's final minutes is to provide some measure of solace to the parents. By the same token, if a court were to award wrongful death damages to relatives for the death of a person who had taken perpetual vows of poverty, one practical effect would be to provide some psychic balm to the relatives.[34]

If one were writing on a blank slate, one might wish to collapse into one statutory vehicle the concepts embodied in separate wrong-

---

31. See, e.g., id. at 909 (dictum).

32. See id. at 912.

33. See, e.g., Mitchell, supra note 30.

34. Cf. Stang v. Hertz Corp., 467 P.2d at 14 (N.M.1970), discussed infra, ¶ 72.03(A), text accompanying note 26 (emphasizing deterrence rationale in wrongful death suit for the death of a nun).

ful death and survival statutes. The statutes of some states in effect do this. But for judges who must seek persuasive solutions for knotty problems of interpretation that arise under dual statutes, it is well to keep in mind not only the theoretical foundation of the legislation but the practical consequences of where the money will go.

Chapter Seventy–Two
ASSESSING INTANGIBLES

Analysis

A large category of tort damages aims to compensate for losses that cannot easily be quantified—surely not so easily as documented medical expenses, and not even so easily as the less certain category of future earnings. This heading of damages, of which "pain and suffering" is the item that generates the most awards, is controversial. A principal basis of criticism lies in the fact that there is no objective dollar measure of these injuries.

¶ 72.01   Categories of Noneconomic Damages

A.   *Pain*

A practical classification of pain divides it into the principal categories of acute and chronic pain, with a collateral category of "chronic pain syndrome" (CPS) presenting special problems. Acute pain, according to the report of the Commission on the Evaluation of Pain, is "of recent onset, most commonly associated with a discrete injury or other trauma." Unless there is an underlying structural problem or disease, acute pain usually "subside[s] as the healing process continues—ordinarily less than six months and usually less than one month."[1]

---

1. Report of the Commission on the Evaluation of Pain, 50 Soc. Sec. Bulletin No. 1, 13, at 22 (Jan. 1987).

By contrast, " '[c]hronic' pain is constant or intermittent pain lasting for long periods of time," with six months being a common benchmark for the minimum. This kind of pain "may be associated with a residual structural defect that persists long after the acute episode." By contrast with acute pain, "which may be conceptualized as a warning that something is wrong and is therefore often a useful symptom, chronic pain may become a problem in its own right—a symptom but not necessarily of an underlying impairment."[2]

Even more difficult to deal with—both medically and legally— is CPS, which "has the added component of certain recognizable psychological and socioeconomic influences." CPS sufferers respond to positive reinforcement of their pain——for example, expressions of concern by others. Their pain may "provide[] a 'legitimate' rationale for quitting an unpleasant work environment" or "the luxury of concerted medical attention." The presence of this kind of "incentive structure" makes "the prospects for spontaneous recovery . . . remote."[3]

Each of these types of pain presumably will present different challenges to courts and juries that must attempt to quantify them. The general challenge to trying to translate assessments of pain into money is evident in the emphasis of the Commission on the Evaluation of Pain "that no one can know the pain of another person." The Commission observed that "[b]ecause science has developed no laboratory tests for identifying and measuring pain, the only available substitute is careful observation of a wide range of behaviors."[4] In seeking to establish principles of review for awards for pain, courts must strike a balance between reliance on objective reports of behavior and recognition of the subjectivity inherent in the fact that pain is highly individualized and unobservable. They also must take into account the potentially counterproductive effects of giving awards for items of damages, like chronic pain syndrome, where the prospect of a damages award may generate incentives for pain behavior.

B. Suffering

"[P]ain and suffering tend to evoke virtually identical behaviors,"[5] and judicial decisions invariably view the two as inseparable, but technically they are different concepts. Suffering is associated with situations in which people "perceive pain as a threat to their continued existence—not merely to their lives or their bodies, but to their integrity as persons." By contrast, "[p]eople may tolerate

---

2. Id. at 22–23.   **4.** Id. at 22.

3. Id. at 23.   **5.** Id. at 21.

great pain without reporting suffering," especially if they know that the pain "does not have dire meaning, that it can be relieved, or that it will be short-lived." A pain patient who has suffered for a long time will have a "pervasive repertoire of mental and physical consequences," including such behaviors as guarding oneself too much, and these behaviors "will require systematic and extensive intervention."[6] Because tort awards lump pain and suffering together, the practical implications of intense or prolonged suffering presumably are to add dollars to an overall total calculated for the combined item.

C.　Fear

Fear is a fairly standard item of tort damages. Besides generating factual issues concerning damages, fear may also be viewed as presenting a question of substantive law, defined as whether the defendant had a duty to the plaintiff with respect to the possibility that the defendant's tortious conduct would cause fear. Some air crash cases present dramatic examples of an issue of damages for fear that at least implicitly presents a question of substantive law. This kind of issue often arises under the technical heading of survival statutes, which have been construed to provide a claim to the personal representative of a dead person for injuries the decedent suffered between the time of a tortious injury and death.[7] The plaintiffs in these cases seek damages representing the fear suffered by victims of fatal crashes when there is evidence that the decedents probably had a few seconds before the crash to consider their fate.

In one case that granted recovery, the court referred to testimony from which jurors could have drawn the inference that the plaintiffs' decedent "apprehended his death" for a period of "at least four to six seconds." Affirming an award of $15,000 for that period of fear, the court declared that "[t]he jury could have reasonably inferred" that the decedent "experienced the mental anguish commonly associated with anticipation of one's own death."[8] In such cases, courts may use several terms to describe the harm. At various times in the decision just summarized, the court refers to "pre-impact fear," "pain and suffering," and "mental anguish."[9]

A rather different question arises in suits for fear of illness ascribed to the plaintiff's exposure to substances that the defendant makes or controls. The defendants in such cases will argue that there should be no recovery for an emotion associated with just a

---

6. Id.

7. See ¶ 71.04(B)-(C) supra.

8. Haley v. Pan American World Airways, 746 F.2d 311, 317 (5th Cir. 1984).

9. Id. at 315–17.

possibility, or even with a probability, of only future harm. However, as discussed above, some courts have viewed this type of fear as an appropriate item for compensation on the theory that the fear itself is a present injury.[10]

D. Capacity to Enjoy Life

An emergent controversial issue is whether an injured person should be able to recover for "loss of the ability to enjoy life" as a category apart from pain and suffering. The issue is especially poignant when the plaintiff is permanently injured but presumably cannot himself sense the loss of enjoyment. The West Virginia Supreme Court opined that loss of enjoyment was a legitimate item of damages in a case involving a semi-comatose accident victim, where the jury had awarded $1,300,000 for that item. Responding to a certified question, the court said that the "loss of capacity to enjoy life is not a function of pain and suffering in the traditional sense of those words since one can lose his eyesight or a limb and be without physical pain." Declaring that damages for the loss of that capacity did not duplicate pain and suffering, the court concluded that "[j]ust as a jury may consider the nature, effect and severity of pain when fixing damages for personal injury, or may consider mental anguish caused by scars and disfigurement, it may consider loss of enjoyment of life."[11]

One must compare a federal appellate court's decision on the merits of the same case. The federal court ruled that the "capacity to enjoy life" was not an allowable damage item under the Federal Tort Claims Act, which bars punitive damages. That court pointed out that the semi-comatose plaintiff could not "use" the money, could not "spend it upon necessities or pleasures," and could not "experience the pleasure of giving it away." The court concluded that since the money could provide the plaintiff "with no direct benefit, the award is punitive."[12]

E. Consortium

A well-established item of tort damages, which takes the name consortium, represents an attempt to quantify intangible family relations. The primary ground for recovery of consortium damages has been the marital relation; however, some courts have extended compensation for consortium to children for injuries to their parents, especially fatal injuries, and to parents for the death of children. In one decision, which went so far as to allow consortium damages for the death of an adult child, the court remarked that "nature recoils from the suggestion that society, companionship

10. See ¶ 49.06(B) supra.

11. Flannery v. United States, 297 S.E.2d 433, 437–38 (W.Va.1982).

12. Flannery v. United States, 718 F.2d 108, 111 (4th Cir.1983).

and love which compose filial consortium automatically fade upon emancipation." The court commented that "[s]ome filial relationships will be blessed with mutual caring and love from infancy through death."[13]

F. Bereavement

Paralleling the consortium category is the classification of bereavement as a separate heading of personal injury damages for survivors of persons whose death was tortiously caused. Some wrongful death statutes specify bereavement in their catalogs of damage items.[14] Courts have pointed out that bereavement differs from loss of consortium—the former being "emotional distress brought on by the decedent's death" whereas the latter refers to lost companionship.[15]

At least theoretically, a concern presented by such refinement of categories is that these separate headings of damages might permit repetitious awards for the same group of mental responses. In mitigation of that concern, it seems plausible that, at least in general verdicts, most juries will lump together various sorts of mental and emotional intangibles rather than piling separate categories one on top of the other. Yet, courts must face the question of whether the more realistic, and legally just, classification system is that of a single category for an integrated cluster of psychological effects or that of a list that allows separate awards for such effects.

G. Intangible death damages generally

Some wrongful death statutes specify categories of noneconomic losses resulting from death; for example, the Virginia statute speaks of "sorrow, mental anguish and solace which may include society, companionship, comfort, guidance, kindly offices and advice of the decedent."[16] Most people would intuitively agree that these things are part of the loss sustained by family members when someone dies. However, where the statute does not specifically identify intangibles of that sort, disputes may arise about whether general statutory provisions for wrongful death should be interpreted to include certain items of damages.

Illustrative of a rather broad view of the appropriate range of wrongful death damages is a federal district court decision in a case involving several deaths caused when a factory exploded. The court awarded damages for the emotional consequences of the event to several relatives. It characterized a $100,000 award to a surviving

---

13. Frank v. Superior Court, 722 P.2d 955, 960 (Ariz.1986).

14. See, e.g., Kan. Stat. Ann. § 60–1904(a)(1) (1994).

15. See Elliott v. Willis, 442 N.E.2d 163, 167–68 (Ill.1982).

16. Code of Va. § 8.01–52.

spouse, who had to view his dying, mutilated wife, as including "mental anguish" as well as "loss of marital companionship, services and society." The court also awarded $50,000 to the decedent's mother, who it described as having "suffered more than the normal grief in the loss of her daughter." Moreover, the court said that a brother was entitled to $5,000, even though there were parts of his testimony that "could be construed as an admission that he suffered no more than normal grief," simply explaining that the brother had "suffered that degree of mental and emotional suffering which entitles him to recover for mental anguish under the wrongful death statutes."[17]

An issue that is symbolic of the complexities of many problems involving intangible losses is whether parents can recover for the wrongful death of a fetus, injured after viability, that is stillborn at term. Some courts have insisted that the language of the wrongful death legislation of their states simply does not include fetuses.[18] Doubtless, courts that hold the line against recovery for the death of a fetus carried to term have in mind the logical slippery slope that liability might create, reaching to such cases as that of the stillborn pre-viable fetus. Ranged on the other side are opinions that stress the inequity of denying liability for the death of a fetus carried to term while allowing recovery for injuries to fetuses before they were viable, so long as they survived to be born alive. These opinions stress that modern medical knowledge diminishes any obstacles to proof of injury that previously may have justified a bar to recovery.[19] In the general field of tort damages, the topic implicates the question of what the true rationales are for recovery for intangible losses, discussed just below.

¶ 72.03 Arguments About Justifications and Rationales

A. The Basic Issue of Propriety

The ultimate question about intangibles as items of tort damages is whether courts should award damages at all for non-pecuniary loss. Because of the large amounts sometimes awarded for pain and suffering, that particular item of intangible damages is controversial both theoretically and practically. On the practical side, some legislatures have expressed a political judgment against high dollar awards for pain and suffering by enacting "caps" on such awards, though no legislature has eliminated pain and suffer-

---

17. Lowe v. United States, 662 F.Supp. 1089, 1098–99 (W.D.Ark.1987).

18. See, e.g., Witty v. American Gen. Capital Distribs., Inc., 727 S.W.2d 503, 504 (Tex.1987) ("the legislature did not intend the words 'individual' or 'person' to be construed to include an unborn fetus").

19. See, e.g., id. at 511–12 (Kilgarlin, J., dissenting).

ing as a category of damages in tort cases. On the theoretical side, those who argue against damages for pain and suffering say that the amount that jurors award under that heading is virtually arbitrary, since pain cannot be readily be quantified. Opponents with an economic bent will point out that there is no legal market under whose auspices people may offer to suffer in exchange for payment.

A contrasting economic approach, supporting awards for pain and suffering, boldly poses the issue of valuation by some macabre exchange mechanism. It is true that this approach is not likely to persuade most people. Indeed, judges have recoiled against the "golden rule" argument, which one court critically characterized as "counsel ask[ing] the jurors to place themselves in the plaintiff's shoes and to award such damages as they would 'charge' to undergo equivalent pain and suffering."[20]

Yet, history is on the side of the advocates of damages for pain and suffering, even if the idea of a market for masochism inspires revulsion. Sources as diverse as twelfth century Jewish texts,[21] Islamic law,[22] and the customs of aboriginal tribes on the island of Luzon[23] support compensation for those and analogous harms, and every American jurisdiction permits awards for pain and suffering.

Although such damages thus represent a well-recognized category of loss, their theoretical justification is not a seamless one, and both supporters and opponents have a range of opinions about the rationale for these awards, apart from their justification as actual compensation. Some judges and commentators rationalize these items of damages as providing a pragmatic, if unprincipled, way for plaintiffs to make up attorneys' fees, which usually come out of tort awards on a contingency percentage basis. Critics assert that awards for pain and suffering represent a masked form of punitive damages. One commentator, generally sympathetic to expanding compensation for injuries, suggested that an appropriate trade-off for giving damages in the absence of fault would be to eliminate awards for "speculative" intangibles.[24]

20. Beagle v. Vasold, 417 P.2d 673, 681–82 n. 11 (Cal.1966).

21. Maimonides, The Book of Torts, Treatise IV, ch.1, at 160 (vol. IX of Yale Judaica Series 1954) (pain as one of a catalog of five items of "effects of ... injury" for which compensation must be paid).

22. See Abdul–Qadir Zubair, An Outline of Islamic Law of Tort 65 (Islamic International Contact, Lagos 1990) (as to damages for qimi, "non-fungible things," with respect to items

for which there is no legislatively fixed sum, it is for judges to decide on "fair and reasonable compensation," and this "is particularly so with claims for loss of amenities and pain and suffering").

23. See Melvin Belli, 4 Modern Trials 67 (1959) (damages to "assuage the mental anguish" caused by divorce or separation).

24. Fleming James, Damages in Accident Cases, 41 Cornell L. Q., 582, 584–585 (1956), discussed supra, ¶ 71.03(I), text accompanying notes 21–23.

Some critics, for example, scholars in the critical legal studies movement, have attacked tort recoveries for a variety of intangibles as involving a "commodification" of human beings.[25] What seems a persuasive response is that intuitively almost everyone believes that these intangibles represent real losses, and that the most practical way to compensate for them is with money. Whether one is considering damages for pain and suffering for living plaintiffs or recovery in death cases for relational or affective losses, such awards may provide the only pragmatic method to vindicate a sense of justice, and also to assure an appropriate level of deterrence.

The deterrence rationale provides an interesting foundation for a decision on an unusual wrongful death issue. In that case, the decedent was a nun who had taken a perpetual vow of poverty, the implication of which was that there had been "no pecuniary injury to a statutory beneficiary." However, in rejecting the defendant's argument that this meant that there could be "no recovery of substantial damages," the court noted that wrongful death statutes had "for their purpose more than compensation." Those statutes, the court said, also were intended "to promote safety of life and limb by making negligence that causes death costly to the wrongdoer."[26] This perspective may soften the objection of those who believe that awarding death damages for the severing of intangible relationships represents a demeaning of personal dignity rather than its vindication.

Arguments over the issue of tort damages for intangibles are part of the more general theoretical debates about whether tort law is preferable to a general social legislation approach, or to complete reliance on first party insurance. The question ultimately involves policy preferences.

B. Reviewing Awards for Noneconomic Damages

1. Generally

Because of the lack of specific benchmarks—for example, bills incurred—courts face an especially difficult task in reviewing awards for noneconomic damages. Such awards represent an attempt to quantify experiences that are extremely personal, and courts bump up against the limits of legal logic in testing them. Here, we seek to identify what appear to be some principal considerations to which judges refer in dealing with these issues.

The case of pain and suffering illustrates judicial efforts to establish standards for review of awards for losses that are not

---

25. See, e.g., Richard Abel, A Critique of Torts, 37 UCLA L. Rev. 785, 789 (1990) (referring to award of damages for "physical pain, disfigurement, loss of bodily function, fear, and damage to emotional relationships").

26. Stang v. Hertz Corp., 467 P.2d 14, 15–17 (N.M.1970).

easily converted into money. One factor in reviewing such awards is the length of time that the plaintiff feels pain or suffers. In litigation involving prolonged episodes of pain, a symbolic practical issue is whether plaintiffs' attorneys may argue to the jury that it should assign a dollar value to pain and suffering for particular units of time—for example, by the day. There is substantial disagreement on this point,[27] but it is clear that where this type of argument is permitted, the dollar amount for each unit of time will tend to decrease as the period of pain lengthens. By comparison, a few seconds of pain—or wrenching emotions analogous to physical pain—may be "worth" a substantial amount of money per unit of time.[28]

Courts often refer to rather abstract verbal formulas in reviewing pain and suffering awards. In seeking to define the boundaries of judicial toleration for dollar amounts, the decisions use such words and phrases as " 'grossly excessive,' 'inordinate,' 'shocking to the judicial conscience,' 'outrageously excessive,' 'so large as to shock the conscience of the court,' " and "monstrous."[29]

Another method of reviewing awards for injuries with intangible features draws on averages of past judicial decisions. Courts are likely to do this in attempting to quantify the value of an objectively definable kind of injury without a specific economic referent, for example, the loss of a limb.

2. *In death cases*

The review of valuations concerning non-economic losses can be particularly challenging in death cases. One strategy for dealing with the unquantifiability of such harms parallels an approach to nonfatal injuries: judges and lawyers may consult recent appellate decisions and reports of jury verdicts in an effort to triangulate the limits that appear tolerable for intangible losses, as well as tangible injuries, associated with loss of life. But especially in the case of awards for loss of affective relationships, this may be a daunting enterprise because of the difficulty of comparing the injuries alleged in the case at issue with descriptions in summaries of prior cases.

Thus, as they do in reviewing verdicts for pain and suffering, appellate courts resort to terms like "shocking to the conscience," "grossly excessive" and "monstrous" as standards for determining whether to reverse a death award or to require a remittitur. In one

---

27. A leading precedent allowing use of the "per diem" technique is Beagle v. Vasold, 417 P.2d 673 (Cal.1966). A principal decision opposing it is Botta v. Brunner, 138 A.2d 713 (N.J.1958).

28. See discussion of Haley v. Pan American World Airways, ¶ 72.01(C) supra, text accompanying notes 8–9 (affir-

mance of $15,000 award for mental anguish in period of four to six seconds in pre-impact fear case).

29. The court catalogues these formulas in Dagnello v. L.I.R.R., 289 F.2d 797, 802 (2d Cir.1961).

such opinion, reviewing an award of $414,000 for a wife's loss of her 51–year-old husband's "counseling and guidance and love and affection," the court commented that it thought the verdict "over-generous." However, the court also said that although it was "left with the uncomfortable feeling that the verdict is too high, we think we would be exceeding the limits of our authority if we were to disturb it."[30]

This discussion simply underlines the problems that courts face in reviewing awards for non-pecuniary loss. However, while pointing out those difficulties, one should note that many cultures, over a millennium and more, have found it quite appropriate to make these awards.

---

30. Huff v. White Motor Corp., 609 F.2d 286, 296–97 (7th Cir.1979).

Chapter Seventy–Three

PUNITIVE DAMAGES

Analysis

A traditional classification divides tort remedies into two major categories. One, discussed above,[1] is compensatory damages, a principal purpose of which is to restore the plaintiff to the position that the plaintiff occupied before an injury. The other, punitive damages—sometimes called "exemplary damages," or more informally, "smart money"—rests on several different rationales. The topic of punitive damages has generated legal and policy controversy, and has been the subject of review by the Supreme Court on several occasions.

¶ 73.01   The Purpose of Punitive Damages

A. *Punishment*

As the word "punitive" implies, a major purpose of this form of damages is to punish. To justify such an award, therefore, the plaintiff must show that the defendant's conduct was particularly culpable or even reprehensible.

---

1. See supra, Chapters 71 (economic damages), 72 (loss of intangibles).

429

B. Deterrence

Another purpose of punitive damages, which overlaps with the rationales for compensatory damages, is deterrence. This goal breaks down into two subcategories. Punitive awards may provide both a club to deter the particular defendant from future behavior of the kind that caused the injury, and a signal to others that will discourage them from conduct of that sort. Viewed from this perspective, the punitive damages remedy has a heightened behavior-controlling effect, but one should note that compensatory damages also serve a deterrence function.

C. Retribution

Closely related to the punishment rationale is retribution, a rationale that itself has two somewhat separable purposes—vindicating both individual plaintiffs and society. In awarding punitive damages, courts seek to endow with moral content the payment of extra money as a way of making clear to the community as well as the victim that justice has been done beyond making the plaintiff as whole as possible.

D. A bridge between civil and criminal law

One may also view punitive damages as serving as a bridge between criminal law and torts. As a civil remedy, punitive awards provide some intermediate punishment and extra deterrence functions without the plaintiff having to meet the relatively stringent due process standards associated with criminal prosecutions. Yet, the fact that the foundations of punitive damages are civil rather than criminal carries the seeds of an argument against the remedy. This argument is precisely that the process for granting punitive damages provides insufficient procedural and evidentiary safeguards to those against whom these awards are, after all, used as punishment.

E. Implications for Attorneys' Fees

An informal justification for awarding punitive damages is that such awards provide a way of helping severely injured plaintiffs make up the cost of their attorneys' fees. This is not a principled reason; it does not fit the underlying logic of the punitive remedy and has no independent justification for the purpose of lawyer compensation. The same argument has been advanced as a rationalization for pain and suffering damages and to justify not subtracting plaintiffs' "collateral sources" from tort awards. With respect to all three issues, the attorneys' fee rationale stretches pragmatism uncomfortably. Concerning punitive damages in particular, one may suggest that this remedy must stand or fall on such mainstream rationales as punishment, deterrence, and retribution.

¶ 73.02   Appropriateness as a Civil Remedy

A fundamental question is whether punitive damages are an appropriate remedy in private civil litigation. A principal argument against punitive damages, as we have noted, is that the remedy allows civil juries to levy what amount to fines for punishment without the safeguards required by criminal and constitutional law that are usually associated with punishment. A strong argument for permitting punitive damages, however, inheres in that very element of such awards. They achieve strong deterrence and some punishment in cases of especially blameworthy conduct, in a way that satisfies the sense of justice of jurors, overseen by judges, without involving the full machinery of the criminal justice process. A practical rationalization of this departure from the requirements of criminal law is that punitive damages result only in an award of money rather than loss of liberty to the defendant, which in many cases is a corporation and therefore not subject to imprisonment.

¶ 73.03   Verbal Standards

Courts have used several verbal standards for punitive damages, with those terms representing a range of views about how culpable a defendant's conduct must be to justify a punitive award. Some courts require that the plaintiff show conduct that verges on the criminal; an important opinion in a products liability case drew from state law the idea that "recklessness that will give rise to punitive damages must be close to criminality."[2]

Other courts use different linguistic tests that are at least as emotive and perhaps no more precise. For example, some decisions require that a defendant's conduct be "outrageous" or exhibit a "conscious or knowing disregard" for the probability of injury. One decision strings together no fewer than nine adjectives in discussing a claim for punitive damages. After summarizing the standard as requiring "malice, vindictiveness, ill-will, or wanton, willful or reckless disregard of plaintiff's rights," it lines up an overlapping set of adjectives in which the complaint alleges conduct that was "intentional, reckless, willful, wanton, gross and fraudulent."[3] Another phrase that has attracted courts, particularly in products liability cases, is "flagrant indifference" to harm.[4] A few courts will drop down the scale of culpability epithets from terms like "conscious disregard" and "flagrant indifference" to allow punitive damages on the basis of gross negligence, a particularly vague

---

2. Roginsky v. Richardson–Merrell, Inc., 378 F.2d 832, 843 (2d Cir.1967).

3. Wangen v. Ford Motor Co., 294 N.W.2d 437, 462 (Wis.1980).

4. See, e.g., Leichtamer v. American Motors Corp., 424 N.E.2d 568, 580 (Ohio 1981).

standard.[5] It is at least clear that simple negligence will not support a punitive award, with courts distinguishing negligence from the "complete indifference" to safety that can be grounds for punitive damages.[6]

In a bizarre case, opposed opinions of the Wisconsin Supreme Court demonstrated both the variety and the flexibility of the verbal standards for punitive awards. The plaintiff in this perhaps unique litigation was an employee of the defendants, who owned and operated a nursing home. The defendants loaned the plaintiff money for dentures, apparently supposing that she would stay with them as an employee for some time. When the plaintiff told the defendants that she was leaving their employment, an argument resulted about how she would repay the loan. One of the defendants then held the plaintiff and the other pulled the upper plate out of her mouth, a direct if brutal assertion of the defendants' apparent belief that they had a right to hold the denture to secure the loan. A majority of the court affirmed a jury award of punitive damages on the grounds that the defendants' conduct was "illegal, outrageous and grossly unreasonable."[7] A dissenter commented that "[u]nless malice is equated with momentary loss of temper or is to be presumed from an act of poor judgment, there is no element of malevolence or vindictiveness." He complained that to allow a punitive award on those facts would mean that "the most trivial of altercations and mildest of scuffles dons the garment of wantonness or recklessness."[8]

¶ 73.04 Judicial Control Over Punitive Damages

A. *Justification for making any award*

Courts exercise at least two levels of control over punitive awards. They must decide, at the outset, whether punitive damages should have been granted at all in a particular case. If they find a punitive award to be justified, then they must review the amount of the award. The question of whether to permit any award of punitive damages depends on whether the defendant's conduct has met the verbal standard of the particular jurisdiction.[9] This, in turn, will largely depend on how the court assesses the defendant's conduct in light of the policy bases of punitive damages, reviewed above.[10]

---

5. See, e.g., American Cyanamid Co. v. Frankson, 732 S.W.2d 648 (Tex.Ct. App.1987).

6. See, e.g., Roth v. Black & Decker, U.S., Inc., 737 F.2d 779, 782 (8th Cir. 1984).

7. Jones v. Fisher, 166 N.W.2d 175, 180 (Wis.1969).

8. Id. at 183–84 (Hansen, J., dissenting).

9. See supra, ¶ 73.03.

10. See supra, ¶ 73.01.

B. *Reviewing amounts of punitive damages*

A slippery and difficult issue for courts, once they have decided that punitive damages are appropriate and a jury has given a punitive award, is how to review the amount awarded. The Supreme Court has wrestled with this problem in several cases, gradually developing criteria for review that take into consideration such factors as the "reprehensibility" of the defendant's conduct, the ratio of punitive damages to compensatory awards, and the penalties otherwise provided by law—for example, regulatory fines—for the type of conduct at issue.

A foundational precedent is *Pacific Mutual Insurance Co. v. Haslip*,[11] which involved an Alabama jury's award of punitive damages against an insurer whose agent misappropriated health insurance premiums that he had collected, with the result that the plaintiffs' policies lapsed. The award was for "more than 4 times the amount of compensatory damages" and "more than 200 times the out-of-pocket expenses."[12] Upholding the judgment, Justice Blackmun's majority opinion emphasized that although the trial court had given "significant discretion" to the jury, "that discretion was not unlimited."[13]

The trial judge's instructions in *Haslip* explained the nature of punitive damages and their function as punishment, and pointed out that it was not compulsory to impose them.[14] Moreover, the courts below had adhered to criteria set out by the Alabama Supreme Court, including whether there was "a reasonable relationship between the punitive damages award and the harm likely to result from the defendant's conduct as well as the harm that actually ... occurred." Other elements of this catalog included the "degree of reprehensibility" of the defendant's behavior, the profitability of the wrongful conduct, the "financial position" of the defendant, and "all the costs of the litigation." The Alabama criteria also identified two mitigating factors—the imposition of criminal sanctions and "the existence of other civil awards against the defendant for the same conduct."[15]

The Supreme Court concluded that these standards provided a "sufficiently definite and meaningful constraint" on punitive awards.[16] Because the trial court applied the state standards, and the Alabama Supreme Court had given the case "appropriate review," the Supreme Court affirmed the award. It said that while

11. 499 U.S. 1 (1991).
12. Id. at 23.
13. Id. at 19.
14. Id.

15. Id. at 21–22.
16. Id. at 22.

the ratio of the punitive award to the other damages was great, it "did not lack objective criteria."[17]

Some critics view lists of factors as unsatisfactory because of the way that they allow juries and courts to pick and choose among those factors in setting or reviewing the amount of an award. However, it would seem that any review of money awards made for the purposes that justify punitive damages—with their moral overtones—will require courts to employ some kind of factor analysis. Another Supreme Court decision illustrates how courts may apply several criteria to the facts of a case to test the alleged excessiveness of an award. In that case, *TXO Production Corp. v. Alliance Resources Corp.*,[18] the Court affirmed a $10,000,000 punitive award for slander of title that was 526 times the amount of the $19,000 "actual damages." Despite the "dramatic disparity" in these figures, the Court could not find the award " 'grossly excessive.' "It cited the harm that the defendant's conduct could have caused to both its "intended victim" and "other victims," the defendant's "bad faith," and "the fact that the scheme employed ... was part of a larger pattern of fraud, trickery and deceit." The Court also mentioned the wealth of the defendant as a factor supporting the award.[19]

The defendant argued that it had been subjected to a "fundamentally unfair procedure," in part because the trial court had told the jury it could consider "the wealth of the perpetrator." The Court thought that this argument had not been properly presented to the state supreme court, but it did "note ... that in *Haslip* we referred to the 'financial position' of the defendant as one factor that could be taken into account in assessing punitive damages."[20]

The Supreme Court focused on limiting principles in its 1996 decision in *BMW of North America v. Gore*.[21] At issue in this Alabama litigation was BMW's repainting of a car that had suffered minor predelivery damage, without advising the dealer that there had been any repairs to the vehicle. The company admitted that the fact it had not disclosed the repairs was in line with a nationwide policy it had followed concerning cars that suffered minor damage during manufacture or transportation.

The jury, which found compensatory damages of $4,000, awarded the purchaser $4,000,000 punitive damages, which the Alabama Supreme Court reduced on remittitur to $2,000,000. In reversing the punitive award, Justice Stevens said that "[p]erhaps the most important indicium of the reasonableness of a punitive damages award is the degree of reprehensibility of the defendant's

---

17. Id. at 23.

18. 509 U.S. 443 (1993).

19. Id. at 460–62.

20. Id. at 462–64.

21. 517 U.S. 559 (1996).

conduct."[22] He pointed out that the defendant's conduct had "evinced no indifference to or reckless disregard for the health and safety of others," and that there was no evidence of "deliberate false statements, acts of affirmative misconduct, or concealment of evidence of improper motive, such as were present in *Haslip* and *TXO*."[23]

Moreover, although Justice Stevens observed that the Court had refused to adopt "a simple mathematical formula" on the ratio of punitive damages to compensatory awards, he described the ratio in this case as "a breathtaking 500 to 1."[24] He also noted that the award was "substantially greater than the statutory fines available in Alabama and elsewhere for similar malfeasance," and said that there appeared to be no "judicial decision in Alabama or elsewhere indicating that application of [BMW's policy on slightly damaged vehicles] might give rise to such severe punishment."[25]

The Ninth Circuit applied the test of *BMW v. Gore* in the spectacular setting of the massive oil spill in Prince William Sound, Alaska, caused by the running aground of the tanker *Exxon Valdez*. Concluding that a $5 billion punitive award was too high, the court parsed several of the *BMW* factors, including these:

▲ *Reprehensibility:* The company behaved reprehensibly because of its awareness of the risk of a major oil spill in the Sound and its knowledge that the captain of the tanker was an alcoholic who drank on board ships. However, factors "reduc[ing] reprehensibility" included the company's compensation of "many people" after the spill. Moreover, it "did not spill the oil on purpose, and did not kill anyone."[26]

▲ *Ratio:* The ratio of punitive damages to the $287 million awarded in compensatory damages was 17.42 to 1, which "greatly exceed[ed]" the 4 to 1 ratio that the Supreme Court had termed "close to the line" in the *Haslip* case.[27] The court also noted that Exxon's other losses in connection with the incident—including

22. Id. at 575.

23. Id. at 576–79.

24. Id. at 582–83.

25. Id. at 584. The Court followed *BMW v. Gore* with a decision requiring appellate courts to "apply a *de novo* standard of review when passing on district courts' determinations of the constitutionality of punitive damages awards." Cooper Indus. v. Leatherman Tool Group, Inc., 532 U.S. 424, 436 (2001). In doing so, the Court reversed a court of appeals decision applying an "abuse of discretion" standard to review of a punitive award in a case involving allegations of false advertising and unfair competition. The Court stressed the comparative "institutional" advantages it perceived appellate courts as possessing, relative to trial courts, with respect to analyzing the difference between juries' punitive awards and "the civil penalties authorized or imposed in comparable cases." See 532 U.S. at 440.

26. In re *Exxon Valdez*, 270 F.3d 1215, 1242–43 (9th Cir.2001).

27. See id. at 1243, referring to Pacific Mut. Life Ins. Co. v. Haslip, supra note 11.

$2.1 billion in cleanup expenses—provided a significant deterrent outside of punitive damages.[28]

▲ By any definition, the punitive award was significantly, even greatly, in excess of potential criminal or civil fines or other penalties.[29]

¶ 73.05 Statistics and Arguments About Effects in Litigation

There have been several statistical studies of punitive damages, focusing significantly on punitive awards in products liability cases but also embracing tort cases more generally.[30] The results of these studies indicate that punitive damages are given relatively infrequently. For example, one survey found punitive damages to have been awarded in only about one per cent of cases where California and Cook County (Illinois) juries gave verdicts for plaintiffs suing for personal injuries.[31] Another study revealed that punitive damages were awarded in 2 per cent of a group of 359 products liability cases, with only four punitive awards being upheld after appeal in a set of 172 federal products cases.[32]

Still another survey discovered only 355 punitive awards in products liability cases over a 25–year period between 1965 and 1990, and reported that if one removed asbestos cases from the calculation, the number of awards decreased in the last six years of that period. The researchers who did that study pointed out that 38 per cent of the people who won punitive awards from juries ultimately collected no punitive damages, and that in cases ultimately resolved on appeal, the average amount of compensatory damages was almost double that of punitive damages.[33]

Despite the relative paucity of punitive awards, however, opponents of punitive damages argue that the very threat of such awards creates socially detrimental disincentives. They claim that entrepreneurs like product manufacturers may refuse to take certain risks in innovation because of the fear of punitive damages, and that, on balance, these decisions are harmful to consumer welfare. Moreover, critics contend that the number of punitive awards reduced or overturned demonstrates that many juries that

28. Id. at 1244.

29. See id. at 1245–46.

30. A summary appears in Michael Rustad, Nationalizing Tort Law: The Republican Attack on Women, Blue Collar Workers and Consumers, 48 Rutgers L. Rev. 673, 689–92 (1996).

31. Mark A. Peterson, et al., Punitive Damages: Empirical Findings 35 (Rand Inst. for Civil Justice 1987).

32. William A. Landes & Richard A. Posner, New Light on Punitive Damages, Regulation, Sept.-Oct. 1986, at 35–36.

33. Michael Rustad and Thomas Koenig, Punitive Damages in Products Liability: A Research Report, 3 Prod. Liab. L. J. 85, 89–91 (1992).

award punitive damages respond to arguments based on passion and prejudice.

¶ 73.06   Particularized Issues Concerning Punitive Damages

A. *Post-event conduct*

Some interesting issues in punitive damages law relate to the legal effect of post-event conduct by the defendant. These issues have arisen with respect to both alleged culpable conduct and attempts at amends.

A case involving the over-radiation of a hospital patient presents an issue concerning allegedly reprehensible misconduct that follows, rather than precedes, the underlying tort that directly caused the plaintiff's injury. Besides complaining that she received far too much radiation—an occurrence the court viewed as due to negligence—the plaintiff in effect alleged that the defendant hospital had concealed the magnitude of the excess radiation. But in denying punitive damages, the court declared that even if that had happened, "later concealment of evidence of negligence does not render the act which constituted the negligence" to be "malicious since, of necessity, the negligent act must have been performed negligently before there can be any concealment thereof." The court commented that "[l]ater acts do not make a former act malicious when it was not malicious at the time that it was done."[34]

A decision concerning commendable rather than culpable post-event conduct exhibits a similar philosophy, holding that a defendant's attempt to act more responsibly after the sued-upon event will not provide a reason to reduce punitive damages. In this case, which involved fatal toxic shock associated with high-absorbency tampons, the district court ordered a remittitur of a punitive award because the manufacturer pledged to remove the offending product from the market.[35] However, the Tenth Circuit said that it was inappropriate to base a remittitur on post-event conduct, emphasizing that the defendant's behavior after the event "had no relevance to the injurious conduct underlying the claim for punitive damages." The appellate court expressed the concern that if it reduced punitive damages, this would encourage "other potential defendants ... to pursue the very behavior that the punitive award here was intended to deter, and thus would discourage voluntary cessation of injury-causing conduct."[36]

---

34. Rouse v. Riverside Methodist Hosp., 459 N.E.2d 593, 597 (Ohio Ct. App.1983).

35. O'Gilvie v. Int'l Playtex, Inc., 609 F.Supp. 817, 820 (D.Kan.1985).

36. O'Gilvie v. Int'l Playtex, Inc., 821 F.2d 1438, 1450 (10th Cir.1987), *rev'g on remittitur issue*, 609 F.Supp. 817 (D.Kan.1985).

B. *Insurance for Punitive Damages*

An important question about the practical ramifications of punitive awards, which inspires plausible arguments on both sides, is whether it is appropriate to permit insurance for punitive damages. Those who favor allowing insurance for punitive awards contend that this is just another form of liability insurance and that the nature of the defendant's conduct should not be relevant to whether the defendant may secure indemnity against civil liability. Opponents of insurability for punitive damages emphasize that the kind of conduct that supports such awards is invariably a type of behavior for which responsibility should inescapably be placed on the tortfeasor. They contend that an extremely culpable wrongdoer should not be allowed to avoid the burden of punishment-based liability by having a third party pay the award. This argument obviously has the most force when the conduct at issue is criminal.

C. *Caps*

An issue currently in the political arena is the question of whether legislatures should impose caps—dollar limits—on punitive damages. Advocates of caps stress the potentially ruinous consequences to defendants who suffer multi-million dollar punitive awards, which often appear to reflect juror sentiments that cannot easily be analyzed or rationally reviewed. Those opposing caps point out that in cases involving outlandish awards, the courts do not hesitate to reduce punitive damages by means of remittiturs. They also argue that it is precisely the potential of very high punitive awards to influence behavior that may have the most salutary effects in deterring egregious misconduct.

[Chapters 74–75 are reserved for supplementary material.]

Part Six

TORT LAW AND ITS NEIGHBORS

Section Thirteen
RELATION TO CONTRACT LAW
Chapter Seventy–Six
TORTS INVOLVING CONTRACTS

Analysis

Although a lawyer's basic training begins with a dichotomy between tort and contract, the twain occasionally do meet. This chapter discusses a set of important issues at the border of tort and contract. At the threshold of contract, these issues arise when a claimant asserts that the defendant committed a tort because of something that the defendant did to prevent a contractual relationship from beginning to form, most starkly the defendant's initial outright refusal to do business with the plaintiff.

Other kinds of litigation occur after the process of contracting has begun or when a contract is already in existence. Sometimes the plaintiff sues the contracting party itself for refusal to perform its obligations—a type of suit that often is difficult to distinguish from a straight breach of contract action. On many occasions, the suit is against a third party for interfering with the plaintiff's relations with a party with whom the plaintiff has a contract or is trying to make a contract.

Important policies are at play in these cases. Plaintiffs often base their cases on notions of basic fairness as well as concepts like disappointment of expectations. Typically, defendants argue that in a free economy, there should be very little judicial interference with the choices of people and firms to decide with whom they will contract, even if such decisions cause significant harm to those who lose contractual opportunities.

This chapter analyzes two principal categories of cases. The first involves suits based on claims that the defendant's refusal to deal with the plaintiff, or to perform a contract, was tortious. In the second group of cases, A sues B because B did something that interfered with A's contractual relationship, or prospective relation, with C.

¶ 76.01　Suits for Refusal or Failure to Contract

A. *Refusals to deal*

1. *Initial rejection of economic relations*

The purest case of refusal to deal arises when the defendant rejects the plaintiff's efforts to establish an economic relationship. In the common law setting, courts are likely to be unsympathetic to claimants who allege that they were damaged by the defendant's unwillingness to do business. They will reason that economic liberty is a fundamental freedom, and that the question of who one wishes to deal with is primarily, and usually solely, for that person to decide. Thus, at common law, the butcher, the baker, and the candlestick maker, as well as the seller of sweatsuits, refrigerators, and automobiles, could refuse for any reason to sell goods to another person—because of that individual's color, or because that person is unkempt, or simply because the seller does not like the prospective buyer personally.

Legislation has produced a substantial set of restrictions on total freedom of contract with respect to choice of business dealings. The Civil Rights Act of 1964 provides a prime example.[1] One may no longer refuse to deal with someone, even as an initial matter, because of that person's characteristics or status, so long as that aspect of the person is protected by law. Obvious illustrations are refusals to provide public accommodations or to sell goods to another person, or to hire him, because of his race. The fact that it has taken legislation to deal with these problems underlines judicial reluctance to compel sellers of goods and services, or prospective employers, to deal with particular parties. However, as will appear below, even in the absence of legislation the courts themselves have identified some situations in which they will hold that refusals to deal or at least to continue business dealings, or interferences with others' contracts by offering a better deal, are improper.

---

1. See, e.g., 42 U.S.C.A. §§ 2000a— 2000a–2 (public accommodations); 2000e–2—2000e–3 (equal employment opportunities).

2. *Refusal to continue doing business*

Courts' reluctance to involve themselves in people's choices about whether to begin commercial dealings with one another carries over into cases in which one party to a business relationship elects not to continue it. In one case, a concessionaire sued the operator of a state park because it did not renew the lease for the concession. In rejecting the action, the court indicated that business persons must stay on their toes in changing environments. It declared that "by failing to anticipate and prepare for the possibility that [the defendant] would not renew or purchase its business," the plaintiff had "seriously damaged its bargaining position, and as it should have expected, rendered itself incapable of negotiating a satisfactory deal."[2]

Yet, even a general belief that courts should not interfere with business decisions has not rigidly excluded all suits for refusals to keep doing business. Courts are especially likely to restrict freedom of contract when a party's refusal to continue a relationship affects important interests of the legal system itself. A good example is a case in which an insurance company canceled a dentist's malpractice insurance after he had testified under subpoena in a malpractice suit against another dentist. In upholding the complaint of the dentist whose insurance was canceled, the court invoked the strong "public policy against intimidating a witness."[3]

B. *Failure to perform a contractual obligation*

A substantial body of tort-oriented law has developed around various instances of the failure to perform contractual obligations. Principal defendants on this stage have been insurers that are accused of failing to defend or refusing to settle lawsuits brought against their insureds.

A leading California decision[4] captures the tensions inherent in claims alleging that insurers tortiously failed to settle cases against their policyholders. In this case, the insurer could have settled a personal injury action brought against its insured within the policy limits of a rather modest policy. Instead, basing its position on what the California Supreme Court called "blind faith" in its own experts' opinions about the merits of the case, the company refused to settle even though its insured offered to pay part of the settlement.

2. Stone Mountain Game Ranch, Inc. v. Hunt, 746 F.2d 761, 766 (11th Cir.1984).

3. L'Orange v. Medical Protective Co., 394 F.2d 57, 60 (6th Cir.1968).

4. Crisci v. Security Ins. Co. of New Haven, 426 P.2d 173 (Cal.1967).

The personal injury case went to trial and a jury awarded a very substantial amount to the plaintiff in that action, far exceeding the insured's policy limits, the result of which was that the insured became indigent and suffered serious physical and emotional consequences. In upholding an award for the insured against the insurer, the California court summarized a spectrum of positions on the obligations of insurers. These included:

1.　Most favorably to the insurer, a requirement that the insured show that the insurer acted in bad faith.

2.　Most favorably to the insured, a rule that the insurer will always be liable when it rejects an offer to settle within the policy limits and the underlying litigation results in an award against the insured above that figure.

3.　A compromise position outlined in a precedent, which the court applied to the case, was that in deciding whether to settle, "the insurer must give the interests of the insured at least as much consideration as it gives to its own interests."[5]

Each of the positions just described has attracted adherents. It is at least clear that when settlement and defense of liability claims involves the relationship of insurer and insured, the courts will not leave business judgments solely to those whose business it is to make those judgments. Undoubtedly, the courts that accept the complaints of insureds in cases of this kind respond to significant imbalances of power between the parties.

C.　Bad faith denial of the contract

A substantial body of case law treats the plaintiff's claim that the defendant's failure to perform a contract was in bad faith. The California Supreme Court has struggled with this question, first recognizing and then rejecting an action in tort for bad faith denial of the existence of a contract. Initially viewing state law as implying "in *every* contract a covenant of good faith and fair dealing,"[6] the court recognized the theory in a case brought by a small contractor that dealt in maritime goods. This plaintiff sued a major oil supplier for refusing to go forward with its expression of intent to sell fuel, on the basis of which the plaintiff had signed a marina lease with a municipality. Ultimately, the court reversed a plaintiff's judgment on the count for breach of the duty of good faith and fair dealing, because of the trial court's failure to instruct on the bad faith requirement. However, it accepted the premise that there was

---

5.　Id. at 176–77, referring to Comunale v. Traders & Gen'l Ins. Co., 328 P.2d 198, 201 (Cal.1958) for the standard under which the insurer must give at least equal consideration to the insured's interests.

6.　Seaman's Direct Buying Service, Inc. v. Standard Oil of Calif., 686 P.2d 1158, 1166 (Cal.1984).

liability for "denying, in bad faith, and without probable cause, that the contract exists."[7]

In a later case,[8] the California court overruled its prior recognition of the bad faith tort. The occasion was a suit by an accounting firm against an oil company for terminating the plaintiff's services, which were originally secured by an engagement letter signed by a law firm that at the time was counsel to the oil company. The jury found in favor of the plaintiff on a count for breach of contract, and, responding to questions, also said that the defendant had "denied the existence of the contract and . . . acted with oppression, fraud, or malice." Giving a relatively small verdict for the breach of contract, the jury awarded a much larger amount in punitive damages, apparently on the tort theory of bad faith denial of the contract.

The supreme court concluded that "a tort recovery [was] unavailable" to the plaintiff, and affirmed an appellate court judgment that reversed the plaintiff's judgment on its tort claim. Summarizing judicial and scholarly criticism of its adoption of the doctrine of bad faith denial of contract, the court referred to the differing purposes of tort and contract remedies.[9] In that connection, it quoted a precedent's description of contract law as " 'encourag[ing] efficient breaches, resulting in increased production of goods and services at lower cost to society.' "[10] The court generally expressed concern about the difficulty of "distinguishing between tortious denial of a contract's existence and permissible denial of *liability* under the terms of the contract." Moreover, it spoke of the "confusion" in interpretation of the bad faith doctrine, as well as the "excessive damage awards" that had resulted from its earlier recognition of the tort.[11]

¶ 76.02   Interference With Contractual Relations

A new order of complexity appears in cases in which the plaintiff claims that the defendant's actions caused harm by interfering with the plaintiff's contractual relationship, or prospective contractual relationship, with a third party. These cases contrast with suits against the party with whom a plaintiff contracted or wished to contract, for the defendant in "interference" cases is an outsider to the relationship the plaintiff claims has been injured. Thus, the plaintiff's action against the "interfering" defendant is

7. Id. at 1167.

8. Freeman & Mills, Inc. v. Belcher Oil Co., 900 P.2d 669 (Cal.1995).

9. See id. at 676–79.

10. Id. at 677, quoting Harris v. Atlantic Richfield Co., 17 Cal.Rptr.2d 649, 653–54 (Ct.App.1993).

11. Id. at 679. The court preserved an exception for suits on "the implied covenant in insurance cases." Id. at 680.

not a claim that might be remedied by a suit by the plaintiff against that defendant for breach of the contract.

In the grandmother of these cases, the 1853 decision in *Lumley v. Gye*,[12] the plaintiff was an opera impresario. He alleged that the defendant, a competitor, had "enticed and procured" a breach of contract by a singer who was under contract to the plaintiff. A majority of the Queen's Bench upheld the action, with one of the majority judges saying that it was "clear law that a person who wrongfully and maliciously, or ... with notice, interrupts the relation subsisting between master and servant by procuring the servant to depart from the master's service ... commits a wrongful act for which he is responsible at law."[13]

There has been a hard-fought struggle over the proper scope of a tort for intentional interference with contract—in many instances over whether it is desirable to have such a tort. The ground of battle is much the same philosophically as that in cases pleaded in tort in which only the contracting parties are the litigants. Again, the plaintiff invokes principles of fairness. Again, the defense draws on the idea that in a free economy, the only appropriate damages for the consequences of any breach of a contract are contract damages, and that it is inappropriate to bring tort into the picture.

The Restatement's analysis of this problem pivots on the concepts of intentional and improper interference.[14] There is some controversy about the verbal standard for intentionality. The California Supreme Court effectively opted for a requirement that the defendant act with "purpose or design" in a case discussed above on the issue of bad faith denial.[15] The plaintiff, a firm that had contracted for oil, sued an oil company for its refusal to supply fuel, which effectively forced the plaintiff to breach a marina lease with a city. In the branch of the suit in which the plaintiff claimed that the defendant had interfered with its contractual relationship with the city, the trial court gave instructions that defined the minimum requirements of intentionality as the defendant's knowledge with substantial certainty that its conduct would disrupt the plaintiff's business relationship. In reversing a plaintiff's verdict rendered on these instructions, the supreme court stressed that there was no evidence that the defendant had a "purpose or design" to cause the

---

12. 2 E. & B. 216 (Q.B. 1853).

13. Id. at 224 (Crompton, J.).

14. These are the baseline requirements of Restatement (Second) of Torts § 766 (1979) ("[o]ne who intentionally and improperly interferes with the performance of a contract (except a contract to marry) between another and a third person by inducing or otherwise causing the third person not to perform the contact, is subject to liability to the other for the pecuniary loss resulting to the other from the failure of the third person to perform the contract").

15. See supra, ¶ 76.01(C), text accompanying notes 6–7, discussing Seaman's Direct Buying Service, Inc. v. Standard Oil of California, 686 P.2d 1158 (Cal.1984).

plaintiff to breach its contract with the city, even though that was a "foreseeable consequence of [the defendant's] action."[16]

Besides the requirement that the defendant act intentionally, the "interference" tort requires that the defendant have behaved "improperly."[17] This Restatement's formulation of the tort sets out an elaborate catalog of factors to which the court is to give "consideration" in determining whether the defendant's conduct was "improper." These range from the defendant's "motive" and the interests of the plaintiff to the "interests sought to be advanced by the [defendant]" and "the social interests in protecting the freedom of action of the [defendant] and the contractual interests of the [plaintiff]."[18]

An interesting presentation of the issue, in which the social interests opposing the interfering behavior are substantial, appears in a case involving an insurer alleged to have engaged in "blacklisting" behavior. The plaintiffs were seamen who claimed that the defendant insurer required vessel owners to pay "exorbitant added premiums" to cover them for the plaintiffs' employment on board ship. The plaintiffs alleged that the defendant had designated them as "high-risk seamen," "not for legitimate risk-related reasons, but because they had filed personal injury claims" against the defendant's insurance companies.[19]

The First Circuit affirmed a part of a temporary injunction issued against the defendant that prohibited it from raising premiums on vessels on which the plaintiffs worked. The court conceded that an insurer was "entitled ... to raise its premiums where legitimate considerations dictate," but observed that the defendant had "relied on few, if any, objective criteria or statistical guidelines" and had "set premiums largely on a subjective, ad hoc basis."[20] Making explicit its concern that the defendant's conduct would discourage access to the legal process, the court declared that "[t]here is no privilege to deter people from exercising their legal rights by penalizing those who do."[21]

In a prior version of this long-running litigation, a state court had affirmed a damage award as well as an injunction, saying that "[e]ven though the plaintiff's 'contract of employment' may be terminable at the will of either party, the plaintiff is still entitled to appropriate remedies to prevent the defendants from unlawfully interfering with his employment."[22] Such decisions make it clear

---

16. Seaman's, 686 P.2d at 1165.

17. Restatement (Second) of Torts § 766 (1979).

18. Id. § 767.

19. Pino v. Protection Maritime Ins. Co., 599 F.2d 10 (1st Cir.1979).

20. Id. at 16–17.

21. Id. at 14.

22. Pino v. Trans–Atlantic Marine, Inc., 265 N.E.2d 583, 588 (Mass.1970).

that in cases where strong public policies intertwine with a contractual relation, courts may find it appropriate to intervene in business judgments, however undesirable that may be as a general matter.

Especially when linked to definable societal interests, such as preserving the right to bring meritorious claims to court, the "interference" tort has carried the moral power to command widespread judicial acceptance.[23] However, there has been trenchant theoretical criticism of the doctrine.

Professor Dobbs, for example, has analogized the development of the tort to Kafka's *The Trial*, saying that "these claims invite courts to judge and punish a state of mind."[24] Dobbs rests his critique, in part, on the philosophical notion that the tort undermines "the standing of all parties involved as autonomous human beings." He observes that if a defendant persuades another to breach a contract with a third person, the defendant is "the persuader but not the decision-maker," for it is the person persuaded "who decides to break off the relation." In cases where the person who terminates the relation has "committed no actionable wrong and is not even liable for breach of contract," then the defendant in an interference case would be held liable "for inducing a perfectly legal act by" the breaching party. In any event, "[i]n all cases [the defendant] is held liable for a decision which he himself did not make." Dobbs concludes that "[a]ny reasonable assessment of accountability must put the blame, if blame there is, on the person who makes the decision, not on one who, without fraud or duress, merely persuades."[25] From a more quantitative perspective, Dobbs argues that interference suits, "even if justified in some cases, may do more harm than good, simply because many innocent defendants will be sued to protect one deserving plaintiff," a statistical hypothesis that he offers as a refinement of the "flood of litigation" argument.[26]

Focusing on considerations of economic efficiency in another critique, Professor Perlman stresses that imposing liability for the interference tort "impairs the inducer's ability to negotiate with the party better able to take advantage of [an] alternative opportunity," whether that is the promisor or the promisee in the original contract. Positing that "[a]n inducer free of personal liability will be free to deal with the better party," Perlman contends that the prospect of tort liability will "undermine[] this freedom by encour-

23. See 2 Fowler Harper, Fleming James and Oscar Gray, The Law of Torts § 6.7 (1986).

24. Dan Dobbs, Tortious Interference with Contractual Relationships, 34 Ark. L. Rev. 335, 346–47 (1980).

25. Id. at 358.

26. Id. at 357.

aging the inducer to negotiate with the promisee [that is, the potential plaintiff in the interference litigation] to avoid the possibility of litigation."[27] In sum, Perlman argues that "tort liability works at cross-purposes with contract policies" because "[c]ontract remedies seem to promote efficiency," but "the addition of inducer liability inhibits efficient outcomes."[28]

Even critics declare that there are some cases in which the law should impose liability for interference with contract or prospective relationships—for example, "[w]here the defendant's act of interference is independently unlawful."[29] The case for liability is also particularly strong when the interference arises from "an act of duress, economic compulsion or undue influence."[30]

From a broad perspective, the battles over the interference tort reflect a more general struggle in tort law. Although most analysts weigh a variety of considerations in examining tort decisions, one may identify two polar positions. On one side is the position that courts often do and should restrict liability to acts that produce inefficient results and to illegal conduct. On the other is the view that tort law does and should operate in terms of a moral calculus that is more capacious, if less precise.

---

27. Harvey Perlman, Interference with Contract and Other Economic Expectancies: A Clash of Tort and Contract Doctrine, 49 U. Chi. L. Rev. 61, 84 (1982).

28. Id. at 128.

29. Id.

30. See Dobbs, supra note 24, at 366–67. Cf. Clark A. Remington, Intentional Interference with Contract and the Doctrine of Efficient Breach: Fine Tuning the Notion of the Contract Breacher as Wrongdoer, 47 Buff. L. Rev. 645 (1999). Professor Remington summarizes his argument, id. at 711–12, as supporting recognition of the tort in cases involving "wrongful" breaches, which he defines as "breaches for which the aggrieved contract party would not have had an adequate remedy in damages or breaches that involved bad faith refusal by the breaching party both to perform and to compensate the aggrieved party."

Another author suggests that the best way to contain the interference tort is to broaden the scope of the specific performance remedy for contract. The expansion of that remedy, he suggests, would permit courts to limit liability for the interference tort "to cases in which specific performance is not a possible contract remedy—those involving personal-service contracts, or, more broadly, relational contracts." This proposal would eliminate the "redundant litigation" that occurs when the promisee sues the breacher and the promisee also sues the inducer. Deepa Varadarajan, Tortious Interference and the Law of Contract: The Case for Specific Performance Revisited, 111 Yale L.J. 735, e.g., at 757–59 (2001).

Table of Cases

A

Aalco Mfg. Co. v. City of Espanola, 95 N.M. 66, 618 P.2d 1230 (N.M.1980)— ¶ **51.02, n. 8.**

Adams v. Cleveland–Cliffs Iron Co., 237 Mich.App. 51, 602 N.W.2d 215 (Mich. App.1999)— ¶ **36.01, n. 10.**

Aiken v. Clary, 396 S.W.2d 668 (Mo. 1965)— ¶ **27.01, n. 5.**

Aikens v. Debow, 208 W.Va. 486, 541 S.E.2d 576 (W.Va.2000)— ¶ **64.01, n. 6.**

Alaskan Oil, Inc. v. Central Flying Service, Inc., 975 F.2d 553 (8th Cir. 1992)— ¶ **64.04, n. 19.**

Albany Urology Clinic, P.C. v. Cleveland, 272 Ga. 296, 528 S.E.2d 777 (Ga. 2000)— ¶ **27.02, n. 15.**

Alexander v. Director, Office of Workers' Compensation Programs, 297 F.3d 805 (9th Cir.2002)— ¶ **54.02, n. 14.**

Allison v. Merck and Co., Inc., 110 Nev. 762, 878 P.2d 948 (Nev.1994)— ¶ **39.04, n. 21.**

Alsteen v. Gehl, 21 Wis.2d 349, 124 N.W.2d 312 (Wis.1963)— ¶ **13.02, n. 23, 25; ¶ 13.03, n. 35.**

Alton Box Bd. Co. v. Pantya, 236 So.2d 452 (Fla.App. 1 Dist.1970)— ¶ **49.04, n. 10.**

Alvis v. Ribar, 85 Ill.2d 1, 52 Ill.Dec. 23, 421 N.E.2d 886 (Ill.1981)— ¶ **33.01, n. 3; ¶ 33.02, n. 5.**

American Bank & Trust Co. v. Federal Reserve Bank of Atlanta, 256 U.S. 350, 41 S.Ct. 499, 65 L.Ed. 983 (1921)— ¶ **14.01, n. 5.**

American Cyanamid Co. v. Frankson, 732 S.W.2d 648 (Tex.App.-Corpus Christi 1987)— ¶ **73.03, n. 5.**

Anderson v. Farmers Hybrid Companies, Inc., 87 Ill.App.3d 493, 42 Ill.Dec. 485, 408 N.E.2d 1194 (Ill.App. 3 Dist. 1980)— ¶ **38.03, n. 16.**

Anderson v. Liberty Lobby, Inc., 477 U.S. 242, 106 S.Ct. 2505, 91 L.Ed.2d 202 (1986)— ¶ **67.03; ¶ 67.03, n. 42.**

Armory Park Neighborhood Ass'n v. Episcopal Community Services in

Arizona, 148 Ariz. 1, 712 P.2d 914 (Ariz.1985)— ¶ **37.03, n. 19.**

Arnold v. Union Oil Co. of California, 608 F.2d 575 (5th Cir.1979)— ¶ **30.03, n. 26.**

Ayers v. Jackson Tp., 106 N.J. 557, 525 A.2d 287 (N.J.1987)— ¶ **49.06, n. 37.**

B

Babb v. Matlock, 340 Ark. 263, 9 S.W.3d 508 (Ark.2000)— ¶ **71.04, n. 28.**

Backes v. Valspar Corp., 783 F.2d 77 (7th Cir.1986)— ¶ **49.04, n. 16.**

Baker v. City of Festus, 418 S.W.2d 957 (Mo.1967)— ¶ **44.03, n. 5.**

Baltimore & O.R. Co. v. Goodman, 275 U.S. 66, 48 S.Ct. 24, 72 L.Ed. 167 (1927)— ¶ **31.02; ¶ 31.02, n. 16.**

Bammerlin v. Navistar Intern. Transp. Corp., 30 F.3d 898 (7th Cir.1994)— ¶ **19.02, n. 10, 12.**

Barbara A. v. John G., 145 Cal.App.3d 369, 193 Cal.Rptr. 422 (Cal.App. 1 Dist.1983)— ¶ **17.02, n. 6.**

Bardy v. Sears, Roebuck and Co., 443 So.2d 212 (Fla.App. 2 Dist.1983)— ¶ **45.01, n. 4.**

Barker v. Lull Engineering Co., 143 Cal. Rptr. 225, 573 P.2d 443 (Cal.1978)— ¶ **19.02, n. 15; ¶ 39.02; ¶ 39.02, n. 6.**

Barnes v. Harley–Davidson Motor Co., Inc., 182 Ga.App. 778, 357 S.E.2d 127 (Ga.App.1987)— ¶ **30.01, n. 13.**

Barr v. Matteo, 360 U.S. 564, 79 S.Ct. 1335, 3 L.Ed.2d 1434 (1959)— ¶ **66.07, n. 28.**

Battalla v. State, 219 N.Y.S.2d 34, 176 N.E.2d 729 (N.Y.1961)— ¶ **59.02, n. 8.**

Bauer v. Piper Industries, Inc., 154 Wis.2d 758, 454 N.W.2d 28 (Wis.App. 1990)— ¶ **31.02, n. 6.**

Beagle v. Vasold, 65 Cal.2d 166, 53 Cal. Rptr. 129, 417 P.2d 673 (Cal.1966)— ¶ **72.03, n. 20, 27.**

C

D

Dagnello v. Long Island R. Co., 289 F.2d 797 (2nd Cir.1961)—¶ **72.03, n. 29.**

Daly v. General Motors Corp., 144 Cal. Rptr. 380, 575 P.2d 1162 (Cal. 1978)—¶ **33.03, n. 14, 15.**

Dang v. New Hampshire Ins. Co., 798 So.2d 1204 (La.App. 4 Cir.2001)— ¶ **31.02, n. 7.**

Darby v. Compagnie National Air France, 728 N.Y.S.2d 731, 753 N.E.2d 160 (N.Y.2001)—¶ **20.01, n. 6.**

Daubert v. Merrell Dow Pharmaceuticals, Inc., 509 U.S. 579, 113 S.Ct. 2786, 125 L.Ed.2d 469 (1993)— ¶ **49.04;** ¶ **49.04, n. 18.**

Day v. Waffle House, Inc., 743 P.2d 1111 (Okla.App. Div. 3 1987)—¶ **63.03, n. 6, 8;** ¶ **63.04, n. 11.**

Demchuk v. Bralow, 404 Pa. 100, 170 A.2d 868 (Pa.1961)—¶ **48.01, n. 3.**

Depue v. Flateau, 100 Minn. 299, 111 N.W. 1 (Minn.1907)—¶ **42.02;** ¶ **42.02, n. 6.**

Desai v. SSM Health Care, 865 S.W.2d 833 (Mo.App. E.D.1993)—¶ **10.02, n. 5.**

De Witt Properties, Inc. v. City of New York, 406 N.Y.S.2d 16, 377 N.E.2d 461 (N.Y.1978)—¶ **45.03, n. 8.**

Diaz v. Oakland Tribune, Inc., 139 Cal. App.3d 118, 188 Cal.Rptr. 762 (Cal. App. 1 Dist.1983)—¶ **69.01, n. 7.**

Dillon v. Legg, 68 Cal.2d 728, 69 Cal. Rptr. 72, 441 P.2d 912 (Cal.1968)— ¶ **61.02, n. 17.**

Dillworth v. Gambardella, 970 F.2d 1113 (2nd Cir.1992)—¶ **30.04, n. 61, 63.**

Dimeo v. Griffin, 943 F.2d 679 (7th Cir. 1991)—¶ **8.02, n. 15.**

DiSalvatore v. United States, 499 F.Supp. 338 (E.D.Pa.1980)—¶ **30.03, n. 27.**

Dockter v. Rudolf Wolff Futures, Inc., 913 F.2d 456 (7th Cir.1990)— ¶ **13.02, n. 14.**

Doe v. Walker, 193 F.3d 42 (1st Cir. 1999)—¶ **21.03, n. 13.**

Dole v. Dow Chemical Co., 331 N.Y.S.2d 382, 282 N.E.2d 288 (N.Y.1972)— ¶ **51.04, n. 20.**

Dopp v. Fairfax Consultants, Ltd., 771 F.Supp. 494 (D.Puerto Rico 1990)— ¶ **8.03, n. 18.**

Dotterweich, United States v., 320 U.S. 277, 64 S.Ct. 134, 88 L.Ed. 48 (1943)—¶ **1.05, n. 27.**

Douglas v. Delp, 987 S.W.2d 879 (Tex. 1999)—¶ **59.03, n. 19.**

Douglass v. Hustler Magazine, Inc., 769 F.2d 1128 (7th Cir.1985)—¶ **69.03, n. 28.**

Downs v. Gulf & Western Mfg. Co., Inc., 677 F.Supp. 661 (D.Mass.1987)— ¶ **30.01, n. 7.**

Dullard v. Berkeley Associates Co., 606 F.2d 890 (2nd Cir.1979)—¶ **45.03, n. 8.**

Dun & Bradstreet, Inc. v. Greenmoss Builders, Inc., 472 U.S. 749, 105 S.Ct. 2939, 86 L.Ed.2d 593 (1985)— ¶ **67.01;** ¶ **67.01, n. 21.**

Duncan v. Rzonca, 133 Ill.App.3d 184, 88 Ill.Dec. 288, 478 N.E.2d 603 (Ill. App. 2 Dist.1985)—¶ **55.03, n. 10.**

Dunnaway v. Duquesne Light Co., 423 F.2d 66 (3rd Cir.1970)—¶ **19.02, n. 9.**

E

East River S.S. Corp. v. Transamerica Delaval, Inc., 476 U.S. 858, 106 S.Ct. 2295, 90 L.Ed.2d 865 (1986)— ¶ **64.04, n. 15.**

Edwards v. Hollywood Canteen, 27 Cal.2d 802, 167 P.2d 729 (Cal. 1946)—¶ **21.03, n. 5.**

Eiseman v. State, 518 N.Y.S.2d 608, 511 N.E.2d 1128 (N.Y.1987)—¶ **57.04, n. 16.**

Elliott v. Willis, 92 Ill.2d 530, 65 Ill.Dec. 852, 442 N.E.2d 163 (Ill.1982)— ¶ **72.01, n. 15.**

Employers Nat. Ins. Co. v. Chaddrick, 826 F.2d 381 (5th Cir.1987)— ¶ **33.02, n. 8.**

Erickson v. Muskin Corp., 180 Ill.App.3d 117, 128 Ill.Dec. 964, 535 N.E.2d 475 (Ill.App. 1 Dist.1989)—¶ **33.02, n. 10.**

Erkson by Hickman v. Sears, Roebuck & Co., 841 S.W.2d 207 (Mo.App. W.D. 1992)—¶ **32.01, n. 5.**

Escola v. Coca Cola Bottling Co. of Fresno, 24 Cal.2d 453, 150 P.2d 436 (Cal. 1944)—¶ **38.01;** ¶ **38.01, n. 4.**

Esposito v. Christopher, 166 Colo. 361, 443 P.2d 731 (Colo.1968)—¶ **63.03, n. 7.**

Estrada v. Jaques, 70 N.C.App. 627, 321 S.E.2d 240 (N.C.App.1984)—¶ **27.02, n. 10.**

Everett v. Bucky Warren, Inc., 376 Mass. 280, 380 N.E.2d 653 (Mass. 1978)—¶ **39.05, n. 32.**

Exner v. Sherman Power Const. Co., 54 F.2d 510 (2nd Cir.1931)—¶ **35.04, n. 21.**

461 TABLE OF CASES

Sturges v. Bridgman, 11 Ch.D. 852 (CA 1879)—¶ **36.01, n. 6.**

Summers v. Tice, 33 Cal.2d 80, 199 P.2d 1 (Cal.1948)—¶ **50.02; ¶ 50.02, n. 6.**

Sundquist v. Madison Rys. Co., 197 Wis. 83, 221 N.W. 392 (Wis.1928)—¶ **59.01, n. 1.**

Suter v. San Angelo Foundry & Mach. Co., 81 N.J. 150, 406 A.2d 140 (N.J. 1979)—¶ **30.02, n. 24.**

Sutphin v. Platt, 720 S.W.2d 455 (Tenn. 1986)—¶ **23.04, n. 14.**

Swartz v. General Motors Corp., 375 Mass. 628, 378 N.E.2d 61 (Mass. 1978)—¶ **38.02, n. 13.**

Swope v. Columbian Chemicals Co., 281 F.3d 185 (5th Cir.2002)—¶ **7.01, n. 20.**

Szabo v. Pennsylvania R. Co., 40 A.2d 562 (N.J.Err. & App.1945)—¶ **65.01, n. 1.**

T

Tackett v. Columbia Energy Group Service Corp., 2001 WL 1463383 (Ohio App. 10 Dist.2001)—¶ **20.01, n. 7.**

Tarasoff v. Regents of University of California, 131 Cal.Rptr. 14, 551 P.2d 334 (Cal.1976)—¶ **57.03; ¶ 57.03, n. 11; ¶ 57.04, n. 15.**

Tavoulareas v. Piro, 817 F.2d 762, 260 U.S.App.D.C. 39 (D.C.Cir.1987)—¶ **67.02, n. 33.**

Taylor v. Burlington Northern R. Co., 787 F.2d 1309 (9th Cir.1986)—¶ **32.01, n. 4.**

Temple v. Wean United, Inc., 50 Ohio St.2d 317, 364 N.E.2d 267 (Ohio 1977)—¶ **38.02, n. 11.**

Tenants Council of Tiber Island–Carrollsburg Square v. DeFranceaux, 305 F.Supp. 560 (D.D.C 1969)—¶ **26.02, n. 10.**

Tennessee v. Garner, 471 U.S. 1, 105 S.Ct. 1694, 85 L.Ed.2d 1 (1985)—¶ **11.03; ¶ 11.03, n. 3.**

The Nitro–Glycerine Case, 82 U.S. 524, 21 L.Ed. 206 (1872)—¶ **19.02; ¶ 19.02, n. 7.**

The Thorns Case, Y.B. Mich. 6 Ed. 4, f. 7, pl. 18 (1466)—¶ **35.01, n. 2.**

The T.J. Hooper, 60 F.2d 737 (2nd Cir. 1932)—¶ **19.03; ¶ 19.03, n. 22; ¶ 23.06, n. 19.**

Thing v. La Chusa, 257 Cal.Rptr. 865, 771 P.2d 814 (Cal.1989)—¶ **61.02, n. 12, 16, 18; ¶ 61.03, n. 19.**

Thomas v. Housing Authority of City of Bremerton, 71 Wash.2d 69, 426 P.2d 836 (Wash.1967)—¶ **26.02, n. 8.**

Thompson v. Nebraska Mobile Homes Corp., 198 Mont. 461, 647 P.2d 334 (Mont.1982)—¶ **64.04, n. 17.**

Thompson v. Southern Pacific Transp. Co., 809 F.2d 1167 (5th Cir.1987)—¶ **49.03, n. 5.**

Thompson v. Thompson, 484 U.S. 174, 108 S.Ct. 513, 98 L.Ed.2d 512 (1988)—¶ **22.02, n. 2.**

Tidler v. Eli Lilly and Co., 851 F.2d 418, 271 U.S.App.D.C. 163 (D.C.Cir. 1988)—¶ **50.02, n. 8.**

Time, Inc. v. Firestone, 424 U.S. 448, 96 S.Ct. 958, 47 L.Ed.2d 154 (1976)—¶ **67.02; ¶ 67.02, n. 26, 38.**

Time, Inc. v. Hill, 385 U.S. 374, 87 S.Ct. 534, 17 L.Ed.2d 456 (1967)—¶ **69.02; ¶ 69.02, n. 11, 14, 17.**

TMI Litigation Governmental Entities Claims, In re, 544 F.Supp. 853 (M.D.Pa.1982)—¶ **64.04, n. 25.**

Tolbert v. Duckworth, 262 Ga. 622, 423 S.E.2d 229 (Ga.1992)—¶ **19.02, n. 5.**

Tolbert v. Gerber Industries, Inc., 255 N.W.2d 362 (Minn.1977)—¶ **51.04, n. 22, 30.**

Trans World Airlines v. Curtiss–Wright Corp., 1 Misc.2d 477, 148 N.Y.S.2d 284 (N.Y.Sup.1955)—¶ **64.04, n. 18.**

Traylor v. Husqvarna Motor, 988 F.2d 729 (7th Cir.1993)—¶ **30.01, n. 8.**

Troncalli v. Jones, 237 Ga.App. 10, 514 S.E.2d 478 (Ga.App.1999)—¶ **8.02, n. 13.**

Truman v. Thomas, 165 Cal.Rptr. 308, 611 P.2d 902 (Cal.1980)—¶ **27.01, n. 3.**

Tufte v. City of Tacoma, 71 Wash.2d 866, 431 P.2d 183 (Wash.1967)—¶ **10.05, n. 15.**

Turcotte v. Fell, 510 N.Y.S.2d 49, 502 N.E.2d 964 (N.Y.1986)—¶ **30.04; ¶ 30.04, n. 34, 36.**

Turner v. American Motors General Corp., 392 A.2d 1005 (D.C.1978)—¶ **39.04, n. 30.**

Twyman v. Twyman, 855 S.W.2d 619 (Tex.1993)—¶ **13.01, n. 2.**

TXO Production Corp. v. Alliance Resources Corp., 509 U.S. 443, 113 S.Ct. 2711, 125 L.Ed.2d 366 (1993)—¶ **73.04; ¶ 73.04, n. 18.**

Tyler, City of v. Likes, 962 S.W.2d 489 (Tex.1997)—¶ **59.03, n. 19.**

U

Union Oil Co. v. Oppen, 501 F.2d 558 (9th Cir.1974)—¶ **64.04, n. 22.**

United States v. _____ (see opposing party)

Index

-A-

Abnormally dangerous activities, ¶ 35.03
Absolute liability
  See also Liability per se
  Designation for ultrahazardous activities, ¶ 35.04
Active-passive distinction, indemnity, ¶ 51.01(A)
Act
  Assault element, ¶ 6.01(A)
  Consent, ¶ 17.01
Activities
  Basis for negligence standards, ¶ 18.01
Administrative economy
  Factor in decisions
    Negligence, ¶ 18.02
    Nuisance, standing doctrine, ¶ 37.03
    Private necessity, ¶ 42.04
Alternative hypotheses
  See subhead under Proof
Alternative liability, ¶ 50.02(C)
Alternatives
  See also Reasonable alternative design
  Negligence, ¶ 19.03(D)
Apartments and condominiums
  Duty, ¶ 57.02
  Exculpatory clauses, ¶ 26.02
  Owners' liability, ¶ 21.03(B)
Apportionment of liability
  See also Comparative apportionment of liability, Contribution, Indemnity
  Generally, Chapter 51
Apprehension
  Assault, ¶ 6.01(C)
Appropriation
  Privacy tort, ¶ 69.04
Assault
  Defined, ¶ 6.01
Assumption of risk
  See Express assumption of risk, Implied assumption of risk

Autonomy
  Duty to act, argument opposing, ¶ 65.02
  Informed consent, ¶ 27.03
  Intentional interference with contractual relations, ¶ 76.02
  Workplace cases, controversy, ¶¶ 30.01(A)(1), 30.03(C)

-B-

Balancing tests
  Detention of alleged shoplifters, ¶ 16.04
  Intentional infliction of emotional distress, ¶ 13.03(A)
  Intrusion, ¶ 8.03(B)
Bargaining of safety
  Worker assumption of risk, ¶ 30.04(C)
  Tool for measuring damages, ¶ 71.03(F)
Barker v. Lull Engineering Co., ¶ 39.02(D)
Battery
  Defined, ¶ 7.01
  Informed consent, ¶ 27.01
Behavior, law's influence on
  See Deterrence
Behavioral effects of law
  See also Deterrence
  Comparative fault, ¶ 33.02(B)
  Defamation, ¶¶ 67.04, 68.05
  Punitive damages, ¶ 73.05
  Informed consent, ¶ 27.04
Bereavement, ¶ 72.01(F)
Bill collection, ¶ 13.02(C)
Bizarre consequences
  Economic loss, ¶ 64.04(C)
  Rescue, ¶ 63.04(C)
Bystander claimants
  Generally, Chapter 61
  Limiting elements, ¶ 61.02

-C-

Capacity to enjoy life

463

Everyday touchings, ¶ 7.01(E)

-F-

Fact and law
    Contributory negligence, ¶ 31.02
    Negligence, ¶ 18.02
Failure to warn
    Generally, products cases, ¶ 38.04(C)
    Defect, relation to, ¶ 39.05(B)
Fact vs. opinion
    Generally, ¶¶ 66.04, 68.02
    Argument distinguished from fact,
        ¶ 68.03
    Common usage or meaning, ¶¶ 68.02,
        68.03
    Contexts of statements, ¶ 68.02
    Distinction rationalized, ¶¶ 68.01,
        68.03
    Fair comment, ¶ 68.04
    Verifiability, ¶ 68.02
Fair comment, ¶ 68.04
Fairness
    Bystander claims, ¶ 61.03(A)
    Circumstantial evidence, ¶ 44.04
    Comparative apportionment of liabil-
        ity, ¶ 51.04(B)
    Comparative negligence, ¶ 33.02(A)
    Foreseeability, ¶ 19.02(C)
    Medical res ipsa, ¶ 45.06(C)(2)
    Private necessity, ¶ 42.03(B)
    Products liability, ¶ 38.05(C)
    Res ipsa, ¶ 45.05(B), (D)
    Settlement, ¶ 54.02(B)
    Statutory violations, ¶ 56.04
    Torts involving contracts, Chapter 76
        introduction; ¶ 76.02
False arrest
    Defined, ¶ 11.01
    Rationales, ¶¶ 11.03, 11.04
False imprisonment
    Defined, Chapter 10 introduction
False light, ¶ 69.03
Fear
    See also Negligent infliction of emo-
        tional distress
    Element of damages, generally,
        ¶ 72.01(C)
    Of illness, ¶ 49.06(B)
Federal Tort Claims Act
    Intentional torts exception,
        ¶ 7.03(B)(1)
Fireman's rule, ¶ 30.03(B)
Fictionalization
    First amendment protection, actual
        malice test, ¶ 69.02
Foreseeability
    See also subhead under Duty
    Bystander cases, ¶¶ 61.02, 61.03(A)
    Economic loss, ¶ 64.02

Foreseeability—Cont'd
    Negligence, generally, ¶ 19.02(C)
    Rescue cases, criticized, ¶ 63.05
Fortuitousness of occurrence,
    Proximate cause lacking, ¶ 55.03
Fraud
    Consent vitiated, ¶¶ 17.02, 17.03
    Media access to business premises,
        ¶ 69.05
    Medical care, ¶ 23.01
Fright
    See Fear, Shock and fright

-G-

Gertz v. Robert Welch, Inc., ¶ 67.01(C)

-H-

Harm
    Alternative requirement for false im-
        prisonment, ¶ 10.05
Harmful contact, ¶ 7.01(F)
Health maintenance organizations
    See Managed care
Honest error in judgment
    Medical cases, ¶ 23.05
Household services, loss of, ¶ 71.01(C)
Human condition
    Limitation of liability, argument for,
        ¶ 61.03(E)
Hyperbole
    Not defamation, ¶ 68.02

-I-

Identification
    Defamation element, ¶ 66.03
Independent contractors
    Employers entitled to indemnity,
        ¶ 51.01(B)
Illegality
    Corruption distinguished, ¶ 14.03
    Intentional interference with con-
        tractual relations, ¶ 76.02
Implied assumption of risk
    Defined, generally, ¶ 30.01
    Primary, ¶¶ 30.04(A)(3), 30.04(B)(1)
    Secondary, reasonable,
        ¶¶ 30.04(A)(5), 32.02(3), 33.03
    Secondary, unreasonable,
        ¶ 30.04(A)(4)
Implied causes of action, ¶ 22.02
Implied consent, ¶ 30.04(A)(1)
Implied warranty
    Historical background of strict liabili-
        ty, ¶¶ 38.01, 38.02
    Obstacles to recovery, ¶ 38.05(G)

Libel
  See also Defamation
  Per se, ¶ 66.06
  Slander distinguished, ¶ 66.02
Libel proof plaintiffs, ¶ 66.01(C)
Licensees, ¶ 20.01(B)
Limits on damages
  Punitive damages, ¶ 73.06(C)
Local standards
  Medical cases, ¶ 23.04
Loss distribution
  See also Loss spreading, Risk spreading
  Private necessity, ¶ 42.04(C)
  Strict liability for activities, ¶ 35.05
  Strict liability for products, ¶ 38.06
Loss spreading,
  See also Loss distribution
  Generally, ¶ 1.04
  Landowners' liability, ¶ 21.04

-M-

Making whole
  See Restoration
Managed care, ¶¶ 23.01, 27.05
Manufacturing defects, ¶ 38.04(A)
Market share liability, ¶¶ 50.02(D), 50.03
Materiality
  Informed consent, ¶ 27.02
Medical care
  See Informed consent, Medical negligence, Medical standards
Medical expenses, ¶ 71.01(A)
Medical monitoring, ¶ 49.06(C)
Medical negligence
  Costs of legal rules, ¶ 48.03
  Res ipsa
    Generally, ¶ 45.06
    Circumstantial evidence and specific acts of negligence ¶ 45.06(B)(3)
  Standard of care, generally, Chapter 23
  Unavailability of testimony, ¶ 48.03
Misuse
  Defect, relation, ¶ 39.05(A)
  Products cases, generally, ¶ 32.01
Moral aspects of tort law
  Battery, ¶ 7.04
  Duty to act, ¶ 65.03
  Implied assumption of risk, ¶¶ 30.02, 30.03(C)
  Intentional interference with economic relations, ¶ 76.02
  Market share liability, ¶ 50.03
  Negligence per se, ¶ 22.05
  Nuisance, ¶ 36.04(C)
  Professional sports, ¶ 30.04(A)(7)
  Proportionality, ¶ 61.03(F)

Moral aspects of tort law—Cont'd
  Public disclosure of private facts, ¶ 69.01
  Rescue, ¶ 63.05
  Strict liability for activities, ¶ 35.05
Motions
  Procedural, generally, ¶ 18.02
Motion to dismiss, ¶ 18.02
Multiple defendants
  See also Apportionment of liability
  Res ipsa, ¶ 45.03
  Theories of liability, ¶ 50.01, 50.02

-N-

National standards
  Medical cases, ¶ 23.04
Necessity, private, Chapter 42
Negligence
  See also Duty, Foreseeability, Standard of care
  Generally, Chapters, 18, 19
  Defined, ¶¶ 19.01, 19.02
  Economic analysis, ¶ 19.02(D)
  Environmental injury, ¶ 36.01(D)
  Evidence, sufficiency, ¶ 43.02(A)
  Multiple goals, ¶ 19.02(E)
  Negated, ¶ 30.01(D)
Negligent infliction of emotional distress
  See also Fear, Shock and Fright
  General mental anguish, ¶ 59.03
  Impact on plaintiff or vehicle, ¶ 59.01
  Shock or fright, ¶ 59.02
  Skepticism about injuries, ¶ 59.03
Negligence per se, ¶ 22.05
New York Times v. Sullivan test
  Defamation,
    Public figures, ¶ 67.01(B)
    Public officials, ¶ 67.01(A)
  False light, ¶ 69.03
  Fictionalization, ¶ 69.02
No duty
  Generally, ¶ 30.01(C)
  Hypothesized explanation for rejection of liability, ¶ 32.02(5)
  Professional sports, ¶ 30.04(A)(2)
No negligence
  Generally, ¶¶ 30.01(D) 32.02(1)
  Sports and recreation, ¶ 30.04(B)(3)
Noncategory torts, Chapter 14
Noneconomic loss
  See subhead Intangibles under Damages
Notice
  Exculpatory agreements, ¶ 26.01
Nuisance
  See Private nuisance, Public nuisance

-S-

†